Economics and Contemporary Issues

Sixth Edition

Michael R. Edgmand
Oklahoma State University

Ronald L. Moomaw
Oklahoma State University

Kent W. Olson
Oklahoma State University

THOMSON
SOUTH-WESTERN

Australia · Canada · Mexico · Singapore · Spain · United Kingdom · United States

Economics and Contemporary Issues, 6e
Michael R. Edgmand, Ronald L. Moomaw & Kent W. Olson

Vice President/Editorial Director:
Jack Calhoun

Vice President/Editor-in-Chief:
Michael P. Roche

Publisher of Economics:
Michael B. Mercier

Sr. Acquisitions Editor:
Peter Adams

Sr. Developmental Editor:
Susan Smart

Sr. Production Editor:
Elizabeth A. Shipp

Executive Marketing Manager:
Lisa L. Lysne

Media Developmental Editor:
Peggy Buskey

Media Production Editor:
Pam Wallace

Manufacturing Coordinator:
Sandee Milewski

Production House:
Rebecca Gray Design

Design Project Manager:
Rik Moore

Internal and Cover Designer:
Jody Gittinger

Cover Images:
© PhotoDisc, Inc.

Printer:
Phoenix Color/Book Technology Park

COPYRIGHT ©2004
by South-Western, a division of Thomson Learning. Thomson Learning™ is a trademark used herein under license.

Printed in the United States of America
2 3 4 5 06 05 04 03

ISBN: 0-324-17193-5

Library of Congress Control Number: 2003100043

ALL RIGHTS RESERVED.
No part of this work covered by the copyright hereon may be reproduced or used in any form or by any means–graphic, electronic, or mechanical, including photocopying, recording, taping, Web distribution or information storage and retrieval systems–without the written permission of the publisher.

For permission to use material from this text or product, contact us by
Tel (800) 730-2214
Fax (800) 730-2215
http://www.thomsonrights.com

For more information contact South-Western,
5191 Natorp Boulevard,
Mason, Ohio 45040.
Or you can visit our Internet site at:
http://www.swcollege.com

Brief Contents

Preface		xiii
To the Student		xxiii
Chapter 1	Economic Growth: An Introduction to Scarcity and Choice	1
Chapter 2	An Introduction to Economic Systems and the Workings of the Price System	27
Chapter 3	Inefficiency: The Pervasive Economic Problem	65
Chapter 4	Competitive Markets and Agriculture	93
Chapter 5	Market Power: Does It Help or Hurt the Economy?	127
Chapter 6	Air Pollution: Balancing Benefits and Costs	153
Chapter 7	Medical Care: Costs Out of Control?	175
Chapter 8	Crime and Drugs: A Modern Dilemma	197
Chapter 9	College Education: Is It Worth the Cost?	227
Chapter 10	Educational Reform: The Role of Incentives and Choice	247
Chapter 11	Social Security: Where Are We? Where Are We Going?	273
Chapter 12	Poverty: Old and New Approaches to a Persistent Problem	293
Chapter 13	Tracking the Macroeconomy	321
Chapter 14	Unemployment: A Recurring Problem	345
Chapter 15	Inflation: A Monetary Phenomenon	365
Chapter 16	Deficits, Surpluses, and Debt: Past, Present, and Future	401
Chapter 17	The Global Economy: Trade	427
Chapter 18	The Global Economy: Finance	443
Glossary		461
Index		469

Contents

Preface xiii
To the Student xxiii

Chapter 1
Economic Growth: An Introduction to Scarcity and Choice 1

International Perspective: China: Economic Growth and Poverty 3
Recent Growth Experiences 3
Sources of Economic Growth 6
   Production Possibilities for the Economy 7
   The Best Combination of Goods and Services: Consumption Versus Growth 10
   Resource Accumulation, Technological Improvements, and Efficiency Improvement 12
   The Importance of Productivity Growth 14
Productivity Growth: What Can We Expect in the "New Economy"? 15
Insights: Were the Good Old Days Really Better? 16
   The Contribution of Capital Intensity Growth: The New Economy? 18
   The Contribution of Technical Change: The New Economy? 18
Economic and Productivity Growth in Various Parts of the World 20
   Growth in Europe and Japan: Catching Up 20
   Developing Countries after 1950: Some Grow, Some Don't 22
International Perspective: Economic Freedom and Economic Growth in Developing Countries 23
Summary 24

Chapter 2
An Introduction to Economic Systems and the Workings of the Price System 27

Market Economic Systems: An Introductory Look 29
What Does an Economic System Do? It Coordinates 32
International Perspective: What Happened in China? 33
   The Division and Specialization of Labor 34
   Economic Coordination and the Market System 36
The Price System as Coordinator 36
   Demand 36
   Supply 39
   Putting the Pieces Together: Demand and Supply 41
Comparative Systems: An Introductory Sketch 44
   The Price System 44
   Information, Rationing, and Motivation in a Market Economy 45
   Information, Rationing, and Motivation in a Command Economy 48
   Systems and Coordination 49
Insights: Can Socialism Use the Price System? 50
Transitions to a Market Economy: Some Experiences 51
   Stable Prices and the Monetary System 51
   Other Economic Reforms 54
International Perspective: Cowboy Capitalism in Russia? 59
   Additional Thoughts on Transition Economies 61
Summary 62

Chapter 3
Inefficiency: The Pervasive Economic Problem 65

Introduction 65
Rules for Achieving Efficiency in Resource Allocation 66
The Competitive Market: An Example of Efficiency in Resource Allocation 66

Market Failure: Inefficiency in the Private Sector	68
Monopoly	*68*
External Benefits	*70*
Public Goods	*72*
External Costs	*72*
Nonexistent Markets	*74*
Incomplete Markets	*74*
Government Failure: Inefficiency in the Public Sector	75
Rent Controls	*75*
Agricultural Price Supports	*76*
Government-Subsidized Medical Care	*76*
Minimum Wage	*78*
Taxes	*78*
Insights: What Does Government *Really* Cost? The Practical Significance of the Efficiency Losses from Taxation	**85**
How Much Efficiency Do We Want?	85
Efficiency Versus Equity: Tax Trade-Offs	*85*
Efficiency Versus Innovation	*86*
International Perspective: Does More Government Mean Less Growth?	**87**
Efficiency and Equity	*87*
Efficiency Offsets to Inefficiency	*88*
Summary	88

■ Chapter 4
Competitive Markets and Agriculture   93

Demand and Supply Analysis	96
International Perspective: OECD Farm Policy: New Zealand Breaks the Mold	**97**
Other Demand Factors	*98*
Other Supply Factors	*101*
How Changes in Demand and Supply Affect Equilibrium Price and Quantity	103
Changes in Demand	*104*
Changes in Supply	*105*
Changes in Demand and Supply	*105*
U.S. Agriculture	106
Economic and Historical Characteristics	*106*
Competitive Markets and Economic Profits	*109*
Insights: What Does It Mean for a Farmer to Break Even?	**113**
U.S. Farm Policy	114
Price Floor	*114*
Output Constraints	*116*
Target Prices and Deficiency Payments	*117*
Insights: The Sugar Program: How Sweet It Is	**118**
Rent Seeking	*119*
Summary	120
Appendix: The Price Elasticity of Demand	**123**

■ Chapter 5
Market Power: Does It Help or Hurt the Economy?   127

Monopoly Analysis	128
Marginal Revenue	*130*
The Marginal Principle	*131*
Monopoly and Competition Compared	*132*
Market Power and Economic Efficiency	135
The Trend in Market Power	*135*
Barriers to Entry	*136*
International Perspective: The Battle Between American and Japanese Automobile Firms	**137**
OPEC: A Few Sellers Acting Like a Monopoly	138
Cartel Formation	*139*
The Determinants of Cartel Success	*140*
Problems of the OPEC Cartel	*141*
Do a Few Firms That Dominate a Market Have Market Power?	*145*
Market Power and Economic Growth	145
Government and Market Power	148
Insights: QWERTY Versus DSK: Can the Market Choose the Right Technology?	**149**
Summary	150

Chapter 6
Air Pollution: Balancing Benefits and Costs — 153

- The Principal Air Pollution Problems — 154
  - Urban Air Quality — 154
  - Acid Rain — 155
  - Global Warming — 155
  - Stratospheric Ozone Depletion — 155
  - Hazardous Air Pollutants — 156
- The Economic Perspective — 156
- **International Perspective: The Total Social Cost of the Automobile: Pollution and Much More — 158**
- Market Failure: Is Government Action Necessary? — 158
- Air Pollution Regulation: The Clean Air Act — 161
  - National Ambient Air Quality Standards (NAAQS) — 161
  - Emissions Limits — 161
  - Restricted Technology — 161
  - New Source Performance Standards — 161
  - Prescribed Fuels — 162
  - Offset Requirements — 162
  - Emissions Trading — 162
  - Prevention of Significant Deterioration — 162
  - Monitoring and Compliance — 162
- Effects of the Clean Air Act on Air Quality — 162
- The Economics of the Clean Air Act: Have We Gone Too Far? — 163
  - Benefits and Costs of the Clean Air Act, 1970 to 1990 — 164
  - Benefits and Costs of the Clean Air Act, 1990 to 2010 — 165
- Cost-Reducing Measures — 166
  - Emissions Taxes — 166
  - Marketable Pollution Permits — 167
- Limiting Global Warming: Emissions Permits in an International Context — 169
- **Insights: Carbon Taxes — 171**
- Summary — 171

Chapter 7
Medical Care: Costs Out of Control? — 175

- The Rising Cost of Medical Care — 176
- Why Health Expenditures Have Increased Relative to GDP — 176
  - The Cost Disease of the Services Sector — 177
  - Population Aging — 178
  - Income Elasticity of Demand for Health Care — 179
  - Increases in Insurance Coverage — 179
  - Technological Change — 180
- **Insights: The Medically Uninsured — 181**
- Is Technological Change in Medical Care Worth It? — 181
- Does the Medical System Provide the Right Amount of Medical Care? — 184
  - Third-Party Payments — 184
  - Physician-Induced Demand — 186
- **International Perspective: Another Hidden Cost of Third-Party Payments — 187**
  - Defensive Medicine — 189
  - Federal Tax Exemption for Health Insurance — 189
- Approaches to Reducing Wasteful Expenditures — 190
  - Managed Care — 190
  - Eliminating the Federal Tax Exemption for Health Insurance — 192
  - Health Care Vouchers — 193
- Summary — 193

Chapter 8
Crime and Drugs: A Modern Dilemma — 197

- Public Goods — 200
  - Government Enforcement of Property Rights — 200
- Crime and Crime Control — 201
  - An Economic Approach to Crime and Crime Control — 202

Insights: Police, Guns, and Crime	**205**
A Comparison of Crime Trends in the United States and England	*206*
Insights: An Introduction to the Scientific Method in Economics	**210**
Drug Legalization: Competing Views	210
Liberty: An Argument for Legalization	*210*
Paternalism: An Argument Against Legalization	*211*
Morality: An Argument Against Legalization	*211*
The Final Analysis	*212*
A Positive Analysis of Drug Policy	212
Does Increased Enforcement Work?	*215*
Unintended But Inevitable Consequences of Drug Prohibition	*216*
Unintended But Perhaps Avoidable Consequences of Drug Prohibition	*218*
Unintended Consequences of Drug Legalization	*219*
Evaluation: Hawks, Doves, and Owls	219
Competing Views in Practice	*219*
International Perspective: Dutch Drug Policy	**220**
Current Policy	*221*
Owlish Criticism	*222*
Insights: Alternatives for the United States	**224**
Summary	224

Chapter 9
College Education: Is It Worth the Cost? — 227

Analyzing the Investment Decision	228
Step One	*228*
Step Two	*229*
Step Three	*229*
Investing in a College Education: Monetary Benefits and Costs	230
Student PVNB and ROR	*232*
Social PVNB and ROR	*234*
Insights: Does Where You Go to School Matter?	**235**

International Perspective: Education and Economic Growth	**236**
Investing in a College Education: Nonmonetary Benefits and Costs	236
Nonmonetary Student Benefits	*236*
Nonmonetary Student Costs	*237*
Nonmonetary External Benefits	*237*
International Perspective: Rates of Return Around the World	**238**
Nonmonetary External Costs	*238*
Is Government Support Necessary?	238
Ensuring That Society Invests Enough in College Education	*239*
Ensuring That Student Borrowing Reflects the Social Risk of Default	*240*
Insights: The Demand for Education	**242**
Increasing Enrollment of Lower-Income Students	*242*
Summary	243

Chapter 10
Educational Reform: The Role of Incentives and Choice — 247

The Nature of the Problem	248
Arguments for Public Support of Schools	251
Insights: Jefferson, Smith, and Public Schools: Standards and Local Control	**253**
The Economics of Student Achievement	254
High-Stakes Testing	256
Insights: Setting Standards for Mathematics Achievement	**257**
The Economics of Investing in High-Stakes Testing	*259*
International Perspective: High-Stakes Testing in Japan	**261**
Investing in More Required Courses	*261*
The Economic Organization of Public Education	262
Decision Making and Markets	*263*
Decision Making and State-Owned Enterprises	*265*
Decision Making and Public Schools	*266*

Alternatives to the Current System of Public Education	268
Summary	270

Chapter 11
Social Security: Where Are We? Where Are We Going? — 273

Principal Features of Social Security	274
Who Pays the Social Security Tax?	276
Social Security and Early Retirement	278
Social Security and Household Savings	278
Individual Rates of Return	279
Is That All There Is to It?	282
The Long-Run Deficit	283
What Social Security Analysts Say	283
Are the Analysts Right?	284
International Perspective: Public Pension Plans in Trouble: The United States Is Not Unique	**285**
What Can Be Done About the Deficit?	286
Benefit Reductions	286
Revenue Increases	287
The Trade-Off for Individuals: Lower Deficits Mean Lower Rates of Return	289
Summary	290

Chapter 12
Poverty: Old and New Approaches to a Persistent Problem — 293

The Scope of the Problem	294
Antipoverty Effectiveness of Government Transfers	297
Insights: The Tide Has Risen, But Most Boats Have Not	**301**
Means-Tested Transfers and Income from Work	302
Food Stamps	302
Earned Income Tax Credit (EITC)	303
Insights: Welfare Reform: Then and Now	**304**
Temporary Assistance for Needy Families (TANF)	305
TANF + Food Stamps + EITC	306
Making Work Pay	307
Unemployment Policy	308
Childcare Assistance	309
Medical Protection	311
Minimum Wage	311
Wage Subsidies	311
Labor Market Discrimination Policy	312
Making Fathers Pay	315
Child Support Assistance	316
Child Support Assurance	317
Summary	317

Chapter 13
Tracking the Macroeconomy — 321

Gross Domestic Product (GDP)	322
Insights: Measured GDP and the Underground Economy	**323**
GDP's Components	324
Consumption	324
Gross Investment	324
Government Purchases	326
Net Exports	326
Nominal GDP, Real GDP, and the GDP Deflator	326
The Nation's Economic Performance	330
Insights: Real GDP and Social Welfare	**332**
Determining the Nation's Output and Price Level	333
Aggregate Demand	333
Aggregate Supply	337
Aggregate Demand and Supply Interaction	338
Insights: The Long Boom	**340**
Summary	342

Chapter 14
Unemployment: A Recurring Problem — 345

Costs of Unemployment	346
Economic Costs	346
Noneconomic Costs	346

Counting the Unemployed	347
Insights: Job Opportunities and Discrimination	**349**
Types of Unemployment	349
Frictional Unemployment	*349*
Structural Unemployment	*350*
Cyclical Unemployment	*350*
Full Employment	351
Policies to Reduce Unemployment	352
Reducing Cyclical Unemployment	*352*
International Perspective: Unemployment in Japan	**355**
Reducing Structural Unemployment	*355*
Reducing Frictional Unemployment	*356*
Unemployment and the Minimum Wage	357
Unemployment in Europe	359
Impediments to Hiring	*360*
International Perspective: More on European Labor Markets	**361**
Impediments to Accepting Employment	*361*
Conclusion	*362*
Summary	362

■ Chapter 15
Inflation: A Monetary Phenomenon 365

Defining Inflation	366
Measuring Inflation	366
The GDP Deflator	*366*
The Consumer Price Index	*366*
Calculating the Inflation Rate	*367*
Recent Experience	*368*
Effects of Inflation	368
The Redistribution of Income and Wealth	*368*
Inflation and Government	*372*
Inflation and Net Exports	*372*
Other Effects	*373*
Money and the Money Supply	374
Money's Function	*374*
The Money Supply	*374*
Insights: Currency Holdings and the Underground Economy	**375**
The Federal Reserve	*376*
Causes of Inflation	376
The Quantity Theory of Money	*376*
International Perspective: Deflation in Japan: The Reemergence of an Old Issue	**378**
Inflation Is a Monetary Phenomenon	*379*
Inflation as a Monetary Phenomenon: Two Qualifications	*380*
Labor Unions, Monopolies, and Inflation	*382*
Inflation and Policy	383
Monetary Policy	*383*
Insights: The Fed as Inflation Fighter	**384**
Fiscal Policy	*385*
Supply-Side Policies	*385*
Incomes Policy	*386*
Summary	388
Appendix: Money Creation and Monetary Policy	**391**

■ Chapter 16
Deficits, Surpluses, and Debt: Past, Present, and Future 401

Budgets and Budget Concepts	402
Historical Budget Perspective	403
Insights: From Deficit to Surplus	**404**
The Public Debt	405
International Perspective: The Relative Importance of Budget Deficits and Surpluses for Various Countries: 1998	**406**
Long-Run Budget and Debt Projections	408
The Incredible Shrinking Surplus	*408*
The Deficit and Debt in the Coming Decade	*410*
The Really Long Run	*412*
Measurement Issues	412
Inflation	*413*
Business Cycles	*414*
Government Investment	*415*
State and Local Government Deficits and Surpluses	*416*
Economic Effects of a Deficit	416
The Keynesian View: A Deficit Can Help to Cure a Recession	*416*

The Modern View: The Strength of the Cure Depends on How the Deficit Is Financed	417
The Burden of Debt	420
Taking Stock	422
Summary	423

Chapter 17
The Global Economy: Trade — 427

U.S. Participation in World Trade	428
Comparative Advantage and International Trade	429
Net Gains from International Trade	432
Insights: The Cost of Saving U.S. Jobs	**434**
Barriers to International Trade	434
Tariffs	*434*
Quotas	*435*
Voluntary Export Restraints	*435*
The Case for Free Trade	436
Decreasing Costs	*436*
Increased Competition	*436*
Diversity of Products	*436*
The Case for Protection	437
Infant Industry	*437*
National Defense	*437*
Save American Jobs	*437*
Cheap Foreign Labor	*438*
Reducing Trade Barriers	438
The Global Approach	*438*

International Perspective: The WTO: An International Conspiracy?	**439**
Insights: Trade Negotiations, Labor, and the Environment	**440**
The Regional Approach	*440*
Summary	441

Chapter 18
The Global Economy: Finance — 443

The Balance of Payments	444
Insights: The United States: The World's Largest Debtor	**445**
Exchange Rates and Their Determination	447
Flexible Exchange Rates	*447*
Fixed Exchange Rates	*450*
The Current International Financial System	452
The Case for Flexible Exchange Rates	452
International Perspective: The Euro	**453**
The Case for Fixed Exchange Rates	454
Should Capital Flows Be Controlled?	454
International Perspective: The Mexican Peso Crisis	**455**
The Asian Financial Crisis	457
Summary	457

Glossary	**461**
Index	**469**

Preface

Economics and Contemporary Issues, Sixth Edition, takes an issues approach to introductory economics. The result is a user-friendly textbook that illustrates how knowledge of economics will help students make more sense of the world. The economy affects us personally and socially. An understanding of the way it works is crucial in personal planning and in making political and social decisions.

This book examines major issues, such as those pertaining to education, medical care, Social Security, unemployment, inflation, and international trade. It provides answers to questions such as: Is education a good investment? What causes inflation? What are the benefits and costs of international trade? It also examines social and political phenomena that will have continued importance in the twenty-first century—the collapse of communism and central planning, the role of government in a modern economy, crime and drugs, poverty, and the failure of some economies to grow.

This textbook maximizes the advantages of the issues approach by examining issues that interest students, while developing core economic principles that provide penetrating insights and a basis for lifelong learning. An economic analysis of contemporary issues will often challenge students' deeply held beliefs about how the world works. Such challenges, combined with the analytical framework provided by economic theory, make this textbook ideal in a curriculum emphasizing critical thinking.

Students who study this textbook will develop an increased interest in economics, seeing it as important in understanding issues that affect them personally, as well as in understanding today's headlines. Experience has shown that students will often study additional economics as a result of using this book.

■ THE INTENDED AUDIENCES

One audience for this textbook is students enrolled in the growing number of one-term issues courses offered by economics departments, often as general education courses. This book contains enough economic theory, however, for the traditional one-term survey course in economics. It is also appropriate for use as a supplement in traditional two-semester principles courses or as a text for the economics part of social science survey courses. If the instructor adds other readings (and ample references are provided on the text's Web site), it can also be used as a core text in an upper-division issues or capstone course.

■ FEATURES

Economics and Contemporary Issues has several features that are important in an issues-oriented text:

- ■ Effective aids to self-learning
- ■ A balanced treatment of microeconomics and macroeconomics
- ■ A basic theory core
- ■ Up-to-date, comprehensive background information on each issue

- Flexibility in the sequencing of topics and issues
- An emphasis on globalization

Effective Aids to Self-Learning

The first route to self-learning is a clear, concise exposition of basic concepts. *Economics and Contemporary Issues* is readily understood by beginning students. Every sentence has been written with them in mind.

To understand economics, students must master its basic vocabulary. To facilitate this, key terms are highlighted when they first appear and defined in three places: the body of the text, the margin, and the glossary. In addition, each chapter ends with a list of the key terms introduced in the chapter as a reminder to the reader.

To help students master the standard tools of economic analysis, there is a judicious use of graphs and tables that are carefully explained both in their accompanying captions and in the text narrative. The initial graphs are constructed from accompanying data to help the beginner master this important tool of economic analysis.

"Insights" and "International Perspective" features are provided to supplement text material and to illustrate the broad applicability of economics. For instance, one feature discusses the well-known coffeehouses in the Netherlands and another asks whether the college a student attends makes a difference in future earnings.

Self-testing is an essential component of self-learning. Each chapter contains review questions (with answers in the *Instructor's Manual*), and a carefully constructed *Study Guide* is available. Each chapter provides a summary of important points.

Most of today's students are computer-literate and familiar with the Internet as a source of information. This text helps the student (and instructor) tap this resource by providing a large number of references to Web sites related to the issues addressed in this book. In addition, this edition provides text adopters with access to InfoTrac® College Edition, a database of more than a million articles. Keywords to help the reader search this database effectively are provided in the margins of the text.

A Balanced Treatment of Microeconomics and Macroeconomics

The analysis of macroeconomic issues is often slighted in issues books. Not in this one. Seven of the 18 chapters cover macroeconomic issues, including national income accounting, unemployment, inflation, the federal deficit and debt, the balance of payments and trade deficits, and economic growth. The microeconomic aspects of agriculture, monopoly power, medical care, crime, pollution, education, Social Security, and poverty are also examined.

A Basic Theory Core

Both the micro and macro parts of this book use a small number of understandable, yet powerful, economic concepts and models.

In the microeconomics chapters, supply-demand and marginal analysis are used extensively. Models of competitive and monopolized markets are developed. The distinctions between social and private benefits and costs are used to analyze market and government failures. Measures of consumers' and producers' surpluses are used to illustrate efficiency gains and losses.

The basic macroeconomics tool is the model of aggregate supply and aggregate demand. Use of this versatile model enables beginning students to understand the forces that determine output, employment, the price level, and the effects of alternative fiscal and monetary policies (such as proposed changes in taxes and the Federal Reserve discount rate).

Up-To-Date, Comprehensive Background Information on Each Issue

Our experience shows that most beginning students know too little about economic history, data, and institutions. An issues course must fill this void by providing the information necessary for understanding the nature and significance of the problems addressed.

Essential information can be provided by both the instructor and the textbook. Although there is no perfect substitute for an instructor who seeks new information and provides it to students, this book simplifies the instructor's quest by providing current and comprehensive background information on each issue and references to additional resources.

Flexibility in the Sequencing of Topics and Issues

This book is structured so that microeconomic principles (and issues) are examined before macroeconomic principles are introduced. Macroeconomic principles and issues can be studied first, however, because they have been designed to be independent of the micro chapters. Instructors who prefer to teach macro first, following an introduction to the market system, can do so by assigning Chapters 1 and 2 and then going to Chapter 13.

Chapters 1 and 2 provide the foundation for Chapters 3 through 12. Chapter 13 provides the foundation for Chapters 14 through 17. A one-term principles survey course could include Chapters 1 through 5, 13 through 17, and other selected chapters to fit the instructor's interests.

An Emphasis on Globalization

Chapter 1 examines economic growth from an international perspective, and the last two chapters analyze international trade and finance. Today, however, most issues have a global dimension, and the book reflects this. In almost every chapter, students will find an "International Perspective" feature or a section dealing with an international dimension of the issue.

■ NEW TO THIS EDITION

Economic problems and issues change rapidly, requiring frequent updating of data and information. For the sixth edition of *Economics and Contemporary Issues*, we have gone back to the drawing board in more than one-half of the chapters to produce a new edition that is truly different from its predecessors. Of course, we have at the same time done the standard things expected in a revision: updating all of the data, tables, and figures; clarifying explanations; and including more examples and illustrations. The boxed material that complements the main text by providing additional "Insights" and "International Perspective" has also been revised and expanded. The number of references to Web sites has been greatly expanded as well, reflecting the growing importance of the World Wide Web as a source of current, comprehensive, and readily accessible information on the issues addressed in this book.

The power of the Internet has been multiplied in this edition by providing text adopters with access to InfoTrac® College Edition, a database of more than a million articles. Keywords are provided in the margins of the text.

CHAPTER 1 ECONOMIC GROWTH: AN INTRODUCTION TO SCARCITY AND CHOICE. We begin the text with an analysis of economic growth, arguably the most important economic and social phenomenon of the last 200 years. The title reflects the fact that even rapidly growing economies are not relieved of the necessity to choose among alternative uses of scarce resources. The relationships between growth, scarcity, and choice are illustrated with the production possibilities curve. The critical role of productivity in the growth process is highlighted, and recognition is given to the development of the "New Economy" as a source of recent U.S. economic growth.

CHAPTER 2 AN INTRODUCTION TO ECONOMIC SYSTEMS AND THE WORKINGS OF THE PRICE SYSTEM. This chapter compares the experiences of the Eastern European transition economies to the benchmark of a competitive market system. This edition places increased emphasis on the importance of property rights and honesty (minimum corruption) in determining the success of the transition to a market economy. The discussion and graphics are simplified by focusing most of the discussion on four representative countries.

CHAPTER 3 INEFFICIENCY: THE PERVASIVE ECONOMIC PROBLEM. This is a new chapter, although it incorporates some of the material that was in Chapter 12 of the previous edition. It identifies inefficiency as an important (rivaling unemployment, inflation, growth, and so forth) and pervasive (endemic to both the private and public sectors of the economy) problem. The problem is illustrated with a number of examples of inefficiency in the private sector, or market failure, and a number of examples of inefficiency in the public sector, or government failure. Most of the examples are illustrated graphically. Efficiency losses and gains are identified and measured as areas in supply and demand diagrams.

CHAPTER 4 COMPETITIVE MARKETS AND AGRICULTURE. As indicated by the change in title (from the former "US. Farm Policy: How Is It Changing?"), this chapter has an increased emphasis on competitive markets. This allows users to downplay agriculture and agricultural policy and expand on the economics of competitive industries. The chapter has a discussion of the 1996 Farm Reform Bill and argues that we are continuing with the failed policies of the last 50 years, but it does not go into detail on the new farm bill. An appendix on the price elasticity of demand has been added.

CHAPTER 5 MARKET POWER: DOES IT HELP OR HURT THE ECONOMY? This analysis of the economics of market power continues to focus heavily on two important contemporary examples, the Microsoft antitrust case and the OPEC oil cartel. Both examples are brought up to date. The role of the OPEC cartel in influencing oil prices at the end of the 1990s is thoroughly discussed.

CHAPTER 6 AIR POLLUTION: BALANCING BENEFITS AND COSTS. This chapter has been completely revised, and more than one-half of the material is new to this edition. The economists' perspective on the pollution problem has been condensed into one supply-demand diagram that illustrates and quantifies the efficiency losses from pollution. This diagram is also used to illustrate how the Coase theorem works. New data are presented on the progress made in reducing air pollution under the Clean Air Act, and there is a new section on the benefits and costs of the Clean Air Act. The section on pollution taxes and emissions permits has been completely revised, using an example that illustrates the cost savings possible with these approaches.

CHAPTER 7 MEDICAL CARE: COSTS OUT OF CONTROL? This chapter has also been thoroughly revised, prompting the change in title from "Health Care Reform: How Much?" in the previous edition. The chapter begins with a new section in which the rising cost of medical care is discussed in terms of Baumol's Cost Disease Theory, population aging, income elasticity of demand for health care, increases in insurance coverage, and technological change. This is followed by another new section in which the benefits and costs of technological change—the primary cause of rising medical costs—are examined. Evidence indicates that the benefits of medical advances far outweigh the costs; other evidence indicates that economic incentives induce Americans to overuse medical care at the same time that they are reaping the benefits of medical advances.

CHAPTER 8 CRIME AND DRUGS: A MODERN DILEMMA. This chapter continues to highlight the economic approach to crime. The primary change from the previous edition is the addition of a discussion of the economics of controlling terrorism.

CHAPTER 9 COLLEGE EDUCATION: IS IT WORTH THE COST? This chapter remains built around a numerical example of the benefits and costs to a typical college graduate from investing in a college education. New diagrams based on this example have been added, however. The discussion of nonmonetary benefits and costs has been condensed, and the section "Is Government Support Necessary?" has been thoroughly revised. A new supply-demand diagram has been added to illustrate why government support of higher education is necessary to achieve the right number of college graduates. A new time series diagram has been added to illustrate how a student loan affects the payoff from investing in a college education.

CHAPTER 10 EDUCATIONAL REFORM: THE ROLE OF INCENTIVES AND CHOICE. This chapter has been thoroughly rewritten, but its purpose remains that of demonstrating how economics can illuminate the debate on reforming U.S. elementary and secondary education. Special attention continues to be given to the role of tougher educational standards and the possibilities afforded by greater reliance on educational choice.

CHAPTER 11 SOCIAL SECURITY: WHERE ARE WE? WHERE ARE WE GOING? Much of this chapter is new. All of the data have been updated to reflect the latest program information, and all of the projections have been changed to reflect the *2002 Annual Report* of the Social Security Trustees. A numerical example has been added to illustrate the principal steps taken to determine Social Security retirement benefits. New time series diagrams have been added to illustrate the benefits and costs of investing in Social Security, and the latest projections of the Social Security Trust Fund. There is a new discussion of the relationships between the Social Security surplus, national saving and investment, and the long-run Social Security deficit. The section on privatization has been rewritten, and a new section has been added to illustrate that the rate of return on Social Security depends on how the long-run deficit problem is solved.

CHAPTER 12 POVERTY: OLD AND NEW APPROACHES TO A PERSISTENT PROBLEM. About two-thirds of the material in this chapter is new. Several time series diagrams have been added to illustrate trends in the official poverty rate, the poverty rates of selected groups, the pre-transfer poverty rate, the antipoverty effectiveness of government transfers, and the relationship of poverty and unemployment. There is a new analysis of the relationship between means-tested transfers and income from work, featuring the separate and combined effects of food stamps, the earned income tax credit, and the Temporary Assistance for Needy Families (TANF) program. New sections have been added on childcare assistance and medical protection for individuals making the transition from TANF to work. The final section throws the spotlight on efforts toward a more effective system of child support.

CHAPTER 13 TRACKING THE MACROECONOMY. The basic text of this chapter continues to be devoted to the elements of measuring national output and the price level. The primary changes in the sixth edition are in the "Insights" features. The feature on GDP and social welfare incorporates a discussion of the economics of terrorism. The material on the underground economy has been thoroughly updated, and there is a new feature on the "long boom"—the nearly uninterrupted expansion in the U.S. economy from 1982–2001.

CHAPTER 14 UNEMPLOYMENT: A RECURRING PROBLEM. The basic aggregate demand–aggregate supply framework of this chapter remains intact. A new "International Perspective" feature on European labor markets has been added.

CHAPTER 15 INFLATION: A MONETARY PHENOMENON. This chapter continues to analyze inflation using both the equation of exchange and the aggregate demand–aggregate supply model. There is a new "International Perspective" feature on the increasingly important problem of deflation in Japan.

CHAPTER 16 DEFICITS, SURPLUSES, AND DEBT: PAST, PRESENT, AND FUTURE. This is the most thoroughly revised chapter in the text. The overall objective of the revision is to address the budget deficit issues currently being debated in Washington, using the concepts and measures featured in that debate. The chapter incorporates a new section on the components of the federal budget that distinguish between different types of deficits and surpluses. There is an expanded historical review of the deficit and recent surpluses, using new time series diagrams. There is another new section that explains and illustrates the relationships between the public debt, the national debt, and the net budget balance. Projections of net budget balances and the public debt are incorporated in the text for the first time, as is a discussion of the controversial issue of how to measure the deficit.

CHAPTER 17 THE GLOBAL ECONOMY: TRADE. This chapter provides updated data, and a new time series diagram of the trade deficit has been added. The most substantive change, however, is the addition of a supply-demand analysis of the gains from trade, using the concepts of consumers' and producers' surpluses. This part of the chapter gives readers a final opportunity to reinforce their knowledge of what economists mean by efficiency losses and gains, and it provides additional support for a policy of free trade.

CHAPTER 18 THE GLOBAL ECONOMY: FINANCE. This chapter also provides updated data, as well as several changes to clarify the exposition of difficult points. As in the previous edition, the chapter contains discussions of fixed exchange rates, flexible versus fixed exchange rates, the European Monetary Union, the euro, and the Asian financial crisis.

■ Supplementary Materials

- **http://edgmand.swlearning.com** is the address of the text's Web site. It provides access to Online Quizzes, CyberProblems, each chapter's list of Suggestions for Further Reading, the Internet addresses for each chapter, Author Updates, links to the EconApps (Economic Applications) Web site, and much more.

- **http://econapps.swlearning.com** is the site of South-Western's dynamic economics Web features: EconNews Online, EconDebate Online, and EconData Online. Organized by topic and searchable by topic or feature, EconApps are easy to integrate into the classroom. EconNews, EconDebate, and EconData all deepen your understanding of theoretical concepts through hands-on exploration and analysis of the latest economic news stories, policy debates, and data. These features are updated on a regular basis. The Economic Applications Web site is complimentary to every new book buyer via an access card packaged with the books. Used-book buyers can purchase access to the site at http://econapps.swlearning.com.

- InfoTrac® College Edition is packaged as an access card with every new copy of the textbook. It is a fully searchable online university library containing complete articles and their images. Its database allows access to hundreds of scholarly and popular publications—all reliable sources—including magazines, journals, encyclopedias, and newsletters.

- The *Study Guide*, revised by Dale G. Bails, Christian Brothers University, contains a list of objectives, review of key terms, quantitative problems, true/false questions, multiple-choice questions, and fill-in questions for each chapter.

- The *Instructor's Manual/Test Bank*, thoroughly revised by Hamid Azari-Rad of SUNY, New Paltz, provides instructors with useful tools for planning their courses and preparing exams. The *Instructor's Manual* includes chapter overviews, teaching objectives, key terms, teaching suggestions, additional references, detailed lecture outlines, and answers to review questions. The *Test Bank* provides a variety of exam questions and problems in true/false, multiple-choice, and essay and discussion formats. Chapters also include critical thinking multiple-choice questions. Both are available—password protected—to instructors on the text's Web site.

- ExamView – Computerized Testing Software contains all of the questions in the printed test bank. This program is an easy-to-use test creation software compatible with Microsoft Windows. Instructors can add or edit questions, instructions, and answers, and select questions by previewing them on the screen, selecting them randomly, or selecting them by number. Instructors can also create and administer quizzes online, whether over the Internet, a local area network (LAN), or a wide area network (WAN).

- The *Instructor's Activity Manual* contains group activities to facilitate understanding of each chapter. Each activity is designated by type, topic, class size, and time needed, and includes instructions and relevant questions. The activity manual is available on the text Web site, password protected, to instructors.

- Encouraging students to use the World Wide Web to further their studies can sometimes be a challenge. *Economics HITS on the Web* is designed to do just that. This supplement offers a reader-friendly

- overview of the various aspects of the Internet and gives students a good grasp on browsing, searching, and communicating online with more than 50 links that are specific to the study of economics.

- The shape, pace, and spirit of the global economy has been greatly impacted by the events that occurred on September 11, 2001. *9/11: Economic Viewpoints* offers a collection of essays that provide a variety of perspectives on the economic effects of these events. Each essay is written by one of South-Western's economics textbook authors, all of whom are highly regarded for both their academic and professional achievements. This unique collaboration results in one of the most cutting-edge resources available to help facilitate discussion of the impact of 9/11 within the context of economics courses.

ACKNOWLEDGMENTS

This book is a joint product of three authors who are long-time colleagues and friends. We did not produce this book alone, however, and we greatly appreciate the contributions of users, colleagues, reviewers, students, and the editorial team at Thomson Learning/South-Western. We appreciate all comments that we receive and rely on them as we make revisions. Please let us know how we can improve our book.

Many of the changes in this edition were made in response to the careful reviews and thoughtful suggestions of Joseph Horton (University of Central Arkansas); John P. Manzer (Indiana University–Purdue University, Ft. Wayne); Melanie Marks (Longwood College); Gary L. Stone (Winthrop University); Randall Holcombe (Florida State University); Daphne T. Greenwood (University of Colorado, Colorado Springs); and Manjuri Talukdar (Northern Illinois University). We are grateful for their help, as well as for the help of the reviewers of previous editions: Michael Applegate (Oklahoma State University); Steven Petty (College of the Ozarks); Michael W. Babcock (Kansas State University); Fred J. Ruppel (Eastern Kentucky University); Gary L. Stone (Winthrop University); Rebecca Summary (Southeast Missouri State University); John P. Blair (Wright State University); Eric Brooks (Orange County Community College); Bruce Domazlickey (Southeast Missouri State University); Robert B. Harris (Indiana University–Purdue University at Indianapolis); Philip J. Lane (Fairfield University); John Merrifield (University of Texas–San Antonio); Paula Smith (University of Central Oklahoma); John Scott (Northeast Louisiana University); Charles Stull (Western Michigan University); Millicent Taylor (University of Southern Colorado); Ugur Aker (Hiram College); Gale Blalock (University of Evansville); James R. Frederick (Pembroke State University); Christopher Lingle (Loyola University–New Orleans); Edwin A. Sexton (Virginia Military Institute); Ranbir Varma (Long Island University); Pauline Fox (Southeast Missouri State University); Neil Garston (California State University–Los Angeles); Doug McNeil (McNeese State University); John Pisciotta (Baylor University); Steve Smith (Rose State College); Barbara Street (Chaminade University–Honolulu); Hyung C. Chung (University of Bridgeport); Emily Hoffman (Western Michigan University); George Murphy (University of California–Los Angeles); Larry Sechrest (University of Texas–Arlington); and Alden Smith (Anne Arundel Community College).

We also gratefully acknowledge the guidance, support, and encouragement provided by the Thomson Learning/South-Western team, including Peter Adams, Susan Smart, Libby Shipp, and Janet Hennies.

They have greatly facilitated the development of this edition. We certainly could not have done it so quickly—or so well—without them.

All of our children have by now reached the age where the preparation of yet another edition does not come at the expense of time spent with them, but our wives—Judy, Julie, and Carol—continue to willingly bear some of the opportunity costs of this project. Their support and encouragement has been an invaluable asset, and they deserve the biggest thanks of all.

Michael R. Edgmand
Ronald L. Moomaw
Kent W. Olson

To the Student

Welcome to *Economics and Contemporary Issues*, Sixth Edition. This book will teach you how the American economy works and how economic incentives and institutions are related to important social problems. In the process of learning these things, you will sharpen your critical thinking skills.

The issues and problems you will study command the attention of concerned citizens and policy makers. Many of them will continue to be important long after you have finished this book; some will, hopefully, fade away. The principles you learn here, however, will help you to understand new problems and issues as they appear.

In examining each issue, we develop and apply the principles essential for understanding its economic dimensions, and then evaluate current and alternative approaches to dealing with it. The first step is the province of positive economics; the second is the focus of normative economics. Positive economics explains and predicts economic phenomena; normative economics selects social goals and evaluates policy alternatives according to how well they achieve these goals. This approach reflects the dual purpose of economics: to discover how the world works and to determine how it can be improved.

The basic normative questions posed throughout this book are whether government action is necessary to solve social problems and, if so, what policies should be adopted. For example, the chapter on air pollution considers whether curbing pollution—a social goal—can be accomplished efficiently by the private sector alone and concludes that it cannot. Existing regulations and proposed policies are then evaluated to determine which of them are most likely to improve the situation. We use a similar approach in examining the other issues. We hope the net result will be a greater appreciation of the strengths and weaknesses of both the private and public sectors of the economy.

To achieve lasting benefits from economics, and to do well in your course, plan to go beyond merely memorizing this material. Learn, in addition, how to apply the principles and models developed in the text. We have attempted to write clearly and concisely so that you will understand the important principles. You will greatly enhance your ability to apply these principles, however, by answering the questions at the end of each chapter and by working through the *Study Guide*, by Dale G. Bails, that has been written to help you master the material.

Finally, no single text can provide all of the information that pertains to the issues that we address. You can learn much more by examining the Web sites we suggest throughout the text, by exploring recent articles using the InfoTrac® subscription that accompanies your purchase of this text, and by accessing the book's Web site at **http://edgmand.swlearning.com**.

CHAPTER 1

Economic Growth: An Introduction to Scarcity and Choice

Outline:

Recent Growth Experiences

Sources of Economic Growth
- Production Possibilities for the Economy
- The Best Combination of Goods and Services: Consumption Versus Growth
- Resource Accumulation, Technological Improvement, and Efficiency Improvement
- The Importance of Productivity Growth

Productivity Growth: What Can We Expect in the "New Economy"?
- The Contribution of Capital-Intensity Growth: The New Economy?
- The Contribution of Technical Change: The New Economy?

Economic and Productivity Growth in Various Parts of the World
- Growth in Europe and Japan: Catching Up
- Developing Countries After 1950: Some Grow, Some Don't

Two truly important documents that provided a basis for economic growth appeared in 1776. Thomas Jefferson's *Declaration of Independence* and Adam Smith's *Wealth of Nations* established guidelines for the growth of political and economic freedom during the next 2 centuries. These masterpieces emerged from ideas associated with the great artistic, political, and religious renewals that awakened Europe, drawing the Middle Ages to a close. The values of the *Declaration of Independence* as implemented and developed in the U.S. Constitution and Abraham Lincoln's Gettysburg Address are beacons of political and economic freedom. As we shall see, these freedoms promote economic prosperity. Drawing from the same awakening, Adam Smith, the pioneering British economist, explained that an economy organized by markets and emphasizing economic freedom promotes the wealth of nations more effectively than one organized by a government plan.

Understanding how individuals interacting in an economy create prosperity has attracted many people to economics because they know that it is the key to improving the human condition. For instance, Alfred Marshall, another eminent British economist, was drawn to study economics by his concerns about poverty, saying, "[I] visited the poorest quarters of several cities and walked through one street after another, looking at the faces of the poorest people. Next, I resolved to make as thorough study as I could of Political Economy."[1] Marshall's "thorough study" resulted in his *Principles of Economics*, an unusual book in two ways. First, it was the dominant economics textbook for several decades at the beginning of the twentieth century, and it still exerts influence. Second, much of its analysis was based on Marshall's own contributions to economics as a discipline. Understanding economics because of its importance for the general welfare continues to fascinate economists. Nobel Prize–winning economist Robert Lucas of the University of Chicago noted the influence on his career of economic growth's ability to extinguish poverty. "Once I started thinking about economic growth," he said, "I could think of little else."

Economic growth has transformed life in industrialized countries. The material standard of living in the United States, for instance, is incomprehensibly higher for the average citizen than it was in 1776. Measures of health, education, longevity, and material goods show vast improvement. The rich and famous 200 years ago enjoyed a material life vastly superior to that of the average person in most dimensions—health, diet, entertainment, housing, education, and so on. Abraham Lincoln's early childhood in a small, windowless cabin with few books and little time for schooling contrasted sharply with the luxurious lifestyle enjoyed by Thomas Jefferson's children at Monticello. Today, most people in the United States have a material standard of living that far surpasses that enjoyed by the wealthy 200 years ago.

The ability of compound growth to raise living standards is immense. *Gross domestic product (GDP)* is one measure of an economy's total output or production of goods and services.[2] Consequently, one measure of the standard of living is GDP per capita (person). Since 1820, GDP per capita in the United States has increased more than 21 times, although the growth rate was just 1.7 percent per year. This is comparable to income rising from $1,500 per person to over $30,000. The growth rate in Japan during this period was higher, 1.9 percent per year. This seemingly similar growth rate was enough to increase GDP per capita in Japan 36 times. In 1820, GDP per capita income in the United States was 100 percent greater than in Japan; in 1998, it was just 36 percent greater. Big oaks grow from small acorns.

Understanding the sources of persistent economic growth is crucial. Why does one country's output grow at 1.5 to 2 percent a year over long periods while another country's output grows at less than 0.5 percent a year or even shrinks? People in the first country prosper and in the second country struggle. From 1820 to 1998, Japan went from low-income status with GDP per capita 1.25 times India to advanced status with per capita GDP 11 times that of India. One country becomes a high-income country, and the other remains low income.[3]

---

[1] As cited in William Breit and Roger Ransom, *The Academic Scribblers* (Fort Worth: Dryden, 1982) Rev. ed., 20.

[2] The GDP concept is developed in Chapter 13. For now, we can view it simply as an output measure. We have adjusted GDP for any general rise in prices or inflation. Because of this adjustment, all of the measures are measures of real activity.

[3] Computed from data in Angus Maddison, *The World Economy: A Millennial Perspective* (Paris: Development Center—OECD, 2001).

INTERNATIONAL PERSPECTIVE

CHINA: ECONOMIC GROWTH AND POVERTY

About 200 million Chinese escaped absolute poverty over a 20-year period beginning in 1978. *Absolute poverty* is defined as a situation where people lack the minimum necessary food, clothing, and shelter to survive and live a healthy life. Millions of others living just above subsistence level in China made substantial improvements in their standard of living over this same period: More people managed to escape dire poverty than in any other 20-year period. Adjusted for inflation, per capita GDP more than tripled from 1978 to 1999. Using the 1985 price level, it increased from about $800 per person to more than $2,700 per person.[a]

An article in *The Economist* put this change in perspective a few years ago by noting that it was equivalent to one-half of the people living in the United States escaping absolute poverty. People in China had much more to eat, were much better clothed, and had many more of life's other necessities in 1991 than in 1978. To quote *The Economist*, "grain consumption of the average Chinese went up by 20%; seafood consumption twofold; pork consumption 2½ times; egg consumption more than threefold. . . . In 1981 each 100 urban households in China averaged less than one colour television among them; ten years later it was 70. In 1981 there were six washing machines for each 100 city households; in 1991 more than 80. . . ."[b]

Adam Smith, Robert Lucas, and Alfred Marshall had it right. Prosperity is heavily influenced by political economy. Rapid economic growth is the only way that this huge number of people could escape poverty. The rest of the current chapter analyzes economic growth, and Chapter 2 considers why some economies prosper and others do not.

[a]Global Development Network Growth Database.
[b]Jim Rohwer, "The Titan Stirs," *The Economist* 325 (11/28/1992), 2.

We hope that you agree that the lessons that we might learn about easing world poverty provide more than enough reason to start our journey in economics with economic growth. Jumping directly into this topic, we will use some concepts that are more thoroughly explained in later chapters. You will acquaint yourself with these concepts here, and as we go through the course, you will grasp them more completely. Initially, we look at several countries' economic growth from 1960 to 1998, emphasizing three points.

1. Economic growth in the high-income countries slowed after 1972 but may have picked up in the United States after 1990.
2. GDP per capita in some countries may be catching up to that in the United States.
3. Some countries are experiencing significant economic growth, but others appeared trapped with low growth rates and low standards of living.

We will discuss the sources of growth in the U.S. context and then expand the discussion to include other countries that have experienced significant economic growth and those that have failed to do so.

INFOTRAC
College Edition

Keywords: *sources of economic growth*
Use your InfoTrac password to look up articles on these topics at
http://www.infotrac-college.com

RECENT GROWTH EXPERIENCES

As seen in Figure 1.1A, since 1960 the United States has had a substantially lower per capita GDP growth rate than China, Korea, and Japan, and a slightly lower rate than Brazil, India, and the United Kingdom.[4]

---

[4]These countries provide a variety of experiences to compare with that of the United States. Japan's economy stagnated in the 1990s, but its overall performance from after World War II to the present has been exceptional. Korea's economy experienced a serious setback in the late 1990s; nevertheless, its performance also has been exceptional. The data underlying Figures 1.1 and 1.2 are from the Global Development Network Growth Database, prepared by William Easterly and Mirvat Sewadeh of the World Bank, and are available at http//www.worldbank.org.

FIGURE 1.1A Annual Growth Rates of Real GDP per Capita: 1960–1999

Since 1960, GDP per capita in China, Japan, and South Korea has grown much faster than in the United States, the United Kingdom, India, and Brazil.

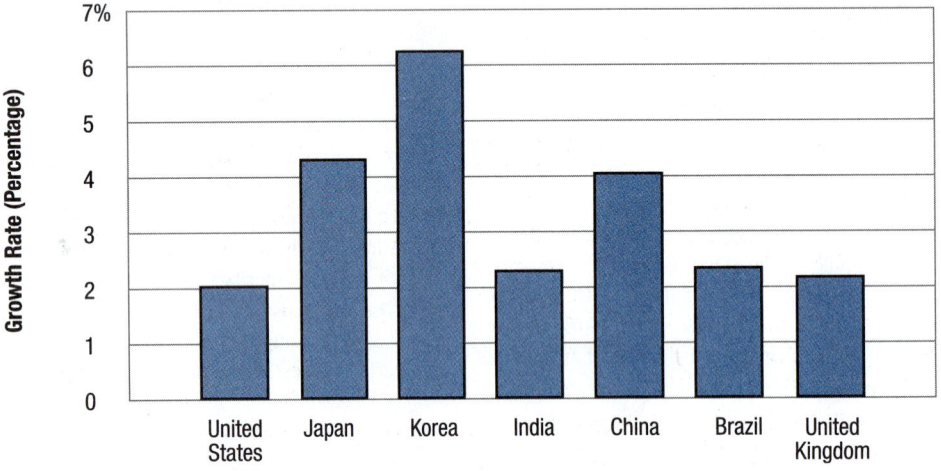

SOURCE: Global Development Network Growth Database, William Easterly and Mirvat Sewadeh, World Bank; available at http://www.worldbank.org/research/growth/GDNdata.htm.

The United States' 2 percent growth rate, however, was greater than its 1.7 percent growth rate from 1820 to 1998, a rate that propelled its citizens to their current living standards. Japan's 4+ percent growth rate and the Republic of Korea's 6+ percent rate show that higher growth rates are possible. The Korean growth rate doubles GDP per capita in about 12 years compared with a 36-year doubling time for the United States.[5] If output per person doubled every 12 years in Korea and every 36 years in the United States, Korea would soon surpass the United States. India, on the other hand, grew slightly faster than the United States, but only for 40 years. It would have to grow at that rate for about 100 more years to reach Korea's current level of GDP per capita, and it would fail to overtake any of the countries shown in Figure 1.1A.

Figure 1.1B shows the growth rates for these countries for three periods: 1960 to 1973, 1973 to 1990, and 1990 to 1999, allowing us to consider changes in growth rates. For instance, four countries—the United States, Japan, Brazil, and the United Kingdom—had significant decreases in their growth rates after 1972. This experience, shared with most industrialized countries, has caused much concern about economic stagnation. Looking at the 1990s, the United States and Japan present the stark alternatives facing other high-income countries: Will their growth accelerate as in the United States or decelerate to low levels as in Japan?

Lower-income countries provide similar conflicting examples. Brazil's growth rate has fallen substantially since 1972, with both India and China enjoying successive increases in their growth rates. Although

---

[5] A useful rule of arithmetic is that the doubling time for something growing at a compound rate can be approximated by dividing the rate into 72. For example, if an investment is earning compound interest of 8 percent, it will double in 9 years.

FIGURE 1.1B Growth Rates: 1960–1973, 1973–1990, and 1990–1999

After 1972, growth rates of GDP per capita slowed in the United States, Japan, the United Kingdom, and Brazil; increased in China and India; and changed little in South Korea.

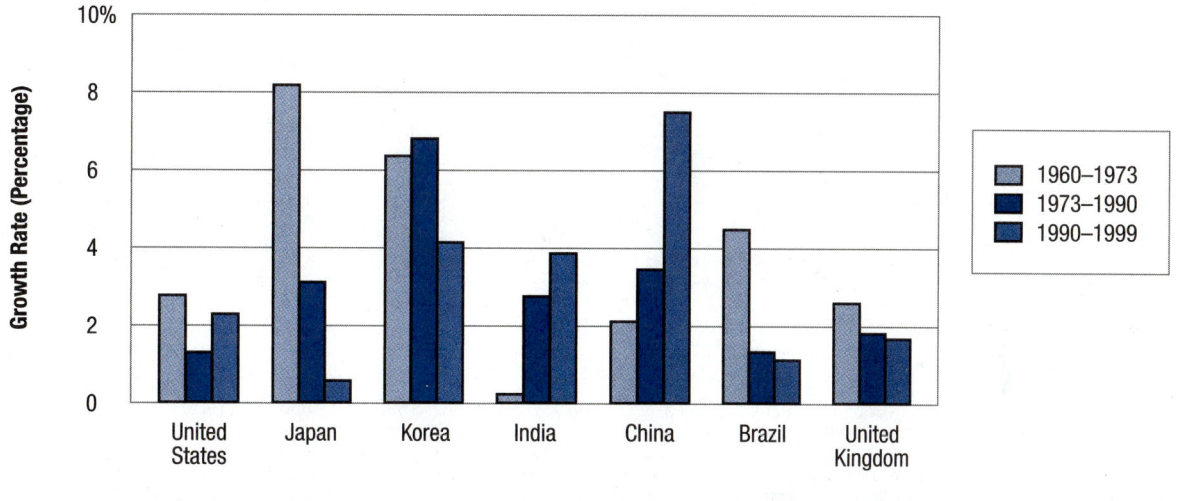

SOURCE: Global Development Network Growth Database, William Easterly and Mirvat Sewadeh, World Bank; available at http://www.worldbank.org/research/growth/GDNdata.htm.

Korea's performance declined in the 1990s, much of this decline was due to what appears to have been a temporary downturn in the late 1990s; its per capita GDP growth appears to have accelerated since 1999 (not shown in the figure).

Can a poor country catch up with the advanced countries? Japan and India were at similar levels of development in 1820. Japan grew 0.3 percentage points faster than the United States during the next 170 years and achieved development similar to that of the United States by 1990. The prospect of gradually becoming a high-income country over a 200-year span, however, gives little hope to current generations. Fortunately, the Japanese experience shows that the process need not take 200 years. In fact, partly because of World War II, the United States' average income advantage compared to Japan's grew until about 1950. In 1820, U.S. per capita GDP was twice that of Japan's; by 1950 it was five times greater. By the 1960s, as Figure 1.2A shows, Japan's GDP per capita was overtaking that of the United States. With its rapid growth rate, by 1990 Japan's GDP per capita was within about $4,000 of that of the United States. If the trends of the 1980s had continued, Japan would—as could be seen by extending the lines in the figure—be close to overtaking the United States. The Japanese experience is not unique; other East Asian countries, such as Korea, also have experienced rapid growth. The figure shows that Korea was closing the relative gap with the United States in the 1960s. In 1960, Korea's per capita GDP was about one-tenth that of the United States; by 1995, it was almost one-half. Japan's economy has stagnated since 1990. With growth continuing and perhaps accelerating in the United States, the U.S. advantage has grown. Similarly, other Asian countries, such as Korea, experienced economic crises in the late 1990s that resulted in the United States' advantage again growing.

FIGURE 1.2A Japan and Korea: Catching Up with the United States?

Until the mid-1990s, GDP per capita in Japan and Korea was catching up with that of the United States.

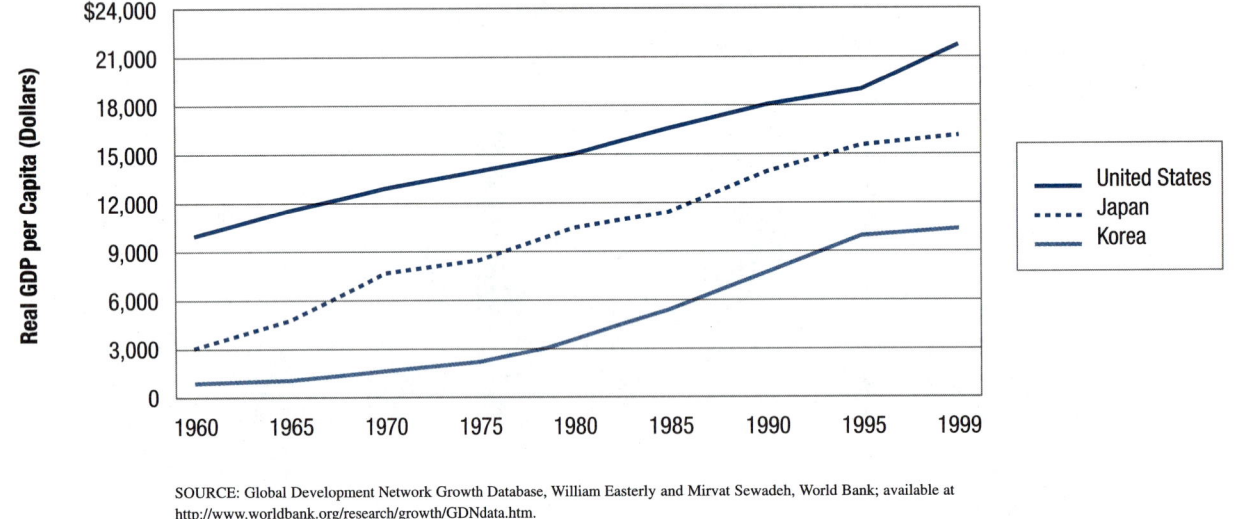

SOURCE: Global Development Network Growth Database, William Easterly and Mirvat Sewadeh, World Bank; available at http://www.worldbank.org/research/growth/GDNdata.htm.

INFOTRAC
College Edition

Keywords: *economic growth in Asia*

Use your InfoTrac password to look up articles on these topics at
http://www.infotrac-college.com

Unfortunately, not all countries have been successful at economic growth since 1960. Figure 1.2B shows GDP per capita for the United States, Brazil, Korea, and China since 1960. Although each country has closed a small part of its relative gap with the United States, the absolute difference between Brazil (China) and the United States continues to grow. China's per capita production has increased about five times since 1960, and Brazil's has more than doubled. Although this is encouraging, it is slow compared with countries such as Korea, which has increased its per capita GDP by a factor of 10. In 1960, Brazil's GDP per capita was larger than Korea's; by 1999, Korea's GDP per capita had more than doubled Brazil's.

In this overview of recent growth in selected countries, at least three questions arise.

1. What are the sources of economic growth in the United States, and what are the prospects?
2. What are the similarities among countries that are successful in growth?
3. What are the similarities among countries that have failed to achieve steady economic growth?

These are big questions, and we can only touch on some of the factors involved.[6] In the next section, we turn to the sources of growth.

■ Sources of Economic Growth

Understanding economic growth requires us to consider society's production possibilities. Economic growth occurs when an economy produce more goods and services, a greater GDP, as time goes by. This section first develops the production possibilities curve and then applies it to economic growth.

---

[6]Answers to these questions are controversial. See the suggested readings at http://edgmand.swlearning.com.

FIGURE 1.2B Low-Income Countries Converging?

Although Korea may be catching up with the United States, Brazil and China are not.

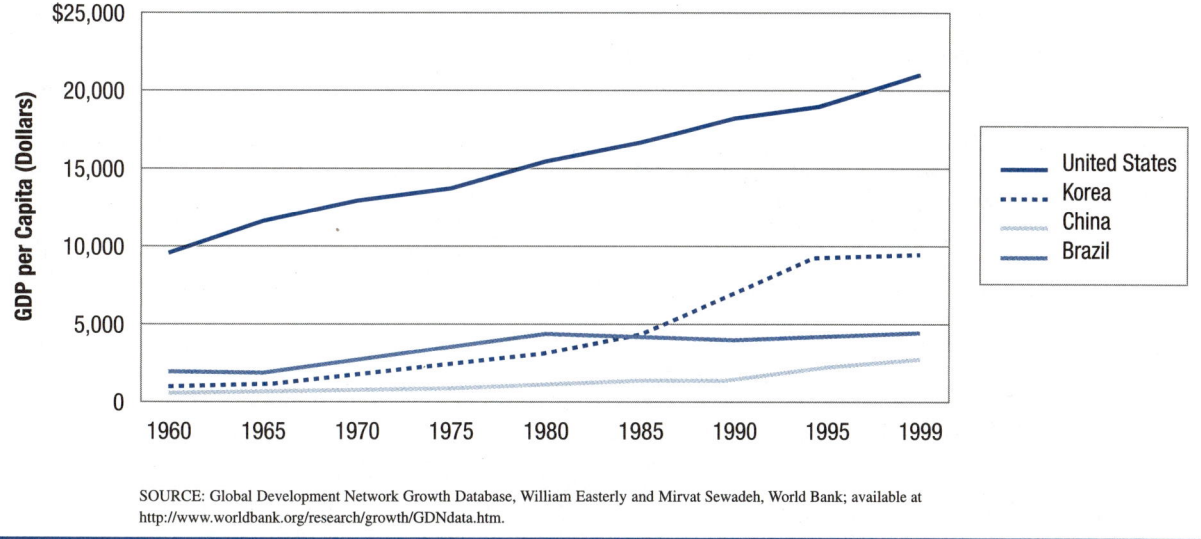

SOURCE: Global Development Network Growth Database, William Easterly and Mirvat Sewadeh, World Bank; available at http://www.worldbank.org/research/growth/GDNdata.htm.

Production Possibilities for the Economy

An axiom of economics is that the resources required to produce goods and services are scarce relative to peoples' aggregate wants for goods and services. The primary resources are land, labor, and capital. **Land** includes all natural resources and raw materials, such as agricultural land and silicon. **Labor** includes efforts and services of people in the production of goods and services. **Physical capital** consists of durable produced goods, such as factories, industrial equipment, highways, and airports. **Human capital** has characteristics of both labor and capital. It consists of the knowledge and skills embodied in people, as applied to the production of goods and services. Like physical capital, it is produced in the economy. Using resources otherwise available for producing current goods and services to produce, say, a new building, produces physical capital. Likewise, applying resources, say, teachers, video equipment, buildings, and the time of students themselves, to students' education produces human capital. *Technology* can be thought of as recipes that show how to use the resources to produce goods and services.

People require food. In a world of *scarcity*, to produce more food, we must produce less of something else. Producing less of something else, say, clothes, releases resources to produce the extra food. Every economic system must choose what goods and services to produce, how to produce those goods and services, and to whom to distribute them. These choices largely determine the growth rate of GDP per capita.

Suppose for simplicity that the choice is between just two alternatives: food and cars. Table 1.1 introduces a useful way to analyze this choice. The economy is assumed to produce only food and cars. We assume that all resources (land, labor, and capital) are fully employed and that the best technology is used. If all resources are used for food production, no cars can be produced and, we assume, 100 million bushels of food is the most possible. Now suppose that we decide to produce 100 thousand cars, which would require

Land – Resources found in nature, such as land, water, forests, mineral deposits, and air.

Labor – All physical and mental abilities used by people in production.

Physical Capital – Man-made, durable items used in the production process, such as factories, equipment, dams, and transportation systems.

Human Capital – The knowledge and skills embodied in people, as used in the production process.

TABLE 1.1	Hypothetical Data for Production Analysis

We assume that (1) the economy produces only cars and food, (2) all resources (land, labor, and capital) are fully employed, and (3) the best technology is used. If all resources are devoted to food production, no cars can be produced. This economy can produce 100 million bushels of food—combination A. If, for example, it chose to produce combination B—100 thousand cars and 95 million bushels of food—resources that could have produced 5 million bushels of food must be transferred to car production. The opportunity cost of the cars is what was given up to produce them: the value of 5 million bushels of food.

	Number of Cars per Year (Thousands)	Bushels of Food per Year (Millions)
A	0	100
B	100	95
C	200	85
D	300	70
E	400	50
F	500	25

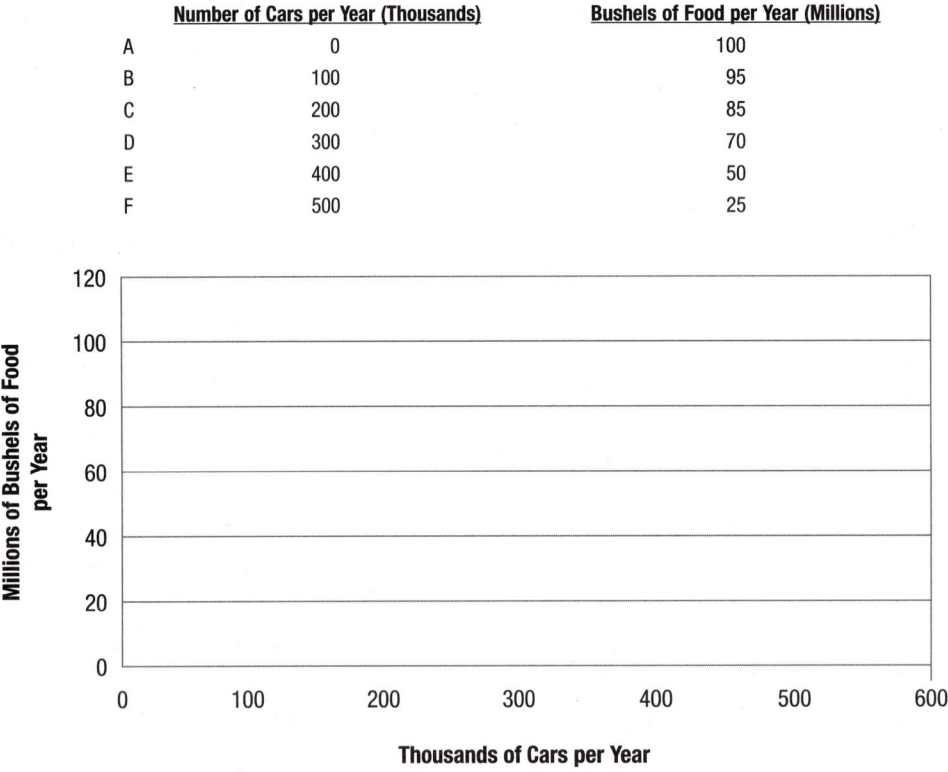

Opportunity Cost – The value of the best alternative sacrificed when a choice is made.

that we take resources from food production and use them for car production. Obviously, to produce the cars implies that we cannot produce as much food—we have taken resources away from food production. If we produce 100 thousand cars, the table, by assumption, shows that 95 million bushels is the most food that can be produced. Consequently, to produce the first 100 thousand cars requires resources that could have produced 5 million bushels of food. The **opportunity cost** of the cars is the value of what is given up to produce them: the value of 5 more million bushels of food, given that you have 95 million bushels. Each combination of cars and food in the table can be produced only if all resources are used with the best technology. Consequently, each combination represents an appropriate use of resources. The best choice from all these combinations depends upon the preferences of the people in the economy.

A diagram makes it easier to understand. Let's summarize the information by plotting it on the chart in Table 1.1, which you may want to reproduce in your notebook. The horizontal axis measures thousands of cars per year, and the vertical axis measures food production in millions of bushels per year. Start by finding one of the points, say, D. To do so, go to the point on the horizontal axis that represents 300 thousand cars and draw a vertical dashed line to the top of the chart. According to the table, if 300 thousand cars are produced, the most food that can be produced is 70 million bushels. Draw a horizontal dashed line from 70 (on the vertical axis) to the right edge of the chart. The intersection of these two dashed lines is point D, representing 300 thousand cars and 70 million bushels. Plot the other points from the table in the same way and connect them with a smooth curve. In your diagram, point A shows the maximum amount of food that can be produced per year—100 million bushels—if all resources are used for food production and the best methods of producing food are used. This curve in your diagram, which you can compare with Figure 1.3, is a **production possibilities curve**. It shows the maximum combinations of the goods or services that can be produced using available resources. A maximum combination is the largest quantity that can be produced of one good for a given quantity of the other good. Each combination on AG assumes full employment of labor, capital, and land and the use of the **best technology**—the technology that requires the fewest resources to produce a given combination of goods and services—in this case, cars and food.

The intervals on the horizontal axis associated with successive moves down the curve from A to B, C, D, E, and F correspond to equal increases in car production: Each interval equals 100 thousand cars. The corresponding vertical intervals measure the reduction in food production for each increase in car production. An examination of Figure 1.3 shows for successive equal increases in car production the corresponding decrease in food production gets larger. An equal increase in car production requires that more food be given up; the **marginal cost** of a car increases as more cars are produced.

Production Possibilities Curve – A curve showing the maximum combinations of two goods or services that can be produced by an economy when resources are fully used and the best technology is applied.

Best Technology – The technology that requires the fewest resources to produce a given combination of goods and services.

Marginal Cost – The opportunity cost of producing an additional unit of a good.

FIGURE 1.3 The Production Possibilities Curve Applied to the Choice Between Food and Cars

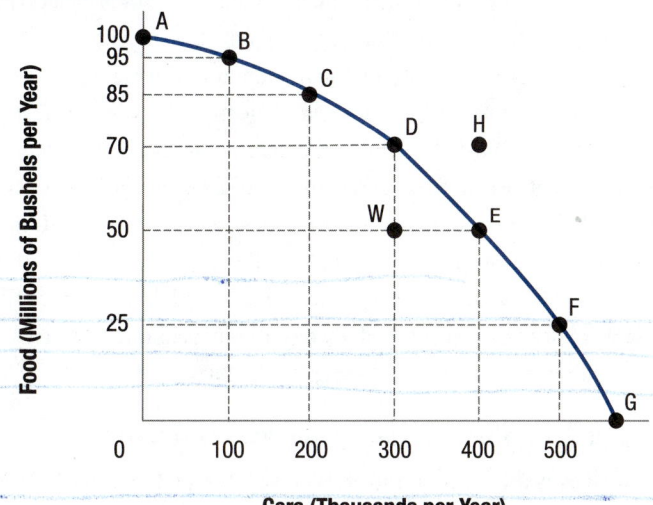

The economy is assumed to produce only food and cars. Along the production possibilities curve, marked by points A to G, resources are used fully, and the best technology is applied. The combinations of food and cars, A to G, are the largest possible combinations. Starting at point A, production of food must decrease by 5 million bushels (from 100 million to 95 million) to produce the first 100 thousand cars. Production of the next 100 thousand cars requires giving up 10 million more bushels of food. The value of food given up with each move down the curve is the marginal cost of cars, which increases with each successive increase in car production.

Marginal cost increases as resources are transferred out of food production and into the production of cars because resources that are particularly suited to food production must be converted to a use, car production, for which they are less well suited. At first, the types of land, labor, and capital that are better suited to car production than to food production will go to expanding car production. Thus, relatively little food production is sacrificed. Eventually, however, car production can be expanded only by taking more fertile cropland, more skilled farm labor, farmers who are especially good at farming, factories that are better suited for making farm implements than cars, scientists who are better at creating fertilizers and pesticides than at developing new methods of combustion, and engineers and construction workers who are better at designing and building farm structures than designing cars. Thus, equal increases in car production require ever-increasing sacrifices of food production.

Marginal cost also increases for equal increases in car production, because the value of a bushel of food increases as more cars and less food are produced. Why? Suppose at combination A (0 cars, 100 million bushels of food) people are well fed. No one places a high value on one more or one less bushel of food. Now consider combination F (500 thousand cars, 25 million bushels). People will now pay more for an additional unit of food, because they are not as well fed. As more cars are produced, an increasing number of bushels of food has to be sacrificed for one more car, and the value per bushel of food sacrificed is greater.

The economy can also be at a point like W inside the production possibilities curve, producing 300 thousand cars and 50 million bushels of food. If so, the economy is operating with waste or inefficiency. Either resources are unemployed or the best technology is not being used. To see the inefficiency or waste, note that the economy could move to point E, making 100 thousand more cars without giving up any food, getting something—more cars—for nothing. The move is made by using previously unemployed resources or switching to best technology.

Point H, a combination of 400 thousand cars and 70 million bushels of food, is outside the curve. Unlike W or any other point on the curve, H cannot be reached, given the available resources and technology. It illustrates **scarcity**, the common situation of all economies, in that with finite resources and a given technology, it is impossible to produce more of everything. In a given year, an economy is limited to points on (or inside) its production possibilities curve. If, for a given amount of one good, people want more of another good than is possible to produce, *scarcity exists and choices must be made*. The production possibilities curve shows that for 70 million bushels of food, the maximum numbers of cars that can be produced is 300 thousand. If everyone wants to have the same amount of food and someone wants one more car(s), scarcity exists. As previously mentioned, economists believe that scarcity—and, therefore, the necessity of choice—is the human condition. To reach point H, the economy must grow either because best technology improves or the economy acquires more resources: land, labor, and capital. The land and labor available to an economy are not influenced much by day-to-day economic decisions. Thus, economic decisions that increase growth are those that increase capital, improve technology, or both.

Scarcity – The common situation for all economies, in which aggregate wants exceed the economy's ability to meet them because of limited resources.

The Best Combination of Goods and Services: Consumption Versus Growth

The best combination of goods and services is the one that fulfills wants as completely as possible. Figure 1.4, which assumes that the economy produces capital goods (tractors) and consumption goods (popcorn) helps clarify what this requires. In the figure, a move down the curve results in an increase in the number

FIGURE 1.4 Production Possibilities and Economic Growth

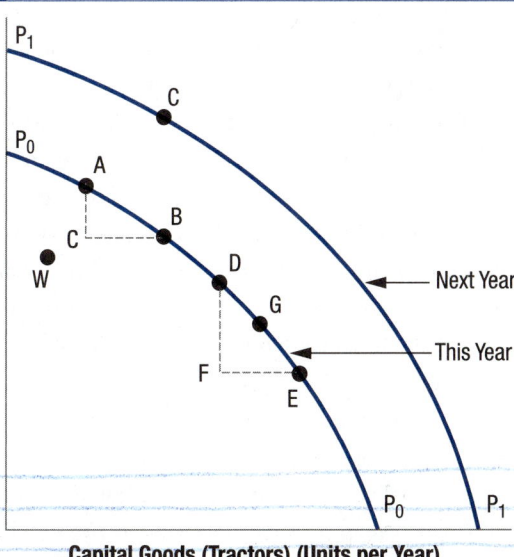

An economy's output can increase if its production possibilities curve shifts to the right, as illustrated by the shift from P_0P_0 to P_1P_1. It can be caused by resource accumulation or technological improvement. Efficiency improvement, a movement from W to P_0P_0, can also result in economic growth.

of tractors (capital goods) produced at the expense of a reduction in the amount of popcorn (consumption goods) produced. The opportunity cost of the tractors is the value of the popcorn not produced. For instance, suppose at A it is necessary to sacrifice 1,000 bushels of popcorn to produce another tractor. The marginal cost of the tractor is the value of the 1,000 bushels of popcorn. What is the **marginal benefit**? In this example, the marginal benefit of the tractor is the value of the increased popcorn that can be produced in the future because more capital equipment—tractors—will be available in the future.

Marginal Benefit – The satisfaction or value received from consumption of an additional unit of a good or service.

It pays to move down the production possibilities curve from A to B and so on—producing more capital goods by sacrificing the production of consumption goods this year—so long as the marginal benefit of increased consumption goods in the future is greater than the marginal cost of a reduction in consumption goods today. Marginal cost increases and marginal benefit decreases as we move down the curve. The move from A to B and the move from D to E increase tractor production by the same amount. Inspection of the figure shows, however, that the sacrifice of popcorn production is greater with the second move. As discussed, some resources are more suited to the production of one type of good; others are more suited to another type. As land, labor, and capital are transferred from the production of consumption goods to capital goods, the first increments transferred will be those with the greatest advantage in producing capital goods. As the process continues, the resources will have smaller and smaller advantages in producing capital goods. Because it takes more resources to produce another unit of the capital good, greater amounts of the consumption good are sacrificed to increase capital good production. Marginal cost also increases because of the reduction in the quantity of consumption goods; with fewer consumption goods, the value of the last unit sacrificed of the consumption good increases. As people give up more popcorn, they become hungrier and hungrier and place a higher value on a little more popcorn. As capital good production increases, more units of the consumption good are sacrificed, and the value of present consumption goods increases.

As more capital goods are produced, the marginal benefit of another tractor (another unit of the capital good) decreases. The increment in the future production of consumption goods—the marginal benefit of the capital good—falls because of declining **marginal product** of capital. The marginal product of capital is the increase in the production of consumption goods that will occur if one more unit of capital is used. Marginal product declines because the increased amount of capital is used with the fixed amount of labor and land. At first, as more capital is available in the future, the extra output of the consumption good will be large because the additional capital allows better use of labor. But, as more and more tractors are added to a fixed labor force and a fixed amount of land, the increases in popcorn production will shrink. There may be no one to drive the new tractor, or there may be no land to plow! Besides the declining marginal productivity of capital, future increments of consumption goods are worth less because a greater amount of consumption goods becomes available in the future.

This analysis identifies, in principle, the best combination of consumption and capital goods to produce. So long as the marginal benefit of an additional capital good is greater than the marginal cost, it increases net benefit (benefit − cost) to produce more capital goods. The value of future consumption gained is greater than the value of the present consumption lost. These values depend both on the amounts sacrificed and gained and on the values that individuals place on present and future consumption. At some combination, marginal benefit just equals marginal cost; this is the best combination. This analysis shows why more growth is not always better: More growth requires a reduction in present consumption.

Marginal Product — The change in output associated with a one-unit change in an input, for example labor.

Resource Accumulation, Technological Improvement, and Efficiency Improvement

Long-term economic growth occurs if an economy increases its capacity to produce GDP—increases its production possibilities. An economy's production possibilities increase if it accumulates more resources: land, labor, and capital. Labor and capital have greater potential for expansion than land, so we will restrict attention to labor and capital growth. Production possibilities also grow if the best technology improves. **Technological improvement** means that the same amount of goods and services can be produced with less labor and capital or equivalently that more goods and services can be produced with the same quantity of labor and capital. Finally, economic growth occurs if an economy moves from using less than the best technology to using better or the best technology. This process, called **efficiency improvement**, also allows more output with a given amount of resources. Economic growth is possible if (1) more resources are accumulated, (2) technology improves, or (3) efficiency improves.

Technological Improvement — An improvement in best technology that allows more output with a given amount of resources.

Efficiency Improvement — A change from less than the best to the best technology. It allows more output to be produced with the same resources.

Figure 1.4 explains the three sources of economic growth using production possibilities curves. In this analysis, the economy produces two goods, a capital good and a consumption good, with two resources, labor and capital. This year's production possibilities curve, P_0P_0, shows the combinations of consumption and capital goods that can be produced if the economy has full employment of its labor and capital and uses the best technology. For instance, it could produce a combination represented by A, which emphasizes the production of consumption goods relative to capital goods. The only ways that this economy could grow, so that it has the potential to produce more of both goods in the next year, would be for it to have more labor and capital resources or for it to experience technological improvement. Thus, resource accumulation or technological improvement could cause the production possibilities curve to shift to P_1P_1, next year.

RESOURCE ACCUMULATION. Resource accumulation consists of increases in the labor force or in the stock of physical or human capital available to the economy. Population growth is the major source of labor-force growth. GDP has to grow faster than population for the average standard of living, GDP per capita, to improve. Just as with the marginal product of capital, the marginal product of labor decreases as more labor is added to a fixed amount of capital. Therefore, population (labor force) growth, with capital and technology fixed, will result in successively smaller increases in GDP. Although labor-force growth causes GDP to grow, it will not cause GDP to grow fast enough to increase living standards. Capital accumulation, on the other hand, can increase living standards because the use of more capital permits an increase in GDP without any increase in the use of labor. Capital accumulation may consist of producing more capital equipment (physical capital) or increasing education and training (more human capital).

Unfortunately, investment in physical and human capital is not free. Suppose that this year the economy is producing at A in Figure 1.4. For a given rate of technological improvement and labor-force growth, assume that capital goods production at A, added to this year's capital stock, is just enough to push next year's production possibility curve to P_1P_1. Now suppose that people believe that this growth is too slow. The only way to have more growth in this circumstance is to increase the production of physical and human capital: to move from A to, say, point B. To have more growth, which increases consumption in the future, it is necessary to sacrifice consumption goods today. Greater economic growth is not necessarily desirable because it means sacrificing in the present for the future.

TECHNOLOGICAL IMPROVEMENT AND EFFICIENCY IMPROVEMENT. Another source of economic growth is technological improvement. Improvements in best technology shift the production possibilities curve: P_0P_0 to P_1P_1 in Figure 1.4. Accordingly, more of both goods can be produced with the same amount of resources. A movement from A to C could occur because of scientific and engineering advances. Examples of advances in science that have expanded production possibilities are numerous. The basic discoveries related to DNA have resulted in improved plant varieties and new drugs. The development of transistors and semiconductors revolutionized calculation and communication. The introduction of the videocassette recorder and player (VCR) transformed the entertainment industry.

New economic institutions are another source of technological improvement. Henry Ford's profitable development of assembly-line (mass) production, Sam Walton's profitable creation of a new way of retailing, and Eiji Toyoda's profitable introduction of flexible manufacturing (the Toyota Production System) are all examples of technological improvements that go beyond what we typically think of as scientific and engineering advances. E-commerce is a recent example. Its rapid introduction and widespread acceptance is transforming the way some people shop. Residents of small towns, including college towns, can obtain goods quickly without leaving their homes. Suppose, in the past, a student or professor would make a 150-mile trip twice a year, especially to buy books. The cost of access to the books each time would be the cost of driving a car 150 miles, say $45, and the value of the driving time, say $60. E-commerce based on new technology and new economic institutions could save this individual up to $105 per trip.

Efficiency improvements are another source of economic growth and are, in some ways, similar to technological improvements. Improvements in efficiency lead to greater output from a given amount of inputs, but they do *not* shift the production possibilities curve. For instance, an economy may be operating inside its production possibilities curve, at a point such as W in Figure 1.4. Failure to use the best available technology is one source of inefficiency. Elimination of such inefficiencies allows the economy to move closer to the production possibilities curve. Such a change means that greater output is obtained from a given amount of resources. (Remember that the production possibilities curve assumes that the amounts of labor and capital are fixed.)

Growth based on technological or efficiency improvements can cost much less than growth based on capital accumulation. Technological improvements can occur as a by-product of investment in human and physical capital. A higher level of education or greater use of capital equipment can lead to scientific discoveries, to discoveries of new ways of doing old tasks, and to new ways of organizing economic activity (for example, e-commerce). Similarly, as educational levels increase, and as firms compete more with firms from other parts of the country and of the world, we may learn about and borrow state-of-the-art production techniques; efficiency will improve. Growth caused by such factors might not require much sacrifice of present consumption. Although not free, sometimes such growth can be close to it. Nevertheless, achieving growth through technical progress is uncertain, and it can be costly because efforts to generate technical progress may fail.

The Importance of Productivity Growth

For over 200 years, people in the United States have seen the average standard of living of the next generation improve. Each generation has had a brighter future. Before then (and now in many parts of the world), each generation faced the same economic prospects. The answer to the question—What changed?—expresses the importance of productivity growth.

> *The change that gave better economic prospects for succeeding generations is that productivity growth increased and continued over the entire period, allowing compensation per hour to increase.*

Growth in productivity or output per hour of labor is important because it limits how fast compensation per hour can grow. Real output per hour, as Figure 1.5 shows, grew at about 3 percent per year from 1960 to 1973. From 1973 to 1990, it grew by about 1.3 percent a year, substantially less than one-half the previous rate.[7] (Although these differences in percentages may seem small, they compound rapidly over a short time period.) Correspondingly and consequently, compensation per hour grew at about the same rate as output per hour—productivity—in both periods, illustrating the close dependence of compensation (wages and benefits) on productivity. Specifically, from 1960 to 1973, real compensation per hour in private business grew at an annual rate of about 3 percent. At this rate, it doubles about every 24 years. Following labor productivity growth downward, compensation growth fell to slightly more than 1 percent per year from 1973 to 1990—about one-third the previous rate—increasing the doubling time to 60 years.

---

[7]To analyze long-run productivity growth, it is necessary to study long time periods so that short-run variations are minimized. Therefore, rather than examining decades, we examine 1960 to 1973, 1973 to 1990, and 1990 to 2001.

CHAPTER 1 ■ ECONOMIC GROWTH: AN INTRODUCTION TO SCARCITY AND CHOICE

FIGURE 1.5 Annual Growth in Hourly Productivity and Compensation

Labor productivity—output per hour—grew at close to 3 percent a year from 1960 to 1973, but at just more than 1 percent from 1973 to 1990. From 1990 to 2001, its growth increased to 2 percent per year. Hourly compensation followed output per hour closely. (Hourly compensation is compensation per hour adjusted for inflation using the relevant implicit price deflator.)

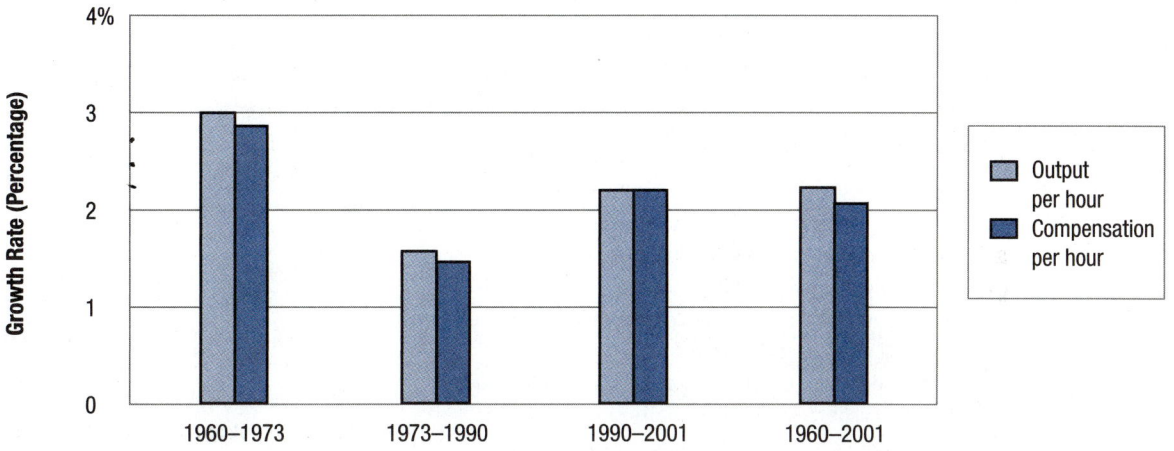

SOURCE: Computed from U.S. Department of Labor, *Monthly Labor Review*, selected issues or data from the U.S. Department of Labor; available at http://stats.bls.gov.

Since 1990, productivity and thus compensation have grown faster—at a 2 percent annual rate. Although this is the same as the average rate over the period since 1960, some observers believe that more rapid growth since 1995 (not shown in the figure) suggests that we are in a "new economy" and expect that we may be at the beginning of a long period of rapid economic growth. In the 1970s and 1980s, many families saw their incomes grow, but for many the growth occurred because more family members were working more hours. Income growth because of higher wages—the experience of the 1950s and 1960s—is much preferred to income growth because of working more hours. What are the chances that we have created a new economy that will provide every increasing opportunity? The answer depends upon what is happening to productivity growth.

■ PRODUCTIVITY GROWTH: WHAT CAN WE EXPECT IN THE "NEW ECONOMY"?

To understand what has happened to productivity growth, we must understand its components. The growth of labor productivity can be divided into one part caused by the growth of capital (human and physical) relative to labor and another part caused by technological and efficiency improvements. Human capital accumulation contributes to growth because it means that workers have greater education and experience. Physical capital accumulation contributes to growth because it means that workers

INSIGHTS

WERE THE GOOD OLD DAYS REALLY BETTER?

In the early 1970s, bookkeepers in most small businesses collected and paid bills using manual calculators, typewriters, and ledger sheets. Letters were typed with electric typewriters, some of which had built-in correction devices. Medical procedures such as cataract removal required long hospitalization and recovery. Cars and televisions required frequent repair. Today, most businesses process information with computers. Laser and other new surgical techniques have reduced recovery time for many surgeries, limiting many previously long-stay procedures to outpatient surgeries. Cars, televisions, and many other goods require much less maintenance and repair.

Individual and family consumption of goods and services has increased substantially since 1970. The average family has more living space with more conveniences—air conditioning, dishwashers, home entertainment systems, and so on. International travel, attendance at cultural events, eating out, and visits to national parks have all mushroomed. A Rip Van Winkle who fell asleep in 1972 would be amazed at the changed production techniques, the greater labor productivity in the service sector, and the increased consumption of goods and services today.[a]

Imagine Rip Van Winkle's surprise if you told him that real earnings per hour had fallen since 1973 and that technical change in the service sector had stopped after 1980. He might question your accuracy or your veracity. Yet the most frequently quoted government statistics on these issues suggest exactly that. What is wrong with this story? As we will discuss in Chapter 15, the problem may be with the way inflation is measured. In December 1996, the Advisory Commission to Study the Consumer Price Index (the Boskin Commission) in a report to the Senate Finance Committee claimed that changes in the consumer price index (CPI) overstate changes in the cost of living by 1.1 percent per year.[b] If the CPI is used to adjust earnings for inflation, real earnings fell by 13 percent from 1973 to 1995. Correcting for the errors in the CPI reported by the Boskin Commission, however, real earnings actually grew by 13 percent. Moreover, instead of falling by 4 percent, real median family income grew by 24 percent. As we argue in Chapter 15, the CPI has several problems that lead to inaccuracies when we use it to adjust earnings for changes in the cost of living.

For instance, if a consumer switches from buying at a department store to buying at Wal-Mart, he will pay lower prices. Even if the service at Wal-Mart is not up to that of the department store, the consumer benefits. He must, or he would revert to the department store. The CPI, however, does not treat as price decreases lower prices that result from switching to a discount store. It also ignored lower gasoline prices associated with shifts to self-service gasoline in the 1970s and 1980s. Presumably it ignores lower prices associated with shopping on the Web.

The tremendous increase in the number of new and improved products also causes the CPI trouble. New products enter the index every 10 or 15 years, depending on the frequency of revision. Microwave ovens and VCRs were commonly used for 10 years before they became part of the index. During that 10 years, quality improved and prices fell by almost 100 percent. These price decreases never affected the CPI because they occurred before the goods were part of the index. Similarly, quality improvements are not fully accounted for in the CPI.

In summary, according to the Boskin Commission, we can add 1 percent per year to wages, earnings, or income, if it has been adjusted by the CPI. U.S. living standards have improved more than some statistics show.

---

[a] See Michael J. Boskin, "Prisoner of Faulty Statistics," *The Wall Street Journal* (December 5, 1996); and W. Michael Cox and Richard Alm, "The Good Old Days Are Now," *Reason* (December 1995).

[b] Advisory Commission to Study the Consumer Price Index, "Toward a More Accurate Measure of the Cost of Living," Report to the Senate Finance Committee, December 1996.

Capital Intensity – The ratio of capital to labor in production; units of capital per unit of labor.

Technical Change – Technological and efficiency improvements combined.

have more capital to work with—more equipment. From this point on, we refer to the growth of human and physical capital relative to labor as growth in **capital intensity** and to technological and efficiency improvements as **technical change**. In Figure 1.6 the height of each bar shows that output per hour (labor productivity) in the private business sector grew at 3, 1.3, and 2 percent per year during the periods 1960 to 1973, 1973 to 1990, and 1990 to 2000, respectively. The bottom part of each bar gives the contribution of increased capital intensity, which was about 1 percentage point per year in each period. Increases in human capital intensity, reflecting a more experienced and better educated labor force, added from 0.2 to 0.4 percentage points to the part of productivity growth due to capital intensity over these periods, with the remainder due to increases in physical capital intensity. Technical change, the top part of the bar, contributed the remainder: 2.1, 0.3, and 0.9 percentage points.[8]

Figure 1.6 provides a visual description of the levels and changes in labor productivity's growth rate and that of its components. The heights of the bars trace a U-shape—labor productivity first falls dramatically, reflecting the growth slowdown that began in the 1970s, and then rises tantalizingly, suggesting that rapid growth may be emerging. Comparing the two components of productivity growth—technical change and capital intensity—we see that the contributions of capital increase slightly from one period to

FIGURE 1.6   **U.S. Productivity Growth and Its Components: 1960–2000**

The figure provides information about the private business sector. Each bar represents a particular time period. The height of the first bar set shows labor productivity growth in the first period. The two segments of the bars show the contributions of technical change and capital intensity to the productivity growth. Moving from the first time period to the second, we see the slowdown in productivity growth. Notice the sharp decline in the contribution of technical change. Notice also that in the first period technical change accounts for more than half of the productivity growth and that in the second period it accounts for much less than half. Movement to the third and fourth bars shows the gradual increase in productivity growth and the contribution of technical change.

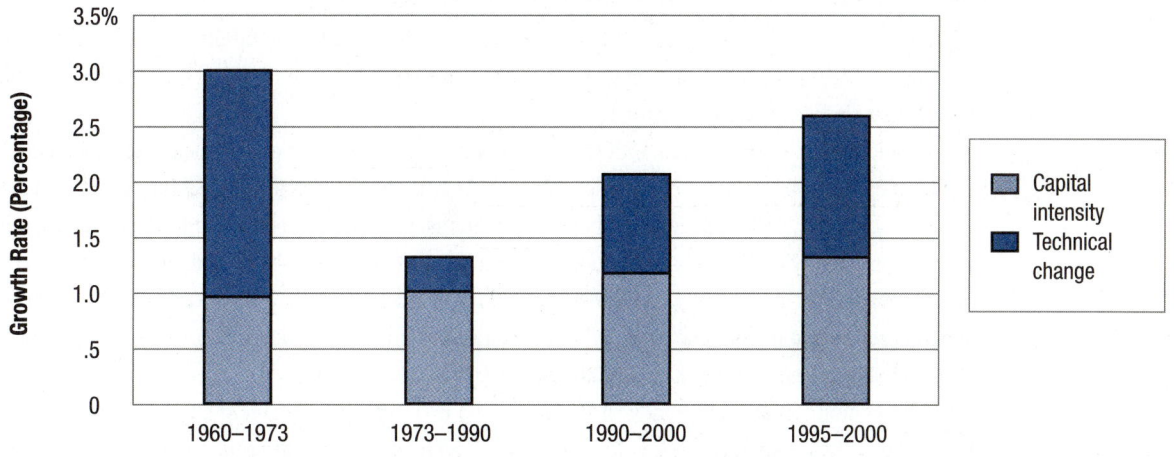

[8]Calculations based on data from the U.S. Department of Labor at http://stats.bls.gov. You may want to visit the Multifactor Productivity Home Page at the Bureau of Labor Statistics, U.S. Department of Labor.

INFOTRAC
College Edition

Keywords: *economic growth and the new economy*

Use your InfoTrac password to look up articles on these topics at http://www.infotrac-college.com

the next, with a definite increase apparent from 1990, and especially, 1995 to 2000. Technical change, on the other hand, makes a substantial contribution to the first period's productivity, a contribution that falls substantially in the 1973 to 1990 period. It then gets larger in the final period, with an extra boost after 1995. The decline in labor productivity growth and its subsequent recovery have largely reflected the behavior of technical change with a small contribution from the behavior of capital intensity.

The Contribution of Capital Intensity Growth: The New Economy?

Information technology (IT) has transformed the workplace and the nature of work in the U.S. economy. This transformation rests on achievements of the semiconductor industry. Moore's Law predicted (in 1965) that the number of transistors per chip would double every $1^1/_2$ to 2 years. Accompanying this essentially correct prediction, semiconductor prices (logic and memory chips) plummeted by 40 to 50 percent a year. Combined with the breathtaking developments in communications technology and associated price decreases, the sharp semiconductor price decreases stimulated an acceleration of investment in IT assets. IT assets, in effect, were substituted for other types of capital assets and for labor across the economy's broad spectrum. The use of IT capital services (computers, software, and communications equipment) grew at almost 20 percent per year from 1995 to 1999, almost doubling the rate of the previous 5 years. Non–IT capital services grew at about 3 percent a year, and labor services grew at about 2 percent. The growth rates imply that labor works with more non–IT capital and substantially more IT capital than in did in 1990 or even 1995. As Figure 1.6 shows, the growth of capital intensity makes an additional contribution to productivity after 1995. Expert economists conclude that an increasing and now large portion of the capital intensity effect on productivity is tied to increases in capital services from IT assets. Labor productivity has grown faster in the 1990s, and particularly after 1995, for two reasons. One is the just discussed increased contribution of capital intensity. The other is the increased contribution of technical change.[9]

The Contribution of Technical Change: The New Economy?

Changes in labor productivity growth caused by fluctuations in technical change limited our prosperity from the 1970s through the early part of the 1990s and may have enhanced it since then. What caused this fall and rise depicted in Figure 1.6?

It is ironic that in the 1970s and 1980s, a period of rapid scientific advances, measured technical change all but disappeared from the U.S. economic statistics. At first, this appears inexplicable, but it reminds us that technical, scientific, and engineering advances, by themselves, are not sufficient to create a dynamic economy. The former Soviet Union had world-class scientists and engineers, but technical change was exceedingly slow because the Soviet economy did not (could not?) incorporate their discoveries into economic growth. Remember also that technical change is more than scientific and engineering advances; technical change is anything that increases output from a fixed amount of resources. Improved or new products based on research and development, greater efficiency in the economy, or improved management techniques might cause it. Numerous explanations for the slowdown have been advanced,[10] including the possibility that

---

[9] See Dale Jorgenson, "U.S. Economic Growth in the Information Age." *Issues in Science and Technology* (Fall 2001, Vol. 18, Issue 1), 42–51.

[10] William E. Cullison, "The U.S. Productivity Slowdown: What the Experts Say," *Federal Reserve Bank of Richmond Economic Quarterly* (July/August 1989), 10–21. This article provides an excellent review of discussion about the productivity slowdown. A more recent look at the issue is Roy H. Webb, "National Productivity Statistics," *Federal Reserve Bank of Richmond Economic Quarterly* (Winter 1998) 45–64.

- Inflation, unemployment, petroleum price increases, and price controls of the 1970s affected the economy's efficiency and caused management to focus on short-term results.
- Increased error in measuring productivity caused the measured growth to be less than the actual growth.
- U.S. business firms by the early 1970s had incorporated much of the new knowledge about products and production developed before and during World War II into their established procedures.

The scientific and engineering advances of the 1960s and 1970s would have their greatest impacts in the information technology sectors, and just like earlier innovations—electricity, the telephone, the internal combustion engine, and assembly-line techniques—they did not have large immediate effects on the economy. By the 1970s, however, the previous innovations that had been reorganizing the economy since the turn of the twentieth century had had their dramatic impacts. We now know that major U.S. industries, such as automobiles, steel, and transportation, had peaked based on the available technologies. Firms and managers had prospered with the existing technologies; they naturally were suspicious of new ones. IBM, for instance, did not anticipate the opportunities presented by desktop computing and did not respond in ways that allowed it to maintain its preeminent position in computing. Similarly, the Big Three American automobile companies (Chrysler, Ford, and General Motors) were slow in adopting new production technologies more appropriate for the economy of the 1980s. Competitive pressure forced IBM and the Big Three to change. The competitive pressure came from Apple, Intel, and Microsoft, on one hand, and Japanese automobiles producers on the other. As the new firms and new technologies forced changes, these U.S. industrial titans suffered significant losses. Restoring rapid productivity growth would require new knowledge and the introduction of new technologies.

Although it was not obvious at the time, by the mid-1980s the IT revolution probably had begun a new wave of economic progress, introducing new technologies and discarding old ones. These new technologies—new knowledge—could have their impacts over a long time period. Perhaps the acceleration of technical change in the mid-1990s will result in rapid productivity growth for an extended period.

The productivity acceleration of the late 1990s, according to a recent study by McKinsey Global Institute (MGI), was not broad based; indeed, it could be credited to six sectors of the economy responsible for only about 30 percent of total output.[11] Some of these sectors are expected—industrial machinery and equipment (primarily computer manufacturing), electronics (primarily semiconductors), and telecommunications—and others—retail, wholesale, and securities brokerage—are surprises. They contributed to aggregate productivity growth in two ways; their productivity accelerated and some of these sectors were high-productivity sectors whose share of the overall economy increased.

Productivity in the semiconductor industry increased rapidly as Intel introduced chips at a faster pace. According to MGI, Advanced Micro Devices' competitive pressure pushed Intel to the faster pace. The computer industry's large productivity acceleration resulted from innovations in the input industries—disks, modems, and microprocessors—that provided the computer industry with higher quality inputs at lower prices. Competition among suppliers resulted in lower prices to the computer assemblers, who, prompted by competition, passed the improvements on to consumers through lower prices. In addition, more complex operating systems and more sophisticated applications led consumers to demand high-performance

---

[11]McKinsey Global Institute. *U.S. Productivity Growth 1995–2000.* Washington, DC: McKinsey Global Institute, 2001.

computers, where productivity gains are magnified. Advances in IT technology have also stimulated productivity growth in the mobile phone segment of the telecommunications industry.

The acceleration of productivity growth in these "high-tech" industries and their larger shares of the economy account for about the same increase in productivity as is attributed to the retail sector (basically Wal-Mart). Wal-Mart's productivity increase, its growing share of the market, and the pressure that it exerts on competitors is an important source of aggregate productivity growth. IT plays a role in Wal-Mart's competitive success, but the "big box" approach to retailing along with supply management and innovative management techniques are also key. (Incidentally, e-commerce had little to do with the productivity increase in retailing) The wholesale sector provided a boost to productivity slightly larger than the retail sector. Again, IT facilitates the improvements, but the big boost comes from warehouse automation.

Outside the semiconductor, computer assembly, and mobile phone sectors, the "new economy" has had dramatic and decisive effect on productivity growth in only one industry, the securities industry. Online stock trading jumped to about 40 percent of all retail stock trades from a base of about zero in 1995. It is only here that the Internet has been absolutely necessary for the advances to take place.

Have the technological advances in the IT sector and the buildup in IT assets been responsible for the productivity acceleration? Certainly, they have played a role. As others have noted, much of the productivity acceleration is found in IT manufacturing and telecommunications. IT investment has facilitated advances in retailing and wholesaling, although competitive pressures have also been important. IT may result in continuing radical transformations such as those found in the securities sector. But other sectors, such as retail banking and the hotel industry, have invested heavily in IT and are not realizing productivity benefits. Whether or not we are in a new period of rapid economic growth due to advancing productivity related to IT investments is still to be determined. The prospects are encouraging, but the existence of the new technology is not sufficient to guarantee the results. Firms and consumers must have incentives to make appropriate choices, and government must provide an economic environment that promotes efficiency.

INFOTRAC
College Edition

Keywords: *economic growth and information technology*

Use your InfoTrac password to look up articles on these topics at
http://www.infotrac-college.com

■ Economic and Productivity Growth in Various Parts of the World

Angus Maddison has provided important insights into productivity in his comparative study of capitalistic development in the advanced industrial nations. He shows both that the U.S. economy is the lead economy operating at the technological frontier and that other industrial countries (the followers) are converging on the U.S. position. Our discussion will compare the U.S. economy with the two largest follower economies, Japan and Western Europe (hereafter, *Europe*).[12] Maddison's data will also be used in examining productivity growth in developing countries.

Growth in Europe and Japan: Catching Up

In 1998, GDP per capita in the United States—in 1990 U.S. dollars appropriately adjusted for differences in purchasing power of different national currencies—was about 45 percent higher than the average for 12

---

[12] Angus Maddison, *Dynamic Forces in Capitalistic Development: A Long-Run Comparative View* (New York: Oxford University Press, 1991) and *The World Economy: A Millenial Perspective*. The specific European countries are Austria, Belgium, Denmark, Finland, France, Germany, Italy, Netherlands, Norway, Switzerland, United Kingdom, Ireland, and Spain.

Western European countries and 33 percent higher than for Japan. Productivity (GDP per hour), a slightly different measure, was over 50 percent less in Japan and 20 percent less in the European countries than in the United States. Although European and Japanese productivity approaches or exceeds U.S. levels in some manufacturing industries, productivity in other sectors is much lower. For instance, retailing in Japan is notoriously obsolete.

With hourly productivity so much lower, why is Japanese per capita GDP as close as it is to that of Europe and the United States? The answer is simple. The average hours worked per worker are much greater in Japan. In addition, a greater proportion of the Japanese population is employed.

The follower countries, however, are converging on the leader. Since 1950, productivity has grown almost 2½ times faster in Japan and more than 1½ times faster in Europe than in the United States. Why? Part of the convergence results from a more rapid growth of capital intensity. The capital stock has grown faster in Europe and particularly in Japan, while employment has grown much faster in the United States. Consequently, capital intensity has increased faster in Europe and Japan. Little wonder that their productivity has grown faster.

Europe and Japan also receive a greater boost to labor productivity growth from technical change—and, in particular, efficiency improvement—than does the United States. Maddison identifies three major sources for their more rapid efficiency improvement: structural effects, technological diffusion effects, and foreign-trade effects.

Earlier in the period, both Europe and Japan had much larger shifts out of agriculture—structural effects—than did the United States. Shifts out of agriculture tend to raise overall productivity. Shifts into the service sector, however, did not cause a relative disadvantage for the United States because Europe and Japan were becoming service economies even faster.

Technological diffusion effects represent technology transfer. In 1950, output per hour in the United States was more than twice the output per hour in other industrial countries. Part of this difference was due to the devastation of World War II in the other countries, but another part was because U.S. producers were more likely to be operating with best technology. Thus, producers in other countries had and have more opportunities for technical change based on efficiency improvement. Since that time, other countries have adopted some U.S. technology and production methods; to a lesser extent, the United States has adopted technology and production methods from other countries. It remains to be seen if rapid U. S. technological improvements will continue to provide other industrialized countries with the opportunity for greater catch-up. Technology and production techniques transfer easily to a country that has an educated labor force and an economy that provides incentives for entrepreneurial activity. Productivity in such a country is unlikely to lag behind the leader for long. The United States is the leader. Other countries are catching up. It is unfortunate, however, that more countries have not provided an economic and political environment that allows them to catch up.

Maddison's final explanation for catch-up is the foreign-trade effect. Freer trade after World War II gave an advantage to follower countries. This advantage, however, cost the United States nothing. It arose because freer trade, first through the European Common Market and continuing through the European Union, for example, increased competition for firms in the smaller economies in Europe. Small economies, like small towns, are fertile ground for monopolies. Monopolies sheltered by international trade barriers lack incentive to become more efficient. In addition, in a small economy a firm may not be

Keywords: *economic growth and OECD*

Use your InfoTrac password to look up articles on these topics at http://www.infotrac-college.com

able to grow large enough to realize the advantages of a large size. With its larger economy, the United States already had the advantage of a large internal market. With freer trade, however, firms in these smaller economies tended to adopt new technologies; carrots and sticks led them to greater efficiency. Carrots are the profits to be earned in other markets. Sticks are the foreign competitors, not unlike a Wal-Mart coming into a small town.

Developing Countries after 1950: Some Grow, Some Don't

In 1950, GDP per capita (in 1990 dollars) in all Latin American countries more than doubled that of African and Asian countries. Moreover, it was slightly higher in African countries than in Asian ones. From 1950 to 1998, GDP per capita grew faster in selected Asian countries than in African and Latin American countries.[13] Growth accelerated in many of these Asian countries between 1973 and 1990, and more than held its own after 1990. In contrast, it declined in Latin America (and selected Latin American countries) after 1973 and ceased in Africa. By 1999, the average level of GDP per capita in these selected Asian countries exceeded the average level of the selected Latin American countries.

As we saw earlier, a number of Asian countries have demonstrated that poor countries can experience rapid economic growth, pulling their populations out of dire poverty. As in any country, growth in GDP per capita in developing economies requires either (1) that labor grow faster than population, (2) that capital grow faster than labor, or (3) technical change. Compared with the past, developing countries enjoy improved health care, resulting in increased life expectancy and accelerated population growth. This more rapid population growth, however, makes it more difficult for labor to grow faster than population or for capital to grow faster than labor. Even with accumulation-based growth becoming more difficult, it is still possible. Much of the growth of the successful Asian economies has rested on resource accumulation.

Moreover, developing countries today have a tremendous advantage compared with countries that grew in the nineteenth century. The advantage is technological catch-up. Their technical change can be due to efficiency improvement rather than technological improvement because the more advanced technology already exists. Their problem is to adapt it to their economies, rather than develop it from scratch. Although this is probably easier than developing new technology, adapting ideas and processes that work in one economy to another can be difficult.

Examining specific countries allows us to be more concrete. In 1950, Korea ($770) and Taiwan ($936) had GDP per capita comparable to that of Ghana ($1,122) and Nigeria ($753) and well below that of Argentina ($4,987) and Chile ($3,821). Since then, Ghana and Nigeria have stagnated, and Argentina and Chile have grown to nearly $10,000. Korea and Taiwan, however, have moved well ahead of these countries—to $13,000 + and $15,000 +. An emphasis on primary and later secondary education for boys and girls is one factor that stands out in the Korean, Taiwanese, and other East Asian success stories. Moreover, as these economies developed, birth rates and population growth rates declined more rapidly than in the comparison countries of Latin America and Africa. With development, the opportunity cost of children increases because of increased opportunities for adults in the labor force. As parental income and education increase, parents invest more in children rather than increasing the number of children that they have. The resulting reduction in the population growth rate, combined with increased labor-force participation,

---

[13]The Asian countries are Bangladesh, China, India, Indonesia, Japan, Korea, Pakistan, Taiwan, and Thailand; the Latin American countries are Argentina, Brazil, Chile, Colombia, Mexico, and Peru; and the African countries are Cote d'Ivoire, Ghana, Kenya, Morocco, Nigeria, South Africa, and Tanzania.

INTERNATIONAL PERSPECTIVE

ECONOMIC FREEDOM AND ECONOMIC GROWTH IN DEVELOPING COUNTRIES

At the beginning of this chapter, we implied that the level and growth of living standards are likely to be higher in economies based on economic freedom rather than centralized government planning. In particular, we suggested that the values of the *Declaration of Independence* and *The Wealth of Nations* promote economic prosperity. Some critics turn this argument on its head. They argue that economic and political freedom are luxuries that only prosperous economies can afford. In short, they argue that prosperity causes economic and political freedom, rather than the other way around.

Several studies have computed indexes of freedom for most of the countries of the world. For example, the Heritage Foundation and *The Wall Street Journal* publish the *Index of Economic Freedom*. Similarly, James D. Gwartney, Robert A. Lawson, and others prepare the *Economic Freedom of the World*, published by the Fraser Institute and other free-market–oriented institutes around the world. These and other indexes show a strong correlation between economic freedom and prosperity. According to the executive summary of the former, "The study demonstrates unequivocally that countries with the highest levels of economic freedom also have the highest living standards. Similarly, countries with the lowest levels of economic freedom also have the lowest living standards."[a] The study by Gwartney and colleagues reaches the same conclusion. These correlations, however, do not prove that economic freedom causes prosperity; it is possible that prosperity leads people to demand more freedom.

To understand what causes what, Gwartney and Lawson, in *Economic Reform Today*, examined their index for developing or low-income countries and identified the 12 (top 10 with ties) countries that had the greatest increase in economic freedom from 1975 to 1990. They were Chile, Jamaica, Malaysia, Turkey, Pakistan, Egypt, Portugal, Mauritius, Singapore, Costa Rica, Indonesia, and Thailand. They also identified those developing countries with the greatest decrease in economic freedom: Panama, Morocco, Algeria, Tanzania, Zambia, Congo, Venezuela, Honduras, Iran, Somalia, and Nicaragua. If economic freedom promotes prosperity, one can reasonably expect developing countries with increases in freedom to experience more growth in a later period than developing countries with decreases in freedom. Consequently, Gwartney and colleagues examined growth rates of these same countries in a later period (1985 to 1994). The countries with the biggest increases in economic freedom showed an average of 4 percent annual growth in real per capita GDP. Real per capita GDP fell at 1.2 percent per year in the countries with the greatest decreases in economic freedom. Thus, increases in economic freedom were followed by higher growth rates in a later period. Although other explanations are possible, this relationship between growth of economic freedom and growth of per capita GDP is consistent with the proposition that well-functioning market economies promote economic growth.

Greater appreciation for these results requires some discussion of the index. Gwartney and colleagues argue that low taxes, secure property rights, free markets, free trade, and price and monetary stability promote growth. The 12 countries that achieved the faster growth rate had several factors in common. They improved their inflation performance, and 11 of the 12 now allow their citizens to hold foreign-currency accounts, making the domestic inflation less harmful.[b] International trade became more important, and its importance (approximately) doubled for countries such as Malaysia, Turkey, and Thailand. Finally, 11 of the 12 countries reduced their highest marginal income tax rates to below 50 percent. The highest marginal tax rate, in Portugal, went from 82 percent to 40 percent. Malaysia's dropped from 50 percent to 34 percent. Gwartney and colleagues concluded that the economic success of Hong Kong and other countries that have well-functioning market economies is "powerful evidence concerning the potency of economic freedom and a market economy as an engine of growth and development."[c]

---

[a]Kim R. Holmes, Bryan T. Johnson, and Melanie Kirkpatrick, "1997 Index of Economic Freedom: Executive Summary," *The Wall Street Journal*, December 16, 1996.

[b]James Gwartney and Robert Lawson, "Economic Freedom and the Growth of Emerging Markets," *Economic Reform Today* 2 (1996) online at http://www.cipe.org.

[c]Ibid.

leads to the labor force growing faster than population. According to Maddison, the successful countries in Asia had several other attributes: (1) Their policies encouraged the establishment of a private business sector and established secure property rights; (2) they encouraged domestic saving and investment; and (3) they invested heavily in education. In short, they accumulated capital—human and physical—rapidly. Moreover, they were open to foreign influences; this openness was expressed in various ways. Asian students studied abroad; foreign ideas and investments were imported into Asia; and Asian firms competed in international markets. This openness to foreign influence made efficiency improvements easier, permitting these countries to move toward the technological frontier. Combining this openness with individual incentives encouraged appropriate adaptation of foreign technology to each country's individual situation. Finally, the governments of the successful countries were able to avoid extreme inflation, while they allowed individual product and labor markets to adjust to changing demand and supply conditions.[14]

The Latin American countries, particularly after 1973, had lower growth rates. Maddison attributes their slower growth to failures in government policy. These countries had erected significant barriers to international trade to protect their domestic industries. Because the firms had protected home markets and were not expected to export, they could (and did) become inefficient and still survive. Additional problems arose because government policies caused extremely rapid inflation. Governments dealt with this inflation with price indexing, price controls, and many regulations instead of halting the inflation. Attempting to deal with the inflation caused additional inefficiencies in resource allocation.

In short, developing countries that are closing the gap with high-income countries follow policies based on the prescriptions laid out by Adam Smith. Essentially, these prescriptions are based on allowing individuals to make economic decisions as they see fit. As for government intervention, these successful economies range from Hong Kong, with limited government intervention, to Singapore, with its stringent regulations requiring that people save substantial amounts of their income. Regardless, they permit a wide scope for individual initiative, and they avoid detailed central plans for their economies.

Summary

Economic growth has raised citizens of the United States, Canada, Japan, and countries of Western Europe to living standards unimaginable just 100 years ago. Per capita income continues to grow in these economies, although at a slower rate than just after World War II. Several other countries, particularly in East Asia, experienced rapid growth beginning in the 1960s and 1970s that has transformed their economies.

The production possibilities curve for an economy helps to explain the sources of economic growth. The curve shows that for a fixed amount of resources and a given technology, an economy has a menu of efficient combinations of output. In particular, it can produce more consumption goods and fewer capital goods or the reverse. If the country wants more rapid growth, it can increase the production of capital goods at the expense of consumption goods. It can sacrifice present consumption for the increased future consumption that increased investment in capital goods allows. The economy can also grow through technical progress: technological and efficiency improvements.

From the end of World War II until the early 1970s, rapid labor productivity growth fed by technical change allowed compensation per hour to grow rapidly in the United States and other industrial countries. From 1973 to the early 1990s, the growth rates of labor productivity, compensation, and technical change fell substantially. The 1990s, with increased competition and the coming of age of technologies, may be the beginning of a new spurt in productivity growth due to technical change.

---

[14]Angus Maddison, "Explaining the Economic Performance of Nations," in William J. Baumol, Richard R. Nelson, and Edward N. Wolff, eds., *Convergence of Productivity: Cross-National Studies and Historical Evidence* (New York: Oxford University Press, 1994), 20–61.

Higher-income countries that have closed the gap with the United States have effective market economies: private property rights, flexible prices, a stable price level, appropriate incentives, and a stable legal system. Lower-income countries that are growing rapidly share these characteristics. Nevertheless, a great variety of economic policies exist in countries that have had sustained economic growth. In addition to promoting education and developing appropriate infrastructure, some countries have applied tariffs and other subsidies to some of their industries. Other countries have remained more hands-off. Few, if any, of the countries that have sustained economic growth for long periods have used a comprehensive central plan.

Key Terms

Land	Production possibilities curve	Marginal product
Labor	Best technology	Technological improvement
Physical capital	Marginal cost	Efficiency improvement
Human capital	Scarcity	Capital intensity
Opportunity cost	Marginal benefit	Technical change

Review Questions

1. Compare the economic growth of Japan, Korea, and the United States since 1960.
2. Define the following terms:
   a. production possibilities curve
   b. technological improvement
   c. efficiency improvement
3. Is a faster rate of economic growth always desirable? Explain carefully, using the production possibilities curve.
4. Use the accompanying graph to answer questions a through d.

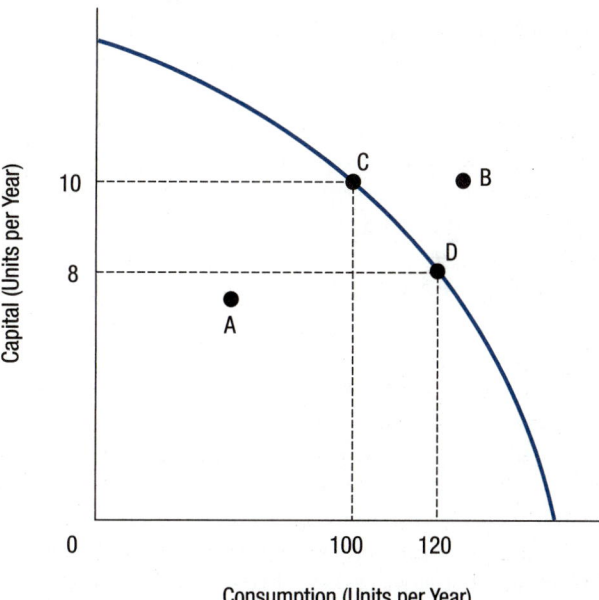

   a. What point would represent a combination of goods and services that cannot be produced with the economy's given resources and technology?

b. What point would represent a combination of goods and services that might be produced if the economy were experiencing unemployment? What else could cause the economy to be at that point?
c. Suppose the economy is currently producing at point C and would like to have the consumption goods represented by point D. What must be given up to obtain the increased consumption goods?
d. Suppose the economy is at point D. What might be done to increase the chances of being at B next year? What are other ways to reach B?

5. Why did compensation per hour not increase as fast after 1973 as it did from 1960 to 1973?
6. According to the box titled "Were the Good Old Days Really Better?" the American standard of living has grown more since the early 1970s than suggested by government statistics that use the CPI to adjust for inflation. Explain.
7. What caused the slowdown in labor productivity growth in the United States after 1973?
8. Explain the sources of increased productivity growth in the United States in the 1990s.
9. "Productivity growth in Japan is greater than productivity growth in the United States because its workers are more productive." Is this statement true or false? Defend your answer.
10. What factors explain why labor productivity in Japan and Western Europe has grown faster than in the United States?
11. According to the box titled "Economic Freedom and Economic Growth in Developing Countries," countries with more economic freedom have higher levels of per capita income. Does this prove that economic freedom causes prosperity? Defend your answer. The box also states that countries with increased economic freedom subsequently experience faster economic growth. Does this give you any more information about economic freedom and economic growth? Explain.
12. Discuss one advantage and one disadvantage that developing countries share as they try to encourage economic growth. What policies have proven successful in promoting economic growth?
13. Go to http://www.swcollege.com/bef/econ_news.html. Choose the Equilibrium category under Economic Fundamentals and choose an EconNews story that interests you. Read the full summary, and answer the questions posed.

Economic Issues on the Internet

– The E. F. Schumacher Society—**http://www.schumachersociety.org**
E. F. Schumacher is the author of *Small Is Beautiful: Economics as if People Mattered* (Harper Collins, 1989), which was first published in 1973. Not everyone agrees that economic growth is desirable. A visit to this site help explain this position.

– Free the World—**http://www.freetheworld.com**
The Web site for the *Economic Freedom of the World* publications and data. See also the *Index of Economic Freedom* at http://www.heritage.org/research/features/index/.

– Freedom House—**http://www.freedomhouse.org**
The Web site for indices of economic and political freedom.

– The International Monetary Fund—**http://www.imf.org**
The IMF is another international agency dealing with economies throughout the world. Its quarterly periodical, *Finance and Development*, often contains material of interest to and accessible by students. It too has working papers, policy papers and data.

– The World Bank—**http://www.worldbank.org**
The World Bank is an international agency focused on economic growth and development throughout the world. Its Global Development Network Growth Database is only one of its many data sets available online. Working papers and policy papers are also available.

CHAPTER 2

An Introduction to Economic Systems and the Workings of the Price System

Outline:

Market Economic Systems: An Introductory Look

What Does an Economic System Do? It Coordinates
  The Division and Specialization of Labor
  Economic Coordination and the Market System

The Price System as Coordinator
  Demand
  Supply

Putting the Pieces Together: Demand and Supply

Comparative Systems: An Introductory Sketch
  The Price System
  Information, Rationing, and Motivation in a Market Economy
  Information, Rationing, and Motivation in a Command Economy
  Systems and Coordination

Transitions to a Market Economy: Some Experiences
  Stable Prices and the Monetary System
  Other Economic Reforms
  Additional Thoughts on Transition Economies

In the late 1950s, Nikita Khrushchev, General Secretary of the Communist Party of the Soviet Union, vowed to Western Europe and the United States, "We will bury you." It was of little comfort that he meant to do so economically. According to the relevant Soviet Economic Plan, by 1980 Soviet industrial production would be greater than the combined production of the capitalist countries, including the United States.

After World War II, many observers, including policy makers in various parts of the world, considered centrally planned *(command) economic systems* superior to *market economic systems*. From this perspective, the Great Depression of the 1930s, in which market economies experienced extreme economic distress, foretold future economic troubles. Those who considered a command economy superior had several reasons: no unemployment; reduced inequality; and the ability to redirect resources from uses deemed unimportant to uses that promoted economic growth. In this view, the economic problem was how to accumulate sufficient industrial capacity to become a modern economy.

A complete comparison of the structures of a command economy and a market economy requires extensive discussion beyond our scope. Our short discussion, however, will help you understand the differences between the two systems. In a command economy, a central plan details the amounts of various goods and services to produce. It sets targets for consumer goods and investment goods. For instance, the plan might call for building apartments in various parts of the country and building a steel mill. It would, of course, have to establish targets for many other activities. Planners in the former Soviet Union set prices and determined production for more than 500,000 different items. The planners had to consider numerous factors, including

- What products people desired
- What products and actions the government desired
- How to produce various products
- Who would receive the products

If more apartments were to be built, the planners would have to decide what size apartments to build, what types of construction to use, where to build them, and who would live in the apartment. They would have to ensure that construction materials, kitchen appliances, furniture, and numerous other resources and products would be available. Moreover, the kitchen appliances would have to fit into the apartment's kitchens. It is doubtful that the planners would provide much variety in terms of the apartment's size, layout, and style. Apartments in the Soviet Union were often described as drab, gray, monolithic, and made from the same pattern.

In a market economy, the same factors—what, how, and for whom—must be considered, but without a central plan. Instead, the market solution results from millions of independent decisions made by individuals. Each individual considers the opportunities available and the costs of different actions and decides on the action that will make her or him better off. Would you expect the planned system to be organized and the market system to be chaotic? Many do. But, in fact, a comparison of market and command economies reveals that market economies do a much better job of delivering the right stuff to the right place at the right time. Imagine the numerous goods and services used in any large city every day. The astonishing fact is that people who are willing to pay the market price can buy almost any good that can be produced and shipped, usually without delay.

Although both command and market systems faced the same economic problem, as the last half of the twentieth century unfolded, market economies increasingly outperformed the command economies. Before World War II, East Germany probably had a slight economic edge over West Germany. Within a few years after the war, the West German economy was providing its residents a better standard of living than was the planned East German economy. By 1990, West German per capita income almost quadrupled that of East Germany. Similar comparisons of communist North Korea to South Korea and communist China to Hong Kong give the same result. Starting from a similar economic and cultural base after World War II, people in the noncommunist countries surged ahead of those in comparable communist countries.

From the end of World War II to the 1980s, the command economies (the Soviet Union and other communist states) and the market economies (the United States and allied states) challenged each other's economic performance. The competition ended with the collapse of the centrally planned systems in the former Soviet bloc. Many of these countries, in turn, are trying to create market economies from the wreckage of their planned ones, and some have succeeded. The collapse of Soviet communism was one of the most important events of the twentieth century; the successful transformation of these command economies to market economies is a central hope of the twenty-first century. According to *The Economist*, "Across the whole region [Central and Eastern Europe and countries formed from the Soviet Union], the possibility and desirability of creating capitalism has now been accepted, even by the laggards." The most decisive reason "has surely been a simple recognition of the superiority of capitalism as an economic system."[1]

INFOTRAC
College Edition

Keywords: *Soviet Union and economic aspects*

Use your InfoTrac password to look up articles on these topics at **http://www.infotrac-college.com**

Because market (capitalist) economies have evolved without anyone actually deciding to create them—like Topsy, "they just grew"—it is sometimes difficult to understand their essential features. We cannot see the trees for the forest. The process of abandoning a command economy—central planning—and creating a market economy provides a laboratory for the study of these features. This chapter uses that laboratory to discuss two fundamental questions: What are the essential characteristics of a market economy system? Why do market systems perform better than command systems? To make the discussion concrete, some of the experiences of former command economies—the transition economies—in transforming themselves are examined.

■ Market Economic Systems: An Introductory Look

The changes countries undertake in trying to establish a market economic system imply much about the system's essential features: private ownership, market exchanges, and market incentives. These countries are establishing a legal system consistent with *private ownership* of most business operations—particularly agriculture, manufacturing, retailing, wholesaling, and business and personal services. They also are allowing individuals to undertake voluntary economic transactions (*market exchanges*); that is, they allow individuals' decisions to establish market prices. Finally, they are using market rewards and penalties as *incentives*: allowing economically successful people to benefit from the wealth they create and unsuccessful people to suffer the consequences of deficiencies in wealth creation.

Relative Price –
The price of one good in terms of another good. It measures what must be given up to obtain a good.

Knowing the price of a good helps people decide if they want to purchase it. Price is most helpful in a purchase decision, when considered in relative terms. A **relative price**, the price of one good in terms of another good, measures what we must give up to purchase an item. It is an exchange value and measures opportunity cost. For instance, if a concert ticket is priced at $30, an individual sacrifices the best alternative use of the $30 to attend the concert. The $30 could be used to buy six movie tickets at $5 per movie or two compact discs at $15 per CD. Let's assume that José, a college student, has decided to spend $30 on one of these three alternatives. José chooses the concert over purchasing two CDs or going to six movies. The relative price of the concert is two CDs, or six movies, or $30. The opportunity cost of the concert is the value of José's preferred alternative, which we assume is two CDs. In deciding between the

---

[1]"After Communism," *The Economist* (December 3, 1994), 27.

concert and the CDs, José compares the expected benefit of owning the CDs to the expected benefit of the concert. If prices change little over time, people become aware of relative prices as measures of exchange values—what they must give up of one thing to obtain another. This information greatly simplifies their decision making. Of course, when price changes, it signals that exchange values have changed.

The information conveyed by a change in market price, say, of concerts, depends upon what happens to prices of other products. Consider three examples. First, suppose that the concert ticket price doubles to $60 and that all other prices stay the same. This price increase might occur if the band becomes more popular. At $60, the sacrifice for a concert ticket would be four CDs. The price increase, therefore, signals that a greater sacrifice—at least the value of four CDs—is required to attend a concert. As a result, fewer people choose the concert. The price change provides the appropriate signal to consumers, telling them the concert now requires a greater sacrifice of other items.

If the average of all prices is increasing rapidly over time, however, prices might be unreliable indicators of sacrificed alternatives. For the second example, suppose that a year later the concert price doubles to $60, that all other prices double, and that José's entertainment budget also doubles—to $60. (If prices continue to rise, this is an example of *inflation*, a continuous increase in the average of all prices over time. Inflation is analyzed in Chapter 15.) José still has the choice of one concert, two CDs, or six movies. Because the cost of the concert in terms of CDs and movies remains the same—two CDs or six movies—he still chooses the concert. If all prices change in the same proportion, relative prices, exchange values, and opportunity costs do not change. Thus, a steady rate of inflation may not seriously damage the usefulness of the price system in summarizing and conveying information.

Often, however, inflation accelerates and decelerates over time and has different effects on prices in different sectors of the economy. After some point, as inflation increases, it becomes more erratic. Erratic inflation prevents people from using past decisions and information as a reliable guide to future decisions. Suppose, for the third example, that the price of movie tickets remains at $5, the price of concert tickets is $60 rather than $30, the price of CDs goes up by a factor of four to $60, and José's budget becomes $60. Relative to concert tickets, CDs now are more and movies less expensive. José now has to recompute the exchange values, to rethink relative prices. The cost of a concert ticket is now either one CD or 12 movies. José might now choose to go to 12 movies. Because of the change in relative prices, José foregoes the concert and purchases the movie tickets. As erratic inflation continues, people must evaluate their alternatives in detail each time they consider a purchase, increasing the cost of information captured from prices. A stable average price level, on the other hand, makes historical prices an excellent source of information and thus reduces decision-making costs.

In addition, a well-functioning market system requires that individuals trust other individuals with whom they deal. A major step in this direction is the establishment of a clear and understandable legal system creating private property rights. The system must create all types of ownership structures: proprietorships, partnerships, and corporations. Besides property law, the legal system must include contract, criminal, tort, and other types of law. Many problems must be dealt with; they include, among others, fraud, theft, counterfeiting, misrepresentation of a product's attributes, and failure to mention safety problems. These laws encourage economic transactions by making the terms of the transaction less ambiguous and more binding. For the legal system to be most effective in promoting prosperity, however, people must generally accept, obey, and understand the laws. If not, more government resources must be devoted to law enforcement, and people will devote more personal resources to protecting their person and their property and to understanding and evading laws and regulations. A market economic system thus becomes less effective because resources are devoted to nonproductive activities, such as tax avoidance and evasion.

No legal system can regulate all situations in which honesty is an important stimulus for good economic performance. Besides formal rules of conduct based on a system of justice, well-functioning economic systems also require informal rules. People must be able to rely on each other's word. For example, suppose that when you asked other people the time of a meeting, some gave you the correct time but others did not. It is hard to imagine a law requiring that we tell each other the correct time. If we cannot rely on an honest answer, however, our lives become terribly inconvenient.

If you have ever bought or sold a used car, you understand the importance of honesty and trust. Suppose you are in the market to buy a used car. You see the exact car that you want in the classified advertisements; you also see one for sale in the used-car lot of a new-car dealer. If you buy the car from the private seller, you will pay a lower price than you would pay the dealer. Moreover, the private seller will receive a better price for his used car than if he had sold it to a dealer. It is a win-win situation. However, even though they might secure a better price in a private one-on-one transaction, many people decide to go through a dealer. Various reasons exist for using the dealer, but one of the important ones is that the dealer must be concerned about the effect of transactions on her reputation. She has an economic incentive to be honest because her good reputation is valuable. On the other hand, if two people are mutually trustworthy, perhaps friends or family, they may bypass the dealer and both parties receive a better price. Of course, misunderstandings associated with business transactions might doom friendships and create family feuds.

To summarize some of the characteristics of a successful market system, we expand on the list in Table 2.1.

- First, a successful market system is one with a system of private property and property rights defined, established, and protected by law. Furthermore, private property must constitute a significant portion of the economy.

TABLE 2.1	Characteristics of a Successful Market System

1. A system of private property and property rights defined, established, and protected by law (private ownership)

2. Flexible prices that fluctuate in response to individuals' voluntary decisions and exchanges (market exchange)

3. Market incentives that are generated by a price system whose rewards and penalties motivate decision makers

4. Reasonably stable prices and a well-functioning monetary system that facilitates voluntary exchange

5. A legal system that is broadly obeyed and a culture that generates a climate of trust

- Second, a successful market system has flexible prices that fluctuate in response to individuals' voluntary decisions and exchanges. Markets and flexible prices allow the economy to be organized based on voluntary decisions and exchanges. Given private property, individuals decide what to produce and consume based on their personal interests and opportunities. They also make career and production decisions based on their interests, opportunities, and talents and in light of what other people will pay for their labor or their products. Having decided what to produce or where to sell their labor, people exchange what they produce or what they earn for goods and services produced by other people. A market economy eases these voluntary exchanges by establishing prices for goods and services that allow individuals to purchase from others rather than directly exchanging what they produce.

- Third, in a successful market economy incentives are generated by a price system whose rewards and penalties motivate decision makers. In such a system, people make careful decisions and exchanges because they are responsible for the consequences. They keep the rewards and bear the costs, giving them incentive to be careful.

- Fourth, a successful market economy has a reasonably stable price-level and a well-functioning monetary system that facilitates voluntary exchange. A well-functioning monetary system makes it unnecessary for people to trade bread for wine; they can sell bread for money and use the money to buy wine. For example, the use of money and prices allows college professors to teach without the bother of students paying them with house painting, baby-sitting, house cleaning, farm products, or whatever students and their families produce. As you well know, students pay colleges money; colleges in turn pay the professors, who buy what they want and can afford. With a stable monetary system and little inflation, prices generate information that simplifies voluntary exchange between individuals; they inform and motivate people in their economic decision making.

- Finally, a market system works best with a legal system that is broadly obeyed and a culture that generates a climate of trust. For this to occur, the legal and judicial systems must clearly and simply define and enforce the economy and society's rules. Moreover, people must generally behave in a mutually trustworthy manner.

INFOTRAC
College Edition
Keywords: *survey and perestroika*
Use your InfoTrac password to look up articles on these topics at
http://www.infotrac-college.com

■ What Does an Economic System Do? It Coordinates

An economic system consists of a set of economic, political, social, and other rules. Given the rules, people make choices that, taken together, determine five interrelated economic outcomes: (1) the methods of production, (2) the quantities of various goods and services produced in an economy, (3) who receives the goods and services, (4) the overall stability of the economy and whether it produces at its capacity, and (5) the economy's growth. The remainder of this section discusses these concepts.

THE METHODS OF PRODUCTION.
How will business firms produce? Will automobile producers, for example, make extensive use of robots, or will they move from assembly-line production to team production? How-to-produce questions are among the easier ones that an economic system deals with, because they are partly answered by engineering considerations.

THE QUANTITIES OF VARIOUS GOODS AND SERVICES PRODUCED IN AN ECONOMY.
How much and what types of food, clothing, and various other products should be produced? Reasonable

INTERNATIONAL PERSPECTIVE

WHAT HAPPENED IN CHINA?

In an International Perspective in Chapter 1 ("China: Economic Growth and Poverty"), we briefly described how economic growth in China since 1978 has lifted more than 200 million people from absolute poverty and raised the standard of living of hundreds of millions of others who were on the brink of absolute poverty. Now let's discuss why this growth occurred.

According to *The Economist* and many other sources, China's initial growth and poverty reduction stemmed from changes in the agricultural sector of the economy. In particular, farmers were given responsibility for a certain parcel of land and given the rights to earn additional income based on their productivity. Prices of agricultural products were allowed to rise. Previously, farmers worked in collective farms, and their incomes were not tied to their work effort. In short, the introduction of market incentives and flexible prices stimulated economic growth. From 1978 to 1984, rural incomes grew by 14 percent a year.

Although farmers received long-term leases on their land, they were not given full ownership. The farmers received rights to the income they could earn from the land and some assurance that they would have these rights for an extended time. Consequently, farmers had some incentive to make improvements in the land that would pay off in the future. They lacked the strongest possible incentive to make the improvements because the land was government owned and the government could assign it to other people or uses. Moreover, the farmer cannot sell the rights to use the land. Consequently, farmers have proven unwilling to make investments whose payoffs might be in the distant future. Unable to sell the land or to transfer it to heirs, farmers cannot be sure that they will reap the rewards of their investments. Perhaps because of this incomplete privatization, growth in China's farm productivity and farm income has slowed since 1984.

SOURCE: Suggested by "The Long March to Capitalism," *The Economist* 344 (11/13/1997), 23–26.

---

answers depend on the talents and desires of the 285 million people and 143 million workers in the U.S. economy. What goods and services are they adept at producing? What goods and services do they wish to consume? The questions are difficult because people do not wish to consume everything they are adept at producing and are not adept at producing everything they want to consume.

WHO RECEIVES THE GOODS AND SERVICES?

The distribution of goods and services also raises difficult issues. To achieve a high level of economic output, people must be rewarded for what they produce so that they have incentive to continue and perhaps to increase their production. Compassion or justice, however, requires that those who cannot produce an adequate amount be taken care of in some way. The contradiction between the distribution of material goods as incentives and their distribution for compassion is troubling. People in most societies are unwilling to accept a distribution of goods and services based entirely on what one produces because some people would not obtain enough to survive. As a result, many people voluntarily give goods and services to the less fortunate (charity) and support government's mandatory redistribution (welfare).

THE OVERALL STABILITY OF THE ECONOMY AND WHETHER IT PRODUCES AT ITS CAPACITY.

Periods of high unemployment or rapid inflation disrupt an economic system. If many people are unemployed, their potential production is lost and can never be recovered. Rapid inflation makes it harder for an economic system to operate. Because an unregulated market system may be subject to recurring episodes of unemployment and inflation, many economists believe that governments must promote economic stability.

THE ECONOMY'S GROWTH. Economic growth in the United States and other industrial countries slowed in the past quarter century. Proponents of the New Economy believe that the slowdown has been reversed, but the evidence is not yet conclusive. Therefore, the relationship between economic growth and economic policy remains on the front burner for high-income countries and remains a fundamental issue for those who would alleviate world poverty. Promotion of economic growth is complex and controversial. As discussed in Chapter 1, economic growth requires sacrificing in the present to provide for the future, making growth a feature of the conflict between generations.

This book introduces you to a market economic system, particularly the U.S. system, and its performance. Although the five economic outcomes listed here are interrelated and difficult to discuss in isolation, different parts of the book emphasize different ones. Economic growth was discussed in Chapter 1. Chapters 3 through 10 explore aspects of what goods to produce. Chapters 3, 10, and 12, focus on distribution: taxes, social security, and poverty. Chapters 13 through 16 deal with unemployment, inflation, and other issues related to the overall economy. Finally, Chapters 17 and 18 examine the international economy.

All of these issues involve the central problem of coordination. We next examine why coordination is so complex in a modern economy. After identifying what an economic system must do—*coordinate*—we discuss how a market economic system does its job. Later, we compare market and centrally planned (command) economic systems.

The Division and Specialization of Labor

As early as 1776, when Adam Smith published his trail-blazing treatise in economics, *The Wealth of Nations*, economists recognized the importance of the division of labor. By the division of labor, Smith meant (1) the specialization of labor in a particular production process—today, that might be the person in a service station who specializes in changing oil—and (2) the specialization of firms in a few activities, such as the automobile service station that does only mufflers. Division of labor implies specialization of economic activity.

Smith argued that the division and specialization of labor gave "modern" economies a tremendous wealth advantage over "traditional" subsistence economies. He illustrated the division of labor in a firm by describing the specialized tasks of workers who produced straight pins. One worker "draws out the wire, another straights it, a third cuts it, a fourth points it, a fifth grinds it at the top for receiving the head; . . . and the important business of making a pin is divided into about eighteen distinct operations, which in some manufactories are all performed by distinct hands."[2] Smith estimated that, in factories with extensive division of labor, the daily production of pins per worker might be 4,800 times the production of a single worker who did all of the tasks.

Although you might think producing a textbook involves no extensive division of labor, both types of specialization are important. The production of this book used the services of tens of thousands of specialized

---

[2]Adam Smith, *An Inquiry into the Nature and Causes of the Wealth of Nations* (Indianapolis: Liberty Press, 1981), a reprint of the edition published by Oxford: Clarendon Press, 1979, Book I, Ch. 1, p. 15.

people and specialized business firms—the many economists who have researched the topics; the editors, publishers, and printers; the loggers and manufacturing employees who produced the paper; the people who invented and produced the computer hardware and software; and so on. The enormous availability of books today would have been unimaginable to monks in the Middle Ages, who manufactured books by hand, copying and beautifully illustrating manuscripts. Dramatically increased division of labor along with new technology has made books incredibly inexpensive today compared to their cost in the Middle Ages.

Smith's insights about the advantages of the division and specialization of labor remain relevant. He discussed three ways that specialization increases the output of goods and services.

First, specialization allows people to become highly skilled in particular tasks. Today, we would say that specialized workers become more skilled through higher education, vocational training, and on-the-job training.

Second, specialization reduces the time wasted as people shift from one task to another. Smith referred to the time wasted by subsistence farmers, who did several jobs in a short time. Time-management experts currently make a similar point. They recommend that workers complete one task—for example, respond to their e-mail—before they switch to another task. By reserving large blocks of time for each task, people avoid losing time because of (1) mental shifting of gears, (2) putting materials away, (3) locating new materials, and so on. The fewer tasks an individual does—that is, the greater the specialization—the more time saved.

Third, Smith observed that specialized workers produced many inventions and innovations in the early Industrial Revolution; because they concentrated on just a few tasks, these workers could see easier ways to do them. Some inventions and innovations today come from people who specialize in invention, itself an example of greater division of labor. Still, specialization aids innovation because a simple task is easier to automate than a complex one. Furthermore, just as in Adam Smith's day, contemporary workers invent and innovate in a search for new and better ways of doing their jobs. As we do our jobs, we gain knowledge. Often that knowledge is tacit—knowledge that we can use but cannot explain easily to others. For instance, an expert at video games cannot use a lecture or a book to teach someone else to play the game equally well. If winning a particular game were important, an expert would choose to play the game rather than use a lecture or book to teach a beginner, even if the beginner had substantially better hand-to-eye coordination. Other people must learn by doing, just as the expert did. Because we cannot easily transfer tacit knowledge to others, the people who have it can make the best use of it. Given the opportunity and the incentive, workers use tacit knowledge to develop new procedures and products that create wealth for their employers, for themselves, and for final users.

Greater division and specialization of labor are not unmixed blessings. The monk responsible for producing a beautiful manuscript had a great feeling of accomplishment. He could see the product of his labor. With increased specialization, many workers cannot see their accomplishments. Work that requires repetitive, monotonous actions leads to worker discontent. Economic systems must balance promoting division of labor with ways of avoiding the negative results of overspecialization.

Specialization based on division of labor is an integral part of any economy.[3] If we specialize, however, we produce more of the few things than we want to use and we produce nothing else. To obtain the

---

[3]Comparative advantage, developed in Chapter 17, is another important source of specialization.

many other goods and services that we want, we must trade, which means the consumption and production of vast numbers of specialized people must be coordinated.

Economic Coordination and the Market System

The coordination of economic activity through prices in a market system relies on *voluntary exchange* between two people. Its appeal rests on a simple idea: It occurs only if each person expects to benefit from the exchange. For the exchange to be truly voluntary, both parties must

1. *Be responsible individuals* who can make rational decisions. An exchange between an adult and a child may not be voluntary because the child is unable to form opinions about the relative values of the items exchanged.
2. *Have reasonable access to information.* Suppose Sam, a doctor, knows that an expensive treatment that cures baldness for some people will not help Eric. Eric has no way of getting this information. If Sam convinces Eric to pay $3,000 for the treatment, the exchange is hardly voluntary.
3. *Have reasonable alternatives to the exchange.* Suppose Chris's one talent is playing the electric cello, and he has applied for a job with Kate's band, which is the only place of employment for a cellist. Chris is in a perilous position. If he has no other way to earn income, any agreement that Chris makes to work for Kate may not be voluntary. Fortunately, we face few situations that offer no alternatives for essential products. (We will discuss monopolies, in which buyers have limited alternatives, in Chapter 5.)

A major exception to the purely beneficial effects of voluntary exchange arises if a third party is negatively and involuntarily affected. Suppose Chris obtains the job with Kate's orchestra but must practice at home for 5 hours a day. If Sara and his other neighbors can hear his practicing, it could cause them involuntary harm. Such involuntary harm is an example of an *external cost*. If such effects are important in particular exchanges, the harm experienced by third parties must be considered along with the advantages gained by the trading parties. A real example is air pollution. Producers and consumers of paper benefit from their voluntary exchanges, but a paper mill's air pollution may harm people who live in its vicinity.

■ THE PRICE SYSTEM AS COORDINATOR

One of any society's most important tasks is to ensure that the quantity produced of any good (such as apartments) is the quantity that consumers purchase. If more apartments are produced than consumers demand, resources are wasted that could produce something else. If fewer apartments are produced than consumers demand, they will be dissatisfied. In this case, too much of something else is being produced and again resources are wasted. In *competitive markets*, which are markets with many buyers and sellers, the interaction of demand and supply determines the quantity of the good produced. This section discusses demand and supply using the market for apartments as a familiar example.

Demand

Consider the market for apartments of a given size and quality in, say, Gotham City. Gotham has a population of 5 million, income is $16,000 per person, and the price of a standard owner-occupied house is $90,000. Assume that population, income, and the house price are three of the four factors that affect how

Quantity Demanded – The quantity of a good that consumers plan to buy at each possible price, holding constant other factors that affect demand.

many apartments people want to rent. The fourth factor is apartment rental price. How many apartments will people plan to rent at different rental prices, holding income, population, and house price constant?

To answer, we develop a *demand schedule* for apartments that shows the consumers' **quantity demanded** of apartments per month at each possible price. The demand schedule exists for given values of *income*, *population*, *house price*, and *other variables*. If any of the values, other than apartment rent, change, the demand schedule changes. If the price of an apartment is $500 a month, Table 2.2 shows that Gothamites demand 400,000 apartments. If the price were $450 a month, they would want 475,000 apartments. Thus, if the price falls from $500 to $450, the quantity demanded of apartments increases from 400,000 to 475,000.

We can summarize the demand schedule in a diagram. Because we use diagrams throughout this book, we have included a chart at the bottom of Table 2.2 for you to practice working with graphs. If you like, transfer the chart to a separate sheet of paper. Note that it has price (rent) per apartment per month on the

TABLE 2.2 Demand Schedule for Apartments in Gotham City

The demand schedule shows the quantity demanded of apartments at each price. For instance, if the price is $500 a month, the quantity demanded is 400,000 apartments per month. At a lower price of $450, the quantity demanded would be greater: 475,000 apartments. The demand schedule exists for a given income, population, and price of a house.

	Price (Monthly Rent per Apartment)	Quantity (Apartments per Month)
A	$500	400,000
B	450	475,000
C	400	550,000
D	350	625,000
E	300	700,000
F	250	775,000
G	200	850,000

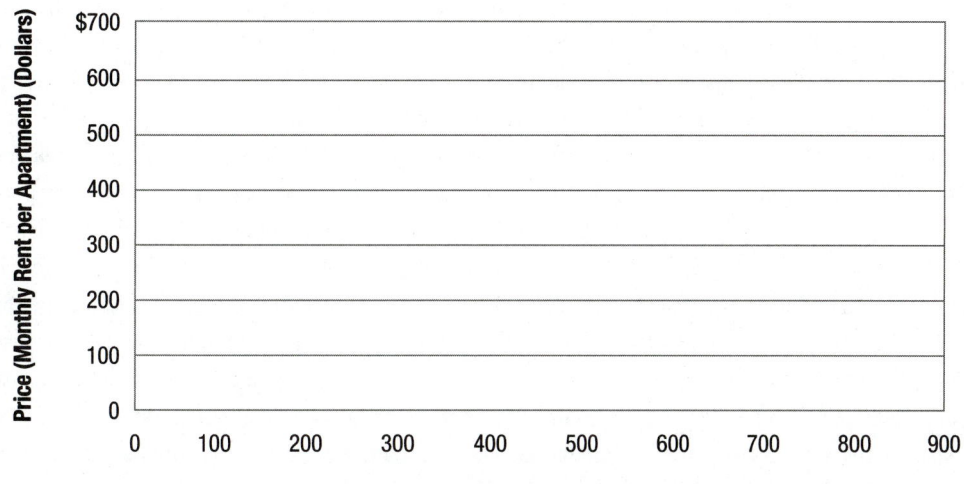

Demand Curve –
A curve (line) showing the quantity demanded of a good for each possible price, holding constant other factors that affect demand.

vertical axis in $100 increments and the number of apartments per month on the horizontal axis in increments of 100,000. Assume that all apartments are of equal size and quality. To draw the **demand curve**, a visual representation of the demand schedule, choose a point from the demand schedule and locate it in your figure. (Note that the demand "curve" can be a straight line.) For instance, at point E in Table 2.2, the price is $300 and the quantity demanded is 700,000. Find $300 on the vertical axis of your diagram and draw a horizontal dashed line at that price all the way across the diagram. Now find 700,000 on the horizontal axis and draw a vertical dashed line from there to the top. The intersection of the two dashed lines is point E on the demand curve. Find another point, maybe point B, in the same way. Because we chose data to trace out a straight line, the two points can be connected to give the demand curve.

Suppose now that the market price is $400. Draw a horizontal dashed line from $400 to the demand curve; at the intersection, draw a vertical dashed line to the horizontal axis. The point where the dashed line hits the axis gives the quantity demanded of apartments: 550,000. The demand curve, therefore, gives the quantity that consumers plan to buy, at each alternative price, assuming the other demand factors remain constant. Of course, only one price can exist at any particular time.

For another perspective on the demand curve, suppose 400,000 apartments are on the market. The **demand price** is the price at which consumers will buy exactly that quantity, the price at which the market would clear. To find it, draw a vertical dashed line from the horizontal axis (start at 400,000) to the demand curve and draw a horizontal dashed line to the vertical axis. The demand price for 400,000 apartments per month is $500 per month. The demand price has an important interpretation. Some consumer will rent the last apartment, the 400,000th, if the actual price is $500 per month. If the actual price were slightly higher, $501 per month, no one would rent the last apartment. It is not worth $501. In other words, the 400,000th apartment is worth at least $500, but no more than $500; thus, it is worth exactly $500. The demand price shows the maximum price that some consumer will pay for the last unit.

Demand Price –
The price at which consumers will just buy the exact quantity on the market. It is the maximum price that anyone will pay for a unit.

Law of Demand –
As the price of some good changes with other factors constant, the quantity demanded for that good changes in the opposite direction.

The demand-price concept helps us to understand the **law of demand**, which is that the quantity demanded of any good is negatively related to its price, holding constant other variables such as population, consumer income, consumer preferences, and the prices of other goods. Figure 2.1, which like your plot is based on Table 2.2, shows that a lower price—$300 rather than $400—results in a larger quantity demanded. Equivalently, the more apartments consumers have, the lower the value consumers place on the last unit rented—the lower the demand price. Therefore, if consumers are to buy more, price must drop. Price must drop because the value of one more unit is less than the value of the previous one. Why? In the market for apartments, the demand price falls because the first apartments are rented by people who place the greatest value on them. If the price is $500, the only people willing to rent apartments are those who value them at a minimum of $500. To persuade more people to rent apartments, people who value them at less than $500 must want to rent them. But that happens only if the price is less than $500.

This will make sense if you think in terms of an individual consumer—perhaps yourself. For instance, as you consume additional scoops of ice cream per day, what happens to your demand price? How much satisfaction does the fourth scoop of ice cream in a day provide compared to the first scoop? Most of us get more satisfaction from the first scoop than from the second, and so on. Because of this diminishing satisfaction, our top price for each additional scoop falls as the number we have already consumed rises. As quantity increases, demand price falls, implying that your demand curve for ice cream has a negative slope. Likewise, the market demand curve, which is made up of all of the individual demand curves, would have a negative slope.

FIGURE 2.1   Demand Curve for Apartments in Gotham City

The demand curve shows the quantity demanded of apartments per month at each alternative price. Only one price can exist at a time, so only one quantity demanded can exist in a particular month. The demand curve is plotted from the demand schedule in Table 2.2. At point E, price is $300 per apartment per month and quantity demanded is 700,000 apartments per month. Put this and other points in the diagram and connect them to reveal the demand curve. If the market price is $400, the demand curve says that the quantity demanded is 550,000 apartments. Or, it says, if 400,000 apartments are on the market, the demand price, the price at which 400,000 apartments could just be filled, is $500.

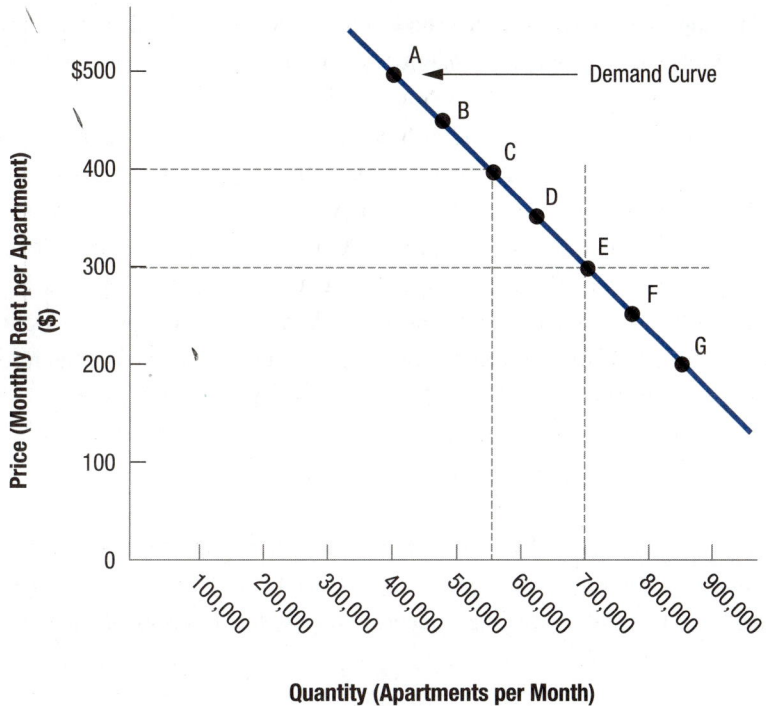

The demand schedule, quantity demanded, the demand curve, demand price, and the law of demand help us to understand one side of a market. To understand market coordination, however, it is also necessary to understand the other side—the supply side.

Supply

To understand the supply of apartments in Gotham City, suppose that construction technology and the prices of land, construction materials, and labor are fixed. Suppose also that the alternatives available to people who might build and place apartments on the market do not change, for example, the profitability of supplying office space. Holding constant these and other variables affecting cost, the number of apartments that landlords plan to supply depends upon the monthly rent that they expect to receive.

The *supply schedule* gives the number of apartments per month that landlords plan to supply at each alternative rental price. Like the demand schedule, the supply schedule exists for the given levels of

Quantity Supplied – The quantity of a good that producers will plan to sell at each possible price, holding constant other factors that affect supply.

Supply Curve – A curve (line) showing the quantity supplied of a good for each possible price, holding constant other factors that affect supply

Supply Price – The price at which sellers will just put a specific quantity of a good or service on the market. It is the minimum price that a seller will accept in return for selling one more unit of a good or service.

other variables—here, *construction technology, resource and materials prices,* and *profitability of other alternatives available to landlords and potential landlords.* Change in any other relevant variable would create a new supply schedule. The supply schedule in Table 2.3 shows that landlords plan to supply 400,000 apartments if the rental price is $300 per month and to supply 475,000 apartments if the price is $350. If the expected price increases from $300 to $350 per month, the **quantity supplied** increases from 400,000 to 475,000.

The **supply curve** is constructed and interpreted in the same way as the demand curve. (Use the supply schedule in Table 2.3 to draw a supply curve, which you can compare with Figure 2.2.) Suppose the market price is $450. The supply schedule or curve shows that the quantity supplied is 625,000. If the market price is $450, landlords would supply any quantity up to 625,000. They will not voluntarily supply more than 625,000.

The **supply price** aids in understanding why landlords are willing to supply less than 625,000 apartments, but not more than that quantity. The supply price—$450—is exactly sufficient to persuade landlords to supply a specified quantity. If the actual price is less than the supply price, say, $449, landlords will not supply the 625,000th apartment because $449 does not both cover the cost of production and provide an acceptable surplus (rate of return). The supply price, $450, is just sufficient to get the last unit to the market. It exactly covers the opportunity cost (which includes an acceptable surplus or rate of return) of producing the last unit. The opportunity cost, in turn, is the value of what the resources—land, labor, construction materials, the owners' contribution, and so on—could have produced in their next best use. The supply price, therefore, is the minimum price that any producer would accept for supplying the last unit. The producer, of course, would be happy to receive a price higher than the supply price for the last unit.

Inspection of the supply curve in Figure 2.2 shows that the supply price increases as quantity increases. This positive relationship shows that the greater the quantity supplied, the greater the opportunity cost of the last unit supplied. An example clarifies why this happens. Suppose that more apartments are built and

TABLE 2.3 Supply Schedule of Apartments in Gotham City

The supply schedule gives the number of apartments per month that landlords would supply at each alternative price. It exists for given values of other variables: construction technology, resources and materials prices, and profitability of alternatives. If the price is $300 per month, the quantity of apartments supplied per month is 400,000. If the price is $350 per month, the quantity supplied is 475,000.

	Price (Monthly Rent per Apartment)	Quantity (Apartments per Month)
A	$500	700,000
B	450	625,000
C	400	550,000
D	350	475,000
E	300	400,000
F	250	325,000
G	200	250,000

FIGURE 2.2 Supply Curve for Apartments in Gotham City

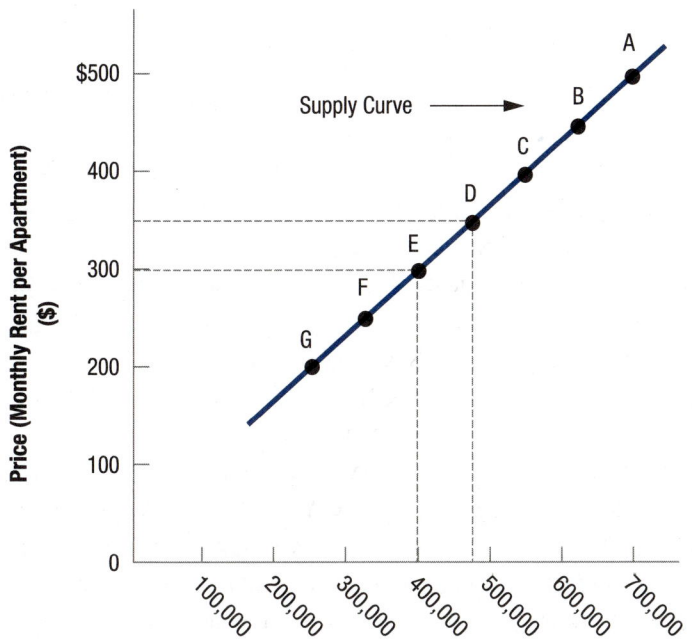

The supply curve shows the quantity of apartments supplied per month at each alternative price. It is plotted from the supply schedule in Table 2.3. At point E, price is $300 per apartment per month and quantity supplied is 400,000 apartments per month. The diagram can also illustrate the supply price. The supply price is the price that must be paid to put a certain quantity of apartments on the market. If 400,000 apartments are on the market, the lowest price that any supplier would accept for the 400,000th apartment is $300. If the price were $299, the 400,000th apartment would not be supplied. The supply price, therefore, is $300.

rented in Gotham City. To do so, workers and materials in Gotham City (and perhaps in other cities) would be diverted from the production of other goods and services. The opportunity cost of these new workers and materials is the value of what they currently produce. Workers and materials would be diverted first from the least valuable of their current uses. Perhaps they are attracted from building yet another amusement park that would just barely be profitable. Both the opportunity cost and wages necessary to attract the new workers might not be much higher than those of the workers currently producing apartments. But as apartment construction increases, workers and materials might be attracted from the construction of new health care facilities that are in greater demand than the amusement parks. Opportunity costs would be higher, and the wage necessary to attract the workers would also be higher. The opportunity cost of producing additional apartments increases because the additional workers must be diverted from uses with increasingly higher values. It is this relationship that leads to the **law of supply**—namely, holding other variables constant, the quantity supplied of a product is positively related to its price.

Law of Supply – As the price of some good changes with other factors constant, the quantity supplied for that good changes in the same direction.

Now we put our understanding of the supply side of the market—the supply schedule, the supply curve, the supply price, and the law of supply—together with our understanding of the demand side. The two parts of a market interact to coordinate the plans of consumers and producers.

Putting the Pieces Together: Demand and Supply

In a market economic system, government does not tell producers how much to produce or what price they will receive for their product. Neither does it tell consumers what they can buy nor what they must pay for products. The decisions about what to buy and sell are coordinated through the laws of supply and demand with no central direction. An astounding fact about market economies, therefore, is that year in and year out producers and consumers simultaneously adjust their production and consumption until they are equal. It is unusual to have excessive stockpiles of fruit or automobiles at the end of a typical year; likewise, few people who are willing to pay for a product cannot buy it. Exceptions occur, however, when producers slip up in planning. For example, during the holiday season, a toy or gadget occasionally becomes unexpectedly popular or else unpopular and either not enough or too much is produced; unexpected shortfalls or stockpiles result. In a market economy, these are exceptions; history shows, however, that in command economies such coordination failures are the rule.

Suppose a supercomputer were programmed to ensure that the vast majority of the 15 million people of the New York metropolitan area would find places they choose to rent and provide the appropriate quantities of other goods (food, clothing, and so on), and that this could be done with little overcrowding of apartments or few vacant ones. We would be amazed and rightly so. Yet a market economy does this every day. How?

Table 2.4 puts the demand and supply schedules from Tables 2.2 and 2.3 together. These schedules show the quantity demanded and supplied of apartments at alternative prices. Individuals in the Gotham City apartment market do not affect the market price. They are like the potato farmer who can produce from fence row to fence row or withhold all of her potatoes from the market without causing the price of potatoes to change. They are also like the shopper who can spend all or none of his money on potatoes, again without affecting the price of potatoes. They are price takers.

TABLE 2.4 **Demand and Supply Schedules for Apartments in Gotham City**

The demand and supply schedules for apartments help us see how the plans of consumers and producers are coordinated in a market economy. Each individual consumer or producer assumes that the market price is outside his or her control, so these consumers and producers adjust their quantity demanded or quantity supplied to the market price. Suppose the market price is $250. Consumers wish to rent 775,000 apartments per month. However, landlords will not place that many on the market. They are willing to supply only 325,000. Excess demand of 450,000 will push price up. As price increases, quantity demanded falls and quantity supplied increases. The originally inconsistent plans of consumers and producers come together as price adjusts. At a price of $400, the plans are exactly coordinated. Quantity demanded equals quantity supplied. The equilibrium quantity exchanged is 550,000 apartments.

Price (Monthly Rent per Apartment)	Quantity Demanded (Apartments per Month)	Quantity Supplied (Apartments per Month)
$500	400,000	700,000
450	475,000	625,000
400	550,000	550,000
350	625,000	475,000
300	700,000	400,000
250	775,000	325,000
200	850,000	250,000

Excess Demand – A situation in which quantity demanded exceeds quantity supplied at a given price.

If the market price is $300 a month, the number of apartments demanded is 700,000 a month and the quantity supplied is 400,000. At $300, the quantity demanded by consumers is greater than the quantity supplied by producers; this is an example of **excess demand**. People want more apartments than are available; landlords notice that they have unsatisfied customers. Someone will ask or offer a higher price (rent). Landlords will find that they are still able to lease their apartments at the higher price. As the price increases, the quantity demanded decreases—the law of demand. In addition, as the price increases, landlords will figure out ways to supply more apartments. The quantity supplied increases, illustrating the law of supply. As price goes up, the quantity that people plan to buy decreases and the quantity that other people plan to sell increases. Initially, the plans of consumers and producers are not coordinated. However, as the price increases, the plans converge. At $400 per month, the quantity of apartments demanded and the quantity supplied are equal—550,000. (Work out on paper what happens if the market price is $450 a month.) The excess demand that exists at the lower price is automatically eliminated if the price of apartments is flexible. The price system *coordinates* the plans of consumers and producers.

Figure 2.3 puts the demand and supply curves of Figures 2.1 and 2.2 together. Suppose the market price is $500 a month. The figure shows that the quantity demanded is 400,000 apartments per month and that the quantity supplied is 700,000 per month. The situation is one of **excess supply** because quantity supplied exceeds quantity demanded. The excess is 300,000 apartments: 700,000 minus 400,000. In the figure, it is measured by the distance from A to B—AB. Many landlords have vacant apartments. Although the apartments are vacant, the landlords must pay taxes and perhaps make mortgage payments. They will

Excess Supply – A situation in which quantity supplied exceeds quantity demanded at a given price.

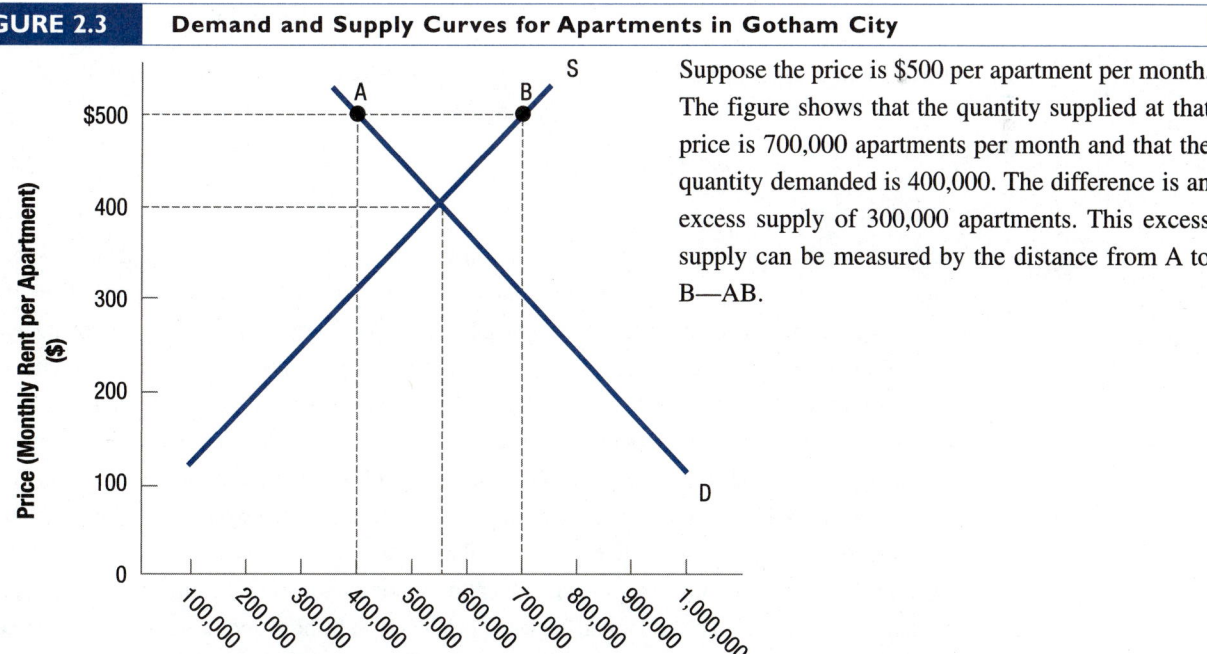

FIGURE 2.3   Demand and Supply Curves for Apartments in Gotham City

Suppose the price is $500 per apartment per month. The figure shows that the quantity supplied at that price is 700,000 apartments per month and that the quantity demanded is 400,000. The difference is an excess supply of 300,000 apartments. This excess supply can be measured by the distance from A to B—AB.

INFOTRAC
College Edition

Keywords: *price, demand, supply*
Use your InfoTrac password to look up articles on these topics at http://www.infotrac-college.com

Equilibrium –
A state of rest for the economy or market. Market equilibrium occurs at the price at which quantity demanded equals quantity supplied. This price is referred to as the equilibrium price, and this quantity is referred to as the equilibrium quantity.

try to entice consumers into the apartments by offering a lower price. The quantity demanded will increase. Some young people, for example, might decide to establish independent households because of the lower price. As the price falls, some landlords might decide to use their buildings for something other than apartments. The quantity supplied decreases.

Suppose the existing price is $300. As an exercise, use Figure 2.3 to explain to yourself why the price will increase. This exercise and the example in the previous paragraph show that *if the price results in excess demand, the price will increase* and *if it results in excess supply, the price will decrease.* The price adjusts until the quantity demanded equals the quantity supplied—until the market is in **equilibrium**. Equilibrium is a situation that will continue indefinitely unless some outside force changes it, which in this context occurs when quantity demanded equals quantity supplied. The price, $400, that equates the quantity demanded and the quantity supplied is the *equilibrium price*. The quantity demanded and supplied (550,000) at that price is the *equilibrium quantity exchanged*.

This emergence of equilibrium is the essence of market coordination. It is the process through which a market system determines how much of each good to produce and how to produce it. Moreover, the market system accomplishes these tasks without a central plan. The essence of a command economy—a planned economy—is that government orders individuals to produce certain goods and services. These orders are laws. In other words, in a command economy people are under legal obligation to obey a central plan. In a market economy, on the other hand, government establishes rules of behavior. Given these rules of behavior, individuals are free to decide what goods to produce and how to produce them.

■ COMPARATIVE SYSTEMS: AN INTRODUCTORY SKETCH

This section discusses coordination through the price system in a market economy and compares it with coordination in a command economy. We will then discuss the transition of former planned economies to market economies.

The Price System

Comparing a market economy to a command economy—capitalism versus centrally planned socialism—is not a matter of comparing no planning with planning. Planning occurs in any economy. The difference is who plans the coordination of economic activity and how plans are enforced. In a command economy, government plans what and how to produce. The plan is enforced by law. In a market economy, individuals plan and laws protect their transactions. As students, you plan your education: courses, major, and graduate school. In a command economy, your choices would not be allowed if they were inconsistent with the plan. Similarly, as consumers, you plan what to buy based on prices, your income, and your preferences. In a command economy, your choices might be frustrated if they were inconsistent with the plan. In the former Soviet Union, you could have afforded and wanted to buy a car, but you might have had to wait 10 years to buy one because the plan did not call for enough new cars. In a market economy, the purchase would be immediate. In the United States, a producer plans how and how much to produce based on expected profitability. In a command economy, the manager of a state-owned enterprise produces according to the central plan and uses materials and techniques imposed by the central planners.

We assume that in a market economy consumers attempt to maximize their satisfaction and producers attempt to maximize their total profits. A competitive market has many consumers and producers. No single consumer or small group of consumers has any noticeable effect on the market price. Consequently, a single consumer does not worry that the price of, say, housing will go up if he buys more housing. In competitive markets, consumers are *price takers*, which means that they accept market prices as given. Given their circumstances, their economic choices are simply how much to consume.

Competitive producers, attempting to maximize their profits, also are price takers. No single housing producer or small group of housing producers has any noticeable effect on market price. Consequently, a competitive producer does not worry that the price of housing may fall if she attempts to sell more.

There are two exceptions. First, suppose a product, such as the Windows operating system, has only a single producer. Microsoft realizes that, holding everything else constant, to increase the planned sales of a new version of Window, it must reduce the planned price. Consequently, a single producer affects the price when deciding how much to sell.

Second, what applies to a single competitive producer does not apply to all producers. In a competitive market, one housing producer does not noticeably affect the price of houses, even by increasing production by 10 percent. If, however, each of 10,000 producers put just 1 percent more on the market, the price would have to fall for all those houses to sell. An individual's decision to produce more or less will have no effect on others' production decisions because no one expects a single producer to affect market price. Likewise, because decisions about what to produce rely on market price, producers do not respond to what another producer does. For instance, suppose that Edward decides to produce 20 percent more houses. His decision does not affect how many houses Venus or other housing producers plan to produce. Consequently, the individual competitive producer is a price taker even though all producers acting together affect market price.

In a competitive market, all participants are price takers. They take market prices as given. Given their circumstances, their economic choices are simply how much to produce and consume.

Information, Rationing, and Motivation in a Market Economy

In a market economy, prices play three roles: They inform, they ration, and they motivate. These roles are crucial in the coordination of consumer and producer plans. The price system informs producers and consumers about underlying changes in the economy. For instance, an increase in price signals to consumers and producers that a good has become more valuable. The price system also provides incentives that motivate consumers and producers to adjust to those changes. These incentives provide the motivation for change: conservation and increased production.

INFORMING. Suppose the apartment market in Gotham City is in equilibrium. In Figure 2.4, the equilibrium price and quantity are P_0 and Q_0. Now suppose the demand curve changes unexpectedly from D_0 to D_1. Perhaps population increases. Notice that we assume that one of the "other" variables has changed, which has caused a change in demand.[4] This demand increase means that, at the same price, people plan

---

[4] We will examine changes in demand and supply in more detail in Chapter 4.

FIGURE 2.4 Effects of Change in Demand in the Apartment Market

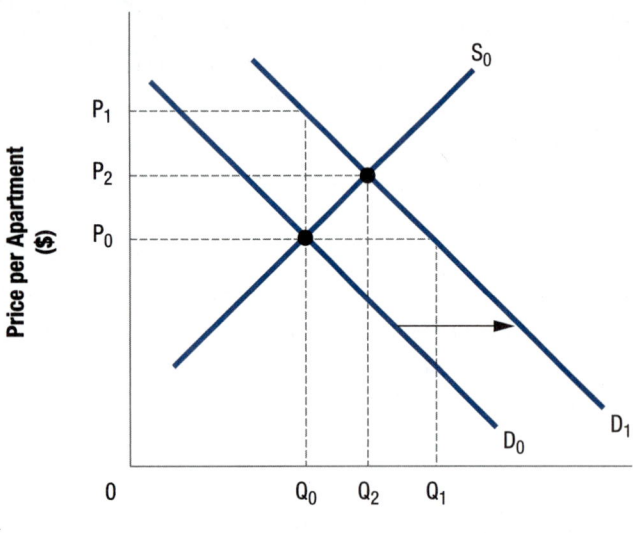

With the demand and supply curves D_0 and S_0, the equilibrium price and quantity in the apartment market are P_0 and Q_0. An increase in demand to D_1 disturbs the original equilibrium. The immediate effect may be no change in quantity and an increase in price to P_1. The increased price rations the original quantity of apartments to consumers who are willing to pay the most for them. P_0, however, is the supply price (opportunity cost) of an additional apartment. With the market price, P_1, above the supply price (opportunity cost), producers can profit by expanding output. Ultimately, the price increase motivates producers to expand output.

to rent more apartments. For instance, at price P_0 people now plan to rent Q_1 rather than Q_0 apartments. In contrast, an increase in the quantity demanded of apartments occurs if price falls and none of the "other" variables change. Because none of the other variables change, demand and the demand curve stay unchanged. For instance, consider the demand curve D_1 in Figure 2.4. The quantity demanded at the price P_1 is Q_0. If consumers in the city face a price of P_2, rather than P_1, their quantity demanded increases from Q_0 to Q_2.

The increase in demand that occurs when population increases might not be immediately obvious to the landlords or tenants. In any city, some people are moving out while others are moving in. An increase in population can occur either when fewer people leave or more people arrive. The immediate effect of the increased demand for apartments may be simply that apartments are leased more quickly and vacancy rates fall. Landlords will find that they can raise prices and tenants will find that they can get an apartment faster if they offer a higher price. The price increase will spread through the market, providing a signal to all participants that apartments are currently more valuable. This information, available to everyone, will generate numerous changes.

RATIONING OF EXISTING APARTMENTS. The increase in demand raises the demand price for the quantity, Q_0 from P_0 to P_1. Excess demand would exist if the price remained at P_0, but landlords discover that some applicants are willing to pay more than the going rate, P_0, for an apartment. The possibility of excess demand for apartments is eliminated as tenants bid up the price to the demand price, P_1. Even if the quantity of apartments supplied does not increase, the excess demand disappears. This price increase *informs* people that apartments have become more scarce. If they expect the price increase to be permanent, the original residents of the town will reduce the quantity they demand of housing. Similarly, the new residents will demand a lower quantity at the higher price than at the lower price. In short, consumers automatically respond to more expensive apartments by reducing the quantity demanded. They conserve because it is to their advantage to do so.

People will choose to live in more crowded conditions, but this does not mean that excess demand exists: It means that increased *scarcity* has caused the equilibrium price to go up. The distinction between excess demand and increased scarcity is important. **Scarcity** is the economic condition common to all societies. It simply means that, in the aggregate, our wants exceed our abilities to meet them. Consequently, we must choose which wants to satisfy. Excess demand, on the other hand, persists only if price cannot adjust.

In short, the price system automatically **rations**, or allocates, an available supply to consumers. This automatic rationing of a good that has become more scarce is a controversial feature of a market system. It means, for example, that the market allocates apartments impersonally. A higher price changes people's consumption plans. Those people who are willing to pay the most for the good obtain it. The rationing of apartments on the basis of willingness (and ability) to pay, however, might result in people living in what others perceive as inadequate housing.

Scarcity –
The common situation for all economies, in which aggregate wants exceed the economy's ability to meet them because of limited resources.

Ration –
To allocate a limited supply of goods and services to people.

Economic Profit –
A rate of earning in excess of the minimum necessary to attract economic resources into a particular use.

PROFIT AS A MOTIVATION FOR INCREASED APARTMENT PRODUCTION. At a price of P_1 (Figure 2.4) and quantity of Q_0, provision of an additional apartment—an increase in quantity supplied—generates **economic profit** because the price is greater than the minimum price necessary to rent the last apartment. The supply price, P_0, just covers the opportunity cost of putting the last apartment on the market. It is important to realize that a minimum acceptable return is part of the opportunity cost. If price equals opportunity cost, therefore, the seller can sell at this price and earn the return necessary to stay in the business. If the market price is above the supply price, some landlord will find it profitable to put another apartment on the market. With the new demand curve D_1, the new demand price, P_1, clears the market if no more apartments are supplied. Because the market price rises above the supply price, however, it will be profitable to build new apartments. The higher price *informs* producers of the possible increased scarcity of apartments. Some landlords will think that the increased scarcity is temporary, but others will take the price change signal as a clue that demand has increased. If market research confirms the demand increase, the possibility of earning profits *motivates* the adventuresome landlord to produce more apartments. Because the demand price is above the supply price, producing more apartments yields a higher return than producing other goods. Quantity supplied increases as existing or new producers put more apartments on the market.

As long as the market price is greater than the supply price, producing more generates more profits. As producers place more apartments on the market, competition increases and the price falls. The increase in quantity supplied moves the market to a new equilibrium with price P_2 and quantity Q_2. The producers compete for the potential profits by producing more apartments. As they do so, price falls; beyond the quantity Q_2, profits cannot be earned by producing more. It is ironic that the pursuit of profits under competitive conditions eventually eliminates the opportunity for additional profits. The first landlord to get additional apartments on the market will make economic profits. The last one will cover costs and get the minimum acceptable return.

The increased demand in the apartment market automatically causes increased demand in input markets. Increases in construction wages, for instance, *signal* greater job opportunities, motivating people to become construction workers. If input prices change, the cost of production of other goods changes. The effect of the increased demand for and, therefore, increased scarcity of apartments ripples into other markets. In each market, as price changes, individuals adapt their plans to new conditions. Price changes are the signals for individuals to consider changing their plans; profits are the motivation.

Information, Rationing, and Motivation in a Command Economy

In a command economy, even if the central planners want to respond to the desires of consumers, adjustment to changes in demand and supply is necessarily slower and subject to larger error than in a market economy. This is because the planners do not allow the price system to play its three roles of informing, rationing, and motivating.

INFORMING. If the demand for apartments in a particular area increases, the central planners could respond, as the market does, by allowing rent to increase. In a situation where the government rather than an impersonal market sets prices, governments are often unwilling to raise price. A price increase would meet political resistance. Furthermore, it is not just in one market that demand and supply changes cause equilibrium price to change. If planners adjusted prices in all markets where the equilibrium changed, it would be incredibly costly both in terms of planning costs and politically. To avoid these complications, planners tend to keep prices constant, making it impossible for price changes to signal and inform.

RATIONING OF EXISTING APARTMENTS. In the former Soviet Union, the state committee on prices set about 500,000 prices. Prices of some products could not be changed without changing other prices. Because it is extremely expensive to set 500,000 prices, prices did not change often. Many prices changed no more than once every 10 years. If prices are not flexible, however, the price system cannot ration available supply. Excess demand and excess supply did not disappear in the Soviet Union, because prices did not adjust. For instance, excess demand for apartments persisted for years. Young couples, even those who could afford separate housing, had to live with their parents and perhaps others in small apartments. Exceptions included Communist Party and government officials. People with political influence got apartments. It was who you knew that counted, not what you would pay, unless you were willing to pay bribes. Similar situations arise in Berkeley and Manhattan, which are examples of the many cities in the United States and throughout the world where laws prevent apartment rents from being raised to market levels.

The market price system, by contrast, is anonymous. An increase in demand causes price to rise automatically and leads the economy to a new equilibrium. Because price increases spring from the adjustments of many individual planners, no single entity can be blamed for the price increase. In a command economy, on the other hand, a price increase must be approved by the central planners who, therefore, are blamed for it.

MOTIVATION FOR INCREASED APARTMENT PRODUCTION. Problems persist in a command economy even if the planners allow prices to rise. Setting new prices takes a long time. The higher prices result in economic profits. In a command economy, however, producers rarely share in these profits, which undermines their motivation to increase production. One reform often tried in command economies is to let producers share in profits so they will be motivated to follow price and profit signals.

Alternatively, the central planners could order the production of more apartments. They first must be sure, however, that the demand increase is permanent. If not, they could make a serious error. In a market economy, if an individual (one of the many planners in the market system) expands production, that person bears the consequences. If the decision is a good one, the person profits. If not, the person bears the loss. Normally, the effects on the market would be inconsequential because one producer has little effect on the entire market. When central planners make a decision, however, they necessarily affect the entire market. If the decision is a good one, the planners receive little credit. (The politicians take the credit.) If they build too many apartments, the error can be easily traced to their planning decision, making it easy to penalize them. As a result, central planners often decide that the risks associated with inaction are less than the risks of significant changes. In other words, for the market producer, it is "heads, I win; tails, I lose." For the central planner, it is "heads, other people win; tails, I lose."

A command economy has limited ability to adjust to economic changes. Political factors limit the price or output adjustments that can be made, and economic changes require enormous amounts of information about the market in question and about related markets. Because planners or production managers rarely profit legally, motivation for change is often political rather than economic. On the other hand, a market economy with decentralized planning based on a price system does not require the large bureaucracy of central planning. It needs no centralized information about individual markets; it has a built-in incentive system.

Systems and Coordination

This discussion of the provision of apartments in different economic systems shows that a market system provides goods to people based on their willingness (including ability) to pay. Command economies are much less successful in coordinating demand and supply. They run into problems of excess demand (shortages) and inequitable allocation based on personal characteristics rather than willingness to pay.

Market systems successfully coordinate economic activity. Price falls in response to excess supply and rises in response to excess demand so as to equate the quantity demanded and supplied of a good. A market system coordinates the interdependent actions of specialized producers and does so without a legally imposed central plan. It fosters the division of labor that is responsible for increasing the "wealth of nations."

INFOTRAC
College Edition

Keyword: *economic central planning*
Use your InfoTrac password to look up articles on these topics at
http://www.infotrac-college.com

Historical experience shows that command economies have great difficulty in coordinating economic activity. They lack a market economy's ability to automatically and inexpensively collect information about consumer wants and production capabilities. Neither do they share the capability to automatically and inexpensively provide incentives and motivation for people to make wealth-promoting decisions. Prices do all of this in a market economy. The next section briefly discusses experiences of some former communist countries in their struggle to transform their command economies to market economies.

INSIGHTS

CAN SOCIALISM USE THE PRICE SYSTEM?

Some leaders of former communist countries want to keep elements of central planning while moving their economies to a price system. Presumably, they are searching for the benefits of the price system—coordination, motivation and incentives, information, and rationing—while maintaining the political power that comes from central planning. Or perhaps they want to maintain the power to reduce income inequality—a major stated goal of socialism.

THE COORDINATION PROBLEM

The early opponents of socialism doubted that a centrally planned economy (CPE) could calculate prices that cleared markets. The ability to clear markets is one of the great achievements of a price system. Indeed, the price system can be thought of as a supercomputer calculating prices that coordinate plans of producers and consumers. Today, some people argue that appropriate ingenuity combined with the great capacity of supercomputers may permit planners in a CPE to calculate prices that result in smooth coordination.

But CPE history is not encouraging. For instance, excess demands for housing and some kinds of food were characteristic of the former Soviet Union. Planners were unable or unwilling to set equilibrium prices. Even if modern computers enable the computation of appropriate prices, central planners may have political reasons for not using them.

THE INCENTIVE PROBLEM

Suppose that a socialist system solves the coordination problem. Can it create incentives that motivate people to respond appropriately—to reallocate resources to consumers' most desired uses? The first step is to calculate prices that reflect opportunity costs. Under central planning, Poland, in Northern Europe, exported semitropical flowers. It priced energy so low that it was profitable to grow flowers in artificially heated greenhouses. The opportunity cost of these flowers was greater than their market price, but they were grown and exported because the subsidized energy prices hid their opportunity cost. Subsidized energy and food prices continue to provide inappropriate incentives in many of the former CPEs.

The second step is to reward people who make appropriate decisions based on the price signals. That is, CPEs must pay people according to the value of what they produce and allow them to make huge profits in return for developing lower cost production methods or new products. Because one purpose of socialism is to narrow wage and income differences, it has difficulty with such an incentive system. In short, socialists are often unwilling to adopt policies that guide people toward economically appropriate behavior.

THE INFORMATION PROBLEM

Giant strides in economic growth in capitalist economies have raised the material condition of ordinary people to heights unimaginable to Adam Smith and Alfred Marshall, two economists who believed that understanding economics was the key to prosperity. This growth has occurred in economies where entrepreneurs respond to market prices that relay appropriate information about profitable opportunities. Relaying appropriate information is the essence of solving the coordination and incentive problems.

Entrepreneurs take the information and develop new processes and products—new information. The price system relays information to potential users about the new processes and products. This transmission of existing information and development of new information are essential for economic growth. Thus far, only societies that have relied on markets for the transmission and growth of information have had sustained economic prosperity.

Perhaps CPEs can solve the calculation and incentive problems, but the information problem is the most challenging. Many economists argue that if the leaders of former CPEs want economies that generate progress, these leaders must abandon the idea of salvaging elements of central planning. Only in economies where the price system relays accurate information have entrepreneurs like Walt Disney, Henry Ford, Bill Gates, and Oprah Winfrey initiated persistent economic growth.

SOURCE: For a detailed discussion, see Don Lavoie, "Computation, Incentives, and Discovery: The Cognitive Function of Markets in Market Socialism," in *Privatizing and Marketizing Socialism*, special ed., Jan S. Prybyla, ed., Richard D. Lambert, *The Annals of The American Academy of Political and Social Science* 507 (January 1990), 72–79.

■ Transitions to a Market Economy: Some Experiences

Centrally planned economies, if they are to become market economies, must bring together five pieces of a market economic system. Unfortunately for these so-called transition economies, these are not five easy pieces, and all of them must fall in place at about the same time. As shown in Table 2.1, to work well, a market economy or price system must have the following:

- Reasonably stable prices and a well-functioning monetary system that facilitates voluntary exchange
- A system of private property and property rights defined, established, and protected by law
- Market incentives that are generated by a price system whose rewards and penalties motivate decision makers
- Flexible prices that fluctuate in response to individuals' voluntary decisions and exchanges (market exchange)
- A legal system that is broadly obeyed and a culture that generates a climate of trust

We will next discuss the progress of several transition economies in terms of these five pieces. Although the collapse and breakup of the Soviet Union happened more than a decade ago, some of these countries have made little progress toward establishing well-functioning market systems. Change continues, and the situation that we describe here may alter by the time you read this. Several countries in Central Europe, including the Czech Republic, Estonia, Hungary, and Poland, have, in effect, created market economies. Others, including Belarus, Kazakhstan, Romania, and Ukraine, have a long way to go. Russia, the largest and most powerful of the transition states, has serious problems. These countries' different rates of transition depend upon history, politics, tradition, and the economic situation when the transition began. Our discussion of transition experiences begins with a comparison of the performance of the economies of two countries: Hungary and Ukraine. We then look at the four other pieces of the puzzle using the Hungary and Slovenia "success" stories and the Russia and Ukraine "adversity" stories.

Stable Prices and the Monetary System

Many countries that abandoned communism did so in part because economic growth had stagnated. Moreover, inflexible prices led to excess demand for many products—apartments, cars, and so on. Excess demand for many consumer products removed much of the incentive for business firms to produce high-quality products. They had no competition. The government had a monopoly on everything produced. Moreover, international trade restrictions eliminated foreign competition. Inflation and unemployment, however, were generally low under central planning. Inflation was low because prices were held down by law, by plan, and by inertia. Prices did not reflect the scarcity of goods and services. Unemployment was low because many people had make-work jobs where the value of what they produced was less than the cost of production.

As prices were freed, the suppressed inflation exploded, hidden unemployment became open, unemployment grew, and production fell drastically. These countries faced extremely difficult and painful economic problems. Initially, they had the pain of the transition without the rewards of a market economy.

Figure 2.5 describes the transition for Hungary and Ukraine. Hungary had an early start in the transition to a market economy. In the early part of the transition, its annual inflation rate rose to more than 30 percent.

FIGURE 2.5 The Transition: Selected Countries

The three panels provide a snapshot of the Hungarian and Ukrainian economies in transition. The first panel shows that Hungary brought inflation down early in the transition, whereas Ukraine's inflation literally exploded off the chart, approaching 5,000 per year at its peak. Moreover, it is more erratic than Hungary's. Perhaps because its transition began earlier, Hungary's output growth rate recovered faster than Ukraines'. Ukraine had deep and sustained output declines; its GDP today is substantially less than it was in 1989. Hungary's output started to grow in 1994 and is currently above its 1989 level. Its unemployment rate reached 12 percent early in the transition and has fallen since then. Ukraine's unemployment did not begin to rise until the mid-1990s, indicating that labor markets had not been liberalized. Since that time, its unemployment has increased.

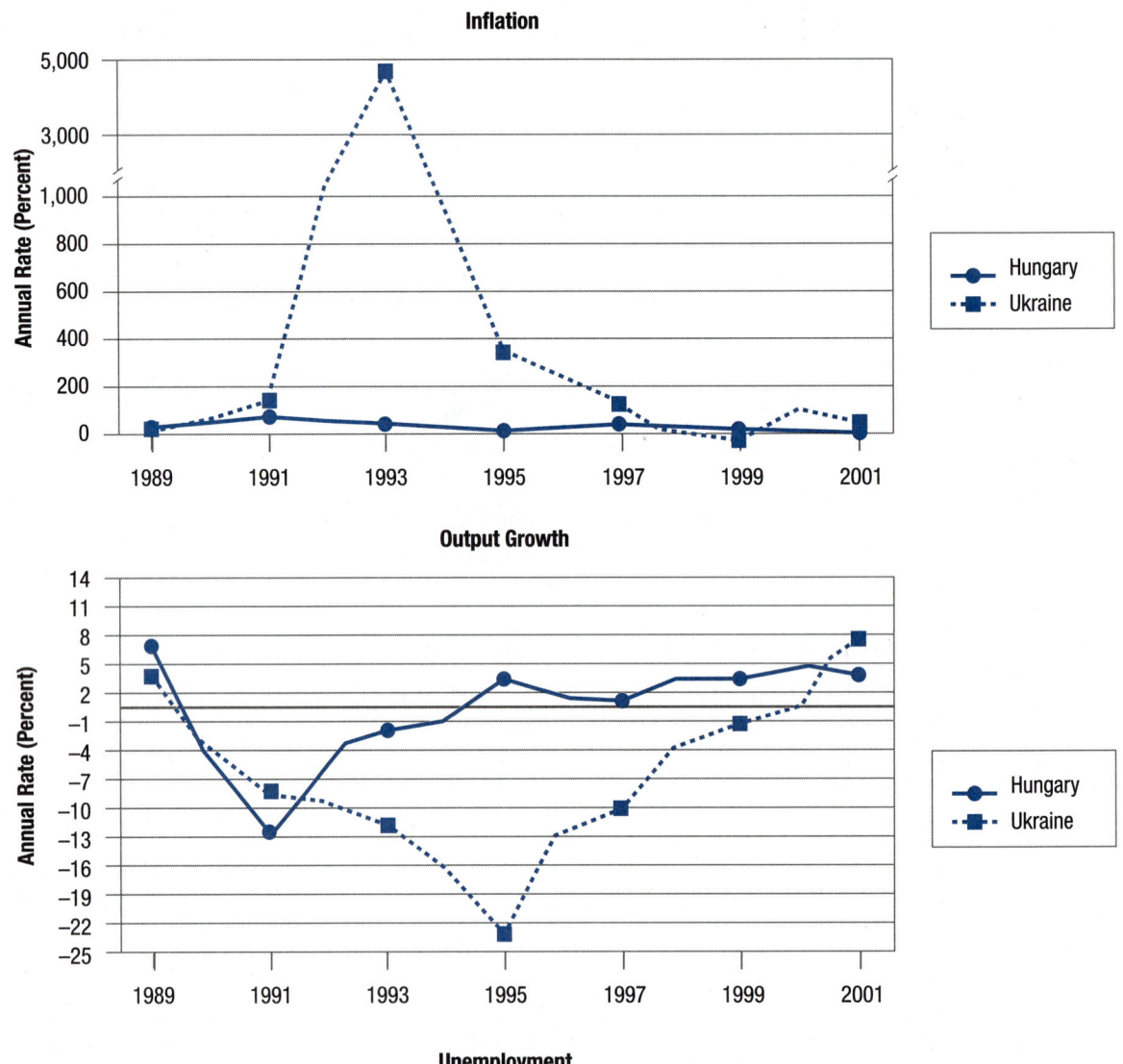

FIGURE 2.5 The Transition: Selected Countries (continued)

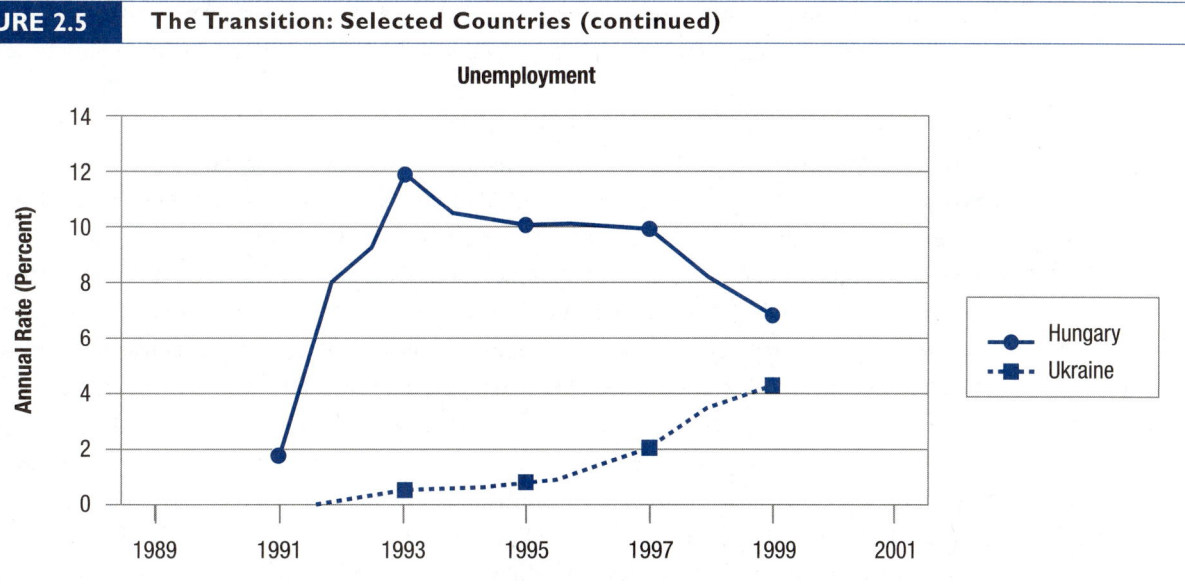

SOURCE: EBRD *Transition Reports*. See http://www.ebrd.com for summaries of the transition reports.

Inflation at this rate damages the information function of prices, but, as Figure 2.5 shows, the annual inflation rate dropped over the decade—with one interruption—to its current rate of about 10 percent.

This rapid inflation, followed by a reduction in the inflation rate, characterizes a successful transition. Hungary quickly removed most restrictions on prices and foreign trade and privatized its business firms. As a result, prices increased and unemployment rose. The huge increase in its unemployment rate and the associated sharp reduction in output was a necessary part of instituting competition and establishing market incentives. For long-term growth, it was necessary to move resources into areas of the economy where they would be more productive. Hungary's output began to grow again by 1994, and its unemployment rate began to fall. Since 1994, as Figure 2.5 shows, unemployment has continued to fall, output has continued to rise, and inflation has generally fallen. The decline in output and the rise in unemployment are characteristics of an economy in transition from central planning to markets. The Czech Republic, Estonia, Poland, and Slovenia among other countries have followed a similar path.

Ukraine has not attempted to reform its economy as quickly as the countries mentioned here. Nonetheless, its inflation rate is, literally, off the chart in Figure 2.5. (To make the chart legible, we did not try to display the huge Ukrainian inflation rate—up to nearly 500 percent per year—in the omitted years.) Although Ukraine liberalized prices sufficiently to have inflation, its unemployment remained at command economy levels through the mid-1990s; the low reported unemployment rates indicate that much unemployment was disguised. Disguised unemployment, in turn, suggests that Ukraine has been slow in transition. Ukraine's output decline was much sharper and lasted much longer than Hungary's. Other countries that have followed a gradual path include Albania, Belarus, Kyrgyzstan, and Romania.

The inflation rate in Russia from 1996 to 2001 ranged between 15 percent and 85 percent. These inflation rates are sufficiently high and variable to continue eroding the price system's ability to coordinate. More significantly, the Russian government has had difficulty providing a monetary framework for market transactions. Many Russian businesses pay their bills and their taxes with what they produce; in short, they pay in kind. "By 1998, [Russian] industry collected as much as 70 percent of its receipts in nonmonetary form, leaving many firms with too little cash to pay salaries and taxes."[5] The complex development and acceptance of direct barter (payment in kind) and of various credit instruments that operated as near monies arises from the history and institutions of the Soviet Union. The electric power company provides one example of how this has happened. Firms that were using electrical power could not or would not pay the power company in rubles. If the firms held bank accounts, the government and the power company could simply take their money directly from the bank. Owners of the firms realized that if they had no bank accounts, they could avoid these involuntary payments, so they stopped using money. Furthermore, many of the firms simply lacked the resources to pay their bills. Because neither would benefit by closing the firms down, both the power company and the government were willing to accept almost anything the firms offered in payment. For example, "automotive fuels, fertilizers, and pesticides were accepted in taxes and distributed to farms in lieu of budget subsidies."[6] If the recipient of the goods in kind had a direct use for the goods, this barter was relatively uncomplicated. However, if the "goods available as in-kind tax payments could not be put to direct use, some way of exchanging them needed to be found; here, the clearing operations become more complicated."[7] One local government was unable to buy medicine for its hospital. It forgave the tax liability of the local power company in return for medicine. The power company, in turn, had previously accepted the medicine as payment from one of its debtors.

The impact on the Russian economy of this reversion to barter is well summarized by David Woodruff: "More quietly and significantly, as many as 60 percent of Russians made a complete or partial retreat from the division of labor, using subsistence farming to minimize their need for the cash that their regular jobs as doctors, engineers, or mine workers could not be counted on to generate."[8]

Other Economic Reforms

The remainder of this section refers to four charts that rank countries on various aspects of the economic reforms necessary to develop a market economy. The European Bank for Reconstruction and Development (EBRD)[9] has rated a country's success in transition from 1 to 4.3 for many categories, with 1 indicating no progress and 4.3 indicating that the country has achieved norms for the category typical of that of "advanced industrial countries." In the tables, the countries are indexed according to ratio of their 2001 GDP to their 1989 GDP times 100. If a country had a GDP of $2 billion in 1989 and $3 billion in 2001, its index number would be ($3 billion/$2 billion) times 100 or 150. Its GDP would have

---

[5]David Woodruff, *Money Unmade: Barter and the Fate of Russian Capitalism* (Ithaca: Cornell University Press, 1999), p. xi.
[6]Ibid., p. 135.
[7]Ibid., p. 135.
[8]Ibid., introduction.
[9]European Bank for Reconstruction and Development (EBRD) Transition Report; selected issues.

grown by [(150−100)/100]: 50 percent. Slovenia's index number, 114, presented immediately below its name in each table means that its GDP (adjusted for inflation) was 14 percent greater in 2001 than in 1989. Similarly, Figure 2.6 shows that Russia, with its index number of 63, had a 37—[(63−100)/100]—percent lower GDP in 2001 than in 1989. The countries are arranged from left to right according to their index numbers in each figure. Most economists would agree that the two countries on the right (Slovenia and Hungary) have progressed farther in transition than the bottom two (Russia and Ukraine).

FLEXIBLE PRICES. Most of the countries of Central and Eastern Europe have allowed the prices of most goods to adjust to demand and supply conditions. Some have freed prices all at once, and others have done it gradually, but almost all have done so. Nevertheless, the ones that liberalized first, the success stories, have had a more successful transition than the remainder. Liberalization here is defined as the year in which a country first had a price liberalization score of 3 and a trade score of 4. A price score of 3 indicates substantial price flexibility, with only prices of "essentials" held down. The trade score indicates substantial trade liberalization with the only restrictions on international transactions being tariffs. The first bar for each country in Figure 2.6 shows the number of years (measured on the right axis) since a country first achieved liberalization. Hungary and Slovenia were considered liberalized at least 8 years ago, while Russia and Ukraine have barely started. The upward drift of the bars as we move to the right in this and the next 3 figures indicates that the countries that have been most successful in restoring their GDP have been the ones that have been most successful in transforming from their old economic system to a market economic system.

| FIGURE 2.6 | **Flexible Prices and Markets: Selected Countries** |

This figure shows that the success stories—Slovenia and Hungary—begin liberalizing earlier than the adversity stories—Russia and Ukraine. The numbers after the country name are index numbers that show the country's GDP in 2000 as compared to its 1989 GDP, which is indexed at 100.

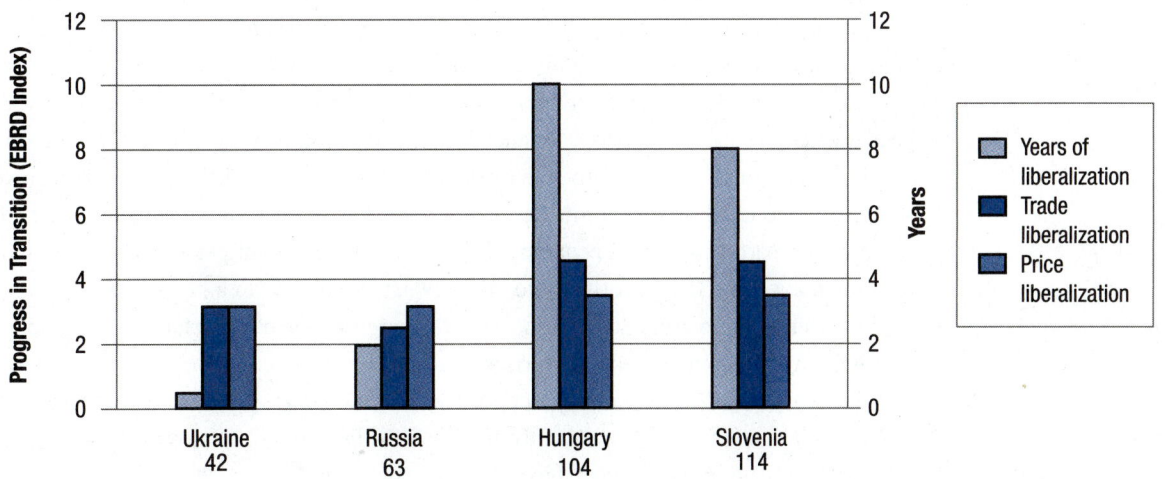

SOURCE: EBRD *Transition Reports*. See http://www.ebrd.com for summaries of the transition reports.

The other 2 bars for each country in this figure index the success that a country has had in trade and price liberalization. According to these rankings, Russia and Ukraine have failed to remove most restrictions on international trade, whereas Hungary and Slovenia have reached the status of "advanced industrial countries." In terms of flexible domestic prices, Hungary and Slovenia are slightly ahead of the other countries. They all, however, have been slow in freeing prices of such items as electricity, energy, and public transportation. These prices have been held down for humanitarian and political reasons. Allowing these prices to increase to market-clearing levels would cause distress and could cause political unrest. Nevertheless, these price controls limit market coordination and impede economic restructuring.

Another factor behind the price scores being below 4 for all of the countries is that the transition countries continue to subsidize their state-owned enterprises (SOEs). One purpose of the subsidies is to prevent unemployment from increasing beyond its already high rates. Another purpose is to ensure that the SOEs continue to provide social services, such as health and education, to their employees, as they did under the previous system. Nevertheless, some SOEs are completely wasteful; the value of what some of them produced under central planning was actually less than the value of the resources that they used. This is probably still true in some transition countries. The transition economies use subsidies to keep inefficient and wasteful state-owned enterprises operating, impeding the economic restructuring necessary to privatize physical capital assets, both directly and indirectly. In a market economy, an enterprise that does not cover its full costs must reduce costs, increase revenues, or shut down. If it is shut down, its resources—land, labor, and capital—are released for use by other enterprises. Although the subsidization of SOEs has interfered with privatization, it has not prevented either the creation of a large private sector in these economies or the establishment of property rights.

THE ESTABLISHMENT OF PRIVATE PROPERTY AND PROPERTY RIGHTS. The creation of private property requires creating private property rights, enticing entrepreneurs to start new business, and transferring SOEs to private ownership. As seen in Figure 2.7, all four countries have made substantial progress in setting up the legal framework for transition. Russia and Ukraine, however, lag the other countries because they are deficient in laws protecting corporate shareholders and those establishing a modern bankruptcy system. Indeed, many transition economies have made little progress in creating legislation to allow private and state enterprises to become bankrupt. Bankruptcy is unpleasant. When it happens, owners lose their property. Financial institutions suffer. Employees of the bankrupt enterprise may lose their jobs. Consequently, the difficulty that the leaders of the transition economies have had in developing political support for modern bankruptcy law is not surprising. Nevertheless, bankruptcy is an important part of a market economy. It is a way that economic resources can be moved from owners who are not using them profitably to other owners who may do a better job.

Although it seems odd to criticize an economy for having too few bankruptcies, the reason for the criticism is simple. Allowing inefficient enterprises and managers to continue to operate prevents the economy from moving to a higher level of production. These shortcomings affect large firms and corporations more than small business firms. Consequently, the small-business sector of most transition economies has emerged with significant private ownership.

Entrepreneurs have created new restaurants, repair shops, small manufacturing operations, and other small businesses that account for significant parts of these economies' private sectors. Similarly, many

FIGURE 2.7   Private Property and Property Rights: Selected Countries

Slovenia and Hungary have complete the transition to private property in terms of small-scale privatization, and Russia is not far behind. Ukraine is last in terms of small-scale privatization, but it is ahead of Russia and close to the others in terms of large-scale privatization. Slovenia and Hungary are also ahead of the two in terms of establishing an effective legal framework.

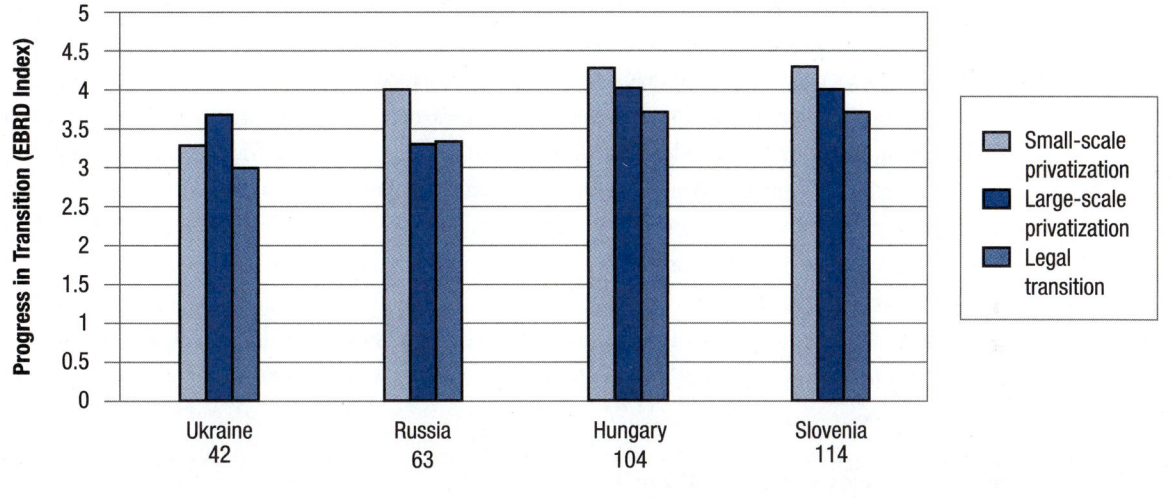

SOURCE: EBRD *Transition Reports*. See http://www.ebrd.com for summaries of the transition reports.

small state-owned enterprises have been transferred to private ownership. The legal system has enabled many private individuals to start new business and to purchase small SOEs and manage them effectively. Figure 2.7 shows that the success stories have reached advanced industrial status in terms of privatizing small business and that the other countries are not far behind

The second aspect of privatization is the much more difficult task of privatizing large SOEs. Imagine a society in which most people are completely unfamiliar with the idea of owning stock in a company like General Motors (GM). Imagine also that the people who currently manage GM were stripped of their authority and that ownership responsibilities were sold to people with absolutely no management or ownership experience. The problems would be enormous. Where would people find the resources to buy stock? How could they choose new managers? How could they know whether their managers were doing a good job? Establishing a corporate culture in these countries is difficult. In addition, many of these large SOEs provided their employees with health care, education, and recreation. Governments are reluctant to privatize such enterprises because the social services would be discontinued and many workers laid off. As Figure 2.7 indicates, large-scale privatization has been slower than small scale. Again, Slovenia and Hungary have made the most progress, with Ukraine next, followed by Russia. The latter countries have only 25 to 50 percent of original state assets in private hands or moving to private hands. Countries with substantial production still taking place in SOEs have much to do to establish market incentives.

INCENTIVES.   For market incentives to work well, prices must reflect cost, and individuals must bear the costs and receive the benefits of their decisions. The interest rate that is charged for loans is an important price because it rations investment funds among competing uses. Suppose you wanted to build a house and planned to borrow the money from a bank to do so. Typically, you would plan to repay the bank on a monthly basis at a rate that would pay off the mortgage in 30 years. Suppose you could borrow the money at zero interest rate. You then decide what house to build and contract for the resources—land, labor, and capital—to do so. Alternatively, suppose that you have to pay 10 percent interest. In this case, you certainly would build a less expensive house, because the total payment for the original one will include repaying what you borrowed plus interest. You will use fewer resources in building your house. In a command economy, interest rates do not reflect cost, and investment decisions are made without concern for cost of borrowing money. Without market interest rates to ration investment funds, the command economy had to so in some other way. The government had to decide what investments to make. Until the transition economies have market-determined interest rates and well-developed financial institutions, it will be difficult for interest rates to provide the appropriate information to investors. As Figure 2.8 shows, only Hungary has made substantial progress toward interest rate liberalization. Russia and Ukraine, in particular, still prevent free adjustment of interest rates and have substantial government involvement in the allocation of investment funds among investors.

The figure also shows that Russian and Ukraine, reflecting the difficulties that they have had in large-scale privatization, are well behind the other countries in restructuring enterprises. To see how this

FIGURE 2.8   Incentives (Selected Countries)

Establishing effective market incentives requires prices that reflect opportunity costs and establishing ownership institutions that link rewards to actions. For interest rates to provide signals of opportunity cost necessary for making sound investment decisions, financial markets must be liberalized. Russia and Ukraine have made little progress in this area and, consequently, cannot rely on interest rates as measures of opportunity costs. Similarly, they are behind Slovenia and Hungary in terms of developing institutions of corporate ownership.

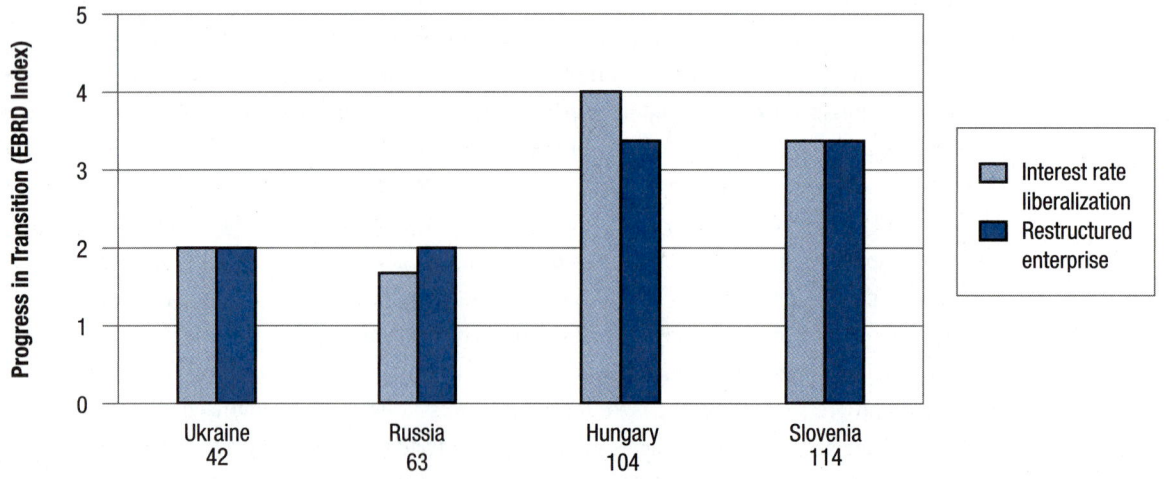

SOURCE: EBRD *Transition Reports*. See http://www.ebrd.com for summaries of the transition reports.

INTERNATIONAL PERSPECTIVE

COWBOY CAPITALISM IN RUSSIA?

Criminal activity in Russia reminds some people of the lawlessness in the Old West. After all, rustling, land grabbing, bank robbing, and other criminal activities are part of the western saga, just like the cowboy. Perhaps a new capitalist economy breeds criminal and gang activity. Certainly Russia has a significant crime problem. Russians might be reassured to know that the chaotic criminal conditions that exist today are just a stage of capitalism.

Numerous gangs operate in Russia. They deal in illegal goods, they smuggle, they bribe government officials, and they force legitimate businesses to pay for protection. They divert resources, such as oil, which they buy at below-world–market prices, from legitimate uses and sell them on the world market. Blackmail, threats, and murder are used to prevent competition or to learn business secrets.

It is an insult to the early settlers, however, to compare contemporary Russian lawlessness to conditions in the Old West. Because law enforcement did not spread west as fast as the settlers, criminal activity probably exceeded the norm in more established parts of the United States. Despite respect for the rule of law derived from a long history of established property law, vigilante groups, consisting of community leaders, operated outside the law. Superficially, this appears like gang activity. Unlike the Russian gangs, however, vigilante groups attempted to enforce the law, not victimize honest citizens.

In the early stages of capitalism in the United States, most prices were unregulated, and few regulations prevented people from doing what they wanted, so long as other people were not harmed involuntarily. Unlike the situation in a command economy or in a society with price controls, unexploited gains from voluntary exchange did not exist and thus could not generate profits for gangs. Government officials lacked the power to prevent profitable activities; consequently, no reason existed to bribe them.

Russian history is different. Bribery of government officials was routine in the Soviet Union, and it was not considered wrong. It was a way to get things done. Evading price controls was also a way of life. As a result, life in the Soviet Union did not generate the respect for and trust of the legal system necessary for capitalism to work well.

In fact, the situation in Russia is more like what began to develop in the United States during Prohibition. Prohibition made gang activity extremely profitable in the 1920s. Criminals profited from selling alcohol, some otherwise honest citizens enjoyed its consumption, and government officials profited by turning a blind eye to the situation.

Gang activity in Russia does not result from an early state of capitalism; it is not cowboy capitalism. Furthermore, it will not automatically go away. The gangs that prospered during Prohibition in the United States outlasted Prohibition by decades. They moved into illegal gambling and drug sales, and they corrupted some labor unions. Furthermore, gang activity can harm an economy as well as the individual victims. As the wealth and power of gangs increase, they are more likely to infiltrate legitimate businesses and labor unions. Investors in industries where gangs are less prevalent will be reluctant to invest in gang-ridden ones. Evidence suggests that areas of southern Italy with the highest growth rates have the lowest crime rates and vice versa. Although this is not conclusive, it is hard to disagree with the scholar who said gangs "can therefore have serious consequences for the economic growth of the legitimate economy. . . . [They] may create monopolies in local enterprises, control entry, . . . [and collect] protection payments. New investment may be discouraged and old investment driven out."

SOURCE: This box was suggested by Annelise Anderson, "The Red Mafia: A Legacy of Communism," Chapter 10 in *Economic Transition in Eastern Europe and Russia* (Stanford: Hoover Institution Press, 1995), p. 343.

relates to incentives, it is necessary to look at one of the major problems of command economies, namely, motivating the managers of SOEs to make sound economic decisions. A central plan might provide a target of a certain number of suits of clothes. The enterprise would be allocated workers and cloth. Without profit as an incentive, managers would have incentive only to make the most suits possible, and so they would make them in one size only—small. Although it might seem unbelievable, such things happen under central planning. Consequently, in transition, it is important to provide the managers of these enterprises with appropriate incentives. This is also why it is so important for the transition economies to privatize their SOEs. If the enterprises are privatized, the owners presumably will be interested in profits.

Different countries have used different schemes to achieve privatization. Managers and workers have been given partial ownership of their enterprises. Citizens have been given ownership shares in enterprises. Enterprises have been sold to foreign investors. In all such situations, the owners want profits. Contrary to what happens in a command economy, firms in market economies earn profits by finding cost-effective ways to produce what consumers want. If managers share in the profits through ownership, performance contracts, or in other ways, they will have an incentive to respond to consumer wants. They will also have incentive to use appropriate production techniques, to monitor workers, and to try to figure out better ways of doing things.

The information in Figure 2.8 indicates that Russia and Ukraine have done little to establish effective institutions that induce large firms and corporations to make decisions profitable for the firm and the economy. In particular, they subsidize big business and inhibit bankruptcy. Slovenia and Hungary, on the other hand, are much less likely to subsidize big business and have developed sound bankruptcy procedures. Recall that bankruptcy is important in a market economy, so that firms that make unprofitable economic decisions lose control of resources, which, in turn, are transferred to better decision makers.

CULTURE THAT ENCOURAGES HONESTY AND TRUST. Each country must develop and enforce a system of contract, criminal, property, and tort law to carry out its economic transformation. Many of these countries have established much of the legal structure important for their transition. As Figure 2.7 shows, the legal transition is not complete, but the countries receive similar ratings. Indeed, the rankings in the figure are closer than in the other figures. The culture necessary to a market economy differs substantially among these countries, as seen in Figure 2.9. This figure presents one ranking of respect for and enforcement of the laws. The rule of law is a measure based on crime rates, judicial effectiveness and predictability, and contract enforcement. The rankings along the vertical axis in this figure are percentiles rankings. Thus, for Slovenia, about 20 percent of all countries in the world rank higher and 80 percent rank lower when considering the rule of law. For Ukraine, on the hand, the numbers are reversed: 80 percent rank higher and 20 percent rank lower. It is not coincidental that Slovenia has progressed so much farther in transition than Ukraine.

Another part of a culture of honesty and trust relates to the use of government for private gain. It measures the frequency of bribes, business corruption, the illegal transfer of state-owned assets to private hands, and so on. As one study put it, "The presence of corruption is often a manifestation of a lack of respect of both the corrupter (typically a private citizen or firm) and the corrupted (typically a government official)

FIGURE 2.9   Culture That Respects Honesty (Selected Countries)

Although the countries are fairly close in terms of the legal transition (see Figure 2.7), Russia and Ukraine rate much lower than Slovenia and Hungary on measures of the rule of law and corruption.

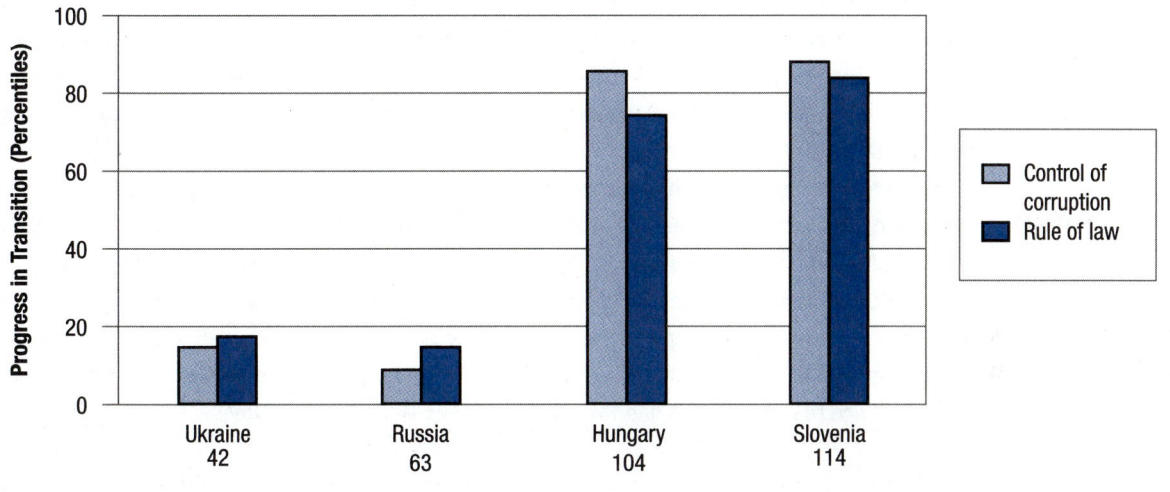

SOURCE: D. Kaufmann, A. Kraay, and P. Zoido-Lobaton, "Governance Matters" *World Bank Working Paper #2196*, 1999.

for the rules which govern their interactions . . . ."[10] Again, in terms of control of corruption, Figure 2.9 shows that the success stories rank much higher than the adversity stories.

These measures of the honesty and trust in the "culture" indicate that individuals or firms doing business in low-rated countries cannot count on the people that they deal with to obey the law and cannot count on the judicial system to enforce it in an equitable manner. The cost of doing business is increased because of the necessity of making contracts as clear and comprehensive as possible. Resources must be used to ensure that contracts are enforced and laws upheld. Moreover, corruption may require that favors be done and bribes be paid. Conflicts that arise out breach of contract often are settled only after costly renegotiations. Usually the business ends up with a less valuable contract. Such actions reduce the security of property rights and inhibit economic activity by domestic and foreign investors.

Additional Thoughts on Transition Economies

Transition economies face diverse experiences on their different paths to market economic systems. They have different starting points. Some have had well-performing economies, and others have decided to change their systems because their economies were doing poorly. Some have had significant private sector

---

[10]D. Kaufmann, A. Kraay, and P. Zoido-Lobaton, "Governance Matters" *World Bank Working Paper #2196*, 1999. The World Bank states that the rule of law, control of corruption, and other governance indicators "reflect the statistical compilation of perceptions of the quality of governance of a large number of survey respondents in industrial and developing countries, as well as non-governmental organizations, commercial risk rating agencies, and think-tanks. They in no way reflect the official position of the World Bank, its Executive Directors, or the countries they represent (http://www.worldbank.org)."

and recent experience with a market economy; others have had neither. Some have had a functioning government; others have had to establish national sovereignty and also a new economic system. In all cases, the transition has caused severe economic problems. Some countries have attempted a quick transition to a market economy, while others have taken a more gradual approach. Although they all have had extremely high unemployment and rapid inflation, some, such as Hungary, have stabilized their economies and created conditions conducive to sustained growth. Others, such as Russia, have a long way to go. Similarly, almost all of the transition economies have freed most prices, but they are reluctant to free the prices of necessities, such as food and shelter. Hungary has one of the freest price systems, and Ukraine has one of the least free.

Similarly, the transition economies recognize the need to improve incentives, particularly for the remaining state-owned enterprises, but they differ in their willingness to adopt market incentives. They have been slow to establish institutional and legal systems, such as bankruptcy law and procedures, to undergird their embryonic market systems. As new economic, legal, and political institutions evolve in the transition countries, they have marvelous opportunities to reap the benefits of market systems, while perhaps avoiding some problems of established market economies. Mounting evidence suggests that the economies that have reformed the fastest have had the most economic growth since 1989.[11]

INFOTRAC
College Edition

Keywords: *transition economies*

Use your InfoTrac password to look up articles on these topics at
http://www.infotrac-college.com

Summary

Market economic systems must have a legal and institutional framework that supports private property and the validity of contracts. These systems work by allowing individuals to make voluntary exchanges; a price system evolves. For voluntary exchanges and a price system to work well in organizing an economy, prices must be free of government control and inflation must be avoided. A market system replaces centralized control with dispersed individual decision making as the method for approaching economic questions. It relies on incentives based on prices to encourage and to motivate people to respond to other peoples' abilities and desires when they choose what to produce and consume.

Division of labor results in specialization that creates a need to coordinate the interdependent actions of the people in an economy. A market economy accomplishes this coordination with a decentralized price system. Understanding basic demand and supply analysis is crucial to understanding this coordination. Prices coordinate by informing producers and consumers about alternatives, by rationing existing supplies, and by motivating people to respond to market incentives. In a command economy, prices are often unable to perform these functions.

Transition economies are making uneven progress in the transformation of their economic systems. Some countries have stabilized their economies, freed prices, established private property rights, developed market incentives, and created the beginnings of legal and institutional systems necessary for a market economic system. Most other countries have freed prices (to one degree or another), but they show great differences in the extent to which they have transformed other elements of their systems.

Key Terms

Relative price	**Quantity supplied**	**Excess supply**
Quantity demanded	**Supply curve**	**Equilibrium**
Demand curve	**Supply price**	**Scarcity**
Demand price	**Law of supply**	**Ration**
Law of demand	**Excess demand**	**Economic profit**

---

[11] Oleh Havrylyshyn and Thomas Wolf, "Determinants of Growth in Transition Countries," *Finance and Development*, June 1999, Vol. 36, Number 2. This issue has several articles on transition countries.

Review Questions

1. What are five characteristics of a successful market economy? Explain.
2. Why is average price stability important in a market system?
3. What are five questions that an economic system must answer?
4. Why is the division of labor important? Why does an increased division of labor make the coordination problem more difficult?
5. State the law of demand and illustrate it with a diagram. Show an example of a demand price on your diagram and explain why it falls when quantity increases.
6. The supply price of corn increases as more corn is produced. Illustrate this fact with a diagram and explain why it happens.
7. The operation of the laws of demand and supply ensures that the market for apartments will be in equilibrium.
   a. Define equilibrium.
   b. Draw a diagram with demand and supply curves. Illustrate the equilibrium price and the equilibrium quantity exchanged.
   c. Suppose the market price is above the equilibrium price. Show the quantity demanded and the quantity supplied on your diagram.
   d. What will happen to cause this market to return to equilibrium?
8. Use a diagram or diagrams to explain how price acts as a signal for consumers and producers and explain how it acts as a motivator.
9. Why is coordination difficult to achieve in a command economy?
10. Draw a demand curve D_0 and a supply curve S_0 for apartments. Show the equilibrium. Now draw a new demand curve D_1 to the right of D_0; the new demand curve is caused by an increase in population. Explain how the price system will operate to signal and motivate producers and consumers to react to this new situation. What is the role of profits?
11. What have transition economies had to do in their attempts to create market economic systems?
12. Compare and contrast the effectiveness of the transition in Hungary with that of Ukraine.
13. According to the box titled "Can Socialism Use the Price System?" what are the three problems solved by the price system?
14. According to the box titled "Cowboy Capitalism in Russia?" is the gang activity in Russia typical of the early stage of capitalism? Discuss.
15. Go to http://www.swcollege.com/bef/econ_news.html. Choose the Comparative Economic Systems category under World Economy and choose an EconNews story that interests you. Read the full summary and answer the questions posed.

Economic Issues on the Internet

- The Adam Smith Institute—**http://www.adamsmith.org**
  As you might expect, a market-oriented Web site with information about Adam Smith and suggested readings for the "New Generation."

- The Brookings Institution—**http://www.brook.edu**
  The Foreign Policy Studies research area at Brookings contains information about Russia, China, and other countries.

- Center on Budget and Policy Priorities—**http://www.cbpp.org**
  This research and policy institute advocates government policies designed to assist low and moderate income people.

- Centre for Economic Reform and Transformation—**http://www.som.hw.ac.uk/cert**
  CERT focuses on academic research that assists in understanding the transition to a market economy.

- European Bank for Reconstruction and Development—**http://www.ebrd.com**
  The EBRD provides financing for projects in transition economies and monitors the progress in transition.
- World Bank—**http://www.worldbank.org/transitionnewsletter**
  The World Bank has data and papers on the transition economies. This URL takes you to the Transition Newsletter, which provides current information.

CHAPTER 3

Inefficiency: The Pervasive Economic Problem

Outline:

Introduction
Rules for Achieving Efficiency in Resource Allocation
The Competitive Market: An Example of Efficiency in Resource Allocation
Market Failure: Inefficiency in the Private Sector
  Monopoly
  External Benefits
  Public Goods
  External Costs

Nonexistent Markets
Incomplete Markets
Government Failure: Inefficiency in the Public Sector
  Rent Controls
  Agricultural Price Supports
  Government-Subsidized Medical Care
  Minimum Wage
  Taxes

How Much Efficiency Do We Want?
  Efficiency Versus Equity: Tax Trade-Offs
  Efficiency Versus Innovation
  Efficiency and Equity
  Efficiency Offsets to Inefficiency

■ INTRODUCTION

Economic Efficiency – An allocation of resources that satisfies wants as fully as possible.

The fundamental premise of economics is that resources are scarce—that the amount available is not large enough to satisfy all human wants. Economists recognize that scarcity cannot be eliminated, but they also believe that its effects can be minimized. This can be accomplished by allocating resources so that wants are satisfied as fully as possible. An economy that does this has achieved **economic efficiency**.

The resource allocation problem has two parts: the allocation of resources in the short run (for example, a year) and the allocation of resources over the long run (for example, across several years). An economy

Static Efficiency — An efficient allocation of resources in the short run.

Dynamic Efficiency — An efficient allocation of resources in the long run.

that allocates resources efficiently in the short run achieves **static efficiency**. An economy that allocates resources efficiently in the long run achieves **dynamic efficiency**. Only a small percentage of the economy's resources, however—primarily nonrenewable resources like minerals, fossil fuels, and timber—pose a long-run allocation problem. Accordingly, we will concentrate on the problem of achieving static efficiency. When we refer throughout this chapter to the simpler term *efficiency*, please remember that it is static efficiency that we have in mind.

You will discover from reading this chapter that the U.S. economy exhibits many instances of inefficiency. You will also learn that inefficiency is a problem that pervades both the private or market sector of the economy and the public or government sector. Inefficiency is an important economic problem. It may, in fact, be public economic enemy number one. As we will explain, the economic losses from inefficiency easily exceed a trillion dollars a year. By contrast, the losses from widespread unemployment are unlikely to be this high, and they occur only once every 5 to 10 years.

■ RULES FOR ACHIEVING EFFICIENCY IN RESOURCE ALLOCATION

The objective of economic activity is to satisfy wants, but economists have no direct measure of the "want-satisfying" power of goods and services. They are forced to work, instead, with proxy measures of the benefits that individuals derive from goods and services. Assuming that benefits can be measured, there is a two-part rule for determining the efficient amount of a good or service. The first part is that the benefits provided by a good or service must be equal to or greater than the costs of providing it. The second part is that the *difference* between the benefits and costs must be as large as possible, or maximized. Properly measured, costs represent the largest possible benefits from other goods and services that must be given up to provide a specific good or service. Given this interpretation, the rule for efficiency in resource allocation is nothing more than the common-sense notion that you are not doing the best you can until you maximize the difference between what you get and what you give up to get it. It takes something more than common sense, however, to determine benefits and costs.

The easiest cases are those of goods and services that are produced and sold in markets where the demand curve provides the information needed to determine benefits and the supply curve provides the information needed to determine costs. We begin our application of the rules for efficiency with two such cases.

■ THE COMPETITIVE MARKET: AN EXAMPLE OF EFFICIENCY IN RESOURCE ALLOCATION

The first case is one in which the amount produced and sold is determined solely by demand and supply. Figure 3.1 illustrates such a market in terms of the demand (D) for, and supply (S) of, apartments for rent in Kansas City. We have added additional labels, however, to the demand and supply curves to facilitate measures of benefits and costs.

The height of the demand curve for each apartment indicates the maximum monthly rent that buyers are willing to pay for that apartment. For example, Figure 3.1 indicates that buyers are willing to pay $800 for the 100,000th apartment, slightly less for the next apartment, $700 for the 200,000th apartment, and so on. Economists use the maximum amount that buyers are willing to pay for a unit of something as a meas-

CHAPTER 3 ■ INEFFICIENCY: THE PERVASIVE ECONOMIC PROBLEM

| FIGURE 3.1 | A Competitive Market for Apartments |

This figure illustrates a competitive market for apartments in Kansas City. Market equilibrium occurs at 450,000 units, where S=D or MB=MC. This is also the number of units where total net benefits are maximized; thus, this market achieves economic efficiency.

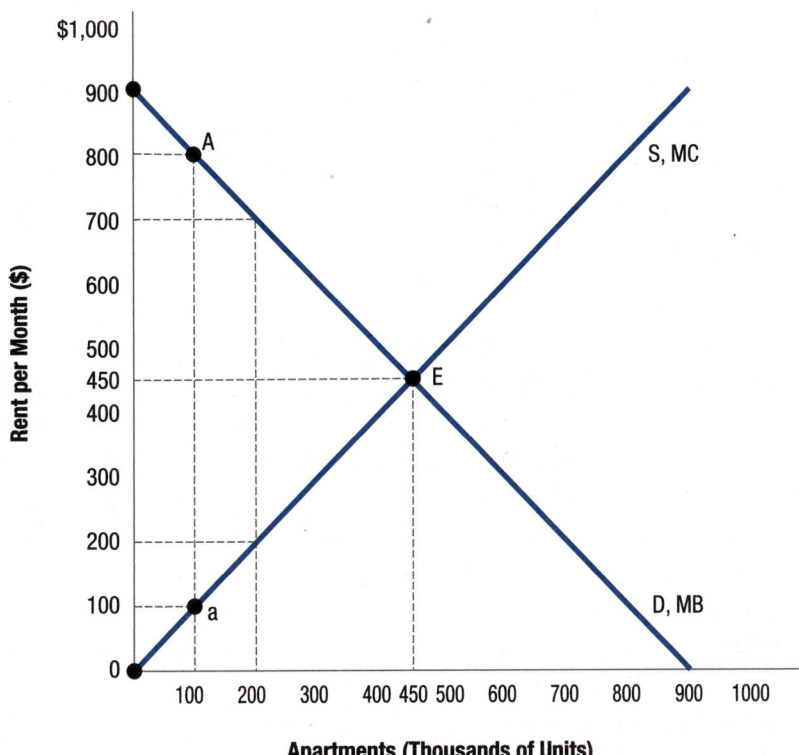

Marginal Benefit Curve –
A curve that depicts the benefits from each additional, or marginal, unit.

Marginal Cost Curve –
A curve that depicts the costs of providing each additional, or marginal, unit.

Total Benefit –
The sum of marginal benefits; also the area under the marginal benefit or demand curve.

ure of the benefit they perceive from buying that unit. Thus, the demand curve for apartments is also a **marginal benefit curve**; it indicates the benefits buyers perceive from each additional, or marginal, unit.

The height of the supply curve for apartments indicates the minimum monthly rent that sellers must receive for each apartment. For example, Figure 3.1 indicates that sellers must receive at least $100 for the 100,000th apartment, slightly more for the next one, $200 for the 200,000th apartment, and so on. Economists use the minimum amount that sellers must receive as a measure of what must be given up, or the cost, to provide each apartment. Thus, the supply curve for apartments is also a **marginal cost curve**; it indicates the costs sellers must receive to provide each additional, or marginal, unit.

The area under the demand curve is a measure of the **total benefit** to buyers. This follows from the fact that the area under the curve between two quantities is the sum of all of the marginal benefits between the two quantities. Thus, the total benefit from the first 100,000 units is $85,000,000—calculated as the sum of two areas under the demand curve: the rectangle bounded by the points $800, A, 100,000 units, and 0 and the triangle bounded by the points $900, A, and $800. The total benefit of all 900,000 units, or

Total Cost – The sum of marginal costs; also the area under the marginal cost or supply curve.

the area under the entire demand curve, is $405,000,000—the area of the triangle bounded by the points $900, 900,000 units, and 0.

The area under the supply curve measures **total cost**, or the sum of marginal costs. Thus, in Figure 3.1, the total cost of the first 100,000 apartments is $5,000,000 (the triangle bounded by the points, 0, 100,000 units, and a). The total cost of the first 500,000 units is $125,000,000—the value of a triangle with a height of $500 and base of 500,000 units.

Total benefits are greater than total costs all the way up to the last, or 900,000th, apartment. (The reader should verify this by calculating the areas under the MB and MC curves.) But efficiency requires provision of the number of apartments where the difference between total benefit and total cost is maximized. This occurs at 450,000 units. This can be confirmed by noting that MB>MC for all apartments up to 450,000 units and that MB<MC for all apartment units beyond 450,000. Thus, each apartment rented up to 450,000 units adds to the difference between benefits and costs. Beyond 450,000 units, however, each apartment yields benefits less than costs, so each additional apartment reduces the total difference between benefits and costs. It follows that the total difference between benefits and costs must be the largest at 450,000 units.

Total Net Benefit – Total benefit minus total cost; also the area between the demand and supply curves.

An alternative way to approach this proof is to realize that the difference between total benefits and total costs is equal to the area between the MB and MC curves. This area, also known as the **total net benefit**, is maximized at 450,000 units, with a value of $202,500,000. This area can be calculated as the value of the triangle bounded by the points 0, $900, and E. Alternatively, it can be calculated that buyers are willing to pay $303,750,000 for 450,000 units (the area under the MB curve) and that sellers must receive $101,250,000 (the area under the MC curve), so the difference determined by comparing total benefits and total costs is also $202,500,000.

Markets that are highly competitive—in which neither buyers nor sellers can influence market price by their individual actions—will automatically clear at the intersection of D and S or MB and MC. Thus, they will automatically achieve efficiency. Based on this test, there is no economic efficiency rationale for government intervention in such markets.

■ Market Failure: Inefficiency in the Private Sector

Market Failure – A situation in which a market fails to achieve efficiency.

There are markets in the economy, however, that do not achieve efficiency. When they do not, they are said to exhibit **market failure**.

Monopoly

Profit – Total revenue minus total cost.

Total Revenue – Number of units sold times price per unit; also the rectangle under the demand curve, where height is the price per unit and base is the quantity sold.

If some market participants have market power in the form of the ability to affect price, the market will exhibit inefficiency. A good example is that of a monopoly, a market in which only one seller exists. As explained in Chapter 5, the monopolist will set the price at the level where its profits are maximized. The profit-maximizing price is normally higher than the price determined by the forces of demand and supply. This makes the monopoly inefficient in the sense that too little is produced and too few resources are allocated to the monopolized market. Alternatively, the monopolist denies consumers the opportunity to buy additional units from which they would reap benefits greater than costs.

Profit is total revenue minus total cost. **Total revenue** is the price per unit times the number of units sold. In Figure 3.2, total revenue is a rectangle under the demand curve. For example, total revenue from

FIGURE 3.2 A Monopolized Market for Apartments

This diagram illustrates the market for apartments in Kansas City, given the assumption that one firm owns all of them. Market equilibrium occurs where profits are maximized, or at 300,000 units. There are efficiency or deadweight losses equal to area MEm.

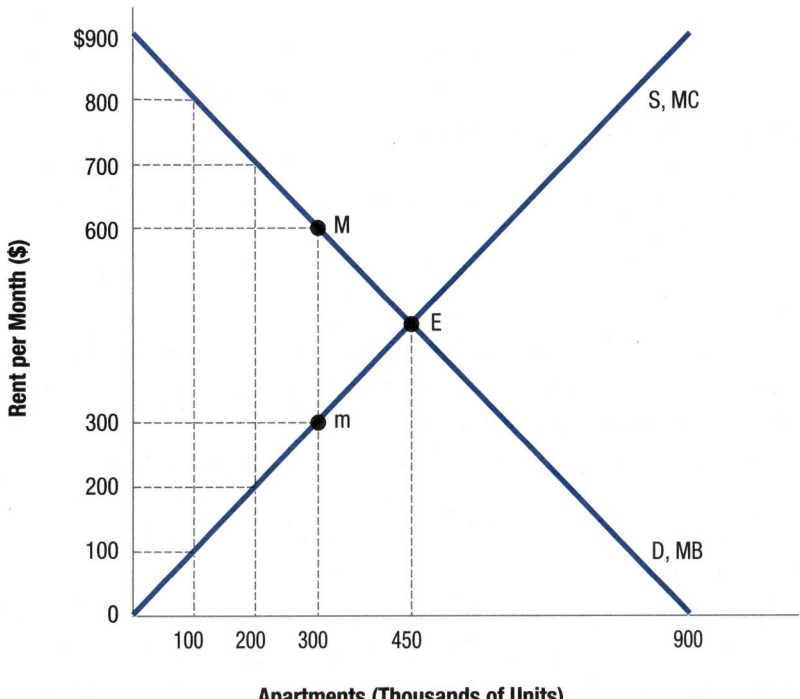

renting 100,000 apartments is $80,000,000—the product of a price of $800 and 100,000 units. This differs from the total benefit of $85,000,000 for these units. The difference between total benefit and total revenue results from the fact that the monopolist charges the same price of $800 for each apartment, rather than a series of prices between $900 and $800 for these apartments.

Continuing with the calculations, the total cost of the first 100,000 units is $5,000,000 (the area under the supply curve). Thus, the profit realized by renting the first 100,000 apartments is $75,000,000. Although this is a lucrative option for the monopolist, it can do much better. Total profit from renting the first 200,000 units is $120,000,000 (total revenue of $140,000,000 minus total cost of $20,000,000), but it is even higher from renting 300,000 units; namely, $135,000,000 (total revenue of $180,000,000 minus total cost of $45,000,000). In fact, profit is maximized by renting 300,000 units at $600 per apartment. If the monopolist were to rent 450,000 units at $450 each, for example, profit would be only $101,250,000 (total revenue of $202,500,000 minus total cost of $101,250,000).

If the monopolist sets the apartment rent at $600 per unit—and it will, because this is the price that maximizes its profits—the number of apartments rented (300,000) will be less than the efficient number

Efficiency Loss – Maximum total net benefits minus actual total net benefits.

Deadweight Loss – Another name for efficiency loss.

INFOTRAC
College Edition

Keywords: *deadweight loss, welfare loss*

http://www.infotrac-college.com

External Benefits – Benefits created in a market that are realized by individuals other than the buyers and sellers.

Marginal External Benefits (MEB) – External benefits on the additional, or marginal, unit.

Marginal Social Benefits (MSB) – The sum of marginal benefits and marginal external benefits.

(450,000). If only 300,000 units are rented, the difference between total benefit and total cost is not maximized. At 300,000 units, total benefit (the area under the demand curve) is $225,000,000 and total cost is $45,000,000, so the difference (or total net benefit) is $180,000,000. However, this is smaller than the difference (total net benefit) of $202,500,000 between total benefits ($303,750,000) and total costs ($101,250,000) at 450,000 units. The difference of $22,500,000 ($202,500,000 minus $180,000,000) between the two total net benefit figures is a measure of the **efficiency loss** due to the exercise of monopoly power. The reader should also recognize that this loss in total net benefits can be calculated directly as the value of the triangle bounded by the points, M, E, and m. Economists often call this loss in efficiency the **deadweight loss** from monopoly pricing.

There are not many pure monopolies, but in some markets a few firms are so dominant that they have market power as a group. Inefficiency occurs in such markets, although to a lesser degree than in the pure monopoly case. The pure monopolies in the United States are firms to which government has given an exclusive franchise to supply a product. The most familiar of these are the public utilities that supply electricity and natural gas. Economists estimate that the efficiency losses from monopoly pricing in the U.S. economy amount to between 0.5 percent and 2 percent of total output, or between $50 billion and $200 billion for a $10 trillion economy. Many of the problems involved in attempting to reduce these losses by government intervention are discussed in Chapter 5.

External Benefits

In the competitive model for apartments in Kansas City, we assumed that the demand or marginal benefit curve provides an accurate measure of all of the benefits realized from the rental units. That may not be the case, however. Suppose, for example, that the apartment buildings are particularly attractive; in fact, they are so attractive that they draw visitors from around the country just to view them. In this case, each visitor realizes benefits from the apartments that are in addition to the benefits realized by the renters of the apartments. Economists call these benefits **external benefits**; they are external to the transaction between buyers and sellers.

It is not easy to determine the value of external benefits in real-world cases because they are not included in demand curves. However, they are not impossible to estimate. In this case, we can approximate them by assuming that the external benefits are at least as great as the cost of the time and travel expenses of the viewers. Suppose that we take a survey of viewers and discover that these costs and expenses average $100 per month per apartment. In the economist's jargon, the external benefit of each apartment—the **marginal external benefit (MEB)**—is $100. In Figure 3.3, these benefits are added to the demand or MB curve of Figure 3.1. The result is a curve labeled MSB, for **marginal social benefit**, where MSB is the vertical sum of MB and MEB; MEB is the vertical distance of $100 between MSB and MB.

With this change, total benefits become the sum of the MSBs, or the area under the MSB curve. Now, the difference between total benefits and total costs, or total net benefit, is maximized at 500,000 units. At this level, total benefits are $375,000,000 (the area under the MSB curve) and total costs are $125,000,000 (the area under the MC curve), so total net benefit is $250,000,000 (area $1,000,B,0). This is more than the total net benefits of $202,500,000 that will be realized when only 450,000 units are built and rented. Most of the extra $47,500,000—$45,000,000 to be exact—will be realized if only 450,000

FIGURE 3.3 A Market for Apartments—With External Benefits

This figure illustrates the market for apartments in Kansas City with the assumed presence of marginal external benefits. The market equilibrium is 450,000 units, where MB=MC. This is less than the efficient quantity of 500,000 units, where MSB=MC. Total net benefits are $2.5 million higher at 500,000 units than at 450,000 units.

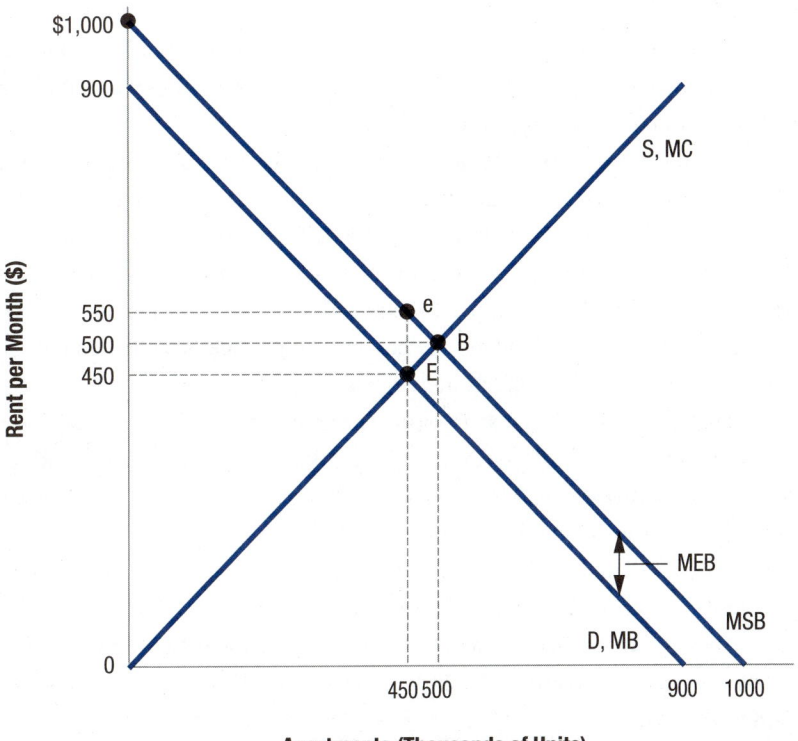

units are rented. The remaining $2,500,000 (area e,B,E) could be realized if renters received a subsidy of $100 a month for each unit rented. The subsidy would increase their willingness to pay for apartments by $100 a unit, inducing them to rent an additional 50,000 units. This may strike you as a bad deal—an extra $2,500,000 in net benefits for a subsidy of $50,000,000 ($100 times 500,000 units). It is not, however, from an efficiency perspective. The government could take the $50,000,000 from taxpayers and transfer it to the renters. The losses of the former would just be offset by gains to the latter, so the net effect of the tax and transfer, alone, is zero. An additional 50,000 units would be rented, however, on which there would be a net gain of $2,500,000. That is, when all gains and losses are added up, there is a net gain for society; that is, taxpayers, renters, and viewers considered together.

This may be a fanciful illustration, but it underscores an important point: Whenever buyers cannot appropriate benefits, the market tends to allocate too few resources to the provision of the good or service. This point applies to less fanciful examples like primary and secondary education and public health.

Primary and secondary education enhance the earning power of the persons educated, but turn them into better citizens as well, to the benefit of others (an external benefit). Public health measures, such as immunization, provide protection to the party immunized, but also some protection to people not immunized (an external benefit).

Public Goods

Public Goods – Goods from which no one can be excluded, even if they pay nothing for their provision.

Goods and services differ in terms of the relative importance of external benefits. External benefits are most important in the case where, if a good is provided to one individual, all other individuals benefit from its provision. Economists call such goods **public goods**.

National defense is the classic example of a public good. It is "public" in the sense that if it is provided at all, it bestows benefits on the public in general. That is, no one can be excluded from the benefits of national security. In such a case, it is likely that each individual will not reveal his or her true willingness to pay, hoping for a "free ride" after other people pay for it. If everyone reasons this way, of course, we will have no national defense even though the aggregate benefits from it may be large. In such a case, there is a clear need for government to levy taxes and use the proceeds to provide what the market cannot provide; that is, for the government to act on behalf of individuals.

Another important example of a public good is basic research. Private firms will undertake basic research provided that they can exclude others from using the knowledge it produces long enough to make an adequate return on their investment. Unlike national defense, it is possible, although difficult, to exclude others from using such knowledge. For example, patent protection can be secured for new discoveries. However, basic research produces fundamental knowledge—knowledge with great potential for creating widespread external benefits—and precluding access to this knowledge through patent protection would cut off some of the external benefits associated with diffusing and utilizing that knowledge. Thus, some form of government support for basic research appears to be required to ensure an efficient allocation of resources to this activity.

INFOTRAC
College Edition

Keyword: *public good*
http://www.infotrac-college.com

External Costs

External Costs – Costs created in a market that are paid by individuals other than the buyers and sellers.

Marginal External Costs (MEC) – External costs on the additional, or marginal, unit.

Marginal Social Costs (MSC) – The sum of marginal costs and marginal external costs.

Now suppose that, as in Figure 3.1, no external benefits are associated with apartments in Kansas City. Assume instead that each apartment burns coal to produce heat and that harmful by-products—pollutants—of coal combustion escape from the apartments and drift across the city. People who are particularly sensitive to these pollutants suffer physically. Some become ill and miss work. Many see the doctor more frequently. Some curtail their outdoor activities. Some buy filtration systems for their homes. The income they forgo, the money they spend at the doctor, the value to them of the activities they give up, and their outlays for filtration systems all are examples of **external costs** imposed by apartment dwellers.

Suppose that we have studied the problem and determined that there is an external cost of $100 per apartment per month, or a **marginal external cost (MEC)** of $100 per unit due to the air pollution created by renters. We examine the effects of this cost on efficiency by adding this $100 to the MC curve in Figure 3.4. The result is a curve lying above the MC curve, labeled MSC for **marginal social cost**—the sum of MC and MEC. MEC is the distance between the MC and MSC curves.

Total costs are now measured as the area under the MSC curve, instead of the MC curve. Given this change, the difference between total benefits (the area under the demand or MB curve) and total costs,

FIGURE 3.4 A Market for Apartments—With External Costs

This figure illustrates the market for apartments in Kansas City with the assumed presence of marginal external costs. The market equilibrium is 450,000, where MB=MC. This is greater than the efficient quantity of 400,000 apartments, where MB=MSC.

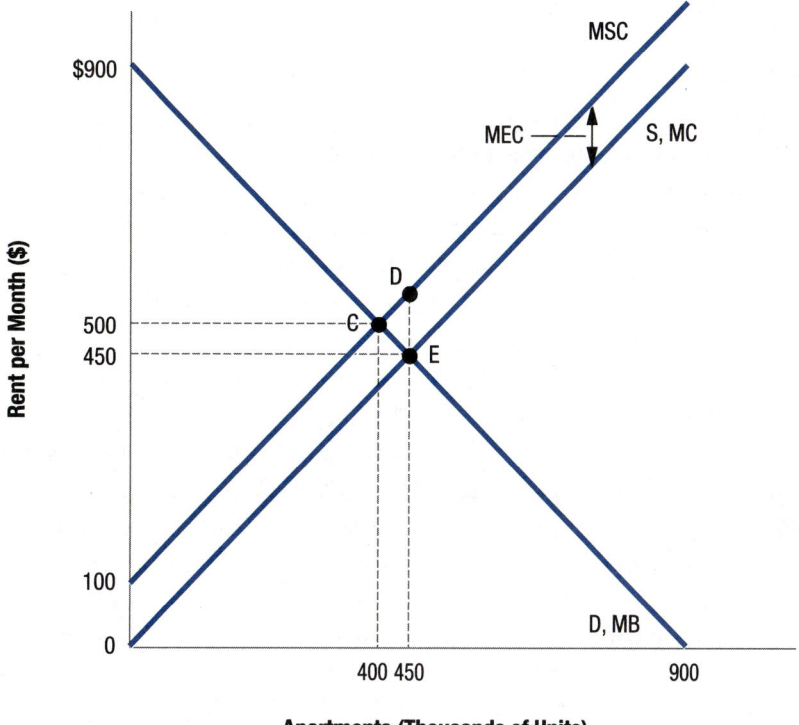

or total net benefit, is maximized at 400,000 units. Total net benefit at this level is $160,000,000 (area $900,C,$100). If 450,000 units are rented, as in a competitive market, total net benefits will decrease by $2,500,000 (the triangle CED) to $157,500,000. Thus, the competitive market solution is marked by inefficiency, characterized by an allocation of too many resources to apartments.

In cases such as this, the government may have to take action to reduce the quantity of apartments rented. They could, for example, levy a tax equal to MEC per unit, as outlined in Chapter 6 for real-world cases of air pollution. If they did, there would be a net gain to society, or an increase in net benefits, of $2,500,000.

Real-world efforts by government to realize net benefits from reducing air pollution are spearheaded by the U.S. Environmental Protection Agency (EPA), operating under the authority of the Clean Air Act. The Clean Air Act establishes a framework for the attainment and maintenance of clean and healthful air quality levels. The Clean Air Act was enacted in 1970 and amended twice—in 1977 and in 1990. A recent study by the EPA estimates that the total monetized benefits (benefits that could be quantified in dollars) of the Clean Air Act realized during the period from 1970 to 1990 range from $5.6 to $49.4 trillion, with

INFOTRAC
College Edition

Keywords: *externalities, pollution*
http://www.infotrac-college.com

Nonexistent Markets – Markets that cannot be organized or created.

a central estimate of $22.2 trillion.[1] By comparison, compliance expenditures, or costs, over the same period were approximately $0.5 trillion. Subtracting costs from benefits results in net benefits ranging from $5.1 to $48.9 trillion, with a central estimate of $21.7 trillion (or nearly $1.1 trillion per year) for the 1970 to 1990 period. These estimates have been the source of considerable debate (see more detailed discussion in Chapter 6), but even if they prove to be too high, we are hardly addressing a trivial problem.

Nonexistent Markets

The situations just discussed—external benefits, public goods, and external costs—are cases in which the probability that markets could develop and provide an efficient allocation of resources is small. These are cases of **nonexistent markets**.

Nonexistent markets characterize two other important events: unemployment and poverty. Life is full of risks—risks that might lead to poor health, death, accidents, fire, inflation, disability, natural disasters, unemployment, and poverty. The market system responds to these risks whenever it can by offering insurance. In some cases, however, it cannot provide insurance. For example, the market does not insure against unemployment and poverty. Suppose people want to purchase insurance against the possibility of becoming unemployed or poor. Would a private insurance firm find it profitable to supply unemployment or poverty insurance? No, because if individuals purchased such insurance, they might decide not to work so hard. To discourage such behavior, insurers would have to monitor behavior to determine if an individual's low income sprang from circumstances beyond his or her control or from shirking. Such monitoring would be difficult, if not impossible, and certainly expensive. Hence, no market exists for unemployment and poverty insurance. Government steps in and provides unemployment insurance and poverty insurance in the form of income support programs. It exacts "premiums" in the form of taxes.

Incomplete Markets

The dilemma that insurance companies would face in covering unemployment and poverty risks resembles that for the risks against which they do insure. Insuring against the risks of any event over which individuals have some control may make them less careful about avoiding the event. For example, having automobile accident insurance may induce policyholders to drive less carefully; having good medical insurance may induce them to risk poor health. Economics refers to cases such as these, where insurance increases the probability that claims will be made or that the claims made will be more expensive, as examples of **moral hazard**.

Moral Hazard – The risk that insurance for an event will increase the probability of the event occurring.

Adverse Selection – Self-selection by policyholders that results in a pool of insured individuals dominated by high-risk individuals.

Moral hazard will flourish only if individual policyholders can shift the increased costs associated with their acts to others who are insured. If individual policyholders assume, however, that they can shift the costs of their actions to others, and act accordingly, the cost of insurance rises for the whole group. This discourages individuals from buying insurance, especially individuals least in need of insurance (for example, those who are more healthy). The market suffers from **adverse selection**—a situation in which self-selection results in an insurance pool of predominantly high-risk individuals—and a situation that adds further to upward pressure on cost. The probability of adverse selection can be so extreme that insurance companies simply will not insure certain groups.

---

[1] U.S. Environmental Protection Agency, *The Benefits and Costs of the Clean Air Act, 1970 to 1990*, October 1997.

Incomplete Market – A market in which the good or service is available to only some of the potential customers.

We call a market of this type an **incomplete market**; the good or service is available but only to part of the population of potential consumers. Government could intervene in these instances by requiring insurance for everyone, thereby reducing the cost per policyholder. A rationale such as this has been used to justify government health insurance, such as Medicare, and government-mandated automobile liability insurance.

Incomplete markets are not confined, however, to insurance. The market for college loans is also incomplete, but for a different reason. College students, as a group, are an attractive pool of borrowers. They will realize high lifetime incomes and experience low rates of unemployment. What is true about the group, however, is not necessarily true about individual members of the group. The superior earning power of college students is no guarantee against the risk that *individual* students will not repay a loan in a timely manner.

The same problem arises with borrowers, in general. Lenders protect themselves against risk of default by requiring collateral for a loan; for example, they retain the titles to cars and houses until auto and home loans are repaid. This protection is unavailable for student loans; that is, students cannot serve as collateral. This makes a loan to a specific individual relatively risky and requires the lender to charge a relatively high rate of interest to cover this risk.

A conflict arises, then, between individual and group risk of default in the market for college student loans; group risk of default is small, but individual risk of default is high. In the absence of a government guarantee against default, the rate of interest charged for student loans would reflect the relatively high individual risk of default. This rate would be higher than the one that reflects the group, or social, risk of default. If students had to pay the individual risk-of-default rate, the level of borrowing would be less than the socially optimal amount of borrowing.

In this instance, a government guarantee against default would provide the necessary collateral, and the government would assume the relatively low risk associated with lending to college students as a group. Defaults would occur, but they could not be eliminated under any conceivable financing arrangement.

■ Government Failure: Inefficiency in the Public Sector

One could hardly develop a balanced view of the U.S. economy's defects by examining only cases of market failure. Numerous instances of government failure exist as well. In a manner parallel to the concept of market failure, government failure occurs whenever government activity is inconsistent with achieving one of the nation's economic goals. Again, we confine our analysis to the goal of efficiency.

Rent Controls

Several local governments in the United States have adopted rent controls, placing an upper limit on rents that landlords can charge. These limits commonly keep rents below the market-clearing, or equilibrium, level. When this happens, landlords supply fewer units than the equilibrium quantity—too few from the perspective of efficiency—resulting in less than maximum net benefits.

These points are illustrated in Figure 3.5, which represents the market for rental units in a city with rent controls. The equilibrium price (rent) and quantity are P_e and Q_e, respectively. The equilibrium quantity is also the efficient quantity. If landlords can charge no more than P_c because of the rent control, they will

FIGURE 3.5 A Market for Apartments—With Rent Controls

This figure illustrates a market for apartments with rent controls. The market equilibrium without government intervention would be at Q_e units, where S=D. This is also the efficient quantity. When rent is limited to P_c, only Q_c units, less than the efficient quantity, are supplied.

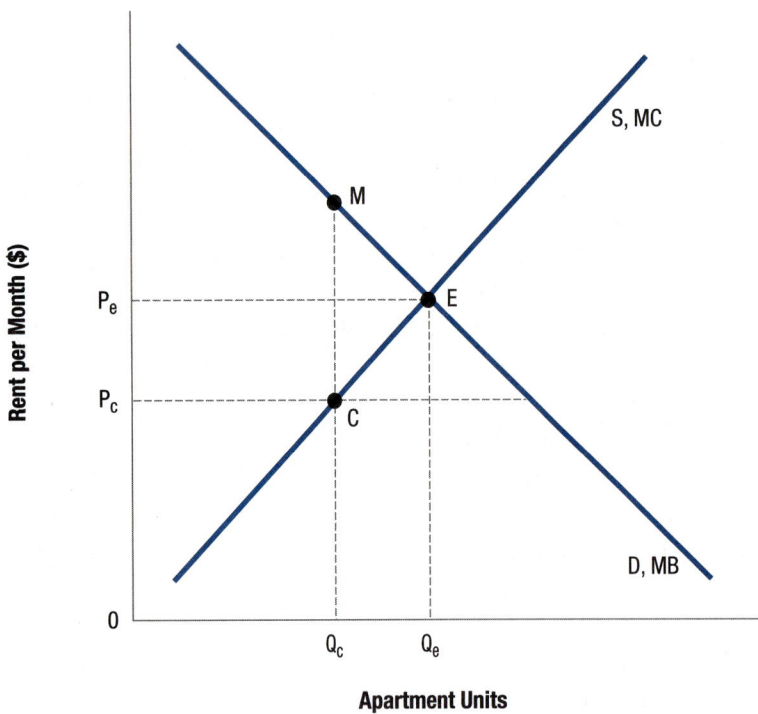

provide only Q_c units. At Q_c, MB exceeds MC, and net benefits are short of the maximum possible by the area CME.

Agricultural Price Supports

As explained in Chapter 4, the U.S. government has a series of programs designed to keep the prices of various agricultural commodities above the market-clearing, or equilibrium, level. Such prices induce farmers to produce more than market-clearing quantities—too much, in fact, from the perspective of efficiency.

These points are illustrated in Figure 3.6, which depicts the market for wheat. The equilibrium price and quantity are P_e and Q_e, respectively. If the government supports the price at P_s, farmers will produce Q_s bushels, a quantity resulting in efficiency losses equal to area ESM.

Government-Subsidized Medical Care

As discussed in Chapter 7, government provides large subsidies to consumers of health care through the federal Medicare and the federal–state Medicaid programs. These programs are designed to improve medical care access for the elderly (Medicare) and the poor (Medicaid). They do so by lowering the cost

INFOTRAC
College Edition

Keywords: farm programs, price supports

http://www.infotrac-college.com

FIGURE 3.6 A Market for Wheat—With a Government-Supported Price

This figure illustrates a market for wheat with a government-supported price. The market equilibrium without government intervention would be at Q_e, the efficient quantity. When the government assures a price of P_s, the quantity supplied becomes Q_s, or more than the efficient quantity.

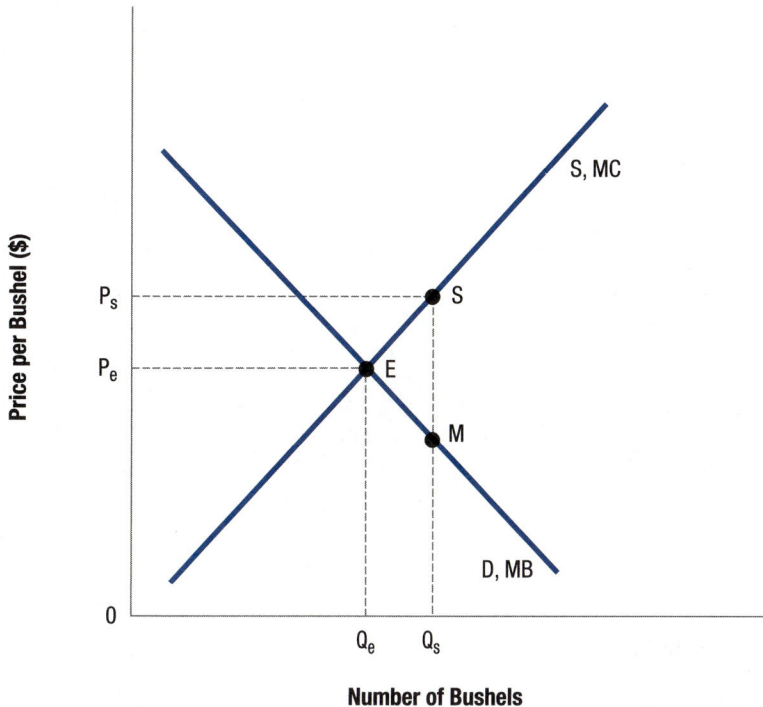

of each unit of medical care received or consumed by Medicare and Medicaid patients. For example, Medicare pays about 85 percent of the costs of a hospital stay, and the patient pays only 15 percent. Medicaid pays all the costs of a hospital stay, and the patient pays nothing.

From the patients' perspective, these cost-sharing arrangements drastically reduce the perceived price of a hospital stay. They make the perceived price—what the consumer must pay for a unit of medical care—significantly less than the marginal social cost of medical care—the amount the consumer and the government together must pay to ensure the production of a unit of medical care. Acting solely on the part of cost that they pay, consumer–patients buy too much medical care.

These points are illustrated in Figure 3.7, which represents the market for medical care. MC is the minimum amount that suppliers must receive to pay the costs of providing each unit. The line P_c represents the amount that consumers pay for each unit. The difference between MC and P_c per unit is the share of costs paid by the government. Consumers will want to buy all units for which the perceived benefit per unit—the marginal benefit—is greater than or equal to P_c. Thus, consumers will choose to buy Q_c, resulting in efficiency losses equal to area ESM.

INFOTRAC
College Edition

Keyword: *welfare loss*

http://www.infotrac-college.com

FIGURE 3.7 A Market for Medical Care—With Government Cost Sharing

This figure illustrates a market for medical care in which government shares part of the cost. The market equilibrium without cost sharing would be Q_e, the efficient quantity. When the government shares or pays part of the cost, consumers perceive a price, P_c, that covers only part of the marginal cost of providing the care. With cost sharing, consumers buy Q_c units, or more than the efficient quantity.

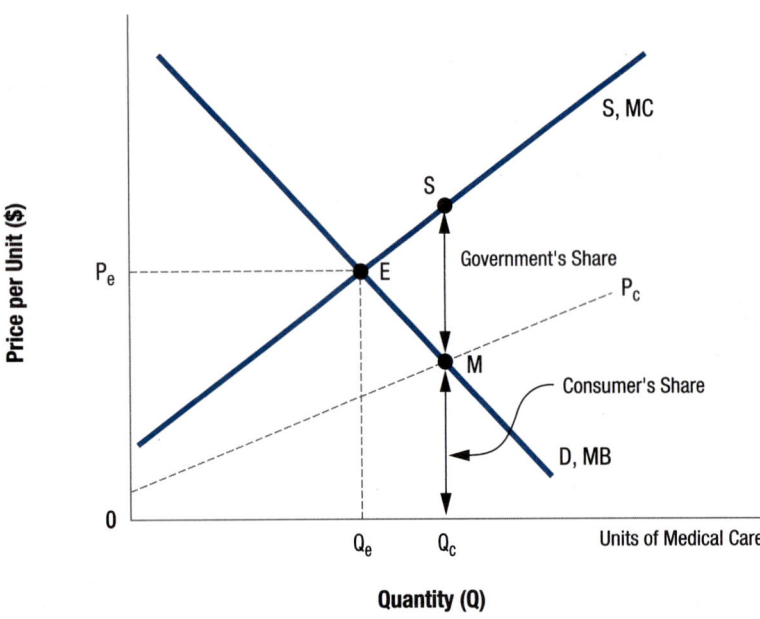

Minimum Wage

The United States has a federal law requiring employers to pay workers in most occupations a minimum wage of $5.15 an hour. The intent of the law is to increase the income of low-wage workers. Whatever its merits in this regard (see the discussion in Chapter 14, which indicates that it is not a very effective strategy for achieving this purpose), it is a source of inefficiency.

This point is illustrated in Figure 3.8, which depicts the market for unskilled labor (the market affected by the minimum wage). The demand or marginal benefit curve in this market reflects the benefits that employers get from hiring additional workers. The supply curve in this market reflects the amount that workers must receive in order to come to work, or the marginal cost (to them) of working. Net benefits are maximized where MB=MC, or at N_e workers hired. If the lowest wage that employers can legally pay, W_m, exceeds the market-clearing wage, W_e, as in this example, there will be less than the efficient quantity of labor hired (N_m rather than N_e) and efficiency losses equal to MEm.

INFOTRAC
College Edition

Keyword: *minimum wage*
http://www.infotrac-college.com

Taxes

The preceding examples deal with how governments spend their money (agricultural price supports, health care subsidies) or require private sector participants to use their resources (rent controls, environmental regulations, minimum wage). The ways in which governments finance their activities are also sources of inefficiency. This is especially true of taxes.

According to Table 3.1, governments collected nearly $3 trillion in taxes in 2000—almost one of every three dollars of income produced that year. Nearly three-fourths (72 percent) of this total consisted of income taxes: the individual income tax, the Social Security payroll tax, and the corporate income tax.

FIGURE 3.8 — A Market for Labor—With a Minimum Wage

This diagram illustrates a labor market in which a legislated minimum wage, W_m, exceeds the equilibrium wage, W_e. Under these circumstances, N_m workers will be hired. This is fewer than the efficient quantity, N_e.

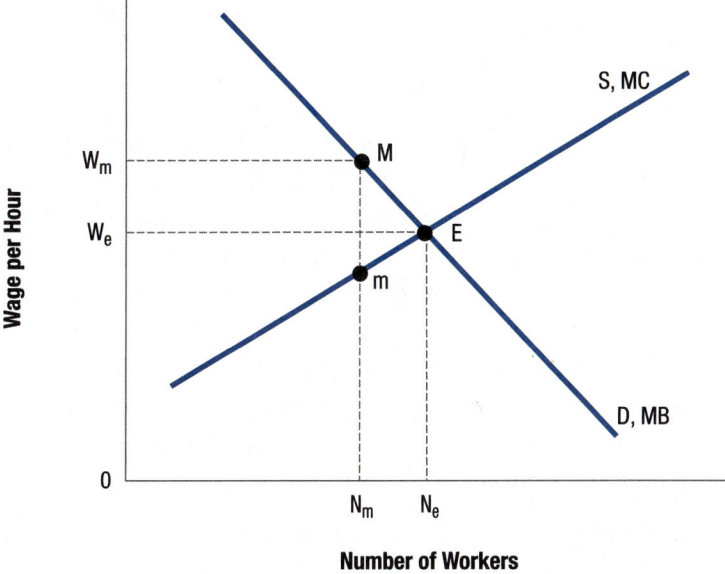

TABLE 3.1 — Tax Receipts in 2000 for Federal, State, and Local Governments ($ Billions)

Type of Tax	Federal Tax Receipts	State and Local Tax Receipts	Total Tax Receipts
Individual income	1,005	216	1,221
Social Security payroll	621		621
General sales		332	332
Property		249	249
Corporate income	207	40	247
Excise and misc.	69	180	249
Total tax receipts	1,902	1,017	2,919

Source: U.S. Bureau of the Census, *Statistical Abstract of the United States: 2001*.

Taxes on sales—the general sales and excise taxes—accounted for 16 to 17 percent of total tax receipts. The state and local property tax provided an additional 8.5 percent of taxes collected.

Regardless of how large these numbers may seem, tax receipts actually understate what taxes really cost. The full costs of taxation are the sum of the amounts reported in Table 3.1 *and* the efficiency losses from taxation. The efficiency losses from taxation are the subject of a huge literature, a full review of which is well beyond the scope of this text. We will illustrate the concept, instead, with a couple of examples.

INCOME TAXES. Taxes collected are the product of the tax rate and the tax base. For example, if the tax rate is 15 percent and the tax base is $1 billion, taxes of $150 million (0.15 × $1 billion) will be collected. Efficiency can be affected by both the size of the tax rate and the design of the tax base.

As noted, there are two principal income taxes: the federal individual income tax and the federal payroll tax for Social Security. Table 3.2 and Table 3.3 display the tax rates that individuals face under each of these taxes. The rates reported are marginal tax rates: the rates on each successive portion of the tax base.

Progressive Tax – A tax with marginal tax rates that increase as the tax base increases.

Regressive Tax – A tax with marginal tax rates that decrease as taxable income decreases.

The individual income tax is an example of a **progressive tax**, one for which the tax rate increases as taxable income increases. The payroll tax is an example of a **regressive tax**, one for which the tax rate decreases as taxable income increases. Taxes on the first $84,900 are used to finance the entire federal Old-Age, Survivors, Disability and Health Insurance (OASDHI) program. Taxes on income over $84,900 are used to provide additional funding for the HI (Medicare) portion only. The law requires employers to withhold one-half of the amounts reported in Table 3.3 from employee paychecks and to match that payment with an equal-size payment of their own. The rates reported in Table 3.3 are the sum of both employee and employer contributions. This method of reporting reflects the dominant view in economics that employers actually shift their half of the tax to employees in the form of lower wages.

An individual's tax bill is determined by applying these marginal rates to income subject to taxation. To see how this works, consider Amy, a single individual with taxable income of $40,000 earned by

TABLE 3.2 Federal Individual Income Tax Rates for 2001 by Filing Status and Tax Base

Single	Married Filing Jointly	Marginal Tax Rate
Up to $27,050	Up to $45,200	15%
$27,501—$65,550	$45,201—$109,250	27.5%
$65,551—$136,750	$109,251—$166,500	30.5%
$136,751—$297,350	$166,501—$297,350	35.5%
$297,351 or more	$297,351 or more	39.1%

TABLE 3.3 Federal Payroll Tax Rates for Social Security in 2002 by Tax Base

Tax Base	Marginal Tax Rate
Up to $84,900 in wages and self-employment income	15.3 %
Over $84,900 in wages and self-employment income	2.9 %

working 2,000 hours at $20 an hour before taxes. She is subject to both the individual income tax and the payroll tax. She must pay a combined rate of 0.303 (30.3 percent) on the first $27,050—15 percent in individual income taxes and 15.3 percent in payroll taxes. The combined marginal rate increases to 0.428 (42.8 percent) on Amy's income from $27,051 to $40,000. Her tax bill consists, then, of $8,196.15 on the first $27,050 (= 0.303 × $27,050) and $5,542.60 (= 0.428 × $12,950) on the next $12,950 ($40,000 − $27,050). Her total income tax bill is $13,378.75. Given this, her income tax bill is 34.3 percent (= $13,378.75/$40,000) of her taxable income. The 34.3 percent is her *average* tax rate, calculated as indicated by dividing the total tax bill by total taxable income.

We have implicitly assumed in this example that the number of hours Amy works is unaffected by the taxes she pays. There are probably many Amys, but the evidence indicates that they are greatly outnumbered by individuals whose decision to work *is* affected by the taxes they pay.

Consider the case of Bill, who is representative of the larger group. Bill's situation is depicted in Figure 3.9. Bill earns a wage of $20 an hour before taxes, represented by the horizontal line drawn at

FIGURE 3.9   **The Effect of Marginal Tax Rates on Hours Worked and Efficiency**

This diagram illustrates the combined effect of the individual income tax and the payroll tax on hours worked by Bill, an individual who works more (less) at higher (lower) wage rates. The before-tax wage, W, is $20 per hour. Given the marginal tax rates faced by Bill (30.3 percent and 42.8 percent), the after-tax wage, W_t, is $13.94 for the first 1,352.5 hours worked and $11.44 for the next 2,125 hours worked. Without the tax, Bill would work 2,000 hours. With the tax, he works only 1,800 hours. The tax creates efficiency or deadweight losses equal to the area ABE. Note that only the higher marginal tax rate affects hours worked.

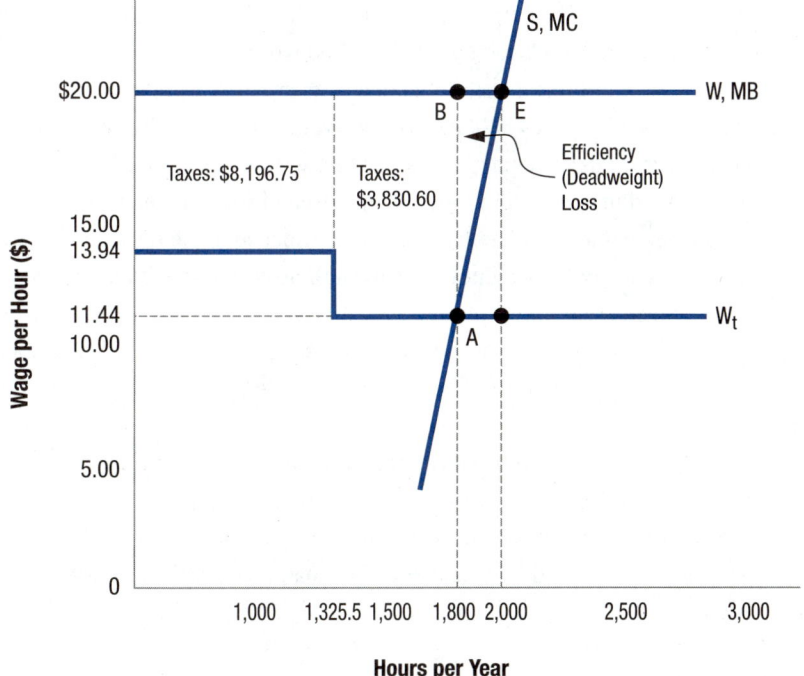

that wage. Bill's willingness to work at various wages is represented by the supply curve (S) for his labor. The upward slope of this curve indicates that he responds to higher wages by working more hours; it also indicates that he responds to lower wages by working fewer hours. In the absence of income taxes, Bill would choose to work 2,000 hours—just like Amy. In the presence of income taxes, however, he will work less. How much less depends on the *marginal* tax rate that he faces. The effects of the marginal tax rates that Bill faces are shown in the curve labeled W_t, which depicts the wage he will receive after taxes. His after-tax wage on the first 1,352.5 hours is $13.94, reflecting a marginal tax rate of 30.3 percent on the first $27,050 in taxable income ($27,050/$20 per hour = 1,352.5 hours). Bill's after-tax wage on the next 647.5 hours (= $12,950/$20 per hour) is only $11.44 ($20 minus taxes of 42.8 percent). Faced with these rates, Bill chooses to work only 1,800 hours per year. Note, however, that the work decision reflects the marginal tax rate of 42.8 percent that he faces.

The government collects $12,027.35 in taxes from Bill: $8,196.75 on income from the first 1,352.5 hours and $3,830.6 from the last 447.5 hours that he works. The 200 hours that Bill chooses *not* to work is a source of inefficiency. This can be seen by recognizing that the wage represents the marginal benefit to Bill from working additional hours and the supply curve represents the marginal cost of working. In the absence of the income taxes, Bill's net benefits would be maximized by working 2,000 hours, because this is where MB=MC. In the face of these taxes, net benefits are less than the maximum amount by the value of the triangle EBA. The value of this triangle, $856 [= (200 hrs × $8.56)/2], is the **efficiency loss from taxation**. This loss is also referred to often as the **deadweight loss from taxation**. In Bill's case, it is about 7 percent [= ($856/$12,027.35)100] of the taxes collected from him. This result illustrates our claim that the cost of taxation exceeds the amount of taxes collected. In Bill's case, it costs an average of $1.07 for every $1.00 collected in taxes. The extra 7 cents is the net benefit per tax dollar that would have been realized on the goods and services produced by Bill if he had worked 200 more hours.

We noted that Bill is more like the typical income taxpayer than Amy. In fact, even Bill reacts to income taxes less than the evidence indicates is likely for the average taxpayer. For example, a widely cited study by Jorgenson and Yun finds efficiency costs of at least 30 cents for each dollar collected.[2] Although there is still some uncertainty regarding the results of empirical studies of this relationship, the president's Office of Management and Budget has enough confidence in the results that they require federal agencies to increase tax costs by 25 percent for deadweight losses when conducting benefit-cost analyses of government programs.[3]

Efficiency can also be affected by the way in which the tax base is determined. The tax base for the individual income tax is equal to income *minus* various deductions, exclusions (also called *exemptions*), and deferrals. The final tax bill is also reduced by various tax credits. The largest of these are listed in Table 3.4.

The effect of these items on efficiency can be illustrated best by focusing on a particular case. The deductibility of mortgage interest is a good, and financially important, example.

Consider Figure 3.10, which depicts the housing decision variables for Bob and Mary. There is the usual downward-sloping demand curve, designated by D and MB. The marginal cost (MC) curve reflects all of

Efficiency Loss from Taxation – The wedge between maximum total net benefits and actual net benefits created by some feature of the tax, such as the marginal rate or exemptions from the tax base.

Deadweight Loss from Taxation – Same as the efficiency loss from taxation.

INFOTRAC
College Edition

Keywords: welfare loss from taxation, deadweight loss

http://www.infotrac-college.com

---

[2]Dale W. Jorgenson and Kun-Young Yun, "The Excess Burden of Taxation in the United States," *Journal of Accounting, Auditing, and Finance* 6, No. 4, Fall 1991, 487–508.

[3]Office of Management and Budget, *Guidelines and Discount Rates for Benefit/Cost Analysis of Federal Programs*, Circular No. A-94, Revised, October 29, 1992.

TABLE 3.4 Federal Individual Income Tax Deductions, Exclusions, Deferrals, and Credits: The Reduction in the Tax Base from Selected Items ($ Billions, 2000)

Item	Amount
Exclusion of employer contributions for medical insurance	76.5
Deduction of mortgage interest on housing	60.3
Deferral of and preferential rate on capital gains	40.5
Accelerated depreciation of machinery and equipment	30.7
Preferential treatment of capital gains at death	27.1
Deductibility of property taxes on houses	22.2
Deductibility of charitable contributions	20.2
Child-care tax credit	19.3
Exclusion of capital gains from home sales	18.5
Exclusion of Social Security benefits for retired workers	18.3

Source: U.S. Bureau of the Census, *Statistical Abstract of the United States:2001*.

FIGURE 3.10 The Effect of Tax Subsidies for Housing on Efficiency

This figure illustrates the effect of federal subsidies for housing provided through the tax code. The subsidies reduce the costs of home ownership from MC to MC_t. They increase the quantity of housing purchased from the efficient level, H_e, to the inefficiently large level, H_t, and create an efficiency loss equal to the area ETS.

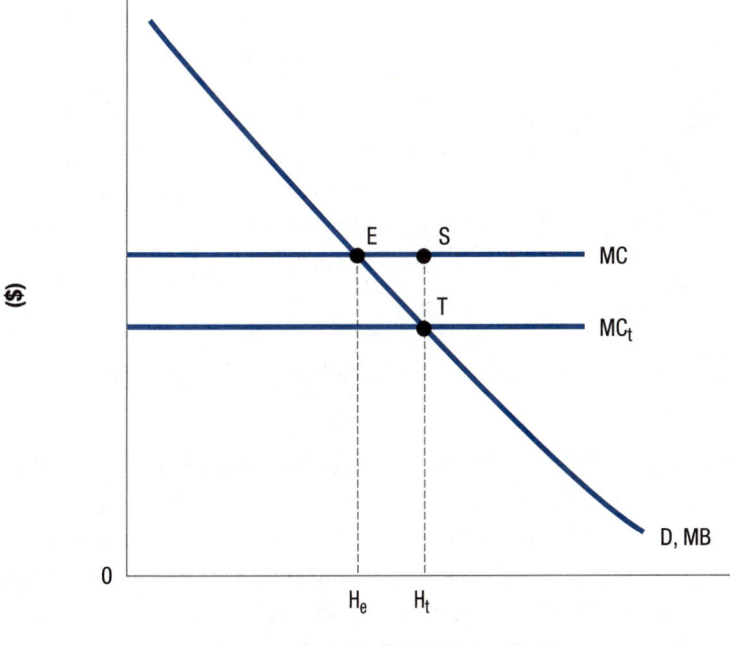

the costs of home ownership, including the interest costs of money borrowed to finance a home mortgage. If interest costs are not deductible, the couple will buy H_e square feet, and net benefits will be maximized. The deductibility of mortgage interest lowers the cost of home ownership, shifting the marginal cost curve down to MC_t. For example, if mortgage interest is $10,000 a year and Bill and Mary's annual income is $75,000, the deductibility feature lowers the tax bill—or cost of home ownership—by $2,750, the value of the deduction times the marginal income tax rate of 27.5 percent that this couple faces.

In the face of the lower cost of home ownership, the amount purchased will increase from H_e to H_t. Bill and Mary will have been induced by this feature of the tax code to buy too much housing, and there will be losses in efficiency equal to the area bounded by the points E, T, and S (the amount by which maximum net benefits are decreased).

The other items in Table 3.4 also induce taxpayers to do too much from an efficiency perspective. For example, the exclusion of employer contributions for medical insurance will induce taxpayers to buy too much medical insurance. Roger Feldman and Brian Dowd[4] have estimated efficiency losses from excess health insurance at 0.9 to 2.9 percent of national output, or $90 billion to $290 billion for a $10 trillion economy. A substantial part of this loss may be attributable to the exclusion of employer contributions for medical insurance. The deferral and preferential treatment of **capital gains** (the difference between the market value of an asset and the purchase price of that asset) will induce taxpayers to earn too much of their income in this form. The accelerated depreciation of machinery and equipment will lower the cost of these items, inducing purchasers to buy too much of them. The deductibility of property taxes on houses and the exclusion of capital gains from home sales will lower the cost of home ownership, just like the exclusion of mortgage interest, and induce taxpayers to buy too much housing. In fact, estimates by Poterba indicate that all of the features of the tax code that favor expenditures on housing create efficiency losses of about $600 per year for someone who owns a $100,000 home.[5]

Capital Gain – The market price of an asset minus the purchase price of that asset.

SALES TAXES. A similar tale can be told for the general sales taxes levied at the state level. The rates associated with these taxes induce taxpayers to spend too little, creating efficiency losses. There are many exclusions from the tax base, however, especially for services, and these exclusions lower the cost of the exempted items relative to the cost of items subject to taxation. This produces a pattern of too much consumption of some items and too little of others. The net result is a system of sales taxation that is characterized by many instances of inefficiency.

Excise taxes—sales taxes applied to narrow classes of items—are also sources of inefficiency. Excise tax rates increase the price of taxed items relative to nontaxed items, inducing taxpayers to buy too little of the taxed items.

THE INDIVIDUAL INCOME TAX AND PERSONAL SAVING. The decisions to work and to consume specific items are not the only decisions affected by taxes. The overall division of disposable income into consumption and saving may also be affected. Individuals have the choice of spending all of their income during the period in which it is received or saving it for future consumption. The amount that they defer to later periods will be influenced, in part, by the interest income that they earn on the por-

---

[4]"A New Estimate of the Welfare Loss of Excess Health Insurance," *American Economic Review* 81, March 1991, 297–301.

[5]James M. Poterba, "Taxation and Housing: Old Questions, New Answers," *American Economic Review* 82, No. 2, May 1992, 237–142.

Insights

What Does Government *Really* Cost? The Practical Significance of the Efficiency Losses from Taxation

In 2000, U.S. governments collected revenues of $2.919 trillion—about 31 percent of the nation's total output. The opportunity cost of government—what the nation actually sacrificed for the goods and services it received from government—was considerably higher, however. You have already met the principal source of the difference: the efficiency loss from taxes on labor income. As noted in the text, this loss probably amounts to around 30 percent of taxes collected from this source of income. Taxes on labor income consist of individual income taxes and payroll taxes paid on wages and salaries. Taxes from these sources were $1.84 trillion in 2000. Thus, the efficiency loss from taxes on labor income was $552 billion. You have also met another important source of the difference between the tax cost and the opportunity cost of government: the efficiency loss from tax deductions that distort the pattern of household spending. We provided an estimate in the text for only a single subsidy, but recent research indicates that spending distortions attributable to all tax deductions could add as much as another 20 percent of income taxes, or $368 billion. You have not yet met a third important source: the efficiency losses due to the taxation of income from investment in business plant and equipment. Recent research indicates that annual costs of this type are in the range of 1 to 2 percent of national output, or $100 billion to $200 billion a year. Adding these numbers together yields total efficiency losses from income taxes alone in the neighborhood of $1,020 billion to $1,120 billion. Although all of these numbers are subject to debate, the opportunity cost of government was probably much closer to $4 trillion in 2000 than it was to the nearly $3 trillion in taxes collected.

---

tion that they save. The individual income tax applies to interest income, so it distorts the choice between present and future consumption, or, what is the same thing, current consumption and saving. This distortion is the source of additional efficiency losses from taxation.

■ How Much Efficiency Do We Want?

We think that it follows from the previous analysis that inefficiency in the U.S. economy is a serious problem. It does not necessarily follow, however, that eliminating inefficiency is always an appropriate strategy. One important reason is that efforts to do so may make the distribution of resources or income more inequitable, and equity is also a desirable economic goal. Another reason is that attempts to achieve efficiency may stifle innovation, and innovation can be an important means of satisfying wants more fully.

Efficiency Versus Equity: Tax Trade-Offs

We have so far ignored the possibility of desirable economic goals other than efficiency. Many people are concerned, however, about who reaps the benefits from and who pays the costs of alternative allocations of resources, or about who pays the tax bill. They want an allocation of resources or a distribution of the tax burden to treat particular individuals or groups equitably or fairly.

Because the tax system is such an important source of inefficiency, there is understandably considerable interest in redesigning it to reduce the efficiency costs of taxation. This could be done, for example, by reducing marginal income tax rates or by eliminating some of the exclusions, deductions, and credits pertaining to this tax. The largest increase in efficiency via rate reductions could be achieved by reducing the higher bracket rates more than the lower bracket rates. This would tend to shift a greater portion of the tax burden, however, to lower income taxpayers, and many people would consider this to be a less equitable distribution of the tax burden. Alternatively, efficiency could be enhanced by taxing income that is currently excluded from the tax base. This could be done, for example, by eliminating the child-care tax credit, but many people would object to this on the grounds that the costs of this change would fall primarily on lower income households. Many trade-offs between efficiency and equity such as these would be involved in any attempts to reduce the efficiency costs of taxation.

Is there a way to determine how far to go in reducing inefficiency? The simple answer is yes—at least in theory. The solution is to assign weights to the individuals who will benefit from and pay for the changes that will be made. If this could be done, the objective would be to make the change only if the weighted sum of the benefits from doing so were equal to or greater than the weighted sum of the costs. Ideally, we would go one step further and design the change so that we maximized the difference between the weighted sum of benefits and the weighted sum of costs.

The weights to which we refer tell us how much satisfaction one individual gets from the marginal dollar relative to other individuals. For example, if, as some believe, a dollar to a poor person is worth more than a dollar to a rich person, a dollar received by or given up by the former would be weighted more heavily than a dollar received by or given up by the latter.

INFOTRAC
College Edition

Keywords: *economic tradeoffs, leaky bucket*
http://www.infotrac-college.com

Suppose that some evidence convinces us that a dollar to a poor person has twice the value of a dollar to a rich person. We could assign any weights to the two groups as long as the value for the poor was twice as large as the value for the rich. A weight of 1 for the poor and 1/2 for the rich would work, but so would 2 and 1, 10 and 5, and so forth. The actual numbers are irrelevant; it is the ratio of the two that matters. These weights could then be applied to changes in the tax burden experienced by the two groups. The difficulty, of course, lies in discovering the appropriate weights. Unfortunately, this has not been done, and the perceived equity costs of increases in efficiency can be a powerful brake on changes that focus primarily on efficiency.

Efficiency Versus Innovation

There are trade-offs, as well, between achieving greater efficiency and more innovation in the economy. This is illustrated in the following case.

As we have seen, efficiency calls for industries in which firms have little market power, and a case can be made for government regulation of firms with market power. The objective of such regulation is to keep firms with market power from charging prices that exceed marginal cost. Chapter 5 develops examples of markets, however, in which prices greater than marginal cost are required to elicit the development of new products. This is especially true of industries that are highly dependent on knowledge and the creation of new knowledge as the basis for growth, such as the computer hardware and software industries and the pharmaceutical industry. The leading firms in these industries must incur large and highly uncertain start-up costs for research and development and production. Prices greater than operating, or marginal, cost must be charged in order to finance the start-up costs required to compete in these industries. There is a clear trade-off in such cases between efficiency and innovation. Both are desirable goals, however, and government regulation that opts for efficiency only exacts too high a price in terms of new product development.

International Perspective

Does More Government Mean Less Growth?

Many economists are concerned that there may be a trade-off between the size of the government sector and the rate of economic growth. More specifically, they fear that more government may mean slower growth. A larger government sector requires higher taxes, and higher taxes may reduce work effort, savings, and investment. A larger government sector may also mean more regulation, and more regulation may require business firms to substitute investment in regulatory compliance for investment in goods-producing plant and equipment. More government need not mean slower growth, however, if it provides more education, research, social infrastructure, and political stability. Theory alone, then, will not help us determine whether more government means slower growth.

Considerable variation occurs across countries in terms of both size of government and rate of economic growth. Accordingly, several researchers have attempted to detect a relationship between government and growth by making cross-country comparisons. In the studies done to date, government's influence on the economy has been represented by either government expenditures or taxes. The research questions whether slower rates of growth have been associated with higher ratios of government spending or taxes to output.

Keith Marsden, using a sample of 20 countries for the period 1970 to 1979, found a statistically significant negative relationship between growth rates and tax shares: On average, a 1 percent increase in the ratio of taxes to output was associated with a 0.36 percent decrease in the rate of economic growth.[a] Charles Wolf and Randy Ross estimated that a 10 percent increase in the ratio of government spending to output was associated with a 1 percent decrease in the rate of growth, using a sample of 27 countries for 1972 to 1982.[b] Daniel Landau's study of the relationship between government expenditures and per capita economic growth shows results similar to those of Marsden and Wolf and Ross.[c] Alternatively, Mancur Olson found no reliable connection between the size of government and economic growth in his study of long-term secular growth,[d] and Frederic Pryor reached a similar conclusion based on his study of a broad range of market-based and command economies between 1950 and 1980.[e] Based on these studies, the evidence of a relationship between the size of government and the rate of economic growth is somewhat ambiguous. This issue is such an important one in making the choice between markets and government, however, that certainly we have not heard the last word from the research community.

---

[a] Keith Marsden, "Links Between Taxes and Economic Growth: Some Empirical Evidence," World Bank Staff Working Paper 605 (Washington, DC, 1983).
[b] Charles Wolf, Jr., *Markets or Governments*, 2nd ed. (Cambridge, MA: MIT Press, 1994), 145–151.
[c] Daniel Landau, "Government Expenditure and Economic Growth: A Cross-Country Study," *Southern Economic Journal* 49, No. 3 (January 1983), 783–792.
[d] Mancur Olson, *The Rise and Decline of Nations* (New Haven: Yale University Press, 1982).
[e] Frederic L. Pryor, "Growth and Fluctuations of Production in OECD and East European Countries," *World Politics* 37, No. 2 (January 1985), 204–237.

Efficiency and Equity

Efforts to achieve greater efficiency do not always create conflicts of the type noted here. There are cases where we could increase efficiency and equity at the same time—or at least be unlikely to reduce equity significantly as efficiency increases.

AGRICULTURAL PRICE SUPPORTS. Although federal farm programs supposedly are designed to attack farm poverty, we argue in Chapter 4 that the evidence clearly indicates that price-support and target-price programs give the biggest benefits to farmers who produce the most and surely have the most wealth. Given this result, it seems possible to reduce some of the inefficiency created by these programs without seriously violating notions of equity.

MINIMUM WAGE. A similar verdict seems in order for the federal minimum wage. A recent study of this subject finds evidence that the minimum wage largely redistributes income among low-income families.[6] Thus, it seems possible to reduce the application of this measure without imposing significant additional costs on low-income families as a group. That is, most of the gainers and losers from such a measure would be in the same income category.

MEDICARE AND MEDICAID. As noted earlier, government-subsidized medical care is an important source of inefficiency. Poor families and individuals benefit significantly, however, from these subsidies through the Medicare and (especially) Medicaid programs. One potential solution to the problem of reducing inefficiency without great harm to the welfare of these groups is to provide them with vouchers that they could use to pay for medical care directly. The vouchers could be issued in a smaller amount than the current subsidy because the existence of too much medical care is evidence that the care is worth less to consumers than the cost of providing it. The vouchers, themselves, would provide consumers of medical care with the incentive and the means to be more careful shoppers.

Efficiency Offsets to Inefficiency

Finally, there are cases in which one source of inefficiency is offset to some degree by other sources of efficiency. Some examples of taxes illustrate this point clearly.

Excise taxes on cigarettes are a case in point. Cigarette smoking is a source of external costs in the form of second-hand smoke. Without excise taxes on cigarettes, there will be too many cigarettes consumed from an efficiency perspective—just like the case of the coal-burning apartments in Kansas City. Application of the excise tax will reduce cigarette consumption, creating efficiency losses from taxation but reducing efficiency losses from second-hand smoke. The two effects may or may not offset each other, but the excise tax certainly works in this instance as a corrective measure. In a similar fashion, the efficiency losses from gasoline taxes may be offset somewhat by reduced efficiency losses from the air pollution associated with oil refining or automobile travel, and the efficiency losses from excise taxes on alcohol may be offset somewhat by reduced efficiency losses from the external costs of alcoholism.

INFOTRAC
College Edition
Keyword: *green taxes*
http://www.infotrac-college.com

Summary

Efficiency in resource allocation is an important economic goal. To achieve efficiency, resources must be allocated so that benefits are equal to or greater than costs, and marginal benefits must equal marginal costs. Competitive markets automatically fulfill these conditions, but there are many instances of inefficiency in the U.S. economy; some are in the market sector (cases of market failure), and some are in the public sector (cases of government failure).

Several cases of market failure were examined. We found the following:

- Monopoly pricing causes too few resources to be allocated to monopolized industries, creating efficiency losses or deadweight losses from monopoly.
- The presence of external benefits from an activity causes too few resources to be allocated to that activity, resulting in efficiency losses.
- Public goods are an extreme version of the external benefits case.
- External costs created by an activity cause too many resources to be allocated to that activity.

---

[6]David Neumark and William Wascher, "Do Minimum Wages Fight Poverty?" *Economic Inquiry*, Vol. 40, No. 3, July 2002, 315–333.

- Markets cannot be created for some products, such as insurance against unemployment and poverty.
- Markets for some insurance products are inherently incomplete because of moral hazard, adverse selection, and differences between individual and social risk.

Several cases of government failure were also examined. We found the following:

- Rent controls cause too few resources to be allocated to markets for rental housing.
- Agricultural price supports cause too many resources to be allocated to agricultural markets.
- Government subsidies for medical care also cause too many resources to be allocated to medical care.
- The minimum wage causes too few workers to be employed.
- The tax system is a primary source of efficiency or deadweight losses, resulting from high marginal tax rates and exceptions to the tax base.

When the various sources of inefficiency are added together, they indicate that inefficiency is a serious problem for the U.S. economy. Efficiency losses easily exceed a trillion dollars a year. In fact, efficiency losses from both external costs and taxation are probably that large by themselves.

It does not follow, however, that eliminating efficiency is a desirable thing to do. There are trade-offs between efficiency and equity and between efficiency and innovation. These trade offs indicate that some inefficiency is desirable, but they also make it difficult to determine exactly how much this might be.

There are some instances in which the trade-off between efficiency and equity is not severe. Agricultural price supports and the minimum wage are cases in point. There may be instances in which policy can be designed to reduce efficiency losses without seriously compromising equity; the case of vouchers for medical care is an example. Finally, there are instances where government intervention that creates efficiency losses of one type reduces efficiency losses of another type, as exemplified by the so-called sin taxes (taxes on cigarettes and alcohol) and gasoline taxes.

Key Terms

Economic efficiency	**Total revenue**	**Nonexistent market**
Static efficiency	**Efficiency loss**	**Moral hazard**
Dynamic efficiency	**Deadweight loss**	**Adverse selection**
Marginal benefit curve	**External benefits**	**Incomplete market**
Marginal cost curve	**Marginal external benefit (MEB)**	**Progressive tax**
Total benefit	**Marginal social benefit (MSB)**	**Regressive tax**
Total cost	**Public goods**	**Efficiency loss from taxation**
Total net benefit	**External costs**	**Deadweight loss from taxation**
Market failure	**Marginal external cost (MEC)**	**Capital gains**
Profit	**Marginal social cost (MSC)**	

Review Questions

1. What do we mean by market failure? By government failure?
2. What conditions must be fulfilled to achieve economic efficiency?
3. Explain how a competitive market achieves economic efficiency automatically.
4. Describe two cases in which the market produces an inefficiently small quantity. Explain why.
5. Describe and explain two cases in which markets produce too much from the perspective of economic efficiency.
6. Explain why the resolution of the problems of unemployment and poverty cannot be left up to the market.

7. Describe and explain two cases in which government policies cause too many resources to be allocated to an activity.

8. In determining the effect of income taxes on individual work effort, the key is the highest marginal tax rate faced by an individual. Explain.

9. A study has been done of a government program that provides the following benefits to, and imposes the following costs on, two groups of individuals:

	Group A	Group B
Benefits	$100 million	$50 million
Costs	$50 million	$75 million

   a. From the perspective of efficiency alone, should the program be undertaken? Why or why not?
   b. Suppose that group A consists of rich people and that group B consists of poor people, and that it has been determined that a dollar to a poor person is worth three times as much as a dollar to a rich person. Should the program be undertaken? Why or why not?
   c. What trade-off is illustrated by part b of this question? Explain.

10. Many communities in the United States experience droughts each year.
    a. Use a supply-demand diagram to illustrate the effects of a drought on the equilibrium price and quantity of water in such a community.
    b. Suppose the city authorities do not allow the price of water to change as indicated in your diagram. Use your diagram to illustrate the effect of such a pricing policy on efficiency.

11. Suppose that the market for apartments for rent in your community is described by the following data:

Rent per Month	Apartments Demanded	Apartments Supplied
$2,000	0	20,000
$1,800	2,000	18,000
$1,600	4,000	16,000
$1,400	6,000	14,000
$1,200	8,000	12,000
$1,000	10,000	10,000
$800	12,000	8,000
$600	14,000	6,000
$400	16,000	4,000
$200	18,000	2,000
$0	20,000	0

   Determine the following:
   a. The equilibrium quantity of apartments
   b. Total benefits at equilibrium
   c. Total costs at equilibrium
   d. Total net benefits at equilibrium
   e. Total revenue at equilibrium
   f. Suppose that Bill Gateway buys all the apartments in your community and engages in monopoly pricing. As a result, the number of units rented falls to 7,000 and the price rises to $13,000. How large is the efficiency loss from monopoly pricing?

12. Use the diagram you have constructed for your answer to question 11 (without Bill Gateway) to illustrate the efficiency losses from air pollution. Suppose that each apartment is heated by coal that produces smoke that impairs health in the community by an average of $400 per apartment per month.

Economic Issues on the Internet

- Taxpolicy.com—**http://www.taxpolicy.com/build.htm**
  Build Your Own Tax Policy in Just 10 Minutes! What are your beliefs about taxation? What kind of tax policy would you design? Take the brief survey.

- Tax Policy & Reform Groups—**http://www.taxsites.com/policy.html**
  Review some alternative tax systems as found on the Web sites. Which system is most interesting to you? How does it differ from the current tax system? Will it increase or decrease efficiency losses from taxation? Will it distribute the tax burden equitably?

- U.S. Department of Commerce, Bureau of Economic Analysis—**http://www.bea.doc.gov**
  Learn more about taxes and expenditures of U.S. governments.

CHAPTER 4

Competitive Markets and Agriculture

Outline:

Demand and Supply Analysis
   Other Demand Factors
   Other Supply Factors
How Changes in Demand and Supply Affect Equilibrium Price and Quantity
   Changes in Demand
   Changes in Supply
   Changes in Demand and Supply

U. S. Agriculture
   Economic and Historical Characteristics
   Competitive Markets and Economic Profits
U.S. Farm Policy
   Price Floor
   Output Constraints
   Target Prices and Deficiency Payments
   Rent Seeking

Appendix: The Price Elasticity of Demand

In the mid-1990s, Congress considered the Freedom to Farm bill and enacted a related law, the Federal Agriculture Improvement and Reform Act of 1996 (the 1996 Farm Bill). After reading in Chapter 2 about formerly centrally planned economies trying to transform themselves to market economies, you might not be surprised to find, say, the Russian legislature considering "freedom to farm," but why was it an issue in the United States? The answer starts with the massive government intervention in production agriculture that arose during the Great Depression of the 1930s. The intervention stemmed, in part, from the fact that poverty was a greater problem in the rural and agricultural sectors of the economy and from the fact that many farmers were losing their farms and their homes in bankruptcy.

From this beginning, federal government intervention in agriculture continued, becoming more expensive and more complex as the twentieth century unfolded. By the early 1990s, government payments to farmers ranged from $10 to $20 billion per year (adjusted for inflation). This amount does not include the higher prices that consumers pay because of government policies, including the inefficiency cost resulting from governmental interference in farmers' decisions. The Organization for Economic Cooperation and Development put the direct and indirect subsidies to U.S. farmers in the early 1990s at between $30 and $35 billion per year. The original conditions of farm poverty and farm bankruptcies, however, no longer provided a reason for government intervention, particularly of the type used by the U.S. government.

The agricultural sector of the U.S. economy is tremendously successful. With only 2 percent of the labor force, it feeds the entire nation with enough left over to account for approximately 10 percent of U.S. exports. Farmers, moreover, are well compensated for their efforts compared with the compensation received by the average American. In 2000, the average income of farm households was slightly above $61,000, about 20 percent higher than the national average for all households. In addition, farming is no longer a peculiarly risky business: A nonfarm business is six times more likely to fail.[1]

Given this situation, the proponents of the 1996 Farm Bill wanted to take government out of agriculture and provide farmers with freedom of choice in terms of what they produced. This bill was expected to reduce direct government payments to farmers to about $7 billion dollars a year through 2002. If the policies had evolved as expected, after 2002 the direct payments to farmers were expected to fall to about $2 billion per year.

The difference between projections and results is dramatic. In 1999, direct payments to farmers amounted to about $20 billion per year and exploded to about $32 billion in 2000. Recall that the hidden costs of these programs add substantially to the total cost. In 2000, about six of 10 farms received no direct government payment. Four farms of 10 received average direct payments of more than $17,000. Fine, you might say: The 40 percent of the farmers who need help get it, and the 60 percent who are doing all right get by on their own. Alas, the productive farms and wealthy farmers grab most of the payments.

Sixty-four percent of all farms are classified as rural residence farms that provide retired people and hobby farmers with a desired lifestyle (and a tax break) or as limited resource farms with sales less than $100,000 per year, assets less than $150,000, and household income less than $20,000. These farmers as a group lose money. How can they continue? As Figure 4.1 shows, these farmers receive all of their income from off-farm sources. Only about 13 percent of total government agricultural payments go to farms in this category. Government payments per household are about $1,500, and household income is about $63,000.

Intermediate farms, consisting of family farms with sales up to $250,000 (exclusive of the rural residence farms), account for 29 percent of all farms and receive about 39 percent of the total government payments. As Figure 4.1 shows, the contribution of farm income to total household income for this group is positive, but small. Off-farm income accounts for over 95 percent of total household income. In this category, household income averages about $44,000, and government payments average about $10,000. Without the government payments, this group too would lose money in agriculture.

Family farms with sales greater than $250,000 a year are classified as commercial farms. Although they account for only 6 percent of all family farms, they receive over 60 percent of total government

---

[1] Brian M. Riedl, "Top 10 Reasons to Veto the Farm Bill," *Heritage Foundation Backgrounder*, No. 1538 (April 27, 2002), available at http://www.heritage.org.

FIGURE 4.1 — Farm Household Income and Government Payments per Farm Household

This figure illustrates the positive relationship between subsidies and size of farm. It also shows that the largest direct payments go to the households with the highest average income.

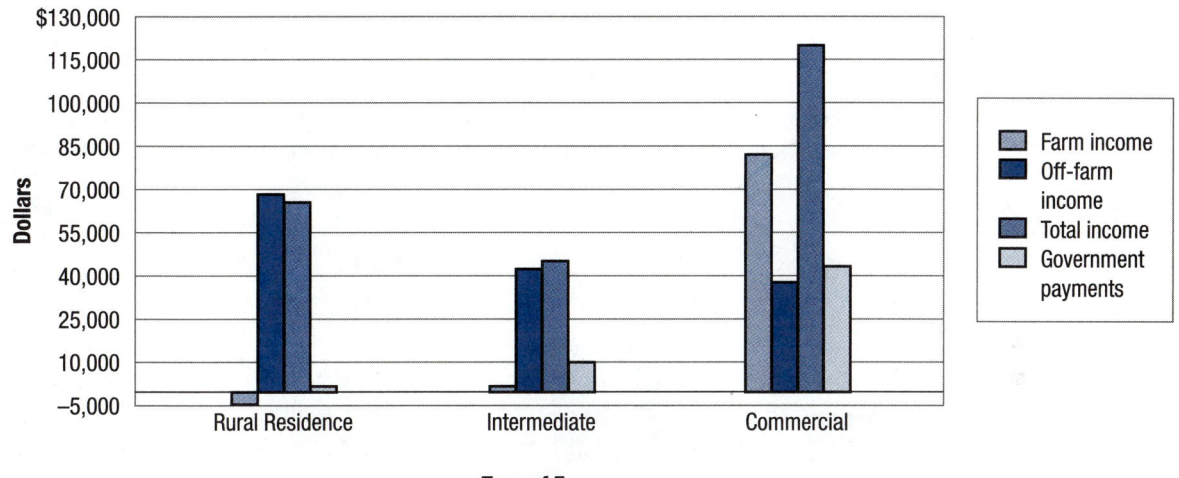

SOURCE: "Agricultural Income and Finance: Situation and Outlook," Resource Economics Division, Economic Research Service, U.S. Department of Agriculture, September 2001; available at http://www.ers.usda.gov.

payments. As Figure 4.1 shows, these farm households receive over $40,000 a year in government payments, even though total household income is close to $120,000 per year.

Figure 4.2 presents information for these three categories for only those farms that participate in the government subsidy programs. As Figure 4.2 shows on the right axis, the rural-residence farms have the lowest participation rate, about 30 percent. As we move to the intermediate and commercial farms, the participation rate increases to about 60 percent and then 70 percent. Similarly, the average payment to each category of farms (on the left axis) increases from about $5,000 to about $17,000, and then to about $62,000.[2] Clearly, direct payments from farm programs are **not** focused on the poor. Just the opposite! The programs are designed in a way that ensures that the largest benefits go to the largest and presumably most wealthy farmers. To be specific, a program that gives taxpayer dollars to Scottie Pippen, David Rockefeller, and Ted Turner can hardly be justified as helping the poor. Yet they, along with such members of congress as Representative Doug Ose, R-Calif, and Representative Marion Berry, D-Ark, receive government payments through the farm programs. Consider also the 500 or so recipients in Stuttgart, Arkansas, who received $150 million from 1996–2000. Surely the subsidies do not have to be that large to lift 500 people out of poverty.[3]

---

[2]"Agricultural Income and Finance: Situation and Outlook," Resource Economics Division, Economic Research Service, U.S. Department of Agriculture, September 2001; available at http://www.ers.usda.gov.

[3]The Environmental Working Group presents details on subsidies received by individuals by zip code, county, and state on its Web site available at http://www.ewg.org/farm.

FIGURE 4.2 Government Payments and Farm Participation Rates by Farm Type

This figure measures on the right axis the percentage of each type of farm that participates in the subsidy programs. Moving to the right moves us to larger and more profitable farms. Thus, the larger the farm, the more likely it is to receive subsidies. On the left axis, it measures the subsidy per participating farm and shows that the larger the farm the greater the subsidy.

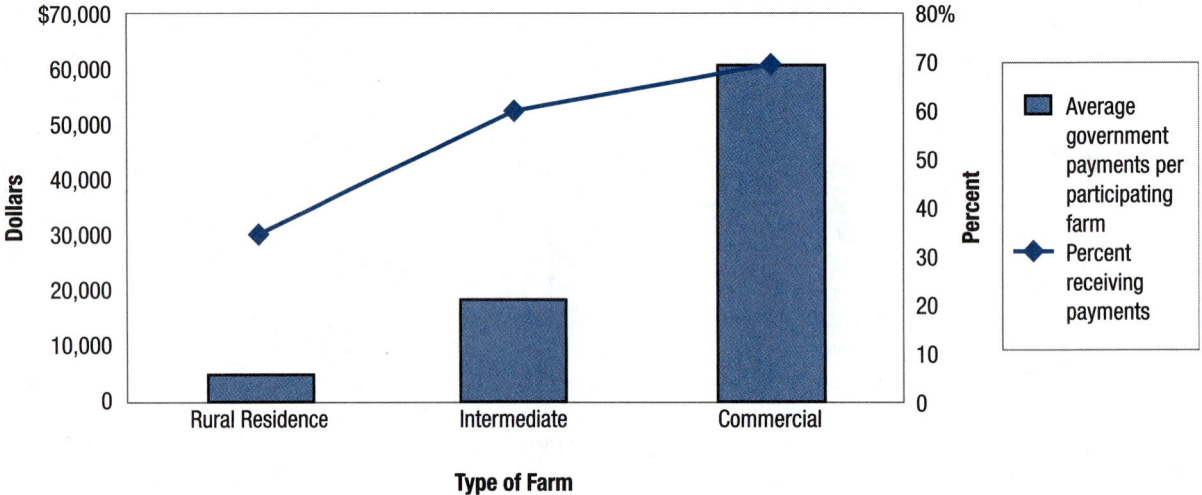

SOURCE: "Agricultural Income and Finance: Situation and Outlook," Resource Economics Division, Economic Research Service, U.S. Department of Agriculture, September 2001; available at http://www.ers.usda.gov.

Government farm programs interfere with farmers' production decisions, increase food costs, provide large subsidies to the wealthy, and do little to help poor farmers. The support that agriculture receives from the average citizen is an example of a program that redistributes income from taxpayers in general to a privileged group, a program that our political system has been unable to reform. To understand the difficulties of reform, we resume our discussion of demand and supply and bring in some political considerations.

■ DEMAND AND SUPPLY ANALYSIS

Demand and supply analysis shows how the market determines what to produce. The law of demand states that, at a lower price, consumers would plan to purchase more of a good—say, milk—during a week.[4] It also states the reverse. At a higher price, consumers would plan to purchase less milk per week. Conversely, the law of supply states that producers of milk would plan to sell less milk per week at a lower price. It also states that, at a higher price, they would plan to sell more. (Our statements about the laws of demand and supply assume that factors other than price of the good stay constant.)

---

[4]In discussing demand and supply, we must include a time dimension. It would be meaningless to say that Nadia has a greater demand for milk than Ivan because she plans to purchase 20 gallons of milk and Ivan plans to purchase 2 gallons. For instance, Ivan may plan to purchase 2 gallons a day, and Nadia may plan to purchase 20 gallons a month. Ivan would have the greater demand.

INTERNATIONAL PERSPECTIVE

OECD FARM POLICY: NEW ZEALAND BREAKS THE MOLD

Farm policy in the United States is not unique. Throughout the industrialized world, farmers have obtained substantial protection from their governments. This protection consists of barriers to free trade that permit domestic agricultural prices to rise above world market prices, price supports, deficiency payments, and various other subsidies. The dollar support per year given directly to producers in the late 1990s for countries in the European Union (EU) was about $12,000; the United States, $20,000; and New Zealand, **zero**![a] These direct payments plus other farm subsidies cost about $300 per capita in the EU, $340 in the United States, and $80 in New Zealand. In the United States, government policy leads to a family of four paying $1,400 to agriculture, in addition to the amount that it pays agriculture for food, clothing, and other products. In New Zealand, government policy requires that family to give up only about $320. A fundamental fallacy—the all-or-nothing fallacy—provides a national security argument for protecting farmers and agriculture.

The argument is simple and persuasive. Food is necessary to survive. Farmers produce food. If domestic farmers go out of business, we may lose our independence, because we would have to rely on foreign countries for life's necessities. This argument, along with the relative and absolute decline in the number of farms and farmers in most developed countries, leads nonfarmers in some countries to want to protect agriculture. The implicit assumption is that if some farms or farmers are going out of business, all farmers are in danger of doing so.

Economic situations are rarely so cut and dried. In the United States, the number of farms and farmers has declined for most of the twentieth century. Does this mean that the United States is in danger of becoming reliant on other, perhaps unfriendly, countries for its food supply? No! U.S. farms are producing more than ever. Only the high-cost farms and the high-cost farmers are leaving agriculture, and as they do, the supply price of U.S. farm products falls. The lower-cost farms and farmers would be able to supply the U.S. market at lower cost. One example of the all-or-nothing fallacy is to think that if one farmer leaves agriculture, all farmers will leave agriculture. They don't. Moreover, as the high-cost producers leave, the remaining producers in the industry are the lower-cost ones.

New Zealand no longer accepts this fallacy, having eliminated all direct producer subsidies. Most of its government expenditures for agriculture are spent on research, disease control, and pest control. Government payments to farmers based on production have essentially been eliminated. New Zealand has also moved away from providing relief payments to farmers because of climatic disasters, encouraging farmers to undertake risk management. New Zealand permits marketing boards to attempt to influence market price, but overall New Zealand's farmers, as we have seen, receive far less per farmer than do farmers in most other OECD countries, and New Zealanders pay far less to support agriculture.

New Zealand has demonstrated that a country can eliminate most agricultural protection without causing a crisis in its agricultural economy. In 1996, the United States started toward a free market in agriculture. The 2002 Farm Bill, however, has reversed that movement, turning policy toward bigger subsidies and ultimately more regulation.

---

[a]Organization for Economic Cooperation and Development, *Agricultural Policies in OECD Countries: Monitoring and Evaluation* (Paris: OECD, 2001).

In a market economy, the laws of demand and supply lead to equilibrium. By definition, equilibrium exists when a situation has no cause to change. A market equilibrium exists when the quantity that people plan to buy at the market price is the same as the quantity that producers plan to sell at that price; no one wants to change behavior. To review the analysis from Chapter 2, suppose that, at the going price, consumers plan to buy more of a good—say, milk—than producers plan to sell. Consumers find their plans frustrated. They cannot buy the amount of milk they want, even though they are willing to pay the price. Producers find that they cannot satisfy their customers. Some consumer is likely to offer a higher price or some producer is likely to ask for one. Either way, the offer will be accepted and the price will increase. According to the law of demand, at the higher price consumers will plan to purchase less. According to the law of supply, producers will plan to produce and sell more. Buyers buy less; sellers sell more. As the plans of consumers and producers converge, the market moves to equilibrium.

If this economic coordination (also discussed in Chapter 2) were accomplished once and for all, the price system's ability to coordinate might not be particularly important. Change, however, characterizes modern economies. New goods and services emerge. Consumers learn about new goods and learn more about existing goods. National population grows. Population grows in some parts of a country and declines in others. These and other changes that affect demand require an economic system to solve the coordination problem again and again.

Similarly, changes in factors affecting supply require the economy to adjust to new equilibriums. Supply is affected by changes in technology, in the prices of resources such as labor, and in the relative profitability of various activities. New production techniques, new goods, and new opportunities will be trademarks of the twenty-first century, just as they were of the twentieth. To understand why agriculture is so heavily subsidized, we must understand competitive markets; the first step is to understand demand and supply.

Other Demand Factors

The maximum amount that consumers are willing to pay for an additional gallon of milk, the demand price, depends on how much they like milk (their preferences) and their income, among other factors. It also depends on the amount of other goods, such as cheese, that they consume, which, in turn, depends upon the prices of other goods. Consequently, the demand for any good—say, milk—depends on factors other than its price: for instance, consumers' preferences, consumers' income, and the prices of other goods.[5] A complete statement of the law of demand is that as the price of some good changes, keeping the other factors unchanged, the quantity demanded of the good changes in the opposite direction.

Decrease in Demand – A situation in which, at each price, consumers plan to purchase less of a good; it is depicted by a leftward shift of the demand curve. It may also be interpreted as a reduction in the value of an additional unit of the good, which emphasizes the downward shift of the curve.

In Table 4.1, columns 1 and 2 present a market demand schedule for milk. Suppose that this demand results when the price of a pound of cheddar cheese is $5, the price of a gourmet chocolate chip cookie is $1.25, and consumers earn $900 per week.

RELATED GOODS. Now suppose that the price of some related good changes: Suppose that the price of a pound of cheddar cheese drops to $3. As a result, consumers purchase more cheese. Eating more cheese, milk is less important for them. Consequently, for any given quantity of milk, consumers will not be willing to pay as much for an additional unit. Its demand price falls. For the sixth gallon of milk, it decreases from $1.75 to $1.25. In Table 4.1, the demand schedule changes from that in columns 1 and 2 to that in columns 3 and 4. This is an example of a **decrease in demand** for milk because of a decrease in the price of a related good, cheese. For any given quantity of milk, consumers place a lower value on

---

[5]To read about some of the other factors that affect demand, such as expected future prices, see James D. Gwartney, Richard L. Stroup, Russell Sobel, and David Macpherson, *Economics: Private and Public Choice* (Cincinnati: South-Western, 2003). Chapter 19 discusses these other factors.

| TABLE 4.1 | Changes in Demand for Milk When Other Factors Change |

The original demand schedule for milk changes to a new demand schedule as other factors affecting demand change. The demand for milk decreases if the price of cheese decreases. The demand for milk increases if consumers' income increases.

Original Demand		Demand with New Cheese Price		Demand with New Income	
Price per Gallon (1)	Gallons per Week (2)	Price per Gallon (3)	Gallons per Week (4)	Price per Gallon (5)	Gallons per Week (6)
$3.50	0	$3.50	0	$3.50	1
3.25	0	3.25	0	3.25	2
3.00	1	3.00	0	3.00	3
2.75	2	2.75	0	2.75	4
2.50	3	2.50	1	2.50	5
2.25	4	2.25	2	2.25	6
2.00	5	2.00	3	2.00	7
1.75	6	1.75	4	1.75	8
1.50	7	1.50	5	1.50	9
1.25	8	1.25	6	1.25	10
1.00	9	1.00	7	1.00	11

an additional unit of milk—that is, the demand price decreases. Another way to see the decrease in demand is to note that for each possible price, consumers plan to purchase less milk. For instance, at the price of $1.25, the planned purchase decreases from 8 to 6 gallons.

The demand curve changes from D_0, the original demand curve, to D_1, as shown in Figure 4.3, which plots information from Table 4.1. The downward movement in the entire demand curve reflects the decline in demand prices. Its leftward movement shows that consumers' planned purchases have decreased.

Suppose the price of cookies increases. The law of demand implies that you now would buy fewer cookies. Assume that consuming cookies enhances your enjoyment of milk. Because you are consuming fewer cookies, milk is less important—the value that you put on an additional gallon of milk declines. Demand decreases, as in Figure 4.3.

The demand for milk reacts the same way to a decrease in the price of cheese and an increase in that of cookies. Two goods are **substitutes** if a decrease in the price of one, say cheese, causes a decrease in the demand for the other, say milk. The price change for one good and the demand change for the other good move in the same direction. In the example in Table 4.1, cheese and milk are substitutes because a decrease in the price of cheese leads to a decrease in the demand for milk. In effect, the cheese substitutes for the milk in consumers' diets.

In contrast, cheese is a **complement** with hamburger if an increase in the price of cheese results in a decrease in the demand for hamburger. This might occur among people who really like cheeseburgers, but do not particularly like burgers without cheese. The price change for one good and the demand

Substitute – A good used in place of another good. An increase in the price of one good results in an increase in demand for the substitute good.

Complement – A good used with another good. An increase in the price of a good results in a decrease in demand for its complement.

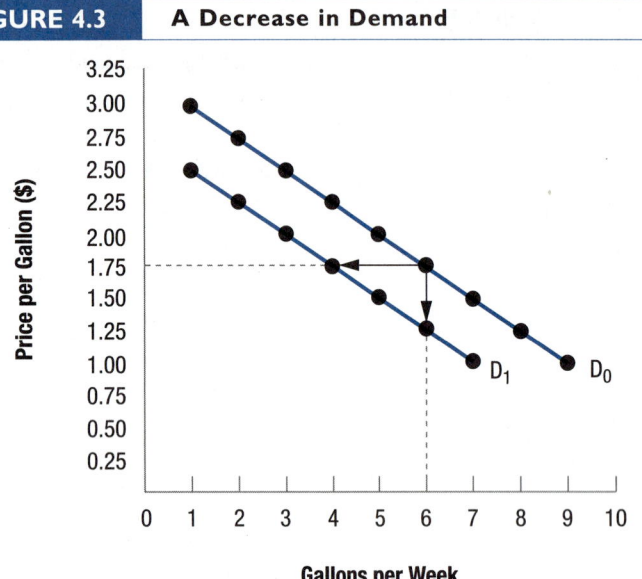

FIGURE 4.3 A Decrease in Demand

The change in demand from D_0 to D_1 is a decrease in demand. At a price of $1.75, the quantity purchased decreases from 6 to 4 gallons per week. Quantity demanded decreases at every price. Alternatively, the demand price for the sixth gallon falls from $1.75 to $1.25. The demand price falls for every quantity.

change for the other good are in opposite directions. Cookies and milk are complements in our example because an increase in the price of cookies leads to a decrease in the demand for milk.

INCOME. Now suppose that each consumer's income doubles. With this increase in income, each consumer might place a higher value on milk. In Table 4.1, the demand schedule resulting from the increased income is shown in columns 5 and 6. Demand has changed. Originally, the fourth gallon of milk was worth $2.25. Now it is worth $2.75. This **increase in demand** means that consumers plan to purchase more at each price. For instance, at the price of $2.25, the quantity demanded is now six gallons; originally, it was 4 gallons.

Figure 4.4 shows the demand change from D_0, the original demand curve, to D_1, the new demand curve. The movement upward in the demand curve shows that, for each quantity, demand price increases. Alternatively, the move to the right shows that, for each price, consumers plan to purchase more.

In this example, the demand for milk increased when income increased. A good for which this happens is a **normal good**, one that consumers purchase more of when their incomes go up. Some goods—perhaps hamburger—are inferior goods. Nothing is inherently inferior about these goods; it is just that as consumers' incomes go up, they place a lower value on **inferior goods**. For instance, if your income goes up, you may decide to eat more steak dinners. If you eat more steak, you will have less room in your diet for hamburger. Thus, the demand for hamburger decreases, implying that it is an inferior good. One can imagine a low-income family that eats very little hamburger. If the family's income increases, it might place a higher value on hamburger—it is a normal good for this family. If its income increases even more, it may now decide to purchase some steak, reducing the value of hamburger. Hamburger has become an inferior good for the family.

Increase in Demand – A situation in which, at each price, consumers plan to purchase more of a good, depicted by a rightward shift of the demand curve. It may also be interpreted as an increase in the demand price, which emphasizes the upward shift of the curve.

Normal Good – A good that consumers purchase more of when their income rises.

Inferior Good – A good that consumers purchase less of when their income rises.

FIGURE 4.4 An Increase in Demand

The change in demand from D_0 to D_1 is an increase in demand. At a price of $2.25, the quantity purchased would increase from 4 to 6 gallons per week; quantity demanded increases at every price. Alternatively, at a quantity of 4 gallons per week, the demand price increases from $2.25 to $2.75. The demand price increases for every quantity.

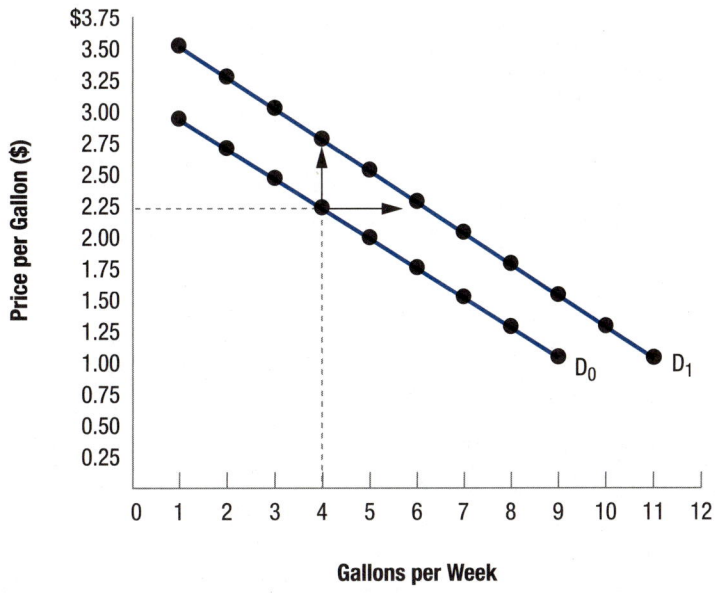

INFOTRAC
College Edition

Keywords: *price cuts and demand*
http://www.infotrac-college.com

Other factors obviously affect demand. One is consumers' preferences. Consumers may change their minds about the benefit received from consuming certain goods. If so, the demand for the goods will change. Demand in a particular market also will change if the number of consumers in the market changes. This is so because market demand is just the sum of the demands of individual consumers. In short, the demand for a good depends upon the price of the good, consumers' income, the prices of related goods, consumer preferences, and the number of consumers.

Other Supply Factors

Just as with demand, factors other than its price affect the quantity of wheat that producers plan to supply; these other factors are those that affect production cost. These include the technology of wheat production, the prices of inputs, (say, fertilizer and labor), and the prices of goods (say, corn) that could be produced instead of wheat. A full statement of the law of supply, therefore, is that a change in the price of a good, keeping these other factors unchanged, results in a change in quantity supplied in the same direction as the price change.

Figure 4.5 shows the market supply curve, S_0, that exists when, for example, the price of fertilizer is $0.25 a pound, the price of labor is $10 an hour, the price of corn is $4 a bushel, and a given technology exists. To find the quantity supplied for each price, choose a price on the vertical axis in Figure 4.5,

FIGURE 4.5   An Increase in Supply

The shift in the supply curve from S_0 to S_1 is an increase in supply. At any price, the quantity supplied increases. For instance, at a price of $2.20 the quantity supplied increases from 5 to 8 bushels per year. Alternatively, at any quantity the supply price decreases. For the fifth bushel, the supply price falls from $2.20 to $1.90.

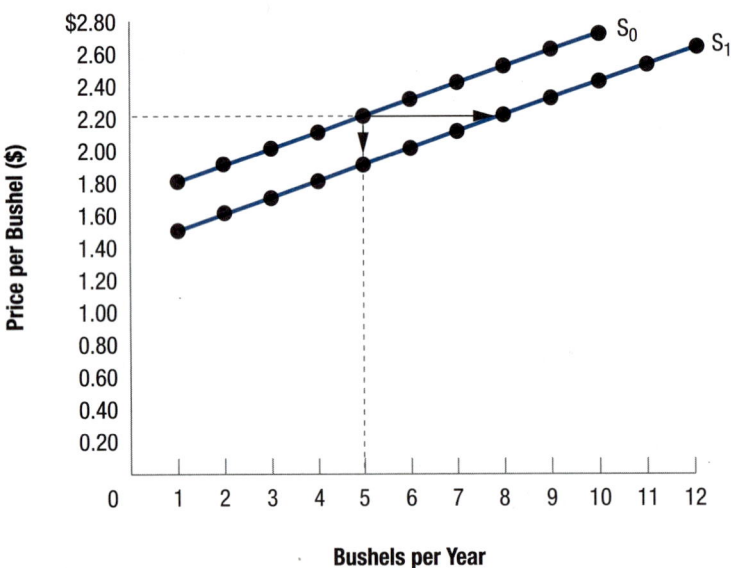

Increase in Supply – A situation in which, at each price, producers plan to sell more of a good; it is depicted by a rightward shift of the supply curve. It may also be interpreted as a reduction in supply price for each quantity of the good, which emphasizes the downward shift of the curve.

say, $2.20. The corresponding point on the horizontal axis gives the quantity supplied, 5 bushels. The supply price for 5 bushels, $2.20, is just sufficient to cover the cost of the fifth bushel.

What happens to the supply curve when other factors change? Suppose technology advances. Perhaps a new strain of wheat is developed that thrives with less fertilizer. Clearly, the cost of wheat production falls. The fifth bushel of wheat produced in the market might now cost only $1.90 rather than $2.20. In other words, the supply price of the fifth bushel falls from $2.20 to $1.90. Because of the cost reduction, a new supply curve, S_1, exists in Figure 4.5 Suppose the price had been $2.20. Before the advance in technology, the quantity supplied was 5 bushels. But now, a profit is earned on the fifth bushel because $2.20 is greater than the new supply price. With the new supply curve, producers supply 8 bushels at $2.20. In fact, with the new supply curve, more will be supplied at each price. The cost reduction leads to a movement of the supply curve to the right. This is an example of an **increase in supply**, where for each price producers plan to sell more.

Now suppose the price of labor rises from $10 to $15 an hour. The cost of wheat production increases. The cost of the fifth bushel of wheat, the supply price, might go from $2.20 to $2.50 (Figure 4.6). With the increase in cost, the supply curve moves up, from S_0 to S_1. With S_0, if the price had been $2.20, the quantity supplied would have been 5 bushels. But with S_1, a price of $2.20 is less than the new supply price of the fifth bushel: Producers will supply only 2 bushels. In fact, the quantity supplied will be less

FIGURE 4.6 A Decrease in Supply

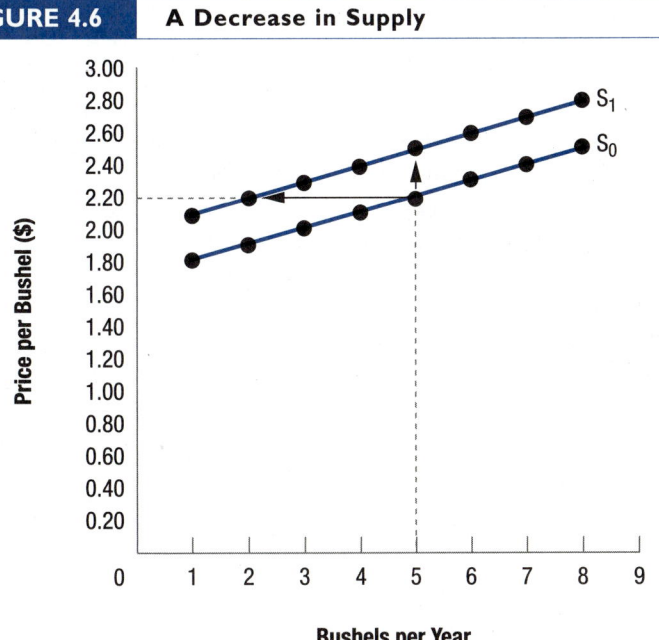

The shift in the supply curve from S_0 to S_1 is a decrease in supply. At any price, the quantity supplied decreases. For instance, at a price of $2.20, the quantity supplied decreases from 5 to 2 bushels per year. Alternatively, at any quantity, the supply price increases. For the fifth bushel, the supply price increases from $2.20 to $2.50.

Decrease in Supply — A situation in which, at each price, producers plan to sell less of a good; it is depicted by a leftward shift of the supply curve. It may also be interpreted as an increase in the supply price for each quantity of the good, which emphasizes the upward shift of the curve.

INFOTRAC
College Edition

Keywords: *price increases and costs*
http://www.infotrac-college.com

at any given price. The cost increase leads to a movement of the supply curve to the left. This is an example of a **decrease in supply**, where for each price producers plan to sell less.

Any farm or any agricultural area can produce different crops. To decide about wheat production, one must consider the profitability of these related crops. For instance, suppose the price of corn goes up. According to the law of supply, the quantity of corn supplied will increase. Farmers find it profitable to increase corn production, which requires transferring some land previously used for wheat to corn. Because corn has become more profitable, the opportunity cost of growing wheat has increased. Because the cost of wheat production is up, the supply price increases; in other words, the supply of wheat decreases, as in Figure 4.6.

In short, the supply of a good depends upon the price of the good, technology, the prices of inputs, and the prices of other goods that could be produced. The law of supply is that the quantity supplied changes in the same direction as the change in the price of the good, assuming that the other supply factors do not change. With our knowledge of what causes demand and supply to change, we now turn to how demand and supply changes affect the equilibrium.

■ How Changes in Demand and Supply Affect Equilibrium Price and Quantity

In Chapter 2, we studied price determination in competitive markets. Competitive markets have many well-informed buyers and sellers. No single buyer or seller has a noticeable effect on market price; buyers

FIGURE 4.7   The Effects of a Change in Demand

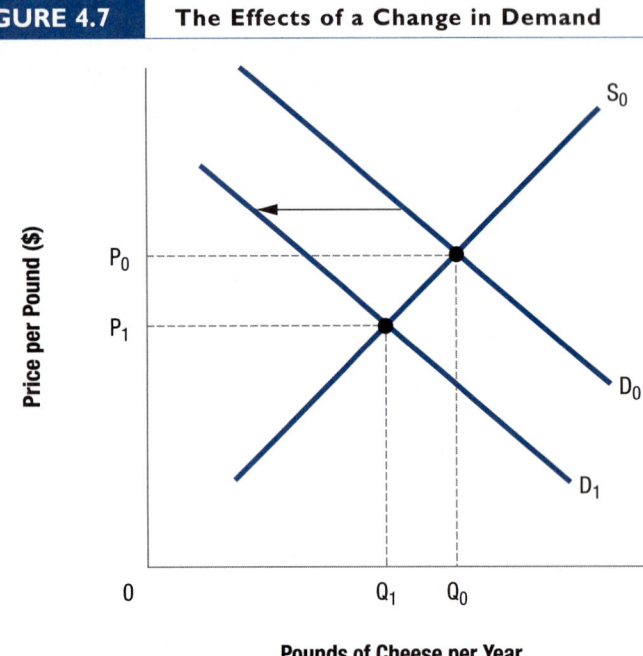

The decrease in demand from D_0 to D_1 creates an excess supply at the original equilibrium price, P_0. This excess supply creates pressure for the price to fall. As the price falls, the quantity supplied decreases. Equilibrium is restored at P_1 and Q_1. Both price and quantity exchanged decrease.

and sellers are price takers. Furthermore, people can participate in competitive markets solely in response to their evaluation of the advantage of doing so. Potential buyers need only consider whether the expected value of a purchase is worth its opportunity cost. Similarly, people can become producers simply because they expect to profit. Government laws and regulations do not prevent voluntary exchanges. How do competitive markets handle changes in demand and supply?

Changes in Demand

Figure 4.7 illustrates the market for cheese. The initial demand and supply curves are D_0 and S_0. As explained in Chapter 2, the equilibrium price and quantity exchanged are P_0 and Q_0. At P_0, consumers plan to purchase Q_0, and producers plan to produce and sell Q_0; equilibrium requires that quantity demanded equals quantity supplied. Suppose now that new medical studies, as they so often do, find evidence of much greater health dangers in eating dietary fat. Cheese is high in dietary fat, so consumers will place a lower value on cheese. Demand, as illustrated in Figure 4.7, decreases from D_0 to D_1. The reduction in demand for cheese causes a price decrease, which in turn causes a reduction in quantity supplied. The old equilibrium was at P_0 and Q_0; the new one is at P_1 and Q_1.

The simplicity of this change conceals the complexity of what is happening. Consumers have decided that cheese is less valuable. They want less at the initial price, P_0: An excess supply develops at this price. Sellers have more cheese than they can sell. With the excess building up, some seller decides to cut price and possibly take customers away from other sellers. Or, some sharp consumer sees the excess building up and offers a lower price to take the cheese off the seller's hands. Without central direction, the price falls. As it falls because of the demand decrease, the quantity supplied falls. As the quantity supplied falls, some inputs are released from cheese production. Some labor resources (people) are forced to find jobs in other industries. Because milk is used in cheese production, dairy farmers start producing less milk. Land that had been used for dairy farming is converted to other agricultural uses. The change in consumer preferences causes resources to be reallocated to products on which consumers now place a greater value relative to cheese. Although the market accomplishes this reallocation automatically, history shows that central planning, such as existed in the former Soviet Union, is often unable to do so.

Notice that the supply curve for cheese has not changed. The quantity supplied has decreased, but no change has occurred in technology, the prices of inputs, or the prices of other goods that might be produced. We sometimes read that a reduction in demand causes a reduction in supply, but that is not true. The correct interpretation is that a decrease in demand (a leftward shift in the demand curve) results in a decrease in price, which causes the quantity supplied to decrease (a movement along the existing supply curve).

Cheese producers and dairy producers may have other responses. They may advertise that cheese is a healthful food, just as beef producers now advertise that beef is a healthful food. They might support research to develop a lower-fat cheese, as pork producers have developed lower-fat pork over the years. These efforts to protect their profits through advertising and research would lead to an improved situation for consumers and producers. In the face of falling prices, however, producers might use a political approach rather than attempting to satisfy consumers' changed demand. They might use political advertising, campaign contributions, and so on to persuade the government to keep the price of cheese at its original level.

Changes in Supply

The impact of an increase in the supply of cheese is also easy to determine. Suppose that workers in the cheese industry receive lower wages. This lowers the cost of producing cheese and its supply price: Supply increases from S_0 to S_1 (see Figure 4.8). The increase in the supply of cheese causes price to fall, resulting in an increase in quantity demanded. The old equilibrium was at P_0 and Q_0; the new equilibrium is at P_1 and Q_1.

Again, much is happening behind the scene. Producers have learned that it is cheaper to produce cheese. Fewer sacrifices are made to produce a pound of cheese, and because its opportunity cost is less, producers are willing to supply more at the going price. Producers try to sell more at P_0, but they fail. Excess supply develops. Again price falls, without a government planner giving any orders. As price falls, quantity demanded increases. As quantity demanded increases, consumers substitute the now cheaper cheese for other foods in their diets. Because of the change in cost conditions, consumers now consume more cheese and less of other foods.

The demand curve for cheese, however, has not changed. The quantity demanded has increased, but no change has occurred in consumer preferences, income, the prices of related goods, or the number of consumers in the market.

Changes in Demand and Supply

The process is somewhat more complicated if both demand and supply change at the same time. Suppose that demand decreases and supply increases. A demand decrease means that consumers wish to buy less at the going price; a supply increase means that producers wish to sell more at the going

FIGURE 4.8 The Effects of a Change in Supply

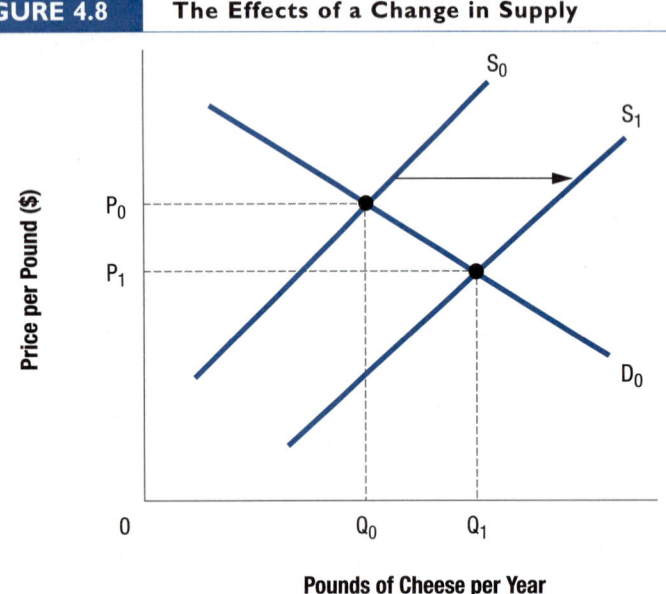

The increase in supply from S_0 to S_1 creates an excess supply at the original equilibrium price, P_0. The price falls in response to the excess supply, causing quantity demanded to increase. The new equilibrium is at a lower price, P_1, and a higher quantity, Q_1.

INFOTRAC College Edition

Keywords: law of supply and demand
http://www.infotrac-college.com

price. As you might expect, whether the amount actually exchanged increases or decreases depends upon the relative size of the two changes. For any quantity, however, consumers now place a lower value on cheese, and producers are willing to accept a lower price for it. Consequently, the price will fall.

In Figure 4.9, the decrease in demand from D_0 to D_1 is a larger change than the increase in supply from S_0 to S_1. Consequently, quantity exchanged decreases from Q_0 to Q_1, but the quantity exchanged would have increased if the supply increase were large enough. Price falls, as it must, from P_0 to P_1.

Price changes for agricultural products occur frequently because of changes in demand and supply. Over time, the prices of many agricultural products, adjusted for inflation, have fallen. This long-term fall in agricultural prices is partially responsible for federal government intervention in agricultural markets.

■ U.S. AGRICULTURE

Political support for U.S. farm policy derives from two sources. One is based on economic and historical characteristics of the industry. The other is based on the political influence of the recipients of farm subsidies. We first discuss the economic and historical characteristics of agriculture that have shaped farm policy. Then we consider the political aspects.

Economic and Historical Characteristics

As the Industrial Revolution progressed through the nineteenth century, household income in the small but growing industrial and urban parts of the U.S. economy surged ahead of household income in the farm sector. In 1840, slightly more than two-thirds of employed workers—3.7 million—were in agriculture. Although the number of workers in agriculture grew until the 1920s, the percentage has fallen since 1800.

FIGURE 4.9 The Effects of Changes in Demand and Supply

The decrease in demand from D_0 to D_1 and the increase in supply from S_0 to S_1 cause an excess supply at the original equilibrium price, P_0. The excess supply causes price to fall. Other factors equal, the increase in supply would also cause quantity to increase. But other factors are not equal. Demand has decreased. By itself, a decrease in demand would cause quantity to decrease. Consequently, quantity might increase or decrease depending on the size of the supply increase compared to the demand decrease. In this example, the demand decrease is larger, so quantity falls.

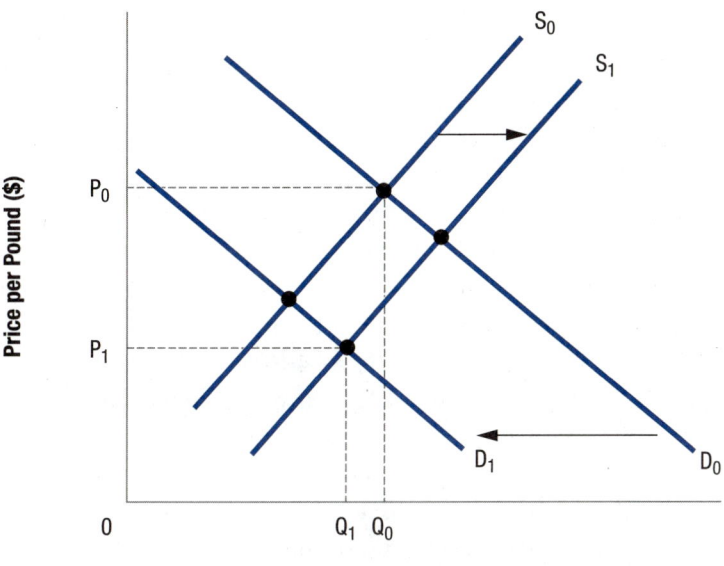

In 1920, more than one-fourth of U.S. workers—11.1 million—were still in agriculture, but since then the percentage of agricultural workers has dropped to about 2 percent, and the number has dropped to less than in 1840—about 2 million. This massive downsizing of agricultural employment was accompanied by large reductions in the number of farms. Price and income instability in agriculture caused by economic fluctuations in the economy and erratic weather at times forced thousands off the farm in a short time.

A substantial exodus from agriculture has accompanied economic development in most countries. Innovations in agriculture and industry, combined with education and research provided through the land-grant university system, have resulted in tremendous technical progress in U.S. agriculture. The supply of agricultural products has increased substantially. The demand for agricultural products—food, in large part—increases with income and with world population, but these increases have not been large enough to offset the large supply increases. First, increases in income do not cause proportionate increases in demand. For instance, if your income doubles, you probably would not double food consumption or the amount spent on food. You probably would not increase your food consumption at all, but you might spend more on food—not by eating more, but by eating better. Second, population has not grown nearly fast enough to counteract the huge increases in supply caused by technical progress. (To test your understanding, draw a diagram that illustrates these demand and supply changes.)

Suppose output per farmer doubles in 14 years, which is within the historical experience. If the number of farmers remains the same, this productivity growth will double farm output. The demand for food must double for farm prices to remain the same. Population and income simply grow too slowly to increase demand that much. If productivity grows rapidly, farm prices must fall, as they have over the past 100 years—about 0.5 percent per year. This price trend, based on farmers' greater ability to produce, is part of U.S. agriculture's success story. The falling prices indicate a greater availability (reduced scarcity) of food. Because the quantity demanded is not very responsive to price changes, prices would plummet if agricultural employment remained the same as productivity increased.

Farmers have responded to this price trend by leaving agriculture. Consider the demand for and the supply of labor in agriculture in Figure 4.10. Suppose now that output per worker has increased, which means that fewer workers can produce the same amount of agricultural products. Furthermore, because the price of agricultural products has decreased, the demand price for a given amount of labor has decreased. Both the productivity increase and the price reduction for farm output cause a decrease in the demand for farm labor from D_0 to D_1. Economic development in the nonagricultural sector affects the supply of farm labor. Growth in manufacturing, services, and other sectors of the economy improves opportunities outside agriculture, increasing the opportunity cost of remaining in agriculture. Thus, the supply of labor to agriculture decreases from S_0 to S_1. As Figure 4.10 shows, the result is necessarily a reduction of labor in agriculture. Because of the tremendous growth of opportunities outside agriculture, the supply decrease is larger than the demand decrease. Thus, wages in agriculture increase.

Farmers have also responded to the falling prices in agriculture by taking high-cost farms and farmland out of agriculture. Farms may be high cost because they have infertile land or adverse weather. In many parts of the country, forests stand on land like this, land that was farmed 75 years ago. Today, farming this land requires too much labor, fertilizer, and other inputs. In other places, buildings stand on land that was used for farming just a few years ago. This land also left agriculture because it is high cost; land has high opportunity cost in agriculture if it has valuable alternative uses. Farming even the most fertile agricultural land is costly if the land is also a prime site for a shopping center.

The tremendous productivity increases in agriculture have been accompanied by an enormous reallocation of labor resources (people) and land away from agriculture. This reallocation occurred in response to market forces and in spite of government farm-support programs. Moreover, the reallocation has left the remaining farm population better off—relatively and absolutely. The median family income among people who call themselves farmers is above the median family income among nonfarmers, and the poverty rate is lower among farmers. Furthermore, the labor and land resources transferred from agriculture are now in more productive uses, increasing the total output of the economy.

The reforestation that has accompanied the land reallocations is a boon to the environment, and the availability of relatively inexpensive farmland for suburban development has resulted in improved housing conditions in urban areas. Although productive, these reallocations can cause pain. Some family farms no longer are viable. Agricultural families see their children migrate to urban areas, breaking the family farming tradition. Some people promote subsidies to agriculture as a way of saving the rural agricultural environment. In terms of population, however, it is too late to save the agricultural environment. Large family farms will continue to be profitable, even if government protection were completely elim-

CHAPTER 4 ■ COMPETITIVE MARKETS AND AGRICULTURE

FIGURE 4.10 The Demand for and Supply of Labor in Agriculture

The initial wage is W_0 and the initial amount of farm labor is L_0. Technical change and falling output price cause a decrease in the demand for agriculture labor. At the same time, economic development in the nonagricultural sector raises the opportunity cost of being in agriculture, causing the supply of labor to agriculture to decrease. The wage for workers in agriculture goes up, although the amount of labor goes down.

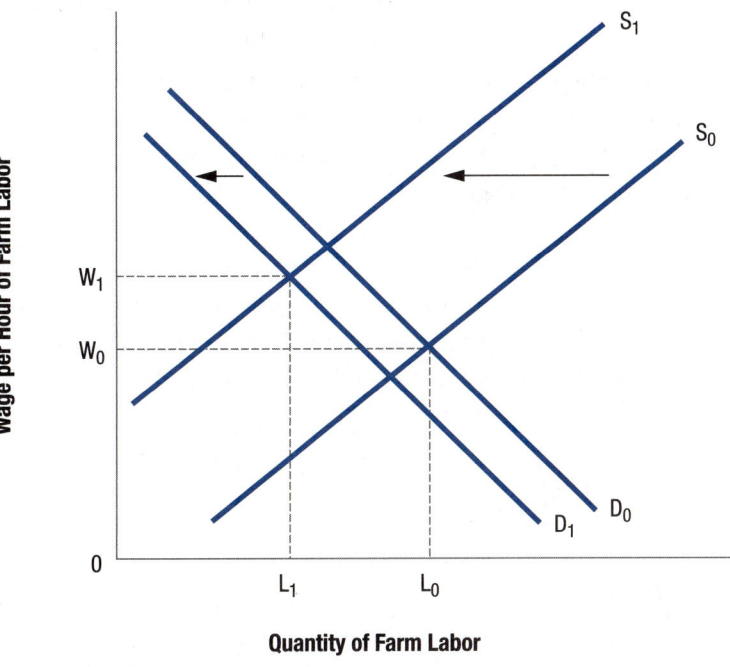

INFOTRAC
College Edition

Keywords: *family farm and economic aspects*
http://www.infotrac-college.com

inated. Their demand for resources and goods and services in rural areas, along with the many other advantages of rural life, would be sufficient to preserve many small towns.

Competitive Markets and Economic Profits

Two elements of agricultural markets are especially important for farmers. First, agriculture is risky; second, agricultural markets are competitive. Long-term changes in demand and supply of agricultural products create steady pressure to leave the farm, short-term events may create crisis conditions.

RISK. Most types of agriculture are risky; income for individual farmers from a single type of agriculture can fluctuate dramatically from year to year. At the beginning of a growing season, farmers make decisions about the use of their land, equipment, and labor in light of expected prices and profit. Often they borrow large amounts to buy land and to plant crops or build an inventory of livestock. The long lag between planting and harvesting crops or buying and selling livestock makes it hard for farmers to be sure they will have output to sell. Disease, pestilence, and localized bad weather (such as hailstorms) can wipe out a farmer's crop or herd. A run of bad luck can cause a farming operation tremendous financial and emotional stress.

Besides this individual risk, farmers also face market risk. Unexpected price decreases because of a reduction in demand or increase in supply occur frequently in agriculture. The supply of farm products responds little to price changes in a particular year—after the potato crop is planted, the farmer has little opportunity to change quantity in response to a price increase or decrease. Nor does the demand for farm products—particularly broad categories of food such as meat, fruit, and vegetables—respond much to price changes. In Figure 4.11 the original demand and supply curves, D_0 and S_0, for vegetables are quite steep. An increase in supply to S_1, perhaps caused by good weather, causes price to fall from P_0 to P_1. Price falls substantially because quantity demanded responds little to price change; thus, quantity exchanged increases only from Q_0 to Q_1. What happens to vegetable farmers' total revenue? Total revenue (price times quantity sold) in the original situation in Figure 4.11 is $0P_0$ times $0Q_0$. It is represented by the area of the rectangle $0P_0R_0Q_0$. In the new situation, the relevant rectangle is $0P_1R_1Q_1$. By inspection, the area of $0P_1R_1Q_1$ is less than that of $0P_0R_0Q_0$. The new rectangle increases in area by $Q_0T_0R_1Q_1$ because more is sold, but the increase is more than offset by the reduction in area $(P_0R_0T_0P_1)$ due to the lower price. Although farmers sell more, they receive less revenue than originally expected because the good weather leads to a large price decrease. Such an unexpected reduc-

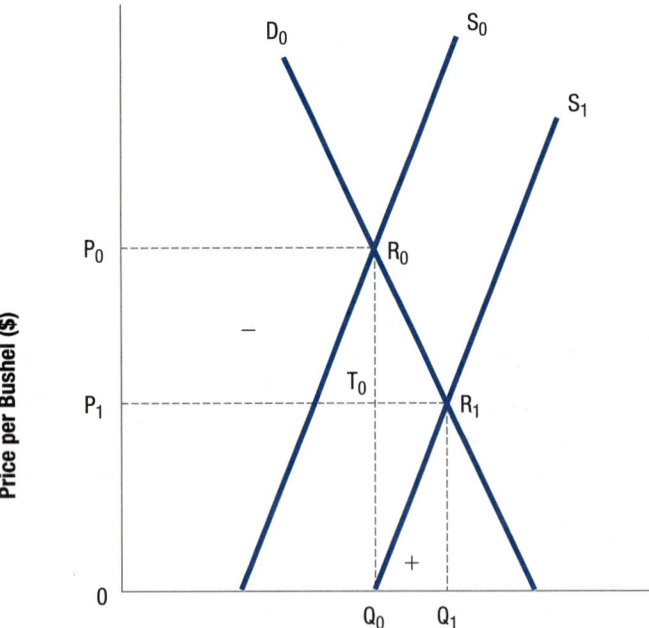

FIGURE 4.11 The Effect of an Increase in Supply

This figure shows a demand curve for which quantity demanded responds little to changes in price. Because of this unresponsiveness, an increase in supply (perhaps caused, ironically, by good weather) pushes price down by relatively more than it pushes quantity exchanged up. In this situation, the total revenue for vegetable producers falls because of the supply increase. Before the supply increase, total revenue is measured by the area of the rectangle $OP_0R_0Q_0$; after, it is measured by the area of $OP_1R_1Q_1$.

tion in price can cause a large reduction in income, making it difficult if not impossible to repay loans and continue operation.

An analysis of an unexpected reduction in demand would show similar results. Because quantity supplied is relatively unresponsive to a price change, a reduction in demand causes a sharp drop in farm prices and farm income. Farmers experienced this during the Great Depression, when agricultural prices fell more than other prices in response to reduced demand. They also experienced it in the late 1990s when the Asian economic crisis reduced the demand for U.S. agricultural products. Moreover, farm products are subject to variation in demand because of foreign trade. Suppose Argentina has a bumper wheat crop. Argentine wheat may displace U.S. wheat in other countries, reducing the demand for U.S. wheat. Farmers face substantial market risk because weather is unpredictable and because quantity demanded and quantity supplied respond little to price changes. The fact that most agricultural markets are competitive magnifies the risk.

INFOTRAC College Edition
Keyword: *crop insurance*
http://www.infotrac-college.com

Competitive Market – A market is competitive if it has many buyers and sellers, so that both buyers and sellers are price takers, and easy entry of new producers, so that new firms enter in response to economic profit and compete that profit away.

COMPETITION. Many agriculture industries—corn, wheat, beef, and poultry—are examples of competitive industries operating in **competitive markets**. In our issues-oriented approach, we emphasize two characteristics of a competitive market:

- A large number of buyers and producers (sellers)
- Free entry of new producers in response to profitable conditions

Pure economic theory also specifies that a competitive market or industry is one in which different producers produce identical (very similar) products and both buyers and sellers have good information about market conditions. The large number of buyers and sellers means that no one individual or small group of individuals can affect market price. The free-entry condition means that profitable industries attract new producers that produce more of the product, until the profits are competed away. Let's use an agricultural example to explain.

Consider the kiwi fruit. This fruit, from China via New Zealand, has exploded in popularity in the United States, but the first California farmers to grow and sell kiwis took a big chance. Such innovative farm products as the Belgian endive and the Ugli fruit have floundered in the U.S. market. The early kiwi farmers were successful; the price received for their product more than covered the marginal cost of production. Figure 4.12 describes the situation. As an approximation, assume that the supply curve for a particular year is vertical—VSR–S_0. Such a supply curve is sometimes called a very-short-run supply curve because it does not allow for adjustments in planned production. We assume that after the production decision is made for a particular year, farmers can do nothing to adjust the amount they sell. (Weather can affect the supply curve by moving it to the left or the right.) With demand curve D_0, the equilibrium price and quantity exchanged are P_0 and Q_0. The price these farmers receive is above their marginal cost of production, C_0, which includes a normal rate of earnings on the investment made by the farmers. (The marginal cost—supply price—is C_0 by assumption.) Therefore, the market price P_0 is above the supply price. This price gives existing farmers **economic profit**, which is a rate of earning greater than necessary to attract resources into the industry. If these farmers are operating at capacity, this situation is stable—they will continue to earn economic profits—until other farmers start growing kiwis.

Economic Profit – A rate of earning in excess of the minimum necessary to attract economic resources into a particular use.

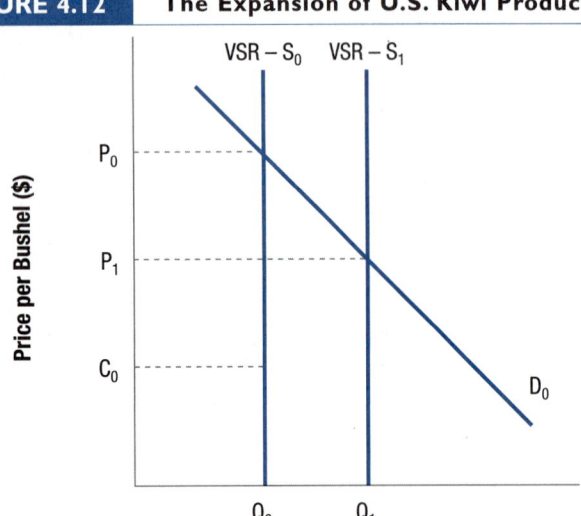

FIGURE 4.12 The Expansion of U.S. Kiwi Production

This figure shows that competitive farmers have incentive to supply food in response to consumer demand. At quantity Q_0, the demand price, P_0, is greater than the cost of producing an additional unit, C_0. Because a producer will receive a price greater than the cost of production for one more unit, some producer will increase profit by doing so. So long as the demand price is greater than the supply price, the very-short-run supply curve will march to the right, causing market price to fall and quantity exchanged to increase.

Other farmers will soon see their kiwi-growing neighbors driving BMWs; or maybe the county extension agent will tell them about kiwis' profitability. As they become aware of the profits, they will invest in kiwi production, which increases supply. So long as the market price is greater than the supply price (marginal cost of production), the very-short-run supply curve will march to the right, as more and more farmers learn of the opportunity. As supply increases, the market price will fall. As more farms are converted to kiwi production, the supply price (marginal cost) will increase for at least three reasons. First, the new farmers and the new land may not be well suited to kiwi production. Second, as more orange groves are converted to kiwi production, the land transferred is likely to be better and better suited to orange production. Third, as more orange groves are converted, the opportunity cost of kiwis (the value of the oranges given up) increases.

Suppose that the very-short-run supply curve advances to $VSR - S_1$, pushing the market price to P_1 and the quantity exchanged to Q_1. Assume also that the supply price (marginal cost) rises to P_1. Because the market price equals the supply price, farmers no longer find it desirable to enter the industry. Supply will stop increasing. With quantity demanded equal to quantity supplied and no economic profits or losses, the market is in equilibrium. No reason exists for any change in this market unless changes occur in other factors affecting demand and supply.

As new farmers began kiwi production, the original ones saw steady erosion of their economic profits. Depending upon how long it takes to establish kiwi production, these profits may exist for a year or two or perhaps as long as 5 years. Farmers who take the risks in producing new crops or have the good luck of being among the first producers, earn their extra rewards during this period. The economic profits eventually will be competed away; latecomers receive only a normal rate of earnings. Economic profits alert people that extra rewards are available to those who risk putting their resources into producing the

INSIGHTS

WHAT DOES IT MEAN FOR A FARMER TO BREAK EVEN?

According to the U.S. Department of Agriculture (USDA), the average wheat farmer in the Northern Great Plains had 527 acres of wheat with costs of about $160 an acre. Can this farm prosper if it just breaks even? Operating costs—seed, fertilizer, and so on—were about $52 an acre. The average farm family provided most of the labor; the cost of labor per acre is, therefore, an implicit cost. The farmer does not directly pay this implicit cost to a third party. It is, however, an important opportunity cost. According to the USDA, this opportunity cost was $11.60 per acre. This opportunity cost is then about $6,000 per year. If the farm business breaks even, the farmer at least has the $6,000. Moreover, suppose the farmer owns the land. In this region, the opportunity cost of land is about $36 an acre; with 527 acres, the farmer also earns about $19,000. The farmer's income would also include an opportunity cost for the investment in machinery and equipment and for the investment in operating inputs—seeds and fertilizer must be purchased and used months before the crop is harvested and sold. Although the USDA does not have the average value of these investments in this report, for farms in the intermediate class the investment might be around $150,000. If the necessary return to keep resources in agriculture is 8 percent, this adds another $12,000. The wheat farmer in the Northern Great Plains who breaks even still generates income: $37,000. Moreover, many of these farmers have off-farm employment, so their family income is even greater.

Suppose we consider the large family farms. If the farmer owns all of the farm business assets, the farm family average investment might be about $1.5 million. If the necessary return is 8 percent, then when this average large farm breaks even, the family earns $120,000 plus the opportunity cost of the labor provided by the family. Farm income is not actually this high because the farmers have borrowed to finance their investment. A farmer who financed half of the investment with an 8 percent loan would have interest cost of $60,000 and a return on the owned part of the investment of $60,000. Because operating a large farm leaves little time for off-farm employment, the opportunity cost of the labor would be well above that for the wheat farmer discussed earlier. Because many commercial farmers own a large proportion of their assets, when they break even, their income is indeed very high.

---

product. Besides their information role, these profits motivate people to take action that benefits other members of society.

Farmers operate in an inherently risky, competitive industry. Competitive markets ensure that economic profit will be competed away. If farming is inherently more risky than other industries, the normal rate of earnings in farming will be greater than the normal rate of earnings in other industries, which compensates farmers for taking greater risks. In addition to the greater compensation, farmers have ways of reducing the risk that they face.

- First, they can buy crop insurance to protect against natural disasters.
- Second, they can diversify. At one time, the wisdom of diversification was explained with an agricultural example: "Don't put all of your eggs in one basket." In the nineteenth century, Ireland depended heavily on one crop—one variety of potatoes—and suffered famine when it failed. South American farmers, who rely on potatoes for subsistence, have diversified for centuries. They developed different varieties of potatoes for different altitudes in the Andes, different weather patterns, and immunities to different diseases. If one failed, another would likely succeed.

- Third, U.S. farmers can use commodity market techniques to reduce their risk.[6]
- Fourth, market participants who are more willing to bear risk may voluntarily assume other participants' risks—for a price, of course. Poultry farmers, for instance, have shifted much of their market risk to large processors such as Tyson and Perdue. Poultry farmers previously suffered unstable incomes because of the variability of input costs and output price. Most poultry farmers now contract with the processors, with most of the payment dependent upon how efficiently farmers convert feed into pounds of bird. The price variability still exists, but the processors, who bear the risk, are more efficient in handling it.

INFOTRAC
College Edition

Keywords: *farm competition, opportunity cost*

http://www.infotrac-college.com

Risk is not unique to agriculture; moreover, people who take on risk get rewarded for it. Producers who can produce in more or less risky industries will only stay in the more risky industry if their earnings are greater. This implies that producers in risky industries have a higher normal rate of earnings. They require a bigger return to stay in the industry. The fact that farmers face risk does not distinguish them from other businesspeople who face risk without the government providing them with price supports.

■ U.S. FARM POLICY

The most visible and costly farm programs have been those designed to increase the price that farmers receive for such commodities as corn, cotton, milk, peanuts, rice, corn, tobacco, and wheat. Although the methods may differ from crop to crop and over time, the basic idea is that the government guarantees a minimum price for the product. The government might

1. Establish a minimum price—a price floor—and take appropriate action to maintain that price
2. Use regulation to control supply and thus support the price
3. Pay the farmer a deficiency payment, which is the difference between the market price and some guaranteed price

Price Floor

Price Floor — A minimum price set by government, below which the market price is not allowed to go.

Price floors have been used extensively for crops, such as corn, rice and wheat. The program is sometimes presented as a way to keep prices up in good years by allowing the government to buy and store some of the bountiful harvest, which in turn would be sold in lean years, increasing availability and reducing price. Although biblical in concept, the program has not worked in this way.

Suppose the government establishes a price floor for corn at P_1 as in Figure 4.13 The equilibrium price is P_0 and the equilibrium quantity is Q_0. The quantity demanded of corn falls from Q_0 to Q_1, but farmers plan to supply Q_2, which is more than consumers plan to buy. An excess supply of corn, as measured by the distance from Q_1 to Q_2, $Q_2 - Q_1$, emerges. To maintain the price at P_1, someone has to buy the excess supply. The government, in effect, does so. Rather than buying the corn, in the typical program the government takes the corn as collateral in a loan to the farmer. The government lends an amount equal to the value of the corn put up as collateral, where the value per bushel is given by the price floor. If the market price stays below the price floor, the farmer defaults on the loan, sticking the government with the corn. The loan is called a *nonrecourse loan*, meaning that the government must accept the corn as

---

[6]These arguments are beyond the scope of this book. For a discussion, see Bruce L. Gardner, *The Governing of Agriculture* (Lawrence, KS: Regents Press of Kansas, 1981).

FIGURE 4.13 Price Floor for Corn

In equilibrium, the price of corn per bushel is P_0 and the quantity exchanged is Q_0. Now suppose the government sets a support price at P_1. Excess supply exists because quantity supplied is Q_2 and quantity demanded is Q_1. The excess supply, $Q_2 - Q_1$, will cause price to return to equilibrium unless something is done. In a price support program, the government buys the excess supply and stores it.

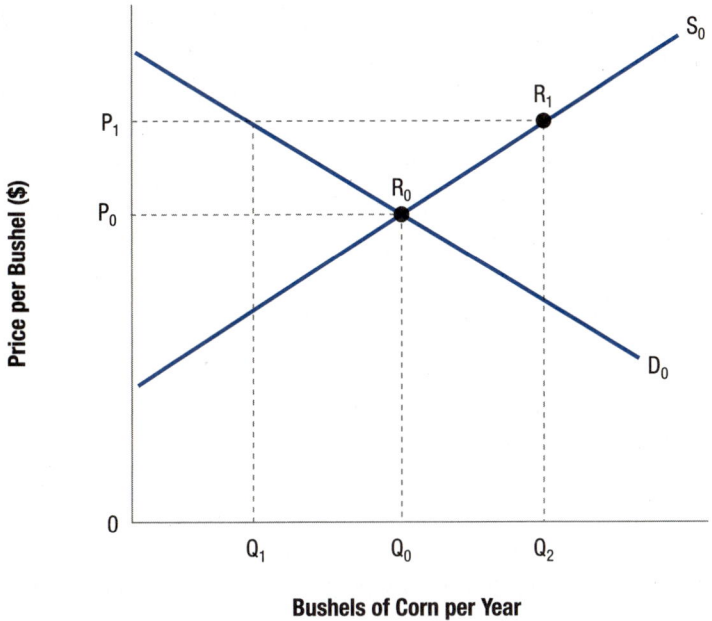

full payment for the loan. The farmer is in a win-win situation. If the market price goes above the floor, she reclaims the corn and sells it at the higher price. If the price stays below the floor, the government takes the corn and the farmer takes the money.

At the equilibrium price and quantity, total expenditures by consumers and total revenues of farmers are measured by the area $0P_0R_0Q_0$. With the price support, the total revenues increase to the area $0P_1R_1Q_2$. To purchase the quantity Q_1, consumers must pay a price higher than the equilibrium price. To buy the excess supply, consumers as taxpayers must pay the support price times the quantity $Q_2 - Q_1$.

Corn farmers earn increased revenue because they sell more at a higher price. Consumers—as direct buyers and taxpayers—spend more but receive less. Part of the cost of the program to consumers is the higher price they pay. Another part is the value of the consumption they give up. A price support program, if effective, eventually results in the government accumulating surpluses, which it must store. If it dumps the surplus on the domestic market during lean years, farmers become unhappy. If it tries to sell it on the world market, it has to subsidize the sale, violating free-trade arrangements and upsetting friendly countries. Storing the excess supply is costly, and giving it away is difficult. Some might be sold, at subsidized prices, to developing countries, which otherwise would not buy it, and some might be given away in school lunch and commodity distribution programs.

Output Constraints

Eventually, the problems of storing the surplus corn created by the price floor above the equilibrium price become too costly politically. Two avenues of escape appear attractive. One is to reduce the storage and disposal problem by requiring or inducing farmers to limit their production. Suppose the government sets a price support of P_1 in Figure 4.14. To participate, farmers must take land out of production, which shifts supply to S_1 and eliminates the excess supply.

Farmers, as we see in the figure, lose the revenue measured by the area of the rectangle labeled A because of the smaller quantity exchanged; however, they gain the revenue indicated by the rectangle labeled B. Inspection of the figure shows farmers gain revenue: the increase in revenue due to the higher price is greater than the decrease due to the lower quantity. This occurs because the change in quantity demanded of corn (in percentage terms) is smaller than the change in price (in percentage terms). In addition to more revenue, the farmers have lower cost because their output is less. Therefore, their net profit would increase. In addition, farmers may be paid for taking their land out of production.

Output constraints appeal to politicians because they shift part of the burden of supporting farmers from taxpayers to consumers without causing excess supply. The costs of the programs are hidden

FIGURE 4.14 Output Constraints for Corn

In equilibrium, the price of corn per bushel is P_0 and the quantity exchanged is Q_0. Now suppose the government wants the price of corn to be P_1. The government can require farmers to take 15 percent of their land out of production in an effort to reduce output by 15 percent. If successful, the supply curve will decrease from S_0 to S_1, which will push the price up to P_1. The government will have established a higher price without causing excess supply. The government need not buy corn or make deficiency payments. Farmers, however, have strong incentives to evade the output constraints in various ways.

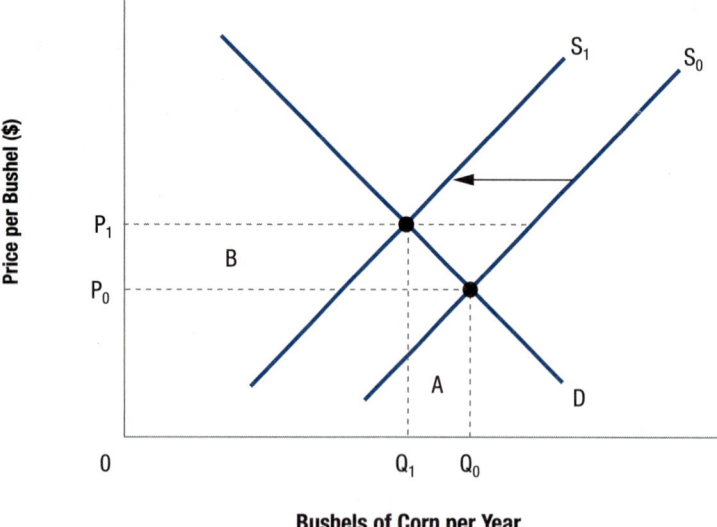

because consumers pay higher prices for many different products rather than taxes for a few large items in the federal budget. Government programs are more popular if their costs are hidden.

Output constraints rarely work as advertised. Suppose the goal of the program is to reduce corn production by 10 percent. At first glance, taking 10 percent of the corn land out of production would seem to be the answer, but this will not work. First, farmers will take their less fertile land out of production. Second, they will farm the remaining 90 percent of their corn land more intensively by using more fertilizers, labor, and other inputs. Presumably, the farmers were farming at the lowest possible cost before any land was taken out of production. Now when they use more inputs per acre of land to produce corn, the opportunity cost of the corn is higher. Thus, the amount of corn produced will not fall by 10 percent, and the attempt to eliminate excess supply or deficiency payments will not succeed. Farmers also resent the bureaucratic controls needed to ensure that they keep the agreement and keep land idle. Moreover, idling good farmland is wasteful. It was not uncommon in the 1960s and 1970s for 50 million acres of U.S. farmland per year to be idle because of farm programs. Paying people not to use their land is politically embarrassing as well as wasteful. A second avenue of escape from political embarrassment is to establish target prices and make deficiency payments.

Target Price – A guaranteed price for a product. The product is sold at the market price, and the government pays the producer the difference between it and the guaranteed price.

Target Prices and Deficiency Payments

Given the problems of storage and disposal, the government may tell farmers that they will be guaranteed a certain price for their crop, say, corn. This guaranteed price is the **target price**. However, the government does not support this price; it does not buy the excess supply produced at the target price.

Farmers decide how much corn to produce on the basis of the target price. In Figure 4.15 with a target price of P_1, farmers plan to produce Q_2 bushels of corn per year. When this amount of corn reaches the

FIGURE 4.15 Target Price for Corn

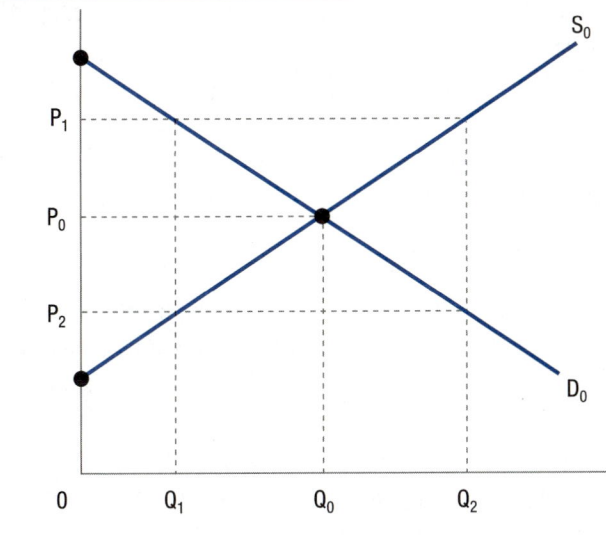

In equilibrium, the price of corn per bushel is P_0 and the quantity exchanged is Q_0. Now suppose the government sets a target price for corn at P_1. Farmers will produce the quantity Q_2 because the government has guaranteed the target price. However, consumers will buy only the quantity Q_1 at that price. Therefore, the target price will not be realized in the market. For consumers to buy the quantity Q_2, price must fall to P_2. To give the farmers the guaranteed price, the government must give farmers $P_1 - P_2$ per bushel as a deficiency payment.

> ## INSIGHTS
>
>
>
> ### THE SUGAR PROGRAM: HOW SWEET IT IS
>
> Sugar is a minor part of U.S. agriculture. More land is used for growing sunflowers than sugar beets and sugarcane. The U.S. price of sugar in 2000 was four times the world price. Because the supply price of sugar in Australia, Brazil, and other countries appropriate for producing sugar increases little with the quantity supplied, U.S. consumers could get all of the sugar they might want at one-fourth to one-half the cost they currently bear. It is estimated that the sugar program costs consumers more than $1.2 billion.
>
> Fairness in sugar production is remarkable by its absence. In 1994, sugar producers received almost $500 per acre in subsidies compared to less than $100 per acre for cotton and less than $50 an acre for corn and wheat. Seventeen of the approximately 1,000 sugarcane growers receive almost 60 percent of the benefits. In the early 1990s, one grower received about $65 million; in 1991, 33 growers received more than $1 million.
>
> The sugar price supports have resulted in a huge increase in cane production in the Florida Everglades. Without this subsidy, this land could not support large-scale agriculture. More than 500,000 acres in this fragile ecosystem have been converted to growing sugarcane.

market, the market price falls to P_2, the demand price for that quantity. There is no excess supply, but the price falls below the guarantee. Now the government must make good its promised target price to farmers. It makes a deficiency payment, which is the difference between the target price and the market price multiplied by the number of bushels of corn that the farmer sells.

The target-price system seems to have several advantages over the price-support system. First, there is no excess supply. Second, no direct export subsidies. Third, consumers avoid paying an elevated price for their corn flakes and other corn products.

The target-price system, however, does not really differ very much from the price-support system, if we examine their basic efforts. Figure 4.15 shows a potential excess supply of $Q_2 - Q_1$, just as if a price support were set at P_1. The output of corn and the amount of money received by farmers are the same under both systems. The excess supply disappears because the price falls to P_2. For the last bushel produced, the supply price is P_1 and the demand price is P_2. Just as with the price-support program, the cost of producing the last unit is greater than its value. Resources that could be used to produce something else are wasted. The government is, in fact, subsidizing buyers to take the potential excess supply off its hands. Thus, the target-price system deals with excess supply by implicitly subsidizing domestic and foreign buyers.

Interference with foreign trade policy happens both with price floors and target prices. If the U.S. price floor is greater than the world price, the United States must impose tariffs, quotas, or other barriers to imports—as is done with the sugar program—so as to keep foreign products out of U.S. markets. Such policies of course fly in the face of the stated U.S. policy of free trade. With other products, the U.S. price floor might equal the world price and create an excess supply. The U.S. government might try to use direct subsidies to foreign buyers to dump the excess supply on world markets. This too is in contradiction to a free trade policy and might violate certain international agreements. As we have seen, a target price system is just an indirect way of subsidizing foreign buyers and can also violate international trade agreements.

Keywords: *price support and agriculture*
http://www.infotrac-college.com

A price-floor system extracts subsidies from consumers for farmers in two ways. First, consumers pay higher prices for farm products. Second, consumers pay taxes so the government can buy the excess supply. A target-price system results in a market price below the equilibrium price. It taxes consumers to pay farmers. With the target-price system, all of the extra money for farmers comes directly from taxpayers, creating two political problems. One, the size of the subsidy is apparent to taxpayers. Two, farmers are clearly receiving government transfer payments—welfare payments.

Rent Seeking

Agricultural policies impose large costs on consumers and create difficulties for politicians and the government. You might wonder why we continue to have such agricultural programs. The answer may be **political rent seeking**. Political rent seeking occurs when people seek economic advantage through government action. It is in contrast to **economic rent seeking**, which occurs when people seek economic advantage by producing new or better products or by producing products at a lower cost and selling for a lower price.

Political Rent Seeking – Attempt by certain individuals or groups to encourage government activity that will result in an economic advantage for them.

Economic Rent Seeking – Attempt by people to gain an economic advantage through production of new or better products or through production of products at a lower cost.

The size of the government giveaway programs to farmers shows that farmers are successful political rent seekers. Their success may seem strange because the farm population is less than 2 percent of the total population. How do farmers have enough political influence to warrant such preferential treatment?

The answer may be that farmers of a particular type, such as dairy farmers, are a small group of producers with a strong interest in getting a higher price for milk. A small increase in the price of milk can generate big profits for dairy farmers, so they are willing to put a lot of time, effort, and money into convincing members of Congress to raise the price of milk. According to political humorist and author P. J. O'Rourke, in the early 1990s the dairy industry contributed $2 million a year to congressional campaigns. Another small group—corn producers—contributes half a million dollars a year.

Legislators weigh the gratitude that dairy farmers will have for a price increase against the reactions of numerous consumers to higher milk prices. Although consumers far outnumber dairy farmers, no single consumer or small group of consumers has a big stake in the price of milk. The increase in the cost of milk results in only a small increase in any single family's cost of living. Even if they are aware of the program and its impact, most families probably will not even be angry enough to write a letter about it to a member of Congress. Few people would make political contributions to defeat legislators simply because they voted to increase the price of milk.

A small group of committed people with a big stake in a desired political decision, like a higher price for milk, has a good chance of obtaining that action. This is so because the cost of the action will be spread over a larger group of people. No single person will bear a large enough cost to attempt to defeat the proposed action. Consumer lobby groups, such as Ralph Nader's various enterprises, do exist, but these groups rarely have the power or resources of an industry lobby group.

The dairy industry is important in many states and makes large donations to many politicians. Not surprisingly, it obtains favorable legislation. The dairy industry is one of many in which the benefits are concentrated in a small group, and the costs are spread over a larger group. Similarly, the 130,000 farmers who receive the bulk of the corn and wheat subsidies are sufficiently concentrated to be a potent political force in several Midwestern states.

In contrast, how do a few thousand rice farmers in a couple of states exert sufficient political influence to obtain government favors? The answer is *logrolling*, which might be defined as members of Congress trading votes to pass legislation of interest to each other. Thus, legislators from rice-producing states vote to support wheat farmers, and, in return, members of Congress from wheat-growing states vote to support rice farmers.

Even if the peanut and rice farmers lack sufficient clout to enact their desired legislation, they can leverage their political influence through logrolling. Will the members of Congress from a state where corn growers have political influence vote for a cotton bill in return for votes for a corn bill from cotton-state representatives? The ability of extremely small agricultural groups to obtain favorable government treatment suggests that they will—that such logrolling occurs.

The logrolling agreements need not be explicit—a wink and a nod will do—because of the way Congress handles farm legislation. Every 5 years or so, Congress considers farm legislation in a single omnibus farm bill. If you want your part of the farm program to pass, you must vote for the whole package.

INFOTRAC
College Edition

Keywords: *farm bill*
http://www.infotrac-college.com

Summary

In this chapter, we first discussed how the laws of demand and supply interact to determine market equilibrium. The equilibrium price and quantity are the price and quantity that coordinate consumers' and producers' plans. The price adjusts until the quantity that consumers plan to buy matches the quantity that producers plan to sell—until quantity demanded equals quantity supplied.

Changes in demand and supply cause the equilibrium price and quantity to change. For instance, an increase in demand means that consumers place a higher value on a particular product. This causes an increase in the equilibrium price and quantity. As price increases, quantity supplied increases.

An increase in supply means that producers can produce at a lower marginal cost. This causes a decrease in the equilibrium price and an increase in the equilibrium quantity. As price decreases, quantity demanded increases.

An increase in demand and an increase in supply both cause equilibrium quantity to increase. However, the demand increase causes price to increase, and the supply increase causes price to decrease. When both changes happen together, we cannot predict what will happen to equilibrium price.

Federal farm programs supposedly are designed to attack farm poverty, preserve the family farm, and stabilize farm prices and income. Although these programs provide large benefits to wealthy farmers, they do not particularly help poor farmers or small family farmers.

Price-support programs and target-price programs give the biggest benefits to farmers who produce the most and thus surely have the most wealth. These programs are expensive for consumers. The price-support programs lead to a large excess supply of farm products. Significant storage costs and waste result. Price-support programs and target-price programs both cause significant problems in international relations.

Farm-support programs appear to exist because small groups of farmers can organize into effective political groups. They use their political influence to seek political rents, and they do so quite successfully.

Key Terms

Decrease in demand	Inferior good	Price floor
Substitute	Increase in supply	Target price
Complement	Decrease in supply	Political rent seeking
Increase in demand	Competitive market	Economic rent seeking
Normal good	Economic profit	

Review Questions

1. What factors will lead to a change in demand? If the good in question is a normal good, briefly explain how each factor will affect demand.

2. Use your knowledge of demand to answer each of the following questions:
    a. How would a freeze in Florida affect the demand for oranges?
    b. The price of coffee falls. How is the demand for coffee affected?
    c. Income falls. How will this affect the demand for beans, an inferior good?
    d. How will a fall in the price of peanut butter affect the demand for jelly?
    e. The media report that red apples are sprayed with a substance that allegedly causes cancer. What would be the likely effect of this news on the demand for apples?
    f. How would an east coast hurricane affect the demand and supply of lumber in the affected area?
3. Briefly describe the difference between a change in quantity supplied and a change in supply. What will cause each of these changes to occur?
4. Use a graph of supply and demand to illustrate each of the following:
    a. equilibrium price and quantity
    b. an increase in demand and its effect on the equilibrium values
    c. a decrease in supply and its effect on the equilibrium values
    d. a relatively small decrease in demand and a relatively large increase in supply and their effect on the equilibrium values
5. Explain in words and use graphs of demand and supply to illustrate what happens to the price and quantity exchanged of each of the following:
    a. new cars, if automobile workers receive a 20 percent increase in wages
    b. compact disc recordings of rock music, if the teenage population increases
    c. bread, if wheat–fertilizer prices increase
    d. fur coats, if conservation laws restrict the number of fur-bearing animals that can be harvested
    e. hamburgers, if strict environmental regulations reduce the profitability of raising cattle and consumers become more worried about the consumption of animal fats
6. Cite and briefly describe some specific examples of the U.S. government farm policy. Explain differences between the effects of price supports and target prices.
7. Suppose the government announced that it was going to treat the agricultural industry the same way that it treats the retail industry. That is, it will eliminate all price-support programs and all deficiency payment programs. What would be the effect on farm poverty? On the number of farmers? On food production? On food prices?
8. Explain the risks involved with farming. Explain why government programs are not necessary for farmers to deal with these risks.
9. Some people argue that no reason exists today for government to be so heavily involved with agriculture. These people believe that agricultural programs exist to satisfy political constituencies. Given that only 2 percent of the U.S. population is in agriculture, how does agriculture gather so much political support?
10. Use Infotrac or some other means to research a particular government program that benefits a specific agricultural crop. Explain how the analysis in this chapter helped you to understand this program.
11. Based on the box titled "OECD Farm Policy," compare New Zealand's farm programs with those of the United States.
12. Explain the all-or-nothing fallacy (see the box on OECD farm policy). Can you think of other examples?
13. Go to http://www.swcollege.com/bef/econ_news.html. Choose the Equilibrium category under Fundamentals and choose an EconNews story that interests you. Read the full summary, and answer the questions posed.

Economic Issues on the Internet

- The Agricultural and Food Policy Center at Texas A&M University—**http://www.afpc.tamu.edu**
  Land-grant colleges and universities provide much research into and about agriculture. Their sites are designed to some extent to help farmers. They also provide much information about agriculture markets and government programs.

- The Cato Institute—**http://www.cato.org**
  The Cato Institute is a market-oriented advocacy and research organization. A "farm bill" search returns numerous sources that are critical of government policies.

- Economic Research Service, U.S. Department of Agriculture—**http://www.ers.usda.gov**
  This site provides official statistics regarding U.S. agriculture and much more. A good source for information about the new farm bill.

Appendix to Chapter 4

The Price Elasticity of Demand

The price elasticity of demand and other elasticity measures are important tools of the applied economist. This appendix presents a brief discussion of demand elasticity. Its purpose is to explain the elasticity coefficient, to discuss the relationship between price elasticity and total revenue, and to discuss the determinants of price elasticity.

■ THE ELASTICITY COEFFICIENT

Coefficient of the Price Elasticity of Demand — The percentage change in quantity demanded divided by the percentage change in price; it is a measure of the responsiveness of consumers to price changes.

The **coefficient of the price elasticity of demand** is the percentage change in quantity demanded divided by the percentage change in price. It shows the responsiveness of quantity demanded by consumers to a price change. It is in percentage terms to make comparisons among different products more meaningful.

The actual calculation of the elasticity coefficient requires a specific formula. In the demand schedule in Table 4A.1, a decrease in price from $2.75 to $2.50 causes quantity demanded to increase from 2,000 gallons per week to 4,000 gallons per week. The percentage increase in quantity demanded is 100 percent. The percentage change in price is about −9.1 percent. Dividing 100 percent by −9.1 percent gives an elasticity coefficient of about −11. The negative sign is usually dropped for convenience.

If the price increases from $2.50 to $2.75, however, quantity demanded falls from 4,000 to 2,000 gallons per week. The percentage decrease in quantity demanded is 50 percent; the percentage increase in price is 10 percent. Dividing 50 percent by 10 percent gives an elasticity of 5. Thus, the elasticity coefficient for the same prices on the demand schedule differs, depending on whether there is a price increase or a price decrease.

To overcome the problem of obtaining different elasticities between the same prices on the same demand schedule, numerous formulas have been developed. A convenient formula is always to use the lowest price and the lowest quantity as the base of the percentage changes in calculating the elasticity coefficient. Between the prices of $2.75 and $2.50, this formula gives the percentage change in quantity demanded as 100 percent and the percentage change in price as 10 percent. The elasticity coefficient is 10, which is between the two coefficients calculated previously.

Price Elastic — Demand is price elastic if the elasticity coefficient is greater than 1.0.

The elasticity coefficient for the prices of $1.00 and $0.75 is the percentage change in quantity (2,000/16,000 times 100) divided by the percentage change in price ($0.25/$0.75 times 100). The coefficient is 0.375. So we have calculated elasticity coefficients greater than 1.0 and less than 1.0. Elasticity coefficients can also exactly equal 1.0. Demand is **price elastic** if the coefficient is greater than one. This means that the percentage change in quantity is greater than the percentage change in price. It is

| TABLE 4A.1 | A Demand Schedule for Milk |

Price per Gallon	Quantity per Week	Total Revenue per Week
$3.00	1,000	$ 3,000
2.75	2,000	5,000
2.50	4,000	10,000
2.25	6,000	13,500
2.00	8,000	16,000
1.75	10,000	17,500
1.50	12,000	18,000
1.25	14,000	17,500
1.00	16,000	16,000
0.75	18,000	13,500

The demand schedule for milk is used to explain the elasticity of demand.

Price Inelastic – Demand is price inelastic if the elasticity coefficient is less than 1.0.

Unit Elastic – Demand is unit elastic if the elasticity coefficient equals 1.0.

price inelastic if the coefficient is less than one. This means that the percentage change in quantity is less than the percentage change in price. If the percentage change in quantity just equals the percentage change in price, demand is said to be **unit elastic**.

■ THE RELATIONSHIP BETWEEN PRICE ELASTICITY AND TOTAL REVENUE

Total revenue is price times quantity. There is a simple relationship among total revenue, price change, and price elasticity. When price changes from $2.75 to $2.50 in Table 4A.1, total revenue increases from $5,000 to $10,000. As we have seen, the percentage increase in quantity is greater than the percentage decrease in price; thus, with the price decrease, total revenue increases. Conversely, when price falls from $1.00 to $0.75, total revenue decreases from $16,000 to $13,500. This happens because the percentage increase in quantity is less than the percentage decrease in price. This example illustrates a general rule. If demand is price elastic and price falls, total revenue will increase. Conversely, if demand is price inelastic and price falls, total revenue will decrease.

Similarly, if demand is price inelastic and price increases, total revenue will increase. Conversely, if demand is price elastic and price increases, total revenue will decrease.

Finally, in the special case of unit elasticity, changes in price will have no effect on total revenue. These relationships among elasticity, price changes, and changes in total revenue are evident in different parts of this book.

■ THE DETERMINANTS OF PRICE ELASTICITY OF DEMAND

The price elasticity of demand is a measure of the responsiveness of quantity demanded to price change. Consumers will be very responsive to price changes under three conditions. One condition is when several substitutes exist for the good whose price has changed. For example, if the price of chicken goes up, other prices unchanged, consumers will find it easy to substitute other meats for chicken.

Conversely, if the good is meat and its price goes up, consumers will find it difficult to adjust their meat purchases to the extent that they could adjust their chicken purchases. Demand will be less elastic for meat than for chicken.

Another condition depends upon the importance of the good in consumer's budgets. Demand will be more elastic the larger the amount that consumers spend on the good. The demand for paper clips is probably price inelastic because consumers spend such a small part of their income on paper clips. Other things equal, the demand for restaurant meals will tend to be more elastic than the demand for paper clips because people tend to spend more per year on restaurant meals.

The third condition depends on how long consumers have to adjust. Demand will be more elastic the longer the time that consumers have to adjust to a price change. The sharp increase in the price of fuel oil used for home heating in the mid-1970s did not have much of an immediate impact on quantity demanded. Given time to adjust, however, people found many ways to reduce the quantity they demanded of fuel oil. They insulated their homes, bought sweaters, found substitute fuels such as wood, and in general conserved energy.

This experience tells us that any future sharp energy price increases will result in a reduction in quantity demanded of energy, and, importantly, the reduction will be larger if consumers expect the price to last for an extended period. Given flexibility and time, energy consumers—both firms and households—will find ways to conserve energy if its price indicates that it is scarcer.

Summary

Price elasticity of demand is an important concept. To calculate the elasticity coefficient, it is important to use a formula that gives the same result for a given price change: increase or decrease. The price elasticity of demand can be elastic, unit elastic, or inelastic. If it is elastic, a price decrease will increase total revenue. If it is inelastic, a price decrease will decrease total revenue. The opposite holds for a price increase. At least three factors affect the elasticity of demand. Demand is more elastic (1) the more substitutes there are for the product, (2) the smaller the amount spent on the product by consumers in a given period, and (3) the longer consumers have to adjust to a price change.

Key Terms

Coefficient of the price elasticity of demand

Price elastic

Price inelastic

Unit elastic

CHAPTER 5

Market Power: Does It Help or Hurt the Economy?

Outline:

Monopoly Analysis
   Marginal Revenue
   The Marginal Principle
   Monopoly and Competition Compared
Market Power and Economic Efficiency
   The Trend in Market Power
   Barriers to Entry
OPEC: A Few Sellers Acting Like a Monopoly
   Cartel Formation
   The Determinants of Cartel Success
   Problems of the OPEC Cartel
   Do a Few Firms That Dominate a Market Have Market Power?
Market Power and Economic Growth
Government and Market Power

Given that government wants to promote economic efficiency and economic growth, appropriate policy toward market power is difficult to prescribe. Economic efficiency, as we will see, requires that market power be minimal; economic growth may require a more permissive view of market power. This tension between efficiency and growth unfolds in U.S. government policy. On the one hand, the United States has laws against firms agreeing to fix prices and laws that prohibit the purchase of one firm by another (the merger of two firms) if the purchase would create significant market power. The European Union and other industrialized countries have similar laws. On the other hand, the United States and other governments grant monopolies—give market power—to firms that invent new products and processes. The purpose of such grants is to provide incentives for research and development and other forms of economic rent seeking. Government discourages the creation of market power through price fixing and mergers of independent firms, but it encourages market power associated with innovations and inventions.

Furthermore, government sometimes helps firms attain market power for reasons other than promoting invention and growth. It does so by helping firms fix prices above the competitive level, restricting new competition, and inhibiting foreign competition. Price floors and import tariffs for agricultural products can be interpreted as government helping firms gain market power.

Firms can earn profits in various ways. Microsoft (MS), in a complex series of events, has established itself in computer software and operating systems. It has done so although many other successful firms (including Apple and IBM) have fought to prevent it. MS has attracted consumers with a product–price combination that they prefer. Much of its success comes from successful economic rent seeking (entrepreneurial behavior). The entrepreneurial behavior of Bill Gates and others such as Mary Kay, Sam Walton, and Oprah Winfrey is responsible for much economic growth and creates large economic profits. As with MS, successful economic activity sometimes results in market power.

Market Power – A situation in which a firm or a few firms can affect the price received for their product, and new firms do not enter the industry in response to economic profit.

Market power exists if firms earn economic profit for long periods without attracting new competitors and without improving their product or reducing their production costs. It does so because it permits a firm or a few firms to set a price higher than the competitive equilibrium price. Market power requires (1) a few firms in control of the product and (2) limitations on the entry of new firms. For instance, in the U.S. tobacco products industries—for example, the cigarette industry—four firms, on average, produce over 90 percent of total U.S. production. These tobacco firms are in a different market situation than the many firms in the furniture industries; in these industries, on average, the four largest firms account for only about 30 percent of U.S. production. As a result firms in the tobacco products industries realize that their output affects market price, whereas a firm in the furniture industries would not normally expect that its output decisions would do so.

Monopoly – An industry with a single producer of a good that has no close substitutes.

Oligopoly – An industry with only a few producers or sellers of a good.

Cartel – An organized group of producers who manage their output and pricing as if they were a monopoly.

This chapter discusses market power and some of its effects on the U.S. economy. A **monopoly**, a single seller of a product with no close substitutes, is the extreme in market power; it chooses its product's price and might be able earn profits without attracting competitors. The chapter explains how monopolies determine price and discusses the source of market power in the U.S. economy. Most U.S. industries with market power are **oligopolies**. An oligopoly consists of a few firms selling the same or similar products. To what extent do oligopolies have market power? To answer this question, the chapter examines **cartels**. A cartel is an organized group of producers who attempt to manage their output and pricing as if they were a monopoly. The chapter first examines market power in terms of efficiency, and then it examines some of the growth aspects of market power.

■ Monopoly Analysis

A monopolist is the sole producer of a good that has no close substitutes. One example is the distribution of electricity and natural gas. The monopoly arises because it is rarely cost-effective to build two or more pipelines or sets of transmission lines to serve the same local market. Currently, in most parts of the country consumers of gas and electricity have only one supplier, and state government regulates it.[1] Other monopoly examples are found in small cities and towns. Throughout the country many such communities have only one provider of first-run movies. A quick Internet search indicates that Frostburg, Maryland; Lexington, Virginia; Davidson, North Carolina; Clemson, South Carolina; and Stillwater, Oklahoma, each have only one first-run theater. College students (and other residents) in these towns apparently have convenient access to only one theater. The theater monopolist's demand curve for attending first-run movies in these towns is the town's market demand curve. In Figure 5.1, the output chosen by the monopolist determines the price that it can receive. If the monopolist chooses to attract a quantity of six moviegoers per week, the demand price, the maximum price at which that quantity can be attracted, is $4. For a larger quantity, seven, the demand price is only $3. Clearly, the more people the monopolist wishes to attract, the lower the maximum price that it can charge. This conclusion is simply a restatement of the law of demand.

INFOTRAC
College Edition

Keywords: *analysis of monopolies*

http://www.infotrac-college.com

Contrast this with the situation facing the competitive firm. A competitive firm can sell as much or as little output as it produces without affecting its price; it is a *price taker*. In contrast, the quantity the monopolist chooses to sell affects price. The monopolist searches for the price that will maximize profit; it is a *price searcher*. Because the monopolist faces the market demand curve, its decision about how much to produce is more complicated than the competitive firm's decision. When it chooses an output, it also chooses a price. In contrast, the competitive firm chooses an output, but the market determines the price.

FIGURE 5.1 The Monopolist Faces the Law of Demand

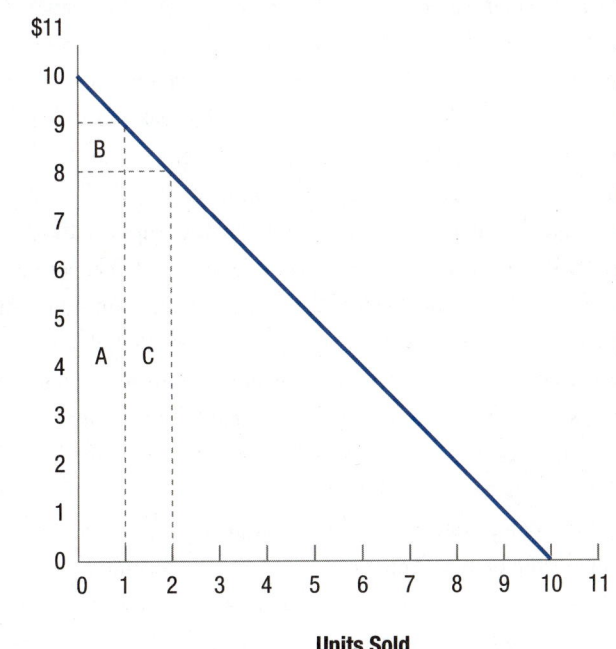

The monopolist is the only seller of the product. It can sell 6 units at $4. Alternatively, it can sell a larger quantity (7) if it accepts a lower price ($3). Suppose the price is $9. One unit is sold, and the total revenue is $9, given by the areas A+B. At a lower price, $8, 2 units are sold and total revenue is $16—areas A+C. Note that at the lower price the monopolist adds area C to total revenue, but must subtract area B. Thus, marginal revenue, the change in total revenue associated with selling an additional unit is the gain C minus the loss B, namely $7.

---

[1] In some places, the sale of electricity and natural gas is being deregulated, and competition is being introduced. To create effective competition, the government must ensure that the owners of the distribution systems provide access to other firms that wish to sell electricity and gas.

Marginal Revenue

Suppose the monopolist faces the demand situation posed by Figure 5.1. At a price of $9, it can attract one moviegoer per week; its total revenue (P×Q) is also $9, which is the sum of areas A and B in the figure. At an $8 price, it can attract two customers per week; its total revenue is $16, given by area C. By producing two rather than one ticket per week, it loses area B and gains area C. It increases its total revenue by $7 per week. This change in total revenue with a unit change in output is **marginal revenue**. Marginal revenue is the private benefit to the monopolist of selling one more ticket.

Marginal Revenue – The change in total revenue associated with a 1-unit change in the output sold by a producer.

For the monopolist, marginal revenue is less than price. This is important because price measures the marginal benefit to some consumer of purchasing one more unit, but it does not measure the marginal benefit to the monopolist of selling one more unit. A monopolist, like anyone else, uses marginal private benefit in decision making. For the monopolist, marginal revenue is less than the demand price and, therefore, the monopolist's marginal benefit of selling one more unit is less than the consumer's marginal benefit of buying it. In deciding how much to produce, the monopolist will value an additional unit less than the buyer values it. Suppose at the current output of widgets,[2] the price of a widget is $35, the marginal revenue to the monopoly producer is $24, and the marginal opportunity cost is $29. If the monopolist were to produce one more widget, it would use resources that would otherwise produce something else worth $29. The consumer would gain a widget, which she values at $35. Any price between $35 and $29 could lead to an exchange that makes both parties better off. If the monopolist has to charge everyone the same price, it will not produce another widget, however, because the monopoly marginal benefit (marginal revenue) is only $24.

It is easy to see why marginal revenue is less than price for the monopolist. When it plans to sell one ticket, it can charge $9. When it plans to sell two tickets, it must charge a lower price ($8) for both the second ticket and the first one. Therefore, with a price of $8 rather than $9, the monopolist's revenue increase is $8 from the second unit sold minus the $1 less for the first ticket; marginal revenue is $7. In comparison, the marginal revenue for a competitive firm is the same as price; the producer's marginal benefit for selling one more unit equals the marginal benefit to the buyer. Suppose the price of wheat is $5 per bushel. A wheat farmer might sell 1,000 bushels per year and receive $5,000 per year. If the wheat farmer instead had sold 1,001 bushels, she would receive $5,005 per year. With a unit increase in the number of bushels sold, the change in total revenue is $5—the price of a bushel of wheat. Marginal revenue equals price for the price taker because the price taker does not have to accept a lower price to sell an additional unit. Price takers, like monopolists, use their marginal private benefit in deciding how much to produce. In a competitive market, however, price takers' marginal benefit is the same as consumers' marginal benefit, but the monopolist's marginal benefit is its marginal revenue, which is less than consumers' marginal benefit (demand price). Because price takers and consumers place the same value on an additional unit, as long as the demand price is greater than opportunity cost, additional units are produced and exchanged. On the other hand, the monopolist—the price searcher—places a lower value than consumers on an additional unit and therefore will choose a quantity to produce where the demand price is greater than the opportunity cost. In contrast, in a competitive industry, the price of an

---

[2]According to the *American Heritage Dictionary of the English Language*, a widget is "1. A small mechanical device or control; a gadget. 2. An unnamed or hypothetical manufactured article." We are using the second definition.

extra unit is the benefit for the consumer and the producer; the market sends both sides of the market the same information about the value of an extra unit.

In Table 5.1, quantity and price are in columns 1 and 2; total revenue is in column 3; and marginal revenue is in column 4. Total revenue is price multiplied by quantity. Marginal revenue is the total revenue associated with a given quantity minus the total revenue associated with the preceding quantity. The total revenue associated with three tickets is the price ($7) times the quantity (3 units), or $21. The total revenue associated with four tickets is $24. Thus, the marginal revenue associated with four tickets is $3, obtained as $24 – $21. If the monopolist decided to sell six tickets rather than five tickets (at $5 per ticket), it would have to lower its price to $4. As a result, total revenue would be $24 rather than $25. The marginal revenue would be negative; it loses $1. It can take in more revenue by selling five tickets than by selling six tickets. As the example shows, marginal revenue decreases as output increases.

The Marginal Principle

To determine the output (tickets sold) that provides the greatest profit to the monopolist, we must include cost. For simplicity, Table 5.1 uses a special cost-output relationship. Marginal cost, the change in total cost with a 1-unit increase in output, is constant at $3 per unit. We assume that for each ticket

TABLE 5.1 Data for the Monopoly Analysis

This table is based on the monopoly's demand schedule and marginal cost schedule. Given price and quantity, total revenue is price times quantity. Marginal revenue is then the change in total revenue with a unit change in output. Given marginal cost, total cost is the sum of successive marginal costs. Profit is total revenue minus total cost.

Q = Quantity per unit of time
P = Price per unit
TR = Total revenue = $P \times Q$
MR = Marginal revenue = $TR_1 - TR_0$
MC = Marginal cost = $TC_1 - TC_0$
TC = Total cost = The sum of successive marginal costs
Profit = $TR - TC$

Q (1)	P (2)	TR (3)	MR (4)	MC (5)	TC (6)	Profit (7)
0	$10	$0	$—	$—	$0	$0
1	9	9	9	3	3	6
2	8	16	7	3	6	10
3	7	21	5	3	9	12
4	6	24	3	3	12	12
5	5	25	1	3	15	10
6	4	24	−1	3	18	6
7	3	21	−3	3	21	0
8	2	16	−5	3	24	−8
9	1	9	−7	3	27	−18

sold the monopolist must pay $3 to the movie producer and that the monopolist has no other costs. The first ticket sold requires the theater owner to pay the movie producer $3, and each succeeding ticket sold requires the same payment: $3. Therefore, the marginal cost of, say, the fourth ticket is $3. The total cost of producing four units is $12—$3 each for the first, second, third, and fourth units.

Marginal Principle – To maximize profits, the producer should choose the output that equates marginal revenue and marginal cost.

The monopolist follows the **marginal principle** in choosing the output that maximizes profit. The marginal principle states that profit will be maximized if marginal revenue equals marginal cost. If marginal revenue is greater than marginal cost, the marginal principle implies that the monopolist should increase output. Because marginal revenue decreases as output increases and because marginal cost is constant, they move toward equality as output increases.

As Table 5.1 shows, following the marginal principle leads the monopolist to an output where marginal revenue equals marginal cost. For instance, at an output of two units, marginal revenue ($7) is greater than marginal cost ($3). So, increasing output from one to two units increases the theater owner's total revenue by $7 and his total cost by $3. Profit increases by $4. At two units, profit is $10, compared to $6 at one unit. At five units, marginal revenue ($1) is $2 less than marginal cost ($3). Decreasing output from five to four units increases profit (by $2).

The profit-maximizing equilibrium may be easier to understand in a graphical analysis. Figure 5.2 shows a demand curve, a marginal revenue curve, and a marginal cost curve.[3] The marginal revenue curve lies below the demand curve. At output Q_1, marginal revenue is Q_1A and marginal cost is Q_1B. Increasing output slightly will increase profit by distance AB. As long as marginal revenue is above marginal cost, increasing output will increase profit. Conversely, if output is greater than Q_2 (say, Q_3), decreasing output will increase profit. In summary, if output is less than Q_2, increasing it will increase profit; if output is greater than Q_2, decreasing it will increase profit. Therefore, the output that maximizes profit is Q_2.

The monopolist will sell its chosen output, Q_2, at the highest price possible, the demand price. This price P_2 is at the point where a vertical line from Q_2 intersects the demand curve. Given these demand and cost conditions, the monopolist will not want to charge a higher price than P_2. A monopolist cannot always increase its profit by increasing price. If the monopolist increases price, it reduces the quantity sold. Beyond a certain price, further increases do not pay.

Monopoly and Competition Compared

In Chapter 2, we discussed some of the characteristics of a market economy; in this chapter and in Chapter 4, we have discussed some of the characteristics of a competitive market. An industry operates in a competitive market if it has (1) many buyers and sellers, so that both buyers and sellers are price takers, and has (2) easy entry of new producers so that new firms enter in response to economic profit and compete that profit away. More theory-oriented approaches add two conditions, namely that (1) firms in the industry produce the same or very similar products and that (2) both buyers and sellers have good information about market conditions. A market economy composed mostly of competitive industries has several notable properties.

---

[3]Here is a useful hint for drawing this diagram. For a straight-line demand curve, the marginal revenue curve is also a straight line. Furthermore, the marginal revenue curve lies halfway between the linear demand curve and the vertical axis. The marginal cost curve is a horizontal line, which is the assumption made in Table 5.1. We use the straight lines for convenience. All of the results discussed would be the same for a curved demand curve and for a curved, upward-sloping marginal cost curve.

FIGURE 5.2 The Monopolist and Economic Efficiency

Following the marginal principle, the monopolist chooses the output Q_2 that equates marginal revenue and marginal cost. It charges the highest price, P_2, consistent with selling that quantity. The marginal cost of the monopolist—under certain conditions—would be the supply curve for the competitive industry. If this industry were to become competitive, the equilibrium price and output would be P_1 and Q_4. Therefore, the monopolist restricts output below the competitive output and charges a price above the competitive price. It makes a profit given by the area P_1P_2MN.

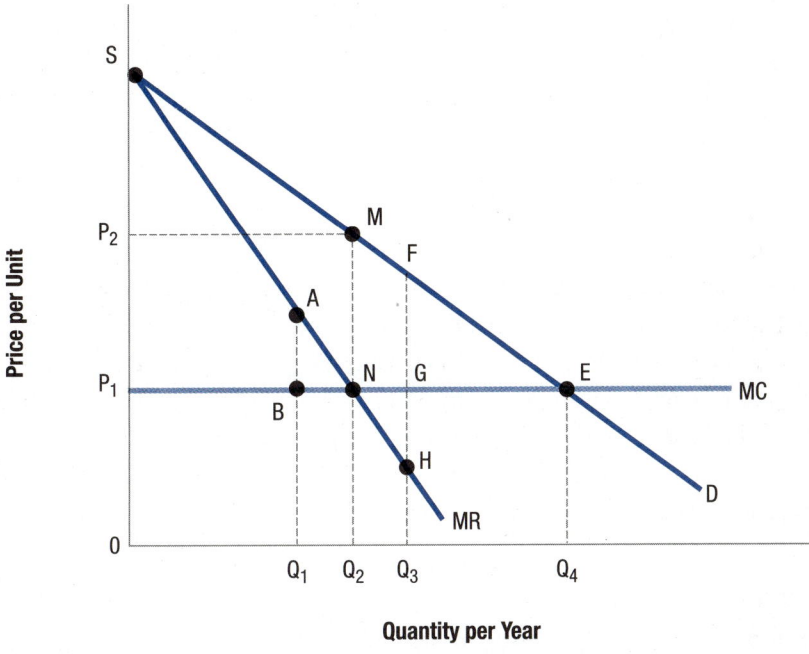

- First, it requires no central planning agency.
- Second, decisions are impersonal; among the many decision makers, no single one has a decisive influence.
- Third, markets are more likely to be in equilibrium than those in a command economy; thus, costs associated with the failure of markets to clear are smaller.
- Fourth, individuals can choose to buy products from or sell their labor to many different sellers and buyers. This freedom to choose limits the power of firms over customers and employees and vice versa.
- Fifth, the more firms in an industry, the less political power each is likely to have. All else being equal, the smaller the number of firms, the more easily they can organize for political rent seeking.

The existence of significant market power alters many of these properties.

- First, it makes markets personal. If the price of refrigerators increases, consumers might blame General Electric or one of the other producers. In contrast, if the price of wheat goes up, consumers do not blame specific wheat producers.

- Second, significant market power limits the freedom to choose. Henry Ford supposedly said that his customers could have any color Model T that they wanted, so long as they wanted black. Only a producer with market power would dare be so unresponsive to consumers' tastes.

- Third, significant market power increases firms' effectiveness in political rent seeking.

Although impersonal markets, free choice, and political factors are important, economists often focus on the purely economic effects of market power. Suppose that the monopoly shown in Figure 5.2 became a competitive industry with no change in the marginal cost curve.[4] The minimum price that some producer would accept for the first unit of output is its marginal cost, P_1. The minimum price would be the same for any additional unit. This minimum price defines the marginal cost curve. Thus, the monopolist's marginal cost curve is the supply curve for the competitive industry. The demand curve also would remain unchanged. Therefore, under competition, price would be P_1, quantity would be Q_4, and economic profit would be zero.

Figure 5.2 suggests that a monopoly causes economic inefficiency. The monopolist restricts output to Q_2, compared to the output of the competitive industry, Q_4. As a result, the monopolist charges more—P_2 rather than P_1. By restricting output and increasing price, the monopolist drives a wedge between the demand price (marginal benefit to consumers) and the supply price (marginal cost of production) of the good. The value of one more unit of the good, the demand price, is greater than the value of the units of other goods given up to produce it—the opportunity cost or supply price. A potential gain from trade exists, but the trade is not made. Therefore, output is less than the **efficient output**.

Efficient Output — The output where marginal social benefit equals marginal social cost.

In contrast, for firms in competitive industries, marginal revenue equals price. In equilibrium, consumers choose the quantity where

- Marginal benefit equals price.

Similarly, producers choose the quantity where

- Marginal revenue equals price equals marginal opportunity cost.

Therefore, in equilibrium

- Marginal benefit equals marginal opportunity cost.

In other words, the value of one more unit just equals the opportunity cost of producing it. Consumers and producers make all trades that have a potential for gain because, in equilibrium, price measures both the value of one more unit and the cost of producing it: Demand price equals supply price.

Some people object to monopoly because of monopoly profit. (Monopoly profit is a type of economic profit because it provides a return greater than the minimum return necessary to keep resources in the industry.) Unlike a competitive firm, a monopolist might earn monopoly profit in equilibrium. Monopoly profit, however, is not a loss to the economy; it is a transfer of income from consumers to the monopolist. People who dislike monopolies because of the profit they earn may be objecting to who earns the profit, not its existence. In fact, a monopolist has no guarantee of a profit. (A monopoly on slide rules probably would not be profitable.)

Perhaps the most fervent complaints about monopoly arise when the good monopolized is extremely important for its users, and its producer makes large profits—"blood money," according to an article in

---

[4] Later in the chapter, we will discuss a situation in which changing a monopolistic industry into one with several firms will change the cost curve.

Scientific American.[5] An obvious example is the monopoly production and sale of breakthrough drugs: for instance, Lipitor, the widely used and highly profitable cholesterol-lowering drug, and Viagara. The possibility exists, of course, that expectation of such profits motivates pharmaceutical companies to undertake the research necessary to discover such drugs. In the next section, we explore the extent and sources of market power in the U.S. economy.

■ MARKET POWER AND ECONOMIC EFFICIENCY

Market power exists when a single seller or few sellers can adjust price or output in pursuit of greater profit and when profit fails to attract new firms into the industry. In the U.S. economy, many industries—such as the aluminum, automobile, beer, and cereal industries; computer-operating systems; and the local telephone service—are dominated by a few firms. We raise three questions about this domination. One, has market power increased in the U.S. economy over the past 60 years? Two, to the extent that market power exists, why is it not eliminated by new competition? Three, does industry domination by a few firms allow them to exercise market power by raising market price?

The Trend in Market Power

Much evidence suggests that market power has decreased—not increased—in the U.S. economy over the past 60 years. It has increased in some industries; for instance, it may have increased in the beer industry as Anheuser-Busch (Budweiser) and Miller have become more prominent. In contrast, it has decreased in the computing industry with the disappearance of IBM's dominance in computer hardware production. William Shepherd's comprehensive study concludes that market power in the U.S. economy fell from 1939 to 1958 and fell again from 1958 to 1980.[6] Competition increased according to Shepherd for three reasons.

- ■ The first reason is increased foreign competition, particularly in the manufacturing sector. As the European and East Asian economies recovered from the devastation of World War II and transportation costs declined, foreign competition became more intense. Government encouraged this greater competition by reducing barriers to foreign trade. As a result, U.S. producers of automobiles, televisions, other electronic equipment, and other products became less able to raise prices without attracting competition. The intensity of global competition has probably increased since 1980, the ending date for Shepherd's study.

- ■ Shepherd's second reason is government deregulation. The transportation sector is much more competitive than it was, because government has eliminated some of its regulations. Interstate trucking, for instance, became more competitive after the late 1970s because no special permission or license beyond safety regulation and such is necessary to begin a freight transport business. Air transportation provides another example. Southwest Airlines, a small local carrier before deregulation, provides significant competition for other domestic airlines. Growing out of the Southwest, it has penetrated California and the mid-Atlantic states, and it is now competing in

---

[5]Tim Beardsley, "Blood Money? Critics Question High Pharmaceutical Profits," *Scientific American* 269 (August 1993) 115–117.

[6]William G. Shepherd, "Causes of Increased Competition in the U.S. Economy, 1939-1980," *Review of Economics and Statistics* 64 (November 1982), 613–626.

New England. Airfares are usually lower at airports serviced by Southwest. This new competition would not have been permitted before deregulation.

- Third, Shepherd cites the federal government policies that made mergers and price fixing more difficult.

A fourth general reason, emerging after Shepherd's study, is the information revolution, which has increased competition in many industries. With easy access to information about prices and markets throughout the country and lower transportation costs, the power of many local monopolies has diminished. Furthermore, business-to-business and business-to-consumer transactions are made with much more information because of the World Wide Web. As part of the information revolution, fiber optics and deregulation have increased competition in long-distance communications. Another communications revolution relates to new products and technologies that provide recorded recreation. Superstations, specialized networks, cable, and satellite dishes have created greater choices among programs, networks, and signal providers. Finally, new manufacturing technologies have allowed firms in some industries to operate at low cost, even at a small output rate.

A recent study suggests that industrial concentration, which can be a basis for market power, began to increase in the 1980s.[7] Although data availability prevented his study from going beyond 1992, Frederic L. Pryor contends that industrial concentration will continue to increase. Although Pryor accepts Shepherd's analysis and finds it likely that changes in technology have reduced the relative advantage of large size, he believes that since 1980, the federal government has become more tolerant of mergers between firms in the same industry. Certainly, the evidence shows that the rate of such mergers has increased since 1980.

Barriers to Entry

Barrier to Entry – Any condition that prevents new firms from entering an industry with the same cost conditions as existing firms.

Natural Monopolies – Monopolies that exist if demand and cost conditions are such that only one firm can survive in an industry.

To the extent that market power persists, it does so because of **barriers to entry** that prevent firms from entering an industry with the same costs as existing firms. These have four major sources. First, technical conditions of production might be such that a technologically efficient factory operating at full capacity supplies most of the market. For instance, the output of a technologically efficient turbogenerator factory would supply about 25 percent of U.S. production. Consequently, just a few firms produce turbogenerators. The technical conditions of production create a barrier to entry.

Some industries are **natural monopolies** because, in a free market, only one firm would survive. Such a monopoly cannot be broken into several firms without causing significant, unnecessary duplication. Imagine breaking a small-town cable television system into five systems. Surely, cost would increase. In this situation, the monopoly with its lower cost may be more efficient than an industry with several firms. Because some natural monopolies produce goods and services of great importance to consumers, government often regulates them and sometimes even owns them. Natural monopolies, however, account for market power in only a few industries.

Second, an existing firm or small group of existing firms might control an essential input and thus have an absolute cost advantage over potential new firms. Firms in the aluminum industry have long had an advantage over potential rivals because they control most of the high-quality, accessible bauxite.

---

[7]Frederic L. Pryor, "New Trends in Industrial Concentration," *Review of Industrial Organization* 18 (2001), 301–326.

INTERNATIONAL PERSPECTIVE

THE BATTLE BETWEEN AMERICAN AND JAPANESE AUTOMOBILE FIRMS

The Big Three of the U.S. automobile industry emerged from World War II with more than 90 percent of U.S. car sales. This dominance continued into the 1970s. By 1991, however, the share had dropped to 63 percent. What happened?

Perhaps Sir John Hicks, a Nobel Prize–winning English economist, had the answer when he declared, "The best of all monopoly profits is a quiet life." Or, as a Chrysler executive said, "The real problem is that the U.S. car industry went to sleep for 20 years."[a]

History suggests that the postwar automobile industry exercised market power. It restricted output, and price increased; costs rose, and quality control faded. The industry was so lucrative that management could enjoy the quiet life. It was easier to share "monopoly" profits with the United Auto Workers, the industry's trade union and its members, than to worry about costs. In addition, management allowed production methods to become obsolete and ignored quality problems. Consumers paid high prices for cars of mediocre quality. Autoworkers and management did well, and stockholders did all right but could have done better.

The energy crisis of the 1970s caught U.S. car producers off guard and increased the demand for smaller cars that got better gasoline mileage. Car imports, particularly from Japan, surged. U.S. firms complained that Toyota and other Japanese firms had a protected home market and were subsidized by the Japanese government.

The Japanese cars, however, had more going for them than gasoline efficiency and perhaps government support. They were of higher quality and were cheaper to produce. Although Japanese wages were lower, the great shock was that the Japanese produced cheaper, higher-quality cars mostly because Japanese management was more effective. Rather than attempting to compete with Detroit's mass production techniques, Toyota's managers developed new techniques of car production. They made assembly-line workers responsible for quality, whereas Detroit's mass production took responsibility away from workers. To Detroit's amazement, a Japanese worker could stop the assembly line if some production problem arose. Stopping the assembly line to prevent the production of defective cars was unheard of in Detroit. U.S. firms expected many newly produced cars to be defective, but the assembly-line workers were not expected or even allowed to do anything about it. In short, the Japanese adopted policies for quality control, inventory, and human relations that led to much greater productivity than U.S. firms could achieve. These improved management techniques are just as much an innovation, and perhaps just as important, as many new products that have been introduced in the past 50 years.

In the 1990s, however, Chrysler (now Daimler-Chrysler), Ford, and GM improved quality and did well, particularly with light trucks (vans, SUVs, and pickups). Their share of car sales did not change much, but they had 73 percent of the car plus light trucks market. Although many factors were involved, competition from other car producers forced the Big Three to improve their products.

---

[a]See John E. Kwoka, Jr., "Automobiles: Overtaking an Oligopoly," in *Industry Studies*, 2d ed., Larry L. Duetsch, ed. (New York: Sharp, 1998), 10. This study provides the basis for much of this discussion.

Third, existing firms in some industries—including the automobile, beer, and cereal industries—develop and maintain market power through product differentiation. A firm whose product is subject to competition from other firms with closely related products has at least one route to market power. If it can convince consumers that its product is superior to the related products, it can raise its price without sacrificing its sales completely. The product may actually be superior, or the firm may merely be convincing. Suppose an existing firm, say, Anheuser-Busch, raises "brand" consciousness sufficiently to develop market power. Existing or potential rival firms may be unwilling or unable to invest in sufficient product development or marketing to recapture part of the Anheuser-Busch market.

Often a barrier to entry for new firms comes from the fourth source of monopoly, the government. The U.S. Postal Service is an example of government-granted monopolies. Nothing in the technology of first-class mail delivery, however, requires that it be one. The government also grants patents to people who invent new products or new ways of producing products, giving them the sole right to produce the product.

Furthermore, government grants protection from new firms in various other ways. For instance, taxes on goods imported from other countries—tariffs—protect domestic producers from foreign competition. Similarly, restrictions on the quantity of goods that can be imported—quotas—protect domestic producers. An example was a restriction on the number of cars that Japan could export to the United States. These restrictions allowed U.S. producers to charge U.S. consumers jacked-up prices. Governments also require that taxicab companies, physicians, and many other firms and professionals have a license to operate. Whatever its purpose, licensing has the effect of excluding unlicensed people from the industry or occupation; it is a barrier to entry.

INFOTRAC
College Edition

Keywords: *barriers to entry*
http://www.infotrac-college.com

Most U.S. industries with market power are oligopolies—consisting of a few firms—rather than monopolies. Can a few market-dominating firms cooperate in choosing output and price? In the United States, such explicit cooperation is illegal. For instance, it is illegal for the owners of gasoline stations in a small town to agree to set a certain price for gasoline. Sometimes, however, the owners can achieve the same result without an explicit agreement. Perhaps they play golf together and simply come to understand that price-cutting is not good manners. We examine this possibility in detail in the next section by studying the Organization of Petroleum Exporting Countries (OPEC) cartel. Although OPEC had its biggest impacts in the 1970s and 1980s, it is still a powerful force affecting us every day through its direct effect on the price of gasoline and other products derived from crude petroleum.

■ OPEC: A Few Sellers Acting Like a Monopoly

Will industry domination by a few sellers allow them to exercise market power by raising price? In the United States, it is illegal for firms to form a cartel and to agree to cut output or raise prices. But suppose it were legal. How effective would such an agreement be? OPEC, an organization of 11 petroleum-exporting countries, provides an excellent case study. (Although OPEC members are countries, not business firms, and may have objectives other than profits, OPEC provides an enlightening example.) In the early 1970s, these countries sold more than 90 percent of all petroleum exported to other countries. Petroleum production in these countries—for instance, Saudi Arabia, Iran, Venezuela, and Kuwait—had been increasing at the same time that production in the largest petroleum-producing and -consuming countries—the Soviet Union and the United States—had begun to decline. In 1970, the average U.S. price per barrel of oil at the well was $3.18. This average price started a roller-coaster ride in 1974 when it rose to $7.67 and reached almost $40 in the summer of 1980. Some respected analysts expected $100-per-barrel prices by 1990, but the roller coaster headed down, with the price falling to $28.52 in 1982, $26.19 in 1983, and $24.09 in 1985 before it fell below $12 for a short time in 1986. Figure 5.3 shows the price of West Texas intermediate crude per barrel from June 1984 to June 2002. Examining the figure shows that from 1987 though 1997 the price tended to be between $18 and $22 per barrel, except

FIGURE 5.3 Monthly Petroleum Prices

This figure shows the price for West Texas crude oil by month from June 1984 to June 2002. The sharp price declines in the mid-1980s and the late 1990s are easily seen. Saudia Arabia caused the first one, and the second may have been caused by cartel instability. The sharp price increase at the time of the Gulf War and the one at the end of the 1990s as the cartel regouped with support form Mexico and Norway also stand out.

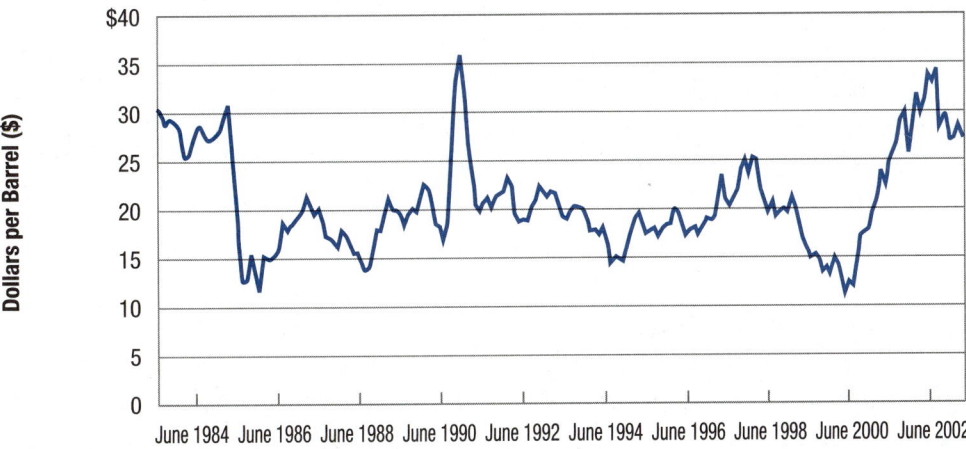

for the period of the Gulf War, where it spiked to $36. In 1998, it fell to about $11 before it again climbed to about $35.

In the mid-1980s, annual petroleum production in the Soviet Union and in the United States had increased compared to the mid-1970s. On the other hand, Saudi Arabia—where petroleum is sometimes cheaper to pump than water in the United States—produced almost 50 percent less in the mid-1980s than it had in the mid-1970s. Other countries with reduced annual production were Kuwait, the United Arab Emirates, and Venezuela, all members of OPEC. Countries with sharply increased annual production were Mexico, the United Kingdom, and Norway, none of which are OPEC members.[8] From 1991 to 1997, as Figure 5.4 shows, non–OPEC and OPEC production increased annually. In 1996, OPEC's production accelerated and received a boost in 1997, when Iraq's production increased, substantially. Prices began to fall in mid-1997 and reached a low of about $12 in mid-1998. The falling prices were followed by a reduction in non–OPEC countries' production. How are these price and production trends related to the OPEC cartel?

Cartel Formation

These changes in petroleum prices and production are consistent with OPEC acting as a cartel. To succeed, a cartel must restrict output and prevent entry of new firms. A successful cartel requires an ACE in the hole: agreement, cooperation, and enforcement.

---

[8]Data can be found in various years' issues of the American Petroleum Institute's *Basic Petroleum Data Book*.

| FIGURE 5.4 | **Petroleum Production** |

This figure gives annual oil production for OPEC and non–OPEC countries in terms of barrels per day. The acceleration of OPEC production in the mid-1990s followed by up-and-down production since then contrasts with the steady upward trend of non–OPEC production.

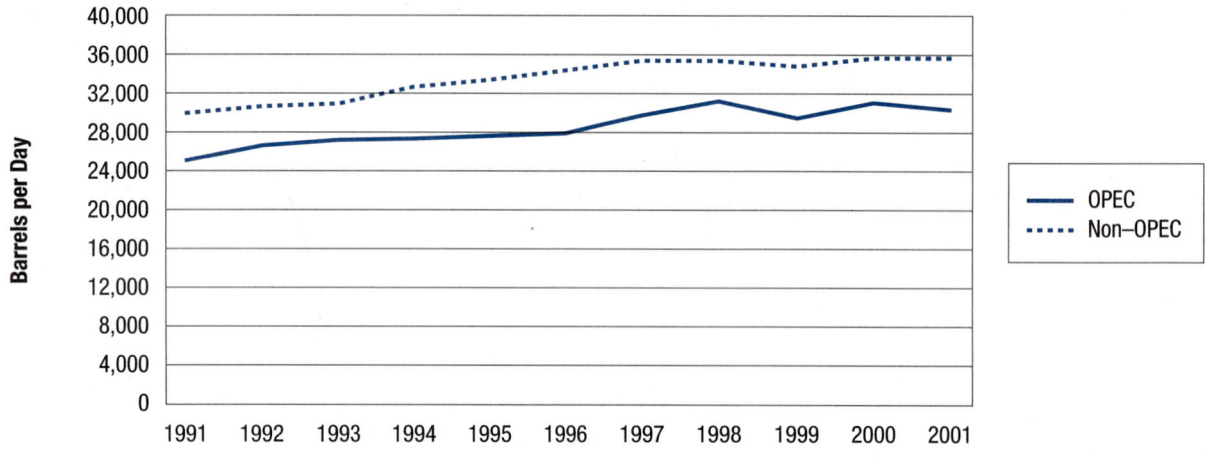

INFOTRAC
College Edition

Keywords: *countries and production management*

http://www.infotrac-college.com

A cartel agreement requires that all important producers *agree* on both total output and the division of that output among cartel members. Its purpose is to restrict output and raise price above the competitive price. The agreement outlines a procedure for solving problems as they arise; it cannot, however, anticipate and solve all possible problems.

In a cartel, the members must continually *cooperate* and come to new agreements as conditions change. If successful, price will be above the marginal cost of production for each member of the cartel. For instance, the price of petroleum in early 2000 was about $25 a barrel in the United States. Some OPEC members can produce and deliver a barrel of petroleum to world markets for less than $5.

Every barrel such a country sells beyond its quota increases its profit by $20. Cheating is very profitable, as it is in any cartel. As long as a cartel member thinks it can cheat—produce more than its quota—without greatly affecting cartel price, it will be tempted to increase its profit by doing so. Therefore, a cartel must be able to *enforce* its agreement.

The Determinants of Cartel Success

All members of a cartel suffer from a split personality. On the one hand, they realize that the maximization of cartel profit is probably in the best interests of each member of the cartel. Thus, they agree to a common policy and cooperate in following and adapting that policy. On the other hand, if other members keep the agreement, each member realizes that it can increase its profit by cheating. Enforcement becomes necessary.

The fewer and more similar the firms, the easier it is to form and operate a cartel. In an industry consisting of two identical firms, the agreement that maximizes cartel profit requires that cartel output be divided evenly between the two firms. For instance, a national market might be split in two. Each firm could keep the profit it earns, and each would earn the same profit.

Furthermore, with only two members, it is easy to determine if the other firm cheats on an agreement. Suppose the market price falls below the expected cartel price. Either demand has decreased or the other member of the cartel is cheating by producing more than the agreed amount.

If cheating occurs, the noncheating firm probably will retaliate by also expanding output. The agreement will break down. Profit will decrease. Neither member wants this to happen. Because each firm can identify the cheater, the agreement may be self-enforcing. With just two identical firms in the industry, no explicit agreement is necessary to reach a cartel-type solution. This is why many economists think that some highly concentrated industries act as if they were monopolies, even in the absence of explicit cartel agreements.

It becomes progressively more difficult to agree on, cooperate with, and enforce a cartel policy (1) as the number of firms in the industry increases and (2) as the firms become less and less similar. With more firms, it becomes more difficult for the agreement to include all or at least most of the major firms in the industry. One problem is the holdout. When Rockefeller Center was being developed in New York City, owners of a small piece of land in its midst refused to sell. Perhaps the owners had some sentimental attachment to the business that they operated on the land. Perhaps they hoped to obtain a much higher price by holding out until the last minute.

A potential member of a cartel might behave in the same way, letting the other firms restrict their output so the holdout will benefit from the higher price without restricting its output. With such a bargaining position, the holdout firm might capture a larger share of the cartel profit. Rockefeller Center was built around the holdout, but continuing cartel success requires that almost all major players participate.

A second problem is that, with more firms, it becomes more difficult to detect cheating. If there are 10 firms in the cartel and the cartel price starts to fall, then either there is a decrease in demand or at least one of the nine other cartel members is cheating. But which? Thus, each firm might think that it could cheat without being detected. As the detection of cheating becomes more difficult, the temptation to cheat becomes overwhelming.

If the firms are dissimilar, agreement also is harder to reach. Suppose there are only two firms, but one is a higher-cost firm. As you might think, to produce a given output at least cost, the lower-cost firm must produce a larger share of total output than the higher-cost firm. In the extreme case, the lower-cost firm would produce all of the cartel output. In this situation, the initial bargaining becomes extremely difficult. The higher-cost firm will insist on a larger profit share than output share in return for accepting the lower output quota. The lower-cost firm will counter that profit shares and output shares should be the same. If the lower-cost firm has a large cost advantage, it may be able to force the other firm to accept and keep an agreement. It may do so by threatening to flood the market with output unless the higher-cost firm cooperates.

Problems of the OPEC Cartel

■ The OPEC cartel has encountered serious problems for at least three reasons. First, there are 11 members of OPEC and 6 to 10 nonmember countries that are important petroleum producers. It currently accounts for less than one-half of world production.

- Second, the demand and supply for petroleum are different when consumers and producers have time to adjust completely to a price change.
- Third, the member countries of OPEC have different and conflicting goals.

OPEC's initial success in the 1970s, measured by the increase in price from about $3 a barrel to more than $30 a barrel in less than a decade, was due to a number of factors. Political upheaval in the Middle East played an important role. OPEC also accounted for more than 90 percent of the world's exports. OPEC, however, did not have significant barriers to entry for new producers. As a result of major petroleum discoveries in Alaska, the North Sea, and Mexico and of numerous successful attempts to squeeze more petroleum out of existing fields, non–OPEC production grew substantially.

The petroleum pessimists in the 1970s thought that the supply of petroleum could be represented by the supply curve S_0 in Figure 5.5. On S_0, an increase in price from P_0 to P_1 does not cause an increase in quantity supplied. However, the pessimists underestimated both the greed and the ingenuity of business owners. The incredible profit potential of $30-a-barrel petroleum attracted a tremendous amount of resources into the industry. Given sufficient time for adjustment—5 to 10 years—the supply curve for petroleum looks more like S_1 in Figure 5.5. The increase in price engineered by OPEC carried the seeds of its own destruction in the supply response of non–OPEC countries. At price P_1, ultimately quantity supplied increases from Q_0 to Q_1.

Just as the petroleum pessimists underestimated supply responsiveness, they also underestimated demand responsiveness to a price change. The pessimists thought that demand responsiveness was almost nil. It is only a slight exaggeration to say that they thought that the demand for petroleum products was vertical. When price increased suddenly and substantially in the 1970s, consumers were not able to adjust their purchases very much—at first. The demand for petroleum could be cut only so much by reducing (1) pleasure

FIGURE 5.5 The Supply of Petroleum

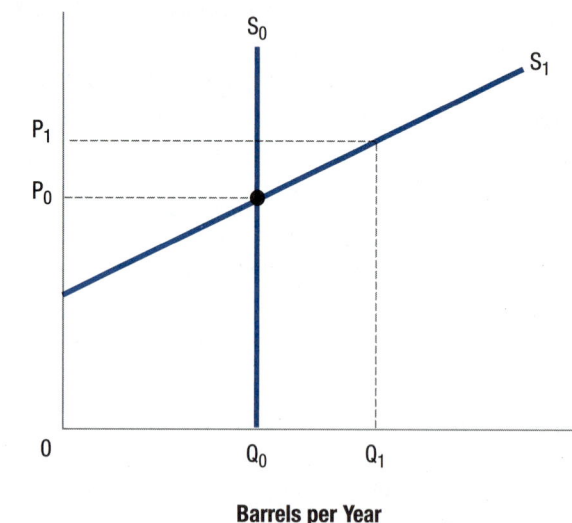

If the supply of petroleum is similar to S_0, raising price does not induce an increase in quantity supplied. Many people believed that OPEC would be successful because they thought S_0 was a good representation of the supply curve for petroleum. It turns out, however, that the supply curve for petroleum is more like S_1 because the price increases engineered by OPEC resulted in big increases in quantity supplied by non–OPEC producers.

driving, (2) home heating in the winter, and (3) home cooling in the summer. Given time to adjust, though, people replaced their cars, furnaces, air conditioners, and houses with ones that were more energy efficient.

Similarly, firms adopted more energy-efficient methods of production. The amount of energy used per dollar of national output fell almost every year in the 1970s and 1980s. Thus, the demand curve for petroleum products—given several years for adjustment—is better represented by D_1 than D_0 in Figure 5.6. Here, an increase in price from P_0 to P_1 ultimately causes quantity demanded to fall from Q_0 to Q_1.

Finally, the OPEC countries differ substantially in terms of their petroleum reserves, their populations relative to their reserves, and in many other ways. They are not similar. Just as in any cartel, each country's self-interest conflicts with the objective of maximizing cartel profit. Countries with large reserves relative to their populations want to stretch their sales of petroleum and their profits over a long period of time. They fear that a low-output/high-price strategy will hasten the demise of petroleum as a major source of energy, preventing them from enjoying petroleum profits in the future.

Countries with large populations and small reserves want to get their profit now with a low-output/high-price strategy. They wish to use their profit to finance economic development and to reduce political tension. They do not care that such a strategy might result in an early replacement of petroleum as a prime source of energy because they will not have any petroleum to sell in the future. The different objectives enhance the always-present incentive to cheat; thus, OPEC is "a confederacy of cheats." According to one magazine, several important producers regularly violate OPEC agreements.[9]

Although OPEC is currently weakened, Saudi Arabia holds it together. Saudi Arabia, the largest producer in OPEC, is a very low-cost producer. Its objective appears to be to establish a cartel price that

FIGURE 5.6 The Demand for Petroleum

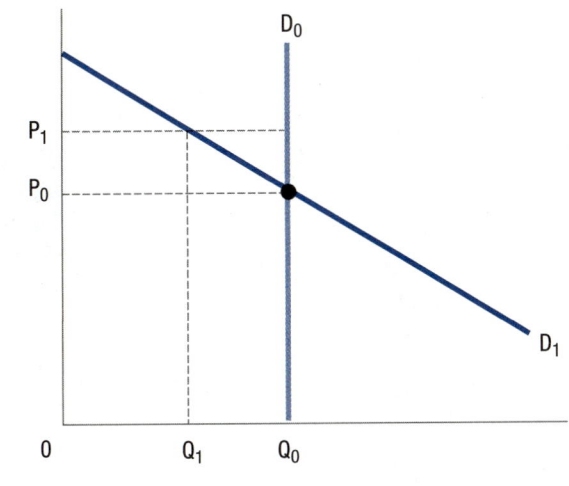

If the demand for petroleum is similar to D_0, raising price does not induce a decrease in quantity demanded. Many people believed that OPEC would be successful because they thought D_0 was a good representation of the demand curve for petroleum. It turns out, however, that the demand curve for petroleum is more like D_1 because the price increases engineered by OPEC resulted in large decreases in quantity demanded after consumers had time to adjust.

---

[9] "A Confederacy of Cheats," *The Economist*, June 10, 1989.

will stretch its profit over a long time. Saudi Arabia is such a large and low-cost producer that it can cause wide swings in the price of petroleum. In the early 1980s, it supported the cartel price by substantially reducing its output. As a result, other countries could cheat with impunity.

In the mid-1980s, Saudi Arabia became an enforcer. It substantially increased its output, driving the price of petroleum temporarily below $10 a barrel. Other cartel members and perhaps nonmembers got the message: Cooperate or the price will stay extremely low. New agreements were reached at a lower price level and a higher output level than existed in the early 1980s. OPEC continues to influence market price, suggesting that it still has market power.[10]

The most recent chapter in the OPEC saga started in 1998, when oil prices had fallen to around $12 a barrel, with Mexico receiving just $7 a barrel for a few shipments. OPEC countries had steadily increased their production, with their share of world production increasing from 30 percent in 1985 to 47 percent in 1998. Late in 1998, Luis K. Tellez, Mexico's energy minister, persuaded the OPEC countries and Norway to cut production. As shown in Figure 5.7, Mexico and Norway's production actually fell in 1998, but OPEC's production grew by about 4 percent. In 1999, however, OPEC played its ACE. Its production fell by almost 5 percent and, in close cooperation Mexico and Norway, again cut their production. Small increases by Russia and other non–OPEC countries could not offset the large production decreases in 1999. By the end of 1998, petroleum prices were rising, and they approached $35 a barrel

FIGURE 5.7 Changes in Petroleum Production: 1998–2001

This figure shows year-on-year changes in production starting in 1998. The assistance and encouragement given to OPEC by Mexico and Norway in 1998 and 1999 contrasts with the production increases for Russia, Mexico, and Norway in 2000 and 2001. The price increases that followed the cuts in 1998 and 1999 show that OPEC, especially if it receives outside cooperation, has significant market power.

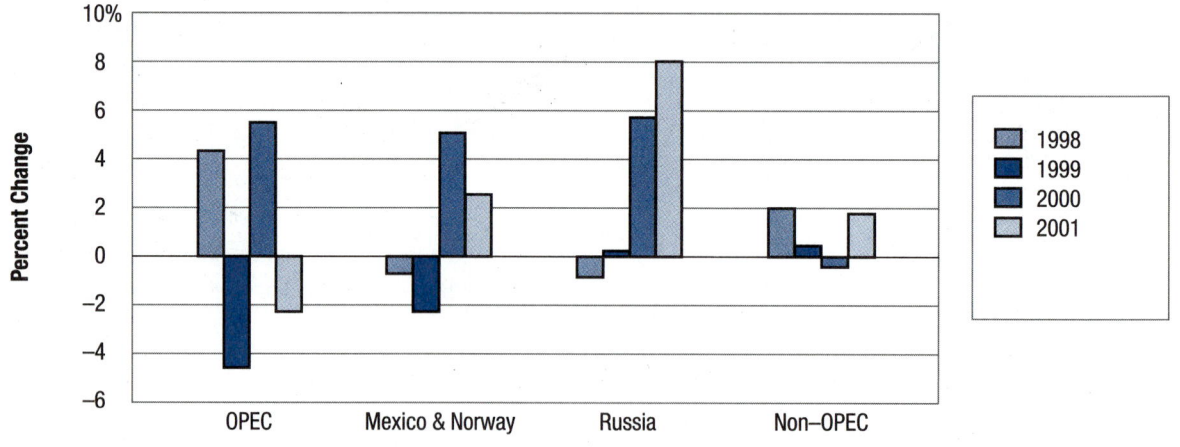

[10]Sargon J. Youhanna, "A Note on Modeling OPEC Behavior 1983–1989: A Test of the Cartel and Competitive Hypothesis," *The American Economist* 38 (Fall 1994), 78–84, finds that OPEC continues to function as a cartel.

by the end of 1999. Large production increases by OPEC, Mexico, Norway, and Russia in 2000 started prices on a downward slide, which OPEC's cuts in 2001 could not overcome. Russia's large production increase in 2001 was largely responsible for OPEC's failure to reverse the 2001 price slide. OPEC's efforts to keep prices in the $25 to $30 range met resistance from countries not in the cartel. Close examination of Figures 5.3, 5.4, and 5.7 suggests that OPEC, when it can reach agreement and receive some cooperation from outsiders, has market power in petroleum. It can, in fact, push prices above $30 a barrel. Whether it can do so for a sustained period is open to question. Two recent magazine articles came to different conclusions. One said, "OPEC cannot maintain $25/bl as a long-term price if demand remains weak. The question is: how far will prices fall?...If demand stays weak, non–OPEC producers could supply all the extra oil the market needs as long as prices remain above their development costs of about $15/bl.... Most likely, the market will stabilise around $18/bl—the average price in the 'nineties.'"[11] In contrast, another one says, "Now, most price pundits are banking on a tighter second half in 2002 to keep prices between $24 and $25 per barrel for the rest of the year."[12] OPEC has market power, but are its agreements sufficiently strong to avoid the problems that cartels face with 10 to 15 players?

Do a Few Firms That Dominate a Market Have Market Power?

Keywords: OPEC and prices
http://www.infotrac-college.com

It is not easy to determine if a few firms that dominate a market have market power. The internal tensions caused by the entry of new producers, by the substitution of other products for the cartel's products, and by dissension and cheating in the cartel itself are not unique to OPEC. Any formal or informal agreement to restrict output and increase price is subject to similar tensions. In the absence of barriers to entry and government enforcement of agreements, formal and informal cartels are likely to be unstable. If government actively discourages cartels, it is even more difficult for them to function. In short, the market power of oligopolies is weaker (1) the greater the number of firms, (2) the more dissimilar the firms, (3) when there is no powerful firm to enforce an agreement, and (4) over time, because of the responses of consumers and other producers to high prices and large profits.

■ MARKET POWER AND ECONOMIC GROWTH

As we have seen, economic efficiency and a dispersion of economic and political power call for industries with little market power. Economic growth, as we saw in Chapter 1, depends upon the development of new products and new methods of production. Knowledge and the creation of new knowledge are the basis for much economic growth and for the growth of many firms. Knowledge-based (high-tech) firms have several features that lead to a monopoly or near-monopoly of their products, that is, to market power. The development of a new medicinal drug or a new operating system for computers has huge start-up costs, and the product developed is essentially knowledge. After the knowledge of how to produce a new drug, operating system, or chip is developed, huge investments in plant and equipment might be required to produce the product. These large up-front costs are a much bigger part of the total cost of producing a drug or a chip than are the direct labor and material costs. Another cost

---

[11]"The Emperor's New Clothes," *Global Markets*, July 1, 2002, Vol. 32, Issue 25, 1.

[12]"Analysts See Steady Oil Price for 2002," *The Oil Daily*, June 24, 2002, Vol. 52.

that knowledge-based firms face is the cost of development projects that fail; failed projects are another cost of the search for new knowledge.

Up-front costs have important implications. For example, as W. Brian Arthur said, "The first disk of Windows to go out the door cost Microsoft $50 million; the second and subsequent disks cost $3."[13] The marginal production cost of successive disks is $3. Similar situations exist for drugs, videos, and CDs. To cover the development cost of these products and the cost of unsuccessful projects, the price of a drug or a software disk must be greater than the marginal production cost.

Firms recover the development costs only if they have discretion in pricing their successful products. To price above production costs, firms must have property rights in the knowledge that underlies the product. If other firms could freely copy CDs or drug formulas, the innovating firm that created the music, the software, or the formula would be unable to raise its price much above production cost; the up-front development costs would not be covered. This is one reason government uses copyrights and patents to give firms monopolies of new products. Even if a firm has this patent or copyright protection, however, it may be unable to capture profits and prevent quick imitation by rivals, unless it uses tactics that attract the attention of regulators. One tactic to secure first-mover advantage is to introduce new products at low prices designed to expand the customer base. Netscape went so far as to give away its software as it was developing its customer base. In these markets, being the first mover and having a superb product is important, but the first mover and the best product may not always win. Arthur cites Prodigy as a first mover in online services and the Macintosh (Mac) operating system as a superb product; neither has become the dominant player in its respective market.

If the initial product is sold cheaply or given away to create a large customer base, the firm must later exploit that customer base to recover its cost. MS presents several examples of how to do this. It has extended its dominant position in operating systems to software by developing word-processing programs, spreadsheets, and other software. In an attempt to capture the software market, MS encourages producers of computers using its Windows operating system to load its software rather than other software on their computers. The idea is that if ultimate consumers can be enticed to learn its software, they will be locked into its products, giving MS a captive market. It is alleged that MS uses persuasion and rebates to entice computer producers to load its software and not its rivals' software on new computers. According to Liebowitz and Margolis, however, MS's most successful applications have been based on superior software; it does not win software battles when its product is inferior.[14] For instance, to extend its position in software, MS attempted to purchase the producer of a popular financial software package so that the package could be part of its bundle. The government discouraged this purchase on monopoly grounds, and MS developed its own financial software, which has not achieved market dominance. Moreover, Liebowitz and Margolis find that in those application markets where MS is dominant, prices fall after it achieves this dominance.

A federal district judge in late 1999 found that MS was a monopolist that harmed consumers and engaged in illegal activities that prevented Netscape from developing a substitute for the Windows oper-

---

[13]W. Brian Arthur, "Increasing Returns and the New World of Business," *Harvard Business Review* 74 (July/August 1996), 100–109. The quote is from p. 103.

[14]For the MS and Mac discussion, see Stan J. Liebowitz and Stephen E. Margolis. *Winners, Losers, and Microsoft: Competition and Antitrust in High Technology* (Oakland, CA: Independent Institute, 1999), 127–129.

ating system. In the summer of 2001, however, the U.S. Court of Appeals (in Washington, DC) overturned much of the district court's decision that Microsoft had illegally bundled Windows and Internet Explorer and had illegally attempted to monopolize the Internet browser market. The appeals court did find MS guilty of monopolization of the operating systems market for PCs. Subsequently, the Antitrust Division of the U.S. Department of Justice along with several states proposed a settlement to the district court. (Some states have not agreed to the settlement.) The proposed settlement calls for MS to provide information that would facilitate competitors' development of software compatible with Windows. Moreover, MS would not be permitted to retaliate against computer manufacturers who put competing software on MS's operating system. This contrasts with the earlier district court decision that called for dramatic changes. It called for a breakup of MS into two or more competing firms or restricting the range of products that it could bundle with its operating system. (As we write, the case is not completely settled. When you read this, you may want additional information.)

INFOTRAC
College Edition

Keywords: *Microsoft antitrust settlement*
http://www.infotrac-college.com

One reason for the legal challenge to MS may be the widespread belief that the Mac operating system is superior to the MS system. Consequently, the harm to consumers arises because we are being locked into an inferior system. The idea is that DOS and then Windows became entrenched, and we are now on an inefficient technological path that the market cannot reverse. In the early 1990s and earlier, MS made decisions that gave it its current dominance. At the same time, Apple made decisions that held the Mac back. This general argument (discussed in the box, "QWERTY Versus DSK") is that the first type of new technology introduced will dominate the market even if a superior product is developed later. This can happen if existing customers are locked into the inferior product and individually do not change to the new product, even when it is in the best interests of all consumers to do so. Although this argument is plausible, Professors Liebowitz and Margolis argue in *Winners, Losers, and Microsoft: Competition and Antitrust in High Technology* that this fails to explain MS's dominance. Rather they argue that the MS DOS systems were chosen over the Mac because, if cost is taken into account, they were superior.

- DOS was cheaper because it took less computing power than the Mac's graphical interface, when computing power was much more expensive than it is now.

- DOS was faster. Most users gained little advantage from the Mac's ease in accessing and learning programs because they used only one program and because limited hard-drive capacity meant that programs ran from floppy drives. Because changing programs required changing floppies, the Mac's advantage was small.

As the graphical interface became more cost-effective, the fact that most users were using DOS did not lock them into DOS. When Windows emerged, they changed, perhaps surprisingly, to it although the Mac system was technically superior to early Windows. Windows became the graphical interface of choice, again, because it was more economical.

- Windows had the advantage of being able to run DOS programs.

- Windows maintained backward compatibility, so upgrading was less costly.[15]

---

[15]See Stan J. Liebowitz and Stephen E. Margolis. *Winners, Losers, and Microsoft: Competition and Antitrust in High Technology* (Oakland, CA: Independent Institute, 1999), 127–129.

MS's success, according to these arguments, is the result of having the superior product in terms of consumer preferences and cost considerations.

An important issue, besides the concern that an inferior product may become the standard, is the question of whether firms that produce an essential product should have unlimited discretion in choosing their price. This issue is well illustrated in the pharmaceutical industry, whose products are often essential and whose firms often have significant market power. Sometimes a firm will have a patent on the only product useful in treating a particular disease. In the late 1980s, Wellcome, a British company, sold AZT, the only drug at that time that helped AIDS patients. It was accused of "profiting from disease" because the annual price for using the drug was $10,000, a price that the company reduced to $3,000 because of political pressure. Even at the lower price, the company may have made as much as 70 percent over the costs of production and marketing.[16] *The Economist* and others recognize that large profits on successful drugs provide incentive for private firms to conduct the risky and expensive research necessary to discover new drugs. In recognition of this incentive role of profits, governments grant patent monopolies to the discoverers of new drugs.

Market power in pharmaceuticals springs from patents, but the patents are necessary to induce private sector research aimed at developing new drugs. Robert Goldberg argues that both government conduct of the research and government regulation of the research would seriously reduce the rate of discovery of new medicines. He uses the experiences of the former Soviet Union and of the United Kingdom to bolster his argument. Governmental pharmaceutical research in the Soviet Union, he notes, was ineffective in producing new drugs. Moreover, he claims that price controls (regulations) have stifled pharmaceutical research in the United Kingdom. In short, he believes that monopoly profits are necessary to induce firms to produce desirable research.[17]

In this discussion of market power and economic growth, we have seen that market power might be an unavoidable consequence of the innovative activity of business firms. Because this innovative activity is essential for continued economic growth, limiting the market power that results from firms finding new products and better ways to produce old products could be self-defeating. A dilemma facing policy makers is what to do about the pricing of new products that are necessary for life and for which we have no close substitutes. These rare situations must be handled on a case-by-case basis. In the next section, we discuss government policy toward market power in other cases.

■ GOVERNMENT AND MARKET POWER

Economists have not reached consensus on government's role in dealing with market power, as they have, for instance, concerning farm policy. The conflicting implications of economic efficiency and economic growth create this lack of consensus. For instance, some economists have criticized and others have supported the U.S. Department of Justice case against MS. Three general principles can guide policy toward market power in a way that reconciles the sometimes-conflicting goals of efficiency and growth. First, government can limit mergers of firms that produce the same or similar products and prohibit price fix-

---

[16] "Profiting from Disease," *The Economist*, January 27, 1990, 17–18.

[17] Robert M. Goldberg, "Race Against the Cure: The Health Hazards of Pharmaceutical Price Controls," *Policy Review* (Spring 1994). For a more balanced view of the issues, see F. M. Scherer, "Pricing, Profits, and Technological Progress in the Pharmaceutical Industry," *Journal of Economic Perspectives* 7 (Summer 1993), 97–116.

INSIGHTS

QWERTY VERSUS DSK: CAN THE MARKET CHOOSE THE RIGHT TECHNOLOGY?

The familiar typewriter keyboard with the letters QWERTY on the top-left row was patented in 1868 by Christopher Sholes. One problem with early attempts at designing a typewriter was that the keys tended to stick; in designing his keyboard, Sholes arranged letters so as to reduce this problem. August Dvorak patented his Dvorak Simplified Keyboard (DSK) in 1936. With newer typewriter technology reducing the sticking problem, Dvorak, a time and motion expert, believed that his new keyboard would increase typing speed. Dvorak convinced many observers that his design was better. Certain economists and engineers have taken the failure of DSK to replace QWERTY as an example of *lock in*, where a superior technology is not adopted because an inferior technology got there first. No one uses DSK because no one uses DSK. In a recent article, one observer says, "The lesson is that the market does not necessarily lead to optimum technologies or efficient outcomes and that close attention to the history of the development of innovation and the institutionalization of 'standards' may be the best way to reveal their inefficiencies."[a] This argument underlies much criticism of Microsoft.

The problem with the argument is that people who have carefully researched the history of the development of the keyboard find no evidence to support the hypothesis that the DSK is superior to the QWERTY keyboard.[b] Liebowitz and Margolis point out that it is not surprising that QWERTY achieved initial domination; early in typewriter history, it passed the market test in competition with many other designs. Moreover, it has maintained its dominance to the present. Indeed, the real surprise would be if DSK were superior and unable to break QWERTY's lock. As Professor Nicholas Economides of New York University says, computer keyboards can be easily and cheaply converted to DSK. It seems that the market has spoken again regarding QWERTY. History shows that if a superior technology is available, huge profits await the entrepreneur that can overcome the old technology. Thus, we saw the rise and fall of the dedicated word processor and of previously dominant spreadsheets and word-processing programs.

Proponents of lock in have yet to find a convincing real-world example of it. Nevertheless, we cannot say that lock in has never occurred nor that it cannot occur in the future. The difficult question is whether lock in is potentially costly enough to warrant government intervention, which boils down to whether profit-seeking entrepreneurs will make more economical choices than vote-seeking politicians.

[a]Dan Krier, "Assessing the New Synthesis of Economics and Sociology," *American Journal of Economics and Sociology* 58 (October 1999), 671.

[b]See Stan J. Liebowitz and Stephen E. Margolis. *Winners, Losers, and Microsoft: Competition and Antitrust in High Technology* (Oakland, CA: Independent Institute, 1999). An interesting question in the sociology of science is why this QWERTY myth has developed and why the findings of Liebowitz and Margolis, first published more than 10 years ago, are so often overlooked.

ing. Second, government can encourage economic rent seeking by granting patents and copyrights and by supporting basic research. Finally, it must discourage political rent seeking so that government itself does not become a source of market power.

U.S. antitrust laws dealing with mergers and price fixing probably satisfy the first principle. They make it even harder for oligopolies to reach formal or informal agreements to exercise market power. These laws, particularly the Clayton and Sherman Acts, prohibit explicit conspiracies to fix prices, divide markets, restrict entry, and engage in other cartel behavior. They also help to maintain the number of firms in an industry by preventing mergers that would increase market power. As Shepherd argues, these laws enhance the tendencies for industries to remain or become competitive. Recall, however, that Pryor contends that antimerger enforcement became much less stringent in the last 2 decades of the twentieth century. Given the federal antitrust laws and the existing structure of industries in the United States, many economists believe that market power is not a major problem in the U.S. economy. They recognize that it exists, but they do not advocate government action—beyond the current antitrust laws—to reduce it.

According to the second principle, government policy should not impede and perhaps should promote economic rent seeking. The tremendous growth in industrial economies in the past 2 centuries depended largely upon the entrepreneur seeking profit. To sustain progress, we must allow prices to relay information about scarcity to entrepreneurs, and entrepreneurs must be allowed to reap profit from their innovations. Two types of remedies were initially considered in response to MS's "monopolization." One type, a conduct remedy, would impose restrictions on the contracts that MS can use in their business dealings. Because it is difficult to specify all of the contractual arrangements that MS might use to increase their profit, these restrictions would probably fail. The other type, a structural remedy, would have involved the forced sale of the Windows source code or some breakup of MS into independent firms. Because MS would be unlikely to receive the full value of its Windows code through a forced sale, this remedy would have had the effect of confiscating MS's intellectual property. As Economides puts it, "this is a serious remedy that takes away the intellectual property of MS. It will severely reduce the incentive for innovation, since dominant firms will no longer be guaranteed with certainty the value of their intellectual property."[18] Instead of breaking up or regulating firms that achieve market power through economic rent seeking, government can play a positive role by increasing the incentive for innovation. As the experiences of General Motors and IBM show, the market power that is created is often temporary. Market power in a market economy is like the mythical gunslinger in the Old West: It lasts only until someone faster comes along.

The third principle implies that government must take care not to make political rent seeking more lucrative than economic rent seeking. Granting patents to innovators must not lead to granting market power to existing firms and interest groups. Political rent seeking—the attempt to gain economic advantage through government action—supports much market power. License systems support the market power of accountants, some cab companies, doctors, real estate dealers, and others. In almost every instance, the license system is requested by the industry or occupation. Moreover, the standards for obtaining and keeping a license are almost always set by the industry or occupation. Rarely does such activity lead to economic progress.

Summary

A competitive economy is efficient because the value of one more unit of any good (marginal benefit) is just equal to the opportunity cost of producing one more unit (marginal cost). If marginal benefit were greater than marginal cost, unrealized gains from trade would exist. This is because the value of the additional unit of a good would be greater than the value of the goods given up to produce it. The monopolist restricts output and raises price above marginal cost. Marginal benefit under monopoly is greater than marginal cost. Thus, monopoly output is inefficient.

The monopolist, however, cannot raise price without limit. When price goes up, output goes down. Charging more and selling less is not always a good strategy. To maximize profit, the monopolist equates marginal revenue with marginal cost.

---

[18] Interview of Nicholas Economides by John Irons of About.com on the judge's "findings of fact" in *U.S. v. MS*, part 3, November 9, 1999. See http://economics.miningco.com/finance/economics or http://www.stern.nyu.edu. The discussion of the MS case is based on this interview.

The U.S. economy is reasonably competitive. Efficiency loss due to monopoly appears limited. Moreover, profit attracts new firms into an industry. In addition, economic rent seeking—innovation—is important in many parts of the economy, in particular the knowledge-based industries.

Monopoly occurs for four reasons: (1) Technology sometimes requires that a firm be so large that it can supply the entire market; (2) a firm might control essential inputs or have other absolute cost advantages; (3) a firm might use advertising and product development to gain a dominant position; and (4) government sometimes encourages monopoly.

The OPEC cartel shows how several firms in an industry might act like a monopoly. Although numerous countries produce petroleum, OPEC has succeeded in restricting petroleum output and raising price. Cooperation, however, is not perfect. Some countries cheat on the cartel agreement by producing more than their share. Enforcement activity by Saudi Arabia has increased OPEC cartel stability.

Analyses of cartels and of OPEC in particular show that agreement among firms—even if it is not an explicit agreement—might lead to the firms exercising market power. Cheating—which increases as the number of firms in the industry increases—and the entry of new firms destabilize such agreements. Government can promote competition through antitrust laws, but it must be careful that it does not unduly impede economic rent seeking.

Economic growth, as well as economic efficiency, is related to monopoly and competition. As they develop new products and processes, knowledge-based firms may achieve significant market power. Doing this on the merits of their products rather than through price fixing and merger may promote economic growth. Even though such firms capture a large market share, government policy, in such circumstances, must recognize that reining in their profit seeking behavior may reduce the incentive to innovate and thus impede economic growth.

Key Terms

Market power
Monopoly
Oligopoly
Cartel
Marginal revenue
Marginal principle
Efficient output
Barrier to entry
Natural monopoly

Review Questions

1. Why does efficient output occur where marginal benefit equals marginal cost? Analyze in detail.
2. If a firm is a pure competitor, marginal revenue and price will be equal. If the firm is a monopoly, marginal revenue will be less than price. Justify these statements.
3. Suppose you are given the information about a monopoly that appears in the following table.

Quantity	Price	Marginal Cost
1	$50	$20
2	45	20
3	40	20
4	35	20
5	30	20
6	25	20
7	20	20
8	15	20
9	10	20
10	5	20

    a. What is the firm's total revenue for each quantity?
    b. What is the firm's marginal revenue for each quantity?

c. What quantity and price should the firm choose to maximize its profits?
d. Suppose the monopolist is currently producing 5 units of the good. What actions should it undertake, and why?
e. Use the information to plot the demand curve faced by the monopolist, the monopolist's marginal revenue and marginal cost curves, the profit-maximizing level of output, and the profits earned by the firm.
4. "A monopolist can charge whatever price it desires for its output." Is this statement true or false? Defend your answer.
5. State and defend the general principle to be followed in maximizing profits.
6. Use graphical analysis to compare and contrast the economic outcome of monopoly with the economic outcome of pure competition.
7. "Because a monopolist can extract a higher price than a firm that is a pure competitor, the monopolist will always earn a profit." Is this statement true or false? Defend your answer.
8. List and briefly discuss the major sources of monopoly in the United States.
9. What is a cartel? What factors help to maintain a cartel? What factors encourage its dissolution?
10. "Profits on drugs are too high. Drug companies should not be allowed to profit excessively from drugs necessary to treat serious diseases." Discuss.
11. Evaluate the following statement: "Because monopoly results in economic inefficiency and in large profits for a few powerful corporations, we should enforce regulations to break up these firms or eliminate their profits."
12. According to the box titled "The Battle Between American and Japanese Automobile Firms," why were the Japanese firms successful in the battle?
13. What are the advantages and disadvantages of government choosing the industry standard for computer operating systems?
14. Assume that Apple's operating systems were and are superior to the MS systems. Explain why DOS dominated the early Mac systems and why Windows dominated later Mac systems. Given Windows' dominant position, how could a new operating system replace Windows?
15. Go to http://www.swcollege.com/bef/econ_news.html and click on Monopoly under the Microeconomics section. Choose an article of interest, read the full summary, and answer the questions. (Some of these questions may go beyond the materials in this course. If you run into such questions, you may want to try to answer anyway, go to a different article, or just answer the ones that seem appropriate.)

Economic Issues on the Internet

– AEI-Brookings Joint Center for Regulatory Studies—**http://www.aei.brookings.org**
   Their "Hot Topics" include the pros and cons of breaking up Microsoft.

– Antitrust Division, U.S. Department of Justice—**http://www.usdoj.gov/atr**
   The place to learn about the Microsoft case and much more.

– Energy Information Administration, U.S. Department of Energy—**http://www.eia.doe.gov**
   This site has information on oil prices and many other aspects of energy markets.

– FamiliesUSA—**http://familiesusa.org**
   Visit this site for one side of the prescription drug price issue, and visit the next site for a different perspective.

– Federal Trade Commission—**http://www.ftc.gov/ftc/economic.htm**
   Visit the FTC to obtain even more information about competition, monopoly, and the federal government.

– Pharmaceutical Research and Manufacturers of America—**http://www.phrma.org**
   Visit this site for one side of the prescription drug price issue, and visit the previous site for a different perspective.

CHAPTER 6

Air Pollution: Balancing Benefits and Costs

Outline:

The Principal Air Pollution Problems
    Urban Air Quality
    Acid Rain
    Global Warming
    Stratospheric Ozone Depletion
    Hazardous Air Pollutants
The Economic Perspective
Market Failure: Is Government Action Necessary?
Air Pollution Regulation: The Clean Air Act
    National Ambient Air Quality Standards (NAAQS)

Emissions Limits
Restricted Technology
New Source Performance Standards
Prescribed Fuel
Offset Requirements
Emissions Trading
Prevention of Significant Deterioration
Monitoring and Compliance
Effects of the Clean Air Act on Air Quality
The Economics of the Clean Air Act: Have We Gone Too Far?

Benefits and Costs of the Clean Air Act, 1970 to 1990
Benefits and Costs of the Clean Air Act, 1990 to 2010
Cost-Reducing Measures
    Emissions Taxes
    Marketable Pollution Permits
Limiting Global Warming: Emissions Permits in an International Context

We live on a small planet with a thin, life-sustaining mantle of air, the quality of which is constantly threatened by economic activities. Millions of urban dwellers endure smog created by factories, power plants, and motor vehicles. Lakes and forests in the eastern United States and Canada suffer from acid rain produced by electric generating plants in the Midwest. Many scientists fear that the Earth will get warmer if we do not control our consumption of fossil fuels. Others contend that the Earth is losing its ozone shield, exposing the planet to greater concentrations of harmful ultraviolet rays.

To counter threats such as these, federal and state governments have adopted an imposing array of laws and regulations. Our focus in this chapter is the federal Clean Air Act. We examine some of the ways in which it has shaped environmental regulation and assess whether it has resulted in improved air quality. We also analyze the costs and benefits of air quality regulation and evaluate ways to reduce the costs of achieving cleaner air.

■ THE PRINCIPAL AIR POLLUTION PROBLEMS

The air pollution problem has several dimensions. The most important of these are (1) poor-quality air in urban areas, (2) acid rain, (3) global warming, (4) ozone depletion, and (5) hazardous air pollutants.

Urban Air Quality

Urban air quality is measured in terms of atmospheric (ambient) concentrations of six common air pollutants: total suspended particulates, sulfur dioxide, carbon monoxide, nitrogen dioxide, ozone, and lead.

Suspended particulates consist primarily of chemically stable substances such as dust, soot, ash, and smoke.

Sulfur dioxide is a pungent, toxic gas with beneficial uses: as sulfuric acid, as a bleaching agent, as a compound in preservatives, and as a refrigerant. It can be harmful to humans, plants, and structures, however, when airborne concentrations exceed critical levels—a problem created primarily by electricity generating plants that burn fossil fuels.

Carbon monoxide is a colorless, odorless, toxic gas produced by incomplete combustion of fossil fuels. It can be a silent killer when an automobile exhaust system is not ventilated properly and a chronic—but less lethal—problem when motor vehicles vent their exhaust gases into urban air sheds.

Nitrogen dioxide emissions are also caused by the incomplete combustion of fossil fuels, primarily by electric utilities and motor vehicles. Urbanites are victimized by nitrogen dioxide when it combines with other elements, such as ozone, to form smog.

Ozone is a form of oxygen with a pungent odor, created naturally in the upper levels of the atmosphere (the stratosphere) by a photochemical reaction with ultraviolet radiation from the sun. In fact, stratospheric ozone shields the Earth from the sun's harmful rays. Ozone is produced commercially and used in disinfectants, deodorizers, oxidizers, and bleaches. It is also produced when volatile organic compounds (chemically unstable hydrocarbons) are emitted from sources such as oil refineries and motor vehicles. As noted, ground-level ozone is a primary ingredient in smog.

Lead is a mineral with many beneficial uses, but it is toxic when inhaled or ingested, even in tiny doses. Lead in the atmosphere used to come primarily from motor vehicles; today, it is largely a by-product of nonferrous smelters and battery plants.

Concern about urban air quality stems largely from its adverse effects on human health, property, safety, and visibility. Research shows that poor air quality contributes to bronchitis, asthma, lung cancer, and emphysema. Air pollutants can cause extensive damage to property, such as autos, houses, commercial buildings and historic structures. Sulfur dioxide and ozone corrode and weaken many materials. Particulates and smog reduce visibility and the amenities associated with a clear vista. High levels of some pollutants, such as carbon monoxide, impair judgment and motor skills, increasing the risk of accident and injury.

INFOTRAC
College Edition

Keyword: *smog*
http://www.infotrac-college.com

Acid Rain

Acid Rain —
A solution of sulfuric acid and precipitation.

Keywords: acid rain
http://www.infotrac-college.com

Acid rain occurs when airborne sulfur dioxide is chemically transformed into a weak sulfuric acid solution that falls to the Earth as part of natural precipitation. Sulfur dioxide emissions come largely from Midwest power plants, and they are transported long distances by the wind currents that flow from west to east in the Northern Hemisphere. Thus, acid rain falls primarily in the eastern United States and Canada.

Some lakes and streams in these regions have become highly acidified, impairing their ability to sustain life, and eastern forests have suffered retarded growth and increased mortality. Acid rain also corrodes materials, erodes and discolors paint, and deteriorates structures.

Global Warming

Greenhouse Gas —
A gas that helps the Earth retain heat from the sun.

As fossil fuels burn, carbon dioxide is released into the atmosphere. The clearing of land (especially heavily forested land) reduces the Earth's capacity to absorb released carbon dioxide. The cumulative effect of burning and clearing has increased the level of atmospheric carbon dioxide.

Carbon dioxide is the principal **greenhouse gas**—a gas that helps the Earth retain heat from the sun. Rays from the sun that reach the Earth are partly absorbed and partly reflected into space. Some of the reflected energy is redirected toward the Earth by greenhouse gases, further warming the planet. Without these gases, the Earth would be too cold for human habitation. If greenhouse gases continue to accumulate, however, the warming they will cause could have serious consequences.

Keywords: global warming
http://www.infotrac-college.com

Slight warming of the Northern Hemisphere has occurred during the past century. If the industrial nations continue to emit greenhouse gases at current rates and today's third world countries industrialize, the atmosphere may get even warmer. Scientists do not currently agree, however, on the likely rate or extent of global warming. Some predict only a slight warming trend, with little impact on the world's climate. Others predict warming sufficient to raise ocean levels and change the location of the world's croplands and forests.

Stratospheric Ozone Depletion

As indicated earlier, ozone is both a beneficial and a harmful gas. It is harmful when present in high concentrations in the lower atmosphere, but it is beneficial when present in the Earth's stratosphere. Ozone in the stratosphere prevents harmful solar ultraviolet radiation from reaching the Earth's surface. A reduction in the protection it provides would increase the incidence of skin cancer and possibly trigger genetic mutations.

When chlorofluorocarbons enter the stratosphere, they trigger a chemical reaction that destroys ozone. Chlorofluorocarbons are used primarily as aerosol propellants, refrigerants, foam-blowing agents, and cleaning solvents. Other gases, principally carbon dioxide and methane, increase the atmospheric concentration of ozone. Scientists are not certain about the effects of these conflicting forces on ozone levels. Measurements taken to date, however, indicate that significant decreases have occurred periodically in the ozone layer over Antarctica. Some computer models indicate a significant decrease in stratospheric ozone with continued growth in the use of chlorofluorocarbons.

Keywords: ozone depletion
http://www.infotrac-college.com

Keywords: *hazardous air pollutants*
http://www.infotrac-college.com

Hazardous Air Pollutants

The air also serves as a medium for transporting thousands of chemicals, many of which may be hazardous to humans, animals, and plants if inhaled or ingested. The Environmental Protection Agency (EPA) targeted 189 of these chemicals for regulation in the Clean Air Act of 1990. The primary impetus for these regulations is evidence that these chemicals impair human health, especially in the form of central nervous system damage and cancer.

■ THE ECONOMIC PERSPECTIVE

As noted earlier, pollution imposes costs on humans, on the ecosystem, and on structures. Some would argue for drastic reductions in pollution in order to reduce these costs. Pollution is largely a by-product, however, of economic activities that produce beneficial goods and services. Economists recognize both the costs of pollution and the benefits of the economic activities that produce it. Accordingly, they argue for reducing pollution only if the costs avoided exceed the benefits given up. Alternatively, they find pollution acceptable only if the benefits from the activities that produce it exceed the costs attributable to the pollution.

The economic perspective can be illustrated with the use of a supply and demand diagram, such as Figure 6.1. The market represented is refined oil products, such as gasoline, kerosene, diesel fuel, and lubricating oils. Producers in this market face an ordinary, downward-sloping demand curve for their products; i.e., additional quantities can be sold only at lower prices. There is an ordinary, upward-sloping supply curve; i.e., additional quantities can be provided only at higher prices. The demand curve is also a marginal benefit (MB) curve—the height of the demand curve at each quantity (or marginal unit) is a measure of the benefit provided by that quantity (or marginal benefit). The supply curve is also a marginal cost (MC) curve—the height of the supply curve at each quantity (or marginal unit) is a measure of the cost of providing that quantity (or marginal cost).

It is critical to recognize that the only costs reflected in the supply or MC curve are those paid by the producers of refined oil products. If oil refining emits pollutants as a by-product, and it does, the costs imposed by those pollutants, such as impaired health and ecosystem damage, are *not* reflected in the MC curve. Economists refer to the costs attributable to pollution as **external costs** to convey the idea that they are external to (do not influence) market transactions between buyers and sellers. Pollution costs attributable to each unit of output are called **marginal external costs (MEC)**. The costs attributable to pollutants should be added to those paid by refiners to portray a complete picture of the costs of oil refining. We have done this in Figure 6.1 by adding marginal external costs to MC. When MC and MEC are added together, all of the costs to society from oil refining are accounted for; hence, the curve labeled MSC—for **marginal social costs**.

Figure 6.1 illustrates constant MEC, or MECs that are the same at each quantity of refined products. We assume this in order to simplify the example. In reality, the MEC of oil refining probably increases as the quantity refined increases.

The quantity of refined oil products will be determined, as usual, by the intersection of the supply and demand or MC and MB curves. Thus, 450 million barrels of refined products will be produced and sold

External Costs – Costs created by producers or consumers, but paid by others.

Marginal External Costs (MEC) – External costs attributable to each additional unit of production.

Marginal Social Costs (MSC) – The sum of marginal costs and marginal external costs.

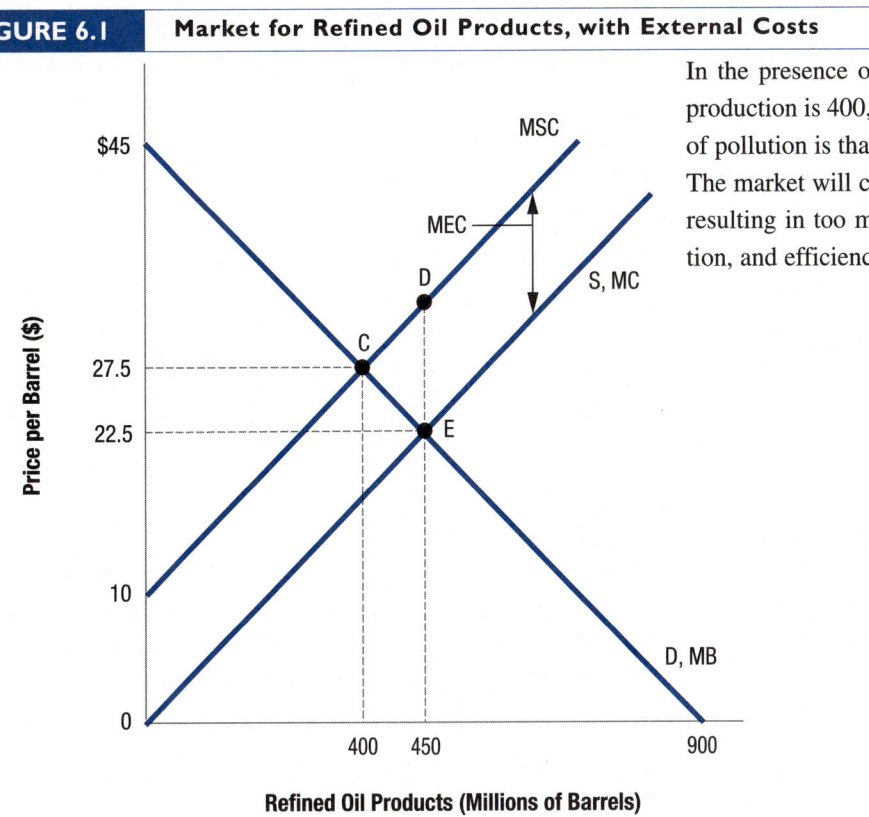

FIGURE 6.1 — Market for Refined Oil Products, with External Costs

In the presence of pollution, the efficient level of production is 400,000 barrels and the efficient level of pollution is that associated with 400,000 barrels. The market will clear, however, at 450,000 barrels, resulting in too much production, too much pollution, and efficiency losses equal to the area CDE.

at $22.50 a barrel. This level of production creates external costs of $4.5 billion—450,000,000 barrels times MEC of $10 per barrel—or the area marked by the end points: O,$10,D, and E. The MECs from the first 400 million barrels are entirely offset by buyers' willingness to pay for both the costs of refining and the MECs associated with refining. This is indicated by the fact that the demand or MB curve exceeds the MSC curve (remember, this curve includes all costs) for all units up to 400 million barrels. For each barrel beyond 400 million, however, MSC exceeds MB, or the social cost per barrel exceeds the benefits per barrel. This means that the market will produce too many barrels of refined oil products—50 million barrels to be exact. Society will lose an amount equal to the area CDE, or $250 million, on these units. Economists call this amount the **efficiency loss from pollution**. To eliminate these losses, the market would have to clear at 400 million barrels, but it will not do so because it is in the interest of both producers and buyers to ignore the costs of the pollutants emitted from oil refineries. (They are external to market transactions, remember.)

It is important to recognize that when both the benefits from economic activity and the costs of pollution are considered, the efficient level of pollution is *not* zero. The level of pollutants associated with 450 million barrels of refined products is too much, but reducing it below the level associated with 400 million barrels would be too little because the social costs saved by doing so would be less than the benefits sacrificed. Social

Efficiency Loss from Pollution – Marginal social cost (MSC) minus marginal benefit (MB), summed over all units produced for which MSC > MB.

INTERNATIONAL PERSPECTIVE

THE TOTAL SOCIAL COST OF THE AUTOMOBILE: POLLUTION AND MUCH MORE

It is widely acknowledged that the privately-owned, gasoline-powered automobile is a major source of air pollution throughout the world. Air pollution costs, however, are just one of several types of external costs attributed to the auto. Others include congestion, noise, accidents, increased vulnerability to recession, and oil-related national security expenditures. All of the world's major oil-consuming nations experience the costs of congestion, noise, accidents, and pollution. All of the major oil-importing countries—such as the United States, Japan, Germany, Italy, France, and the United Kingdom—are susceptible to the costs associated with increased vulnerability to recession. These countries and others devote part of their national security expenditures to ensuring the continued flow of oil from unstable sources of supply.

Anyone who drives in a major urban area of the United States experiences firsthand the congestion that normally occurs during morning and evening rush hours. It has been estimated that these urban drivers annually waste between 1 and 2 billion hours stuck in traffic, and that the delayed delivery of goods and lost employee time amounts to a cost of $100 billion per year. However, such costs are not confined to the United States. In Thailand, Bangkok's workforce loses an average of 44 days in traffic each year, costing the country several percentage points in potential gross domestic product (GDP). It has also been estimated that each driver in central London during peak traffic hours costs all other drivers on the highway about 80 cents per mile in wasted time.[a]

Consider also the economic costs to the oil-importing nations when they suffer an unanticipated oil cutoff. Oil prices suddenly increase, causing recessions. In fact, the largest decline in U.S. real GDP during the post–World War II era, 4.1 percent from 1974 to 1975, was initiated by a reduction in oil exports from the Middle East. The impact of this action reverberated far beyond the United States as total world GDP dipped about 6 percent below its trend value. Such outcomes can be blamed only in part on the world's love affair with the automobile—imported oil is used for many purposes other than transport; however, the world's appetite for gasoline heightens its vulnerability to oil supply disruptions.

The world is also vulnerable to oil supply disruptions. The politically volatile countries of the Persian Gulf produce about one-fourth of the world's oil and sit atop two-thirds of the world's known oil reserves. The U.S.–Iraq war and its aftermath provide vivid evidence of the need for the United States and its allies to spend money to protect their interests in secure oil supplies from this region. The bill for this war—paid partly by the United States and partly by

---

costs saved on each barrel are indicated by the MSC curve, and benefits sacrificed are indicated by the MB curve. Clearly, for units less than 400 million, the amount sacrificed (MB) exceeds the costs saved (MSC).

Pollution is not only inevitable in a market economy, but some pollution is acceptable, as in the case just reviewed. Some pollutants could be so harmful, of course, that the beneficial effects of economic activity are not sufficiently large to warrant producing any of them. This may be the case, for example, of lead used in motor fuels, but it is hard to develop a very long list of pollutants that fall in this category.

■ MARKET FAILURE: IS GOVERNMENT ACTION NECESSARY?

The case just examined is an example of market failure—a situation in which private decisions coordinated through the market produce inefficiency. Many economists believe that government action, such as regulation, is necessary to correct market failures. Other economists question, however, whether gov-

INTERNATIONAL PERSPECTIVE (continued)

its allies—came to more than $50 billion, and it appears that maintaining readiness for future action will cost billions more each year.

The difficulty with these costs is that, because they are external costs, consumers of gasoline and other oil products ignore them. The challenge to policy makers, then, is to find ways to impose these costs on consumers. Economists have suggested a variety of ways to do this. Here we look briefly at three of them: (1) congestion pricing, (2) parking cash-outs, and (3) higher gasoline taxes.

Congestion pricing involves imposing a fee on vehicles that use the central city. Singapore has used a congestion pricing scheme since 1975, and officials are either planning or considering such schemes in Chile, France, Norway, the United Kingdom, the United States, and several other countries.[b]

Solo commuters are a principal cause of the pronounced congestion in central cities. Solo commuting is greatly facilitated when employers provide free parking for their employees. U.S. employers offer free parking because the Internal Revenue Code allows them to deduct any costs of employer-provided parking as a business expense and lets workers deduct the benefits from their taxable income, up to $155 per month. As a result, 95 percent of automobile commuters receive free or subsidized parking. *Parking cash-outs* require employers who provide free parking to offer a travel allowance worth the value of the parking space as an alternative. Employees who choose the less expensive options of car-pooling or public transit can pocket most of the allotted amount. Los Angeles County substituted travel allowances for free parking in 1990 and experienced a 40 percent decrease in the demand for parking.[c] The Internal Revenue Code could be modified to require all employers who currently provide free or subsidized employee parking to offer such a substitution.

Gasoline taxes in the United States average about 40 cents per gallon. They average $1.68 per gallon in Japan, $2.35 in the United Kingdom, $2.66 in Germany, $2.86 in France, and an astounding (to Americans) $3.64 per gallon in Italy. Although American travelers to these countries are puzzled by this practice, its purpose is clear: Officials in these countries have acted aggressively to reduce dependence on imported oil by levying higher gasoline taxes. As a by-product, they have also reduced the air pollution attributable to automobiles. So they have, in effect, charged automobile users more fully for the social costs of the automobile by shifting the costs from those who are not responsible to those who are.

[a]The data in this paragraph come from Marcia D. Lowe, "Reinventing Transport," in Lester D. Brown et al., *State of the World*, 1994 (New York: Norton, 1994), 80–98.
[b]Kenneth A. Small, "Urban Traffic Congestion: A New Approach to the Gordian Knot," *The Brookings Review*, Spring 1993.
[c]Lowe, "Reinventing Transport," 96.

---

ernment regulation is necessary to achieve a cleaner environment. They argue that government need only establish and enforce property rights to the natural environment.

Proponents of the latter view argue that the atmosphere is used excessively for waste disposal because polluters avoid paying a price to use it for this purpose. Normally, a market price for a particular use of a resource can be established only with a clear **property right**—a legally defined and enforceable right to use property in specific ways. A market for alternative uses of the atmosphere has never developed as have markets for other natural resources because the atmosphere is a **common property resource**—a resource that is the property of all. In the absence of the right to use property exclusively, no markets for particular uses of the resource are possible.

Ronald Coase, a winner of the Nobel Prize for Economics, recognized this aspect of the pollution problem and argued that a market in uses of the atmosphere would be established if the right to exclusive use, including the right to transfer that privilege to others, was given to some private party. He demonstrated

Property Right — A legally defined and enforceable right to use property for specific purposes.

Common Property Resource — A resource that is the property of all.

Coase's Theorem — The thesis that the assignment and enforcement of property rights can lead to the efficient level of pollution.

that such a policy would yield the efficient level of pollution regardless of whether the use right was assigned to a polluter or to an environmentalist.[1]

We can illustrate **Coase's theorem**, using the information in Figure 6.1. If producers have the right to use the natural environment for waste disposal, they will choose to produce at 450 million barrels, where S=D or MC=MB. Would they be willing to produce less? Only if the amount that victims of pollution would pay them to reduce production is at least as large as the amount that they would accept. The maximum amount that victims of pollution would be willing to pay oil refiners for reducing pollution is equal to the damages they suffer from pollution, or MSC minus MC. How much compensation would producers require in order to reduce pollution? In order to reduce pollution, they would have to reduce production of refined oil products. If they reduced production below 450 million barrels, they would save costs equal to the MC of each barrel, but they would also sacrifice revenues equal to the amount they could charge for each unit. The maximum amount they could charge is the same as the amount buyers are willing to pay, or the MB on each unit. Thus, they would be willing to reduce pollution only if they received the difference between what they could charge, MB, and what they would save, MC.

Starting at 450 million barrels, the victims of pollution are willing to pay more per barrel to have production reduced (the distance between MSC and MC) than the minimum amount required as compensation by producers (the distance between MB and MC). This is the case for all barrels between 450 million and 400 million. Below 400 million barrels, however, the minimum compensation required for reducing production (MB−MC) exceeds the maximum victims will pay (MSC−MC). In theory, then, if victims could bargain freely with producers, they could pay producers enough to reduce production to the efficient level.

We can also use Figure 6.1 to illustrate the case in which property rights have been bestowed on the victims of pollution. Here we start with a clean environment or zero pollution. Zero pollution means zero production of refined oil products. Now the relevant questions are How much are producers willing to pay victims for the right to produce (and pollute)? How much compensation will victims require from producers? The maximum amount that producers would be willing to pay victims for the right to produce a unit of refined oil products is the difference between MB and MC—the difference between the maximum price they could charge buyers if they increased production by an additional unit and the cost of producing each unit. The minimum amount that victims would accept is MEC—the value of the damages they would suffer from each unit produced. The maximum amount that producers would be willing to pay (MB−MC) exceeds the minimum amount that victims would accept (MSC−MC) for all units up to 400 million. Thus, if producers could bargain freely with victims, they could pay them enough to secure the right to increase production to the efficient level.

If the world worked like this, the government would not need to intervene to eliminate excess pollutants. (They would have to award property rights and enforce them, of course.) It probably works this way only if the number of producers and victims is relatively small; smallness in numbers is required for the bargaining necessary for the affected parties to negotiate a mutually satisfactory payment arrangement. Real-world cases of air pollution most often involve too many affected parties for Coase's solution to work. Thus, some kind of government regulatory activity appears necessary as a means of achieving a cleaner environment.

INFOTRAC College Edition
Keywords: *Ronald Coase, Coase Theorem*
http://www.infotrac-college.com

---

[1] Ronald Coase, "The Problem of Social Cost," *Journal of Law and Economics*, Vol. 3, No. 2 (October 1960), 1–44.

■ AIR POLLUTION REGULATION: THE CLEAN AIR ACT

INFOTRAC
College Edition

Keywords: *Clean Air Act*

http://www.infotrac-college.com

The Environmental Protection Agency (EPA) is the principal regulator of air pollution in the United States. Its basic authority comes from the Clean Air Act of 1963, as amended in 1965, 1970, 1977, and 1990. It is impossible to summarize neatly all the important features of the Clean Air Act; it is too long and too complicated and has been greatly expanded by administrative directives. We will focus instead on the principal regulatory tools or concepts upon which the EPA relies to carry out its regulatory responsibilities.

National Ambient Air Quality Standards (NAAQS)

Ambient Concentrations – Concentrations of pollutants in the atmosphere.

The NAAQS are the upper limits permitted for concentrations in the atmosphere (**ambient concentrations**) of the six common air pollutants described earlier: particulates, sulfur dioxide, carbon monoxide, nitrogen dioxide, ozone, and lead. The limits have both a physical and a time dimension. For example, the standard for ozone is violated when the average hourly concentration is 0.12 parts per million or more for more than one day per year.

The EPA believes that concentrations exceeding the NAAQS pose a significant health risk. The law requires that the NAAQS be set and achieved without consideration of costs. The law also requires that they be applied uniformly across the country.

Emissions Limits

The NAAQS govern concentrations in the atmosphere after pollutants have been released or emitted. The law also fixes limits on the amounts of certain pollutants that may be emitted from various sources. Limits have been placed on emissions of carbon monoxide, nitrogen dioxide and hydrocarbons from automobiles, on emissions of toxic chemicals from industrial and commercial sources, and on emissions of sulfur dioxide and nitrogen oxides from electric generating plants.

Restricted Technology

The Clean Air Act requires not only that certain standards be attained or limits observed; it also places restrictions on the technologies that may be used to achieve them. For example, it requires automobile manufacturers to install catalytic converters with a minimum life of 100,000 miles. Vapor recycling equipment must be installed on new cars, and gasoline stations in areas where NAAQS for ozone are exceeded must install vapor-recovery devices on fuel-dispensing hoses. Stationary sources of pollution are subject to a variety of restrictions on the technologies they may use for pollution control. The resulting patchwork of permissible technologies is a source of great uncertainty to manufacturers, a major administrative burden for the EPA, and a source of excessive costs of air pollution regulation.

New Source Performance Standards

New commercial and industrial facilities—those established after a law is enacted—are often subject to more stringent technology restrictions than old facilities—those established before a law is enacted. The more exacting new source performance standards are a powerful incentive to keep older and more costly plants in operation longer.

Prescribed Fuels

The Clean Air Act also prescribes certain fuel requirements for motor vehicles. Gasoline stations in areas where ambient concentrations of carbon monoxide exceed EPA standards must sell oxygenated gasoline. Officials in areas that fail often to meet ozone standards must develop and implement plans for increasing the percentage of motor vehicles powered by alternative fuels, such as methanol, compressed natural gas, liquid petroleum gas, and electricity.

Offset Requirements

Areas that fail to meet the ozone and carbon monoxide standards can accommodate new sources of pollution, such as new factories, but only if the pollution from new sources is offset by reductions in pollution from existing sources. In fact, the offset must exceed the addition. The ratio of offsets to additions ranges from 1.1 in areas that barely violate the standards to 1.5 in areas with serious air quality problems like Los Angeles.

Emissions Trading

Emissions Reduction Credit — A credit for reducing emissions more than required by regulations.

The offset policy has stimulated development of markets in **emissions reduction credits**. Emissions reduction credits are earned by reducing emissions below the legally required level. For example, suppose that an oil refinery is required to reduce its emissions of sulfur dioxide by 100 tons per year and that it can reduce its emissions by 200 tons at reasonable cost. If it does so, it would receive emissions reduction credits for 100 tons of sulfur dioxide. These credits can be sold to firms seeking offsets for new sources of emissions.

Prevention of Significant Deterioration

To prevent air quality from deteriorating, the Clean Air Act also establishes limits on increases in pollution in areas that did not violate the NAAQS when they were established. In fact, the limits on additional pollution are stricter for areas that started with better air quality.

Monitoring and Compliance

The nature and significance of the air pollution problem varies greatly from place to place. Assuming that state and local authorities have greater knowledge of local conditions than federal officials, Congress has given state pollution control agencies the responsibility for issuing pollution permits, for monitoring sources of pollution, and for ensuring compliance with the standards.

■ Effects of the Clean Air Act on Air Quality

The 1990 Clean Air Act Amendments require the EPA to conduct periodic, scientifically reviewed studies to assess the benefits and costs of the Clean Air Act (CAA). Two such studies have been published so far: *The Benefits and Costs of the Clean Air Act, 1970 to 1990* and *The Benefits and Costs of the Clean Air Act, 1990–2010*. In the first of these studies, the EPA estimated changes in emissions and air quality attributable to the CAA prior to 1990; that is, they isolated the effect of the CAA from other factors that could have produced changes in emissions or air quality. In the second of these studies, the EPA forecasted the additional changes in emissions and air quality that were likely to occur as a result of the

CAA Amendments of 1990, again abstracting from the effects of other factors that might change emissions or air quality.

Table 6.1 summarizes the EPA's estimated and projected percentage reductions in emissions achieved by the end dates of the two time periods.

Emissions of primary particulates were reduced 75 percent in the first 2 decades, due to vigorous efforts to reduce visible emissions from smokestacks. The projections for 1990 to 2010 indicate that most of the easy reductions of particulates have been achieved. Sulfur dioxide emissions are significantly lower in both periods, primarily due to electric generating plants installing stack scrubbers or switching to lower sulfur fuels (low-sulfur coal and natural gas). Nitrogen oxide emissions were reduced during the first time period mostly because of the installation of catalytic converters and other technologies on motor vehicles. Caps on nitrogen oxide emissions from electric generating plants account for most of the reduction expected in this pollutant in 1990 to 2010. The reduction in volatile organic compound (VOC) emissions, 1970 to 1990, was due primarily to the application of motor vehicle emissions control technologies. This is still the primary source of VOC reductions in 1990 to 2010, although there is significant assistance in the future from commercial sources. Most of the reductions in carbon monoxide emissions over the 40-year period are also attributable to motor vehicle emissions control technologies. Lead emissions reductions were due largely to the phase-out of leaded gasoline.

■ THE ECONOMICS OF THE CLEAN AIR ACT: HAVE WE GONE TOO FAR?

This is an impressive record and an encouraging forecast, but the EPA's own data hardly indicate complete control over emissions of the common pollutants (lead excepted). Moreover, despite improvements in air quality since 1970, nearly 40 percent of the total population still lives in counties with air that fails to meet all of the NAAQS; acid rain still poses a problem in some areas of the United States and Canada; and the stratospheric ozone problem is far from solved. Given this view, some would argue that we have not done enough to reduce emissions. Emissions reduction is not a costless endeavor, however; for example, substantial outlays are required for emissions control technologies. Given this view of the issue, some would argue that we have gone too far—that the costs of achieving emissions reductions have been too large.

Economists attempt to resolve the issue by conducting benefit-cost analyses. The two studies by the EPA—*The Benefits and Costs of the Clean Air Act, 1970 to 1990* and *The Benefits and Costs of the Clean Air Act, 1990–2010*—reflect the kind of work that needs to be done.

TABLE 6.1 Estimated and Projected Reductions in Emissions of Criteria Pollutants Attributable to the Provisions of the Clean Air Act (in Percent)

Time Period	Particulates	Sulfur Dioxide	Nitrogen Oxide	Volatile Compounds	Carbon Monoxide	Lead
1970–1990	75	40	30	45	50	99
1990–2010	4	31	39	35	23	

SOURCE: EPA, *The Benefits and Costs of the Clean Air Act, 1970 to 1990* and *The Benefits and Costs of the Clean Air Act, 1990–2010*.

Benefits and Costs of the Clean Air Act, 1970 to 1990

BENEFITS. The lower emissions of pollutants attributable to the CAA from 1970 to 1990 translate into lower ambient concentrations of sulfur dioxide, nitrogen oxides, particulate matter, carbon monoxide, ozone, and lead. These lower concentrations yield a variety of benefits derived from improvements in human health, increased visibility, reduced soiling of items and structures, increased worker productivity, increased agricultural output, and ecological improvements.

Improvements in human health are the most important source by far of the benefits estimated by the EPA. Lower concentrations of pollutants mean fewer (1) cases of premature death, chronic bronchitis and other respiratory illnesses and symptoms, hypertension, strokes, heart disease, and impaired IQs and (2) fewer hospital admissions. Increased visibility, reduced soiling, increased worker productivity, and increased agricultural output are much less important sources, but the EPA was also able to estimate the benefits from these sources. They did not estimate the benefits of any ecological improvements, although this is a potentially significant source of benefits.

The benefits from all of these factors are subject to uncertainty, so the EPA produced a range of estimates. Table 6.2 presents the EPA's mean or central estimates of the benefits produced over the entire 1970 to 1990 period. All estimates were corrected for inflation and for differences in time of occurrence (by discounting benefits; see Chapter 9 for a fuller explanation of this procedure).

COSTS. Consumers, businesses, and governments all incurred higher costs to comply with the Clean Air Act. The costs of providing goods and services (and their prices) were higher due to requirements to install, operate, and maintain pollution control equipment, to report regulatory compliance, and to invest in research and development of new control technologies. Governments incurred costs of designing and implementing regulations and monitoring regulatory compliance. The EPA estimated total compliance costs for the 20-year period—adjusted for inflation and time of occurrence—at approximately $523 billion.

This is not the end of the cost story, however. Some of the expenditures on environmental compliance displaced productive investments. These decreases in investment reduced the nation's capital stock and labor productivity and eventually reduced the rate at which the economy grew. Thus, compliance costs

TABLE 6.2 Total Estimated Benefits from the Clean Air Act, 1970 to 1990

Source of Benefit	Total Value, 1970 to 1990 (Billions of Dollars)
Fewer premature deaths	$17,971
Fewer cases of chronic bronchitis and other respiratory problems, and decreased productivity	3,495
Reduced losses in IQ points	399
Fewer cases of hypertension	98
Fewer hospital admissions	57
Reduced soiling damage	74
Increased visibility	54
Increased agricultural production	23

SOURCE: EPA, *The Benefits and Costs of the Clean Air Act, 1970 to 1990*, ES-7.

should be supplemented with an estimate of the value of GDP foregone because of the lower rate of growth attributable to environmental compliance.

The EPA did not produce estimates of GDP foregone in its study of the 1970 to 1990 period, but a widely-cited study by Jorgenson and Wilcoxen[2] concludes that the growth rate of real GDP was reduced by about 0.2 percentage points annually from 1974 to 1985 as a result of the costs of all environmental rules. This appears to be a small effect—and it is. Our calculations indicate that if real GDP had grown at a rate that was 0.2 percentage points higher than the actual rate each year between 1970 and 1990, the nation would have produced only an additional $327 billion of goods and services (corrected for time of occurrence) over the entire time period.

When environmental regulation increases compliance costs, it also increases the costs and prices of goods and services produced by affected firms. This increase in prices lowers the buying power of workers' wages, or what is the same thing, the reward from working. They will react by decreasing hours worked, imposing an additional cost on society that the EPA has not accounted for. Although there is some evidence that this cost, by itself, is substantial, currently available empirical estimates of this cost are inconclusive.

Given Jorgenson's and Wilcoxen's estimate, however, total costs of the CAA for the 1970 to 1990 time period are $523 billion, plus some portion of the $327 billion they estimate. (Remember, Jorgenson's and Wilcoxen's results pertain to more than air pollutants alone.) This is certainly a large number, but it is dwarfed by the $22.2 trillion in total benefits (the sum of the benefits in Table 6.2). The EPA would appear to have a solid basis for arguing that, as of 1990, the regulations imposed by the Clean Air Act had a net beneficial impact on the economy.

Benefits and Costs of The Clean Air Act, 1990 to 2010

The second issue that the EPA addresses in its benefit-cost analyses is whether the 1990 amendments to the CAA are likely to yield benefits greater than costs over the period 1990 to 2010. Because the amendments are additional regulations, they would be expected to have a smaller impact on both benefits and costs than the regulations cumulated up to 1990. This expectation is confirmed by the estimates reported in Table 6.3.

Criteria Pollutants – Pollutants that are subject to the National Ambient Air Quality Standards (NAAQS).

Table 6.3 reflects the EPA's separation of the 1990 amendments into two types: (1) changes in the regulations aimed at reducing criteria pollutants and (2) changes in the regulations designed to reduce stratospheric ozone. The **criteria pollutants** affected by the 1990 amendments are particulates, sulfur

TABLE 6.3 Benefits and Costs of the 1990 Amendments to the Clean Air Act, 1990–2010

Program	Total Benefits	Compliance Costs	Real GDP Foregone	Total Costs
Criteria pollutants reduction	$680 B	$170 B	$106 B	$276 B
Stratospheric ozone reduction	$500 B	$27 B	$17 B	$44 B
	$1,180 B	$197 B	$123 B	$320 B

SOURCE: All figures except real GDP foregone are calculations based on data provided in EPA, *The Benefits and Costs of the Clean Air Act, 1990–2010*. Real GDP foregone estimates are based on our assumption that the ratio of real GDP foregone to compliance costs is the same in 1990–2010 as in 1970-1990.

[2]Dale W. Jorgenson and Peter Wilcoxen, "Environmental Regulation and U.S. Economic Growth" *RAND Journal of Economics*, Vol. 21, No. 2, (Summer 1990), pp. 314–340.

dioxide, nitrogen oxide, carbon monoxide, and ozone in urban air sheds. The 1990 amendments aim to reduce stratospheric ozone by restricting chlorofluorocarbons and other volatile organic compounds.

Although the gap between benefits and costs is not nearly as large as it is for the 1970 to 1990 period, projected benefits still exceed projected costs by nearly 4 to 1, even after adding an estimate for GDP foregone from productive investment displaced by compliance costs.

Conventional economics shows that environmental regulation does not cause the widespread negative economic effects that are feared by some critics. These results do *not* necessarily mean, however, that we have the efficient level of environmental regulation.

We have efficiency in environmental regulation when *total benefits from regulation exceed total costs* and when the *marginal benefits from regulation equal the marginal costs*. The EPA's estimates clearly indicate that the total benefits from regulation exceed the total costs, but, by themselves, they cannot tell us if we have too little or too much regulation. The fact that benefits exceed costs in the aggregate also does not rule out the possibility that there may be ways to reduce the costs of environmental regulation. Annual costs of the CAA are probably in the neighborhood of $60 billion a year—certainly a worthy target for cost reduction.

INFOTRAC
College Edition

Key words: *environmental cost-benefit analysis*

http://www.infotrac-college.com

■ COST-REDUCING MEASURES

Economists have identified several ways to reduce the costs of environmental regulation without reducing environmental quality. The two that have received the most attention are (1) emissions taxes and (2) marketable emissions permits.

Emissions Taxes

One of economists' favorite solutions to pollution is an excise tax on emissions of pollutants, commonly called a *Pigovian tax* after its originator, the late British economist A. C. Pigou. An **emissions tax** regulates the level of pollution by establishing a price that emitters must pay per unit of emissions.

Emissions Tax — A tax charged polluters for each unit of pollutants emitted.

A numerical example will show how an emissions tax works and how it can lower the costs of achieving a cleaner environment. Suppose that four coal-fired electric generating plants, each owned by a different firm, are initially unregulated. Each plant emits 4 tons of sulfur dioxide per day. Each of the plants could eliminate its sulfur dioxide emissions, but at widely varying costs per ton, as indicated in Table 6.4. The variation in cost per ton reflects factors such as differences in age of plant and access to low-sulfur coal.

Suppose now that the regulators have determined that if total emissions are greater than 8 tons, there will be unacceptable harm to humans, plants, structure, and animals. To achieve this goal, they simply limit each plant to 2 tons and monitor emissions to make sure that they do not exceed 2 tons. In order to comply with the limit, each plant is forced to reduce pollutants by 2 tons. The cost to them of doing this is indicated in Table 6.4 in the columns labeled MAC. MAC stands for **marginal abatement cost**. In the language of environmental economists, a ton that is abated is not emitted. Thus, MAC is the cost of *not* emitting, or eliminating, each successive ton of pollutants. With the 2-ton limit enforced, each plant abates 2 tons. This costs plant A $300, plant B $600, plant C $900, and plant D $1,200, as indicated in row 6 of Table 6.4. Total cost is the sum of these costs, or $3,000 per day.

Marginal Abatement Cost — The cost of abating or eliminating an additional unit of pollutants.

TABLE 6.4   Effects of Imposition of a Pollution Tax of $500 per Ton of Pollutants

	MAC Plant A	MAC Plant B	MAC Plant C	MAC Plant D	Total Cost
First ton abated (MAC_1)	$100	$200	$300	$400	
Second ton abated (MAC_2)	$200	$400	$600	$800	
Third ton abated (MAC_3)	$300	$800	$900	$1,200	
Fourth ton abated (MAC_4)	$400	$1,200	$1,200	$1,600	
Tons abated with uniform emissions limit of 2 tons	2	2	2	2	
Total cost of abatement with uniform emissions limit of 2 tons	$300	$600	$900	$1,200	$3,000
Tons abated with tax of $500 per ton emitted	4	2	1	1	
Total cost of abatement with tax of $500 per ton emitted	$1,000	$600	$300	$400	$2,300
Taxes remitted to government	$0	$1,000	$1,500	$1,500	$4,500

At this point, the EPA's chief economist comes forward and suggests a way to reduce total cost. He argues that the government can achieve the same level of abatement (8 tons), but at lower total cost, if it lets the plants emit what they want, but at the cost of a tax of $500 per ton for each ton that they emit. Each plant will now abate a ton only if the MAC of doing so is less than the tax. If the MAC exceeds the tax, they will not abate, but emit and pay the tax. Applying this decision rule to the data in Table 6.4, we find that the responsibility for abatement shifts to the plants with the lowest MAC; plant A abates 2 more tons and plants C and D abate 1 fewer ton each. Total cost falls from $3,000 per day to $2,300 per day as a consequence. Although total costs fall, total outlays by the 4 plants for pollution control increase from $3,000 to $6,800—$2,300 in abatement costs and $4,500 in pollution taxes. Moreover, the costs of pollution control increase for each plant. Pollution taxes are actually a transfer from the 4 plants to taxpayers in general. Thus, they are not part of the opportunity cost of pollution control and society is better off by $700 when abatement costs fall from $3,000 to $2,300. The fact that pollution taxes would hit polluters in the pocketbook, however, generates considerable opposition to their adoption.

INFOTRAC
College Edition

Keywords: *Pigovian taxes, pollution taxes*
http://www.infotrac-college.com

Marketable Pollution Permits

Suppose that the plant owners have a lot of political influence and that they are successful in stifling passage of legislation that authorizes the $500 pollution tax. Another economist steps forward with another policy that she claims will accomplish the same things as the pollution tax, but at no cost to any of the plants. She suggests that each plant simply be issued 2 permits, each of which allows a plant to emit 1 ton of pollutants, but that the owners of the permits be allowed to sell them to others. She suggests, that is, the use of **marketable pollution permits**. Now the permit owners have to decide whether to hold or sell. If they hold a permit, they save on abatement costs. If they sell a permit, they assume additional abatement costs. What will they do? Their choices are outlined in Table 6.5.

Marketable Pollution Permit – A permit that can be bought and sold that allows a polluter to emit a specified quantity of a pollutant or pollutants.

When the permits are issued, and before any exchange of permits takes place, each plant emits 2 tons of pollutants and abates 2 tons. Total cost at this point is the same as it was in the pollution tax case; namely, $3,000 per day (line 6). With the possibility of exchange, or permit transferability, the owners of each

TABLE 6.5 Effects of Transferable Permits

	MAC Firm A	MAC Firm B	MAC Firm C	MAC Firm D	Total Cost
First ton abated (MAC_1)	$100	$200	$300	$400	
Second ton abated (MAC_2)	$200	$400	$600	$800	
Third ton abated (MAC_3)	$300	$800	$900	$1,200	
Fourth ton abated (MAC_4)	$400	$1,200	$1,200	$1,600	
Tons abated with 2 nontransferable permits	2	2	2	2	
Total cost of abatement with 2 nontransferable permits	$300	$600	$900	$1,200	$3,000
Maximum amount would pay for first permit	$200 ($MAC_2$)	$400 ($MAC_2$)	$600 ($MAC_2$)	**$800** ($MAC_2$)	
Minimum amount would accept for first permit (MAC_3)	**$300** ($MAC_3$)	$800 ($MAC_3$)	$900 ($MAC_3$)	$1,200 ($MAC_3$)	
Maximum amount would pay for next permit	$300 ($MAC_3$)	$400 ($MAC_2$)	**$600** ($MAC_2$)	$400 ($MAC_1$)	
Minimum amount would accept for next permit	**$400** ($MAC_4$)	$800 ($MAC_3$)	$900 ($MAC_2$)	$800 ($MAC_1$)	
Permits sold	2	0	0	0	
Permits bought	0	0	1	1	
Tons abated with transferable permits	4	2	1	1	
Total cost of abatement with transferable permits	$1,000	$600	$300	$400	$2,300

plant must decide how much they are willing to pay for a permit, if they contemplate buying, and how much they are willing to accept for a permit, if they contemplate selling. There will be an exchange or transfer of permits if someone is willing to pay more than someone else is willing to accept.

Let's work through the possibilities one permit at a time. Given the starting point of 2 tons abated, the maximum amount that all plants would be willing to pay for another permit (the first one traded) is what it would cost them to abate the ton themselves. That is, they would pay no more to emit the ton (buy a permit) than the MAC of that ton—i.e., the MAC of the second ton abated. The minimum amount that they would accept is the MAC to them of the third ton; this is what it would cost them for abatement if they sold a permit. Under these conditions, plant A will sell a permit to plant D at some price between $300 and $800. Whatever they may agree to in this range will make both parties better off if the exchange is made. Once the exchange has been made, plants A and D have to make a new calculation. Plant A is now abating 3 tons, and plant D is now abating 1 ton. Plant A is now willing to pay no more for another permit than the MAC, to them, of the third ton. Plant D is now willing to pay no more than the MAC, to them, of the first ton. Plants B and C are still willing to pay the MAC, to them, of the second ton. Plant A is willing to accept no less for a permit than the MAC of the fourth ton; plants B and C are still willing to accept no less than the MAC of the third ton; and plant D is willing to accept no less than the MAC of the second ton. Under these conditions, Plant A will sell another permit, this time to plant C.

The possibilities for exchange have now been exhausted. Plant A ends up abating 4 tons; plant B, 2 tons; plant C, 1 ton; and plant D, 1 ton. This is the same outcome as would be achieved with a pollution tax of $500 per ton, and the total cost is also the same as in that case. All parties, except the government, are as well off, or better off, than they were when no exchange of permits took place.

Given their apparently equivalent ability to reduce total cost without imposing taxes, regulators in this country have opted for transferable permits over pollution taxes. In a fashion similar to our example, the EPA has issued emissions permits for sulfur dioxide to electric generating plants in two phases of a program to reduce acid rain. These permits allow electric generating plants in the aggregate to emit only one-half of the sulfur dioxide that they were emitting before the program was initiated. The EPA estimates that the exchange of sulfur dioxide permits for money will save $1 billion in costs (out of $5 billion) of complying with the acid rain provisions of the Clean Air Act. Economists have hinted, also, at large potential savings from using transferable permits for emissions of carbon dioxide and toxic chemicals.

Transactions Costs – The costs of finding willing buyers and sellers and negotiating a mutually acceptable price.

The transferable permit is an effective regulatory tool, but it is not perfect. Its Achilles heel is **transactions costs**—the costs of finding willing buyers and sellers and negotiating mutually acceptable prices for emissions permits. Both buyers and sellers face transactions costs, and they can be large enough to wipe out the margin between what buyers are willing to pay and sellers are willing to accept. Another problem with transferable permits is the government's practice of allocating them free of charge. This practice not only gives the recipients a valuable piece of property for nothing, but the government foregoes the opportunity to raise revenues—revenues that could be used to reduce other taxes.

INFOTRAC
College Edition

Keywords: *tradeable emissions permits, emissions permits*

http://www.infotrac-college.com

Pollution taxes are not defect-free, either. The primary difficulty they pose is the determination of the correct tax; i.e., the tax that just induces producers to emit pollutants at the level desired by regulatory authorities. In case you did not notice it, we were able to specify a tax in the previous example that was just right, but we had all of the information that we needed to do this—a luxury that the real world rarely permits. Taxes do provide government with money that can be used to reduce other taxes, but they have no advantage over transferable permits in this regard if the permits are auctioned off instead of awarded free of charge.

■ LIMITING GLOBAL WARMING: EMISSIONS PERMITS IN AN INTERNATIONAL CONTEXT

Increasing concerns about the prospects for global warming, and its possible consequences, led to a United Nations conference on the problem in Kyoto, Japan, in late 1997. Delegates from the industrialized countries agreed to reduce carbon dioxide emissions in their countries, although the United States has yet to sign the agreement. Given expected growth in the use of fossil fuels, the Kyoto Accord would require a 15 to 25 percent reduction in projected 2010 emissions. More than 130 of the world's less-developed countries—including Brazil, China, India, and Mexico—were exempted from the agreement, largely on the grounds that they could not afford to reduce carbon dioxide emissions.

The Kyoto protocol would be expensive for the United States. In fact, some estimates indicate that GDP in 2010 could be as much as 5 percent lower as a result of the changes required in the economy to achieve the Kyoto target. As should be clear from the previous analysis, however, U.S. costs can be minimized by using emissions permits to allocate the responsibility for emissions reductions across U.S. emitters. The cost of the protocol can be further reduced by using emissions permits to allocate the responsibility for emissions reductions across countries.

Table 6.6 illustrates the value of trading permits between countries. Currently, eliminating carbon dioxide emissions probably costs more in developed countries than it does in developing countries because the developed countries must sacrifice higher-valued goods and services to achieve lower emissions than will the developing countries. The data in Table 6.6 reflect this assumption.

In the absence of an international agreement, suppose that the levels of economic activity were such that 9 tons of emissions were produced—6 by the developed country and 3 by the developing country. Next, suppose that an international agreement is crafted with an emissions target of 6 tons. A Kyoto-like protocol would require the developed country to reduce emissions from 6 tons to 3 tons and leave emissions at 3 tons in the developing country. The cost of this protocol is the cost in the developed country of reducing emissions by 3 tons, or $1,800 ($300 for the first ton, $600 for the second, and $900 for the third).

Suppose, instead, that the international agreement allowed six marketable pollution permits for 1 ton each, with three permits going to the developed country and three permits going to the developing country. In this instance, the developed country would have an incentive to buy permits from the developing country and the developing country would have an incentive to sell. The developed country would be willing to pay up to $900 for the first marketable permit, because it would have to pay this cost anyway to abate pollution without the permit. The developing country would be willing to sell a permit for no less than $100 because it would have to pay this cost to reduce emissions by 1 ton if it sold a permit. The price paid would be somewhere between $100 and $900. A similar argument can be made for the developed country purchasing a second permit from the developing country, with a sales price somewhere between $200 and $600. They would not trade a third permit because the maximum price the buyer is willing to pay ($300) equals the minimum price the seller is willing to accept ($300). After the two permits change hands, however, the costs of reducing emissions falls from $1,800 to $600. The sale of the permits also transfers money from the developed countries to the developing countries, with the amount transferred depending on the sales prices that are established for the two permits.

TABLE 6.6 — Costs per Ton of Eliminating Carbon Dioxide Emissions

The developed and developing countries differ in terms of their costs of eliminating carbon dioxide. This provides an opportunity for the developed countries to purchase emissions permits from the developing countries.

	Cost per Ton of Eliminating Emissions	
Tons per Day	Developing Country	Developed Country
First	$100	$ 300
Second	200	600
Third	300	900
Fourth	400	1,200
Fifth	—	1,500
Sixth	—	1,800

Insights

Carbon Taxes

As noted in the text, the Kyoto protocol is designed to reduce carbon dioxide emissions. One way to accomplish this is to levy a carbon tax—a tax on different fuels based on the amount of carbon they contain.

A carbon tax is advocated as a cost-effective means of dealing with the problem of global warming. Such a tax would directly raise the price of fossil fuels—especially oil, natural gas, and coal—and the products derived directly from them, such as gasoline and electricity. This increase would encourage energy conservation and the use of relatively cleaner energy sources, such as solar and wind energy. The net result would be less carbon dioxide emitted to the atmosphere.

Economists have estimated the carbon taxes required to reduce carbon dioxide emissions to various target levels. Generally, they fall in the $100 to $400 per ton range. Manne and Richels estimate, for example, that a $250 tax per ton of carbon will be required to reduce long-run U.S. carbon emissions by 20 percent.[a]

The Congressional Budget Office calculates that a tax of $100 per ton of carbon amounts to $60 per ton of coal, $1.63 per thousand cubic feet of natural gas, $13 per barrel of oil, and 30 cents per gallon of gasoline.[b]

Carbon taxes in the $100 to $400 range would raise enormous amounts of revenue. A tax of $100 per ton, for example, would raise about $200 billion per year in the United States—about 2 percent of gross domestic product. Governments could choose to levy a carbon tax but offset the revenues raised by lowering other taxes, such as personal or corporate income taxes. Although this would appear to simply offset the effects of one tax with effects from another, it is possible that a revenue-neutral carbon tax would have net beneficial effects. Not only would the carbon tax reduce the distortion created by people's failure to consider the external costs associated with fossil fuel use, but reducing income taxes would reduce the adverse effects these taxes have on incentives to work and invest. Unfortunately, imposition of the carbon tax, itself, would also distort the work decision, so the net effect of these tax interactions is uncertain.

Carbon taxes also appeal to government officials who want to reduce the nation's trade deficit. As the carbon tax raises the price of oil, American consumers and producers would reduce the quantity they buy, from both domestic and foreign producers.

In spite of uncertainty regarding tax interactions, there is a lot of support for a carbon tax. The lineup of forces favoring a carbon tax, however, would not necessarily ensure passage of authorizing legislation. Forces opposing the tax are bound to be powerful, as it would have an adverse impact on the coal, oil, gas, and automobile industries. Higher energy prices could also trigger falling GDP and rising unemployment. Consumer groups could join the opposition because at least part of the tax would be passed on to them in the form of higher prices. We probably will witness a spirited and protracted debate if the carbon tax rises to the top of the policy agenda.

---

[a]Alan S. Manne and Richard G. Richels, "CO_2 Emissions Limits: An Economic Cost Analysis for the USA," *The Energy Journal* 11, No. 2 (1990), 51–74.

[b]Congressional Budget Office, *Carbon Charges as a Response to Global Warming: The Effects of Taxing Fossil Fuels* (Washington, DC: Congressional Budget Office, 1990), iv.

Summary

The five important air pollution problems are (1) poor air quality in urban areas, (2) acid rain, (3) global warming, (4) ozone depletion, and (5) hazardous air pollutants.

Air pollution is a source of concern primarily because of its harmful effects on human health. It also damages plants, animals, and property, and it impairs visibility.

Air pollution is an inevitable by-product of economic activity; it can be eliminated only at great cost in terms of goods and services foregone. It should be reduced, from an economic perspective, but only so long as the reduction in marginal external costs is greater than or equal to the reduction in marginal benefits. Alternatively, pollution is acceptable as long as the marginal benefit from an activity that produces pollution is greater than or equal to the marginal social cost—which includes the cost attributable to pollution—of that activity.

Private sector decision makers expand economic activities to the point where marginal social cost exceeds marginal benefit because they ignore the marginal external cost of pollution. This behavior produces excess pollution.

The presence of excess pollution is evidence of market failure. Market failure suggests the need for government regulation of economic activity. The Coase Theorem raises the possibility that government regulation is unnecessary; i.e., that government should confine itself to establishing and enforcing property rights to the environment. The conditions under which this prescription would suffice do not prevail in the real world, however.

Government has played an active role in establishing and enforcing regulations that constrain economic activities and choices that affect air quality, principally through the authority established by the Clean Air Act. The Clean Air Act establishes ambient air quality standards, emissions limits, restrictions on pollution abatement technology, constraints on motor fuel sales in certain areas, procedures for the trading of emissions credits and pollution permits, and an extensive federal–state partnership for implementing the act.

There is evidence that the Clean Air Act improved air quality prior to 1990 and that it will produce further improvements in air quality from 1990 to 2020. There is also evidence that the improvements achieved prior to 1990 produced benefits greatly in excess of costs and that the 1990 amendments to the CAA will produce benefits greater than costs, although by a much smaller margin. This evidence does not prove, however, that we have the right amount of environmental regulation.

Economists have suggested two principal approaches to reducing the costs of environmental regulation: (1) emissions taxes and (2) marketable pollution permits. If information were free, both approaches would reduce the costs of pollution abatement by the same amount.

Key Terms

Acid rain
Greenhouse gas
External costs
Marginal external costs (MEC)
Marginal social costs (MSC)
Efficiency loss from pollution

Property right
Common property resource
Coase's Theorem
Ambient concentrations
Emissions reduction credit
Criteria pollutants

Emissions tax
Marginal abatement cost
Marketable pollution permit
Transaction costs

Review Questions

1. According to this chapter, what are the five most important air pollution problems? Briefly discuss them.
2. Explain and distinguish between the following concepts. Use specific examples, if needed.
   a. marginal cost
   b. marginal external cost
   c. marginal social cost
3. "Generally, we would not expect the efficient level of pollution to be zero." Using graphical analysis, explain why this statement is true.
4. Suppose that a market for refined oil products is described by the following data:

Price per Gallon	Quantity Demanded (Gallons)	Quantity Supplied (Gallons)
$2.00	0	20,000
$1.80	2,000	18,000
$1.60	4,000	16,000
$1.40	6,000	14,000
$1.20	8,000	12,000
$1.00	10,000	10,000
$0.80	12,000	8,000
$0.60	14,000	6,000
$0.40	16,000	4,000
$0.20	18,000	2,000
$0.00	20,000	0

Suppose, also, that there are external costs of $1.00 per gallon associated with each gallon produced. Illustrate and determine the following:
   a. the equilibrium quantity of refined oil products
   b. the efficient quantity of refined oil products
   c. total costs of pollution
   d. efficiency losses from pollution

5. Using the diagram you have created for your answer to question 4, identify
   a. the quantity that would be produced if oil refiners (producers) were given property rights to the environment
   b. the quantity that would be produced if victims of pollution (victims) were given property rights to the environment
   c. the maximum amount that victims would pay producers to reduce production (and pollution) and the minimum amount that producers would accept
   d. the maximum amount that producers would pay victims to increase production and the minimum amount that victims would accept

6. What are the principal features of the Clean Air Act?
7. Has the Clean Air Act improved air quality? Explain.
8. Has the U.S. gone "too far" in reducing air pollution? Explain, citing relevant evidence.
9. Briefly explain why an emissions (Pigovian) tax reduces the cost of achieving cleaner air, using the example of the four plants developed in the chapter.
10. Briefly explain why marketable emissions permits reduce the cost of achieving cleaner air, using the example of the four plants developed in the chapter.

Economic Issues on the Internet

- Cleaning the Air—http://www.cato.org/pubs/regulation/reg19n4c.html
  Authors Robert Crandall, Fredrick Rueter, and William Steger criticize the EPA's cost-benefit analysis of air quality regulation on the grounds that it is based on unreliable data on emissions in their article, "Cleaning the Air: EPA's Self-Assessment of Clean-Air Policy." They also note that it focuses entirely on the total benefits and the total costs of pollution abatement, whereas it is necessary to measure the marginal benefits and costs of pollution abatement to determine whether the regulations are specified at an appropriate level. They also suggest that the EPA overstated the health benefits of improved air quality and understated the costs of complying with EPA regulations.

- Council on Environmental Quality—**http://www.whitehouse.gov/ceq**
  The CEQ produces annual reports that provide informative discussions of the nation's pollution problems and efforts to achieve a cleaner environment.

- The Economics of Climate Change—**http://www.senate.gov/~epw/105th/jorg0710.htm**
  In this 1997 testimony before the Senate Committee on Environment and Public Works, Dale Jorgenson, an economist at Harvard, argues that an international agreement on carbon dioxide emissions is desirable even though the expected benefit from this policy is relatively small. He proposes use of a carbon tax to reduce carbon dioxide emissions in the United States.

- Environmental Protection Agency—**http://www.epa.gov**
  The EPA Web site provides access to a wealth of information on environmental regulations and to the results of research related to these regulations.

- Global Change—**http://www.globalchange.org**
  This Internet site is devoted to the discussion of global warming and ozone depletion. It contains an astonishing variety of links to resources on these issues.

- The Kyoto Protocol—**http://www.epinet.org**
  Authors Dean Baker and James Barrett suggest that the introduction of international emissions permit trading would provide an improvement over the existing Kyoto protocol in their article "Cleaning Up the Kyoto Protocol." May 21, 1999. EPI Issue Brief #131. Under their plan, developing countries could finance badly-needed capital investment by selling emissions permits to developed economies. Developed economies would also gain by being able to sell clean technologies to developing economies.

- Resources for the Future—**http://www.rff.org**
  This private think tank provides state-of-the-art studies of research on natural resources and the environment.

Chapter 7

Medical Care: Costs Out of Control?

Outline:

The Rising Cost of Medical Care
Why Health Expenditures Have Increased Relative to GDP
   The Cost Disease of the Services Sector
   Population Aging
   Income Elasticity of Demand for Health Care
   Increases in Insurance Coverage
   Technological Change

Is Technological Change in Medical Care Worth It?
Does the Medical System Provide the Right Amount of Medical Care?
   Third-Party Payments
   Physician-Induced Demand
   Defensive Medicine
   Federal Tax Exemption for Health Insurance

Approaches to Reducing Wasteful Expenditures
   Managed Care
   Eliminating the Federal Tax Exemption for Health Insurance
   Health Care Vouchers

Problems of the medical care system are among the most difficult on the public policy agenda. Public complaints about the system are numerous. In spite of the world's highest expenditures for medical care, about 15 percent of the population is without health insurance—the essential ticket for accessing the system. Many who are insured are at risk of losing insurance coverage if they change jobs, or at risk of higher insurance costs if they contract an expensive disease. The dominant concerns about the U.S. medical care system, however, are that it costs so much money and that future medical care costs promise to be even higher.

In 1950, Americans spent 4.4 percent of national output for health care. In 2001, national health expenditures absorbed 14 percent of national output—close to 1 in every 7 dollars. Government analysts project expenditures equal to 17 percent of national output by 2011. Growing alarm over this trend has spawned a host of proposals in Congress for health care reform. Our objective in this chapter is to examine the economic basis for this reform effort.

■ THE RISING COST OF MEDICAL CARE

Table 7.1 illustrates how national health expenditures (NHE) grew from 1980 to 2000, and how the actuaries at the Centers for Medicare and Medicaid Services (CMS) project that they will grow from 2001 to 2011. NHE grew at an annual average rate of 11 percent between 1980 and 1990, while gross domestic product (GDP) grew at only 7.6 percent per year. As a result, NHE increased from 8.8 percent of GDP to 12 percent. The growth in NHE continued to outpace the growth in GDP until 1993—in fact, by enough that NHE as a percent of GDP was higher in 1995 than in 1990. GDP grew faster than NHE from 1993 to 1998, and NHE as a share of GDP fell from 13.4 to 13.1 percent. The system reverted to its earlier form in 1999 and 2000, however, causing analysts to predict a continuation of the historical trend for the next decade. NHE and GDP are projected to grow at annual rates of 7.3 percent and 4.8 percent, respectively. As a consequence, NHE are expected to be 17 percent of GDP by 2011.

For the period as a whole, the ratio of NHE to GDP grows at an annual average rate of 2.1 percent. If this trend were to continue beyond 2011, health care would account for 1 of every 3 dollars spent in the U.S. economy by 2040. Continuation of this trend may not be inevitable, but it is easy to see why reasonable people can be alarmed about where we might be headed.

INFOTRAC College Edition

Keywords: *health expenditures, medical costs*

http://www.infotrac-college.com

■ WHY HEALTH EXPENDITURES HAVE INCREASED RELATIVE TO GDP

National health expenditures equal the amount spent for all health care (HC) goods and services. GDP equals the amount spent for all goods and services (AGS). The amount spent, or expenditure, for a good or service is the product of the price per unit (P) and the number of units, or quantity (Q), purchased. Thus,

TABLE 7.1   National Health Expenditures, Selected Years, 1980–2011

Year	National Health Expenditures ($ Billion)	Gross Domestic Product	Expenditures as Percent of Gross Domestic Product	Expenditures per Capita (Dollars)
1980	245.8	2795.6	8.8	1067
1990	696.0	5803.3	12.0	2738
1995	990.3	7400.4	13.4	3698
2000	1299.5	9872.9	13.2	4637
2001	1423.8	10201.5	14.0	5039
2005	1902.2	12227.5	15.6	6519
2011	2815.8	16589.8	17.0	9216

SOURCE: Centers for Medicare and Medicaid, Office of the Actuary, January 2002.

(7.1) $$NHE = PHC \times QHC$$

where PHC is the average price of health care and QHC is the average quantity of health care, and

(7.2) $$GDP = PAGS \times QAGS$$

where PAGS and QAGS are the average price and quantity of all goods and services, respectively.

It follows that

(7.3) $$NHE/GDP = (PHC \times QHC) / (PAGS \times QAGS)$$

Equation 7.3 implies that NHE/GDP will increase if PHC increases relative to PAGS; that is, if the average price of medical care increases relative to the average price of all other goods and services. NHE/GDP will also increase if QHC increases relative to QAGS, if the average quantity of medical care increases relative to the average quantity of all goods and services.

The Cost Disease of the Services Sector

There is a good reason to expect that PHC will increase faster than PAGS. The health care sector is part of the services sector of the economy. The services sector is widely believed to suffer from Baumol's **Cost Disease of the Services Sector**.[1]

Cost Disease of the Services Sector – A theory developed by William Baumol that explains why costs in the services sector of the economy will rise faster than costs in the rest of the economy.

Baumol divides the economy into two sectors: (1) the technologically-progressive, capital-intensive sector that exhibits rapid growth in output per labor hour or productivity and (2) the labor-intensive sector that exhibits slow growth in labor productivity. Wages will grow rapidly in the capital-intensive sector as workers are rewarded for productivity increases. Wages will follow suit in the labor-intensive sector as employers find that they have to match what workers can earn in the capital-intensive sector in order to recruit new employees and retain existing workers.

Wage competition between the two sectors leads to costs that grow faster in the labor-intensive sector. To see why, consider this equation:

(7.4) $$\text{LABOR COST PER UNIT OF OUTPUT} = \text{LABOR HOURS PER UNIT OF OUTPUT} \times \text{WAGE PER HOUR}$$

or, the same thing:

(7.5) $$\text{LABOR COST PER UNIT OF OUTPUT} = \text{LABOR PRODUCTIVITY} \times \text{WAGE PER HOUR}$$

There is a direct relationship in equation 7.5 between the wage per hour and labor cost per unit of output; that is, increases in the hourly wage increase labor costs per unit of output. There is an inverse relationship in equation 7.5, however, between labor productivity and labor cost per unit of output; that is, an increase in labor productivity *reduces* labor cost per unit of output. This happens because an increase in labor productivity is the same thing as a *reduction* in labor hours per unit of output.

---

[1] William J. Baumol, "Health Care, Education, and the Cost Disease: A Looming Crisis for Public Choice," *Public Choice*, Volume 77; 1993, 17-28; also William J. Baumol, "Macroeconomics of Unbalanced Growth: The Anatomy of Urban Crisis," *American Economic Review*, Volume 62, 1967, 415–426.

It follows that, if wages are rising at roughly the same rate in both sectors of the economy but labor productivity is increasing faster in the capital-intensive sector, labor costs will rise more slowly (faster) in the capital-intensive (labor-intensive) sector. Given that labor costs are by far the most important component of costs in both sectors, total costs per unit will rise faster in the labor-intensive sector. In a demand-supply context, cost increases shift the supply curve up (or to the left) relative to the demand curve, resulting in increases in prices. Thus, the slower growth in productivity in the labor-intensive sector eventually shows up in the form of faster increases in prices in this sector.

Readily available data indicate that the price of medical care has been increasing relative to prices in general, as the "cost disease" theory suggests. Thus, the increase in the relative price of medical care can be expected to explain some of the increase that has occurred in NHE. To determine how much that might be, it is necessary to separate the influence of this factor from all of the other factors that have increased NHE. This has been done by the Harvard economist David Cutler. He finds that the increase in the relative price of medical care explains about 18 percent of the increase that occurred in NHE between 1940 and 1990.[2]

Refer once more to equation 7.3. If, as Cutler's findings indicate, increases in PHC relative to PAGS explain only part of the increase that has occurred in NHE/GDP, but NHE/GSP has increased (and it has, of course), it follows that increases in QHC must have also exceeded increases in QAGS.

There are several reasons to expect an increase in QHC over time. Chief among these are the following:

- The aging of the population
- The relatively high income elasticity of demand for health care
- Increases in insurance coverage
- Technological change

Population Aging

Other things equal, the quantity of health care purchased can be expected to increase as a result of population growth, but this is also true of purchases of other goods and services. Thus, there is no assurance, a priori, that QHC will increase relative to QAGS as a result of population *growth*. Population *aging*, on the other hand, is expected to make QHC grow relative to QAGS.

Health care spending increases with age because older people tend to have more medical needs than younger people. Thus, average health care spending per person for the population as a whole will rise as the average age of the population increases. The magnitude of the effect of population aging on NHE depends on how steeply spending per person increases with age and the rate at which the population ages.

Keywords: *population aging*
http://www.infotrac-college.com

Contrary to popular belief and concern, empirical studies indicate that population aging is a very minor factor behind the increases that have occurred in NHE. For example, both Cutler and Newhouse find that population aging explains only about 2 percent of the increase that occurred in real health expenditures per capita between 1940 and 1990.[3] Apparently, differences in spending by age are not large enough and the U.S. population is not aging quickly enough to make aging a major cost driver. For certain categories of health care services, such as cardiovascular services, aging may be a more important factor, of course, than it is for all types of services combined.

---

[2]David M. Cutler, "Technology, Health Costs, and the NIH," National Institutes of Health Roundtable on the Economics of Biomedical Research, 1995.

[3]David M. Cutler, "Technology, Health Costs, and the NIH," National Institutes of Health Roundtable on the Economics of Biomedical Research, 1995; Joseph P. Newhouse, "Medical Care Costs: How Much Welfare Loss?" *Journal of Economic Perspectives*, 1992, 6:3, 3–21.

Income Elasticity of Demand for Health Care

U.S. households have experienced significant increases in income at the same time that health care expenditures have been rising so rapidly. It is reasonable to assume that at least some of the increase in expenditures that has occurred is a result of deliberate choices by households to spend a portion of their growing incomes on health care. The effect of increases in income on household purchases of health care is captured by the income elasticity of demand for health care. The **income elasticity of demand (IED)** is a measure of the change in the quantity demanded (or amount purchased) of a specific good or service as a result of a change in income, expressed in percentages. Applied to health care:

Income Elasticity of Demand (IED) – The percentage change in the quantity purchased of a good or service resulting from a given percentage change in income.

Inferior Good – A good with an income elasticity of demand less than zero.

Superior Good – A good with an income elasticity of demand greater than one.

(7.6) $\quad$ IEDHC = Percent Change in QHC / Percent Change in Income.

If the value of IEDHC were negative, health care would be an **inferior good**—one for which quantities purchased actually fall as income increases. A number of estimates indicate, however, that IEDHC is greater than zero. In fact, there is good evidence that IEDHC exceeds 1.0. If so, health care is a **superior good**—one for which quantities purchased not only increase as income increases, but at a faster rate than the increase in income.

To understand the implications of this finding, consider Table 7.2. To generate the numbers in this table, it is assumed that disposable income (DI—household income after taxes) is initially $5 trillion, and that NHE are initially $500 billion or 10 percent of DI. The remainder of DI is spent on all other goods and services (AOGS). It is also assumed that IEDHC = 1.4. Given this value for IEDHC, an assumed increase of $5 trillion in DI—100 percent—will produce an increase in QHC of 140 percent. An increase of 140 percent of $500 billion is $700 billion. Thus, the assumed increase in DI will increase QHC from $500 billion to $1,200 billion, or from 10 percent of DI to 12 percent of DI.

Suppose, further, that DI is three-fourths of GDP (DI = 0.75 GDP). Then, when QHC = 0.10 DI, QHC = 0.10(0.75 GDP), or QHC = 0.075 GDP. And, when QHC = 0.12 DI, QHC = 0.12(0.75 GDP), or QHC = 0.09 GDP. Thus, when IEDHC>1, increases in income increase the share of GDP devoted to health care.

David Cutler and Joseph Newhouse estimate that 5 percent (Cutler) to 18 percent (Newhouse) of the increase in real per capita health care expenditures (i.e., QHC per capita) from 1940 to 1990 can be attributed to increases in income.[4]

INFOTRAC
College Edition

Keywords: *elasticity, income elasticity*

http://www.infotrac-college.com

Increases in Insurance Coverage

Health insurance is the passkey to accessing the health care system. There is substantial evidence that people with health insurance receive more care, more frequently, than people without health insurance.

TABLE 7.2	Effect of an Increase in Disposable Income (DI) on Quantity of Health Care (QHC) Purchased			
DI $B	QAOGS $B	QAOGS %DI	QHC $B	QHC %DI
5,000	4,500	90	500	10
10,000	8,800	88	1,200	12

[4]Ibid.

The number of people with health insurance has grown significantly over the last 50 years. Thus, it is reasonable to expect that some of the increase in QHC is due to increases in insurance coverage. In his empirical study of health care costs, David Cutler finds that 13 percent of the increase in real health care expenditures per capita (QHC per capita) from 1940 to 1990 can be attributed to increases in insurance coverage. Newhouse estimates that increases in insurance explained 10 percent of the growth in QHC per capita over the same period.[5]

Technological Change

If you have been keeping score to this point, you will have noticed that there is still a significant unexplained portion of the increase that has occurred in health care expenditures. Economists believe that technological change explains most of the remainder.

It is important to define medical technology. Medical technology encompasses practically all aspects of medicine: medical devices, pharmaceuticals, the way physicians perform surgeries and practice medicine, and its organization. We often think of technology solely as equipment or hardware. However, technology also includes the means by which various inputs, including labor, capital, and information, are combined to deliver health care, the organizational systems within which health care is provided, and management information systems.

New technology normally increases costs because it increases the "intensity" of care; i.e., it expands the opportunities for providing more services (more QHC) to patients. Even when new technology could reduce unit costs, it often increases health care expenditures by increasing the number of patients to whom the technology is applied.

It is difficult to measure the influence of medical advances on health care spending, but economists have devised some promising techniques. One of these is the "residual" approach. In the residual approach, one uses statistical techniques to measure the influence of all the factors other than technological change that might account for health spending increases, such as those we have already considered. After this is done, the portion of total spending that is not explained by all other factors—**the "residual"**—is generally attributed to technological change. Using this approach, Cutler attributes 49 percent of the increase in real health care spending per capita (in our terms, QHC per capita) from 1940 to 1990 to technological change. Newhouse also uses this approach and finds that 70 percent of real spending increases during this period can be attributed to technological change.[6]

These findings underscore the importance of medical advances, but they probably overstate their independent influence on health care expenditures. Most economists (Cutler and Newhouse included) believe that advances in medical technology and health care expenditures are determined simultaneously by market forces, with a major boost from health insurance. In this view, technological change affects the demand for medical care and insurance, and the levels and terms of insurance coverage affect the nature of technological development and its diffusion over time. Technological change also affects supply by its impacts on productivity, and ultimately the costs of medical care. Together, these demand and

The Residual – In a health expenditures context, the proportion of health expenditures that cannot be attributed to factors other than technology.

---

[5] Ibid.
[6] Ibid.

INSIGHTS

THE MEDICALLY UNINSURED

The high costs of health care and the likelihood that most families and individuals need at least some health care have made access to health insurance crucial. For those ineligible for government health care programs, health care insurance in the United States is closely linked to the workplace. Eighty-five percent of the population under age 65 has some type of health insurance, 92 percent of which is employment-based and only 8 percent of which is private insurance that is not employment-based. The 15 percent with no insurance translates into 40 million people.

It is common, but inaccurate, to attribute lack of insurance to weak or no attachment to the workforce. More than 80 percent of the 40 million uninsured have some connection to the workforce, either as workers or as dependents of workers. The key to lack of workforce coverage seems to be the size of a firm's labor force. The likelihood that a worker will not be covered is inversely related to the size of the firm, measured by number of workers (that is, the fewer the number of workers, the greater the probability of no insurance). The problem is not lack of availability of health insurance to small firms, but the fact that the cost of health insurance per employee is much higher for small firms than for large firms. The higher costs stem from significantly higher insurance administration costs per employee and the higher risk of loss associated with small pools of employees.

Some groups have advocated that either the federal or state governments mandate employer-provided health insurance. Unfortunately, this would increase the cost of insurance coverage for small firms as insurers take on the greater administrative burden of small groups and the higher risks associated with small groups of employees. The increase in costs to employers would result in some increase in unemployment, especially among low-wage workers. In this sense, mandated health care insurance would have effects similar to the minimum wage, discussed in Chapters 12 and 14.

Such a program of mandated insurance might require a supplementary program of subsidies to firms that truly cannot afford it without firing employees or going out of business. This may greatly reduce the political prospects for mandated insurance, including the so-called play-or-pay schemes that would require employers either to "play" by providing insurance or to "pay" by remitting a tax, the proceeds from which would be used to provide government-financed insurance coverage.

INFOTRAC
College Edition

Keywords: *medical technology, medical expenditures*

http://www.infotrac-college.com

supply factors determine aggregate expenditures. In practical terms, this means that changes in demand for medical care, fueled by advertising of drugs and technological developments that promise improved quality of life, increase the demand for insurance. Increases in insurance coverage increase consumers' willingness to pay for new drugs and technologies, and aggregate health expenditures increase. This provides increased earnings to manufacturers of new drugs and technologies; increased earnings stimulate research, development and production of the next generation of products; and the cycle begins anew.

■ IS TECHNOLOGICAL CHANGE IN MEDICAL CARE WORTH IT?

If Cutler and Newhouse are right about the importance of medical advances as a source of rising health care expenditures, and the primary objective of policy is to slow the rate of increase in those expenditures, then the obvious policy prescription is to do something to slow the rate of technological innovation and technology diffusion. Before we adopt policies of this type, however, we should consider the possibility that technological change in health care is worth it; i.e., that it produces benefits greater than costs.

There are two primary sources of benefits from medical advances: reduced mortality or increased life expectancy, and reduced morbidity or enhanced quality of life. Up to now, economists have been much more successful in valuing increases in life expectancy than in valuing enhancements in the quality of life.

David M. Cutler and Srikanth Kadiyala of the National Bureau of Economic Research have analyzed life expectancy in the United States and found that it improved fairly steadily throughout the last century.[7] Life expectancy at birth in 1900 was less than 50 years; today, it is 77 years. Gains prior to 1950 can be explained largely by reductions in infant mortality and infectious diseases. The former are due to improved diet, sanitation, housing, and education. Reductions in infectious diseases are largely due to the development and diffusion of effective pharmaceutical weapons. Since then, the gains in life expectancy are closely associated with declining mortality among the elderly, chiefly from advances made in treating heart disease and strokes. In fact, death rates from cardiovascular diseases, both among the middle-aged and the elderly, have fallen to half of what they were in the mid-1960s.

To a large extent, then, the value of improved health care technology is linked to the increase in life expectancy due to medical advances in treating cardiovascular illness. The economist's task is to estimate the value of the extra years of life produced by these advances.

Value of a Life — The value people put on their own lives, inferred from what they must be paid to incur small but predictable increases in the risk of death.

The starting point is to estimate the **value of a life**. The dominant approach to this in economics is to infer the value people put on their own lives from what they must be paid to incur small but predictable increases in the risk of death. As an example of how this works, suppose that moving from a job in retail sales to housing construction increases a worker's chance of a fatal accident by one in 5,000 each year. In other words, if 5,000 workers made the move, expected on-the-job fatalities would increase by one per year. Suppose further that employers would have to pay each worker an extra $1,000 annually to accept the higher-risk employment. The group would gain $5 million, then, as compensation for the death that will occur. The value that they, and their employers, place on a life, therefore, is $5 million.

Once this value is established, it is necessary to determine what it means in terms of the average value of an additional *year* of life. A typical adult thinking about the previous choice might have about 40 years left to live. If so, that adult is implicitly valuing her life at about $125,000 per year. A large number of studies have used a methodology like this to assess the value of years of life. A rough consensus is that a year of life is worth about $75,000 to $150,000. As a rough midpoint, one could use a value of $100,000 for a year of life.

According to the study by Cutler and Kadiyala, the average American 45 years of age can expect to live 4½ additional years today over 1950 solely because cardiovascular disease mortality has declined. Suppose that 3 years of this is a result of medical advances, with the rest being due to behavioral changes. If each additional year of life is worth $100,000 per year to the person affected, the benefit from medical advances totals $300,000. The additional years of life are tacked onto the end of life, however, so they will not be realized until around 30 to 35 years later. These are *future* values. To determine what they are worth to the 45-year-old, we must determine their *present* value—value to the individual at age 45.

This is done by discounting each future value as follows:

(7.7) $$PVLY_{45} = FVLY_t / (1+i)^{t-45}$$

---

[7] "The Economics of Better Health: The Case of Cardiovascular Disease," (summary) in *Exceptional Returns: The Economic Value of America's Investment in Medical Research*, Lasker Charitable Trust/Funding First, May 2000.

where PVLY is the present value of a life year at age 45, FVLY is the future value of a life year in year t, $(1+i)^{t-45}$ is the discount factor, and i is the discount rate.

Table 7.3 shows how this equation is applied in the case where the additional life years are delayed until ages 76, 77, and 78, or for 31, 32, and 33 years. We use i = 0.02 or 2 percent, the real rate of return on long-term U.S. government bonds realized historically. The net result of discounting is to reduce the value of the additional life years from $300,000 to $159,186.

These benefits must be compared to the increased costs due to medical advances. The typical 45-year-old can expect to spend (most of it paid for by insurance or public programs) about $40,000 in present value on cardiovascular disease over their remaining life. Virtually all of this is for medication, surgeries, and other long-term therapies that were not available in 1950.

Clearly, the present value of the benefits from these medical advances is greater than the costs. For every $1 spent, there is a return of around $4. This is a higher return than most anything a business could hope to realize and higher than most government activities (college education may be an exception—see Chapter 9). Advances in cardiovascular disease treatment have surely been worth it for the 45-year-old in this example.

Kevin Murphy and Robert Topel of the University of Chicago have applied methods similar to these to the entire population for the period 1970 to 1990.[8] They estimate that the additional life years attributable to reduced mortality from cardiovascular disease over this period are worth over $31 *trillion* in present value for the population as a whole. They estimated, further, that the additional life years attributable to reduced mortality from all sources over this time period are worth nearly $57 trillion. Although not all of these benefits can be attributed to medical advances, they are so large that it is hard to escape the conclusion that medical advances have been well worth the investment. Besides, these are lower-bound estimates; they include nothing for any improvements that have occurred in morbidity or quality of life.

INFOTRAC
College Edition

Keywords: *medical research and returns, economic benefits of medical research*

http://www.infotrac-college.com

Moreover, Murphy and Topel estimate that potential future gains are also very large: They estimate that the benefits of reduced mortality from eliminating cancer would be worth roughly $47 trillion, and the benefits of reduced mortality from eliminating heart disease would be worth about $48 trillion. They figure that even modest progress in reducing mortality from these diseases would have great value. For example, a 10 percent reduction in cancer deaths would be worth over $4 trillion. In fact, even a $200 billion research program on cancer would be worthwhile if it reduced cancer deaths by only as little as 1 percent.

TABLE 7.3 Determination of the Present Value of Additional Life Years from Medical Advances in Cardiovascular Disease

FVLY	Years Value Delayed	Discount Factor	PVLY
$100,000	31	$(1.02)^{76-45} = (1.02)^{31} = 1.848$	$100,000/1.848 = $54,112
$100,000	32	$(1.02)^{77-45} = (1.02)^{32} = 1.885$	$100,000/1.885 = $53,050
$100,000	33	$(1.02)^{78-45} = (1.02)^{33} = 1.922$	$100,000/1.922 = $52,029
$300,000			$159,186

---

[8]"The Economic Value of Medical Knowledge," September 2001, authors' Web site—http://gsbwww.uchicago.edu/fac/kevin.murphy/teaching/medical-knowledge.pdf.

■ Does the Medical System Provide the Right Amount of Medical Care?

These results suggest that the conventional wisdom about the need to control rising medical costs may be wrong or, at least, poorly informed. However, conventional wisdom does contain some truth. Americans overuse medical care at the same time that they are reaping huge benefits from medical advances. In a word, the total benefits from medical care undoubtedly exceed the total costs of medical care, but there are many instances where the marginal benefits are less than the marginal costs—a situation that we argued in Chapter 6 also fits U.S. environmental regulation.

A good medical care system uses medical services that are appropriate, but avoids using them too much. Substantial research has examined whether the U.S. medical system does well by this criterion. The universal conclusion is that it does not. A lot of medical care is provided in situations where it is of little or no value. This is particularly true of intensive surgical procedures.

The Dartmouth Atlas Project has shown that medical spending in different areas of the country varies enormously, without substantial differences in health benefits.[9] They have estimated that medical spending could fall by 20 percent if unnecessary care, especially surgical procedures with low value, were eliminated.

Another way to look at overuse of care is to determine if patients meet medical criteria for the care they receive. A large number of RAND studies over the past decade have examined the appropriateness of the use of various medical and surgical procedures.[10] These studies rated all of the indications for performing a given procedure and then used those ratings to determine whether the procedures were performed for "necessary," "appropriate," "inappropriate," or "equivocal" reasons. Generally, a procedure was considered to be "appropriate" if the patient's expected health benefits exceeded the expected health risks by a substantial margin.

Overall, the RAND studies indicate that significant proportions of procedures are performed for inappropriate reasons. The rates of inappropriate use range from a low of 2 percent for coronary artery bypass surgery and cataract removal to a high of 32 percent for carotid endarterectomy. The rates of equivocal use also vary dramatically, ranging from 7 percent for coronary bypass surgery to 38 percent for coronary angioplasty. On average, it appears that one-third or more of all procedures performed in the United States are of questionable benefit.

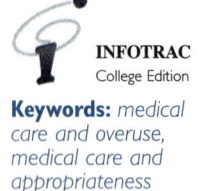

INFOTRAC
College Edition

Keywords: *medical care and overuse, medical care and appropriateness*

http://www.infotrac-college.com

How is this possible? We will examine the principal reasons, but the key is the effect of reimbursement for medical care. We get a lot from medical care because we pay a lot for providing very intensive—and expensive—services. Paying more for intensive services gets a lot of these services provided, both when they are valuable and, unfortunately, also when they are not. The corollary of paying more for intensive care is paying less for routine care. These services are underprovided, even though they may improve health greatly.

Third-Party Payments

Health care is somewhat unusual in that patients (consumers) pay directly for only a fraction of its cost. Much of the tab is paid, instead, with third-party payments.

---

[9]*The Dartmouth Atlas of Health Care 1999*, Center for Evaluative Services, Dartmouth Medical School.
[10]*Assessing the Appropriateness of Care: How Much Is Too Much?* Rand Health Research Highlights, Santa Monica: Rand Corporation, 1998.

CHAPTER 7 ■ MEDICAL CARE: COSTS OUT OF CONTROL?

Third-Party Payment – A payment made directly to the provider of a good or service by a party other than the buyer.

A **third-party payment** is a payment made directly to the provider of a good or service by a party other than the buyer. The principal "third parties" in the health care market are private insurance companies and government agencies. Table 7.4 shows that third-party payments were 85 percent of the $1,299.5 billion spent on national health care in the United States in 2000.

When third-party payments are involved, consumers pay directly for only part of health care costs. They pay out-of-pocket cost equal to the difference between the full cost of the health care received and the third-party payments for that care. According to Table 7.4, out-of-pocket payments amounted to $199.5 billion, or 15 percent, of national health care expenditures in 2000.

The effect of third-party payments can be explained with an example of the market for hospital care. As illustrated in Figure 7.1, this market reflects the demand for, and the supply of, hospital care, measured in hospital days.

According to survey data produced from the *National Hospital Indicators Survey*, 302,674,000 days of hospital care, including both in-patient and out-patient care, were provided in the United States in 2000 at an average cost of $1,228 per day. Private parties paid 15 percent of health care expenditures in 1998. However, out-of-pocket payments for hospital care were only 3.2 percent of expenditures for hospital care, or about $39 a day.

As indicated in Figure 7.1, patients demand approximately 303 million hospital days when they pay only $39 a day. Hospitals receive $1,228 per day: $39 from the patient and $1,189 from third-party payers. Patients would have demanded fewer hospital days, of course, in the absence of third-party payments. To determine exactly how many, we would need to know the exact shapes of both the demand and supply curves for hospital care. We do not know the exact shape of the supply curve, but we assume that it is horizontal at $1,228. We do not know the exact shape of the demand curve, either, but estimates by Manning,

TABLE 7.4 National Health Care Expenditures in 2000 by Type of Payment and Source of Funds, Billions of Dollars and Percent

Type and Source of Payment	Amount of Payment ($Billion)	Percent	
Out-of-Pocket Payments	194.5		15.0
Third-Party Payments			
Private health insurance	443.9	34.2	
Other private funds	73.8	5.7	
Total Private Third-Party Payments	517.7		39.8
Federal government	411.5	31.7	
State and local governments	175.7	13.5	
MEDICARE	224.4	17.3	
MEDICAID	202.7	15.6	
Total Public Third-Party Payments	582.2		45.2
Total Third-Party Payments	1,104.9		85.0
Total Health Care Expenditures	1,299.5		100.0

SOURCE: U.S. Health Care Financing Administration, http://www.hcfa.gov/stats.

FIGURE 7.1 The Effect of Third-Party Payments on Hospital Care

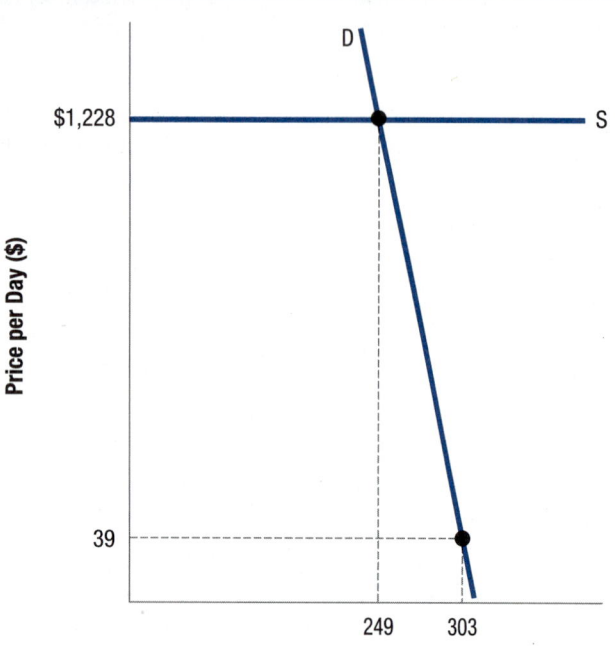

Consumers pay an out-of-pocket price of $39 per hospital day, at which they demand 303 million days. If they were charged the full cost of each day, they would purchase 249 million days at $1,228 per day—the price and quantity at which quantity demanded equals quantity supplied. Moving from the out-of-pocket price to the full-cost price would reduce costs of hospital care by $66.3 billion (54 million days × $1,228 per day).

et al, of the relationship between changes in the price of hospital care and the quantity of hospital care demanded indicate that it would intersect the assumed supply curve around 249 million hospital days.[11]

In the absence of third-party payments, the market for hospital care would clear at the intersection of supply and demand, or at 249 million hospital days. Thus, with third-party payments, consumers purchase an extra 54 million hospital days, increasing health care expenditures by $66.3 billion. The extra 54 million days are a vivid example of "too much" health care.

The preceding case illustrates the effect of third-party payments on expenditures for hospital care. Third-party payments also create additional expenditures other types of health care. Generally, however, excessive demands for other types of health care, such as visits to doctors' offices, surgery, and dental care, are less than in the case of hospitalization because the third-party payments are lower for other types of health care. The out-of-pocket payments for physicians' services, dental care, nursing home care, and drugs in 1994 were 19, 49, 37, and 62 percent, respectively.[12]

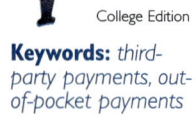

INFOTRAC
College Edition

Keywords: *third-party payments, out-of-pocket payments*

http://www.infotrac-college.com

Physician-Induced Demand

The excess demand created by third-party payments is a good example of how consumer behavior can be affected by monetary incentives. Consumers are merely responding rationally to the incentive of a

---
[11] W. G. Manning, J. P. Newhouse, N. Duan, et al., "Health Insurance and the Demand for Medical Care: Evidence from a Randomized Experiment," *American Economic Review*, 77 (June 1987), 251–77.

[12] *The Health Care Financing Review* (Spring 1996), 233.

International Perspective

Another Hidden Cost of Third-Party Payments

We have noted in the text and in Figure 7.1 that third-party payments induce health care consumers to demand an inefficiently large amount of care, resulting in costs that are excessive from a social perspective. This happens with third-party payments because only a small part of the health care cost is imposed on buyers; the remainder is paid by third parties. Just the opposite effect can occur, however; that is, third-party payments can impose costs on consumers that are not shared by third parties, as seems to be the case in Canada.

In Canada, most health care is paid for entirely by national health insurance. Thus, if the government were willing to pay for it, consumers would continue to consume health care until the benefit perceived on the last unit was zero. (In Figure 7.1, this is where the demand curve would cut the horizontal axis.) The government is not willing to pay, however, for this much health care.

The result of the government expenditure limit is that the quantity of health care demanded often exceeds the quantity of health care supplied. In the face of such excess demand, patients often find that they have to wait for hospital and physician services.

Steven Globerman studied the problem of waiting for health care in British Columbia. He found that all patients together waited a total of 868,408 weeks for 10 types of hospital admissions in 1989 and that many of them experienced significant difficulty either at work or at home because of their untreated condition. To put a cost on waiting, Globerman estimated the value of productive time lost. He did this by first multiplying the total time lost waiting by the percentage of patients experiencing difficulty while waiting, giving him an estimate of the amount of productive time lost. He then multiplied this number by average weekly industrial earnings in British Columbia in 1989. The resulting number—his estimate of the value of the productive time lost due to waiting—turned out to be about 0.2 percent of British Columbia's gross provincial product.

Undoubtedly, some cost is associated with waiting for hospital services in the United States, although we know of no estimates. There appears to be little waiting so far at least, on the part of insured patients, but the spread of managed cost may have changed this situation. In most cases, the waiting is probably concentrated on the uninsured, who must surmount the barriers to accessing hospital care imposed by the inability to pay.

SOURCE: Steven Globerman, "A Policy Analysis of Hospital Waiting Lists," *Journal of Policy Analysis and Management* 10 (Spring 1991), 247–262.

---

reduced price, and the excess hospital care is a reflection of consumer choice. The outcome may not be socially desirable, but the consumer is still sovereign.

In the real world of health care, the doctor often makes the purchasing decision for the patient. Because the doctor normally recommends a course of action, and the patient is presumably free to approve or disapprove, the consumer is ultimately sovereign in the sense that he has the final authority over health care expenditures. Most patients have little knowledge of medicine, however, so they often simply accept a physician's recommendation. This gives doctors considerable freedom to exercise their own preferences. At the very least, it affords them the opportunity to use their superior knowledge to persuade patients that particular services are necessary. If they use this opportunity to enhance their own income by prescribing health care that is ineffective or unnecessary, the doctor-patient relationship is a source of excessive health care expenditures.

We call ineffective health care prescribed by physicians to increase their own wealth **physician-induced demand**. Such health care could be eliminated without materially impairing health; thus, it wastes resources.

Physician-Induced Demand — Clearly ineffective health care prescribed by physicians to increase their own wealth.

At least three conditions are necessary for physician-induced demand. We have already touched upon two of these: (1) asymmetric information (physicians have information that is superior to patients' information) regarding the efficacy of health care alternatives and (2) physicians' desire to increase their own wealth. In addition, physicians' income must depend directly on the amount of health care that they prescribe. The first two conditions are surely present in the United States, although physicians as a group are undoubtedly motivated by more than money. The third condition is present where physicians practice fee-for-service medicine; that is, where a fee is charged for each service provided.

Recognition of these conditions has prompted a search for evidence of physician-induced demand. When experts evaluated medical records to determine if certain procedures are prescribed more often than warranted by risk-benefit considerations, they found indications that as much as one-third of certain common procedures (coronary bypass surgery, coronary angiograms, pacemaker insertions, carotid artery surgery, and upper gastrointestinal endoscopy) are inappropriate or of equivocal value.[13] Enormous variation also appears in care across different areas of the country and across countries. Phelps attributes most of the observed variation to differences in physician practices.[14]

Physician-induced demand does not necessarily cause variations in physician practices or the use of inappropriate procedures. The cause could be the inherent uncertainty of diagnostic medicine and variations in training and skills of physicians. Medicine, after all, is not an exact science, and honest differences of opinion arise within the medical community about the effectiveness of various procedures.

Economists have also identified several potential limits to the pure exercise of physician preferences:

1. *Potential competition.* Between 1965 and 1990, the number of physicians grew by nearly 110 percent while the U.S. population grew by only 28 percent. Observed patterns of physician location indicate clearly that doctors have been unable to hold onto their market share in the face of this increase in supply.[15]

    This factor may moderate the exercise of physician-induced demand, just as the appearance of new foreign competitors reduces the market power of U.S. automobile manufacturers.

2. *Information monitoring by patients.* Many patients have some knowledge of the conditions for which they seek medical care and advice, and this knowledge is becoming easier to obtain over the Internet. If physicians suggest care that deviates significantly from what patients expect, they may not consent to the suggested care. Instead, patients may seek advice from other physicians. Such patient self-monitoring constrains physicians in their pursuit of wealth.

3. *Second opinions.* Third-party payers may require second opinions before they agree to pay for expensive medical care. The threat of alternative diagnoses may make physicians more conservative in the care that they prescribe.

4. *Satisfaction maximization.* Maximizing satisfaction may be more important to doctors than maximizing wealth. If so, the amount of work—and income—that physicians create for themselves is probably less than the amount that they could create.

---

[13]David M. Cutler, "A Guide to Health Care Reform," *Journal of Economic Perspectives*, 8, No. 3, Summer 1994, 14–15.
[14]Charles E. Phelps, *Health Economics*, New York: HarperCollins, 1992, Chapter 3.
[15]This is Phelps' conclusion in *Health Economics*, 186–192.

5. *Physician ethics.* Some physicians may simply consider it unethical to prescribe care that has questionable beneficial effects.

Keywords: *physician-induced medical care*

http://www.infotrac-college.com

Cromwell and Mitchell estimate that each 1 percent growth in the number of surgeons has resulted in only one-tenth of a percent growth in surgeons' services.[16] Rossiter and Wilensky found a similar effect for all physician types.[17] These results suggest that physician-induced demand is hardly even a minor source of increased spending for health care, perhaps for the reasons just noted.

Defensive Medicine

The U.S. legal system provides compensation to patients who can prove that they have been victims of medical malpractice. Doctors buy malpractice insurance as protection against the financial consequences of medical malpractice suits. The cost of malpractice insurance may have increased the rate at which doctors practice **defensive medicine**—medical care given to reduce the risk of a malpractice suit. The problem with defensive medicine is that this may be care with little value to the patient. The likelihood of this practice is increased in the presence of third-party payments; physicians are less reluctant to prescribe treatment of questionable value when they know their patients are not paying full cost.

Defensive Medicine – Medical procedures performed to reduce the risk of a lawsuit.

Defensive medicine need not be wasteful, however. It may result in higher quality care or a reduction in the number of high-risk procedures. Each of these outcomes provides value to patients.

Keywords: *defensive medicine, malpractice insurance*

http://www.infotrac-college.com

According to some physicians, defensive medicine is a major factor in the growth of their medical costs. The most widely cited estimate, however, indicates that it explains less than 1 percent of all medical expenditures.[18]

Federal Tax Exemption for Health Insurance

Employers pay for a significant fraction—more than 80 percent—of the health insurance premiums of workers in the United States. Good evidence indicates, however, that they shift the cost to employees in the form of lower wages.[19] If this is the case, why don't employees just purchase their own insurance? They don't because their cost is lower if their employer pays for it. This happens because the federal income tax code exempts employee compensation received in the form of health insurance from the federal individual income tax.

The size of the exemption depends on the size of the insurance premium paid and the employee's marginal federal income tax rate. The marginal tax rate is the tax rate levied on the last dollar of taxable income. Currently, there are five marginal, or bracket, rates: 15, 28, 31, 36, and 39.6 percent.

Suppose an individual in the 28 percent tax bracket has an insurance policy for which her employer pays a premium of $1,800 a year. If the worker were to buy the insurance herself, she would have to earn enough income before taxes to pay for both the insurance premium and her taxes on that income. In this example, she would have to earn $2,500 to realize the $1,800 after taxes to pay the premium

---

[16] Jerry Cromwell and Janet B. Mitchell, "Physician-Induced Demand for Surgery," *Journal of Health Economics* 5, 1986, 293–313.

[17] Louis F. Rossiter and Gail R. Wilensky, "Identification of Physician-Induced Demand," *Journal of Human Resources* 19, 1984, 162–172.

[18] Roger Reynolds, John A. Rizzo, and Martin L. Gonzalez, "The Cost of Medical Professional Liability," *Journal of the American Medical Association*, May 22–29, 1987, 257, 2776–2781.

[19] Phelps, *Health Economics*, 297.

[$1,800 = $2,500 − (0.28 × $2,500)]. A worker in the 36 percent bracket would have to earn $2,812.50 to buy the $1,800 policy. This means that the employee-provided $1,800 policy would cost the 28 percent taxpayer $2,500 and the 36 percent taxpayer $2,812.50. Alternatively, both taxpayers enjoy exemptions from taxes worth $700 and $1,012.50, respectively; their employer lowers the cost to them of health insurance by 28 and 36 percent, respectively.

Net Cost of Health Insurance – The difference between the subsidized cost of insurance and the value of claims paid.

To understand the value of these exemptions, it is necessary to understand how they affect the net cost of health insurance to the individual. The **net cost of health insurance** is not the same as the insurance premium. The net cost is the portion of the premium that the individual does not recover in the form of expected insurance benefits; it is the portion that covers costs and provides insurance company profits. The net cost of insurance varies inversely with the size of the group insured, with larger groups paying a smaller cost per dollar of benefits. The net cost ranges from 5 percent to 8 percent of benefits for employee groups of more than 1,000 to as much as 40 percent of benefits for groups of 10 or fewer. The average net cost of insurance is 15 to 25 percent of benefits.

The bottom-line cost to the individual is the difference between the net cost of insurance and the value of the tax exemption. Given the net costs just indicated and current marginal income tax rates, the exemption drastically lowers health insurance cost for most insured workers. In fact, the net cost is negative for many workers.

INFOTRAC
College Edition

Keywords: *income tax exemption for health insurance*
http://www.infotrac-college.com

Given a downward-sloping demand curve for health insurance, the income tax exemption will increase the quantity of health insurance purchased.[20] An increase in the quantity of health insurance will increase the quantity of medical care demanded. In fact, Phelps estimates that the tax exemption for health insurance increases the demand for medical care by 10 to 20 percent among the under-age-65 population.[21]

■ Approaches to Reducing Wasteful Expenditures

We have completed our review of the principal sources of excessive health care spending in the United States. Although we have examined each source separately, they are all part of a system in which those who are responsible for health care costs—patients and providers—bear little direct responsibility for cost reimbursement. The key to cost reduction is to make patients and providers more responsible for the costs of their choices. This can be done in many ways, three of which are managed care, eliminating the tax exemption for health insurance, and health care vouchers.

Managed Care

Managed Care – Health care that is reviewed by someone other than the patient or provider to determine whether the right services are being provided and whether the cost of provision is minimized.

As health care costs became a larger part of the cost of doing business in this country, business firms began pressuring insurers to find a way that they could save money on health care costs. The solution chosen was **managed care**. Managed care is a general term for a number of different types of health insurance organizations. Health maintenance organizations, or HMOs, are the best-known of the managed care organizations, but they are only one variety. There are also preferred provider organizations (PPOs), point of service plans (POSs), independent practice associations (IPAs), and others.

---

[20]Phelps, *Health Economics*, 300–302.
[21]Ibid.

Managed care insurers pay less to medical care providers than did traditional insurers. They do so through lower rates negotiated with providers. Traditional insurers did not negotiate lower rates because they believed that doctors would be unwilling to see their patients at lower rates. Managed care insurers do not strive for universal access to providers; they pick and choose with whom they want to contract. In return for lower prices, insurers provide patients. Lowering physician payments is an attractive way to save money because there is little that doctors will do about it. Doctors are trained primarily to practice medicine. If, in order to see patients, physicians must accept a reduction in income, they will do so and continue to practice. Some doctors retire early, and others move into administrative jobs to avoid pay cuts, but the vast majority of doctors do not have that option.

Managed care also saves money through restrictions on what services are provided, coupled with financial incentives for physicians to provide fewer services. Restrictions on services are accomplished by a process called **utilization review**. Managed care insurers use this process most aggressively to reduce hospital utilization and costs. They require second opinions before nonemergency admissions and withhold payment if they are not received. They monitor length of stay to see where extra days might be trimmed—and they trim them. Utilization review is also practiced at the physician level. Routine tests are scrutinized for need, as are referrals to specialists.

Utilization Review — A process used to determine if the medical care prescribed by a physician is appropriate.

Financial incentives have reinforced these restrictions. In addition to lowering fees, managed care creates financial incentives for providers to provide fewer services. Some primary care physicians (general practitioners, internists, pediatricians) receive a fixed payment per patient. They must cover the costs of all medical services provided out of that amount. Thus, they lose money when more care is provided. Similar systems are in place at some hospitals.

Because different insurers use different payment schemes, reimbursement for services is a tangled web for providers. Physicians might be paid a fixed rate for some patients, a discounted fee for others, and a target payment for specific services for some or all of their patients. Most doctors probably have only a vague idea of how much they earn for each patient they treat.

Doctors are still paid more for doing more, but significantly less than under the traditional fee-for-service system. Managed care is in some ways more generous to patients than what came before it.

In exchange for tighter restrictions on utilization, managed care offers lower out-of-pocket payments. Most managed care plans charge very low fees—$5 or $10—per physician visit, substantially below what people paid in traditional policies. This is done in the hope that it will increase preventive care, thereby reducing the incidence of higher cost health episodes. The goal of managed care is to limit use of the system when patients access it, not to keep them away from it.

Managed care has virtually taken over the part of the medical system that is financed by private insurance; currently, nearly 95 percent of privately insured people are in managed care plans. Traditional insurance is largely confined to Medicare patients, although managed care is even making inroads among this population in some states (and must be used by Medicare patients in a handful of states).

Managed care has had a major impact on the health care system. As noted earlier, after decades of medical cost increases that exceeded GDP growth, medical care costs rose less rapidly than GDP from 1993 to 1998, and much of the slowdown in cost increases can be credited to managed care. Unfortunately, it now appears that the savings from the adoption of managed care may be largely one-time savings (as many health care economists predicted); medical costs have been rising since then at a faster rate than GDP is growing.

Monetary savings are not the only concern, of course. If managed care saves money but adversely affects health outcomes, the cost savings might not be worth it. Managed care has changed the type and intensity of treatment provided in some settings, but not, apparently, at the expense of effective outcomes. The worst fears that people have about managed care seem to be overblown, but patients still do not like what they perceive to be managed care's intrusions on their freedom of choice.

Less high-tech care is provided under managed care, but there is more routine and chronic disease care. On balance, these two incentives roughly cancel each other. People are neither better nor worse off in managed care, but the change is not ideal. Over the longer term, the incentives in managed care could be quite damaging. The lower rate of use of intensive care in areas with greater managed care enrollment raises the significant issue of whether managed care will have an adverse effect on new innovations. As noted earlier, these innovations have produced enormous benefits, and it would be bad policy to discourage further innovation.

INFOTRAC
College Edition

Keywords: *cost-savings of managed care, outcomes of managed care*

http://www.infotrac-college.com

Eliminating the Federal Tax Exemption for Health Insurance

We have already explained how the federal tax exemption for employer-provided health insurance increases the demand for health insurance. In so far as this insurance is the traditional fee-for-service variety, the tax exemption indirectly severs the cost-payment linkage for health care. Elimination of this exemption has been proposed to Congress many times, most recently as part of President Clinton's health care reform package, but Congress has refused to do so.

The exemption was granted initially to encourage employer-provided insurance as a means of helping workers secure the lower premiums that come with group purchases of insurance. Many in Congress may believe that the elimination of the exemption would undo this advantage. The exemption tends to benefit primarily workers in larger firms, and they can secure favorable premiums, anyway, because of their numbers. In fact, the exemption may not have had anything to do with the development of the employer-provided insurance market; that can be attributed largely to the competition among insurers for clients that look more profitable based on their experience rating. Take the exemption away, and they would still be the most profitable risk pools.

Thus, two problems arise with the exemption: (1) It leads to excessive health care spending and (2) it is unnecessary as a means of increasing the availability of low-cost insurance. But that's not all. Because its value to workers rises with the marginal tax rate, the exemption provides a greater subsidy to higher-income workers than to lower-income workers. This pattern violates most notions of equity. In addition, the subsidy contributes to the federal deficit by the same amount as equivalent direct federal expenditure. This is not a trivial effect; the exemption amounted to more than $76 billion in 2000.

This is a formidable array of problems. Why, then, does the exemption persist? Probably because it provides a subsidy to the purchase of health care from which thousands of insurance companies, thousands of hospitals, hundreds of thousands of doctors, millions of businesses, and scores of millions of workers benefit. Together they form an almost irresistible force against significant political change. Given the rapidly rising concern about the level of health care spending, we may be closer than ever to the time when economics will triumph over politics on this issue.

Health Care Vouchers

Voucher – A coupon for a good or service that is used as a means of payment.

One possible way to reduce overspending for health care without denying benefits to program recipients would be to replace the current system of reimbursement with a system of vouchers. Their use has been suggested most often for Medicare and Medicaid patients. **Vouchers** are coupons that the recipient can use to pay for something, in this case health care at hospitals or doctors' offices chosen by the recipient. Alternatively, the individual could be required to use the voucher to purchase a conventional health insurance policy or to participate in a lower-cost managed care system. In fact, the voucher program could be tailored to encourage recipients to choose managed care by providing a slightly larger voucher for those who do.

The government could save costs by issuing vouchers for a smaller amount than it currently spends. Economists argue that this could be done without materially reducing beneficial health care to the recipients because they would be faced with a greater share of the costs of their own care and make better health care choices. Proponents of vouchers also stress that their use would enhance price (and cost) competition by health care providers for Medicare and Medicaid patients.

Critics of vouchers stress that they may not work as intended because recipients may make poor choices of health insurers or providers. Some proponents answer that, if this was a problem, the government could provide accurate information about the merits of alternative insurance policies and providers. A similar role for government, however, was rejected as part of the ill-fated Clinton health care reform proposal.

INFOTRAC
College Edition

Keywords: *medical vouchers, Medicare vouchers, Medicaid vouchers*

http://www.infotrac-college.com

Summary

The focus of this chapter is on the rising cost of medical care in the United States. Except for a 5-year period in the middle of the 1990s, national health expenditures (NHE) have increased steadily relative to GDP. Official projections indicate, moreover, that NHE will grow from 14 percent to 17 percent of GDP in the next decade, and past and projected trends imply that NHE could constitute one-third of GDP by 2040.

NHE have increased relative to GDP because of the Cost Disease of the Services Sector (which has driven up health care prices relative to prices in general), population aging, income elastic demand for health care, increases in insurance coverage, and technological change. Technological change is by far the largest source of rising NHE, accounting for 50 to 70 percent of the increase in real NHE per capita between 1940 and 1990.

If the objective is to hold the line on NHE as a percent of GDP, it would be foolish, however, to do so by stifling technological change. Although technological change is cost-increasing, recent studies indicate that the payoff from medical advances has been enormous, considering increases in life expectancy alone. This is especially true of medical advances in treating cardiovascular disease. Economists estimate, moreover, that the payoff from further small reductions in heart disease and cancer are so large that even very expensive research campaigns would be worth it.

This does not mean, however, that all health care expenditures are worth it. The total benefits from health care can be greater than the total costs, but we can still be wasting money by spending it on care for which the marginal benefits are less than the marginal costs. In fact, studies show that medical spending varies across the country without commensurate variation in outcomes and that there is substantial overuse of intensive procedures.

Blame for overuse can be assigned to four factors: third-party payments, physician-induced demand, defensive medicine, and the federal tax exemption for health insurance. Third-party payments are the most important of these, followed by the federal tax exemption. Physician-induced demand and defensive medicine account for very little of the overuse observed.

Payment by the patient of only a small part of the cost of health care at the point of purchase induces the consumption of too much health care. Small out-of-pocket prices characterize all types of health care, but especially hospital care and physicians services. They are a significant source of excessive spending.

Some suspect that physicians have induced patients to overconsume health care. Several checks on physician-induced demand, however, keep it from becoming an important source of excess health care spending. Existing evidence of ineffective and inappropriate care cannot necessarily be attributed to independent, self-serving practices of physicians.

Physicians purportedly prescribe unnecessary procedures as a defensive measure against possible malpractice lawsuits. The costs associated with this practice, however, probably do not exceed 1 percent of health care costs.

Employer-provided health insurance enjoys a substantial subsidy in the form of a federal tax exemption of health insurance premiums. This exemption stimulates the purchase of more insurance and indirectly induces consumers to buy health care of questionable value.

The core problem is that patients and doctors are responsible for generating costs but different decision makers, insurance companies, and governments pay the bill. Three options for improving the cost-payment linkage are managed care, eliminating the federal tax exemption for employer-provided insurance, and health care vouchers. Managed care has resulted in significant cost-savings without adversely affecting outcomes, but it appears that this is a one-time savings and that consumers greatly dislike the restrictions on their freedom of choice that they perceive are imposed by managed care insurers. The federal tax exemption for employer-provided health insurance induces excessive health care spending and provides a larger subsidy to higher-income employees. Nevertheless, it enjoys considerable political support. Vouchers harness the cost-cutting power of consumer choice and may be an effective means of reducing Medicare and Medicaid expenditures.

Key Terms

Cost Disease of the Services Sector	**Value of a life**	**Managed care**
Income elasticity of demand (IED)	**Third-party payment**	**Utilization review**
Inferior good	**Physician-induced demand**	**Voucher**
Superior good	**Defensive medicine**	
The residual	**Net cost of health insurance**	

Review Questions

1. Briefly describe the relationship between national health expenditures (NHE) and GDP over the period 1980 to 2011.

2. Explain how the Cost Disease of the Services Sector works in the case of health care, using equation 7.4 or 7.5.

3. Explain how the income elasticity of demand for health care (IEDHC) increases the quantity of health care and NHE/GDP, using equation 7.6.

4. Suppose that the risk of dying in an automobile accident is reduced by 1 in 10,000 through the use of front seat air bags and that 10,000 auto buyers choose to purchase these air bags as an option at a price of $250. What is the implicit value of a life to these buyers? Explain how you got your answer.

5. Suppose that a year of life is worth $150,000 and that a new treatment for diabetes increases life expectancy for a 40-year-old woman by 2 years. Suppose, further, that the treatment will cost $50,000 in present value per woman. If the discount rate is 3 percent ($i = 0.03$) determine if this treatment is worth the cost.

6. According to the analysis of economic efficiency in Chapter 3, there is a two-part test for determining if the allocation of resources is efficient: Are total benefits greater than total costs? Are marginal benefits equal to marginal costs? Explain how this two-part test helps to explain the apparent paradox of the high payoff from medical advances and the substantial overuse of medical procedures documented by the Dartmouth and Rand research teams.

7. What do we mean by "too much" health care? Illustrate and explain briefly how low out-of-pocket prices for hospital care cause too much hospital care to be produced.

8. Carefully define physician-induced demand. Can it explain the large amount of ineffective and inappropriate care? Why or why not?
9. "Defensive medicine is one of the primary causes of excessive health care spending." Is this statement true or false? Justify your answer.
10. How can the federal tax exemption for health insurance make the net cost of an insurance policy negative?
11. What are the key elements of managed care? Evaluate managed care in terms of its effect on the rate of increase in health care expenditures.
12. In theory, vouchers should reduce excess health care spending. Explain why.

Economic Issues on the Internet

- Centers for Medicare & Medicaid Services (CMS)—http://cms.hhs.gov

  The Centers for Medicare & Medicaid Services (formerly known as the Health Care Financing Administration) is charged with administering Medicare, Medicaid and child health insurance programs. This Web site contains extensive information about these programs and a large collection of health care statistics and data related to these programs. One of the nice features of this site is its provision of online health care indicators, including a medical sector price index, a hospital price index, and a prescription drug price index.

- Funding First—http://www.fundingfirst.org

  Exceptional Returns: The Economic Value of America's Investment in Medical Research, Funding First, May 2000. Summarizes recent studies that find exceptional returns to America's investment in medical technology.

- Rand Corporation—http://www.rand.org

  Assessing the Appropriateness of Care: How Much Is Too Much? Rand Health Research Highlights, Santa Monica: Rand Corporation. Contains a summary of the research conducted at Rand on measuring the appropriateness of medical care. Nontechnical and accessible to the general reader.

- Urban Institute—http://www.urban.org/pubs/hinsure/winlose.htm

  "Tax-Preferred Medical Savings Accounts and Catastrophic Health Insurance Plans: A Numerical Analysis of Winners and Losers," Nichols, Len M., Marilyn Moon, and Susan Wall. This April 1996 Urban Institute study examines the economic implications of the introduction of medical savings accounts combined with catastrophic health insurance plans. Their study indicates that replacing current insurance systems with such a plan would reduce medical expenditures by 4 to 6 percent.

CHAPTER 8

Crime and Drugs: A Modern Dilemma

Outline:

Public Goods
  Government Enforcement of Property Rights
Crime and Crime Control
  An Economic Approach to Crime and Crime Control
  A Comparison of Crime Trends in the United States and England
Drug Legalization: Competing Views
  Liberty: An Argument for Legalization

Paternalism: An Argument Against Legalization
Morality: An Argument Against Legalization
The Final Analysis
A Positive Analysis of Drug Policy
  Does Increased Enforcement Work?
  Unintended But Inevitable Consequences of Drug Prohibition

Unintended But Perhaps Avoidable Consequences of Drug Prohibition
Unintended Consequences of Drug Legalization
Evaluation: Hawks, Doves, and Owls
  Competing Views in Practice
  Current Policy
  Owlish Criticism

In his *Wealth of Nations*, Adam Smith considered the role of government in a market economy. He believed that government must provide national defense, establish an exact system of justice, and ensure the availability of certain public works and institutions. These objectives may not be adequately or efficiently met unless government is involved. Although national defense is self-explanatory, Smith's ideas about an exact system of justice and about public works require some explanation. According to him, an exact system of justice amounts to "protecting, as far as possible, every member of the society from the injustice or oppression of every other member of it . . . ." Public works and institutions consist of (1) laws and infrastructure, such as roads and canals, that facilitate commerce; (2) institutions for the education of the young; and (3) institutions for the instruction of people of all ages. In this context, the educational institutions contribute to the wealth of nations through their effect on commerce. Smith argued, however, that users of the public works and institutions should be expected to pay at least some of the expenses based on the amount used.

The framers of the U.S. Constitution intended to perfect the union that had been established by the Articles of Confederation so as to "secure the blessings of liberty to ourselves and our posterity." The Preamble says that federal government responsibilities are to "establish justice, insure domestic tranquillity, provide for the common defense, [and] promote the general welfare." It is, at least, arguable that the Preamble is consistent with Smith's ideas of the proper roles of government: national defense, internal order, and undertaking those public works that promote commerce. It should not be surprising that a view of government similar to Smith's bubbled up in eighteenth-century America. Jefferson, Madison, and others were directly influenced by Smith and indirectly because they were steeped in the same philosophers.

In a similar vein, Paul Johnson, a British historian, once told Margaret Thatcher that governments "might quite properly do all kinds of things, such as run schools and build roads, but there were only three things they were compelled to do. The more of the optional things they did, the more likely it was that they would neglect the three essentials. So what were the three? They were external defence, internal order, and the maintenance of an honest currency. These things must be done by government because nobody else could do them."[1] Johnson went on to say that governments often failed to provide "an honest currency"; in other words, Johnson argued that governments often cause inflation, a topic that we discuss in Chapter 15. Although the British government currently provides an "honest currency," Johnson believes that it is doing a bad job with the second duty, maintaining internal order.

A majority of U.S. citizens, according to opinion polls, also believe that federal, state, and local governments are not doing a good job in fighting crime, which is one aspect of "maintaining internal order." Recent surveys (2000) show that 59 percent of the population believes that governments should spend more on crime control. This percentage has varied between 59 and 75 percent since 1983 (see Figure 8.1). The highest figure, 75 percent, was in 1994. Surveys show that until quite recently, more people believe that governments in the United States spend too little on crime control than believe they spend too little on dealing with drug addiction or with improving education. The reason for the concern about crime is evident in other polls, which find that over one-third of the population fears walking at night in some areas within a mile of their home. This percentage increased from 40 percent in 1989 to 47 percent in 1994 and has since dropped to less than 35 percent.[2]

Figure 8.1 shows the high percentage of the population that believes that governments spend too little on crime control. It also shows the rapidly increasing expenditures (in inflation-adjusted dollars) from 1983 to the present, which failed to reduce people's concerns about the amount spend on crime control until the mid 1990s. Figure 8.1 shows that the property crime rate (theft, burglary, and motor vehicle theft) has fallen steadily since 1983, again with little apparent effect on people's desire to spend more on crime

---

[1] Paul Johnson, "The Real Job of Government: External Defence, Internal Order and an Honest Currency," *The Spectator* 283 (October 9, 1999): 27.

[2] The data used in the introduction are from Kathleen Maguire and Ann L. Pastore, eds. (various years) *Sourcebook of Criminal Justice Statistics* [online]. (Washington, DC: U.S. Department of Justice, Bureau of Justice Statistics). Current version is available at http://www.albany.edu/sourcebook.

FIGURE 8.1 Selected Crime Facts

Until the mid 1990s, rapidly growing expenditures on crime control had little effect on the public's perception that too little is spent on crime control. Nevertheless, the expenditure growth may have influenced the reduction in property crime rates that occurred throughout the period and the reduction in violent crime rates that began in the mid-1990s.

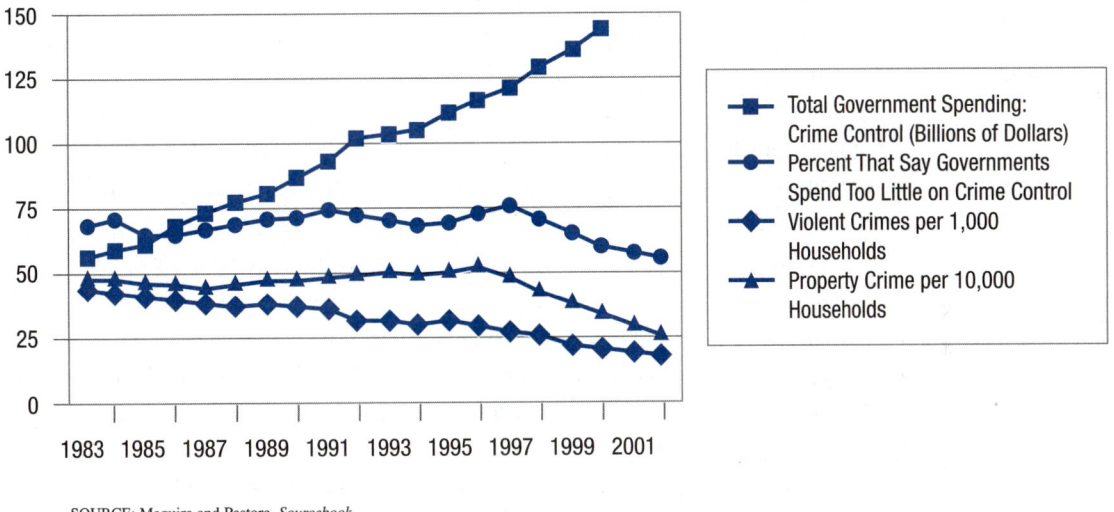

SOURCE: Maguire and Pastore, *Sourcebook*.

control. The figure also shows that violent crime rates (murder, rape, robbery, and aggravated and simple assault) increased from the mid-1980s to the mid-1990s. Since the mid-1990s, the violent crime rate has fallen, which suggests that people's fears about crime began to ease with the decreases in violent crimes.[3]

Crime rates are so high in the United States, at least in part, because of the illegal markets for various drugs. These illegal markets cause much property crime and personal violence. Although the casual use of illegal drugs—as well as alcohol and nicotine—has declined from its peak in the 1970s, frequent users of marijuana, cocaine, and, increasingly, heroin continue to create profitable, but illegal, markets. Violence is endemic on the supply side of these markets. On the demand side, heavy users of illegal drugs often support their habits by committing property crime that are often accompanied by violence.

This chapter explores government's role in crime and drug control. It focuses on Adam Smith's exact system of justice and the Constitution's goal of establishing justice and ensuring domestic tranquillity. First, it discusses crimes in which one person uses force to violate another person's rights. Second, it discusses the so-called victimless crimes created by criminalizing voluntary transactions between two people (for example, a marijuana sale). In both cases, the rationale for government action is discussed. The chapter then discusses drug policy. In subsequent chapters, we discuss the government's role in secondary and college education, which relates to another of the Smithian roles of government and perhaps to the general welfare clause of the Preamble.

INFOTRAC
College Edition

Keywords:
crime and drugs and government

http://www.infotrac-college.com

[3]These crime rates are computed from victimization surveys, which ask people if they have been victims of crimes; victimization rates probably provide the best evidence about crime rates over time because they are more accurate than crimes reported to the police.

■ Public Goods

Public Good – A good that is nonexcludable and nonrival.

Nonexcludable Good – A good that is impossible or extremely difficult to exclude nonpayers from consuming.

Nonrival Good – A good that one person can consume without reducing the amount available for others to consume, such as a feeling of security in a safe city.

Understanding the concept of a *public good* is important to an understanding of the role of government in crime and drug control. Public goods provide a rationale for government's role in the economy. A **public good** has two characteristics. One characteristic is that a public good is a **nonexcludable good**; preventing or excluding people from consuming it is difficult. For instance, if a strong police effort makes streets safe, it is difficult to restrict the feeling of security to people who voluntarily pay for the police effort. In contrast, it is easy to restrict the use of a private good, such as a candy bar, to people who pay for it. Thus, a public good is nonexcludable and a private good is excludable.

The other characteristic is that a public good is a **nonrival good**; an individual can consume a public good without reducing the amount available to other people. To continue the example, if the streets are safe, the fact that one person is enjoying the safety does not reduce the feeling of security available to anyone else. Again, in contrast, if one person eats a candy bar, a private good, other people cannot consume it. Thus, a public good is nonrival and a private good is rival. In summary, a public good is nonexcludable and nonrival; a private good is excludable and rival.

The government may be able to provide a public good more effectively than the private sector for at least three reasons. First, it is costly to exclude people from the benefits of a public good. In the secure-streets example, a private supplier would have to identify when people are enjoying the secure streets and bill them for the security in much the same way that an electric utility sends a monthly utility bill. Monitoring people's street use would be more costly, however, than monitoring their electricity use. Government provision of secure streets, on the other hand, requires that citizens pay taxes, but this payment does not vary with use, which frees the government from measuring it.

Second, in addition to the opportunity costs of the resources used for measuring street use, monitoring the use of some public goods may create privacy costs. Few people want a private firm or government recording where they go or whom they visit.

Third, private provision of a public good, like security or national defense, may be economically inefficient. The opportunity cost of providing security for one more person is zero; the good is nonrival. Nevertheless, a private firm would charge an additional user a price greater than its zero marginal cost. The market price would be greater than its zero supply price. Therefore, too little of the good would be used. If the government finances the public good through taxation, the price to an additional person of consuming security is zero. No one is excluded from the public good by its price. Because the marginal cost of providing the good is also zero, the zero price leads to efficient use of the public good. People consume it up to the point where marginal benefit equals the zero marginal cost.

Government Enforcement of Property Rights

As discussed in Chapter 2, a decentralized market economy requires a government to establish and enforce property rights. An individual with property rights in a good has an exclusive right to use or sell the good within certain constraints. Property rights allow the voluntary transactions of a market system to work well. Dave is more likely to buy a car from Joanna if he feels fairly sure that it will not be stolen or that the government will not take it. Imagine an economy in which the government does not establish and protect property rights. Individuals must protect their own property. With no government protection of property, more theft would occur. To counter the theft, individuals would use more resources to protect their property.

In this imaginary economy, if Hugh is skilled in protecting his property, he makes it easier for other people to protect theirs. To see how this might happen, suppose people in a neighborhood earn a reputation for protecting their property well. Some people in the neighborhood could take advantage of that reputation. For instance, imagine that Hugh and a few other people organize a neighborhood watch. Missy, who lives in the neighborhood, could receive some benefit from the watch without participating in the program. If she acts in this way, she is a *free rider*. A **free rider** uses goods or services provided by others without paying for them. Hugh and his colleagues may not be able to collect any fees or volunteer work from some of the people whose property rights they are inadvertently defending. People have a tendency to be free riders. Free riders will reason that the neighborhood watch is going to exist and provide protection whether they contribute or not, so why contribute?

Free Rider – An individual who uses goods or services provided by others without paying for them.

Hugh and his colleagues will try to prevent free riding by concentrating on protecting their own property. For instance, they will put security locks on their doors but not on the free riders' doors. They may have security patrols only on their own property. By their mere presence in the neighborhood, however, security patrols provide some protection to the free riders' property as well, even though the level of protection will be less than the efficient level. The marginal social benefit of the protection equals the marginal private benefit to Hugh (and his colleagues) plus the marginal benefit to the free riders. Hugh and his colleagues, who pay all of the cost, will expand protection to the point where their marginal private benefit equals marginal cost. However, marginal social benefit is greater than their marginal private benefit. Therefore, Hugh will not expand protection to the efficient level (marginal social benefit equal to marginal cost). If the free riders were willing to share the cost, Hugh would be willing to supply more protection, but the essence of free riding is to avoid paying.

It is cheaper to have a single agency provide security for a town instead of having several types of neighborhood watch groups. Rather than having security patrols concentrate on particular pieces of property, it is probably cheaper and as effective to provide security for the entire town. In other words, monopoly provision of property rights protection may be cheaper than the alternative of individuals providing their own protection.

Another point is that property rights protection requires use of force: *coercion*. Rather than allowing individuals to decide what type of force to use to protect their rights, many people believe that coercive powers should be reserved for representative government.

Finally, because providing property rights protection to one more person does not increase cost, charging for it is inefficient. One more person can consume property rights without reducing their availability to everyone else. In other words, the establishment and enforcement of property rights is a public good because exclusion is difficult and it is nonrival.

■ CRIME AND CRIME CONTROL

Gary Becker, the Nobel Prize–winning economist and sociologist, was one of the first economists, and perhaps the most influential, to analyze crime and its control using the basic tools of economic analysis.[4] Becker and many other economists are willing to assume that criminals, just like law-abiding citizens, are

---

[4] Gary S. Becker, "Crime and Punishment: An Economic Approach," *Journal of Political Economy* 76 (March–April 1968) 169–217.

systematic evaluators of the feasible choices before them. These economists also assume that people are willing to substitute among goods. The implication is that, given a large enough compensation, many people will take actions that they ordinarily would not choose to take. For instance, a person who says, "You cannot pay me enough to live in New York City" or "You cannot pay me enough to live in Stillwater, Oklahoma" almost always means that the market wage in the city is not high enough to induce her to live in that city. Offered a large enough compensation, these people would be willing to live in the other city. In other words, many people are willing to substitute more material goods (greater monetary compensation) for the amenities that they give up by moving to a less desired city.

These systematic evaluators compare the cost and benefit of undertaking a particular action, and they act if the marginal benefit is greater than the marginal cost. Under given conditions, some people find that the marginal benefit of a criminal act is greater than the marginal cost; they commit the crime. Other people choose not to be criminals because they anticipate that benefits will be less than costs, including any psychological costs. Because people are willing to substitute, an increase in the expected benefit of a crime or a reduction in the expected cost will lead more people to crime. Conversely, if the benefit decreases or the cost increases, some criminals will decide to drop their criminal career.

Economists also think of individuals as creative and resourceful.[5] For instance, when tax rates go up, many people become creative in finding legal ways to avoid the tax. In general, when laws are changed to restrict behavior, people respond by figuring out ways around the restriction. Jensen and Meckling discuss peoples' response to the 55-miles-per-hour highway speed limit imposed by the federal government in the 1970s.[6] CB radios and radar detectors became more popular. To avoid the penalties associated with speeding, people searched for better devices to reduce the costs of their traffic violations. The demand for such devices fell when the speed limit was raised to 65 miles per hour and more in some states. In this section, we explore the implications of the economic approach to crime and crime policy.

An Economic Approach to Crime and Crime Control

An individual commits a crime, according to the economic approach, when the expected marginal benefit of the crime is greater than the expected marginal cost. The marginal benefit is the material or psychological reward coming from the crime. The marginal cost is the material or psychological cost of the decision. This general analysis is applicable to any situation. It is more suitable, however, for some issues than for others. The economic approach is particularly useful in analyzing property crime and the illegal behavior of consenting adults in undertaking illegal voluntary actions—prostitution, use of illegal drugs, and illegal gambling. Crimes of violence associated with these crimes also suit this analytical approach. The economic approach may be less useful, however, in analyzing murder, rape, and other acts of violence from which the perpetrator receives only psychological benefit.

An economic approach to crime control implies that government can control crime, particularly property crime, because it can create conditions in which crime does not pay. According to this approach, crime decreases if potential criminals believe their chances of getting away with, say, a bank robbery

---

[5]Michael C. Jensen and William H. Meckling, "The Nature of Man," in Michael C. Jensen, *Foundations of Organizational Strategy* (Cambridge: Harvard University Press, 1998), Chapter 1.

[6]Ibid.

have decreased. They will hesitate if they think that, upon getting caught, they are more likely to receive a speedy trial and, upon conviction, a harsh punishment. Besides making crime less profitable, government can reduce crime by jailing criminals. First, imprisonment raises the cost of crime, making the choice less attractive. Second, it reduces the supply of crimes because some of the people most likely to commit crimes have been locked up. This works because

1. Offenders tend to repeat their criminal activity.
2. An imprisoned criminal is not immediately replaced by a new offender.
3. Imprisonment does not increase after-prison criminal activity.

Because property rights protection is a public good, it can be more efficiently provided by government. Crime control is one part of property rights protection. Government, through the political process, is responsible for determining how much crime control to provide. Everyone benefits from crime control, but, because it is a public good, many people would not voluntarily pay full value for it. As free riders, people reason that they will get the crime control because other people will pay for it. If everyone reasons this way, however, we will have too little crime control. To overcome this free-rider problem, people agree to let the government tax them and to use the resources gained from taxation to provide the crime control.

If government can, in fact, control crime, the allowed amount of crime is a political decision. Why do we decide to allow so much? Figure 8.2 shows the marginal social benefit and cost of reducing the crime rate through crime control. As the amount of resources used for crime control increases, the number of crimes and therefore the probability of being a victim decrease. The marginal social benefit of reducing crime and the probability of being a victim decrease as the crime rate decreases. The feeling of security

FIGURE 8.2 The Efficient Level of Control: Crime or Terror

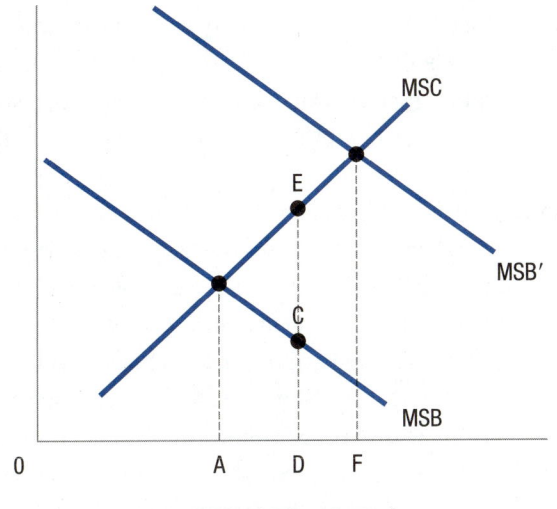

Equating the marginal social benefit and cost of crime control gives the efficient level. Because the marginal social benefit is positive at that level, the efficient level of crime control does not result in elimination of crime—additional benefit results from additional crime reduction. The additional benefit is less than the additional cost. Interpreting the analysis in terms of terrorism control, the terrorist crimes of September 11, 2001, could have had the effect of shifting MSB to MSB'. The efficient level of terrorist control then increased, causing marginal social cost to increase along MSC.

increases as the probability of being a crime victim decreases, say, from 63 percent to 62 percent for a particular time period. The feeling of security also increases as that probability decreases from 3 percent to 2 percent. Most people would not value the second decrease as much as they value the first decrease; in other words, people would be willing to pay more for the decrease from 63 to 62 percent than for the decrease from 3 to 2 percent. If the chances of being a victim are already low, a given reduction in the probability of being victimized would be worth less.

The marginal social cost of reducing the probability of being a victim increases as the amount of crime control increases, as shown in Figure 8.2. The marginal social cost increases for three reasons. First, to reduce crime, more resources must be devoted to crime control. As more resources are devoted to crime control, their opportunity cost increases. These resources must be pulled from other government programs, such as defense, AIDS research, and aid for the homeless—or from taxpayers' pockets.

Second, it takes more resources to reduce crime by a given amount if the crime rate is already low than to reduce it by the same amount if the crime rate is high. The first stage of crime reduction is easy: Catch the incompetent criminals. As the crime rate decreases, however, only the most talented or the luckiest criminals will be in business. It will be more difficult to deter the more talented criminals.

Third, as the amount of crime falls, reducing it further eventually requires an assault on our freedom. By and large, U.S. citizens and their representatives prefer one type of mistake in our judicial system to another. Specifically, we believe punishing the innocent is a worse mistake than not punishing the guilty. Our unwillingness to accept confessions that police obtain by trickery or threat might be interpreted as a way of protecting the innocent. If we had less respect for civil rights, the conviction rate for crimes could increase. The crime rate might drop, but many people believe that the cost would be too high.

The intersection of the marginal social benefit and marginal social cost curves in Figure 8.2 gives the efficient level of crime control and, implicitly, the efficient level of crime. An increase in crime control from A to D reduces everyone's chance of being a crime victim. At D, the marginal social benefit is DC, which is the value that people would place on the increased security and reduced crime rates. The extra cost of an increase in crime control (of a lower crime rate) is DE. This marginal social cost includes the opportunity cost of using more resources for crime control, including the value of lost freedom, if any. Given the circumstances, the crime rate associated with D is too low. It costs more than is gained to increase crime control from A to D.

Just as it suggests that it is possible to spend too much on crime control, the analysis suggests that it is possible to spend too much on antiterrorist actions. Suppose we change the horizontal axis in Figure 8.2 to Quantity of Terrorism Control. Before the terrorist attacks of September 11, 2001, point A might measure the efficient quantity of terrorist control in the United States. The attacks and threats of further attacks changed the perceptions of the threat of terrorist activity and can be interpreted as increasing the marginal social benefit of control from MSB to MSB'. Now at A, the marginal social benefit is much greater than the marginal social cost. Small increases in expenditures on control now have a greater benefit than cost. More expenditures on control are desirable until the control level reaches F.

Several obserations are relevant. First, the increase in the marginal social benefit of control occurs because people believe the world is a more dangerous place than they previously believed. Second, at quantity F, marginal social benefit is greater than it was before the attacks. The fact that MSB is greater implies that people feel less secure than they did before the attacks, even with the increased expenditures on terrorism control. Given the available techniques of control, it is too costly or perhaps impossible to achieve the previous level of security. Third, although the marginal social cost curve has not changed, marginal social cost has increased along the existing marginal social cost curve. The increased resources going to antiterrorism activities have a opportuntity cost that increases as the resources devoted to control increase. The extra government use of resources comes at the expense of other government programs or of private spending. In addition, a large nonmonetary cost is imposed on people. Every airline passenger pays a higher time cost for any given flight. Moreover, people are subjected to the indignities of searches of their belongings and their person. In addition, some freedom has been sacrificed with the increased probability of being held on suspicion of terrorism without the customary legal rights. Finally, as more resources are devoted to terrorism control, more effective ways to control terrorism might be developed. We can also expect technological change that will reduce the cost. This combination of learning by doing and development of new technology may shift the marginal social cost curve to the right, allowing us to be safer at a lower cost.

INSIGHTS

POLICE, GUNS, AND CRIME

Recent information supports the economic approach. New York City, which experienced more than 2,000 murders in 1990, had only one-fifth that many in 2002. Crime rates of all kinds in New York City have plummeted. Associated with this decrease in crime in New York has been (1) an increase of 7,000 police officers, (2) a doubling of the New York prison population, (3) focus on efficient management of the NYPD, and (4) aggressive use of police power to arrest people for minor violations that had in the past been overlooked. For instance, someone who drinks in public or writes graffiti is now more likely to be arrested and required to produce identification, which allows the officer to check for other violations. In short, New York City provides an example of more—and more aggressive—police activity, possibly leading to reduced crime rates.

A statistical study of crime across the United States also supports the economic approach. This study reports that violent crime rates decrease in states that permit their residents to carry concealed handguns. If potential victims might be armed, the expected cost of crimes against people goes up. In turn, criminals may switch to crimes where they are less likely to meet armed resistance. Their study also finds that counties with higher arrest rates per violation have lower crime rates. In response to the possibility that an armed citizenry might lead to more accidental deaths, the study finds that states that introduce concealed-handgun laws have no increase in accidental deaths.

Although these examples are not conclusive, they are consistent with an economic approach to crime. Moreover, they provide an excellent example of the rising cost of crime control. For example, living in a city that harasses people for minor violations can be unpleasant. Encouraging the police to be more aggressive may lead to more incidents of police brutality and to actual or perceived discrimination. A well-dressed jaywalker is likely to escape police attention, whereas a less well-groomed young man is likely to be hassled. Similarly, even if we believe that allowing people to carry concealed handguns reduces the violent crime rate, we also may believe that a society that cannot control crime in other ways is not the ideal society. In short, increased crime control runs into increasing marginal social cost.

SOURCES: John J. DiIulio, Jr., "Arresting Ideas: Tougher Law Enforcement Is Driving Down Urban Crime," *Policy Review* 74 (Fall 1995); and John R. Lott, Jr., and David B. Mustard, "Crime Deterrence, and Right to Carry Concealed Handguns," *Journal of Legal Studies* 26 (January 1997).

INFOTRAC
College Edition

Keywords: *economic aspects of crime*

http://www.infotrac-college.com

This analysis suggests that we have so much crime and so many terrorists acts because they are costly to control. Control may be costly because many people are willing to be criminals or terrorists. Or it may be costly because of the problems, such as poor economic prospects in some inner cities, rural areas, and other parts of the world.

A Comparison of Crime Trends in the United States and England

The economic approach provides a framework useful in understanding the causes of falling U.S. crime rates. A crime occurs when a person decides that the benefit from committing the crime outweighs the cost. Let's assume a crime of tax evasion that pays each taxpayer who commits it $50,000. Let's also assume 1,000 potential tax evaders. Suppose the only cost of the crime is the psychological cost to the criminal. Different people place a different value on being honest. Assume that 300 people choose to commit the crime. The other 700 people value their honesty at more than $50,000. One way to reduce the number of tax evaders is to convince some of the 300 people to place a greater value on honesty. This example implies that one way to reduce crime is to have "better" people; unfortunately, we do not know how to persuade people to place a greater value on honesty. An implication of this example, however, may be that somehow improving the economic and social environment for children is a long-term strategy for crime control.

A direct way to increase the cost of the crime is to use government resources to arrest the criminal, to convict the criminal, and to impose punishment, including incarceration. Increased enforcement and better opportunities in the legal sector of the economy also increase the costs of crime. Because the cost to the criminal increases with the opportunities available, a well-educated person with good job skills faces a higher cost of crime than does a person with poor job skills. Again, the analysis implies that the economic and social environment helps determine whether people become criminals. In particular, people in an economy with good employment opportunities face higher costs of crime.

A comparison of crime trends in the United States and England (including Wales) provides insights about criminal behavior. It may be surprising to learn that (with the exception of murder and rape) crime rates are lower in the United States than in England. More remarkably, English crime rates have remained stable or increased since 1981, while almost all types of U.S. crime rates have fallen. The two panels of Figure 8.3 illustrate these trends for assault and burglary.

The following summarizes the data in these charts and also data from other sources. (We cannot extend the data for Figures 8.3 and 8.4, which are from a careful study of the period 1981 to 1996 that compared crime in the United States with that in England and Wales. We do, however, use later data to show that the relative crime trends in the two countries have not changed.)

1. The English assault rate was about even with that of the United States in 1981 but more than doubled the U.S. rate in 1995. After 1995, the English assault rate continued to increase, while the U.S. rate continued to fall.
2. The English burglary rate was just 40 percent of the U.S. rate in 1981 but it was 75 percent greater than the U.S. rate in 1995. Although the English burglary rate leveled, the U.S. rate continued to fall.
3. The U.S. murder rate was 8.7 times that of England in 1981 and was 5.7 times the English rate in 1996. The U.S. murder rate continued to fall and the English rate continued to increase. By 2000, the U.S. murder rate was about 4 times the English rate.
4. The U.S. rape rate was 17 times that of England in 1981 and was 3 times the English rate in 1996. Although we do not have comparative data on rape after 1996, we have victimization rates for sex-

FIGURE 8.3A Trends in the Assault Rate

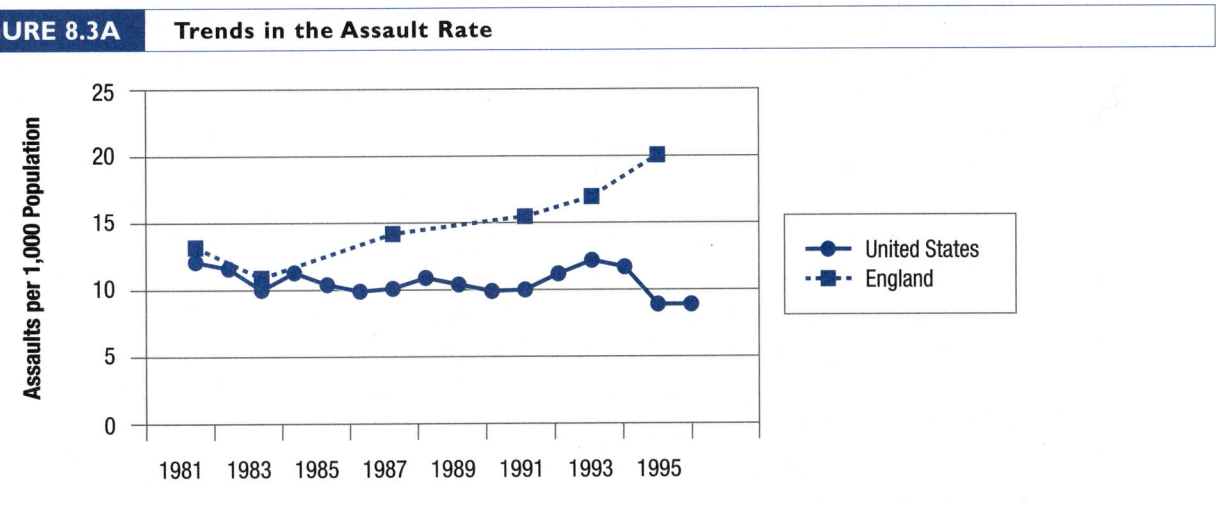

FIGURE 8.3B Trends in the Burglary Rate

Assault and burglary rates are increasing in England and falling in the United States. English assault and burglary rates are now higher than the U.S. rates.

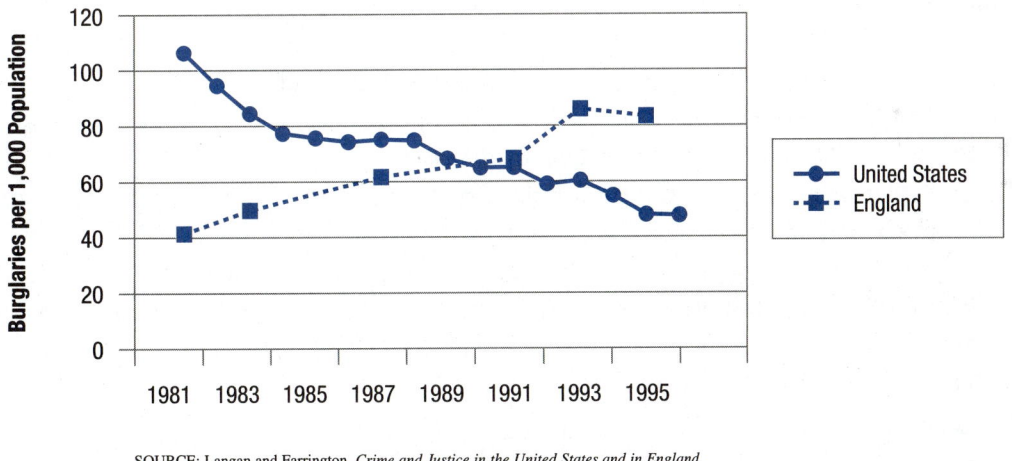

SOURCE: Langan and Farrington, *Crime and Justice in the United States and in England.*

ual incidents, which are defined as offensive sexual behavior and sexual assaults (rape, attempted rape, and indecent assaults). These rates have been falling since 1988 for the United States and rising for England. By 1999 the U.S. rate of sexual incidents was below that of England and Wales.[7]

---

[7] See *Crime and Justice in the United States and in England and Wales, 1981–1996* by Patrick A. Langan and David P. Farrington, Bureau of Justice Statistics, U.S. Department of Justice (October 1998), NCJ 169284, available at http://www.ojp.usdoj.gov/bjs. These results, except for murder and rape, are drawn from victimization surveys, which are probably more reliable than data drawn from police reports. An international victimization survey, the *2000 International Crime Victims Survey* available at http://www.unicri.it/icvs/index.htm, was used to extend the data to 1999. Homicide data through 2000 are available at Gordon Barclay and Cynthia Tavares, "International Comparisons of Criminal Justice Statistics 2000," Issue 05/02, July 12, 2002, available at http://www.homeoffice.gov.uk/rds/pdfs2/hosb502.pdf.

Examining similar data, James Q. Wilson implies that reduced punishment in England and increased punishment in the United States is at least part of the explanation for the changing situation.[8] Certainly, the expected cost of crime is greater in the United States than in England. Days at risk combines the probability of being convicted of crime with the time served if convicted to develop an expected cost of crime based on the economic approach. As seen in Figure 8.4, the risk of days served for assault and burglary is greater in the United States than in England; moreover, the risk has been increasing in the United States and falling in England.[9] Figure 8.4 when compared with Figure 8.3 shows that increases in the costs of crime are associated with reductions in crime rates and that decreases in cost are associated with increases in crime. (A more thorough study would be required to demonstrate the conclusion. The example simply illustrates an approach that economists use to support their theoretical arguments.)

Morgan Reynolds argues that the cause of falling crime rates in the United States is obvious. He points out that in 1950 the probability of going to prison for committing a serious crime was 5.3 percent. It fell to 1.3 percent in 1970 and rose slightly to 1.6 percent in 1980. He attributes the rising crime rates over that period to the reduced probability of significant punishment. The probability of doing time increased to 2.4 percent by 1990 and 2.9 percent by 1997. More generally, a restored confidence in community policing, zero tolerance for minor criminal acts, additional prosecutors, and more prison space led to more people serving longer sentences.[10] By 2000, the number reached 2 million. The rate of imprisonment in the United States is 5 to 20 times greater than in other industrial economies.[11]

Although Reynolds credits the reduced crime rate to the massive increase in the number of people imprisoned, not everyone shares that view. Everyone agrees that it is costly to imprison so many people. In addition, many criminologists believe that a fourfold increase in the number of American prisoners has had little effect on the crime rate. In addition to the increased chance of punishment, criminologists attribute falling crime rates to the following factors:

- Reduction in drug use or stabilization of drug markets
- Demographic and population changes that reduce the number of people in crime-prone categories (e.g., young males)
- A stronger economy and improvements in social and economic conditions
- Greater police visibility through wider implementation of problem-oriented or community-oriented policy
- Community- and youth-oriented programs that promote safer schools and neighborhoods
- Gang abatement programs
- A collective conscience shift toward greater civility and mediation[12]

It is unlikely that any single cause of changing trends in crime rates will be identified. Nevertheless, one important difference in the determinants of crime between the United States and England over this period is in punishment. The United States increased the severity of punishment, and England reduced it.

INFOTRAC College Edition
Keywords: *causes of crime, research of causes of crime*
http://www.infotrac-college.com

---

[8] James Q. Wilson, "Criminal Justice in England and America," *Public Interest* (Winter 1997), 3–14.

[9] See *Crime and Justice in the United States and in England and Wales, 1981–1996* by Patrick A. Langan and David P. Farrington, Bureau of Justice Statistics, U.S. Department of Justice (October 1998), NCJ 169284, available at http://www.ojp.usdoj.gov/bjs.

[10] Morgan Reynolds, "Will Building More U.S. Prisons Take a Bite Out of Crime?" *Insight on the News*, June 7, 1999.

[11] "United States Prisoners: More Than Any Other Democracy," *The Economist* (March 20, 1999), 30.

[12] Dale Steffensmeier and Miles D. Harer, "Making Sense of Recent U.S. Crime Trends, 1980 to 1996/98," *Journal of Research in Crime and Delinquency* 36 (August 1999), 235–274.

FIGURE 8.4A Days at Risk for Assault

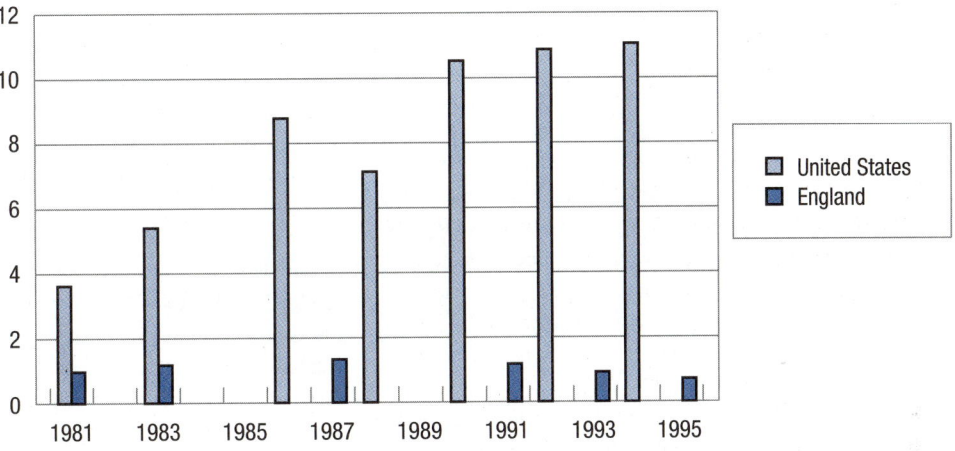

FIGURE 8.4B Days at Risk for Burglary

Days at risk of serving prison time for assault and burglary are greater in the United States than in England. The increasing risk of punishment for assault and burglary in the United States mirrors the falling victimization rates, as does the decreasing risk of punishment in England mirrors the rising victimization rates.

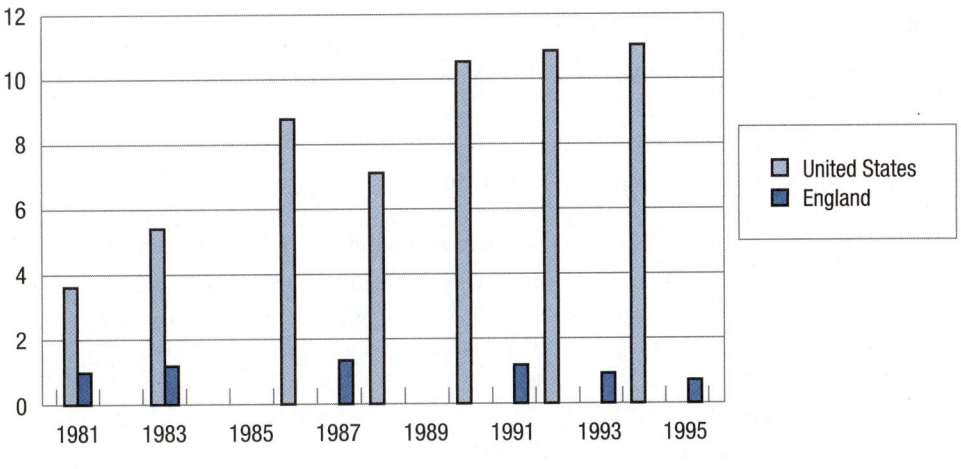

SOURCE: Langan and Farrington, *Crime and Justice in the United States and in England.*

Part of the pattern of U.S. crime rates and punishment relates to illegal drugs. The peak of the cocaine epidemic occurred at about the same time as the peak in the murder rate. In the next section, we examine the interrelationships between drugs and crime.

INSIGHTS

AN INTRODUCTION TO THE SCIENTIFIC METHOD IN ECONOMICS

The discussion of the economic approach to crime and crime control can be used to illustrate one way that economists attempt to gain a scientific understanding of real-world phenomena. This approach uses a logical model based on restrictive assumptions. It then uses the model to derive hypotheses to be tested scientifically. Finally, data are collected that are used in statistical procedures to see whether the hypothesis is consistent with the real world information.

In our model we assume that individuals are systematic evaluators. We then discuss the costs and benefits of crime to the criminal. In the discussion we conclude that if the cost of crime increases, the individual is less likely to commit crime. As we discussed, the definitions of benefits and costs are broad and include more than just monetary benefits and costs.

The next step is to collect data about the hypothesis in question, namely that an increase in the cost of crime to an individual will reduce the number of crimes committed, other things equal. The data collected show the assault and burglary rates in the United States (Figure 8.3) and England and Wales from 1981 to 1996 and the severity of punishment (Figure 8.4). For this to be a valid comparison, the data from both countries must measure the same phenomena. Making the data consistent was a major research project.[a] Assuming the data are consistent, we then look for an association between the observed trend of increased crime in England and Wales and decreased crime in the United States and the severity of punishment. The increased severity of punishment in the United States and the reduced severity in England and Wales are consistent with the hypothesis. Our study, however, is not comprehensive enough to establish the hypothesis. Recall that we assumed in our model that other things affecting the benefits and costs of crime are held constant in the experiment. Examples of the things that must be held constant are listed at the end of the section in the main text. In laboratory experiments, the experimental design holds the other factors constant; in this approach to testing hypotheses in economics, statistical techniques must be used. Finally, although we have shown an association between crime and punishment, we have not established causation. Sophisticated statistical techniques are used by economists to develop empirical support for propositions from economic theory.

[a]Langan and Farrington, *Crime and Justice in the United States and in England.*

■ DRUG LEGALIZATION: COMPETING VIEWS

In any year, more than 10 percent of all arrests reported to the FBI are for prostitution, drug abuse, gambling, and drunkenness (not including driving while intoxicated). These arrests are for voluntary transactions between buyer and seller that have little direct effect on anyone outside the transaction. Why do we make voluntary transactions crimes? In particular, why do we expend so much of our crime-fighting resources in combating the drug trade?

Liberty: An Argument for Legalization

Some people argue that illegal drugs should be legalized. They argue that each responsible individual should have the freedom to engage in any voluntary transaction, as long as it does not impose substantial, involuntary harm on a third party. To John Stuart Mill, the nineteenth-century economist who made this argument, individual liberty was an extremely important value. Similarly, Milton Friedman, an advocate of drug legalization, says, "I believe that adults—by this I mean people whom we regard as responsible, and as a practical matter this means people who are neither insane nor below a certain age—should be responsible for their own lives. . . . People's freedom to make their own decisions is my fundamental objective."[13]

The argument that people should be allowed to make their own decisions is subject to two qualifications. One qualification is that children should not have this freedom. If, say, cocaine were legal, the argument requires that children be forbidden to use it until they reach a certain age. Indeed, it may require strong policies to ensure that children do not use it.

The second qualification is that people should not be allowed to sell themselves into slavery. If you sell yourself into slavery, you relinquish your freedom to make your own decisions. The question then arises of whether dependence on drugs—alcohol, cocaine, or what have you—implies that drug users are selling themselves into slavery. The evidence shows that drug dependence is a powerful force that ruins many lives. Nevertheless, evidence also suggests that the ideas that most drug users become addicts or even that all addicts continue to be users until they die are wrong. An unqualified acceptance of the liberty argument implies the legalization of such drugs as cocaine, heroin, and marijuana.

Paternalism: An Argument Against Legalization

John Kaplan rejects Mill's libertarian principle that would allow people to engage in self-destructive activity in the absence of involuntary harm to others. He argues that people can through government "morally attempt to keep others from likely harm even though they themselves are foolish enough to take the risk. After all, Mill's view that all adults must be assumed to know their own best interest is certainly contrary to fact, as most of us see it."[14] Opinion polls support Kaplan's argument; only a small percentage of the U.S. population—usually less than 5 percent—strongly favors legalizing all drugs.

Public opinion is not completely consistent. The large majority in favor of prohibiting such dangerous drugs as cocaine and heroin opposes prohibiting alcohol and nicotine. We know that alcohol and nicotine are responsible for more deaths and illnesses and that alcohol is related to more crime than all of the prohibited drugs combined. Of course, if we legalized the prohibited drugs, they might generate more problems than alcohol and nicotine.

Morality: An Argument Against Legalization

William J. Bennett, Irving Kristol, and James Q. Wilson, along with many other social scientists, argue that government has a responsibility for prohibiting the use of mind-altering drugs, regardless of (1) whether such drug users are fully responsible and (2) the absence of involuntary harm to others. Wilson flatly states, "Drug use is wrong because it is immoral, and it is immoral because it enslaves the mind and destroys the soul."[15] In this view, the possibility that marijuana or any other drug may be of limited danger to health is irrelevant. The immorality of drug use is in its purpose, which, in this interpretation, is to withdraw from society and civilization.

For people who take this position, the immorality implicit in the use of mind-altering drugs resolves the seeming contradiction in the failure to prohibit nicotine. Although the use of tobacco is arguably as dangerous,

---

[13]Milton Friedman, "Stop Taxing Non-Addicts," *Reason* (October 1988), 24.

[14]John Kaplan, *The Hardest Drug: Heroin and Public Policy* (Chicago: University of Chicago Press, 1983), 104. This book includes an excellent discussion of these issues.

[15]As quoted by "Reclaiming the War on Drugs," *Empower America*, brochure, October 1996. See also James Q. Wilson, "Against the Legalization of Drugs," *Commentary* (February 1990), 23–28.

medically, as the use of various controlled substances, it does not debase life; it only shortens it. According to Wilson, drug users lack such virtues as self-control, sobriety, and the ability to delay gratification. The immorality lies in the effects of drug use on the moral character and on the subsequent harmful effects on society.

The Final Analysis

The inconsistent treatment of alcohol (a mind-altering drug), nicotine, and cocaine suggests that our drug laws do not follow from Mills' or Friedman's libertarian argument, Kaplan's paternalism argument, or Wilson's morality argument. Kaplan tempers his position by stating that the general argument that government should not interfere in basically private behavior is sound practical advice. He simply concludes that the cost of legalization is greater to society than the cost of prohibition. Similarly, Friedman makes his case more persuasive by arguing that drug prohibition causes more harm to innocent third parties than the harm that would be caused to third parties by legalization. In short, both Kaplan and Friedman take a pragmatic approach to drug policy, attempting to weigh the costs and benefits of various actions. Wilson's position, however, leaves no room for a pragmatic analysis.

■ A POSITIVE ANALYSIS OF DRUG POLICY

To analyze the effects of prohibiting a drug such as cocaine requires an alternative. For simplicity, suppose that cocaine is available on demand from government-owned stores. The price paid includes a substantial government tax. Thus, the alternative is similar to the legal situation for liquor in some states. Assume that the supply curve is flat, S_0 in Figure 8.5. This supply curve is the market marginal cost of cocaine. Including a heavy rate of taxation, this marginal cost might be on the order of $20 per gram. Initial users might get 50 doses per gram. Therefore, the cost per dose could be as low as 40 cents.[16] The demand curve,

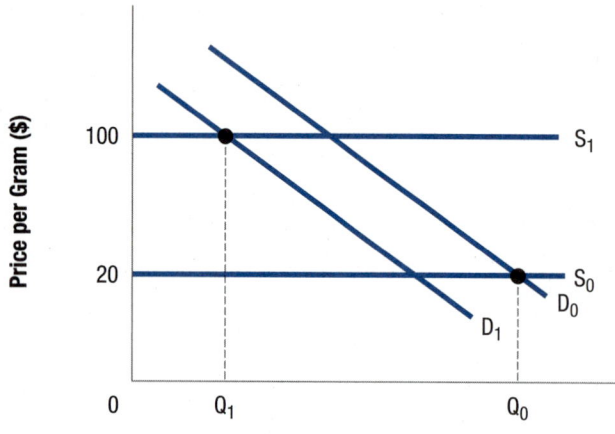

FIGURE 8.5   The Effect of Drug Prohibition on Drug Use

The supply and demand curves, S_0 and D_0, show the market for cocaine when cocaine is legal. Prohibition causes supply to decrease to S_1 and demand to decrease to D_1. Price goes from $20 to $100 per gram, and quantity exchanged falls from Q_0 to Q_1.

---

[16]See John Kaplan, "Taking Drugs Seriously," *The Public Interest* (Summer 1988), 41.

in Figure 8.5, as usual holds several factors constant: the price of other drugs, income, the method of distribution, laws, and consumer preferences.

Now suppose new laws make cocaine and other drugs—except alcohol and nicotine—illegal. Assume that possession and use of the illegal substances would be a felony. Furthermore, selling these substances would be an even more serious felony.

In the new situation, assume the method of distribution matches the one observed in the United States today. A cartel buys cocaine in other countries and exports it to the United States. Presumably, this cartel chooses an output that maximizes profit. After the cocaine arrives in the United States, the cartel distributes it to wholesalers throughout the country. These wholesalers distribute it to city wholesalers, who, in turn, may distribute it to another level of wholesalers, and so on until it reaches local retailers. The several layers of distribution protect the importers and large wholesalers from detection by the authorities. The large difference between the price they pay for their raw material—coca leaves—and the price they receive for their product—cocaine—is partly due to monopoly restriction of output. The price differential also partly reflects extra compensation that the sellers require to cover the cost, including risk of punishment, of evading the drug laws.

Each level of distribution includes compensation for the risk of supplying an illegal product. Additional risks exist for distributors closer to the street. Retail distributors trying to claim a particular neighborhood market sometimes kill other distributors and bystanders.

As the transactions progress beyond the well-organized deals between large wholesalers, the system of property rights established by organized crime disintegrates. Organized crime imposes stiff penalties for stealing rather than buying a major shipment of drugs from a large wholesaler. The penalty—death—is more severe than the penalty imposed by law for, say, hijacking a truckload of whiskey. The retailer and the wholesalers close to the retailer, however, cannot call on a large organization to enforce their property rights. Deals at this level are made through openings in bulletproof doors. Thus, two factors cause the large increase in cost and, therefore, large decrease in supply of cocaine in the United States. One factor includes the cartel system of smuggling cocaine into the United States. The other factor is the risk of punishment for distributing an illegal product and the risk associated with a lack of government-enforced property rights. As a result, if cocaine becomes illegal, the supply curve in Figure 8.5 shifts to S_1.

Demand also changes—from D_0 to D_1—when the product becomes illegal. First, it may decrease because many people avoid illegal activities. This effect may be offset, however, by other people who enjoy violating the law. Second, it will decrease because the deterioration of property rights under the illegal system raises the nonprice costs of buying the good. It is now more difficult to find a supplier of the good. To buy the good, you must deal with people who may murder you if you fail to pay. If you develop a reliable connection at the street level, your connection may be arrested and out of circulation at any time. Then you must go through the dangerous process of finding another supplier. Third, it will decrease because of the legal penalties associated with possession and use. Fourth, it will decrease because of the risk of buying a product in an irregular market. The customer has little recourse if the product purchased is not what it is supposed to be. (This point is comically illustrated by a widely-reported arrest of a cocaine buyer. The buyer reported to the police that he had been sold fake cocaine. The police investigated and found that the substance contained only a small amount of cocaine. Nevertheless, the cheated buyer was arrested for possession.) It may be contaminated with toxic substances used to dilute it. It may be a cocaine look-alike. Many heroin overdoses, some deadly, occur from taking substances of inferior quality or unknown purity; the same is likely true of cocaine overdoses.

The effects of changes in supply and demand are easy to see in Figure 8.5. The price increases from $20 to $100 per gram, and the quantity exchanged decreases from Q_0 to Q_1.

The experience of people who have tried to reduce their use of cocaine supplements the economic analysis. People who have requested treatment for cocaine dependence either through hot lines or clinics have reported spending, on average, from $450 to $800 per week on cocaine. Extremely heavy users have spent as much as $2,000 to $3,000 per week. According to one survey, almost 50 percent of the people who called a cocaine hot line said they had sold cocaine to finance their habit. About 25 percent of them stole at work, and about 35 percent stole from families and friends. About 15 percent had lost their jobs because of cocaine, and about 30 percent had lost their spouses. The illegal use of cocaine clearly involves substantial cost to other people in the economy. In particular, cocaine abusers are similar to heroin abusers in how they finance their habit. If they are unable to support their habit legally, they often resort to crime to support it.[17]

It seems clear that drug prohibition reduces drug use and drug abuse because both demand and supply decrease. A major exception might arise if drug pushing is an important route to drug dependence. The drug pusher supposedly entices people—sometimes young people in the school yard—into drug abuse. This is similar to the approach that tobacco companies used when they distributed free cigarettes on college campuses: Hook a customer, and you may have one for life, albeit a shortened life. This may have been a good strategy for a tobacco company that expected to remain in business for a long time, but it seems less apt for drug dealers. Dependence on heroin or cocaine requires more than a couple of doses. Giving drugs away means less for the dealer–user with no certainty of a future payoff. Furthermore, the target customer might be an undercover drug agent. Even if the pusher creates a dependent customer, either the pusher or the new user might be arrested before the pusher profits on the initial investment. Drug pushing seems to be an investment with little payoff because buyer–seller relationships are so unstable.

In fact, heroin and cocaine use spread like an epidemic. Availability is the key. If people have access to and use heroin, they share their knowledge and their drugs with their friends. Heroin use begins much like a sexually transmitted disease: A friend infects a friend, and, with some promiscuity, the disease soon spreads through a social network.[18]

Cocaine use apparently is similar. One study, for example, found that almost 90 percent of the initial use of cocaine took place at a party or other informal social event. About 70 percent of new users obtained it from friends or relatives. Only 5 percent of the new users obtained it from dealers.[19] Kaplan concludes that the drug pusher is a myth. If this is correct, making drugs illegal results not in dealers pushing drugs on nonusers, but in reducing their general availability and young people's exposure to them.

---

[17]See Mark S. Gold, Andrew M. Washton, and Charles A. Dackis, "Cocaine Abuse: Neurochemistry, Phenomenology, and Treatment," 142–143; and Sidney H. Schnoll et al., "Characteristic of Cocaine Abusers Presenting for Treatment," 173–176 in *Cocaine Use in America: Epidemiologic and Clinical Perspectives*, eds., Nicholas J. Kozel and Edger H. Adams, National Institute on Drug Abuse, Research Monograph 61, U.S. Department of Health and Human Services (Washington, DC: Government Printing Office, 1985).

[18]See Kaplan, *The Hardest Drug*.

[19]Dale D. Chitwood, "Pattern and Consequences of Cocaine Use," in *Cocaine Use in America*, ed. Kozel and Adams, 114–115.

Does Increased Enforcement Work?

Laws against selling and possessing certain drugs reduce their use by reducing supply and demand. The relatively larger reduction in supply leads to a price increase. The law of demand, then, implies that the quantity of drugs purchased decreases further along the new demand curve. Some economists argue, however, that increased enforcement will not work. They say that the quantity demanded of illegal drugs responds little to price; therefore, an increase in price caused by increased enforcement leads to only a small decrease in quantity. Total expenditure for drugs could increase. Drug dealers would be better off—except, of course, for the ones caught.

THE EFFECTS OF POLICIES TO REDUCE SUPPLY. If the drug is sold in a market with significant monopoly power, increased enforcement will reduce cartel profits. Because of the monopoly by the cartel, any increase in cost caused by greater enforcement will reduce the cartel profits.

Different customers, however, may have different responses to a price increase. Over any significant period of time, say, 6 months, almost every user will decrease cocaine consumption. Figure 8.6 shows the demand curve, D_c, for a casual user of cocaine. If price goes from P_0 to P_1, the quantity demanded falls from Q_0 to Q_c. The percentage reduction in quantity is greater than the percentage reduction in price; quantity demanded responds vigorously to the price change. As the figure shows, the casual user spends less; the shaded area labeled A measures the reduction in expenditure because quantity demanded is less. The increase in price leads to an offsetting increase in expenditure measured by the shaded area labeled B. Because the area of A is greater than the area of B, the net effect is for the casual user to spend less when price goes up. Given that the objective of the law is to reduce cocaine use, the increased enforcement works. The user, of course, may substitute other substances for cocaine: alcohol, heroin, or marijuana, for instance.

FIGURE 8.6 Demand Curves for a Casual and a Dependent Cocaine User

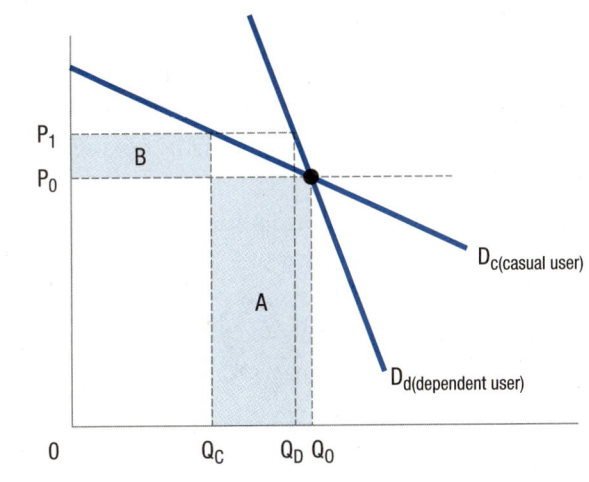

If the price of cocaine goes from P_0 to P_1, the casual cocaine user reduces quantity demanded from Q_0 to Q_c. The percentage reduction in quantity demanded is greater than the percentage increase in price. The casual user reduces expenditures on cocaine by the amount represented by shaded area A (due to lower quantity demanded) and increases expenditures by the shaded area B (due to higher price). By inspection, it is clear that the net effect is a reduction in expenditure. The dependent user, on the other hand, reduces quantity demanded from Q_0 only to Q_D and, by inspection, increases expenditure.

Figure 8.6 also shows the demand curve, D_d, for a dependent user of cocaine. If price goes from P_0 to P_1, the quantity demanded falls from Q_0 to Q_D. But this user is dependent. The higher price reduces quantity demanded only slightly. Here, the percentage decrease in quantity is smaller than the percentage increase in price. The dependent user buys slightly less cocaine if price increases, but spends more. (Using the steeper demand curve, can you identify the areas that represent the expenditure reduction because of a reduced quantity and the expenditure increase because of an increased price?)

Many people would attack drug use and abuse in this country by going after the foreign sources. However, cultivation of coca or opium poppies is possible and profitable over a large part of the world. Coca and opium poppies are traditional crops in many countries. It is unlikely that the U.S. government can convince or afford to bribe farmers in all parts of the world to grow other crops. The implicit position of these farmers is that if U.S. consumers do not want the product, they need not buy it. This, by the way, is the same position that the U.S. government and U.S. tobacco companies take with regard to U.S. exportation of cigarettes.

Similarly, production and distribution of illegal drugs are profitable and easy to conceal. Although increased enforcement can raise the cost of producing and distributing drugs, it is not clear that any acceptable policies can eliminate their supply. If an answer to drug use and abuse exists, it probably lies on the demand side.

THE EFFECTS OF POLICIES TO REDUCE DEMAND. The second way that the laws work is by reducing demand. The effect of increased enforcement is to make the buyer–seller relationship less certain. Buyers and sellers both get arrested. New connections must be made. Particularly with increased enforcement, a new connection—buyer or seller—may be an undercover officer. Given the increased risk, some of the more reliable sellers leave the market. Also because of the increased risk, others may choose to deal in a more concentrated form of the drug. With greater enforcement, the product becomes more variable in purity and more subject to adulteration with toxic substances, leading to more overdoses, deaths, and serious illnesses. These effects will decrease the demand of users and potential users for the drug, but it is a harsh way to reduce demand. It brings to mind a quote from the Vietnam War: "We had to destroy the village to save it."

Many people argue that a better way to reduce demand is through education about the dangers of drug use and abuse. We certainly agree that young people need accurate information about all drugs—legal and illegal. If the opportunity cost of enforcement is a reduction in benefits from education about drugs, a careful study of alternatives would be important.

Social conditions may also be important determinants of drug use and abuse. Some drug use, no doubt, stems from the tendency of young people to take risks. Another part stems from the boredom and alienation experienced by suburban youth. The poverty, despair, and chaos of inner cities also contribute to drug use. A society without inner-city poverty, suburban alienation, and risk-taking youth probably would have a lower demand for drugs. But do we know how to change such social conditions enough to make a large and timely effect on drug use? The economic analysis of drug prohibition, on the other hand, suggests that it works. It reduces use, and increased enforcement of the laws reduces use even more.

Unintended But Inevitable Consequences of Drug Prohibition

Many people argue that drug laws and their increased enforcement have important undesirable and inevitable consequences. First, drug prohibition creates criminals where there were none. Ten percent of

INFOTRAC
College Edition

Keywords: *control of narcotics*

http://www.infotrac-college.com

the population above the age of 11—more than 20 million people per year—commit crimes simply by using illegal drugs. Almost 1 million people are arrested for drug use each year. The law, intended to protect potential users by keeping them away from drugs, makes criminals out of more than 10 percent of the adult population.

Furthermore, the drug user consumes products that are unsafe because they are exchanged in illegal markets and because our government at times sprays the raw material with toxic substances. Of course, the illegal drugs also are unsafe because of their chemical properties. It is an open question, however, whether the more common illegal drugs would be more dangerous, if legal, than alcohol or nicotine. A significant part of the health problems related to drug use is a result of the drug laws.

Another undesirable consequence is that some users commit numerous property crimes in order to buy drugs. In fact, as discussed earlier, increased enforcement—which causes a price increase—may lead to increased crime because dependent users spend more for illegal drugs at higher prices. Many drug users commit crimes. In 1997, 19 percent of all state prisoners and 16 percent of all federal prisoners reported that they committed their crime to get money for illegal drugs. This was up from 16 and 10 percent, respectively, in 1991. We might assume that these people would not have committed their crimes if their drug of choice could be purchased legally.

It is sometimes argued that drug use causes crime in addition to the crimes committed to get money for drugs. Although they do not mention getting money to buy drugs, many other state and federal prisoners were using alcohol or other drugs at the time of their offense. Does this mean that drug use causes crime? Would crime rates increase if more people were using drugs that are currently illegal? We cannot be sure, but it is not correct simply to assume that these people would not commit felonies if they were sober. Many drug-using criminals were criminals before they were drug users.

In addition, prohibition has created opportunities for many people to earn large incomes as drug dealers. For youth—especially those in the poor areas of large cities—the quickest way to a BMW is through dealing illegal drugs. This opportunity would decrease if drugs were legal. At the wholesale and import level, drug prohibition is a bonanza for organized crime. The profit from drug dealing is enormous; almost all of it is available because of drug prohibition.

Large profits in illegal drugs also lead to corruption of public officials. Police officers realize that their salaries are low relative to the earnings of some drug dealers. Moreover, the police know that many citizens see nothing wrong with drug use. In such circumstances, bribes may entice some police officers, judges, prosecutors, prison guards, and other public officials into corruption. The drug war, as currently prosecuted, may lead to police corruption in other ways. The police have the right to confiscate any assets they think are linked to drug dealing. These assets can include your money, your house, and your car. Suppose you are stopped for a traffic violation. If they find the slightest evidence of an illegal substance in your car, the police can confiscate it. If your assets are confiscated, to retrieve them you must prove that they were not somehow obtained from or involved in illegal drug transactions. It is sometimes difficult to prove a negative. Moreover, in some instances, the police keep the assets or a portion of the assets for use of the police department. This creates an obvious incentive for improper police behavior. Although the courts have not ruled such action unconstitutional, many people believe that it diminishes our constitutional liberties. Finally, if any of us condone illegal drug activity, respect for the law diminishes.

In short, drug prohibition causes a link between drug use and crime. If drugs were available legally, crimes committed to finance drug use would decline. Our experience with outlawing products and establishing price controls has taught us that such laws will be broken. Thus, the link between drug prohibition and crime is undesirable but arguably inevitable.

Unintended But Perhaps Avoidable Consequences of Drug Prohibition

Several unintended but perhaps avoidable consequences of the drug laws affect this country. One may be an increased use of cocaine at the expense of marijuana. Cocaine is an inherently more dangerous drug than marijuana. Periods of extensive cocaine use lead to depression, sexual problems, convulsions, unconsciousness, and death.[20] Babies with low birth weights, brain damage, and malformations are a tragic consequence of crack cocaine use by pregnant women.

Ironically, increased enforcement of drug laws may have increased the attraction of cocaine relative to marijuana. The price of cocaine per gram is much higher than the price of marijuana. It is much easier to smuggle a million dollars' worth of cocaine than to smuggle a million dollars' worth of marijuana. The greater weight and bulk of marijuana make it easier to detect in transit than cocaine. The penalties for smuggling or wholesaling cocaine were, at times, not much greater than for smuggling or wholesaling marijuana. Therefore, the laws and more aggressive enforcement of the laws have caused the supply of marijuana to decrease more than the supply of cocaine.

Changes in retail prices of cocaine and marijuana support this analysis. From 1981 to 1988, the street price per pure gram of cocaine fell by more than one-half: from about $280 to about $120 for a small purchase. From 1988 to 1997, it fell by another 20 percent. The price of heroin per pure gram followed the same pattern. Unlike the prices of the two hard drugs, the price of marijuana increased from about $2.50 per gram to about $7 from 1981 to 1988. Its price seems to have stabilized since 1988.[21]

Another unintended and related consequence of increased enforcement of the drug laws may have been the development and widespread use of crack cocaine. The crack epidemic was related to the increased purity of street cocaine. One reason for this increased purity is that the penalty for dealing cocaine is similar whether the cocaine is 35 percent pure or 70 percent pure, making it relatively more profitable to deal in the purer or more concentrated product. Whatever the dangers of cocaine and whatever its addictive properties, it is clear that the more concentrated the product, the greater these dangers. Moreover, crack cocaine is smoked, which means that its effects are almost immediate compared to the slower effects of inhaled cocaine. The immediate reinforcement obtained from smoking crack is one of the reasons for its greater addictive properties.

Yet another unintended consequence of increased enforcement of drug laws is recruitment of teenagers and preteenagers into selling drugs. These children are lured by the fame and fortune of successful drug dealers. Drug dealers use these children for street activities with a high risk of arrest. This keeps the dealers out of jail, while the children arrested in these high-risk activities receive mild treatment from the courts. Thus, tragically, children become valuable gang members. It is ironic that current drug enforcement

---

[20]Chitwood, "Patterns and Consequences of Cocaine Use," 121–124.

[21]See *Drug and Crime Facts* at http://www.ojp.usdoj.gov/bjs/drugs.htm and *What America's Users Spend on Illegal Drugs: 1988–2000* (Prepared for Office of National Drug Control Policy, Prepared by Abt Associates, Inc., Cambridge, MA) December 2001; available at http://www.WhiteHouseDrugPolicy.gov.

is leading young people into drug dealing, when everyone agrees that one goal of drug policy should be to keep young people away from drugs.

Another consequence of current drug policy is the siphoning of resources from fighting nondrug-related crime. Almost everyone would agree that a basic premise of crime control is to protect people from involuntary harm. Our drug control policies run counter to this premise. First, as we have seen, drug prohibition creates numerous crimes that result in involuntary harm to innocent bystanders. Second, using so many resources for drug control almost inevitably drains resources from crime control. Effective deterrence requires a high probability of being caught combined with a quick trial and sure punishment if convicted. Clogging the courts and prisons with drug offenders reduces the probability of being caught, swiftly convicted (if guilty), and surely punished for nondrug crimes. In short, the opportunity cost of drug prohibition is high.

Keyword: *decriminalization*

http://www.infotrac-college.com

Unintended Consequences of Drug Legalization

Many people argue that significant third-party effects of drug use exist. If prohibition reduced alcohol consumption, legalization of alcohol has had significant third-party effects. The legalization of cocaine and other illegal drugs presumably would have similar effects.

First, alcohol abuse by pregnant women has caused many children to suffer from fetal alcohol syndrome. Certainly, this effect of alcohol use is an unintended consequence. If the elimination of prohibition leads to increased use of drugs by pregnant women, an increased incidence of birth problems is an unintended consequence.

Second, drug (alcohol) abuse has led to the breakup of many families and to serious problems for many families that do not break up. This is another unintended consequence of drug legalization. Some people might argue that these first two unintended consequences are confined to the family unit and thus are not third-party effects, but the effect on children must be of concern to the rest of society, and specifically to government.

Third, alcohol abuse has been responsible for the deaths of many innocent individuals in automobile accidents. Here is a clear third-party effect that requires government action. For instance, scarce police resources must be used to keep drunken drivers off the highways.

Keywords: *economic aspects of drug abuse, health aspects of drug abuse*

http://www.infotrac-college.com

Fourth, alcohol abuse means that we have more automobile accidents and higher automobile insurance rates for everybody. We also have more illness and higher medical insurance rates for everybody. Presumably, the legalization of illegal drugs would have similar effects on automobile and health insurance.

■ EVALUATION: HAWKS, DOVES, AND OWLS

This analysis of the relationship between crime control and drug control could lead to a pessimistic conclusion. If we continue to follow the current policy, drug-related crime levels will remain high. Drug users, drug dealers, and some public officials will engage in criminal acts. On the other hand, if we legalize drugs, many more people—including young people—will become drug users and abusers. Can we find a middle ground?

Competing Views in Practice

Peter Reuter stereotypes the debate between the advocates of strict prohibition, such as William Bennett, and those of legalization, such as Milton Friedman, as one between hawks and doves. According to him,

INTERNATIONAL PERSPECTIVE

DUTCH DRUG POLICY

Drug policy in the Netherlands differs from that of the United States in significant ways. The Dutch drug policy emphasizes risk reduction for individual drug users, their neighborhoods, and the general society. Possession, distribution, production, advertising, and international trade of all drugs, except for medicinal or scientific purposes, are illegal. So far, this sounds like U.S. drug policy, but the application is different. Dutch law explicitly distinguishes between soft drugs, such as marijuana, and hard drugs, such as cocaine and heroin.

Dutch law permits nonenforcement if to do so is in the public interest. Using this expediency principle, official Dutch policy is that the possession of small amounts of soft or hard drugs for personal use will not be prosecuted. Regulations permit the establishment of coffeehouses and other retail sites for the sale of marijuana for personal use. Coffeehouses are strictly regulated. Advertising, hard drugs, nuisances, sales to persons younger than 18 years of age, and large quantities sold per transactions are strictly prohibited.

The Dutch rationale for decriminalizing retail sale and use of marijuana is straightforward. The government argues that marijuana, unlike heroin and other hard drugs, does not create an unacceptable risk for users. Moreover, the government rejects the gateway hypothesis, by which the use of marijuana for physiological or psychological reasons leads to hard drug use. The Dutch position is that it is all but impossible to prevent people, including young people, from obtaining marijuana. Experience in the United States, which has had strong enforcement of its harsh drug laws, may confirm the Dutch position. Consequently, the Dutch argue, obtaining and using marijuana in a legal, controlled environment is better for young people than obtaining and using it in an illegal, uncontrolled environment where, Dutch authorities believe, young people are much more likely to be introduced to hard drugs. This argument implies that if marijuana is a gateway drug in the United States, the gateway is through illegal purchase rather than use.

The effect of Dutch policy on drug use and abuse is not easily determined. The best evidence suggests that as more coffeehouses opened, marijuana consumption among young people increased substantially, either because consumption became more accepted or because coffeehouse owners were able to increase the demand for their product. Nevertheless, young peoples' use of marijuana in the Netherlands is less than in the United States.

Furthermore, the incidence of hard drug addiction in the Netherlands is no higher than in other European countries and in the United States. Dutch tolerance of marijuana does not obviously increase the demand for hard drugs. The Dutch also follow a harm-minimization policy in the treatment of hard drug users. Needle exchanges are available, and methadone, a heroin substitute, is freely available to addicts on a maintenance basis. Although addicts are encouraged to reduce methadone use, it is not required. Moreover, methadone clients may use alcohol and other drugs in moderation. This program is designed to inhibit the addicts' health deterioration and perhaps to allow them to function in society. With this approach, only about 12 percent of the diagnosed Dutch AIDS patients were intravenous drug users, compared to about 24 percent in the United States and 38 percent in Europe, in general. Again, little, if any, evidence exists that this nonpunitive approach has caused any substantial increase in addiction.

The Netherlands' more lenient drug policy is something for citizens and policy makers to consider. One pertinent question is whether soft and hard drug use is greater in the Netherlands than it would be under alternative policies. It apparently is no greater than in the United States. Other factors being equal, however, what might be the effect of changing U.S. drug policy? This is a question to be answered by positive analysis. Another pertinent question is, what should be the objective of U.S. drug policy? This normative issue turns on one's ideas about liberty, pragmatics, and morality.

SOURCES: *Drug Policy in the Netherlands: Continuity and Change*, Ministry of Health, Welfare, and Sport, Utrecht, The Netherlands, http://www.minvws.nl; and *Dutch Cannabis Policy*, Fact Sheet 1, Netherlands Institute for Alcohol and Drugs, Utrecht, The Netherlands, http://www.trimbos.nl.

hawks perceive the drug problem as one of values—users and sellers care nothing about right and wrong. Drug use, according to hawks, implies a concentration on short-term benefits and a lack of concern for others. Hawks consider drug use an evil that requires tough enforcement of prohibition as a means of restoring fundamental values. Reuter points out that, in addition to the crime and violence inherently associated with prohibition, hawkish policies may threaten constitutional guarantees. For instance, surveys show that a majority of adults agree that searches of a known drug dealer's house should not require court-approved search warrants.

Doves, according to Reuter, believe that the greatest drug problems are those associated with prohibition, not use. They are particularly concerned about the violence inflicted on third parties and about the threat to constitutional guarantees of freedom. Doves believe that if adults have appropriate information, they will make informed choices about drugs and that government and society should not interfere. Reuter fears, however, that dovish policies risk a large increase in drug use and abuse.

According to Reuter, owls—Kaplan seems to fit—believe that the drug problem is one of drug abuse, addiction, and associated disease.[22] In their view, drug use and abuse results from bad social conditions. Although owls would retain prohibition, bold, demand-side intervention is the core of their policy. Rather than minimizing drug use or minimizing enforcement costs, owls want the lowest level of enforcement compatible with keeping initiation down and encouraging the dependent to seek treatment. Drug control is also not the only goal, and higher drug use may be accepted in return for better performance with respect to some other social goal, such as reduced spread of HIV infection.

Current Policy

Hawks, doves, and owls agree that an important goal is to keep young people away from drugs. Marijuana use by young people peaked about 1980 with a somewhat later peak for older people. Recent surveys indicate that marijuana and other illicit drug use is increasing, but it remains below the peaks of the late 1970s.

Hawks presumably would argue that punitive drug policy is responsible for reducing drug use. As discussed in the introduction to this chapter, governments have funneled more resources into enforcing prohibition. This policy has made it risky to use and to sell illegal drugs. One estimate is that marijuana users face a 2 percent chance per year of being arrested. As may be appropriate for a more dangerous drug, the annual arrest risk for a cocaine user is 6 percent. Similarly, cocaine dealers have a four times greater chance of being arrested in a year of dealing—40 percent—than do marijuana dealers.

The greater enforcement effort directed at cocaine reflects a perhaps owlish conclusion that cocaine is more dangerous than marijuana. It is owlish because the concern relates to the mental and physical health risk to the user; recall that hawks perceive the danger as the risk to society of a collapse of values due to narcissistic drug use.

Economists often analyze a program's effectiveness assuming that it has a fixed budget. Suppose that a drug program were given the approximate $19 billion that the federal government spent on drug control in 2002. Including state spending, total government spending in 2002 may be close to $40 billion.

---

[22]Peter Reuter, "Hawks Ascendant," *Daedalus* 121 (Summer 1992.). Reuter, a self-proclaimed owl, denies that the imagery is loaded. Based on his reading of *Winnie-the-Pooh*, Owl is "learned (he can misspell long words) but unrealistic and self-deluded," fn. 8, 48.

Is this the efficient amount—the amount where marginal social benefit equals marginal social cost? We do not know; furthermore, it is extremely difficult to find out.

Consequently, the policy question often becomes whether the amount allocated is used most effectively. For instance, is the split between marijuana and cocaine control appropriate? The answer depends on whether the *equimarginal principle* is satisfied. The equimarginal principle requires that in the allocation of a fixed budget the last dollar spent on one activity should yield the same marginal benefit as the last dollar spent on any other activity. For instance, if the last dollar spent on marijuana enforcement yields a marginal benefit of 3 dollars and the last dollar spent on cocaine enforcement yields a marginal benefit of 8 dollars, too much is being spent on the former. A dollar taken away from marijuana enforcement causes benefits to fall by 3 dollars. Switching this dollar to cocaine enforcement yields a benefit of 8 dollars for a net gain of 5 dollars. As this switching continues, marginal benefit will fall for cocaine enforcement and rise for marijuana enforcement until the marginal benefits are equalized.

Owlish Criticism

Owls argue that enforcement still concentrates too much on marijuana. They believe that marijuana is less dangerous to the individual than cocaine. Hawks might respond that marijuana is as dangerous to social values as other illegal drugs and that the danger to the individual is less significant for social policy. Owls and hawks, therefore, because of different objectives, disagree about the allocation of the enforcement budget. Owls emphasize harm minimization to individuals, whereas hawks emphasize minimization of illegal drug use.

Reuter argues that the hawks are ascendant. First, he cites increased enforcement budgets, increased severity of laws, and increased punishment for drug possession and sale. As further evidence, he cites the unwillingness of the U.S. government to allow the therapeutic prescription of marijuana to people with AIDS, cancer, and glaucoma. Reuter suggests that the main reason for this prohibition, and the prohibition of heroin's use for pain relief for the terminally ill, is to signal that these drugs have no redeeming social value.

Similarly, HIV infection spreads partly because drug addicts share needles. To combat its spread, several European countries, including Britain, the Netherlands, and parts of Switzerland, have syringe-exchange programs. Syringe exchange is almost taboo in the United States, perhaps because it would imply that the HIV costs of needle sharing are greater than the costs of a recognition of evils worse than heroin use.

If hawkish drug policy were necessary in the successful termination of the drug epidemic of the last decade or in the reduction of drug use by youth, owls might believe that the hawkish policy is appropriate. But was it necessary? If so, why does the epidemic show signs of a recurrence?

Education, a demand-side policy, may have contributed to the declining use of drugs by young people in the 1980s. Figure 8.7 shows large changes in attitudes regarding the legalization of marijuana. In 1980, between 40 and 45 percent of the people ages 18 to 29 favored the legalization of marijuana. By 1990, this dropped, with less than one-fourth of this age group favoring it. Why the change? Part of it may be attributable to the unrelenting war on drugs. Certainly another part may have been attributable to drug education in homes, churches, and schools (DARE programs, for instance); to a greater concern for health; and to public service announcements in the mass media ("Just Say No"). By 2000, however, the percentage of young people favoring legalization had climbed to 41 percent.

Similarly, marijuana use by college students, along with the use of other illicit drugs, alcohol, and cigarettes, declined until the early 1990s. (Figure 8.8). Along with young people's attitudes about legalization of marijuana, however, the use of marijuana, cigarettes, and cocaine increased later in the 1990s,

FIGURE 8.7 — Percentage of Young Adults Who Agree That Marijuana Should Be Legalized

This figure shows that in the 1980s young people became less willing to legalize marijuana use, but in the 1990s they became more willing.

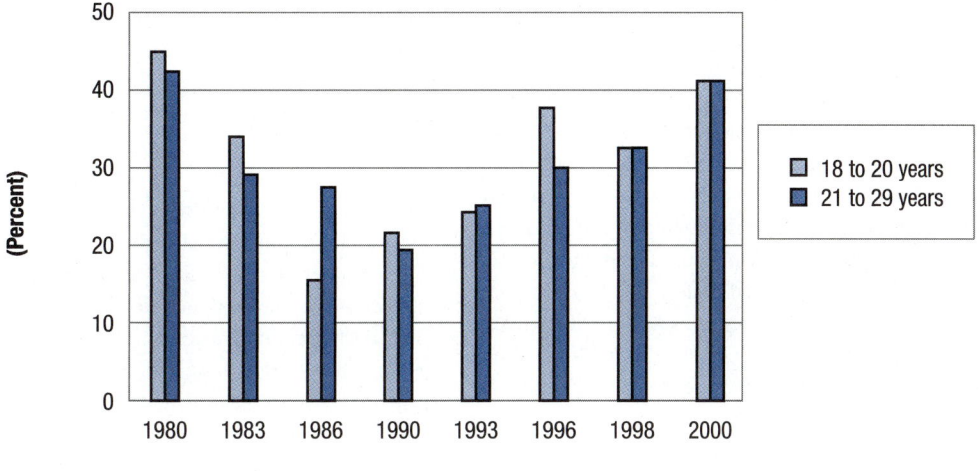

SOURCE: Maguire and Pastore, *Sourcebook*.

FIGURE 8.8 — Percentage of College Students That Used Various Drugs over the 12 Months Prior to the Survey

Young people reduced their use of drugs—legal and illegal—in the 1980s, but now their use is increasing.

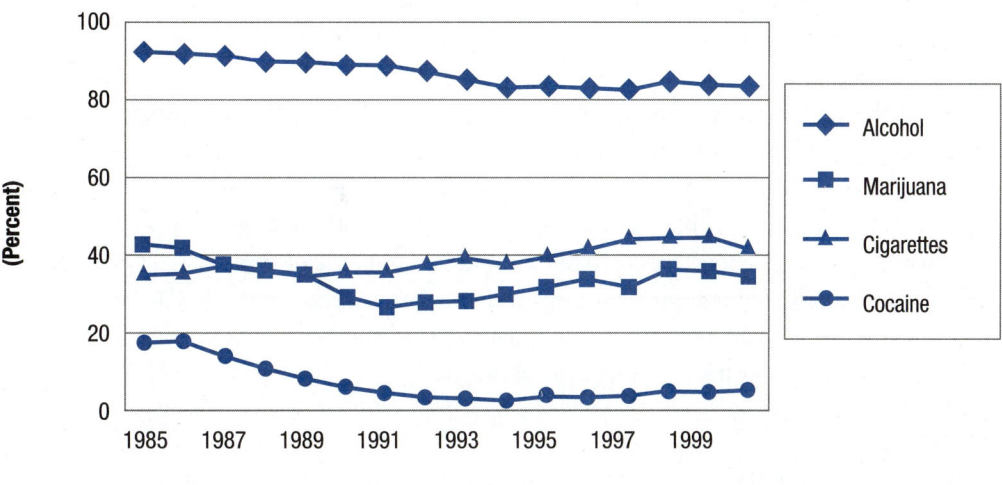

SOURCE: Maguire and Pastore, *Sourcebook*.

INSIGHTS

ALTERNATIVES FOR THE UNITED STATES

Drug policy in the United States remains hawkish. According to the Department of Justice, in 2002 the federal government spent approximately $19 billion on drug control. State governments spent about the same amount. According to the National Center on Addiction and Substance Abuse at Columbia University, states spent almost $80 billion dollars dealing with substance abuse (both legal and illegal). The federal expenditures on control consisted (in round numbers) of $6 billion on treatment and research, $10 billion on domestic law enforcement, and $3 billion on efforts to reduce the imports of illegal drugs into the United States. The equimarginal principle requires that the last, say, $1 million spent on each of these categories should yield the same marginal benefit. Owls believe that this condition is clearly violated.

An analysis of prices shows that efforts to reduce the production of coca leaves and opium, the raw materials for cocaine and heroin, can have only a small effect on the street price in the United States. It is not hard to see why. The coca leaf necessary to produce just over 2 pounds of cocaine costs about $300, but the cocaine might then sell for about $150,000 on the street in $100 units. If the raw material price goes up by $1,000, the street price would only have to go to $100.67 to pass the full cost to the customer. In other words, tripling the price of the raw material would at most push the price up by only 0.67 percent. Similarly paying a pilot half a million dollars to fly 500 pounds into the United States costs $1,000 per pound. If increased enforcement caused the pilot to require $1,000,000 for the flight, the cost only goes up by $1,000 a pound. Because the cost for 2 pounds goes up by $2,000, the necessary increase in the street price (based on this calculation) would be 2×0.67—less than 2 percent. Because the increased efforts to reduce imports of coca leaf have had little effect on price or availability, reducing the effort to limit foreign imports would have little effect on cocaine use. In other words, the marginal benefit of an additional $1,000,000 spent to reduce imports is quite low. The marginal benefit of spending an $1,000,000 on treatment, on the other hand, is much higher. Even if the objective is to reduce cocaine consumption, reallocating funds to treatment or demand reduction would appear to have more effect on consumption than the marginal funds spent on reducing imports. The equimarginal principle, discussed in the text, provides a useful way to thing about drug control.

SOURCE: Suggested by Peter Reuter, "The Limits of Supply Side Drug Control," *The Milken Institute Review*, 2001, 3(1):14-23.

---

while alcohol use stabilized. These patterns suggest that neither education programs nor the war on drugs have had consistent effect on the drug-using behavior of young people.

Nevertheless, hawks argue for a continuation of current punitive drug policies. Without it, they believe that drug use would be even higher. Owls oppose legalization, but they would reduce the punitive nature of current policy and reorient it toward education and treatment. They also would make greater distinctions between types of drugs and enforcement measures. They believe that the current expenditures would yield greater benefits if they were reallocated. Neither hawks nor owls have convincing explanations for the recent upsurge in drug use.

Summary

Free riders can consume public goods without paying for them because it is difficult to prevent people from using public goods. Furthermore, it is inefficient to exclude people from using public goods because the marginal cost of one more user is zero. The existence of public goods provides a rationale for government action in the economy because it is often inefficient for the private market to supply public goods. Imagine the results if national defense were provided through a private market.

One type of crime, broadly defined, occurs if one person violates another person's property rights. The provision of a system of property rights is an important responsibility of government and is an example of a public good. The enforcement of property rights—crime control is an example—is also a public good. Therefore, crime control is an important responsibility of government. The efficient level of crime occurs when the marginal social benefit of crime control equals its marginal social cost.

Drug prohibition is a major cause of crime. A simple way to reduce drug-related crimes is to legalize drugs. Obviously, if drugs were legal, most direct drug crimes—possession and sale—would be eliminated. Furthermore, crimes committed to obtain money to buy illegal drugs would decrease because legal drugs could be cheaper than illegal drugs. Finally, the corruption of public officials that accompanies illegal drug markets would be eliminated.

With the huge profits eliminated from illegal drug markets, inner-city youth would have less incentive to become criminals. Gang activity and indiscriminate violence would decrease in the inner city.

On the other hand, drug legalization would increase the supply of such drugs as cocaine and heroin. Demand also would increase because of legalization, so drug use would increase. If it is true that cocaine use is more dangerous than marijuana use, a possible strategy would be to relax marijuana prohibition and strengthen cocaine prohibition. The debate over drug policy in the United States will continue.

Key Terms

Public good
Nonexcludable good
Nonrival good
Free rider

Review Questions

1. Which of the following would be classified as a public good and why?
    a. clean air
    b. universities
    c. national defense
    d. a loaf of bread
2. Why are public goods generally provided by the government rather than by private firms?
3. Have you ever had a free-rider problem in a group project? How did you resolve it?
4. Because of high crime rates, crime prevention is often a political issue. Do these high rates imply that government should increase crime prevention activities? Defend your answer.
5. Describe recent crime trends in the United States. Why have U. S. crime rates fallen?
6. Describe recent crime trends in England and the United States. Why have crime rates fallen more in the United States than in England?
7. Analyze the theory of crime as presented in the text and in the box titled "Police, Guns, and Crime." Is this theory useful for short-term crime control? For long-term control? Discuss.
8. Some people argue that marijuana and other illegal drugs should be legalized, because people should have the freedom to do as they please. They also argue that downloading and reproducing music should be illegal. Are they being inconsistent?
9. Government restrictions on drug use seem inconsistent with the way alcohol and nicotine (both drugs themselves) are treated. Why do you believe we see this inconsistency?
10. How might the legalization of cocaine affect its market price and quantity? Use graphical analysis to aid in your answer.

11. Why is the cost of drugs likely to increase and the demand for drugs likely to decrease in the face of prohibition?
12. "Making drugs illegal results in dealers pushing drugs on nonusers." Is this statement true or false? Defend your answer.
13. What are the pros and cons of drug laws and their increased enforcement?
14. People come to different conclusions about the desirability of Dutch drug policy. How can people look at the same situation and come to different conclusions?
15. The chapter argues that current drug laws ensure that drug-related crimes will continue. On the other hand, legalization would ensure increased drug use and abuse. Could any actions be undertaken to improve the situation?

Economic Issues on the Internet

- Common Sense for Drug Policy—**http://www.csdp.org**
  Another informative site oriented toward changing U.S. drug policy.

- The Media Awareness Project—**http://www.mapinc.org**
  This site is a worldwide network dedicated to drug policy reform. It informs public opinion and promotes balanced media coverage. This site contains massive amounts of information. It does not support the war on drugs.

- The National Center on Addiction and Substance Abuse at Columbia University—**http://www.casacolumbia.org**
  This site is focused on substance abuse and its costs.

- National Criminal Justice Reference Service—**http://www.ncjrs.org**
  NCJRS is a federally funded resource offering justice and substance abuse information to support research, policy, and program development worldwide. Extensive information on crime and justice.

- Office of National Drug Control Policy—**http://www.whitehousedrugpolicy.gov**
  This is a site that supports current drug policy. It too contains massive amounts of information.

CHAPTER 9

College Education: Is It Worth the Cost?

Outline:

Analyzing the Investment Decision
    Step One
    Step Two
    Step Three
Investing in a College Education: Monetary Benefits and Costs
    Student PVNB and ROR
    Social PVNB and ROR

Investing in a College Education: Nonmonetary Benefits and Costs
    Nonmonetary Student Benefits
    Nonmonetary Student Costs
    Nonmonetary External Benefits
    Nonmonetary External Costs
Is Government Support Necessary?
    Ensuring That Society Invests Enough in College Education

Ensuring That Student Borrowing Reflects the Social Risk of Default
Increasing Enrollment of Lower-Income Students

Americans have long viewed a college education as a ticket to a better life. It is, however, an expensive ticket. Currently, four years in a public college or university costs the typical student almost $71,000. The largest part of this, about $53,000, is the money the student could earn if she did not attend college. The remaining $18,000 pays for tuition, fees, books, and transportation. Receipts from tuition and fees, however, cover only a fraction of college operating costs; more than $40,000 comes from other sources, such as government appropriations, grants and contracts, scholarships, gifts, and endowment income. Accordingly, society (the student and all others) will invest almost $111,000 in the typical 4-year public college education.

Given these costs, it is easy to understand why students, parents, taxpayers, and legislators wonder if a college degree is "worth it." As we will show in this chapter, however, a college degree yields high rates of return—for both students and society. On the one hand, these results suggest that it pays for students to invest in college education. On the other hand, the high rate of return for students raises a question: If a college education is such a good investment for them, why should they get government support? The short answer (which we will explain in detail) is (1) to ensure that society invests enough in college education, (2) to ensure that students borrow enough to finance their college education, and (3) to increase college enrollment by students from lower-income households.

■ ANALYZING THE INVESTMENT DECISION

As noted, the typical college student (and/or the student's family) invests a lot of money in acquiring a college education. We are interested in determining whether this is a wise investment. Properly made, however, the decision to invest in a college education is relatively complex. Thus, we begin with a simplified example that illustrates how investment decisions, in general, are made.

Imagine that your friend, Tom, offers you the opportunity to invest in his new enterprise, Tom's Tops, a business that will make and sell customized T-shirts, sweatshirts, tank tops, and so on. Tom asks you to invest $1,000 today and another $1,000 one year from today. In return, he promises to pay you $700 two years from today, $950 three years from today, and $902 four years from today. You are certain that Tom will pay you these amounts on these dates, but you are uncertain whether this is a wise investment.

Making your decision requires the following three steps:
1. Identify and estimate the costs (C) you expect to pay and the benefits (B) you expect to receive, and list them by date.
2. Adjust your estimates of C and B for date of occurrence.
3. Compare the adjusted Cs and Bs, using an investment decision rule.

Step One

The elements of the first step are displayed in Table 9.1, which lists each of the expected costs and benefits according to the time (t) at which they will be made or realized. The present date, or "today," is designated by $t=0$. One year from today is designated by $t=1$, two years from today by $t=2$, and so on. The investment decision itself is to be made at $t=0$, or today.

Given the elements in Table 9.1, a little addition quickly indicates that expected benefits ($2,552) are greater than expected costs ($2,000). Before you jump to conclude that you should invest in Tom's Tops, however, you must adjust each of the benefits and costs for time of occurrence.

TABLE 9.1   Benefits and Costs of Investing in Tom's Tops

t	B	C
0	0	$1,000
1	0	$1,000
2	$700	0
3	$950	0
4	$902	0

Step Two

To understand why the second step, adjustment for time of occurrence, is necessary, consider the following example. Suppose that you are offered the choice between receiving $1,000 today or $1,000 one year from today. Which would you choose? Unless you are quite unusual, you would choose $1,000 today because you can invest the money today and end up with more than $1,000 a year from now. How much more depends upon the return on your investment. If you put the money into a savings account that pays an interest rate, i, of 5 percent, you will have $1,050 a year from now. Thus, $1,000 today has the same value to you as $1,050 one year from today, or, put differently, $1,050 one year from today is worth only $1,000 to you today.

Future Value (FV) – The value at a future date of a sum of money now.

Present Value (PV) – The value now of a future sum of money.

As the example points out, the **future value (FV)** of a sum of money is larger than the **present value (PV)** of that sum. Formally,

$$(9.1) \quad FV_t = PV_0(1+i)^t$$

where t may be any value equal to or greater than 0, and the 0 subscript denotes the present.

Alternatively, the present value of a sum of money is less than the future value of that sum, or

$$(9.2) \quad PV_0 = FV_t/(1+i)^t$$

Discount Factor – The value of the divisor, $(1+i)^t$, used to discount a future value.

Applied to the current example, $1,050 = $1,000 (1.05)^1$ and $1,000 = $1,050/(1.05)^1$, where $1,050 is the future value at t = 1, and $1,000 is the present value at t = 0. Equation 9.2 indicates that the future value of an amount of money must be divided by a **discount factor**, $(1+i)^t$, to determine what that future amount is worth to the investor today.

Present Value Decision Rule – A rule used to determine if an investment is financially sound; an investment is financially sound according to this rule if the sum of the present value of benefits is equal to or greater than the sum of the present value of costs.

Table 9.2 shows the results of applying equation 9.2 to the data in Table 9.1. Columns 1, 2, and 5 in Table 9.2 are the same as the three columns of Table 9.1. Column 3 in Table 9.2 depicts the value of the discount factor for each value of t from 0 to 4 when the value for i is 0.05. Column 4 contains the present values of the benefits (PVB) listed in column 2. For example, PVB_t for t = 2 is $700/(1.05)^2$ or $700/1.103 (=$635). Column 6 contains the present values of the costs (PVC) listed in column 5.

Step Three

The first two steps in the investment evaluation are now complete. The third step is to decide if the investment is worthwhile. We can apply two investment decision rules for this purpose. The first is the **present value decision rule**. According to this rule, an investment is worthwhile if the sum of the present value of

TABLE 9.2 Benefits and Costs of Investing in Tom's Tops, Adjusted for Time of Occurrence

t	B	$(1+i)^t$	PVB_t	C	PVC_t
0	$0	1.000	$0	$1,000	$1,000
1	0	1.050	0	1,000	952
2	700	1.103	635	0	0
3	950	1.158	820	0	0
4	902	1.216	742	0	0
			$2,197		$1,952

benefits (PVB) exceeds or equals the sum of the present value of costs (PVC). This is equivalent to the rule that the sum of the *present value of net benefits* (PVNB, where PVNB = PVB − PVC) must be greater than or equal to zero.

We easily apply this decision rule to the data in Table 9.2 by adding columns 4 and 6 and comparing them. The sum of the PVBs, $2,197, clearly exceeds the sum of the PVCs, $1,952. Alternatively, the PVNB is greater than zero, or $245 (= $2,197 − $1,952). Thus, according to both versions of the present value decision rule, the investment in Tom's Tops is worthwhile.

Rate of Return Decision Rule – A rule used to determine if an investment is financially sound; an investment is financially sound according to this rule if the rate of return on the investment is equal to or greater than the rate of return on the best alternative use of funds.

The second decision rule is the **rate of return decision rule**. According to this decision rule, an investment is worthwhile if the rate of return on the investment is greater than the rate of return on your best alternative. To apply the second decision rule, you must be able to calculate the rate of return. The **rate of return (ROR)** is the discount rate, r, which makes the sum of the PVCs *equal* to the sum of the PVBs, or which makes PVNB = 0. That is, you must substitute r for i in the discount factor and solve the following equation for the value of r:

(9.3) $[\$1,000/(1 + r)^0] + [\$1,000/(1+r)^1] = [\$700/(1+ r)^2] + [\$950/(1+r)^3] + [\$902/(1+r)^4]$

If several time periods are involved, as in this investment, the value of r can be determined fastest by using a financial calculator or a computer program that calculates rates of return. We have relieved you of this task and already determined that the solution value for r in equation 9.3 is 0.10, or 10 percent.

Rate of Return (ROR) – The discount rate, r, at which the sum of the present value of costs is equal to the sum of the present value of benefits.

This solution is confirmed by the data in Table 9.3, where the sums of the PVBs and PVCs are determined using r = 0.10 in the discount factor in column 3. Note that at this discount rate, the sums of both the PVBs and the PVCs are $1,909, so PVNB = 0. If 10 percent exceeds the rate you could earn on the best alternative use of the funds you lend to Tom, this investment is worthwhile. In our example, you should make the investment in Tom's Tops if the savings account is your best alternative, because you would earn only 5 percent on the savings account.

■ INVESTING IN A COLLEGE EDUCATION: MONETARY BENEFITS AND COSTS

Monetary Benefits and Costs – Benefits and costs valued in dollars.

Now let's use this framework to determine the payoff for a typical student and for society from investing in a college education. The first step, identifying and estimating the benefits and costs by date, is far more complicated that it was for the investment in Tom's Tops. Benefits and costs fall into two general classes: monetary and nonmonetary. **Monetary benefits and costs** are those that can be easily valued

TABLE 9.3   Confirmation of a 10 Percent Rate of Return from Investing in Tom's Tops

t	B	$(1+r)^t$	PVB_t	C	PVC_t
0	$0	1.000	$0	$1,000	$1,000
1	0	1.100	0	1,000	909
2	700	1.210	579	0	
3	950	1.331	714	0	
4	902	1.464	616	0	
			$1,909		$1,909

Nonmonetary Benefits and Costs – Benefits and costs not valued in dollars.

Social Benefits – Benefits that accrue to all individuals; applied to college education, benefits to students and nonstudents.

Social Costs – Costs paid by all individuals; applied to college education, costs to students and nonstudents.

Student Benefits – Benefits of a college education to students.

Nonstudent Benefits – Benefits of a college education to nonstudents.

Student Costs – Costs of a college education paid by students.

Nonstudent Costs – Costs of a college education paid by nonstudents.

in dollars. **Nonmonetary benefits and costs** are those that are difficult or impossible to value in dollars. The procedures we have outlined here can be applied only to monetary benefits and costs.

The principal monetary benefits and costs are listed in Table 9.4. The broadest measures are of social benefits and social costs. **Social benefits** are benefits that accrue to both students and nonstudents. Similarly, **social costs** are costs that are paid by both students and nonstudents. The benefits that accrue only to students are called **student benefits**. The benefits that accrue to nonstudents are **nonstudent benefits** of a college education. **Student costs** are costs paid by students (including those financed by their families). **Nonstudent costs** are costs paid by nonstudents.

The principal monetary student benefit is the increase in lifetime earnings after taxes attributable to a college education. If the student is a recent high school graduate, this benefit is equal to lifetime earnings after taxes with a college degree, minus lifetime earnings after taxes with a high school diploma. Taxes are deducted from earnings because students do not directly benefit from the taxes levied on their earnings. The taxes that should be deducted are those based on earnings. The most important of these are federal and state individual income taxes and the payroll tax for Social Security.

The extra taxes collected from the lifetime earnings of college graduates are used to finance government expenditures that provide benefits—primarily to nonstudents. The benefits from these expenditures are the principal monetary nonstudent benefits from college education.

The principal monetary student costs are student outlays for net tuition (tuition minus the value of scholarships and fellowships received), fees, books and transportation, and earnings foregone after taxes. Earnings foregone are equal to what students could earn after taxes if they were not attending college minus the earnings after taxes they receive from a job while in college. Because the typical college student works only part-time, earnings foregone are substantial.

The principal monetary nonstudent costs are outlays made by federal and state governments in the form of appropriations, grants and contracts, and scholarships. A small share of monetary external costs is paid by private sources, primarily in the form of gifts and income from endowments.

Estimates of these benefits and costs can be used to determine both the PVNB and the ROR from investing in a college education. Actually, we can make two types of estimates. The first type produces

TABLE 9.4 Monetary Benefits and Costs of a College Education

SOCIAL BENEFITS
  Student Benefits
    Increase in earnings, after taxes
  Nonstudent Benefits
    Benefits from government programs financed by increase in tax revenue
    Benefits from education financed by nonstudent private sources

SOCIAL COSTS
  Student Costs
    Net tuition, fees, books, and transportation
    Earnings foregone, after taxes
  Nonstudent Costs
    Costs paid by government
    Costs paid by nonstudent private sources

Student Rate of Return (ROR) – Rate of return realized by students from investing in a college education; the discount rate at which the sum of the present value of student benefits is equal to the sum of the present value of student costs.

Social Rate of Return (ROR) – Rate of return realized by students and nonstudents from investing in a college education; the discount rate at which the sum of the present value of social benefits is equal to the sum of the present value of social costs.

the PVNB and the ROR from the student's perspective—*the student PVNB* and the **student ROR**. These are determined using estimates of student benefits and student costs. The second type produces the PVNB and the ROR from a social perspective—the *social PVNB* and the **social ROR**. These are determined using estimates of social benefits and social costs.

Student PVNB and ROR

In this section, we illustrate how investment decision analysis can determine the student PVNB and ROR for a typical college freshman enrolling in a public 4-year college in 2000.

The student costs and benefits defined here are illustrated in Figure 9.1 for a student who enters college at age 18, graduates at age 22, and works until age 65. Student costs are represented by the negative values labeled C. They consist of student outlays for net tuition, fees, books and transportation, and student earnings foregone after taxes. The increase in lifetime earnings after taxes—or student benefits—is represented by the positive values labeled B. The student in this example is one who will earn the average real wage (the actual wage less inflation) of college graduates projected by the U.S. Census Bureau for 1997–1999 college graduates and who would have earned the projected average real wage of high school graduates.[1] Figure 9.1 reflects these projections, less a deduction for income and Social Security taxes.

We know from the example of Tom's Tops that these costs and benefits must be discounted to obtain the time streams of PVC and PVB. Figure 9.2 shows how discounting affects the investment picture.

FIGURE 9.1 | Annual Costs and Benefits to a "Typical" College Graduate from Investing in a College Education

The typical college graduate incurs costs while in school, as depicted by the negative portion of the line, and reaps benefits after graduation, as depicted by the positive portion of the line.

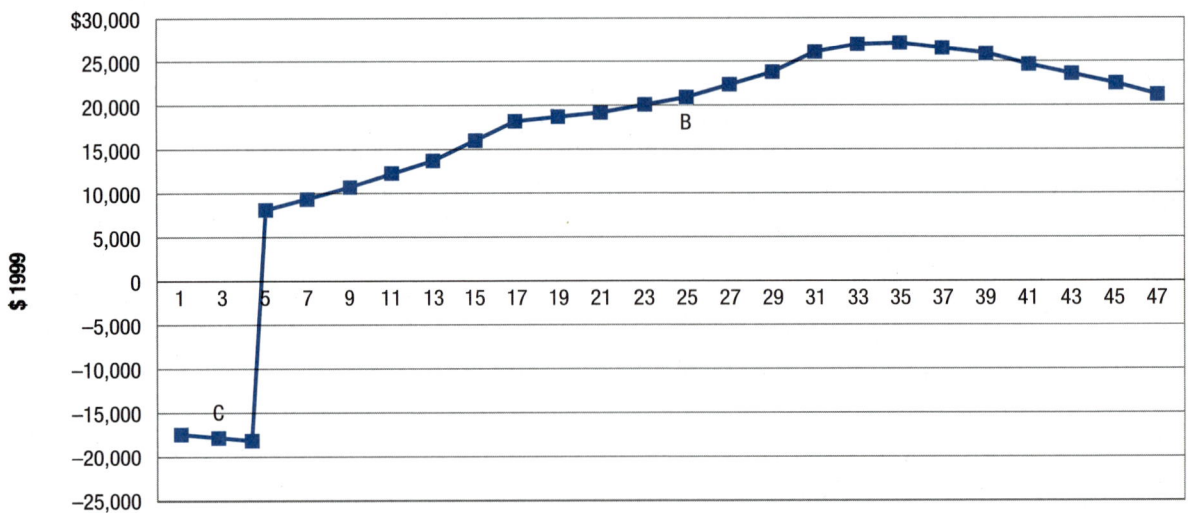

[1]*The Big Payoff: Educational Attainment and Synthetic Estimates of Work-Life Earnings*, Current Population Reports (July 2002), 23–210.

FIGURE 9.2 Annual Present Value of Costs and Benefits to a "Typical" College Graduate from Investing in a College Education

Discounting reduces both the costs and benefits from investing in a college education, the effects of which can be seen by comparing the present value of costs, PVC, and costs, C, and the present value of benefits, PVB, and benefits, B.

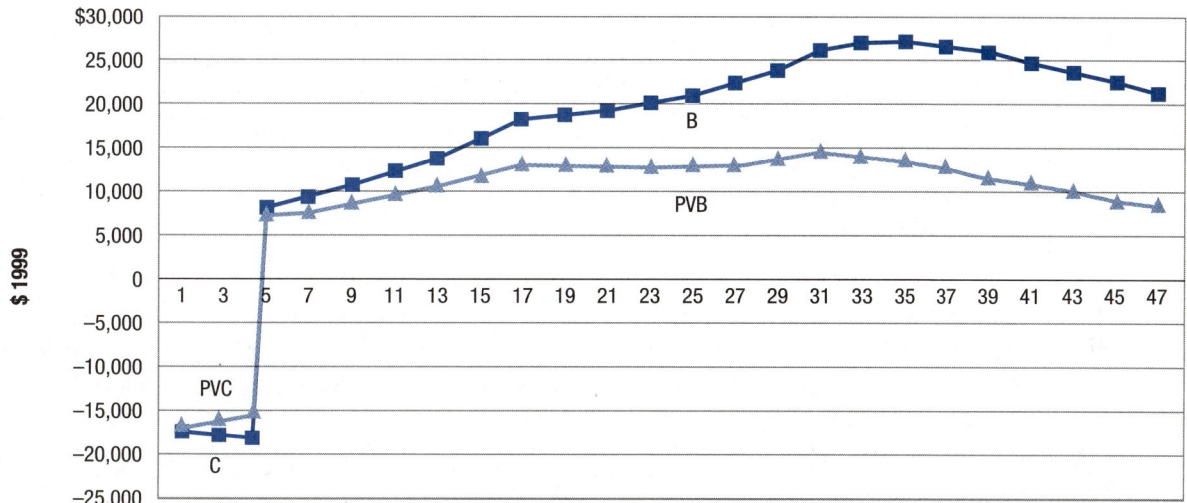

The general pattern is a reduction in both C and B that increases with increases in the number of years after high school graduation.

This adjustment reflects the use of a particular discount rate, of course. The appropriate discount rate is the rate of return that the typical student could earn on a comparable investment. In this case, the comparable investment should be one that is long term and relatively risk-free, such as long-term bonds of the federal government. The real rate of return realized on this asset over the last 50 years—2 percent—is the rate that we have used for discounting the costs and benefits of a college education.

It seems obvious to us from a visual inspection of Figure 9.1 that the area between the B line and the horizontal axis greatly exceeds the area between the C line and the horizontal axis. The former is equal to student benefits summed over all the years following college graduation and the latter is equal to student costs summed over all the years while the student is in college. Thus, the net benefits of a college education clearly appear to exceed zero.

It also seems obvious to us from a visual inspection of Figure 9.2 that the area between the PVB line and the horizontal axis greatly exceeds the area between the PVC line and the horizontal axis. The former is equal to the present value of student benefits summed over all the years following college graduation, and the latter is equal to the present value of student costs summed over all the years while the student is in college. Thus, it appears that the PVNB of a college education clearly exceeds zero.

Both of our impressions are confirmed by the actual estimates reported in Table 9.5. The net benefits for the typical college graduate from investing in a college education are $776,267 and the PVNB are

$420,287. Given that PVNB>0, the rate of return from investing in a college education will exceed the discount rate (2 percent). It certainly does so; our calculations indicate a real rate of return of 14.27 percent.

Given these results, investing in a college degree appears sound from the student's perspective. This is a hypothetical example, however, for a typical college student. Is this example representative? Is the rate of return on a college education typically this high? The answer appears to be "yes," as indicated by the summary in Table 9.6 of rates of return reported in the economics literature. The rate of return will not be as high as in our example, however, for the large number of graduates who end up in jobs after graduation that individuals with a high school diploma could fill. Students who perform poorly while in college, who take little mathematics, or who study majors leading to low-paying jobs should also expect to earn a lower real rate of return.

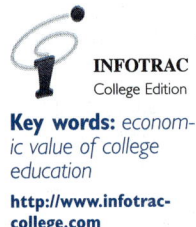

INFOTRAC
College Edition

Key words: *economic value of college education*

http://www.infotrac-college.com

Social PVNB and ROR

As noted previously, the social rate of return is based on a comparison of social benefits and social costs. As illustrated in Table 9.4, the social costs easily valued in dollars are the student costs already examined, plus costs paid by nonstudents. Social benefits consist of (1) the student benefits already estimated, (2) the benefits produced by the government expenditures financed by the increase in income and Social

TABLE 9.5 Estimated Real Monetary Student Benefits and Costs from Investing in a College Education

Real student benefits	$847,155
Real student costs	70,888
Net tuition, fees, books, transportation	15,737
Earnings foregone after taxes	52,865
Real student net benefits	776,267
Present value of real student benefits	487,755
Present value of real student costs	67,467
PV of real student net benefits	420,287
Real student rate of return (%)	14.27

TABLE 9.6 Estimated Rates of Return from a Bachelor's Degree

Year	Average Rate of Return (%)	Number of Studies
1939	15.0	3
1949	11.6	5
1959	12.3	12
1969	13.0	10
1973	11.7	6
1980	16.5	1

SOURCE: Larry L. Leslie and Paul T. Brinkman, *The Economic Value of Higher Education* (New York: Macmillan, 1988), 47, 73.

INSIGHTS

DOES WHERE YOU GO TO SCHOOL MATTER?

The results of the rate of return studies reported in Table 9.6 should encourage high school graduates who are trying to decide whether to invest their time and money in a college education. However, prospective students must decide where, as well as whether, to go to college. Before they decide where to go, they may want to know whether a degree from an elite college is worth more than a degree from a less prestigious one.

The lack of attention to this question is surprising, given the voluminous literature on the rates of return from investing in a college education. Nevertheless, finding the necessary detailed individual and institutional information is difficult.

Fortunately, this situation is about to change as more data become available from the National Longitudinal Study of the High School Class of 1972. In fact, the results of a recent study based on these data provide interesting answers to the question of whether college reputation makes a difference in terms of postcollege earnings. James and colleagues found that the choice of school can provide a slight advantage in later earnings, but only if one is fortunate enough to graduate from a selective private Eastern institution.[a] They found a much larger earnings advantage associated with a student's choices and achievements while in college, regardless of the institution. The choice of major is important, with higher earnings advantages to engineering majors and to business majors who function as managers after college, as opposed, for example, to education majors, especially if they function as teachers after college. A significant payoff follows from taking lots of math, regardless of major. The biggest payoff of all, however, is for a high grade-point average. Apparently, what matters most is not which college or university you attend, but what you do while you are there.

[a]Estelle James, Nabeel Alsalam, Joseph C. Conaty, and Duc-Le To, "College Quality and Future Earnings: Where Should You Send Your Child to College?" *American Economic Review* 79 (May 1989), 247–252.

Security taxes paid by college graduates, and (3) the benefits produced by funds provided by private nonstudent sources. Benefits from government expenditures vary in terms of the ease with which they can be valued in dollars, but they cannot, in general, be easily valued—nor can the benefits produced by funds provided by private nonstudent sources. We resort, instead, to the assumption that the benefits from these two sources are equal to the revenues provided. This is probably an underestimate of the benefits from privately-provided funds. Why would they be provided voluntarily unless the providers perceived benefits at least as great as costs? We do not know how good this assumption is as an estimate of the benefits from publicly-provided funds.

Our typical college graduate will earn $3,158,996 and pay $723,410 in income and Social Security taxes. Our typical high school graduate will earn $1,796,868 and pay income and Social Security taxes of $208,436. The difference in taxes—$514,974—is our estimate of the nonstudent benefits from publicly-provided funds. Nonstudents will pay $3,320 for each college graduate from private funds. Thus, nonstudent benefits from both public and private sources will total $518,294.

On the cost side, public sources will provide $37,200 per graduate, and private nonstudent sources will provide $3,320. Thus, nonstudent costs will be $40,520 for the typical college graduate.

Given that the nonstudent benefits greatly exceed the nonstudent costs, it would appear that a college education is worth a lot more from a social perspective than it is from a student perspective. The real social ROR is only 14.5 percent, however, or just 0.23 percentage points higher than the real student

INTERNATIONAL PERSPECTIVE

EDUCATION AND ECONOMIC GROWTH

This chapter indicates that a college education is a major contributor to the income of individual graduates. Likewise, economists' estimates indicate that education has made major contributions to growth in national income. Studies based on "growth accounting" indicate that investment in education at all levels tends to explain directly about 15 to 20 percent of recorded growth in U.S. national income, and that higher education accounts for about one-fourth of this effect.[a] Another 20 to 40 percent of income growth generally is attributed to growth in knowledge and its application, and higher education is believed to contribute importantly to this process.

---

[a]The leading developer of the art of growth accounting was Edward F. Denison, who produced several estimates of the contribution of education to economic growth. For a good review of his work, see "Accounting for Slower Growth: An Update," in J. Kendrick, ed., *International Comparisons of Productivity and Causes of Slowdowns* (Cambridge, MA: Ballinger, 1984).

Keywords: *social value of college education*

http://www.infotrac-college.com

ROR. This is a consequence of differences in the timing of the nonstudent benefits and costs. The nonstudent costs must be paid up front while the nonstudent benefits are delayed. The wait involved for benefits greatly reduces their present value.

■ INVESTING IN A COLLEGE EDUCATION: NONMONETARY BENEFITS AND COSTS

Up to now, we have emphasized the benefits and costs that we can value in dollars, but additional benefits and costs may be attributed to a college education. We have excluded them from our PVNB or ROR calculations because we lack reliable estimates of their value in dollars. Relevant examples exist, however, in all four benefit and cost categories.

Nonmonetary Student Benefits

Robert Haveman and Barbara Wolfe have examined a number of education benefits commonly left out of PVNB and ROR calculations, some of which may be attributable to a college education.[2] According to them, education enhances the value of leisure. Better-educated parents improve their children's intellectual development, occupational status, and future earnings. Education produces improved health. Education enables people to make better choices among consumer goods, locations, jobs, and prospective mates. Education also increases the returns people realize from savings, and the educational experience itself is a source of satisfaction to many students.

Their discussion suggests that these effects are important sources of benefits. In their 1984 study, they estimated that parents place a value of $300 to $1,800 on the contribution that each additional year of the parents' college education makes to the intellectual development of each of their children. They also esti-

---

[2]Robert H. Haveman and Barbara L. Wolfe, "School and Economic Well-Being: The Role of Non-Market Effects," *Journal of Human Resources* 19, No. 3, 1984, 382; and "Accounting for the Social and Non-Market Benefits of Education," in John F. Helliwell, ed, *The Contribution of Human and Social Capital to Sustained Economic Growth and Well-Being: International Symposium Report*, Organization for Economic Cooperation and Development (2001), 221–250.

mated that parents are willing to pay $360 annually per additional year of college for its effect on their attainment of desired family size and child spacing. They calculated that an additional year of college is worth $100 per year in terms of its effects on improved consumer decisions. They also estimated that the value of better health that an additional year of education produces is worth up to $3,000 per year. The lower rate of smoking among college graduates is an example of how college education contributes to better health.

Keywords: *social benefits of education*
http://www.infotrac-college.com

Haveman and Wolfe do not claim that their estimates are definitive. They do suggest, however, that benefits not easily valued might be as valuable as benefits from increased earnings. Clearly, if estimates such as these were included in the PVNB and ROR calculations, both the student and social payoffs would be larger.

Nonmonetary Student Costs

Some other effects that are hard to value in dollars are nonmonetary student costs. One important example is the cost that comes from overeducation. Overeducation occurs when college graduates end up working at jobs for which they believe they are overqualified. Tsang and Levin argue that overeducation may lead to job dissatisfaction, adverse workplace behavior, deteriorating health, and lower productivity.[3] If the dollar values of these effects were counted as part of the cost of college education, both the student and social PVNBs and RORs would fall.

Keyword: *Overeducation*
http://www.infotrac-college.com

Nonmonetary External Benefits

We categorize three primary types of nonmonetary external benefits: *research spillovers*, *knowledge spillovers*, and *community benefit spillovers*. Essentially, each of these is a benefit of a college education not captured by the student and not easily valued.

The nation's colleges and universities are major producers of research, the benefits of which often widely diffuse, or spill over among the populace at large. Most of these benefits, however, are by-products of education for advanced degrees or separately contracted activity. Thus, the external benefits from research produced solely as a consequence of providing a bachelor's degree—the focus of this chapter—are likely to be small.

A college graduate with a bachelor's degree acquires a stock of knowledge that not only serves as the basis for personal earnings but may enhance earnings prospects of others. The specific knowledge a college graduate acquires may also spur better personal decisions by others and contribute to better community decisions, as well. Thus, the college graduate's general knowledge produces benefits that spill over into society at large.

We know of no estimates of the value of these effects. The general role of the stock of knowledge in the economic growth process appears important enough, however, that it has stimulated the development of a whole new branch of economic inquiry. As the results of this research accumulate, they will quite likely indicate that the social rate of return from college education is higher than we have come to expect on the basis of what we currently know.

Colleges and universities may also provide a variety of events or experiences for both students and nonstudents. Art shows, musical programs, plays, public addresses, and athletic contests provide bene-

---

[3] Mun S. Tsang and Henry M. Levin, "The Economics of Overeducation," *Economics of Education Review* 4, No. 2 (1985), 93–104.

INTERNATIONAL PERSPECTIVE

RATES OF RETURN AROUND THE WORLD

Investment in education is almost universally accepted as worthwhile. In fact, the value of investing in education has been confirmed by studies of rates of return around the world. The following table summarizes the social rates of return estimated in many of these studies, arranged by region and level of education.

The table depicts rates of return on investment in primary, secondary, and tertiary education. Tertiary education is advanced (postsecondary) education, including college education. The estimates reported in this table indicate that investment in education is a productive use of society's resources throughout the world. It promises relatively higher rates of return, however, in lesser-developed countries and at lower levels of education. The higher rates in lesser-developed countries reflect the relatively greater shortage of educated people at all levels in these countries.

The rates in this table are probably high enough to justify investment in education at all levels throughout the world, but they do indicate that the less-developed countries should give a high priority to achieving universal primary and secondary education.

Average Social Rate of Return on Investment in Education by Geographical Region and Level of Education (Percentages)

	Level of Education		
Region	Primary	Secondary	Tertiary
Africa	26	17	13
Asia	27	15	13
Latin America	26	18	16
Developed countries	NA	11	9

Notes: African countries included are Ghana, Kenya, Uganda, and Nigeria. Asian countries included are India and the Philippines. Latin American countries included are Mexico, Colombia, Venezuela, Chile, and Brazil. Developed countries included are the United States, the United Kingdom, Canada, the Netherlands, and Belgium. No information was available on the rate of return to investment in primary education in the developed countries because these countries lack a large enough group without a primary education to serve as a control group.

SOURCE: George Psacharopoulos, "Returns to Education: A Further International Update and Implications," *Journal of Human Resources* 20 (April 1985), 583–604.

fits that spill over into the local or regional community. Although benefits from events such as these can be quantified through admission fees, we know of no general estimates of their magnitude.

Nonmonetary External Costs

Some external costs of college education not valued in dollars include, for example, the extra demands a college or university may place on local schools, police and fire departments, and community social services, or extra local traffic congestion. Including these costs in PVNB and ROR calculations would lower both the social PVNB and social ROR.

■ IS GOVERNMENT SUPPORT NECESSARY?

Our estimates for a typical college graduate suggest a social rate of return high enough (14.5 percent) to justify using society's resources to invest in college education. In fact, the high social rate of return suggests that we should allocate an even bigger share of national resources to college education. That is, national output would be higher if we diverted resources from other uses and devoted them to college education.

A high student rate of return (14.27 percent) indicates that a large share of high school graduates should be earning college degrees. Some economists would argue, in fact, that investing in a college education is such an attractive option to students, per se, that government support for students and educational institutions is unnecessary. To determine whether this is the case, we examine three rationales often advanced for government support of college education:

1. To ensure that society invests enough in college education
2. To ensure that student borrowing reflects the social risk of default
3. To increase enrollment of lower-income students

Ensuring That Society Invests Enough in College Education

As noted earlier, the student ROR is almost as large as the social ROR. This implies that students would voluntarily invest in as much college education as society desires because it is worth as much to them as it is to society. This is not be the case, however, when an adjustment is made in the real student ROR for the costs covered by government.

The student ROR is dependent upon the percentage of the total cost of a college education that students must pay. Currently, tuition and fees cover only about 25 percent of the total operating costs of public 4-year institutions, and federal and state governments pick up about 63 percent of the tab. If government support were withdrawn, students would face the prospect of higher tuition and fees. At the same time, however, withdrawal of government support would permit a reduction in taxes, so students could expect lower taxes in exchange for higher tuition.

A reduction in taxes would increase the student ROR, while an increase in tuition and fees would reduce the student ROR. We expect the student ROR to fall when lower taxes are exchanged for higher tuition and fees, because the student must pay the tuition and fee increase much sooner than the benefits from the tax cut will be realized. This is, in fact, what happens for our typical college graduate. The **student rate of return without government support** is only 11.36 percent. Under these circumstances, students would underinvest in college education, and a government subsidy would be necessary to achieve the desired level of investment.

We have constructed Figure 9.3 to illustrate why students would underinvest and how a subsidy can be used to correct for this problem. This figure depicts the investment choice in terms of the demand for and supply of college degrees. The downward-sloping demand curves indicate that students want more degrees the lower the price. The upward-sloping supply curves indicate that more degrees will be provided the higher the price.

The two demand curves indicate that the demand for college degrees also depends on the expected rate of return from investing in a college degree. The expected rate of return for D_{stud} is 11.38 percent—the student rate of return without a government subsidy. The expected rate of return for D_{soc} is 14.5 percent—the social rate of return. The supply curve labeled S_{soc} reflects the marginal cost to society of producing college degrees.

If students were required to pay all the costs now paid by government, the market would clear at the intersection of D_{stud} and S_{soc} and there would be Q_{stud} degrees produced. The socially efficient number of degrees, however is Q_{soc}, where D_{soc} and S_{soc} intersect. Thus, the market would produce too few degrees. To achieve Q_{soc}, the government could provide a subsidy to students equal to the difference between S_{soc} and S_{sub}, lowering the price or tuition enough to induce students to buy Q_{soc} degrees.

Student Rate of Return without Government Support – The student rate of return from investing in a college education when government pays none of the cost.

FIGURE 9.3   Effect of a Tuition Subsidy on College Degrees

This figure illustrates that students would invest in too few college degrees if they had to pay the full costs of a college education. Under these circumstances, they would perceive D_{stud} and S_{soc} and invest in Q_{stud} degrees, or fewer than the efficient number of degrees, Q_{soc}. Government could ensure investment in Q_{soc} by providing a subsidy equal to $S_{soc}-S_{sub}$.

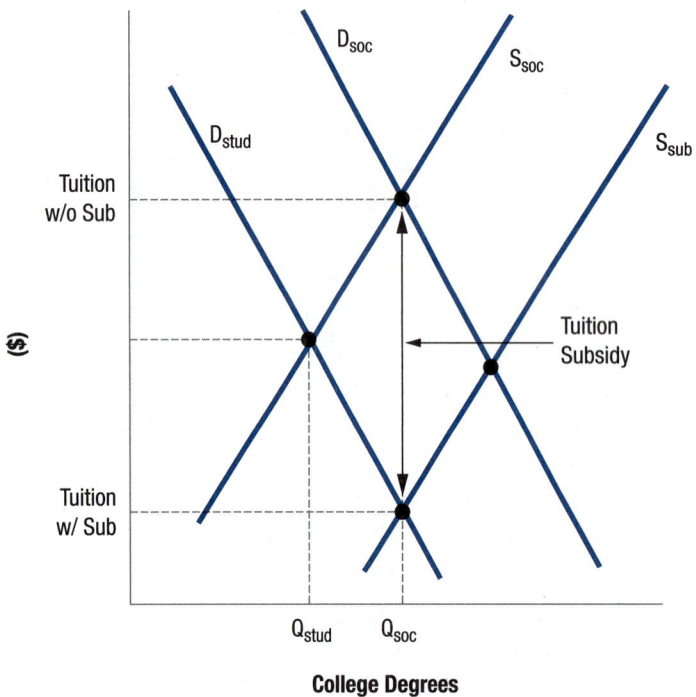

Ensuring That Student Borrowing Reflects the Social Risk of Default

In the school year 1999–2000, college students at all levels borrowed over $42 billion to finance the costs of a college education. More than 60 percent of bachelor's degree recipients graduated with some debt. In fact, the median debt owed at graduation was over $17,000, nearly as much as the typical college graduate spends on tuition, fees, books and transportation.

Figure 9.4 shows how loan finance affects the present value of costs and benefits for the typical college graduate who borrows enough to cover all of the costs of tuition, fees, books and transportation ($18,024). Loan finance has three effects. First, proceeds from the loan reduce costs while in college. Second, these costs, plus interest on the loan, are shifted to the future. As illustrated in Figure 9.4, future loan costs offset part of the PVB from investing in a college education. In this example, we assume that the borrower will pay back the loan over the first 10 years following graduation. The loan behind the picture is not subsidized—interest accumulates while the student is in school—and the borrower's interest rate is 8.25 percent, the average rate charged on federal college loans in 2000. Third, the loan changes the student rate of return. In this case, the student rate of return actually increases from 14.27 percent without the loan to 14.97 percent with the loan—a consequence of changing the timing of costs.

FIGURE 9.4 Effect of Loan Finance on PVC and PVB

College student loans reduce costs while the student is in school, as indicated by the difference between PVC with loan finance and PVC without loan finance. The loan is repaid after the student graduates, in effect reducing the PVB for the period over which loan payments are made. The repayment effect is illustrated by the difference between "PVB Without Loan Finance" and "PVB Without Loan Finance Minus Loan Payments" for the first 10 years following graduation.

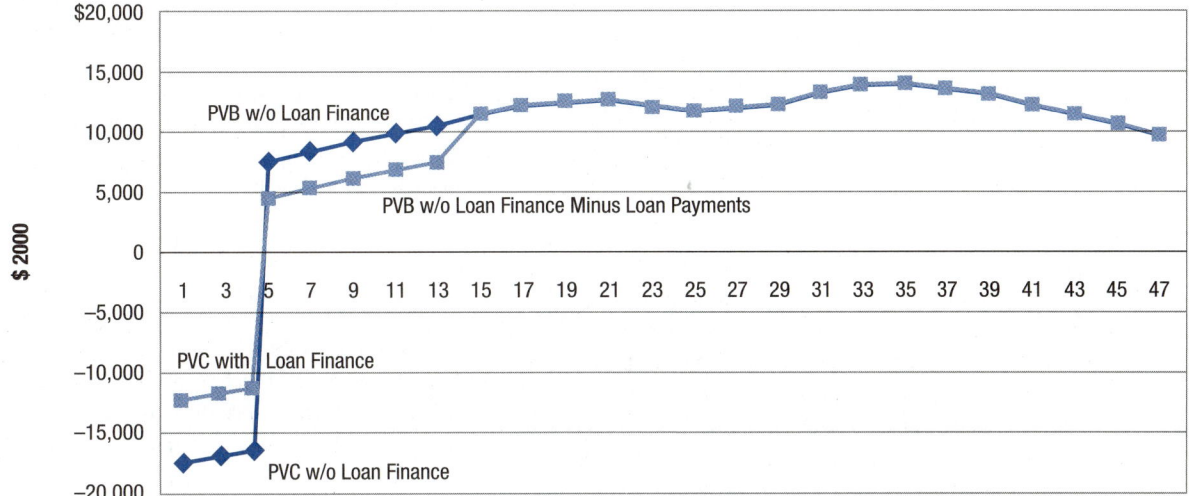

The federal government provided $38 billion of the $42 billion borrowed in school year 1999–2000, and the median debt owed the federal government, alone, upon graduation was over $15,000. Given that there is such a highly developed credit market in this country, how is such a large presence of the federal government in the market for student loans justified?

College students, as a group, constitute an attractive pool of borrowers. They will realize higher lifetime incomes than nongraduates and also experience lower rates of unemployment. What is true about the group, however, is not necessarily true about individual members of the group. The superior earning power of college students is no guarantee against the risk that *individual* students will encounter financial difficulty and be unable to repay a loan in a timely manner.

The same problem arises, of course, for many individuals with whom lenders do business. Lenders normally protect themselves in these instances by requiring collateral for a loan; for example, the lender owns the title to a car or house until the loan on each is repaid. Student loans have no such protection; that is, students cannot serve as collateral. This makes a loan to a specific individual relatively risky and requires the lender to charge a relatively high rate of interest to cover this risk.

Conflict arises, then, between individual and group risk of default in the college student loan market; group risk of default is small, but individual risk of default is high. Lacking a government supply of funds (or government guarantee against default), financial terms for student loans (interest rate, payment

Insights

The Demand for Education

The fact that a college education represents a sound investment for individuals does not necessarily mean that students decide to attend college solely, or even primarily, based on estimated rates of return. In fact, the evidence indicates that they are strongly influenced by the same factors—such as the price of the good or service itself, consumer income, and the prices of related goods and services—that determine their demand for other goods and services such as food, housing, and health care.

Higher education is subject to the law of demand; that is, a higher price, in terms of net tuition and fees (after a deduction for scholarships and fellowships) is associated with a smaller number of students enrolled. In fact, Leslie and Brinkman found this relationship confirmed in 25 studies of the demand for higher education.[a] According to their calculations, enrollment in U.S. higher education in 1982 could be expected to drop about 2.1 percent for each $100 increase in net tuition.

The demand for higher education is also affected by the income of students and their families. For example, in their seminal study of the demand for education in the United States, Campbell and Siegel found that the influence over time of tuition on enrollment was apparent only after controlling for changes in income.[b] Their findings have been confirmed repeatedly, recently by economists studying the determinants of enrollment in public colleges in New York, New Jersey, and Pennsylvania; these economists determined that a 1 percent increase in income in these states increases the demand for public higher education by 1.67 percent.[c] These economists also found a relationship between the demand for public education and the price of private higher education. A 10 percent increase in the price of private colleges increased the demand for public higher education by 2.8 percent in the three states.

Information such as this on the determinants of the demand for higher education should be of great interest to officials of both public and private colleges who are responsible for determining tuition and financial aid policy. Proper application of this kind of information would enable them to predict the effects of certain policy changes on enrollment and institutional revenues more accurately.

---

[a]Larry L. Leslie and Paul T. Brinkman, "Student Price Response in Higher Education," *Journal of Higher Education* 58, No. 2 (1987), 181–204.

[b]Robert Campbell and Barry Siegel, "The Demand for Higher Education in the United States 1919–1964," *American Economic Review* 57 (1967), 482–494.

[c]Cindy Kelly and Suzanne Tregarthen, "Price Plays Key Role in College Selection," *The Margin* (Fall 1991), 60.

---

deferral period, and repayment period), would reflect the relatively high individual risk of default. If students had to borrow on these terms, they would borrow less than they would from a government source offering loan terms that reflect the relatively low social risk of default.

Increasing Enrollment of Lower-Income Students

One argument often invoked to justify government support for college students is that it increases the enrollment of lower-income students. This section examines the principal types of support, the federal Pell grant and state government appropriations, to determine how well they have accomplished this objective.

PELL GRANTS. The Pell grant program provides cash assistance directly to college students, based on their own and their parents' income and assets. It is the largest government program providing grants directly to students—nearly $8 billion in 2000.

The Pell grant is an income-tested transfer payment—one in which the payment falls as income rises. Pell grants are not confined, however, to students from low-income families. First, students from families with middle-class incomes are eligible. Second, the grant award tends to be larger for students attending more expensive schools, and attendees at these institutions are more likely to come from higher-income families. Third, some students from higher-income families establish independent status so that they can qualify for a Pell grant on the basis of their income instead of their parents' income. Nevertheless, the proportion of students receiving Pell grants generally declines as family income rises.

The Pell grant lowers the net cost, or price, of a college education. The law of demand (see the box "The Demand for Education") predicts that this will result in an increase in enrollment. The available evidence indicates that this has been the case, although the Pell grant has failed to appreciably increase the number of lower-income enrollees. The primary reason appears to be that the grant covers only part of the total cost of a college education and that low-income families lack the means to finance the remainder or are reluctant to borrow enough to make up the difference.

STATE APPROPRIATIONS. The largest source of support to college students is money appropriated by state legislatures to state colleges and universities. The institutions use these funds to cover a large share of their costs and pass this cost coverage along to students in the form of lower tuition. Thus, state appropriations provide indirect tuition support. Indirect tuition support is so large, in fact, that it reduces tuition by more than 70 percent. If each 1 percent reduction in tuition increases enrollment by 0.3 percent (a number consistent with the studies cited in "The Demand for Education" box), the indirect tuition support provided by state appropriations increases enrollment by 21 percent.

The concern here, however, is with how this support is distributed across income classes. Most likely, a large part of the support goes to middle- and high-income students. This pattern follows from the structure of higher education. Public institutions of higher learning are arranged according to a 3-tiered structure in many states: junior colleges, 4-year colleges, and comprehensive universities. Educational costs increase more than tuition in moving from the junior colleges to the comprehensive universities; thus, the more comprehensive the institution, the greater the indirect tuition support. Students from lower-income families are overrepresented in less comprehensive institutions and underrepresented in more comprehensive institutions. Thus, indirect tuition support is related directly to family income. So, although indirect tuition support increases enrollment, the enrollment increase is likely to be concentrated more heavily on middle- and upper-income students.

Summary

A college education is a large investment both for students and society. In this chapter, we explain how economists evaluate college education as an investment—from both the student's and society's perspectives.

We determine the soundness of an investment by comparing its benefits and costs. Social benefits and social costs are the broadest measures of benefits and costs. Social benefits are the sum of student benefits and nonstudent benefits. Social costs are the sum of student costs and nonstudent costs. Some benefits and costs are easy to value in dollars; some are not. The former are called monetary benefits and costs; the latter are referred to as nonmonetary benefits and costs.

The principal monetary student benefit to a college graduate is his or her increase in lifetime earnings after taxes. Monetary student costs are composed of outlays for net tuition, fees, books, transportation, and earnings foregone while in college. The principal monetary nonstudent benefit is represented by the increase in taxes associated with increased lifetime earnings. The principal monetary nonstudent costs are the funds provided by federal and state governments and income from private nonstudent sources.

We illustrate how benefits and costs are measured and compared, using an example for a hypothetical public college student who earns a bachelor's degree in 4 years. Data for such an individual yield a real rate of return for the student of 14.27 percent and a real rate of return for society of 14.50 percent.

Many nonmonetary benefits and costs accompany a college education. Examples are easy to come by, but currently available estimates of monetary value are not widely enough accepted to warrant their inclusion in rate of return calculations.

The estimates based on monetary benefits and costs alone indicate underinvestment in college education by both students and society. The high student rate of return, however, raises the issue of need for government support of higher education.

If government support for colleges and universities was withdrawn entirely, and if the money now spent by governments for this purpose was given back as a tax reduction, college students would face both higher tuition and higher after-tax earnings. The effect on tuition outweighs the effect on after-tax earnings, however, and the net effect is a lowering of the student rate of return to 11.38 percent. Because this is well below the social rate of return, government support would be necessary to realize all socially justified investment in college education.

Governments provide several types of support to student borrowers. Government loans are necessary to correct for market failure resulting from a difference between private and social risk of default.

We examined the Pell grant program to determine whether it is likely to increase access to higher education for lower-income students. The Pell grant is structured to provide more aid to lower-income students, and it has increased college enrollment by this group, but not by much.

Indirect tuition support in the form of state appropriations was also evaluated. The typical pattern of indirect tuition support increases lower-income students' access to a college education, but it probably increases access even more for middle- and upper-income students.

Key Terms

Future value (FV)
Present value (PV)
Discount Factor
Present value decision rule
Rate of return decision rule
Rate of return (ROR)

Monetary benefits and costs
Nonmonetary benefits and costs
Social benefits
Social costs
Student benefits
Nonstudent benefits

Student costs
Nonstudent costs
Student rate of return (ROR)
Social rate of return (ROR)
Student rate of return without
    government support

Review Questions

1. Using the following data and an interest rate of 5 percent (.05), calculate the sums of the PVBs and the PVCs. Also determine the rate of return:

t	B	C
0	$ 0	$3,000
1	1,100	0
2	1,210	0
3	1,331	0

2. Explain why benefits and costs must be adjusted for time of occurrence.

3. Explain the nonmonetary student costs and student benefits of a college education. Do they appear to raise or lower the student rate of return on investing in a bachelor's degree? Explain.

4. What distinguishes calculations of the student rate of return from calculations of the social rate of return? Which is likely to be larger? Explain why.

5. Explain why, if governments were to withdraw their support for college education (along with the taxes raised to provide this support), too little money would be invested in college education.

6. Explain the difference between individual and social risk in the market for student loans. What are the implications of this difference for public policy? Illustrate your answer.

7. "The provision of indirect tuition support has substantially increased lower-income students' access to higher education." Is this statement true or false? Defend your answer.

8. Evaluate government loan programs as a means of providing financial support to college students.

Economic Issues on the Internet

- College for All?—**http://www.ed.gov/pubs/CollegeForAll/index.html**
  The National Library of Education, in its January 1999 survey article "College for All? Is There Too Much Emphasis on Getting a 4-Year College Degree," suggests that although the return to education is reasonably high for those who have high levels of academic ability, the expected return is quite low for students with low levels of academic ability.

- Debt Burden After College—**http://nces.ed.gov/pubs2001/quarterly/fall/post_debt.html**
  Susan P. Choy examines the debt burden of college graduates four years after the completion of college. In her article "Debt Burden Four Years After College," she finds that approximately 50 percent of all 1992–1993 college graduates had relied on borrowing to finance part of their education; that students who had borrowed larger amounts were less likely to immediately enroll in post-baccalaureate educational programs; and that monthly loan payments were approximately 5 percent of monthly income.

- Education Statistics—**http://nces.ed.gov**
  The *Digest of Educational Statistics* provides an extensive collection of statistics. You may find information on college costs, educational enrollments, earnings by level of education, and many other related issues.

- Effects of College Quality on Occupational Status of Students—
  http://www.stanford.edu/group/ncpi/documents/pdfs/5-06_collegequality.pdf
  Authors Eric Dey, Leslie A. Wimsatt, Byung-Shik Rhee, and Ellen Waterson Meader examine the return to college quality using long-term data on individual earnings in their working paper "Long-Term Effect of College Quality on the Occupational Status of Students." They conclude that the effect of college quality is not found to be a statistically significant determinant of lifetime earnings.

- Human Capital and Poverty—**http://www.acton.org/publicat/randl/**
  Author Gary S. Becker discusses the returns to education in this January/February 1998 issue of *Religion & Liberty*. In "Human Capital and Poverty," he argues that the rate of return to education has been increasing in recent years for a variety of reasons. Becker suggests that differences in educational investment is a primary reason for differences in rates of economic growth across countries.

- Investment in Education—**http://www.house.gov/jec/educ.htm**
  The Joint Economic Committee, in its January 2000 study "Investment in Education: Private and Public Returns," examined the private and public returns to investment in education. It found that there are relatively large returns to education but that they vary substantially by college major field.

- U.S. Department of Education, National Center for Education Statistics—**http://nces.ed.gov**
  A Web site that provides a wealth of data on the demographic and financial aspects of college education.

- Wages and the University Educated—**http://stats.bls.gov/opub/mlr/1997/07/art1full.pdf**
  College graduates have been increasingly filing jobs that were previously filled by high school graduates. In their study "Wages and the University Educated: A Paradox Resolved," authors Frederic L. Pryor and David Schaffer suggest that this outcome is related to the level of "functional literacy" of college graduates; i.e., that high school jobs are filled primarily by college students who do not possess high levels of reading, writing, or analytical skills. Pryor and Schaffer find that the return to a college degree is substantially higher for college students with higher levels of functional literacy.

Chapter 10

Educational Reform: The Role of Incentives and Choice

Outline:

The Nature of the Problem
Arguments for Public Support of Schools
The Economics of Student Achievement
High-Stakes Testing
   The Economics of Investing in High-Stakes Testing
   Investing in More Required Courses

The Economic Organization of Public Education
   Decision Making and Markets
   Decision Making and State-Owned Enterprises
   Decision Making and Public Schools
   Alternatives to the Current System of Public Education

Education is becoming increasingly important as the economy's dependence on knowledge and technology increases. The increased monetary return to a college education over the last quarter of the twentieth century reflects this increasing importance. The falling real wage of high school dropouts and high school graduates with no college is another indicator of education's importance in the modern economy. Perhaps in response to the increased return to education, state and federal governments have been pouring resources into K–12 (kindergarten through high school) education. Unfortunately, these increased resources have had little, if any, effect on the academic performance of high school seniors. Because of public education's familiarity and importance, we have strong but conflicting opinions about it. For instance, many people would say that the improvements in education depend upon obtaining more resources to raise teachers' salaries and to reduce class size; whereas others would say public schools are well provided with resources, but they use the resources inefficiently.

In this chapter, we consider some of the evidence that suggests that the U.S. public school system does not perform as well as those in comparable countries. The chapter uses simple quantitative analysis to examine the alleged failures of public schools and then uses basic economics to analyze some of the problems of and proposals for K–12 education.

■ THE NATURE OF THE PROBLEM

Evidence that U.S. public school performance is not the best in the world comes from international comparisons of the math and science achievement of high school seniors at the end of their K–12 education. According to the U.S. Department of Education, the Third International Mathematics and Science Study (TIMSS), the most recent one, "is a fair and accurate comparison of mathematics and science achievement in the participating nations. The students who participated in TIMSS were scientifically selected to accurately represent students in their respective nations." In particular, "Because the high enrollment rates for secondary education in the United States are typical of other TIMSS countries, our general population is not being compared to more select groups in other countries." The study concludes, "The performance of U.S. students in mathematics and science at the end of secondary school is among the lowest of those countries participating in TIMSS. This is true for all students as well as for students in advanced mathematics and physics."[1]

Figure 10.1 arranges the United States and a random sample of the other 21 countries included in the TIMSS by their math achievement scores with the highest score on the left. The figure shows that the math and science performance of U.S. high school seniors was below all but one of the countries randomly selected for the table. (The complete results show that the United States was 20th of 22 in math achievement and 17th of 22 in science achievement.) Furthermore, advanced students in the United States performed poorly compared to advanced students in other countries. To be specific, students in other countries outperformed U.S. students in physics in 14 of 16 countries and in advanced mathematics in 11 of 16 countries.

Why do high school graduates in other countries outperform U.S. high school graduates? It is not because other countries spend more per pupil. The United States spends more per pupil than any other country included in Figure 10.1. (Of all the countries listed in footnote one, only Switzerland spends more per pupil than the United States.) Figure 10.2 shows most of the countries from Figure 10.1, again arranged by their math scores. The second variable is per pupil spending; an examination shows no apparent relationship between the math scores and per pupil spending. The United States, which spends the most, has the lowest math score, and the Netherlands, which spends much less, has the highest score.

Figure 10.3 offers further evidence that the United States cannot fix public schools by throwing money at them. Since 1969, spending per pupil in United States has doubled, but achievement scores, represented by

---

[1]The quotes are from the U.S. Department of Education. National Center for Education Statistics, *Pursuing Excellence: A Study of U.S. Twelfth-Grade Mathematics and Science Achievement in International Context*, NCES 98–049. Washington, DC: U.S. Government Printing Office, 1998. Available at the National Center for Education Statistics Web site at http://nces.ed.gov/fastfacts. The countries are Australia, Austria, Canada, Cyprus, Czech Republic, Denmark, France, Germany, Hungary, Iceland, Italy, Lithuania, Netherlands, New Zealand, Norway, Russian Federation, Slovenia, South Africa, Sweden, Switzerland, and the United States.

FIGURE 10.1 International Comparisons of Math and Science Achievement

Countries are ranked by math achievement from left to right. The figure shows that U.S. students perform less well in math and science than students in comparable countries.

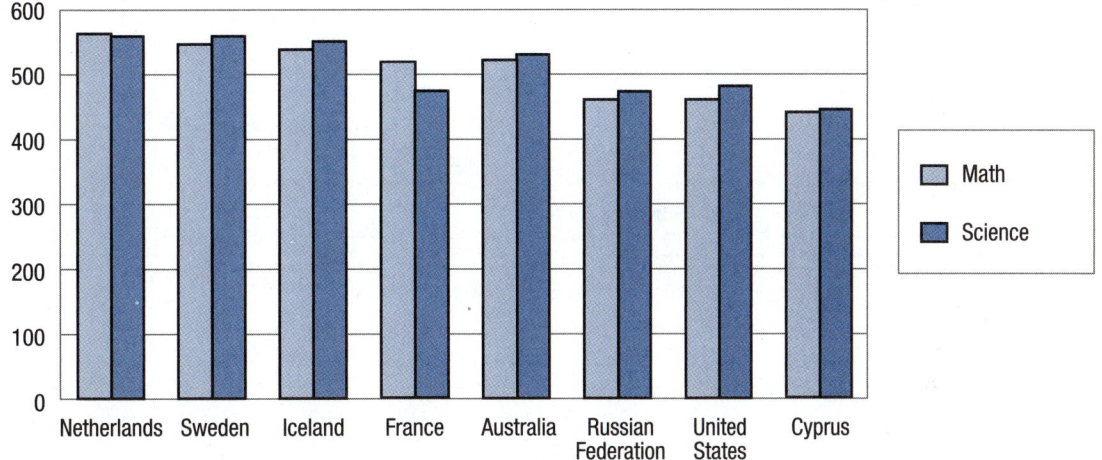

SOURCE: Third International Mathematics and Science Study of 1994–1995 as presented in the 1998 *Digest of Education Statistics*, published by the National Center for Education Statistics, available at http://nces.ed.gov.

FIGURE 10.2 Math Scores and Per Pupil Spending (Selected Countries, 1995)

Countries are ranked by math achievement from left to right. The second bar for each country is per pupil spending. Although math achievement falls moving to the right, per pupil spending shows no trend. The United States with the highest per pupil spending has the lowest achievement score. (Note that the achievement scores from Figure 10.1 have been divided by 10 and that per pupil spending is in hundreds of dollars to make the two measures comparable.)

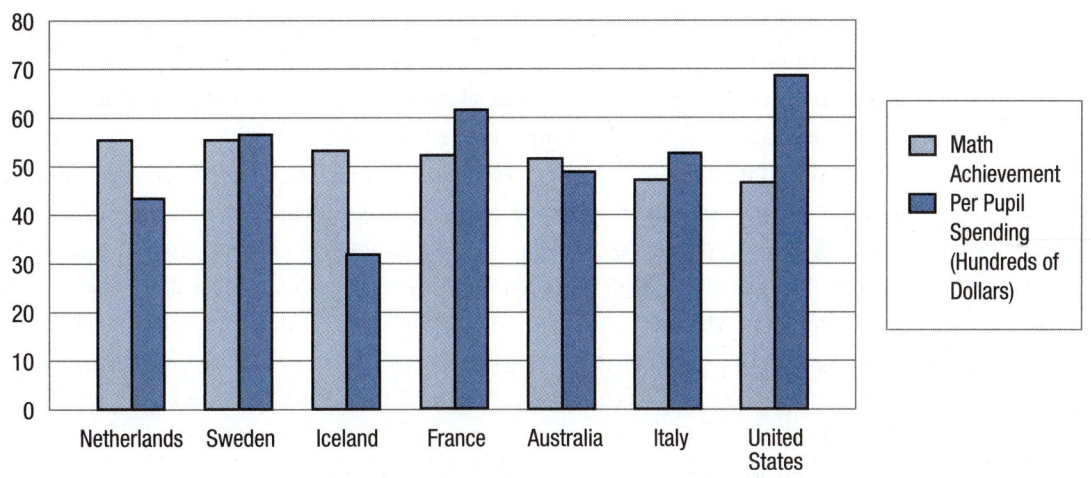

SOURCE: National Center for Education Statistics at http://nces.ed.gov.

FIGURE 10.3 Trends in Per Pupil Expenditures and Mathematics Achievement of 17-Year-Old Students

We see in this figure that the increase in per pupil spending shows no accompanying increase in math achievement. (Note that the achievement scores compared with Figure 10.1 have been multiplied by 10 to make the two series comparable.)

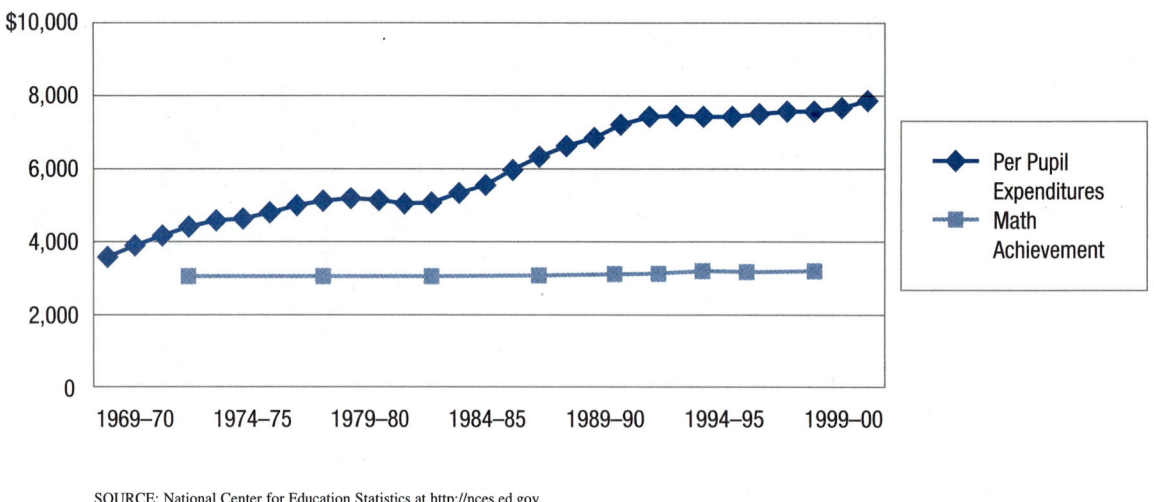

SOURCE: National Center for Education Statistics at http://nces.ed.gov.

math achievement in the figure, have been flat. The tentative conclusion is that we are spending more with no accompanying increase in student achievement. Eric Hanushek and Steven Rivkin have studied the growth in expenditures per pupil from 1970 to 1990. Over this period, rising real wages for teachers and falling pupil–teacher ratios pushed cost per pupil up. The reduction in the number of pupils per teacher alone was large enough to cause the real expenditure per pupil to grow at a 1.4 percent annual rate.

One reason that the decline in the pupil–teacher ratio failed to produce increased achievement could be that more instructional resources were devoted to special education. Even after adjusting for this factor, however, the pupil–teacher ratio fell, but as we see in the figure, achievement did not increase. The conclusion that fewer pupils per teacher is not associated with improved learning outcomes is consistent with the conclusion of many empirical studies, which find that smaller class size and fewer pupils per teacher have no consistent positive effect on achievement.[2]

The upward trend in per pupil expenditures and the flat trend in achievement suggests inefficiency in resource use. Eric Hanushek, a leading authority on K–12 education among economists, summarizes our knowledge in this way. "Studies of class size and pupil–teacher ratios, of teacher education, and of teacher experience give little if any support to policies of expanding these resources . . . it is useful to clarify precisely what is and is not implied by the data. Perhaps the most important fact to underscore is that this finding does **not** [our emphasis] imply that all schools and teachers are the same. Quite the contrary. Substantial evidence suggests that there are large differences among teachers and schools. The

---

[2] Eric A. Hanushek and Steven G. Rivkin, "Understanding the Twentieth-Century Growth in U.S. School Spending," *Journal of Human Resources* 32 (1997), 35–69, provides the information discussed in the previous two paragraphs.

simple fact remains that these differences are not related to teacher salaries or to other measured resources devoted to the program."[3]

Hanushek and other economists who have studied public education would probably agree with Thomas Jefferson that "The truth is that the want of common education with us is not from our poverty, but from the want of an orderly system. More money is now paid for the education of a part than would be paid for that of the whole if systematically arranged."[4]

In this chapter, we consider government's role in K–12 education. After discussing the arguments for public support of K–12 education, we develop a model of student achievement. With this model, we show that student achievement improves if its marginal benefit increases or its marginal cost decreases. From this perspective, achievement tests can be used to increase the benefits of achievement to students, and improved instruction may result in reduced costs to them.

Keywords: *education and international and achievement*
http://www.infotrac-college.com

■ Arguments for Public Support of Schools

Thomas Jefferson, a pioneering education advocate, argued that universal primary education would provide external benefits to society and that such education should receive government support. For instance, in a letter to George Washington, Jefferson wrote, "It is an axiom in my mind that our liberty can never be safe but in the hands of the people themselves, and that, too, of the people with a certain degree of instruction. This is the business of the state to effect, and on a general plan."[5] Moreover, in another letter he wrote, "If the condition of man is to be progressively ameliorated, as we fondly hope and believe, education is to be the chief instrument in effecting it."[6]

We can all agree with Jefferson that K–12 education and college education generate external benefits, and at the same time some can argue that K–12 education does not require government support to achieve the efficient amount. With low high school graduation rates, say, 50 percent of the relevant population, the marginal social benefit may be greater than the demand price—marginal external benefits exist. A slight increase in the high school graduation rate then generates benefits to other people as well as for the graduating individual, whose benefit is measured by her demand price for education. But suppose a 90 percent graduation rate. The external benefit of a slight increase in the graduation rate might then be zero. In Figure 10.4, marginal social benefit is greater than marginal private benefit (demand) from 0 to F. At F and beyond, marginal external benefit is zero, so MSB=MPB=D. Now suppose that supply is S_1. Given the demand situation, the equilibrium quantity of education—the quantity that would be purchased in a market economy—is E_1. But at E_1, MSB is greater than MPB, which in turn equals S=MSC. Marginal social benefit is greater than marginal social cost, so the people in the economy would be better off if

---

[3] Eric A. Hanushek, "Conclusions and Controversies About the Effectiveness of School Resources," *FRBNY Economic Policy Review* 4 (1998), 17–28.

[4] Thomas Jefferson to Joseph C. Cabell, 1820. ME 15:291. Jefferson did not, however, think that state-controlled and state-provided education was the answer. "Education is here placed among the articles of public care, not that it would be proposed to take its ordinary branches out of the hands of private enterprise, which manages so much better all the concerns to which it is equal; but a public institution can alone supply those sciences which, though rarely called for, are yet necessary to complete the circle, . . . " Thomas Jefferson: 6th Annual Message, 1806. *The Writings of Thomas Jefferson*, Memorial Edition, Lipscomb and Bergh, eds. (Washington, DC, Vol. 3, 1903–1904), 423. See http://etext.virginia.edu/jefferson/quotations for this and other Jefferson quotes.

[5] Thomas Jefferson to George Washington, 1786. ME 19:24.

[6] Thomas Jefferson to M. A. Jullien, 1818. ME 15:172.

FIGURE 10.4 The Efficient Level of Education

In this figure, the marginal social benefit (MSB) is greater than the marginal private benefit (MPB) of education from 0 to F, implying that the marginal external benefit (MEB) of education is positive. The MEB gets smaller with increasing levels of education. For levels of education greater than F, MSB=MPB. Because MPB is the same as demand, the market equilibrium quantity of education, when supply is S_1, is E_1. The market equilibrium E_1 is not efficient because MSB>MSC(marginal social cost). One way to reach the efficient level of education in this case is for government to subsidize education. With supply S_2, market equilibrium is E_3, which is efficient because MSB=MSC. Because MEB declines, the market equilibrium is efficient in some circumstances and not in others.

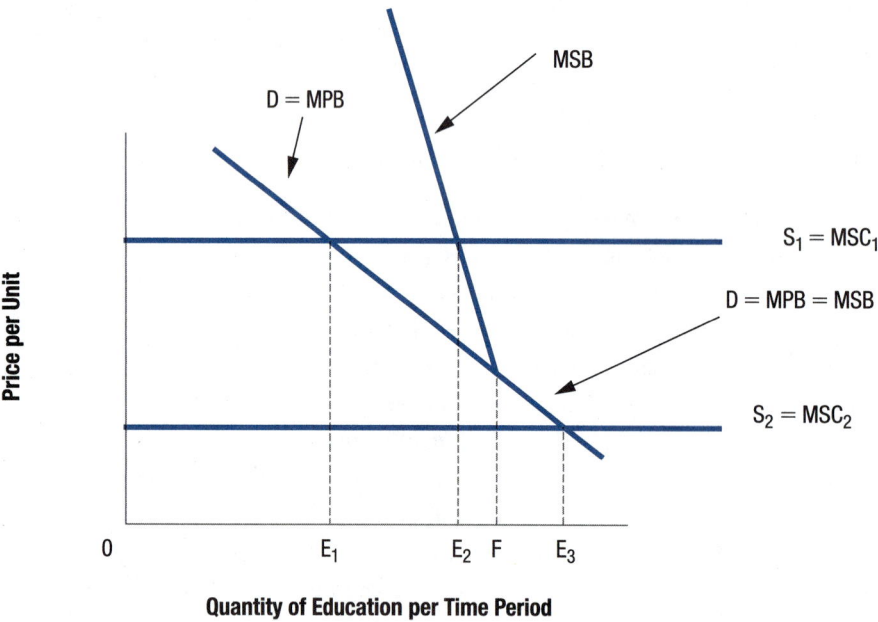

Keywords: federal government and education

http://www.infotrac-college.com

more education were produced. The efficient level is, in fact, E_2. Unless education is somehow required or made more inexpensive, not enough education is produced. With the supply curve at S_2, however, the equilibrium quantity is E_3. It is also the efficient quantity. External benefits of education exist, but at the margin they are exhausted at F. If supply is S_2, private benefit—the demand price—is high enough to call forth the efficient level of education without government subsidies. The seeming contradiction between the existence of external benefits and the market operating efficiently is resolved by noting that at the equilibrium quantity, E_3, marginal external benefits are zero; one more unit adds nothing to the total external benefit because the total external benefit is at a maximum.

In a modern economy that is moderately wealthy, the case for supporting higher education or even high school education on the basis of marginal external benefits may be weak. The private benefit of education may be sufficient to evoke an educational level that exhausts marginal external benefits. Nevertheless, citizens support tuition subsidies for higher education, and they provide universal K–12 education with no tuition charge. Why? Equality, or the ideal of equal opportunity, may provide the answer. Some people argue that justice exists in a market economy because it is organized around voluntary exchange. Given the initial

INSIGHTS

JEFFERSON, SMITH, AND PUBLIC SCHOOLS: STANDARDS AND LOCAL CONTROL

Adam Smith and Thomas Jefferson were advocates of public education. Smith believed that government could facilitate or even require that everyone obtain "the most essential parts of education . . . to read, write, and account . . . [moreover government can establish] in every parish or district, a little school" where even the poorest family could send their children with the expense of the school shared between the family and the government.[a]

For almost half a century, Jefferson promoted his general plan for education in the state of Virginia. His original proposal was that county government would use tax revenue to finance a 3-year education for all (free) children and would assist talented students from families too poor to pay for the child's education beyond the third year. Any other student could continue beyond 3 years, provided only that tuition was paid. Counties and divisions within counties would establish and control the schools.

Both Smith and Jefferson were reluctant to make even primary education compulsory because to do so would interfere with parents' freedom. They entertained the idea, however, that individuals without the abilities conferred by primary education should be deprived of the full rights of citizenship. Even so, neither provided unequivocal support for zero tuition for all students as a way to give everyone a chance to meet the citizenship criteria. Jefferson was willing to compromise on his government-financed 3-year education, if that was necessary to establish a version of universal education. He believed that the well-to-do opposed his plan for free tuition because they would be paying for the education of the poor. In one letter he said, "The modification of the law, by authorizing the alderman to require the expense of tutorage from such parents as are able, would render trifling, if not wholly prevent, any call on the country for pecuniary aid."[b]

Jefferson and Smith apparently would have had no problem with a mixed system of K–12 education that included private schools, home schooling, and public schools dependent at least in part on tuition. They did, however, have standards. To obtain "the honours of graduation," Smith said, "it is not necessary that a person bring a certificate of his having studied a certain number of years at a publick school. If upon examination he appears to understand what is taught there, no questions are asked about the place where he learnt it."[c] In his 1779 proposal to the Virginia General Assembly for the "General Diffusion of Knowledge," Jefferson provided for county-appointed overseers responsible for ensuring that the local school met standards set by the College of William and Mary.

Jefferson advanced two arguments for universal education. One was that the experiment in self-government could work only if all people were literate and numerate. Jefferson's other objective was to ensure that the most talented students were educated beyond the primary level. He would provide public support for the most talented students from poor families, so that they could advance their education. Jefferson's purpose was to create an aristocracy based on merit and talent rather than inheritance. He did not want to waste the abilities of talented but poor students. As he put it, "By . . . [selecting] the youths of genius from among the classes of the poor, we hope to avail the State of those talents which nature has sown as liberally among the poor as the rich, but which perish without use if not sought for and cultivated."[d]

Although Jefferson favored government support for education, he was convinced that what we would call K–12 education should **not** be subject to state control. "If it is believed that . . . elementary schools will be better managed by the governor and council, the commissioners of the literary fund or any other general authority of the government than by the parents within each ward, it is a belief against all experience. Try the principle one step further, and . . . commit to the governor and council the management of all our farms, our mills and merchants' stores. No, my friend, the way to have good and safe government is not to trust it all to one, but to divide it among the many, distributing to every one exactly the functions he is competent to."[e]

---

[a] Adam Smith, *An Inquiry into the Nature and Causes of the Wealth of Nations* (Indianapolis: Liberty Press, 1981), a reprint of the edition published by Oxford: Clarendon Press, 1979, Book II, Ch. 5, 785.
[b] Thomas Jefferson to Joseph C. Cabell, 1816. ME 14:413.
[c] Smith, *Wealth of Nations*, 764–765.
[d] Thomas Jefferson: Notes on Virginia Q.XIV, 1782. ME 2:206.
[e] Thomas Jefferson to Joseph C. Cabell, 1816. ME 14:420.

Commutative Justice – A norm for a market economy based on voluntary exchange. Voluntary exchange means exchange of equal market value.

Distributive Justice – Equality among people, providing a norm of equal opportunity, with the hope that equal opportunity combined with commutative justice will move people toward equality.

INFOTRAC
College Edition

Keywords: *public schools and economic aspects*

http://www.infotrac-college.com

distribution of wealth and ability, people interact voluntarily, taking actions that they believe will increase their well-being. According to Henry Simons, late of the University of Chicago, "Such justice connotes exchange of equal values, as measured objectively by organized markets."[7] Simons refers to justice emerging from voluntary exchange as **commutative justice**, and he believed it important both for economic efficiency and for fairness. Commutative justice by itself, however, is not complete for Simons; **distributive justice** or equality, for him, is another important goal of the good society. Simons concludes therefore that "Equality of opportunity is an ideal that free societies should constantly pursue, even at much cost in terms of other ends. . . . Inequality . . . is overwhelmingly a problem of investment in human capacity, that is, in health, education, and skills. It can hardly be scratched by possible redistributions of wealth . . . . Save as the bride of liberty, equality is pale and deadly dull, if not revolting. But the ultimate liberty is that of men of equal power."[8]

Taxpayers may support public education because of its perceived external effects including its effects on economic growth, or they may do so to promote equal opportunity. Regardless, for any given level of education, obtaining it at the lowest opportunity cost is desirable, just as it is achieving any level of environmental quality. Many analyses of the cost-effectiveness of K–12 education, including our section, "The Nature of the Problem," are like Hamlet without the Prince of Denmark—they omit the students. In the next section, we resolve this problem by considering students' incentives to excel.

■ THE ECONOMICS OF STUDENT ACHIEVEMENT

What explains the level of student achievement? Although economics cannot provide all the answers, it provides a way of thinking about it. The economic perspective is that students (or the parents of young children) make choices about academic achievement much as they make other choices. They assess the benefits and costs of academic achievement, and the chosen level of achievement reflects perceived benefits and costs. More specifically, it assumes that students compare the marginal benefits and costs of additional achievement, aim for higher achievement if the marginal benefits exceed the costs, and aim for lower achievement if the marginal costs exceed the marginal benefits.

For the typical student, additional achievement requires additional time spent on learning, which has a rising marginal opportunity cost: the value of the next best alternative use of his time. It is rising because at higher levels of achievement it takes more time to generate an equal increase in achievement and because the additional time allocated to achievement comes from increasingly valuable uses of that time. Better jobs, better chances of receiving college scholarships, and better chances of being admitted to a desired college are among the perceived benefits from additional effort. The greater the level of achievement, however, the less the marginal benefit of additional achievement. For instance, if you aim for a particular test score to qualify for a scholarship, any achievement in excess of that score may have a much lower marginal benefit. Students will work harder as long as the benefits they expect from additional effort are greater than the costs of their best foregone opportunity.

The relevant costs and benefits are those perceived by individuals. Individual costs will differ because of differences in individual ability and alternative opportunities. Individual benefits will differ because of

---

[7]Henry Simons, *Economic Policy for a Free Society* (Chicago: University of Chicago Press, 1948), 4.
[8]Ibid., 6–7.

FIGURE 10.5 The Chosen Level of Achievement: The Student Perspective

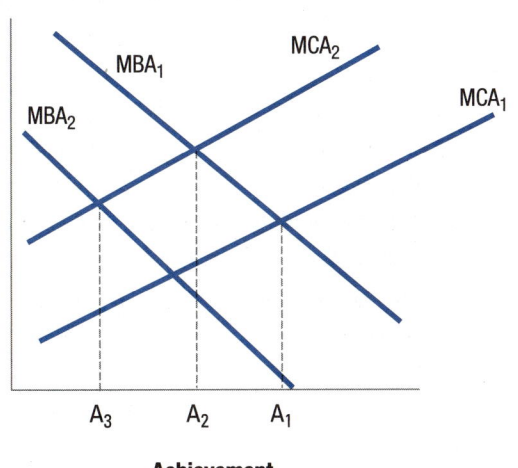

From the perspective of the student or the student's family, the marginal benefit of achievement (MBA) for the student decreases with increases in achievement, and the marginal cost of achievement (MCA) for the student increases with achievement. With the curves MBA_1 and MCA_1, the chosen achievement level will be A_1. An increase in marginal benefit, illustrated by the shift of the MBA curve from MBA_2 to MBA_1, and a decrease in marginal cost, illustrated by the shift of the MCA curve from MCA_2 to MCA_1, results in increased achievement.

individual differences in aspirations, knowledge, and experiences. Given a relatively wide distribution of individual abilities and alternative opportunities, and the inherent difficulty in raising test scores at the margin, aggregate student achievement is subject to increasing marginal cost, as illustrated by the marginal cost of achievement (MCA_1) curve in Figure 10.5. Given a wide distribution of individual aspirations, knowledge, and experience, aggregate student rewards from additional effort are subject to decreasing marginal benefit, as illustrated by the marginal benefit of achievement (MBA_1) curve in the figure.

At low levels of achievement the marginal benefit of increased achievement is greater than the marginal cost. In this situation, the decision maker (family or student) chooses to increase achievement, implying greater student effort. As achievement increases, its marginal benefit falls and its marginal cost increases, implying that at some point, MCA exceeds MBA. If so, student effort and achievement will be reduced. The equilibrium level of student achievement, A_1, occurs where $MCA_1 = MBA_1$.

Figure 10.5 also shows that this model can explain a downward drift in test scores. Suppose A_1 is the equilibrium level of achievement historically. An increase in perceived costs of academic achievement, shifting the MCA curve from MCA_1 to MCA_2, would reduce the equilibrium level to A_2. If the increased costs are accompanied by a decrease in perceived benefits that shift the MBA curve from MBA_1 to MBA_2, the equilibrium decreases farther to A_3.

An increase in MCA can reflect either an increase in the opportunity costs of achievement or an increase in the difficulty of learning. The opportunity costs increase with increases in the value of the alternative uses of the time that would be required for studying. An example for older students is the increasing reward from student part-time employment. Another is the lure of television. MCA also may increase because of school policies that make it more costly for students to learn. For instance, peer pressure to not succeed academically may increase in response to widespread adoption of grading practices that rank students against each other instead of against an absolute scale of achievement.

A decrease in MBA means that the perceived rewards from achievement have decreased. A decrease could occur if college admission becomes less selective and employers place a smaller value on in-school achievement. Students may also aspire to imitate individuals whose success appears to have little to do with academic achievement, such as entertainers, sports stars, or drug dealers. All of these factors can weaken the link between achievement and the consequences of achievement, or what is the same thing, reduce the perceived MBA.

The model implies that achievement increases if the MBA curve increases (moves to the right) or the MCA curves decrease (move to the right). To improve performance, ways must be found to increase the marginal benefits of achievement relative to its marginal costs. One way might be to reduce the number of hours teens can legally work. This would reduce the opportunity cost of achievement, shifting the MCA curve from MCA_2 to MCA_1 and increasing the level of achievement, from A_2 to A_1, as in Figure 10.5. Another idea is to make driving privileges contingent upon a minimum level of academic achievement. This would increase the perceived benefits of achievement, shifting the MBA curve from MBA_2 to MBA_1, and increasing the level of achievement, say, from A_3 to A_2, as in Figure 10.5. A third option is to improve instruction for K–12 education, another way of shifting MCA_2 to MCA_1.

Although the first two ideas might seem fanciful, laws relating to them have been proposed in many state legislatures. The option that has captured the spotlight for now, however, is called high-stakes testing. We will explain this option and use the model of student achievement just developed to see if it makes sense.

■ HIGH-STAKES TESTING

The skills developed in school are important keys to success, both on the job and in college. Many U.S. high school students, however, do not choose to achieve at high levels. The half who do not attend college seldom perceive a connection between performance in school and immediate prospects for a job. For the half who attend college, high school performance has little effect on admission, except for those seeking to enter the most selective colleges. Perhaps as a result, half of those who attend college fail to graduate, in part because they enter college with insufficient knowledge and skills.

High-Stakes Testing – Focuses on achievement testing with demonstration of achievement important for completing high school and for subsequent employment opportunities and college admission.

High-stakes testing is one way to strengthen the connection between school performance and prospects for employment and college. With high-stakes testing, students take achievement tests and their test scores apply to grade promotion, high school graduation, employment, and college admission. Most students are currently tested in each course and do well enough to be promoted from grade to grade and to graduate. Course grades are averaged to obtain a grade point average (GPA), which determines class rank. Both GPA and class rank are often used as criteria for college admission. Some high school students also take the American College Test (ACT) or Scholastic Aptitude Test (SAT), and their scores also apply to college admission. Thus, we have a widespread system of testing in this country, and test scores may affect grade promotion, graduation, and college admission (although not often employment). This system differs considerably, however, from high-stakes testing.

High-stakes testing uses *achievement tests* designed to determine the degree to which a test taker has mastered a broad subject area, not specific course content. The tests are *universal tests*; that is, all students take them at a certain grade level. They use *absolute performance standards*, not relative performance standards such as "curves." A passing grade is established without reference to how others do on the test. The subject matter of the tests is similar to that used in achievement tests in other countries; thus, the tests are *internationally referenced*. Finally the tests are *analytically oriented*, rewarding analytical and problem-solving skills more than memorization.

INSIGHTS

SETTING STANDARDS FOR MATHEMATICS ACHIEVEMENT

The development of standards for elementary and secondary school mathematics provides a good example of the tests envisioned for high-stakes testing. Responding in the mid-1980s to difficulties created by the failures of the New Math, the National Council of Teachers of Mathematics (NCTM) began an extensive review of the state of basic mathematics. After much preliminary discussion, they decided to develop national standards and devised an elaborate consensus and review process that ultimately involved thousands of math teachers. In 1989, they published national standards that required a dramatic change in teaching and learning mathematics. Instead of computation and memorization of abstractions, the new standards emphasize problem-solving, hands-on activities, and the development of mathematics as a way of thinking and reasoning. The new standards set high expectations for all children instead of dividing them into groups that are or are not college bound. The NCTM standards have been widely, although not universally, accepted. They are changing teacher education, because new teachers are expected to learn to teach them. They are changing the way mathematics textbooks are written, with more attention to problem-solving and real-world applications. They are changing the nature of assessment, reinforcing the movement away from standardized multiple-choice tests and toward performance assessments that probe for explanations, interpretations, and understandings. Students who would have traditionally been tracked into remedial math or consumer math are doing algebra, geometry, and even calculus; they have demonstrated that they can learn much more than educators heretofore thought possible.

Achievement tests are not standardized tests of general ability, such as the SAT exam. They concentrate on the core principles of a subject. Students prepare for them by taking specific courses and studying specific materials, but the courses and materials are carefully designed to teach these principles. Properly designed, these courses and materials provide students with a clear understanding of what they must know and do to succeed on the achievement tests.

High-stakes testing would establish high expectations for all students, regardless of family income and location, instead of the different standards for different students that have long characterized the U.S. educational system. Proponents of achievement tests for everyone argue that the traditional practice of allowing students to choose watered-down courses (commercial math versus algebra, for example) effectively denies them equal opportunity to succeed in the workplace of the future or in higher education. High-stakes testing would severely limit this practice.

The absolute grading scale associated with high-stakes testing is an external standard; that is, a standard imposed by state or national authorities. Adoption of such a standard would strengthen the incentives of students and teachers to work together toward a common goal. Without an external standard, teachers might judge individual students relative to their classmates. Students perceive this and apply peer pressure to discourage classmates from "wrecking the curve." An external standard, by contrast, unites teachers and students in a common objective: to perform well.

The labor market for skilled workers is international, and U.S. students find themselves increasingly in competition with workers from other countries. Thus, the standards that prevail in U.S. high-stakes testing should equal those in the countries whose students have been outperforming U.S. students.

The labor market of the future will also require a larger share of the workforce to have more problem-solving ability. The proponents of high-stakes testing recognize this and argue for courses, texts, and tests that better prepare students to be problem-solvers. Under high-stakes testing, students would develop the ability to put core principles to work in solving real-life problems.

The other part of high-stakes testing involves raising the stakes. Simply put, this requires that test scores have consequences: that they affect events of high value to students, such as promotion, graduation, college admission, and employment. Diplomas certifying different achievement levels and transcripts displaying course grades and achievement test results would make high school performance more meaningful. Such information would be useful for colleges and employers; with increased information about students' performance, colleges and employers would give it greater weight in admission and employment decisions.

U.S. educators and government officials have responded to the relatively poor performance of U.S. students primarily by requiring them to take more courses in "solid" subjects, such as math and science. Taking more courses is not sufficient to ensure that students will learn enough to match the performance of students in other countries. According to studies by Becker, Rosen, and Steinberg, increased student effort is essential, and significant increases in effort are unlikely without the prospect of greater rewards from studying than students now perceive. As they and many others put it, why study harder?

- It is highly unlikely that a student will have to repeat a course or a grade.
- Graduation from high school, by itself, is sufficient for admission to a large majority of colleges.
- Colleges and universities are willing to correct deficiencies through remedial courses.
- Employers do not use school performance as a criterion for hiring.[9]

If they are right, ways must be found to require underperforming students to repeat courses or grades, to implement performance-based college admission criteria, to put the colleges and universities out of the remedial education business, and to encourage use of student performance data as a criterion for employment.

One way to raise the stakes is to use achievement test scores rather than course grades to make grade promotion and graduation decisions. As noted previously, good grades do not necessarily mean mastery of a subject when grading relies on relative rather than absolute performance. Although the transition is proving painful, six states have implemented policies linking promotion to achievement test scores. Eighteen states currently require adequate performance on some type of standard exam for high school graduation, and six more are in the process of doing so.

Many students who want a college education will exert more effort to achieve higher test scores if the scores determine college admission. Many public colleges and universities base admissions on ACT scores, high school grade point averages (GPA), and rank in high school graduating class, and they have raised the minimum required for each of these in recent years. Success on the ACT exam requires students to understand and apply the core principles of several basic subjects. Consequently, the ACT exam is an achievement test that can serve as a useful substitute until appropriate achievement tests are developed based on the competencies that states expect high school graduates to have.

Students who plan to enter the labor force directly from high school will also exert more effort to achieve higher test scores if employers use them as a criterion for hiring. Employers currently do not make much use of measures of high school performance, apparently because a graduate's GPA is not

---
[9]William E. Becker and Sherwin Rosen, "The Learning Effect of Assessment and Evaluation in High School," *Economics of Education Review* 11 (1992), 107–118. Laurence Steinberg, "Standards Outside the Classroom," in Diane Ravitch, ed., *Brookings Papers on Education Policy* (1998), 319–158.

an accurate indicator of the desired skills and abilities. Again, achievement tests could change employers' practices.

The Economics of Investing in High-Stakes Testing

High-stakes testing appears to be a "good thing," but it can be achieved only at additional cost to both students and society. Is it worth it? Like all such questions in economics, the answer depends on the additional costs and benefits associated with the activity.

The effect of high-stakes testing is illustrated in Figure 10.6. From the students' perspective, high-stakes testing increases the benefits of academic achievement. The higher the payoff in terms of promotion, graduation, employment, and college admission, the higher the benefits per unit of achievement. Thus, the adoption of more rigorous tests—tests that measure achievement and are universal, internationally referenced, and analytically oriented—shifts the MBA curve from MBA_1 to MBA_2. As students and their families recognize the increased benefits of achievement, students will incur the costs necessary to move to higher achievement levels: from A_1 to A_2.

The improved achievement, however, is gained at other costs. States and local districts must bear the cost of developing, implementing, and grading the achievement tests. To be high-stakes tests, they must be valid measures of the degree to which students have mastered the relevant material. It is crucial that the tests be well-designed and focus on analytical ability rather than memorization or rote procedures. Only if the tests are validated will colleges and employers rely heavily on them.

At this time, many states have multiple-choice achievement tests. Although such tests have the advantage of being easy to grade, they also are limited in their ability to measure students' analytical knowledge of a field. The tests are also subject to manipulation by the state and by teachers. The greater the

FIGURE 10.6   The Effect of High-Stakes Testing on Student Achievement

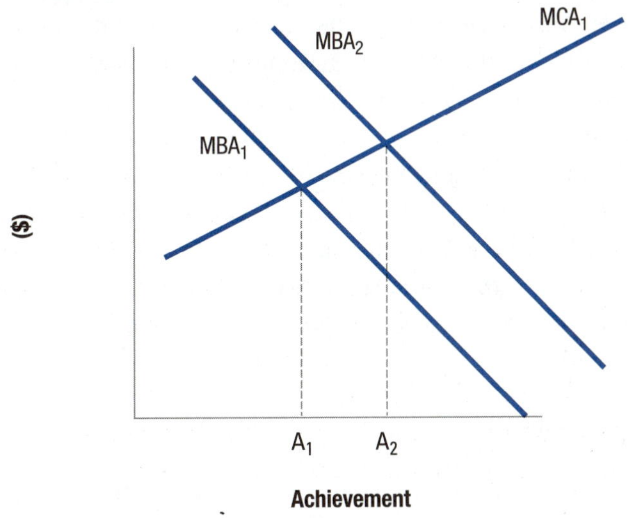

High-stakes testing and its acceptance by colleges and employers shifts the marginal benefit of achievement to the right. At the original achievement level, marginal benefit is now greater than marginal cost. Because achievement is now perceived as more valuable, students find it worthwhile to incur higher opportunity costs and reach the new chosen achievement level, A_2.

stakes for the teacher or the school, the greater "temptation to skew the reports . . . 'whether [in the words of the legislative report] by intentionally falsifying data, or simply stretching the rules to create more favorable data.'"[10] Numerous reports exist of teachers, sometimes prompted by school administrators, actually helping students cheat on standardized tests.[11] Administrators in many school districts stretch the rules on universality, conveniently placing low-performing students in special education categories that exempt them from the test.[12]

In addition to cheating and fudging the data, administrators and teachers might distort the curriculum in an attempt to increase the pass rate. In Texas, many schools use a couple of months before the achievement test to drill students on techniques to pass the test. Math and English classes, and sometimes other classes, ignore the normal curriculum and "teach to the test." If the test was less predictable and more analytical, normal teaching practices would "teach to the test" without distorting the curriculum.

Two questions arise: (1) Will high-stakes testing increase the level of achievement, as predicted in Figure 10.6? (2) If so, will the additional benefits from higher achievement exceed the additional costs?

THE EFFECT OF HIGH-STAKES TESTING ON ACHIEVEMENT.

High-stakes testing is such a new concept in the United States that we lack data needed to determine its likely effect on academic achievement. One exception is a 1996 study by John Bishop, which analyzed the relationship between students' state of residence and SAT scores.[13] He concludes that New Yorkers have done significantly better on the SAT, particularly the math portion, than have students of the same race and background living in other states. He attributes this to New York's use of the Regents' Examinations. The New York Regents' Exams are curriculum-based achievement tests with modest "stakes"; exam scores account for about half of the final course grades, and they influence the type of graduation diploma received. This is encouraging evidence to proponents of high-stakes testing because the stakes in the New York case are so modest, but it is not a sufficient basis for proceeding with widespread adoption of much more rigorous stakes.

INFOTRAC
College Edition

Keywords: *high-stakes testing*

http://www.infotrac-college.com

THE BENEFITS AND COSTS OF HIGHER ACHIEVEMENT.

Unfortunately, the evidence on the prospective benefits and costs of higher achievement sheds little additional light on the economic viability of high-stakes testing. There is a hint or two that high-stakes testing would produce significant benefits in the form of additional earnings, but no evidence on the extra costs that might be required to produce new tests, texts, courses, teaching techniques, and more effective.teachers.

John Bishop, in another study, has estimated that an increase of one standard deviation in General Intellectual Achievement test scores has been associated with a 3 to 4 percent difference in post–high school earnings. Murnane, Willett, and Levy have found that an increase of one standard deviation in mathematics test scores has been associated with an even larger increase in post–high school earnings differentials: 3 to 7.4 percent for males and 8.5 to 15.5 percent for females.[14]

---

[10] Peter Schrag, "Too Good To Be True," *The American Prospect*, January 3, 2000, 48.

[11] Labi Nadya, "When Teachers Cheat," *Time*, December 20, 1999, 86.

[12] Schrag, op. cit.

[13] John A. Bishop, "Signaling, Incentives, and School Organization in France, the Netherlands, Britain, and the United States," in Eric A. Hanushek and Dale W. Jorgenson, eds., *Improving America's Schools: The Role of Incentives* (Washington, DC: National Academy Press, 1996), 111–146.

[14] John A. Bishop, "The Productivity Consequences of What Is Learned in High School," Cornell University School of Industrial and Labor Relations, Working Paper 88–18, 1989. R. J. Murnane, J. B. Willett, and F. Levy, *The Growing Importance of Cognitive Skills in Wage Determination*, Graduate School of Education, Harvard University, Cambridge, MA, 1992.

INTERNATIONAL PERSPECTIVE

HIGH-STAKES TESTING IN JAPAN

To examine the effects of high stakes on achievement, we must go outside the United States for models. The classic case is that of Japan. Japanese students get significantly better results on achievement tests, and many observers attribute this to the high requirements for passing and the stakes associated with a passing grade; namely, admission to the best colleges and entry to the best careers. In fact, the stakes are so high that Japanese parents are not willing to leave educational outcomes for their children solely dependent on what happens in school, and they see to it that they attend cram schools to attempt to get an edge on other students in the preparation for the national exams.

These estimates probably understate the additional earnings to be realized from high-stakes testing. There are three reasons. First, they are based on data from a low-stakes environment. Second, they do not reflect the earnings differentials realized through college attendance. Better high school performers are more likely to attend college, to earn scholarships, to graduate from college, and to enjoy higher-paying careers. Third, they do not reflect the earnings attributable to on-the-job training. Better high school performers will reap larger earnings differentials from on-the-job training whether they attend college or not. We believe, therefore, that the true earnings differentials from the higher achievement associated with high-stakes testing would be much larger than indicated by the Bishop and Murnane/Willett/Levy studies cited previously. We do not know, however, how these differentials would compare to the extra costs associated with high-stakes testing. We do know, however, that the cost per pupil of a well-designed high-stakes testing program is much lower than the cost per pupil of a meaningful reduction in class size.[15]

Investing in More Required Courses

The United States has been slow to develop achievement tests with significant stakes. Individual states have typically chosen, instead, to "raise the bar" by requiring more courses as a condition for graduation, especially in the areas of math and science. Economists question whether this widely adopted policy is likely to be effective or cost-effective.

Economists who question its *effectiveness* are skeptical that requiring more courses will do much to raise overall achievement unless accompanied by demanding achievement tests and higher stakes. In Figure 10.6, the initial equilibrium level, A_1, will change only if the marginal benefit or marginal cost curve changes. Simply requiring more courses is unlikely to affect perceived benefits. Forcing the student to take more required classes might even raise the marginal cost of education and achievement for individual students. Coupling achievement tests with more required courses could prevent students and teachers from meeting the requirement with watered-down courses or curve-based grades and provide students and teachers with incentives to achieve. The local school or school district could then determine the curriculum necessary to foster an environment in which the achievement goals of students and their parents are met.

Although it is not the same thing, the more-required-courses movement provides a valuable opportunity to learn more about the potential effectiveness of high-stakes testing. The variety of practices

---

[15]See Sybil Eakin, TECHNOS Interview: Caroline M. Hoxby *Technos: Quarterly for Education and Technology* (Summer 2001), 10 (2), 4.

among the states is a source of data on different combinations of higher requirements and higher stakes. We predict larger increases in achievement in states that raise the stakes when they raise requirements than in states where the increases in requirements outpace increases in stakes.

Economists who question the *cost-effectiveness* of the more-required courses also raise the issue of whether the government should specify this, or any, particular approach to higher achievement. They would favor public determination of the appropriate minimum level of achievement, but then allow individual schools the freedom to determine how they are going to achieve this and other goals they may have. This would create an environment in which individual schools could experiment with alternatives to increasing required courses and perhaps find alternatives more effective at the same cost (or less costly for a given level of effectiveness). This approach has been successful in lowering the costs of environmental regulation (see our discussion of this approach and cost-savings achieved in Chapter 6).

This approach works well in the private sector because the quest for cost reduction gives the regulated parties incentives to find less-expensive alternatives. Because government regulators lack the knowledge about, say, specific factories' pollution circumstances, and because they have little or no incentive to reduce costs for the regulated firms, regulators are unable and unwilling to find more cost-effective solutions.

Keywords: *educational tests and measurements*
http://www.infotrac-college.com

An obvious objection to the analogy is that market incentives are absent from public K–12 education; therefore, state regulations and school-district regulations are necessary to ensure that the public education system is responsible to its clientele. Although the objection's premise is true, the conclusion does not necessarily follow. Incentives could be introduced. Privatization of the public school system would provide those incentives and could be productive just as privatizing agriculture in China (discussed in Chapters 1 and 2) increased its productivity. Although privatization may appear radical, it is odd, as Nobel Prize economist Milton Friedman says, to trust one of our most important functions to government provision at the same time that we encourage formerly socialist countries to privatize such basic functions as the supply of food. In the next section, we consider the economic organization of public education.

■ THE ECONOMIC ORGANIZATION OF PUBLIC EDUCATION

Hanushek and other economists conclude that the public schools waste a significant part of their resources. If so, we could attain the current achievement levels at lower cost, or we could attain higher levels for the same cost. If we interpret an improved learning environment or improved teaching as reducing the student's opportunity cost of achievement, Figure 10.7 shows how we expect an improved economic organization of public education to increase achievement. It shifts the marginal cost of achievement, moving the equilibrium from A_1 to A_2.

Keywords: *resources for public schools*
http://www.infotrac-college.com

A discussion of other government enterprises that have wasted resources helps in understanding the current organization of U.S. public education and how it might be changed. The only enterprises that can survive significant inefficiency for long periods are government-protected monopolies that receive government subsidies. Let's consider as our example the large state-owned enterprises (SOEs) in China and in the former Soviet Union. To understand the organizational problems of SOEs, we will first analyze how markets organize a private economy. From this analysis, we will derive three principles of economic organization and show that SOE organization is inconsistent with the principles. Finally, we will analyze the U.S. public school system in the 50 states, which, by analogy, consists of 50 SOEs.

FIGURE 10.7 The Effect of Teaching Effectiveness on Student Achievement

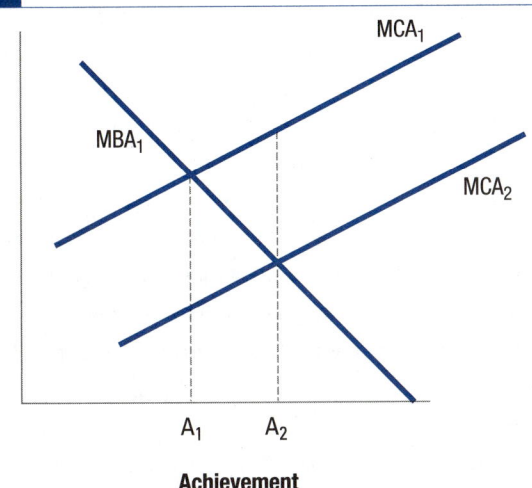

The original marginal benefit and marginal cost curves are the same as in Figure 10.6. Improved teacher effectiveness shifts the marginal cost of the achievement curve to MCA_2. Students choose to increase their achievement from A_1 to A_2 because the costs of doing so have declined. Figures 10.6 and 10.7 show two different ways of increasing achievement.

Decision Making and Markets

To understand why SOEs perform so poorly compared to private enterprises, we can analyze private-enterprise decision making in a market economy and learn why market enterprises perform better. Suppose Alfonso has inherited land with buildings in Vienna, Austria. Alfonso, a Californian, did not know that he had an Austrian relative and he speaks no German. Alfonso can easily locate certain information about the land—its area, its location, the sizes of any buildings, and the portion that is covered by a structure—but other information, such as the quality of the building; how to navigate Austrian laws, regulations, and bureaucrats; and the pros and cons of alternative uses of the property, is more difficult to transmit. The information that is easy to transmit we call **general knowledge**, and the information that is hard to transmit we call **specific knowledge**. Profitable decisions about using the property require specific knowledge; consequently, if Alfonso is going to make a "good" decision, he must spend time in Vienna, learn German, and gain an understanding of the Viennese economy. If the bequest stipulates that Alfonso must retain ownership of the property and manage it himself, he can either make the best decision possible given the general knowledge or he can bear the cost of developing the specific knowledge and then decide. Neither alternative is as likely to lead to the best use of the land or to Alfonso gaining as much wealth as he would if he could get the specific knowledge without cost. Alfonso's situation resembles that of the head of a state department of education, the CEO of a large corporation, or an industry planner in Beijing: He does not have the specific knowledge necessary to make good decisions for the dispersed units of his organization.

If Alfonso has inherited the right to sell the land along with the right to use it, he has another alternative. He can sell it to someone who has the specific knowledge. Actually, he would sell the right to make decisions about the land and to obtain income from it. Selling the decision rights to the highest bidder reduces the chance of a bad decision being made, and it minimizes the costs of using specific knowledge by shifting (at low cost) the decision to someone who has the knowledge. An auction, for instance,

General Knowledge – Knowledge that is easy to transfer to another person, including people in another part of the organization or the economy.

Specific Knowledge – Knowledge that is costly to transfer to another person and is particularly costly to transfer to someone in another part of the organization or the economy.

could sell, or *assign*, the decision rights to the person who believes that she has the most useful specific knowledge. Let us say that Helga places the highest bid and acquires the decision right.

The market also automatically *evaluates* decisions. In private market transactions, each party to the transaction is trying to make the best possible decision. In market transactions between individuals and small firms, the objective is to increase profit or, more generally, to increase individual well-being. In earlier chapters, we learned that voluntary transactions benefit both parties and that they are efficient, increasing net social benefits. Alfonso's decision to sell the Viennese property to Helga will likely make Helga and him better off and result in the property being devoted to the most profitable use. Given Alfonso's lack of specific knowledge, he has probably made the most profitable decision for himself. But how do we know that Helga has made the right decision? We do not. The market, however, will provide an automatic evaluation. If she is successful, her venture will be profitable, and if she is so inclined she can leverage this investment into a bigger one. With successive investments, her wealth increases. Helga, like other entrepreneurs, might make mistakes. If her decision to buy Alfonso's property is not profitable, someone else might buy the decision rights over the property, perhaps at a bankruptcy sale. The crucial point is that the market will automatically evaluate the decisions and make appropriate adjustments.

Finally, Alfonso, Helga, and other participants in the Viennese property market have incentives to make good decisions. If their decisions increase wealth, they can command additional resources or they can use their wealth for various types of consumption. Conversely, if their decisions decrease wealth, they will command fewer resources and have reduced consumption choices. The market, therefore, automatically *rewards* wealth-maximizing decisions.

The market process that we have just described illustrates another way that the price system economizes on information cost. In Chapter 2, we discussed how the price system summarizes and generates information. Here, we see that markets can make it unnecessary to transfer information, because they transfer decision authority to people who have the specific information. In situations where specific information is important, markets exemplify three important organizing principles. They

- Assign decision rights
- Evaluate the profitability of decisions
- Reward profitable decisions

Knowledge of various types can be costly to transmit, and thus, be specific knowledge. *Tacit knowledge*, which might be learned on the job through trial and error, is one type that is costly to transmit. The idea is that it is knowledge that is difficult to put in words. For instance, the knowledge about how to ride a bicycle is hard to transmit verbally. The development of the automatic bread machine provides another example of tacit knowledge. Matsushita, the Japanese electronics company, decided to produce an automatic bread maker. Given the idea, their engineers had an easy time creating the machine. The only problem was that the bread turned out poorly. To figure out how to make good bread, Matsushita apprenticed a couple of engineers to one of the best bakers in Tokyo. Although the engineers had studied the theory of making bread and had collected information from bakers, not until they became personally and directly involved in making bread did they understand how to design the bread machine.[16]

---

[16]Ikujiro Nonaka and Hirotaka Takeuchi, *The Knowledge-Creating Company: How Japanese Companies Create the Dynamics of Innovation* (New York: Oxford University Press, 1995).

Although *local knowledge* based on particular characteristics existing at a particular time is not necessarily tacit, it may also be costly to transmit. Let's suppose that an engineering firm designs a steel plant. It could send the blueprints to a construction manager, and she could build the plant following the blueprints. The steel firm could then take control of the plant and begin production. In contrast, some successful steel firms bring together the engineering firm, the construction firm, and the steel firm's customers and employees to plan and carry out the project. As one steel executive put it, he uses a design engineering firm, but "At the same time, we have a lot of local knowledge about where things are, how things work, so we have an active role in projects."[17] One steel firm puts the new plant's general manager in charge of the construction. Because the prospective general manager will be evaluated on the plant's performance, she has an incentive to adopt changes in the plant's construction that would improve future profits. Moreover, she has the authority—the decision right—to make changes in the construction project without consulting her boss. Steel firms that have decentralized decision rights in this way have built plants whose actual capacity exceeded the engineering capacity by 25 percent. For every four plants that it builds, this company, in effect, gets a fifth one free.

Other types of knowledge that are difficult to transmit are scientific knowledge and assembled knowledge. *Assembled knowledge* is knowledge developed in an organization, as its members interact. For instance, the workers at Monarch Marking Systems in Ohio had significant specific knowledge about their manufacturing process. By making workers responsible and rewarding them for cutting costs, Monarch Marking reduced floor space requirements by 70 percent, reduced past-due shipments by 90 percent, and doubled productivity.[18]

The crucial element in these examples is that people in one part of an organization have important knowledge that is costly to transmit to other decision makers. By realizing the importance of the specific knowledge, these business firms were able to tap into it.

Because specific knowledge is important in organizations, the three important organizing principles exemplified in markets provide the framework for an **economic approach to organization**. To summarize these principles, we note that markets automatically

Economic Approach to Organization – An approach that mimics the market in designing a profit or nonprofit organization. In particular, it assigns decision rights to people who have relevant specific knowledge, evaluates those decisions in relation to the organization's objective, and rewards decisions that advance the objective.

- *Assign* decision rights to individuals with the most useful specific knowledge, or, if cheaper or more profitable, they *transfer* the specific knowledge to people who already have the decision rights. In either case, decisions are made by people who have the relevant specific knowledge.
- *Evaluate* decisions, using profitability as the performance measure.
- *Reward* good decisions by providing good decision makers with more resources that can be used for consumption or investment.[19]

Decision Making and State-Owned Enterprises

In a centrally planned SOE, such as public education in California or a steel mill in China, decisions, by definition, are made at the center. These decisions can be well informed regarding general knowledge and

---

[17] John Schriefer, "Completing Mill-Construction Projects Faster and Smarter," *New Steel*, July 1, 1996, 48.

[18] "Firm Shelves Empowerment as Workers Focus on Projects," *The Wall Street Journal*, October 17, 1997.

[19] Over the last three decades of the twentieth century, Michael C. Jensen of Harvard University and William H. Meckling, late of the University of Rochester, wrote several papers about specific knowledge and organizational design. These papers have been reprinted in Michael C. Jensen, *Foundations of Organizational Strategy* (Cambridge: Harvard University Press, 1998). See also James A. Brickley, Clifford W. Smith, Jr., and Jerold L. Zimmerman, *Managerial Economics and Organizational Architecture*, 2nd ed. (Chicago: Irwin, 2001).

specific knowledge available at the center, but they cannot be well informed about specific knowledge that is dispersed throughout the system. It is too costly to transfer all of the relevant specific knowledge to the center. In large organizations, both private and state-owned, centralized decision making is costly because it fails to use dispersed specific knowledge or because it expends resources attempting to transfer specific knowledge to the center. The alternative is to decentralize by assigning the decision rights to people in the field who have the specific knowledge.

Any goal-oriented organization, SOE or private, must evaluate the success of its transactions. The transactions can be either internal ones affecting resource allocation or external ones between people in the organization and outsiders. If large organizations decentralize decision rights, they must develop means to evaluate employees' decisions. Large private organizations presumably use the same evaluation measure that markets use: profit. But a large private organization usually lacks the market's *automatic* procedures for evaluating decision profitability. Consequently, if it decentralizes decision making, it must use scarce resources to develop and use an evaluation system. A large SOE has an additional disadvantage in evaluation: It typically rejects profit as an evaluation measure.

As with evaluation, if SOEs and large private organizations decentralize, they must develop procedures—rewards—that induce employees to make the appropriate decisions. The market rewards good decisions automatically with wealth and its accompanying opportunities, which appeals to the self-interest of creative people, striving to advance their careers. In recent years, large private organizations in the United States have attempted to mimic market rewards, using various kinds of incentive pay. SOEs also could use rewards similar to those automatically produced in the market. In practice, however, SOE managers tend to compensate employees with little regard to whether their actions advance the organization's goals.

In short, SOEs violate the three principles of an economic approach to organization. Many decisions made at the center are made without using the dispersed specific knowledge of many employees. They also are reluctant to use market-like evaluation systems or provide market-like rewards. State departments of education and school districts, particularly large ones, have organizational problems similar to those of SOEs.

Decision Making and Public Schools

A state department of education (SDE) is, in effect, the central planning office of a state-owned enterprise. It establishes ground rules for the curriculum, chooses textbooks, establishes detailed qualifications for teachers, provides substantial funding, sets standards, perhaps establishes high-stakes testing, and assesses the effectiveness of local schools or school districts. An SDE is apt to be politicized and be responsive to special-interest groups as well as to school children and their parents. Special-interest groups usually include the teachers' unions, environmental organizations, and other organizations promoting ideological and religious ends. The resulting conflicts are detrimental to learning and provide grounds for agreeing with Thomas Jefferson that "If it is believed that . . . elementary schools will be better managed by . . . any . . . general authority of the government than by the parents within each ward, it is a belief against all experience."[20]

---

[20] See the box "Jefferson, Smith, and Public Schools: Standards and Local Control" for the quote.

Following SDE guidelines, a local school district (LSD) board hires the district superintendent and with him oversees the physical plant, plans new construction, oversees the hiring of principals and teachers, and participates in salary determination. LSD superintendents often serve at the pleasure of the school board, which in turn is elected. Superintendents naturally will be concerned with satisfying the LSD board and the SDE. Although school board members are typically not professional policiticians, their objectives may differ from what parents want for their children. Given the political influences on both the state and the school district, what satisfies the school board and the SDE may not be what the parents and students desire.

ASSIGNMENT OF DECISION RIGHTS. Politicians, state bureaucrats, and local administration place two burdens on effective decision making in K–12 education. First, they have decision rights over such issues as curriculum, teacher qualifications, and textbook selection, thus restricting the decision rights of principals and teachers, who have huge amounts of useful specific knowledge regarding these issues. For instance, regulations often prevent principals from employing staff they feel sure would do an excellent job in the classroom. SDEs and teacher unions impose certification requirements that interfere with the judgment of local administrators in efforts to discourage potential teachers and reduce the supply of teachers. If certification requirements contributed to better teaching, they would have benefits as well as costs. Unfortunately, no consistent evidence indicates that advanced degrees in education lead to better teaching. SDEs and colleges of education benefit because these requirements increase the demand for their services. Teacher unions promote the requirements for the same reasons that other unions impose certification requirements on their members. As a result, some people who might be excellent teachers never even apply for positions because the cost of certification is too great.

Similarly, centralized textbook selection creates an environment that politicizes textbook choice, creating two problems. First, a teacher, school, or school district cannot use a book not approved for purchase. Second, K–12 textbook writers focus on obtaining adoptions in key states. To do so, they focus on satisfying the majority of the textbook committee. An innovative textbook that only a small percentage of the teachers or schools want to use is unlikely to be chosen by a state textbook committee. Consequently, textbook authors have little incentive to innovate.

The second burden on decision making is the large number of objectives that state politicians and bureaucrats and, to a degree, local bureaucrats impose on principals, teachers, and schools. Academic objectives may include equal opportunity to all students to achieve their potential, or focus on the most talented students, or focus on students with special needs. Nonacademic objectives might include promoting community service, providing sex education, developing a drug-free America, saving the environment, and winning athletic championships.

EVALUATION. Just as superintendents and principals are responsible to elected and appointed politicians, teachers are responsible to their supervisors. Once a teacher achieves tenure, however, he receives only cursory evaluation from his supervisors. Short of moral turpitude, it is unusual for a teacher to be dismissed or even to be reprimanded effectively. This is not because tenure makes it impossible to dismiss a teacher based on performance evaluation, although union protections and tenure do make it costly to do so. A big part of reason is that, having earned tenure, most teachers are no longer subject to serious evaluation.

Keywords: *teacher evaluations*
http://www.infotrac-college.com

Teachers' unions aim to ensure that all teachers are treated the same way. For instance, in the typical LSD all teachers with the same college degree, say M.S., and the same years of experience receive the same salary. Their performance is irrelevant in their salary determination. Consequently, the supervisors have little incentive to conduct serious evaluations. Evaluation and performance critiques are difficult and can create personal tensions. If they have no effect on salary, it is simply easier to avoid serious evaluations. Without a history of evaluations, it is difficult to document poor performance.

REWARD SYSTEM. In addition to making evaluations irrelevant, the reward system does not encourage excellence. As Adam Smith said, "It is in the interest of every man to live as much at his ease as he can; and if his emoluments are to be precisely the same, whether he does, or does not perform some very laborious duty, it is certainly in his interest, at least as interest is vulgarly understood, either to neglect it altogether, or if he is subject to some authority which will not suffer him to do this, to perform it in as careless and slovenly manner as that authority will permit."[21]

Given that teachers operate in a system where city hall and state government interfere with their professional judgment and impose numerous mandates that require them to spend time on activities of little academic merit, it is surprising how effective most teachers are in making achievement easier for students. In fact, most teachers perform much better than the Adam Smith quotation implies that they would. The reason, of course, is that many teachers teach because they want to help students achieve, but they perform well in spite of the organizational structure rather than because of it. Moreover, some teachers are demoralized because their excellent performance is not rewarded in systematic ways.

Because public school teachers lack the right to make certain education decisions and because objectives are fuzzy, they may with some justification believe that they should not be evaluated and rewarded on the basis of their students' academic progress.

The organization of schools violates the three organizing principles:

- By not assigning the teachers appropriate decision rights, the organization is unable to use teachers' specific knowledge about learning.
- No simple way exists for parents and students to evaluate teachers.
- Because rewards are the same for all teachers regardless of their performance, spending resources on evaluation would be in vain.

Keywords: *merit and pay and teachers*
http://www.infotrac-college.com

Competition and choice provide an alternative to the current public school system.

Alternatives to the Current System of Public Education

Competition among schools and choice for parents provide an approach to public school reform. Evidence from a 1993 survey shows that the parents of most of the students in private schools were "very satisfied" with the schools and their academic standards. In contrast, the parents of less than half of the students who attended assigned public schools were "very satisfied." The survey showed that parents who had choice among public schools or had chosen schools by their choice of residence were more satisfied than parents whose children attended assigned public schools.

---

[21]Adam Smith, *An Inquiry into the Nature and Causes of the Wealth of Nations* (Indianapolis: Liberty Press, 1981), a reprint of the edition published by Oxford: Clarendon Press, 1979, Book II, Ch. 5, 760.

Higher income obviously provides greater opportunity to attend private schools, but it also provides better choice among public schools because it provides greater choice among places to live. About one-half of the students from families with a $30,000 income or less attend assigned public schools based on where their parents reside, which in turn is not chosen based on the local school system. Only 30 percent of students from high-income families attend assigned public schools.[22] This information implies that children in higher-income families obtain the "presumably" better education their parents desire. Caroline Hoxby's empirical studies reinforce the point. She concludes that "parents who have greater choice are more involved in their children's schooling. Parents' influence on school policy, which is greater when choice is greater, will reflect, on average, their stated preferences for tougher curricula and stricter school atmospheres."[23]

Why are parents and students more satisfied if they have choice among schools, such as private or charter schools? (A charter school is one that establishes particular goals and operates without the centralized bureaucratic controls that hamper most public schools. The SDE requires them to meet certain standards, but provides them leeway with regard to how they do so and with regard to other objectives.) To succeed, the teachers in a private or charter school must offer a product that parents demand. Because parents are more likely than politicians, education bureaucrats, and teachers to emphasize the well-being of their children, they would choose and evaluate schools that focus on their children's basic education and preparation for life after high school. For some children, this would be a college preparatory curriculum; for others, it would be a curriculum focused on desirable vocational education. All graduates would have to meet certain state standards. Competition among schools would lead to a variety of educational programs well suited for their clientele, just as competition between colleges and universities does.

Keywords: *educational vouchers*
http://www.infotrac-college.com

The introduction of competition and choice for K–12 education could be accomplished with a system of vouchers used at existing public schools and independent public schools—charter schools—or at the two types of public schools and at private schools. By allowing parents to spend vouchers and additional money at such schools, consumer evaluation of the schools would work like consumer evaluation of other goods and services. To succeed, schools would have to provide students the educational experience their parents demand. We believe that parents would choose schools on the basis of their reputation in motivating students to succeed academically and in motivating their own children. Parents have specific knowledge about their children that is invaluable in matching them with appropriate educational programs. Along with the parents, teachers develop specific knowledge about themselves and about their students that allows them to develop effective pedagogic techniques.

Keywords: *charter schools*
http://www.infotrac-college.com

With the schools competing for students, their principals would evaluate teachers on their success with students. We have good reason to believe that good teachers make learning easier for many students. Although quantitative measures such as experience and degrees are not particularly useful in identifying good teachers, principals and other teachers can identify them. If the principal is evaluated and rewarded by the ability of her teachers to motivate learning, the principal has the incentive to seriously evaluate teachers and use her specific information to identify and reward good teaching.

---

[22]Data from National Center for Education Statistics at http://nces.ed.gov/index.html. See *The Condition of Education* (various years), and *The Digest of Education Statistics* (various years).

[23]Caroline M. Hoxby, "What Do America's 'Traditional' Forms of School Choice Teach Us About School Choice Reforms?" *FRBNY Economic Policy Review* 4 (March 1998), 56.

Some economists have long argued that competition among the providers of education will lead to existing public schools improving their performance.[24] Caroline Hoxby has studied the effects of existing competition (1) among suburban school districts, (2) within school districts, and (3) between private and public schools. She concludes that "public schools can and do react to competition by improving the schooling they offer and by reducing costs. They are not passive organizations that allow their students and budgets to be withdrawn without responding. Realistic increases in the competition they face produce significant improvements in students' test scores, educational attainment, and wages."[25]

The inefficiency of the U.S. public school system is, we argue, largely a result of its organization and lack of competition. Like other SOEs, it lacks clearly specified objectives and it is much too centralized. Because the system is a public system with multiple and sometimes conflicting objectives, it is difficult for the decision makers to know and take the appropriate action. People who have much specific knowledge about particular students and the operation of a particular school—parents, teachers, and principals—lack sufficient authority to make decisions that they are best able to make. The people with the greatest stake in the operation of the public school system—students and parents—rarely have a meaningful role in its evaluation. The teachers and principals who, along with students, make up the system can discern no clear relationship between their performance and their rewards. When administrators and teachers see a link between performance and rewards, they respond. Quoting Hoxby again, "[P]ublic schools' responses do not depend just on whether they lose students; the responses also depend on the fiscal rewards and penalties attached to gaining or losing students. When competition has little fiscal implication, a public school is less likely to react. When cost competition is weakened by a large price wedge (like that between public and private schools), public schools reduce costs less than they do when cost competition is on a more level playing field (like that between two similar public school districts)."[26]

Summary

Critics of public K–12 education in the United States complain that U.S. high school graduates perform less well than high school graduates in other countries with a similar standard of living. The United States spends more per pupil on education than almost any other country, but even as expenditures have increased, performance on math and science achievement tests, if anything, has declined.

Thomas Jefferson was an early proponent of universal education. He believed that such education is necessary to preserve liberty and to improve living standards. Given the current level of education in the United States, it is likely that external benefits of K–12 education are zero, suggesting that government subsidization is unnecessary for economic efficiency. Equal opportunity provides a firmer basis for government subsidy than does economic efficiency.

If the critics are justified in their concern about the relatively poor performance of U.S. high school graduates, the solution to the poor performance problem requires that we understand the determinants of student achievement. Imagine that students and their parents choose an achievement level based on the marginal benefits and marginal costs of achievement to them. This perspective suggests that achievement will increase if the perceived marginal benefits increase or the perceived marginal costs decrease. The widespread adoption of high-stakes testing could increase marginal benefits. High-stakes testing implies universal achievement tests that certify that an individual

---

[24]Milton Friedman, *Capitalism and Freedom* (Chicago: University of Chicago Press, 1962), Ch. 6, "The Role of Government in Education."

[25]Caroline M. Hoxby, "What Do America's 'Traditional' Forms of School Choice Teach Us About School Choice Reforms?" *FRBNY Economic Policy Review*, 4 (March 1998), 55.

[26]Ibid., 55.

has a certain level of understanding about the subjects tested. To set high stakes, these tests must have consequences, such as opportunities for employment and for higher education.

In this context, schools and teachers facilitate learning by reducing the marginal costs of achievement. For an organization or an economy to perform well, decisions must be made by people with appropriate information. Appropriate information is often specific information, which means that it is costly to transmit. Consequently, to use specific information effectively, the people who develop it must use it. In a market, decision-making rights are assigned to people based on their willingness to pay for them. If a person has specific information that makes a certain decision right valuable, that person can purchase the right. Markets automatically evaluate these decisions, using profit as a criterion, and they automatically reward good decisions with the profit.

Like any other organization, managers of a school system must decide who makes decisions, how the decisions are evaluated, and how they are rewarded. State departments of education often control decision rights that may more appropriately be assigned to principals and teachers at local schools. By centralizing decision rights, the state ignores much specific information held by principals and teachers. As a political organization, the public education system responds to politicians and bureaucrats, and to that extent, it is less responsive to students and parents. The centralization of decisions made at the state level and in large local school districts combined with teachers' unions makes it difficult to evaluate local decision makers—teachers and principals—and to reward their performance. Some school districts' clientele—parents and students—have little opportunity or incentive to evaluate the district's performance because they are trapped in the district. Higher-income families have a greater incentive to evaluate the district's performance because they have greater flexibility about where they live and for them private schools are more practical. Consequently, suburban schools and private schools, which are subject to competition, do a better job of satisfying their clientele.

Key Terms

Commutative justice
Distributive justice
High-stakes testing
General knowledge
Specific knowledge
Economic approach to organization

Review Questions

1. What does the chapter identify as the problem or problems with U.S. public schools?
2. The chapter discusses two possible rationales for government support of education. What are they? Evaluate them.
3. The model of academic achievement presented in this chapter suggests that high school and college students choose a level of academic achievement that is a compromise between achievement and other goals. For what other goals have you sacrificed a small amount of academic achievement? What changes would lead you to place a higher value on academic achievement?
4. What are the four characteristics of high-stakes testing, and why is each characteristic important?
5. Suppose high-stakes testing results in greater achievement. If so, does that mean it is the preferred education reform?
6. Some states require students to take additional mathematics and science courses. Will this lead to U.S. students performing at the same level as students in other countries? Why or why not?
7. Which of the following is specific knowledge and which is general knowledge and why?
    a. the distance to Washington, DC
    b. the ability to ride a bicycle
    c. the U.S. Bill of Rights
    d. the ability to read a map

e. the way to win at poker
f. the plot of *Romeo and Juliet*

8. This chapter suggests that giving parents more control over their children's education would be to the children's advantage. Do you agree? If not, why not. If so, does this imply that home schooling is a method of education superior to education in a school system? Explain.

9. Specific knowledge of profitable opportunities are scattered throughout the economy or throughout a business firm. How does a market economy make use of specific information? How does a business firm managed from the top down make use of specific information?

10. What are the three elements of an economic approach to organization?

11. Think of your introductory economics class as an organization. Suppose the professor's objective is to have the highest average score on a standardized test of any introductory economics class of about the same size and composed of similar students. Who has the relevant decision rights in the class? What are the roles of evaluation and rewards in attempting to achieve the objective?

Economic Issues on the Internet

− Education Week on the Web—**http://www.edweek.org**
Online newspaper covering hot topics in education in the United States and internationally. Pulls stories from top U.S. newspapers in the Daily News section. Also has special reports on issues such as charter schools, school choice, and technology in the classroom.

− National Education Association—**http://www.nea.org**
A site that gives perspective of this teacher's organization on public policy issues related to public education.

− OECD Programme for International Student Assessment (PISA)—**http://www.pisa.oecd.org/index.htm**
Web site for a new international test to compare students across industrialized countries.

− U.S. Department of Education - Research & Stats—**http://www.ed.gov/index.jsp**
Source for U.S. government reports and evaluations of education in the United States.

CHAPTER 11

Social Security: Where Are We? Where Are We Going?

Outline:

Principal Features of Social Security
Who Pays the Social Security Tax?
Social Security and Early Retirement
Social Security and Household Savings
Individual Rates of Return
Is That All There Is to It?
The Long-Run Deficit

What Social Security Analysts Say
   Are the Analysts Right?
What Can Be Done About the Deficit?
   Benefit Reductions
   Revenue Increases
The Trade-Off for Individuals: Lower Deficits Mean Lower Rates of Return

Growing old in America often brings a reduction in family income. The situation would be far worse, however, without Social Security. Social Security was established in 1935 to provide income to retired workers. It is now, however, the country's largest income-maintenance program. In addition to retirement benefits, Social Security also provides benefits to the survivors of workers who die, to workers who become disabled, and to the elderly for medical care (Medicare).

As used in this chapter, however, the term *Social Security* means only the old-age and survivors insurance (OASI) portions of Social Security. Together they account for a little more than half of Social Security expenditures. Most of the remainder is for Medicare, a program that is examined in Chapter 7.

The problem that worries the public the most is the possibility that Social Security will run out of money. We will examine this issue and explore some of the things that might be done to avoid such an outcome. But this is not the only problem associated with Social Security. According to some economists, Social Security reduces the nation's labor supply and household savings, and produces a woefully low rate of return. Each of these problems will also be examined in this chapter.

■ Principal Features of Social Security

OASI is the country's largest government expenditure program. In 2000, outlays exceeded $377 billion. They were financed largely by a Social Security payroll tax of 10.6 percent on earnings up to $80,400. Half of the tax was levied on employers, and half of it was deducted from employee paychecks.

The Social Security payroll tax is the second largest source of federal government revenue, exceeded only by the individual income tax. Revenues from the payroll tax are deposited in the OASI Trust Fund. Benefits and administrative costs are paid out of the trust fund. Balances remaining in the fund are invested in long-term U.S. Treasury bonds. At the end of 2001, the fund contained $1,072 billion, enough to pay less than 3 years' benefits and expenses. Retirement funds with balances that can cover future benefits and expenses for only a short period of time are essentially **pay-as-you-go funds**. The expectation with such funds, including the OASI Trust Fund, is that annual revenues will always be sufficient to cover annual outlays. Private retirement funds are normally **fully funded**; that is, fund balances are sufficient to cover benefits and expenses for many years.

Pay-as-You-Go Fund – A fund with a balance that can cover future benefits and expenses for only a few years.

Fully-Funded Fund – A fund with a balance that can cover future benefits and expenses for many years.

Social Security provides periodic benefit payments to retirees based on earnings averaged over most of a worker's lifetime. Benefit determination begins with the record of actual annual earnings on which the Social Security payroll tax has been levied. Earnings realized before age 60 are then adjusted or "indexed" to account for changes in average national wages between the year the earnings were realized and age 60.

The indexing procedure uses equation 11.1:

$$(11.1) \qquad IE_t = E_t \, (ANW_{60}/ANW_t)$$

Indexing Factor – A ratio of average national wages in two different years used to index actual annual earnings.

where IE_t is the indexed value of earnings realized in year t, E represents past earnings, t is the age at which the earnings were realized, ANW is the average national wage, and ANW_{60}/ANW_t is the **indexing factor**—the ratio of the average national wage at age 60 to the average national wage in the year when the earnings were realized. To see how the equation works, consider an individual who earned $10,000 at age 40 (t = 40). Assume that the average national wage when the individual was age 60 is $39,800 and that the average national wage when the individual was 40 is $15,000. The value of the indexing factor is 2.653 ($39,800/$15,000) and the indexed value of these earnings is $26,530. In determining Social Security benefits, the $10,000 realized at age 40 is considered to be equivalent, then, to $26,530 realized at age 60. The indexing factor, 2.653, is equal in value to $(1.05)^{60-40}$. Thus, application of this indexing factor is equivalent to crediting the retiree with a 5 percent rate of return per year on taxes invested at age 40 in Social Security.

Average Indexed Monthly Earnings (AIME) – Actual average monthly earnings for the highest 35 years of earnings, adjusted by an indexing factor.

After all of the indexed earnings are determined, Social Security adds the 35 years of highest indexed earnings and divides this amount by 420 (the number of months in 35 years) to determine the **average indexed monthly earnings (AIME)**. It then applies a formula to the AIME to arrive at the basic bene-

Primary Insurance Amount (PIA) – Monthly Social Security benefits at the normal retirement age.

fit, or **primary insurance amount (PIA)**. The PIA, plus an inflation adjustment starting at age 62 (explained below), is the amount a person would receive at the normal retirement age. The normal retirement age depends on when a person is born. It is 65 years for people born before 1938. It is 65 years and two months for people born in 1938, 65 years and 4 months for people born in 1939, 65 years and 6 months for people born in 1940, and it is scheduled to increase gradually each year until it reaches 67 for people born in 1960 or later.

The formula for determining the basic benefit or PIA reflects the year a person was born. For someone born in 1940—a person who will be 62 in 2002—the PIA formula is

(11.2) $\quad \text{PIA} = .9 \text{ (First \$592 AIME)} + .32 \text{ (\$592} < \text{AIME} < \text{\$3567)} + .15 \text{ (AIME over \$3566)}$

Table 11.1 shows the results of calculations based on this formula for three hypothetical retirees. The first is a low-wage worker who earned $230,000 while working. Application of the average wage index to actual earnings would yield indexed earnings from 1.8 to 2.0 times higher than actual earnings. We assume in this case that they would be $420,000, an amount that falls in the expected range. Division of indexed earnings by 420 gives AIME of $1,000. Application of the PIA formula to this AIME yields $533 in the first bracket (.9 × $592) and $131 in the second bracket [.32 × ($1,000 − $592]. The third bracket does not apply in this case. The net result is a PIA or initial monthly Social Security benefit upon retirement of $664.

INFOTRAC
College Edition

Keywords: *Social Security benefits, Social Security benefit formula*
http://www.infotrac-college.com

The second and third workers have higher lifetime earnings, higher indexed earnings, higher AIME, and higher PIA. The ratio of PIA to AIME falls, however, as AIME increases. The behavior of the PIA/AIME ratio indicates that the Social Security PIA or benefit formula produces more generous benefits to lower- than to higher-income retirees. This is not a mistake; it conforms to Congressional intent to deliberately provide a safety net for the elderly poor. Estimates indicate that more than 45 percent of the elderly would have incomes below the federal poverty line in the absence of Social Security. With Social Security, however, the poverty rate for the elderly—10.5 percent—was less than the poverty rate for the population as a whole—12.7 percent—in 1998.

The benefits noted in Table 11.1 are for single workers who will retire at their normal retirement age. They may retire as early as age 62, but if they retire before the normal retirement age, Social Security benefits are permanently reduced by an **early retirement penalty**. The early retirement penalty reduces the PIA by 0.536 percent per month for each month an individual born in 1940 retires before the normal retirement age. This percentage falls gradually to 0.50 percent per month as the normal retirement age approaches 67 years.

Early Retirement Penalty – The amount by which Social Security benefits are reduced for people who retire before the normal retirement age.

Benefits are 50 percent larger for a retiree with a spouse, provided that the spouse does not qualify for a larger benefit on the basis of his or her own earnings record. Social Security retirees also receive additional benefits for dependents.

TABLE 11.1 Determination of Initial Social Security Benefits (PIA) for Three Individuals Born in 1940 and Retiring at Normal Retirement Age (65 Years, 6 Months)

Actual Earnings	Indexed Earnings	AIME	1st Bracket	2nd Bracket	3rd Bracket	PIA	PIA/AIME
$230,000	$420,000	$1,000	$533	$131	$0	$664	0.66
$580,000	$1,050,000	$2,500	$533	$611	$0	$1,144	0.46
$1,400,000	$2,520,000	$6,000	$533	$952	$365	$1,850	0.31

Inflation Indexing – Annual upward adjustment in Social Security benefits to cover the increase in the consumer price index.

Delayed Retirement Credit – The amount by which retirees' benefits are increased for each year that retirement is delayed up to age 70.

Social Security benefits are indexed for inflation, increasing each year at the same rate as the consumer price index (CPI). **Inflation indexing** begins the year a person reaches 62 and continues throughout the remainder of the person's lifetime.

Workers who delay retirement beyond the normal retirement age receive extra Social Security benefits when they do retire. Their benefits increase by a **delayed retirement credit** of 8 percent for each year that retirement is delayed, up to age 70.

Finally, income from Social Security receives more favorable treatment in the federal tax code than income from private retirement funds. Private retirement income is subject to federal income taxation. Only part of Social Security benefits is subject to taxation, however, and then only if earnings after retirement exceed tax-exempt levels.

■ WHO PAYS THE SOCIAL SECURITY TAX?

As noted previously, OASI is financed primarily by a 10.6 percent tax levied on taxable payroll (essentially wages and salaries, less nontaxable fringe benefits). The law requires employers to collect half of the tax through a payroll deduction and to remit twice that amount to the federal government. Thus, it appears that workers pay half of the tax and employers pay the other half. Economic theory is consistent with this view, but it is also consistent with the case where employers shift their portion of the tax to workers.

Substitution Effect of a Wage Decrease – The decrease in hours worked because of a fall in the wage rate.

Income Effect of a Wage Decrease – The increase in hours worked to replace the decrease in income resulting from a wage rate reduction.

Figure 11.1(a) of the labor market illustrates the latter possibility. Wage rates and hours worked in the labor market are determined by the supply of, and demand for, labor. Although the vertical supply curve indicates that changes in the wage rate do not affect hours worked, the wage rate actually has two potential effects on hours worked. On the one hand, reductions in the hourly wage, or hourly reward from working, induce individuals to work fewer hours. This **substitution effect of a wage decrease** causes workers to substitute leisure for work. On the other hand, a reduction in the hourly wage will reduce the size of the employees' paychecks, which may induce them to work more hours to make up the reduction in the hourly wage. If it does, there is an **income effect of a wage decrease**. The net effect of a change in the wage rate on hours worked depends on the relative strengths of the two effects. In this case, there is no net effect on hours worked. This could be either because the two effects offset each other, or because both of them are unimportant.

The demand curve for labor indicates the value of the output produced by each hour of work. In the absence of the payroll tax, the demand for labor is D_1, the supply of labor is S_1, and the equilibrium wage rate and hours worked are W_1 and H_1, respectively. The total value of output produced is the sum of the values produced by each hour of labor, or the area under the demand curve, $A+B+C+D+F$. Workers receive earnings equal to the wage rate times the number of hours worked, or the area $C+D+F$. Employers claim area $A+B$—the remaining value of output produced—in the form of rent, interest, and profits.

The payroll tax is imposed on employers; that is, they must make the total tax payment to the federal government. From their perspective, therefore, the tax reduces the maximum amount they are willing to pay for each hour of labor. The maximum amount they are willing to pay for labor in the absence of the tax is the value produced by each hour of labor. In Figure 11.1(a), this is the amount indicated by the height of the demand curve at each hour of labor. Imposition of the OASI payroll tax reduces the amount employers are willing to pay by 0.106 of that height. This effect is indicated in Figure 11.1(a)

FIGURE 11.1 Effect of the Social Security Payroll Tax on Hours Worked Under Different Labor Supply Conditions

The payroll tax lowers the demand for labor from D_1 to D_2. In Figure 11.1(a), the tax does not change the number of hours worked, and workers pay all of the tax in the form of a reduced wage. In Figure 11.1(b), the tax reduces the number of hours worked and employers and workers both pay some of the payroll tax.

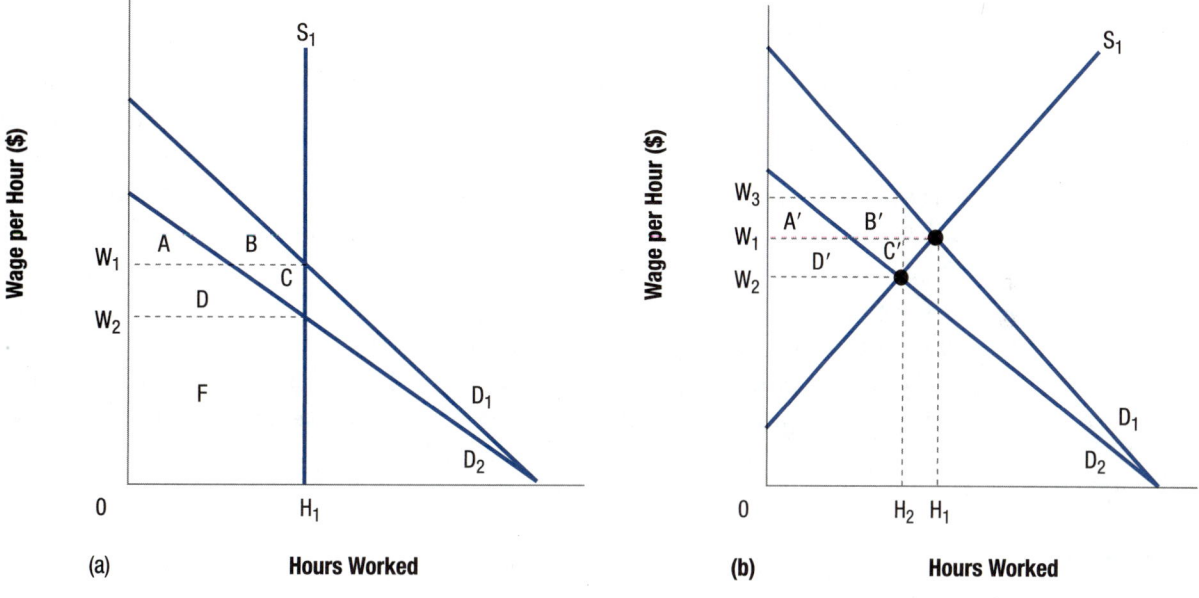

by comparing D_1 (willingness to pay without the tax) and D_2 (willingness to pay with the tax). The height of D_2 is everywhere 0.894 of, or 0.106 less than, D_1.

After the tax is imposed, a new equilibrium forms at W_2 and H_1. No change occurs in the number of labor hours, but the wage rate falls by the same percentage as the payroll tax rate. Labor's earnings fall to area F only. Employers' income, A+B, remains the same as before the tax, and the government collects tax revenues equal to C+D, which just happens to be the amount by which labor's earnings fall. Thus, the full burden of the tax falls on labor.

Another possibility is illustrated in Figure 11.1(b). The labor supply curve in this figure is positively sloped, indicating that the substitution effect of a reduction in the wage rate is stronger than the income effect. The pretax equilibrium is at W_1 and H_1, as in Figure 11.1(a). Imposition of the tax changes the equilibrium to W_2 and H_2; that is, the tax decreases the wage rate realized by workers and reduces the number of labor hours. Total taxes collected are equal to the product of the tax per hour of labor, $W_3 - W_2$, and the number of hours of labor, H_2, or the area A'+B'+C'+D'. Employees pay half of the tax, or C'+D', and employers pay the other half, or A'+B'. This case is probably what Congress assumed would happen when they wrote the law requiring only half of the payroll tax to be deducted from worker's wages.

It is important to determine which view is correct. If the labor supply curve is vertical, the payroll tax has no effect on hours worked, but it places a large burden on workers and reduces the rate of return they

Keywords: *Social Security payroll tax and incidence, Social Security payroll tax and who pays*

http://www.infotrac-college.com

will realize from Social Security. If the labor supply curve is upward-sloping, the payroll tax reduces hours worked, but a smaller burden of the tax falls on workers and they will realize higher rates of return from Social Security as a consequence. We believe that the weight of the evidence favors a supply curve that is vertical, or nearly so, and that the primary effect of the payroll tax, therefore, shows up as lower individual rates of return on Social Security.

■ Social Security and Early Retirement

History reveals a strong trend toward reduced labor force participation by older people. Since 1950, the labor force participation rate (the percentage of a certain population in the labor force) for men age 65 and older has fallen from 41.4 percent to less than 15 percent. Various factors have probably contributed to this trend: rising income, growth in private pensions, increased availability of government transfers, and changing lifestyles, to name a few. Social Security has probably been a major contributor, as well.

The most disturbing aspect of this trend is the large number of workers who retire early; nearly a third of Social Security beneficiaries leave the workforce before age 65. It is impossible to determine on the basis of theory alone if Social Security induces early retirement. On the one hand, the prospect of Social Security benefits encourages early retirement. On the other hand, Social Security discourages early retirement by exacting a penalty for early retirement, and it encourages later retirement by providing a delayed retirement credit. Overall, the evidence indicates that Social Security does induce people to retire earlier; the lure of more immediate benefits appears to outweigh the effects of the early retirement penalty and the delayed retirement credit.

Keywords: *Social Security and early retirement*

http://www.infotrac-college.com

For many years, policy makers showed little concern over this effect of Social Security. In fact, one of Social Security's original purposes was to provide older workers with enough income to leave the labor force and make way for younger workers who were having difficulty finding work during the Great Depression. Today, however, Social Security faces the prospect of a long-run deficit in the OASI Trust Fund. In this context, early retirement is a problem instead of an opportunity. It not only reduces the labor supply and potential output, it also hastens and deepens the long-run Social Security deficit.

The early retirement penalty just offsets the extra years during which early retirees will be drawing benefits. Thus, total lifetime Social Security benefits are unchanged by the decision to retire early. The fact that early retirees do so anyway indicates that they consider themselves better off. This makes many economists reluctant to advocate policies to reverse the trend toward early retirement.

Wealth Substitution Effect – The reduction in household savings caused by the substitution of Social Security wealth for other types of wealth.

Social Security Wealth – The present value of Social Security benefits minus the present value of Social Security taxes.

■ Social Security and Household Savings

The fact that many retirees depend so heavily on Social Security suggests to some economists that the prospect of Social Security benefits may induce people to save less of their preretirement income. If they do save less, private investment drops, resulting ultimately in a smaller potential output.

Social Security will reduce savings if workers believe that Social Security will provide them with enough retirement income that they can spend a larger share of their preretirement earnings. If this happens, economists say that Social Security has a **wealth substitution effect**—an effect that induces workers to substitute **Social Security wealth** (the present value of Social Security benefits less the present value of Social Security taxes) for other types of wealth, such as private pensions.

Induced Retirement Effect – The increase in household savings to offset early retirement induced by Social Security.

Economists also recognize, as already noted, that the prospect of Social Security benefits may induce workers to retire earlier. This **induced retirement effect** of Social Security should increase savings; that is, workers will attempt to save more each year while working to make up for the years when they will not be working.

The net effect of Social Security on savings depends on the relative strength of these two effects. This can be determined only by empirical analysis. Martin Feldstein is well known for his empirical studies of the relationship between Social Security and household savings. In the latest of several studies, Feldstein analyzed annual U.S. data from 1930 to 1992, and found that each dollar of Social Security wealth resulted in a decrease in household savings of $0.028.[1] This result indicates that the wealth substitution effect outweighs the induced retirement effect, but not by much. Closer examination, however, reveals cause for concern.

Social Security wealth was more than $14,000 billion in 1999. Multiplying this number by Feldstein's impact of 0.028 implies that Social Security wealth reduced household savings by $392 billion. This implies that investment and the nation's capital stock were $392 billion less than they would be in the absence of Social Security. Because each dollar increase in the capital stock supports about a third of a dollar increase in potential output, Social Security may have reduced potential output in 1999 alone by as much as $130 billion.

If Feldstein's estimate is correct, the negative effect of Social Security on savings is important indeed. Other studies, however, have produced different results. Munnell, for instance, found a negative effect of Social Security on savings, but only about one-sixth as large as Feldstein's.[2] Leimer and Lesnoy found that Social Security wealth may actually increase savings, depending on how it is estimated.[3] More recently, Bernheim and Levin, using new measures of expected Social Security benefits, found that expected Social Security wealth reduced the savings of single individuals by $1.21 for each dollar of Social Security wealth, but that it had no effect on the saving behavior of couples.[4]

Given the mixed results of the empirical research, we cannot be certain how much Social Security affects household savings. It seems premature, however, to rule out the possibility of a negative impact.

But this does not necessarily mean that potential output will fall. It will, as explained earlier, if the lost savings would have been used to finance productive investment. It will not if the lost savings are used to finance investments in human capital development—e.g., to acquire a college education. Empirical studies have not yet considered this possibility.

INFOTRAC College Edition

Keywords: *Social Security and saving*
http://www.infotrac-college.com

■ INDIVIDUAL RATES OF RETURN

Social Security benefits, like most good things in life, are not free. The typical retiree pays Social Security taxes over a working lifetime of 40 to 50 years and receives 15 to 20 years of retirement benefits. This elicits considerable interest in comparing benefits received with taxes paid or "contributions"

---

[1] Martin Feldstein, "Social Security and Saving: New Time-Series Evidence," *National Tax Journal* 64 (1998), 151–164.

[2] Alicia H. Munnell, *The Future of Social Security* Washington, DC: The Brookings Institution, 1977.

[3] Dean R. Leimer and Selig D. Lesnoy, "Social Security and Private Saving: New Time-Series Evidence," *Journal of Political Economy* 90 (June 1982), 606–629.

[4] B. Douglas Bernheim and Lawrence Levin, "Social Security and Personal Saving: An Analysis of Expectations," *American Economic Review* 79 (May 1989), 97–102.

made. Actual comparisons vary by individual, but calculations for representative individuals sufficiently convey the general results.

Let us examine the prospects for a typical college freshman, using monetary benefits and costs. Our subject is a person born in 1982 who enters college in fall, 2000, at age 18; graduates in 2004; and faces the real (inflation-adjusted) earnings profile illustrated in Figure 11.2. This is the same earnings profile for college graduates used in Chapter 9 to determine the rate of return from investing in a college education.

During college, our student expects to work part-time, earning $5,200 per year. The first job after graduation is expected to provide a wage of $40,261, the average real wage (in $2002) paid a new college graduate in 2005. The real wage is expected to rise rapidly throughout the next 33 years, reaching a peak of $90,601 at age 55. We then expect it to fall slightly to $90,163 by age 64. Given this earnings profile, the typical college graduate is projected to earn real wages of $2,986,695 from age 23 through age 64.

Our graduate will pay Social Security taxes of 5.3 to 10.6 percent of projected wages, depending on how much of the burden of the employers' share of the payroll tax falls on workers. Following retirement, our graduate will receive real Social Security benefits of $24,300 (in $2002) per year for 20 years (the expected remaining lifetime at age 65). Figure 11.3 illustrates the profile of projected taxes and benefits, assuming that all of the burden of the payroll tax falls on workers. Total taxes—the area between the horizontal axis and the tax line—are $316,589, and total benefits—the area between the horizontal axis and the benefits line—are $486,000.

FIGURE 11.2	Real Wages of a Typical College Graduate

This figure illustrates how the real wages of a typical college graduate increase immediately following graduation (year 5) and continue to grow throughout much of the individual's working lifetime.

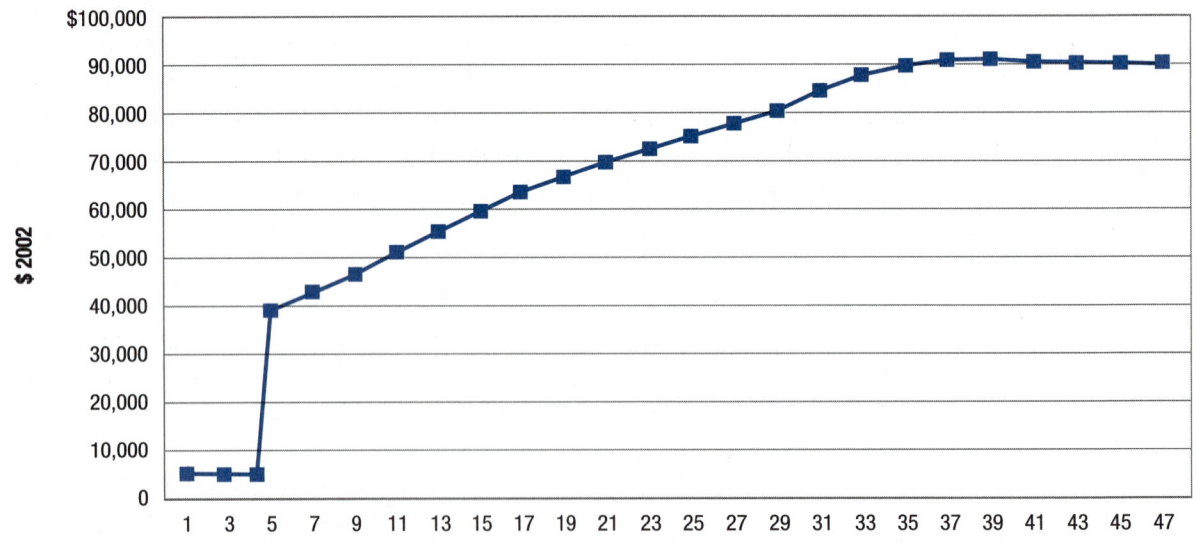

FIGURE 11.3 Social Security Taxes and Benefits for a Typical College Graduate

This figure illustrates projected real Social Security taxes (−) and benefits (+) for a typical college graduate. Taxes are collected for the 4 years the student is in school and the 42 years while the graduate is in the workforce. Benefits are received for 20 years following retirement at age 65.

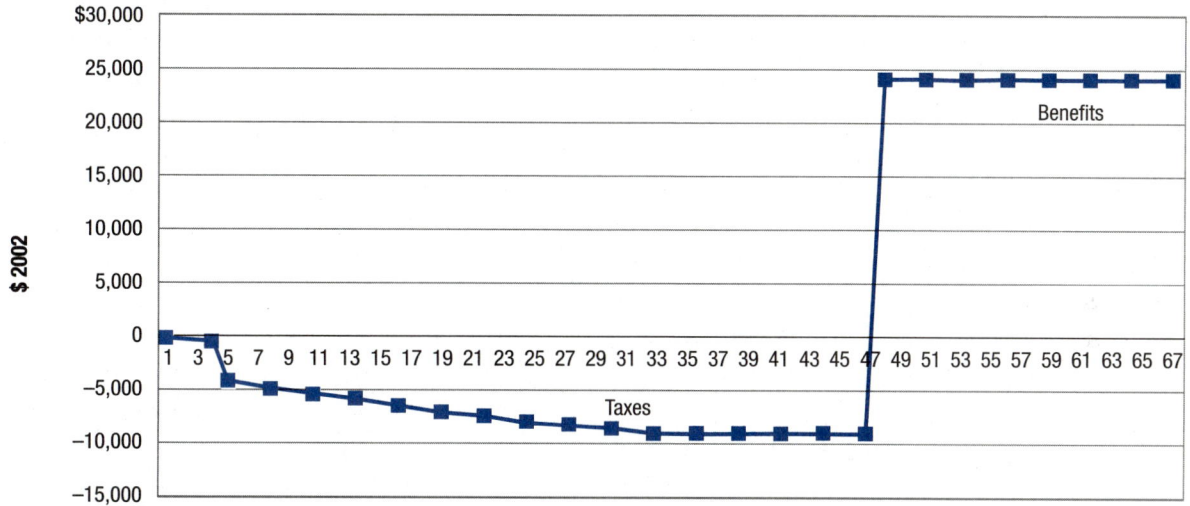

Based on this projection, it appears that an investment in Social Security is worth it. The reader who has studied Chapter 8, however, knows that the tax payments and benefits must be adjusted for date of occurrence by discounting them at an appropriate rate of interest. Discounting is done to determine the present value of taxes and benefits. Figure 11.4 shows the effect of discounting at a 2 percent real rate of interest—the same rate we used in Chapter 8 to discount the costs and benefits attributable to investing in a college education. According to our calculations, the sum of the present value of taxes is $197,352, and the sum of the present value of benefits is only $159,971. The real rate of return is only 1.24 percent. If the student/worker's best alternative is the 2 percent real rate of return earned historically on long-term government bonds (the rate we used for discounting, based on the assumption that this is the best alternative comparable to Social Security), the investment made in Social Security is not worth it.

The verdict is somewhat better if the student/worker bears the burden of only the half of the Social Security payroll tax that is deducted from the paycheck. In this case, the real rate of return is 3.48 percent, significantly better than the 2 percent alternative.

Table 11.2 summarizes the estimates we have made for the typical college graduate, arrayed according to the portion of the Social Security payroll tax that the worker actually bears. The portion borne by the worker may be somewhere in between these two rates, of course. According to the analysis we have reviewed, however, we lean toward the 10.6 percent case.

| FIGURE 11.4 | Effect of Discounting on Value of Social Security Taxes and Benefits |

This figure shows the effects on taxes and benefits from discounting both at 2 percent per year.

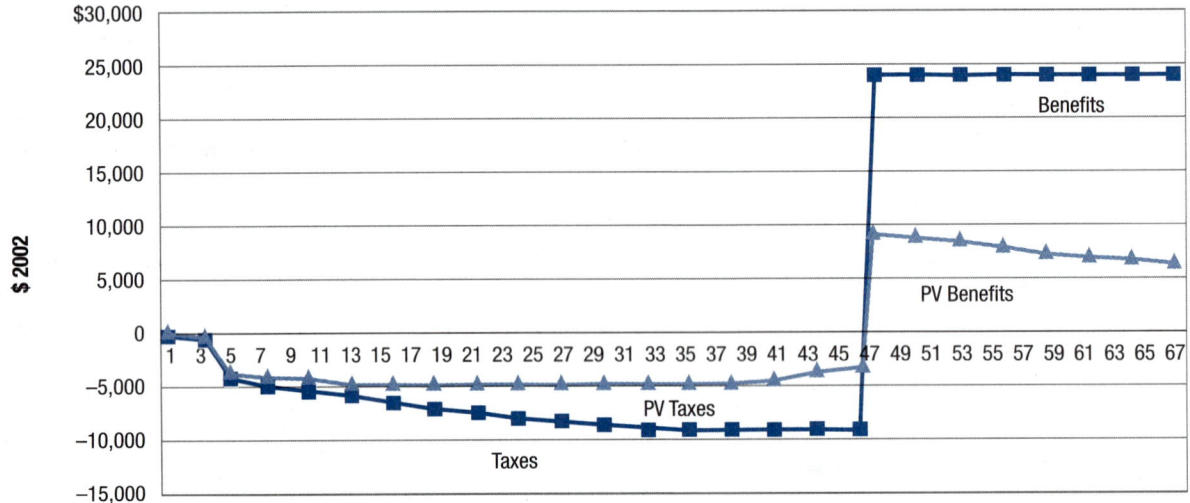

| TABLE 11.2 | Estimates of Social Security Taxes and Benefits for a Typical College Graduate, by Percent of Payroll Tax Borne by Worker |

	Worker Pays 10.6% of Payroll Tax	Worker Pays 5.3% of Payroll Tax
Sum of real earnings subject to tax	$2,986,695	$2,986,695
Sum of real taxes paid	$334,854	$167,427
Sum of real benefits received	$485,998	$485,998
Sum of real net benefits	$151,144	$318,571
Sum of present value of real taxes paid	$197,352	$96,741
Sum of present value of real benefits received	$159,791	$159,791
Sum of present value of real net benefits	-$37,561	$63,050
Real rate of return (percent)	1.24	3.48

■ Is That All There Is to It?

No; Social Security retirement benefits have some characteristics with obvious value to "investors" that are not represented in our calculations. Without Social Security as an investment option, individuals would presumably invest more in private alternatives such as stocks and bonds. Compared to these alternatives, Social Security retirement benefits do not fluctuate like the income and capital gains from

Risk Reduction Benefit – The value of the lower risk of loss of Social Security benefits relative to the risk of loss of income from private securities.

Inflation Protection Benefit – The value of the inflation indexing of Social Security benefits.

INFOTRAC
College Edition

Keywords: *Social Security and rate of return*

http://www.infotrac-college.com

private securities, and they maintain their purchasing power in the face of inflation. That is, Social Security's old-age insurance reduces the income and inflation risk to which individual investors would otherwise be exposed.

Real rates of return on private securities are typically higher than the rates we have calculated, but income from private securities is subject to considerable variation or risk. Individual investors are willing to assume additional risk if they receive a rate of return that includes a risk premium. The size of the required risk premium varies by type of investment, but premiums in the neighborhood of 3 to 4 percent are often mentioned. If Social Security is free of income risk, a **risk reduction benefit** of this magnitude should be *added* to the real rate of return on Social Security.

Investors should be willing also to pay more for a security that provides protection against inflation. Given the few investments that are indexed for inflation, there is little market evidence of the value of this protection. That which is available suggests that an **inflation protection benefit** in the neighborhood of 1 percentage point should be added to the real rate of return on Social Security for the inflation protection it provides.

The bottom line is that the real rate of return from an investment in the Social Security retirement program is likely to be closer to 5 percent than it is to the 1 percent we have calculated in our example.

■ THE LONG-RUN DEFICIT

The question most often raised about Social Security is whether it will be able to provide future generations the benefits they have been promised. Projections produced by Social Security analysts for the 2002 *Annual Report of the Board of Trustees* indicate that, if expected revenues do not increase or if expected benefits do not decline, the balance in the OASDI Trust Fund will eventually fall to zero. After that time, Social Security will be able to pay only a part of future obligations. Most economists agree, but some believe that the Social Security analysts are wrong. Let us examine both points of view, starting with that of the Social Security analysts.

What Social Security Analysts Say

In determining long-run prospects for Social Security, Social Security trustees rely on 75-year projections of income and expenditures prepared by Social Security analysts or actuaries. Because the future cannot be predicted with certainty, they project Alternatives I, II, and III. The assumptions underlying Alternative I produce the most optimistic projection of trust fund surpluses; those underlying Alternative III produce the most pessimistic projection. Congress currently relies on Alternative II, the "best estimate" projection, as the guide for long-run planning.

According to Alternative II projections in the 2002 annual report, the future for Social Security looks both promising and bleak. The promising aspect is that the OASDI Trust Fund will have an annual surplus for another 15 years. Starting in 2017, however, annual expenditures will begin to exceed annual receipts, and the Trust Fund will begin to shrink. Annual tax receipts, combined with annual interest earnings on U.S. Treasury securities and income from redemption of these securities, will be sufficient to pay annual expenditures for several years, but Trust Fund balances at the end of each year will become progressively smaller. Finally, in 2041, all of the securities owned by the Trust Fund will have been redeemed, and the Trust Fund will be exhausted (see Figure 11.5).

FIGURE 11.5 OASDI Trust Fund Balance After 2001

The OASDI Trust Fund has a balance of $1.4 trillion in 2002. The balance will grow to $7.2 trillion in 2026 and then decline rapidly. The Fund will become exhausted in 2041.

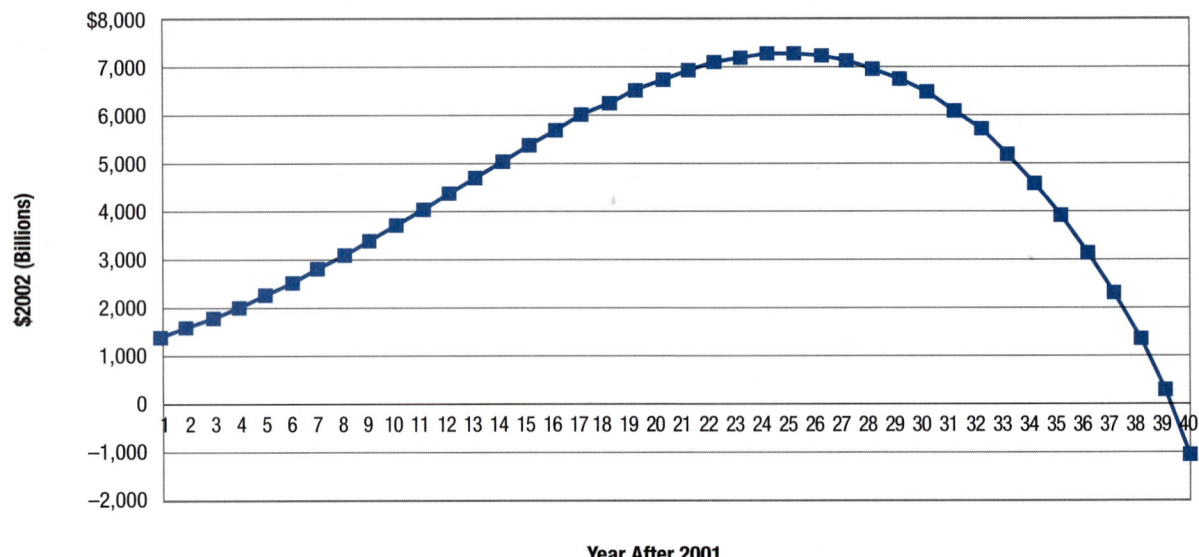

Payroll taxes and other tax income will continue to flow into Social Security after 2041, but they will be insufficient to pay all promised benefits and expenses. Initially, they will cover only about 75 percent of benefits and expenses. By the end of the projection period, 2077, annual income will cover only about 66 percent of benefits and expenses. Thus, although Social Security can provide benefits to future generations, without changes it will fall short.

Are the Analysts Right?

The Alternative II projection of the Social Security analysts relies on assumptions about key economic and population variables. The two most debatable are the fertility rate and the rate of growth in real GDP.

Fertility Rate — The average number of children born to women in their lifetime.

The **fertility rate** is the average number of children born to a woman in her lifetime. Historically, fertility rates in the United States have fluctuated widely. The rate decreased from 3.3 at the close of World War I to 2.1 during the Great Depression. Accordingly, some have described this as a "baby bust" era. The fertility rate rose dramatically after World War II, reaching 3.7 in 1957. This trend fueled the population growth of the "baby boom" generation of 1945 to 1965. This was followed by another "baby bust" of even greater dimensions than that following World War I. Fertility rates after 1965 plunged as low as 1.7 in 1987 and recovered only to 1.9 to 2.05 in the last decade.

Past trends in the fertility rate play an important role in determining expected balances in the Trust Fund. The expected surpluses for the next two decades reflect the large number of baby boomers in the labor force supporting the smaller number of baby busters who preceded them. The expected deficits in

INTERNATIONAL PERSPECTIVE

PUBLIC PENSION PLANS IN TROUBLE: THE UNITED STATES IS NOT UNIQUE

The combination of an aging population and a maturing pension scheme spell long-run difficulty for the U.S. Social Security system. The United States has lots of company, however, and in some ways is even better off than other developed countries, at least according to the numbers in the table.

In 1990, the present value of Social Security pension promises in the United States amounted to about 90 percent of GDP, or nearly $5 trillion. As you know from reading the text, receipts from the payroll tax and other sources will not accumulate fast enough at currently legislated rates to pay all of these obligations. Other countries appear in worse shape, however; Canada, Germany, Japan, and the United Kingdom owed more than 100 percent of GDP in 1990 to current and future retirees, and in France and Italy the obligation exceeded 200 percent.

In order to meet these obligations in the future, each of these countries must find additional revenues, reduce benefits, or both. One revenue possibility is the adoption of a once-and-for-all increase in taxes. Had these countries done this in 1990, the increase required to avoid a long-run deficit would have ranged from 1.1 percent of GDP in the United States to 5.3 percent of GDP in Italy. One benefit-reduction possibility would be to adopt an increase in the normal retirement age. Had these countries used this policy in 1990, the increase required to avoid a long-run deficit would have ranged from 4 years in the United States to a whopping 16 years in Canada.

These options do not exhaust the possibilities for these countries to deal with the long-run deficit in public pension plans, of course, but they do illustrate some of the tough choices to be made. Americans who lament this fact may feel fortunate to know that the task may be easier for the United States than for other countries.

Means of Financing Pension Liabilities

Country	Tax Increase as % GDP	Increase in Retirement Age (Years)
Canada	4.4	16
France	4.0	8
Germany	3.6	11
Italy	5.3	10
Japan	4.3	9
United Kingdom	3.5	12
United States	1.1	4

SOURCE: World Bank, *Averting the Old Age Crisis* (New York: Oxford University Press, 1994), 159.

INFOTRAC College Edition

Keywords: *Social Security Trust Fund, Social Security projections*

http://www.infotrac-college.com

the Trust Fund after the next two decades reflect how the Social Security beneficiary rolls will swell with retiring baby boomers and how much labor force growth will slow in response to the second baby bust.

The Social Security analysts' intermediate projection assumes a long-run fertility rate of 1.9. Some demographers believe that the rate will be higher. If they are right, future Social Security deficits will be smaller. The impact of higher fertility rates on the deficit, however, is not great: According to the 1999 annual report of the trustees, each 0.1 percentage point increase in the fertility rate reduces the long-run imbalance in the Trust Fund by only about 5 percent. Thus, solving the deficit problem would require an increase of 2.0 points (from 1.9 to 3.9) in the fertility rate. Because hardly anyone believes that such an increase is likely, most criticisms of the analysts' assumptions have been focused elsewhere.

Economists raise questions most often about the assumed rate of increase in real gross domestic product (GDP)—the key to the projected growth in real taxable payroll. Social Security actuaries expect the economy to grow at an average annual real rate of growth of around 1.8 percent for the next 75 years. This is sharply lower than the average rate of growth achieved over the past 40 years.

According to data in the 1999 annual report, a 1.2 percentage point increase in the annual rate of growth in real GDP would be sufficient, by itself, to eliminate the long-run imbalance in the Trust Fund. A 3 percent rate of growth would be well within historical experience, and some economists believe that the long-run growth rate will be at least this high. If it is, the long-run deficit is unlikely.

■ What Can Be Done About the Deficit?

In the broadest sense, eliminating the long-run deficit will require either reduced benefits or increased revenues, or some of both. Because it is well outside the scope of this chapter to consider all of the many ways to do this, we will concentrate, instead, on explaining a few widely discussed approaches.

Benefit Reductions

Among the approaches that might be used to reduce benefits are

- A reduction in benefits, starting now
- A reduction in benefits, starting after OASI Trust Fund assets are exhausted
- The use of a more accurate measure of inflation to index benefits
- A change in the method used to index the preretirement earnings of middle- and upper-income retirees
- An increase in the normal retirement age

REDUCE BENEFITS, STARTING NOW. According to the 2002 annual report, the long-run deficit in the OASI Trust Fund will average 1.54 percent of taxable payroll over the entire 75-year projection period. Thus, the deficit could be avoided if benefits were reduced by an amount equal to 1.54 percent of taxable payroll each year, starting in 2002 and continuing until 2077. This method would exact a relatively small annual cost per retiree; 1.54 percent of taxable payroll in 2002 is equivalent to about $170 per retiree.

REDUCE BENEFITS, STARTING IN 2042. If action on benefits is delayed until the OASI Trust Fund has exhausted its assets, the required annual reduction in benefits will be much larger, starting at 25.5 percent in 2042 and increasing to 33.8 percent by 2080. A strategy of waiting to solve the problem until the problem is imminent would not only exact a large cost at that time, but also impose it exclusively on future generations.

INFOTRAC
College Edition

Keywords: *cost of living and Social Security*

http://www.infotrac-college.com

USE A MORE ACCURATE MEASURE OF INFLATION TO INDEX ANNUAL RETIREMENT BENEFITS. Many economists believe that the consumer price index (CPI), as currently measured, overstates the increase in the cost of living. A recent study by the Advisory Commission to Study the Consumer Price Index, chaired by Michael Boskin of Stanford University, estimated that the bias may exceed 1 percentage point per year.[5] Because the CPI serves as the basis for indexing Social Security benefits, correction for this bias would reduce future benefits. Although small on an annual basis, such a correction would have a substantial effect on the deficit because it would be compounded over a long period of time. Each

---

[5]Advisory Commission to Study the Consumer Price Index, *Toward a More Accurate Measure of the Cost of Living*, Final Report to the Senate Finance Committee, December 1996.

0.1 percent reduction in the CPI, initiated in the near future, would reduce the Social Security deficit by 6 percent. Thus, a correction of 1 percent could reduce the deficit by 60 percent.

CHANGE THE METHOD OF INDEXING PRERETIREMENT EARNINGS OF MIDDLE- AND UPPER-INCOME RETIREES. Currently, benefits for new retirees are determined by indexing earnings realized before age 60 for increases in the average annual wage between the year the earnings are received and the year when the retiree turns 60. This method of indexing increases the real value of initial benefits because the average annual wage grows faster than the CPI. Thus, some have suggested instead that Social Security earnings be indexed only for inflation. This could be done by indexing actual earnings for the increase in the CPI, instead of the increase in the average annual wage. If this policy were adopted and applied only to new middle- and upper-income retirees, it would reduce the long-run deficit by 60 percent. The exemption of low-income retirees from this policy would preserve the safety net already built into the Social Security benefit formula.

INCREASE THE NORMAL RETIREMENT AGE. Given past and expected future increases in life expectancy, an argument can be made for an increase in the normal retirement age as a means of reducing the long-run deficit. The life expectancies for males and females at age 65 have already increased 3.8 and 5.0 years, respectively, since the inception of Social Security and are expected to increase another 4.4 years for males and 4.3 years for females by 2075. In an earlier effort to avoid a Social Security deficit, Congress passed legislation that will change the normal retirement age. According to that legislation, the normal retirement age is scheduled to increase two months per year from 2003 to 2008, to remain constant at age 66 from 2008 to 2019, and then to increase again, starting in 2020, at the rate of two months per year, reaching age 67 in 2025. Some observers believe, however, that this is too small an increase in the normal retirement age. If the normal retirement age was increased uniformly by two months each year from 2003 to 2033 and indexed thereafter to increases in life expectancy, the projected deficit would fall by about 45 percent. This would actually produce changes in both benefits and revenues. Raising the normal retirement age reduces benefits per retiree by reducing the number of years each can draw benefits, but it also increases revenues by increasing the number of years each retiree pays taxes.

Revenue Increases

Some approaches that could increase revenues are

- An increase in taxes, starting now
- An increase in taxes, starting after OASI Trust Fund assets are exhausted
- An increase in investment, financed by the Social Security surplus
- The privatization of Social Security

INCREASE TAXES, STARTING NOW OR IN 2042. As noted earlier, the long-run deficit could be eliminated by adoption of a uniform reduction in benefits equal to 1.54 percent of taxable payroll between 2002 and 2077, or by a 25.5 to 33.8 percent reduction in benefits over the period 2042 to 2077. Increases in taxes of similar magnitudes would have the same effects on the deficit.

INCREASE INVESTMENT, FINANCED WITH THE SOCIAL SECURITY SURPLUS. We noted previously that a 1.2 percent increase in the annual growth rate of real GDP would be enough, by itself, to eliminate the long-run Social Security deficit. We also noted that the OASI Trust Fund will experience an annual surplus for the next 15 years. This series of surpluses provides an opportunity to increase investment and potential real GDP. Whether this opportunity is seized or not depends on how the President and Congress shape the federal budget as the Social Security surpluses occur.

Under current law, Social Security surpluses must be invested in U.S. Treasury securities, thereby providing income to the Treasury. If there is no federal budget deficit, this income is used to retire Treasury securities as they come due, reducing the amount that the Treasury would otherwise borrow to finance the national debt. In the event of a federal budget deficit, this income replaces money that the Treasury would otherwise borrow to finance the deficit. In both cases, the Social Security surplus reduces the Treasury's demand for loanable funds, indirectly increasing the supply of loanable funds available for private investment. Use of these funds by the private sector will result in a larger real GDP, larger taxable payroll, larger Social Security tax collections, and a smaller long-run Social Security deficit.

If Congress elects to increase the budget deficit (or reduce a budget surplus), however, because Social Security surpluses provide a convenient way to finance the increase (reduction), the effects just described may or may not be realized. A larger budget deficit (smaller surplus) could occur as a result of either an increase in spending or a reduction in taxes. If spending increases or tax reductions increase the nation's capacity to produce, the long-run Social Security deficit would be smaller, just as it would be if the Social Security surplus was used to reduce the national debt or to finance a preexisting budget deficit. If the spending increases or tax reductions do not increase the nation's capacity to produce, the Social Security surplus will not reduce the long-run Social Security deficit. To ensure that the Social Security surplus reduces the long-run Social Security deficit, the spending increases should be concentrated on capacity-increasing investments in areas like education, training, and infrastructure, and the tax cuts should be the type that increase saving and investment.

PRIVATIZING SOCIAL SECURITY. Privatization has several possible meanings. In the broadest sense, it means the acquisition of private securities for the purpose of producing retirement income. Here we consider the case where Social Security, itself, is privatized. This would occur if the projected Social Security surpluses were used to buy private securities, rather than U.S. government securities. The principal benefit of **privatization** to Social Security would be higher interest income. Private securities produce significantly higher income, albeit at greater risk, than the long-term Treasury bonds Social Security must acquire. According to a recent study by Cochran, the real annual return on Standard and Poor's 500 stocks for the 1947 to 1996 period was 9.5 percent, while long-term Treasury bonds yielded only 1.8 percent after inflation.[6]

Privatization – The investment of Social Security trust fund balances in private securities.

The increased income from private securities would increase the Social Security Trust Fund. The long-run Social Security deficit would shrink but would not disappear, even if *all* the projected Social Security surpluses were invested in private securities. Privatization would reduce the size of the tax increase or benefit reduction required to avoid the long-run deficit, but not to zero. The projected Social Security deficit is simply too large to be eliminated solely by investing projected surpluses in private securities.

---

[6]John Cochran, "Where Is the Market Going? Uncertain Facts and Novel Theories," *Economic Perspectives*, Federal Reserve Bank of Chicago 21 (1997), 3–37.

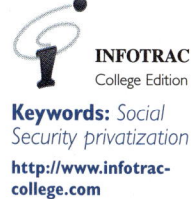

Keywords: *Social Security privatization*
http://www.infotrac-college.com

Social Security retirees, or workers subject to the Social Security payroll tax, would gain from privatization because they would face lower expected increases (decreases) in taxes (benefits). The private sector investors who are crowded out of the securities market by Social Security would lose, however. Privatization would, in effect, transfer wealth from private investors to Social Security retirees and workers. Privatization would function as a "hidden tax" on private investors.

The prospect of losses by competing investors may generate political opposition to privatization, but it would probably pale by comparison to the opposition from those who fear the greater income risk associated with private securities than with government bonds. Because private securities are subject to greater risk than long-term Treasury bonds, this raises the specter that a prolonged market downturn will jeopardize the Social Security Trust Fund, and that prospect, alone, may be enough to blunt political support for privatization.

■ THE TRADE-OFF FOR INDIVIDUALS: LOWER DEFICITS MEAN LOWER RATES OF RETURN

Our calculations of the rate of return reflect the unstated assumption that the long-run deficit problem will somehow be solved without imposing additional taxes on, or reducing the benefits of, our typical college graduate. This is unlikely to be the case; our graduate will be expected to pay his or her share of the costs associated with the options just discussed. If this happens, there will be an effect on the rate of return.

Table 11.3 summarizes the rates of return expected under various scenarios and payroll tax rates borne by the worker. If the deficit problem could be solved at no cost to the worker, we get the results reported earlier and repeated in column 2. If taxes were increased immediately and sustained throughout the projection period for all Social Security beneficiaries, including our typical college graduate, the rate of return would fall compared to the no-cost option (compare column 3 with column 2). This is as expected, given that there are no offsetting increases in benefits. As shown in Table 11.3, the rate of return would also fall if either the required tax increase or benefit reduction were delayed until 2043 (columns 4 and 5). The rate of return for the delayed tax increase exceeds that for the delayed benefit increase because our typical college graduate has his/her taxes increased for only a few years while working but benefits reduced for all years while retired. Judged by the effect on the rate of return only, then, the individual

TABLE 11.3 Rates of Return on Social Security, by Type of Fix for the Long-Run Deficit and Tax Rate Borne by Worker

Tax Borne by Worker (1)	No Cost to Worker (2)	Permanent Tax Increase (3)	Delayed Tax Increase (4)	Delayed Benefit Reduction (5)
Tax rate	ROR	ROR	ROR	ROR
10.6	1.24	0.79	1.13	0.17
5.3	3.48	3.05	3.16	2.49

should prefer the strategy of delaying the tax increase. Under such a strategy, the bulk of the tax increase is actually paid by subsequent generations.

Summary

In this chapter, the term *Social Security* refers to the federal Old-Age and Survivors' Insurance (OASI) program that provides benefits to retired workers and to their survivors.

Social Security is financed by payroll taxes that are deposited in a trust fund. The benefits paid from this fund reflect taxes paid, normal retirement age, age at retirement, changes in the average national wage prior to age 60, marital and family status, and indexing for inflation. The ratio of Social Security benefits to average indexed earnings is higher for lower-income retirees than for higher-income retirees, and Social Security makes a major contribution to reducing poverty among elderly Americans.

The Social Security payroll tax appears to be borne largely by workers, unlike Congress intended. The shifting of the employer's share of the tax to workers reduces the rate of return workers can expect on contributions made to Social Security.

The prospect of Social Security benefits appears to induce many workers to retire early, even though they are penalized for early retirement and rewarded for later retirement. This makes it more difficult for Social Security to provide adequate long-term financing for Social Security benefits.

The prospect of Social Security wealth appears to induce households to save less, although the evidence of this effect is not clear-cut. If it has this effect, Social Security wealth is large enough to produce a significant reduction in household savings, investment, and potential real GDP.

The real rate of return on contributions to Social Security by the typical college graduate is probably less than 2 percent, even under the unrealistic circumstances in which fixes for the projected long-run deficit are made at no cost to our typical worker. Estimates of the real real rate of return would be higher if Social Security were credited with the benefits provided by protection against income and inflation risk.

Social Security analysts project that the OASI Trust Fund will run annual surpluses for about 15 years, but that Trust Fund balances will fall thereafter and become exhausted in 2042, after which Social Security will be able to pay only 67 to 75 percent of the benefits prescribed by current law. Not all economists agree, however, with the analysts' assumptions, especially those relating to the annual rate of growth in real GDP.

If the analysts are right, ways must be found to either reduce promised benefits or to increase expected revenues. Benefits could be reduced by adopting an immediate and sustained reduction in annual benefits of 1.54 percent of taxable payroll, by reducing benefits by 25 to 33 percent starting in 2042, by the application of a more accurate measure of inflation to indexation of benefits, by a change in the method used to index the earnings of middle- and upper-income retirees, and by an increase in the normal retirement age. Revenues could be increased by a uniform increase in taxes, starting now, by increases in taxes starting after Trust Fund assets are exhausted, by the adoption of policies that increase the rate of growth of real GDP, and by the privatization of Social Security. One policy that would increase the rate of growth is to employ future Social Security surpluses as a means of increasing savings and investment. This will occur if the surpluses are used to reduce the national debt, to increase public investment in education, training, and infrastructure, or to finance capacity-increasing tax cuts.

Privatizing Social Security could help solve the long-run deficit problem, but it would not eliminate the deficit by itself. A privatization strategy would have to be accompanied by either a tax increase or a benefit reduction in order to accomplish that objective. Privatization transfers wealth from individuals who would normally buy private securities to Social Security beneficiaries and taxpayers. Privatization also exposes Social Security to income risk.

Finally, we present some additional calculations of the rate of return that show that the fixes examined for the long-run deficit problem will reduce the rate of return on Social Security. This is to be expected because the various fixes either impose additional taxes on our typical worker or reduce prospective benefits.

Key Terms

Pay-as-you-go fund
Fully-funded fund
Indexing factor
Average indexed monthly earnings (AIME)
Primary insurance amount (PIA)
Early retirement penalty
Inflation indexing
Delayed retirement credit
Substitution effect of a wage decrease
Income effect of a wage decrease
Wealth substitution effect
Social Security wealth
Induced retirement effect
Risk reduction benefit
Inflation protection benefit
Fertility rate
Privatization

Review Questions

1. Explain how and why actual earnings are indexed to determine Social Security retirement benefits.
2. Explain how Social Security provides more generous returns to the poor than to the rich, using the concepts of the PIA and AIME.
3. "The Social Security payroll tax appears to be paid largely by workers, unlike Congress intended." Explain how this can be, using a diagram to illustrate your answer.
4. In theory, Social Security may or may not induce people to retire early. Explain.
5. In theory, Social Security may or may not induce people to save less. Explain.
6. If Social Security does induce people to save less, it only reduces savings by less than three cents for each dollar of Social Security wealth. Surely, this is a negligible effect. Do you agree or disagree? Explain.
7. Given benefits and costs that can be measured in dollars, Social Security pays only a 1 to 2 percent real rate of return for the typical college graduate. Is it *really* this low?
8. "All economists agree that Social Security is going to run completely out of money by 2042." What parts of this statement are true and what parts are false? Explain.
9. It is often said that the long-run deficit in Social Security can be eliminated at relatively low cost if the problem is addressed right away, but that the cost will be quite high if we wait to address the problem. Provide an example or two from the chapter that illustrate this point.
10. "The long-run deficit in Social Security could be eliminated by a series of small changes that spread the cost out over the population and over time." What, if any, such combinations were implied in the discussion in this chapter? Explain.
11. One way to reduce the long-run Social Security deficit is to increase the rate of growth in real GDP. Explain why, and explain how the appropriate use of the projected Social Security surplus over the next decade or so will lead to this result.
12. Explain why privatization, alone, cannot eliminate the long-run Social Security deficit.
13. What do you think is most likely to really be the real rate of return on Social Security? Explain, referring in your answer to the estimates presented in this chapter.

Economic Issues on the Internet

- Social Security Administration—http://www.ssa.gov
  The Board of Trustees of the Federal Old-Age and Survivors Insurance and Disability Insurance Trust Funds present a thorough review of the past, present, and future of the Social Security trust funds. Contains 75-year projections.
- Social Security Advisory Board—http://www.ssab.gov/actionshouldbetaken.pdf
  The article *Social Security: Why Action Should Be Taken Soon* outlines the case for not delaying actions required to avoid the long-run deficit.

CHAPTER 12

Poverty: Old and New Approaches to a Persistent Problem

Outline:

The Scope of the Problem
Antipoverty Effectiveness of Government Transfers
Means-Tested Transfers and Income from Work
   Food Stamps
   Earned Income Tax Credit (EITC)
   Temporary Assistance for Needy Families (TANF)

TANF + Food Stamps + EITC
Making Work Pay
   Unemployment Policy
   Childcare Assistance
   Medical Protection
   Minimum Wage
   Wage Subsidies
   Labor Market Discrimination Policy

Making Fathers Pay
   Child Support Assistance
   Child Support Assurance

In 1962, Michael Harrington wrote a book, *The Other America*. The "other Americans" were the poor who lived in a land of plenty, primarily out of sight and out of mind. Harrington's work stirred the conscience of many Americans, including President John F. Kennedy, who directed his Council of Economic Advisers to study the problem. After Kennedy's assassination, President Lyndon Johnson embraced the issue and, in his State of the Union address in 1964, declared "war" on poverty.

In the next decade, the federal government introduced new antipoverty programs and expanded old programs. According to the federal government's official measure, the U.S. poverty rate fell from 17.3 percent in 1965 to 11.1 percent in 1973, and government initiatives have been credited with much of this success. The successes of this decade were short-lived, however. The poverty rate started to grow in 1974 and has remained above the 1973 level since then. It did fall steadily from 1992 to 2000, reaching 11.3 percent in 2000—just a little above the 1973 level—but it increased to 11.7 percent in 2001.

Some interpret this as a sign that we are losing the war on poverty, although they do not necessarily agree on the causes of our failure. Some attribute it to cutbacks in government assistance to the poor. Others argue that this assistance is the wrong kind or is focused on the wrong people. Still others contend that government assistance actually increases the poverty rate by inducing recipients to work less. Finally, some claim that the official poverty data overstate the poverty problem, and that more accurate measures actually show that we have come closer to winning the war than is commonly acknowledged.

There is, in short, no universal agreement among economists about the extent or causes of poverty in the United States. Not surprisingly, they also disagree about what we should do to reduce poverty further. This accounts, perhaps, for the wide variety of approaches to solving the poverty problem in the United States. Some are old and time-tested; some are new and yet to pass the test of time. This chapter is designed to provide you with a primer on what has been attempted, what is currently being done, and what might be done next.

■ THE SCOPE OF THE PROBLEM

Individuals are poor whenever their resources are insufficient to provide what society considers an acceptable minimum standard of living. There are, however, many possible definitions of resources and acceptable minimum standards of living. Thus, there are many possible measures of poverty. The most frequently cited measure is the official poverty measure. According to this measure, a **poor person** is one who lives in a family with a gross money income below the official poverty threshold. The **official poverty threshold** is the annual cost of a nutritionally adequate diet multiplied by three. This multiplier is based on the idea that the poor should not have to spend more than one-third of their income for food—the proportion that they did spend for food when the official poverty measure was developed in the early 1960s.

The government adjusts the poverty threshold each year for changes in the consumer price index (CPI). The poverty threshold also increases (though not uniformly) as family size increases. In 1959, the official poverty threshold for a family of four was $2,973. To compensate for price increases between 1959 and 2001, the government increased this threshold from $2,973 to $18,104. In 2001, the poverty threshold ranged from $9,039 for a single individual to $36,286 for a family of nine or more.

The other half of the official measure of poverty—resources available—is the gross (before tax) money income reported to the Census Bureau in its periodic surveys of income. **Gross money income** includes earnings before taxes, interest, dividends, and private and government cash transfers, such as alimony and child support payments, Social Security benefits, unemployment benefits, and payments from the Temporary Assistance to Needy Families (formerly Aid to Families with Dependent Children) program. If a family's gross money income is less than its relevant poverty threshold, all members of that family are counted as poor.

Figure 12.1 shows the number of people in poverty each year from 1959 through 2001, according to the official measure. Nearly 40 million people were poor in 1959. The number of poor people declined significantly from 1959 to 1969 to 24 million and remained around 25 million until 1978. From 1979 to

---

Poor Person – A person who lives in a family with income below the poverty threshold

Official Poverty Threshold – The annual cost of a nutritionally adequate diet multiplied by three.

Gross Money Income – Earnings (before taxes), interest, dividends, and private and government cash transfers, such as alimony and child support payments, Social Security benefits, unemployment benefits, and payments from TANF.

| FIGURE 12.1 | Number of People in Poverty, 1959–2001 |

The history of poverty in the United States, according to the official measure of poverty, can be described as a series of trends: a rapid decline in the 1960s, followed by stability in the 1970s, a significant increase in the early 1980s, a small decline in the last half of the 1980s, a rapid increase in the early 1990s, and a large decrease since then.

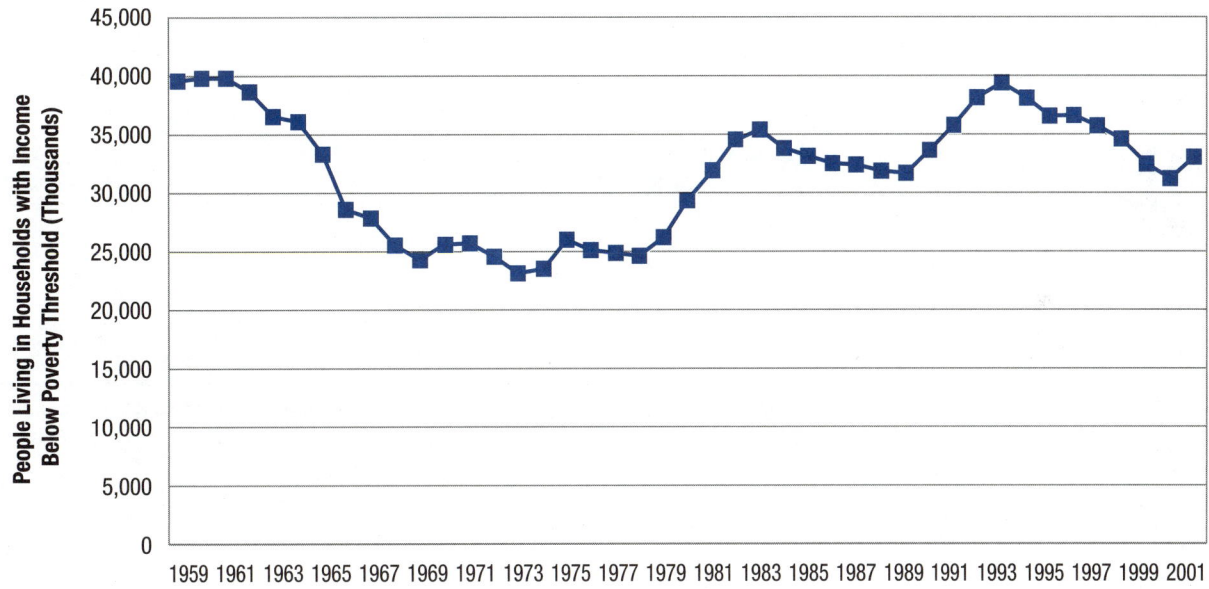

1993, the number of poor people trended generally upward, nearly reaching the 40 million mark again at the end of this period. After 1993, the poverty population plummeted, reaching a low of 31 million in 2000. The number of poor people rose again in 2001, to 32.9 million.

Poverty Rate – The number of poor people divided by the U.S. population.

The number of poor people divided by the U.S. population yields the **poverty rate**. Figure 12.2 illustrates how the poverty rate has behaved from 1959 to 2001. The trend in the poverty rate is similar to the trend in the poverty population from 1959 to 1979. From 1980 through 1993, the poverty rate varied between 13 and 15 percent, averaging 13.8 percent. It fell to 11.3 percent in 2000 and increased slightly to 11.7 percent in 2001. The poverty rate is now roughly where it was at its historic low in the 1970s. Some would interpret this as lack of progress in solving the poverty problem. Others would cite the fact that the U.S. population has grown by over 100 million people since 1959 (from 178 million to 281 million) and argue that we have done a remarkable job in holding the line on poverty.

INFOTRAC
College Edition

Keywords: *poverty in the United States, historical poverty data, poverty trends*
http://www.infotrac-college.com

The biggest success story has been the reduction in the poverty rate for people age 65 and older, as illustrated in Figure 12.3. In 1967, the poverty rate for the aged was more than twice that of the all-ages poverty rate (the same measure as the official poverty rate). By 1982, however, the poverty rate for the aged had fallen below the all-ages poverty rate, where it has remained ever since.

| FIGURE 12.2 | Official Poverty Rate, 1959–2001 |

The official poverty rate fell rapidly from 1959 to 1973. It has never been as low as it was in 1973, although it came close in 2000.

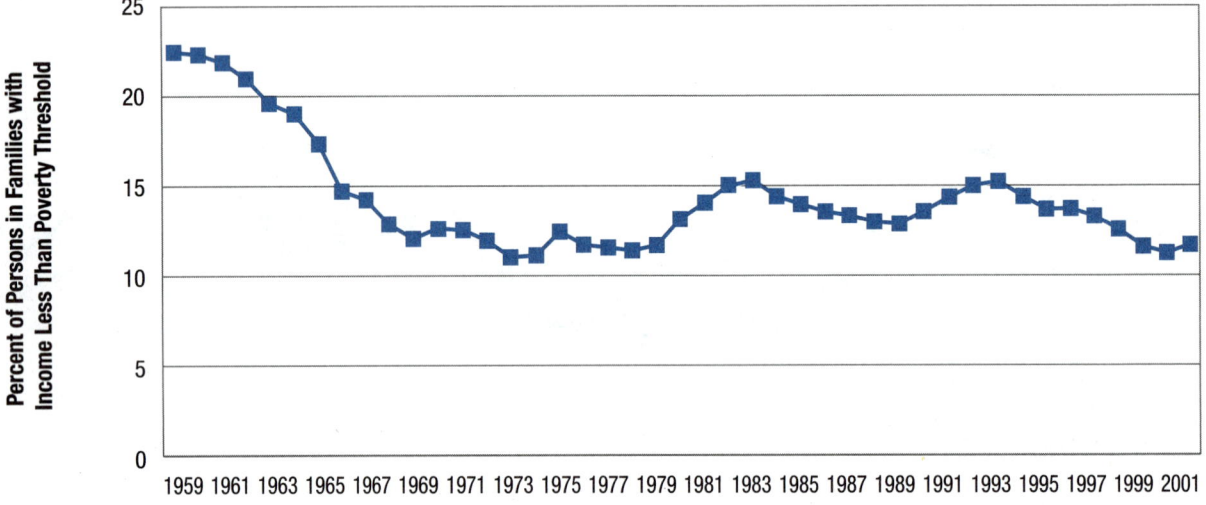

| FIGURE 12.3 | Poverty Rate, All Ages and 65 Years and Over, 1966–2001 |

Thirty-five years ago, the poverty rate for the elderly was more than twice as high as the poverty rate averaged over people of all ages (the official poverty rate). By 1982, the elderly poverty rate had fallen below the all-ages poverty rate, where it has remained ever since.

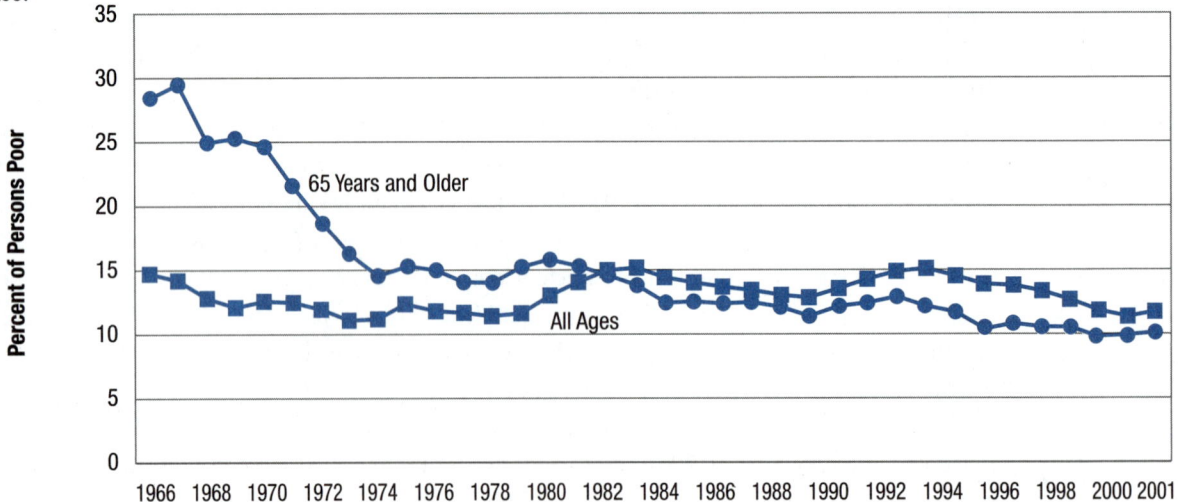

There has been a significant reduction in the poverty rate for persons living in female-headed families, as illustrated in Figure 12.4. Progress here has been concentrated in two time periods: 1959 to 1979 and 1991 to 2001. Racial minorities have also fared relatively well in the last decade, as illustrated in Figure 12.5.

■ ANTIPOVERTY EFFECTIVENESS OF GOVERNMENT TRANSFERS

The official poverty rate reflects the number of people who are poor *after* they receive various government cash transfers. As we will see, government cash transfers significantly reduce the number of people who are poor according to the official measure of poverty. The actual poverty rate is even lower than the official rate, however, if the value of various government noncash transfers is added to the measure of income that is used to determine the official poverty rate.

Table 12.1 provides a list of the principal government transfers that benefited the poor in 2001. All of these programs would be on most people's list of antipoverty programs, except Social Security. Social Security is not normally thought of as an antipoverty program, but it has played an important role in reducing the poverty rate of the elderly below that of the population in general (Figure 12.3). According to a study based on census data,[1] Social Security reduces the proportion of elderly people living in poverty from nearly one in two to fewer than one in eight. They found that in 1997, nearly half of all elderly people—47.6 percent—had incomes below the poverty line before receipt of Social Security benefits. After receiving Social Security benefits, only 11.9 percent remained poor.

FIGURE 12.4 **Poverty Rate, Persons Living in Female-Headed Households, 1959–2001**

The poverty rate for people living in female-headed families has fallen from 50 percent in 1959 to less than 30 percent in 2001.

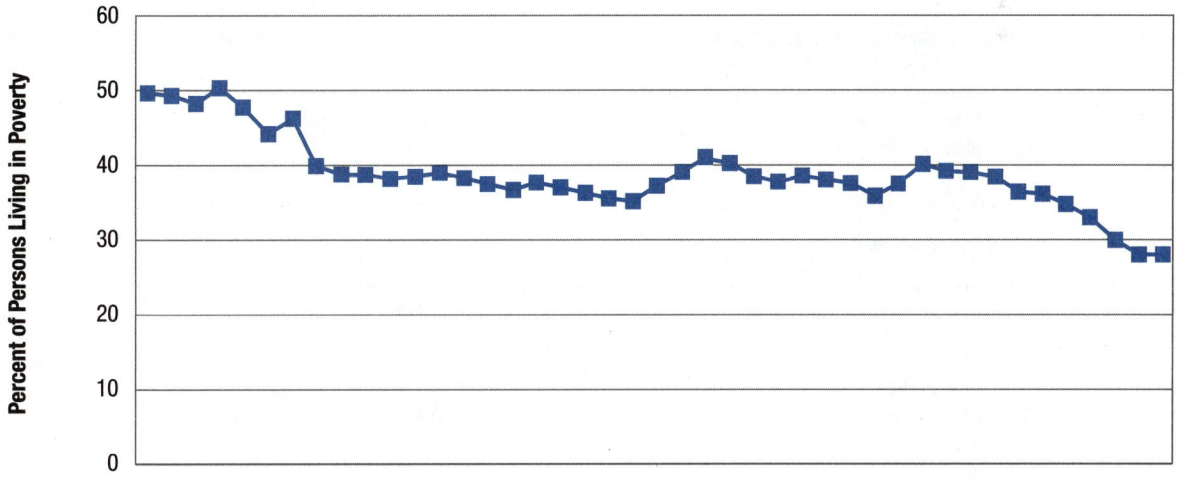

[1] Kathryn Porter, Kathy Lavin, and Wendell Primus, *Social Security and Poverty Among the Elderly*, Center for Budget and Policy Priorities, April 1999.

| FIGURE 12.5 | Poverty Rates by Race, 1973–2001 |

The poverty rates for people living in black and Hispanic households fell both absolutely and relative to the poverty rate in white, non-Hispanic families in the 1990s.

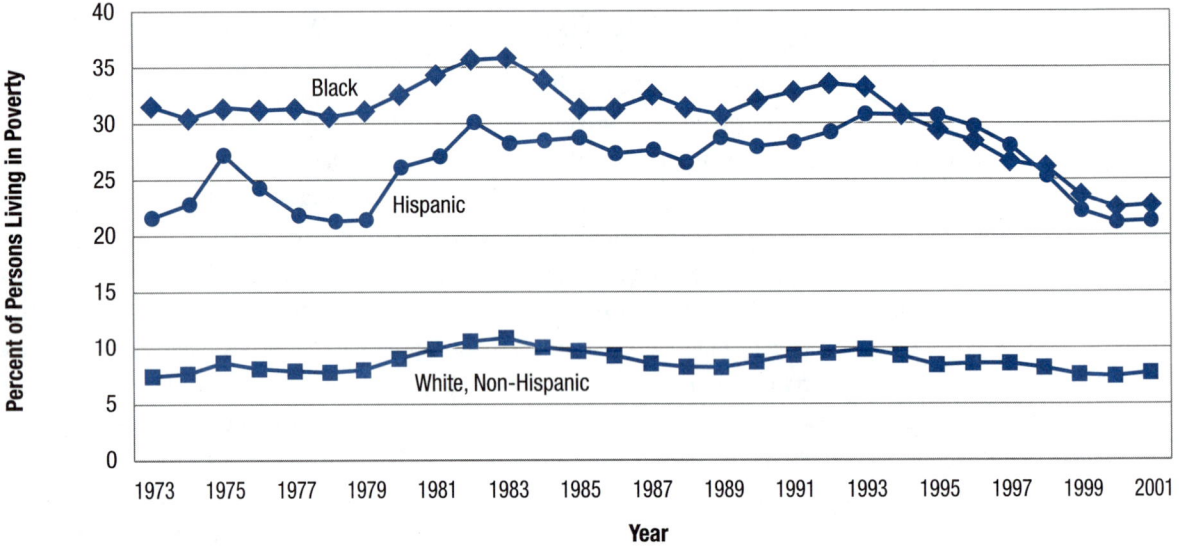

| TABLE 12.1 | Principal Government Transfers Benefiting Lower-Income Families, 2001 ($ Millions) |

Cash Transfers		
Social Security		$440,543
Supplemental Security Income (SSI)		30,561
Earned Income Tax Credit (EITC)		26,123
Temporary Assistance for Needy Families (TANF)		
Federal Government Bloc Grant	16,689	
State Government Funds*	8,345	
		25,034
Total Cash Transfers		**$522,261**
Noncash Transfers		
Medical Care		
Medicaid—Federal Government	$129,419	
Medicaid—State Government	96,666	
Total		226,085
Food Assistance		
Food Stamps	20,058	
Women, Infants, Children (WIC) & Child Nutrition	14,241	34,299
Housing Assistance		25,119
Child Care and Child Support		8,645
Energy Assistance		2,000
Total Noncash Transfers		**$296,148**
Total Cash and Noncash Transfers		**$818,409**

SOURCE: U.S. Office of Management and Budget, *Budget of the U.S. Government, 2003, Historical Tables*, except *, which is authors' estimate.

Pre-Transfer Poverty Rate – An estimate by the Census Bureau of what the poverty rate would be without the income provided by government cash transfers, except the earned income tax credit (EITC)

INFOTRAC
College Edition

Keywords: pre-transfer poverty, post-transfer poverty, government transfers and poverty
http://www.infotrac-college.com

The antipoverty effectiveness of government cash transfers can be determined by comparing the pre-transfer poverty rate with the official poverty rate. The **pre-transfer poverty rate** is an estimate by the Census Bureau of what the poverty rate would be without the income provided by the cash transfers in Table 12.1, except the earned income tax credit (EITC). Figure 12.6 shows that government cash transfers have been a uniformly important factor in reducing poverty throughout the period 1979 to 2001 (the data on pre-transfer poverty begin in 1979). In the absence of income from government cash transfers, the poverty rate would have averaged 21.1 percent; with the income from government cash transfers, the poverty rate averaged 13.5 percent. Government cash transfers reduced the average poverty rate by 7.6 percent, or nearly 36 percent of the pre-transfer level.

As Table 12.1 indicates, government also transferred a large amount of economic resources in the form of noncash transfers in 2001, especially for medical care, food, and housing. It has, in fact, been allocating significant amounts of money to these purposes for several decades. Government also levies taxes on income received by the poor—the Social Security payroll tax and state and local income taxes—although the income tax bill is reduced by the EITC. Taxes, per se, increase the poverty rate, the EITC reduces it, and noncash transfers also reduce the poverty rate. Figure 12.7 shows that the poverty-reducing impacts of noncash transfers and the EITC are stronger than the poverty-increasing impact of taxes. The net effect of the adjustment for taxes, the EITC, and noncash transfers has been to reduce the poverty rate below the official poverty rate throughout the period 1979 to 2001 by an average of 2.8 percent per year.

Table 12.2 shows the effects of taxes and transfers on the poverty population in 2001. It is clear from this table that government programs have had a significant effect on the poverty population, led by the

FIGURE 12.6 Pre-Transfer and Official Poverty, 1979–2001

This figure compares the official poverty rate with the pre-transfer poverty rate. It indicates that the poverty rate would be 7 to 8 percentage points higher in the absence of government cash transfers.

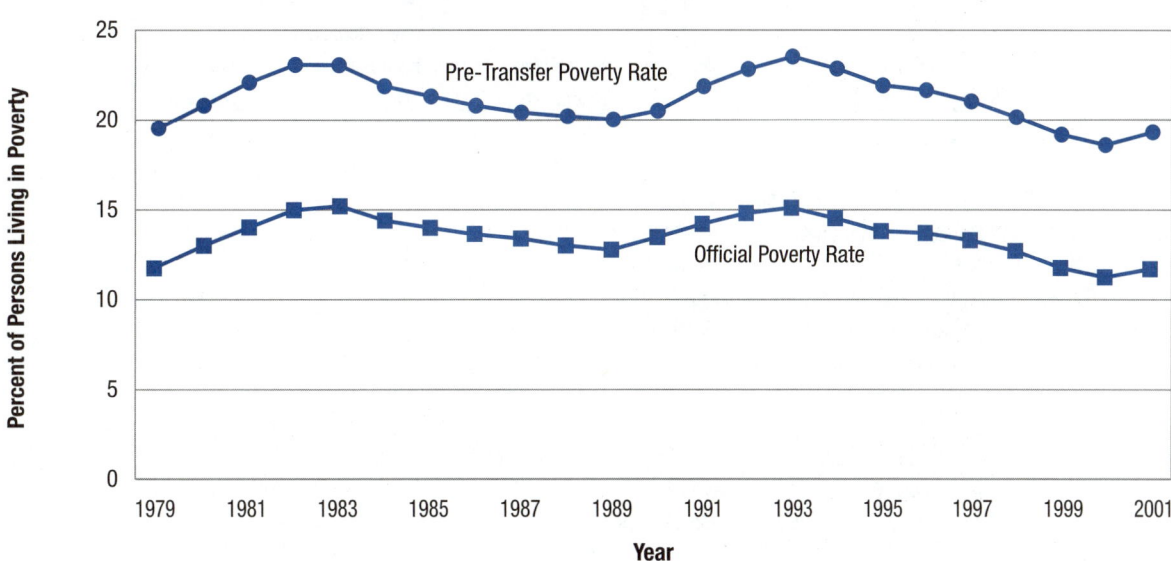

FIGURE 12.7 Poverty Rate Before Cash Transfers, Official Poverty Rate, and Poverty Rate After Taxes and Cash and Noncash Transfers, 1979–2001

This figure shows that the poverty rate would be 7 to 8 percentage points higher in the absence of government cash transfers, but also that the poverty rate would be 2 to 3 percentage points lower than the official rate if noncash transfers and taxes were included in the measure of household resources.

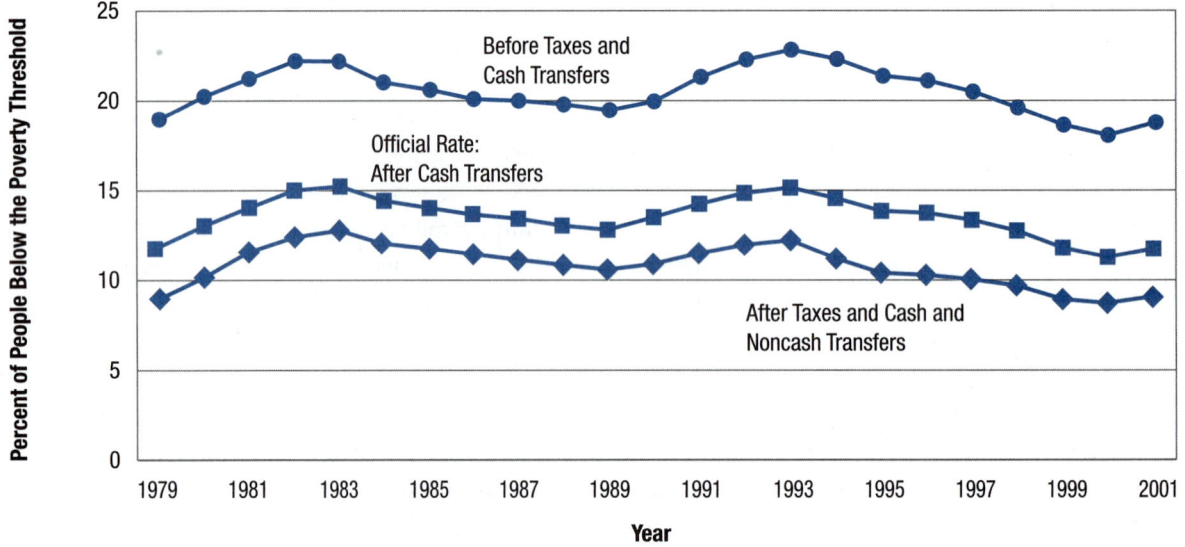

TABLE 12.2 Effect of Taxes and Transfers on Poverty, 2001

	Persons Poor (Thousands)	Persons Removed from Poverty (Thousands)	Poverty Rate (Percent)
Before Taxes and Transfers	52,073		18.5
After Taxes	51,791	282	18.4
Social Security and Income Taxes: +3,377			
Earned Income Tax Credit: −3,659			
Net Effect of Taxes: −282			
After Non–Means-Tested Cash Transfers	32,651	19,140	11.6
e.g., Soc. Sec., Unem. Comp., Workers Comp.			
After Means-Tested Cash Transfers	30,400	2,251	10.8
e.g., SSI, TANF			
After Noncash Transfers	25,332	5,068	9.0
e.g., Medical Care, Food, and Housing Assistance			
Total Removed from Poverty by Taxes and Transfers		26,741	

SOURCE: U.S. Census Bureau, *Historical Poverty Tables—Poverty by Definition of Income.*

INSIGHTS

THE TIDE HAS RISEN, BUT MOST BOATS HAVE NOT

Real national output in the United States has grown dramatically since the Johnson administration launched the "war on poverty" in 1965, averaging nearly 2.8 percent per year. The nation's distribution of income has become significantly more unequal, however. For example, the share of total money income received by the richest quintile has increased from 43.8 percent to more than 49 percent, while the share going to every other quintile has fallen. To describe it metaphorically, the tide has risen, but most boats have not.

A flurry of research in recent years has focused on the subject of growing income inequality. Much of it concerns the nation's labor markets and the distribution of wages. According to this research, real earnings growth did indeed slow in the 1970s and 1980s relative to earlier decades, and earnings became less equally distributed.[a] One apparent factor in this trend is the economic shift from goods production to services production. Industries involved in producing services typically have paid lower wages and exhibited more variation in their wage structures than industries involved in producing goods. Increased wage inequality has also marked the goods-producing industries, however, so other explanations must be sought.

One of the more popular explanations focuses on the growing gap between the earnings of well-educated and poorly-educated workers, presumably spurred by faster-growing demand for skilled workers. The nation's trade deficit also may have added to the problem because a greater proportion of unskilled labor produces this country's imports than its exports. Many of these imports could have been made by low-skilled workers in this country but were made abroad, reducing the demand for unskilled domestic workers.

The declining influence of unions on wage-setting practices also may have played a role. Less-skilled workers have typically received significant wage benefits from union membership. The maturing of the baby-boom generation (individuals born in large numbers between 1945 and 1965) probably had some effect, as it flooded the labor market with record numbers of younger entrants, driving down their wages relative to those of older workers.

Finally, some of the increased inequality in family income is undoubtedly caused by changes in family composition. Married-couple households as a proportion of all households has fallen dramatically in the last 30 years, to be replaced by single-parent family households and nonfamily households, groups that have traditionally exhibited greater inequality of income than married-couple households.

Economists are carefully examining these and many other possible explanations of the growing inequality in the distribution of income. What they find may matter a great deal in the design of future social and economic policy.

---

[a]Gary Burtless, "Has Widening Inequality Promoted or Retarded U.S. Growth?" Unpublished manuscript, April 22, 2002. Available from The Brookings Institution Web site.

---

poverty-reducing power of non–means-tested cash transfers. It is also clear from Table 12.2 that the EITC has more than offset the effect of the payroll and income taxes on individuals.

Some interpret the poverty rate after adjustments for all transfers and taxes as evidence that the poverty problem has been solved. Others do not, citing the relatively high poverty rates that still prevail in female-headed, black, and Hispanic families. Still others argue that we have not solved the poverty problem as long as we have a fifth of the population living in pre-transfer poverty. They believe that we have failed to provide a meaningful solution to poverty to the degree that people live in families where the adults are unable to earn enough money to escape poverty without government transfers.

■ MEANS-TESTED TRANSFERS AND INCOME FROM WORK

A thorough examination of why the pre-transfer poverty rate hovers near 20 percent of the population is well beyond the scope of this book. Some economists argue that part of the problem lies, however, with government transfers, themselves. On one hand, they provide the means to escape poverty. On the other hand, they provide incentives to the poor to do less to earn their own way out of poverty. This is especially true of the **means-tested transfers**, those in which the transfer falls as a recipient's means or income increases.

A working poor adult is potentially eligible for a package of means-tested transfers, including TANF, food stamps, the EITC, Medicaid, and federal housing assistance. We will focus on the benefits from TANF, food stamps, and the EITC in this section because they vary inversely with income and they are widely available as a package. Benefits from housing assistance also vary inversely with income, but only about 20 percent of poor families receive housing assistance. Benefits from Medicaid are extremely important to the poor, but they do not vary inversely with income.

Means-Tested Transfer – A transfer that decreases in value as a recipient's means or income increases.

Food Stamps

The food stamp program (FSP) helps people buy food. Over 80 percent of recipients receive food stamp assistance by using special ATM-like debit cards in grocery stores. The program is funded primarily by the federal government, but administered through local welfare offices. To be eligible, gross household income cannot exceed 130 percent of the relevant poverty line for the particular household.

The food stamp program is a means-tested transfer program—one in which the amount of the transfer or benefit tapers off as the recipient's means or income rises. The transfer does not taper off, however, until a participant's gross income exceeds a deduction to cover essential needs. Gross income is income from before-tax earnings and non–means-tested transfers (such as Social Security benefits).

Basic Benefit – The benefit paid by a means-tested transfer program when gross income is zero.

Deduction for Essential Needs – An allowance for essential needs that is disregarded in determining benefits from a transfer program.

Table 12.3 illustrates how monthly food stamp benefits vary with gross income for a family of 3 in 2002. The family's basic benefit is $366. The **basic benefit** is the amount they receive when their gross income is equal to or less than the **deduction for essential needs** (sometimes called the *income disregard*): $134.0 in 2002. For gross income greater than the deduction, benefits fall as gross income rises. When gross income is $200.0, benefits are $346.2. Thus, an increase in gross income from $134.0 to $200.0, or $66.0, results in benefits falling from $366.0 to $346.2, or $19.8. The ratio of the decrease in benefits to the increase in income is −0.30 (= −19.8/66). This ratio is called the **benefit reduction rate**. As the computations in the remainder of the table show, it is equal to −0.30 (or a 30 cent decrease in benefits for each one dollar increase in gross income) over the entire range in gross income from $134.0 to $1,354.0. When gross income reaches $1354.0, benefits are zero. The level of gross income where benefits are equal to zero is called the **break-even gross income (BEGI)**.

Benefit Reduction Rate – The decrease in benefits paid by a means-tested transfer program when gross income increases.

Break-Even Gross Income (BEGI) – The gross income at which benefits become zero in a means-tested transfer program.

The benefit (B) at each level of gross income (GI) greater than the deduction (GI greater than $134 in this example) can be determined by solving the benefit equation

(12.1) $$B = BB - BRR\,(GI - D)$$

where BB is the basic benefit, BRR is the benefit reduction rate, and D is the deduction for essential needs. For example, if BB = $366, BRR = 0.30, D = $134, and GI = $1,000, then B = $366 − 0.30 ($1,000 − $134) = $106.20.

TABLE 12.3 Determination of Food Stamp Benefits for a Family of 3 in 2002

Gross Income	Deduction	Benefits	Change in Benefits	Change in Gross Income	Benefit Reduction Rate
1	2	3	4	5	6
$ 0.0	$134.0	$366.0			
134.0	134.0	366.0	$ 0.0	$134.0	0.0
200.0	134.0	346.2	−19.8	66.0	−0.3
300.0	134.0	316.2	−30.0	100.0	−0.3
400.0	134.0	286.2	−30.0	100.0	−0.3
500.0	134.0	256.2	−30.0	100.0	−0.3
1000.0	134.0	106.2	−150.0	500.0	−0.3
1354.0	134.0	0.0	−106.2	354.0	−0.3

SOURCE: Author's calculations based on food stamp information from the Social Security Administration.

The break-even gross income (BEGI) can be determined by substituting BEGI for GI and solving equation 12.1 when T = $0. That is, equation 12.1 becomes $0 = BB − BRR (BEGI − D). Solving this equation for BEGI yields

(12.2) $$BEGI = (BB + D(BRR)) / BRR$$

Using equation 12.2, BEGI = $1,354 when BB = $366, D = $134, and BRR = 0.30.

Target Efficiency – The degree to which transfer program benefits are confined to the poor.

INFOTRAC
College Edition

Kewords: *food stamps, food stamp program*

http://www.infotrac-college.com

The break-even gross income is an indicator of the **target efficiency** of a transfer program—the degree to which program benefits are confined to the poor. In general, the lower the break-even gross income relative to the poverty threshold, the greater the target efficiency. In this case, the monthly break-even gross income of $1,354 is 115 percent of the 2002 monthly poverty threshold of $1,178 for a family of 3. Thus, some food stamps were provided to families that were not poor.

Food stamps provide both food and income support. The income support aspect of the food stamp program is reflected in its focus on monthly income, facilitating relatively quick changes in benefits when income changes. The food stamp benefit serves as a supplement to a family's other resources, usually Supplemental Security Income, TANF, and earnings. In at least 14 states, TANF families receive more each month in food stamps than in TANF cash.

Earned Income Tax Credit (EITC)

The federal tax code has provided an earned income tax credit (EITC) since 1975. As the label implies, this is a credit against income tax liability. To be eligible, the taxpayer must have dependents and a relatively low adjusted gross income (AGI—income from all sources less adjustments to income, such as excess employee business expenses and contributions to individual retirement accounts—IRAs). The credit is refundable; taxpayers may receive a credit even if their tax liability is less than the credit. Nine states have also adopted EITCs in the last 5 years.

For a worker with two or more children in 2001, the federal credit was

- 40 percent of AGI over a phase-in range from $0 to $10,020
- $4,008 for AGI over a maximum payment range from $10,020 to $13,090

INSIGHTS

WELFARE REFORM: THEN AND NOW

In 1996, President Clinton signed a Republican-sponsored bill, the Personal Responsibility and Work Opportunity Reconciliation Act, called "historic" welfare reform legislation by its proponents. Politics often makes strange bedfellows, but the nation's long record of failure to reduce its welfare rolls bred bipartisan support.

With the stroke of Clinton's pen, the federal government reduced its planned financial commitment to the poor and appeared to bow out of an active role in solving the nation's poverty problem. Planned federal expenditures for various poverty programs were reduced by $56 billion over the next 6 years. To ensure that this expenditure reduction target was met, the federal programs, Aid to Families with Dependent Children (AFDC) and Job Opportunities and Basic Skills (JOBS), were changed from entitlements to bloc grants to the states. The resulting program was renamed Temporary Assistance for Needy Families (TANF). Since its inception, each state has received a fixed sum of money each year from the federal government. The amount given to each state reflects what they received under the old AFDC program prior to passage of the 1996 law, and it has come with a lot of strings attached.

In order to continue to receive federal support, each family head on welfare must find work within 2 years or face the loss of benefits. A lifetime limit of 5 years was also imposed on all recipients of welfare benefits. Each state is also subject to new federal regulations as a condition of the federal bloc grant it receives. Within 5 years, at least 50 percent of a state's welfare recipients must be working at least 30 hours per week. To appreciate the magnitude of this task, consider that in 1995 only 3.7 percent of the women on AFDC worked full-time. In fact, to hit the federal target, the states had to find jobs for more than 2 million people.

By some estimates, up to one quarter of the nation's welfare recipients are virtually unemployable. Reasons include unwillingness to work, difficulty in retaining jobs, chronic mental or physical problems, lack of basic skills, and serious language deficiencies. The average recipient has the reading and math skills of a typical eighth-grader, and 30 percent have basic skills below the minimum of all women in the lowest-skill occupation (household workers).[a]

In spite of these difficulties, Wisconsin, which cut its welfare caseload by 44 percent between 1987 and

INFOTRAC
College Edition

Keywords: earned income tax credit, earned income credit

http://www.infotrac-college.com

■ $4,008 minus 21.06 percent of AGI over a phase-out range for AGI greater than $13,090

Thus, the benefit equation for the AGI phase-in range from $0 to $10,020 is

(12.3) $$B = 0.40 \,(\text{AGI})$$

For a taxpayer with AGI of $5,000, the EITC would be $2,000 (i.e., B = 0.4 × $5,000).

The benefit equation for AGI over the maximum payment range from $10,020 to $13,090 is

(12.4) $$B = \$4{,}008$$

Thus, for a taxpayer with AGI of $12,000, the EITC would be $4,008.

The benefit equation for the phase-out range of AGI greater than $13,090 is

(12.5) $$B = \$4{,}008 - 0.2106 \,(\text{AGI} - \$13{,}090)$$

where the phase-out rate of 0.2106 plays the same role as the benefit reduction rate in equation 12.1. Thus, a taxpayer with an AGI of $20,000 would have an EITC of $2,553 [i.e., $2,553 = $4,008 − 0.2106 ($20,000 − $13,090)]. The break-even EITC can be determined by solving equation 12.5 for AGI when B = $0. This occurs at AGI = $32,121 [i.e., $0 = $4,008 − 0.2106 ($32,121 − $13,090)].

INSIGHTS (continued)

1996, showed that the targets can probably be met. But the Wisconsin approach was to spend more, not less, on the poor, investing millions in job training, health benefits, childcare, and other support. The Wisconsin experience indicates, moreover, that preparing a person to leave the dole for good usually takes about 18 months of support—only then do the savings begin. Robert Haveman claims, in fact, that no inexpensive way exists to do the task right. For those who might think otherwise, he asks them to consider all the support that unaided families give their children before they finish their education and embark on the path to a meaningful career.[b]

Not all states wanted to or could afford to take the Wisconsin route. The federal bloc grants were sufficient for the first 4 years of the program, judging by the fact that not all available federal money was spent. That was not the case in 2001, however, nor is it expected to be in 2002, in the aftermath of a recent recession and substantial budget difficulties at the state level. Problems in funding TANF have appeared, especially in states with relatively high unemployment rates, few welfare recipients currently working, and large immigrant populations. The urge to simply deny welfare benefits may grow on the part of state officials in order to keep from cutting other state programs.

Howard Chernick and Andrew Reschovsky estimated that, over the course of several years, states would respond to the imposition of bloc grants for welfare by reducing benefit levels by about 20 percent.[c] They expected total welfare spending to decline by more than this as more stringent eligibility constraints and lower benefits reduced the number of beneficiaries. Fortunately, this "race to the bottom" did not occur. Apparently, as long as state economies are doing reasonably well, there is a willingness to provide funds to facilitate the transition from welfare to work. State support for TANF may be in harm's way in a recession, but it should not be assumed that reduced support suggests dissatisfaction with the aims of the 1996 welfare reform law.

[a]Robert Haveman, "From Welfare to Work: Problems and Pitfalls," *Focus* 18 (1), Special Issue (1996), 21–24.
[b]Ibid.
[c]Howard Chernick and Andrew Reschovsky, "State Responses to Bloc Grants: Will the Social Safety Net Survive?" *Focus* 18 (1), Special Issue (1996), 25–29.

Although it is obvious from the relatively high break-even EITC that the program provides benefits to families that are not poor, about a third of the EITC goes to families with incomes below the poverty line.

Temporary Assistance for Needy Families (TANF)

TANF is the nation's safety net program for low-income families. TANF is financed by the federal government through bloc grants to the states. The amount given to each state is based on how much the state received from the federal Aid to Families with Dependent Children (AFDC) program in the middle 1990s, just before TANF was established as a replacement for AFDC. Each state is allowed to design and implement its own TANF program, including benefit levels and criteria for eligibility. States must spend at least 75 percent of the amount they were spending from their own funds on AFDC in 1994.

TANF households are limited to 5 years of support in a lifetime, but states may impose shorter lifetime limits. TANF recipients are required to engage in work or "work activities," such as job training, looking for work, or schooling. States may refuse to provide additional benefits to families who have additional children while on TANF assistance.

The basic transfer varies widely, ranging from a low of $120 per month for a family of 3 in Mississippi in 2001 to a high of $577 per month in New York. States may disregard some of the income received from work in figuring monthly benefits. They may also treat certain expenses associated with the transition from welfare to work as disregarded income, such as childcare and transportation. The states vary greatly in the level and composition of disregards.

It is difficult to generalize about TANF, given the existence of 51 different programs (the 50 states and the District of Columbia). The Urban Institute has completed a study for 12 states, however, that examines how TANF affects household income and the benefit reduction rate as a family of 3 attempts to move from welfare to work.[2] The 12 states are Alabama, California, Colorado, Florida, Massachusetts, Michigan, Minnesota, Mississippi, New Jersey, New York, Texas, and Washington.

For these 12 states in 1998, the basic benefit (BB) averaged $459 a month, deductions or disregards (D) averaged $200 a month, and the benefit reduction rate (BRR) averaged 0.60. Table 12.4 shows how TANF benefits fall as gross income rises for these basic parameters of the program. As noted in the bottom line, TANF benefits become zero at a gross income of $965 a month—about 82 percent of the poverty line for a family of 3.

The underlying TANF benefit equation, for GI greater than or equal to D, is

$$(12.6) \qquad B = \$459 - 0.60 \, (GI - D)$$

When B = $0 and D = $200, GI = $965.

TANF + Food Stamps + EITC

Given the low break-even gross income for TANF payments, they are not large enough, even in conjunction with earnings, to elevate the typical working welfare family above the poverty line. Working welfare families are also eligible, however, for food stamps and the EITC.

Table 12.5 shows effective marginal tax rates for a family of 3, in which the family head earns progressively more income from work. Three sources of additional income from work are considered: moving

INFOTRAC College Edition
Keyword: *TANF*
http://www.infotrac-college.com

TABLE 12.4 Determination of TANF Benefits for a Family of 3 in 2002

Gross Income	Deduction	Benefits	Change in Benefits	Change in Gross Income	Benefit Reduction Rate
1	2	3	4	5	6
$ 0.0	$200.0	$459.0			
200.0	200.0	459.0	$ 0.0	$200.0	0
300.0	200.0	399.0	−60.0	100.0	−0.6
400.0	200.0	339.0	−60.0	100.0	−0.6
500.0	200.0	279.0	−60.0	100.0	−0.6
965.0	200.0	0.0	−279.0	465.0	−0.6

SOURCE: Authors' calculations based on information in Gregory Acs, Norma Coe, Keith Watson, and Robert Lerman, "Does Work Pay? An Analysis of the Work Incentives Under TANF," The Urban Institute, Occasional Paper Number 9, July 1998.

---

[2]Gregory Acs, Norma Coe, Keith Watson, and Robert Lerman, "Does Work Pay? An Analysis of the Work Incentives Under TANF," The Urban Institute, Occasional Paper Number 9, July 1998.

TABLE 12.5	Effective Marginal Tax Rates for a Family of 3 Receiving TANF, Food Stamps (FS), and EITC in Median State, 1997		
Transfer Package	From No Work to 20 Hours @ Minimum Wage	From 20 Hours to 35 Hours @ Minimum Wage	From 35 Hours @ Minimum Wage to 35 Hours @ $9.00 per Hour
TANF, FS, EITC	0.12	0.28	0.65

SOURCE: Gregory Acs, Norma Coe, Keith Watson, and Robert Lerman, "Does Work Pay? An Analysis of the Work Incentives Under TANF," The Urban Institute, Occasional Paper Number 9, Table 4, July 1998.

from a state of "no work" to 20 hours of work per week at the minimum wage, from 20 hours of work at the minimum wage to 35 hours of work per week at the minimum wage, and from 35 hours per week at the minimum wage to 35 hours per week at $9.00. The effective marginal tax rate is the change in welfare payments and net tax liability resulting from a change in earnings. In this example, welfare payments consist of TANF payments and food stamps, and net tax liability is taxes paid after the deduction of the EITC. Workers moving from no work to part-time work at the minimum wage experience a loss in TANF payments and food stamps and increased tax liabilities that exceeds the gain in the EITC by 12 cents per dollar of earnings. In the transition from part-time to full-time work at the minimum wage, the loss in TANF and food stamps and increased tax liabilities exceeds the gain in EITC by 28 cents per dollar of earnings. In the transition from full-time work at the minimum wage to full-time work at $9.00 an hour, the net effect is a loss of 65 cents for each additional dollar earned.

These results indicate that the package of benefits working welfare families receive is structured to penalize participants less for working part-time at low wages than for working full-time at higher pay.

This result is not surprising. Throughout the minimum wage earnings range, the BRRs for TANF and food stamps are largely offset by deductions for essential needs and the EITC. The increase in earnings from $5.15 an hour (the minimum wage) to $9.00 an hour places the worker in the range, however, where the EITC begins to decline, reducing its power to offset the BRRs for TANF and food stamps.

The bottom line is that the core antipoverty programs probably do not discourage heads of low-income households from working—at least, not at minimum wage jobs. They may, however, discourage them from seeking work at higher pay. Whether the net effect of these incentives increases or decreases poverty in the United States has not yet been determined by empirical studies.

INFOTRAC
College Edition

Keywords: *TANF and work incentives, EITC and work incentives*

http://www.infotrac-college.com

■ MAKING WORK PAY

AFDC was transformed into TANF in an attempt to increase the degree to which the poor work their way out of poverty by gainful employment. TANF does this largely by requiring single mothers to find a job and by establishing a lifetime limit on the duration of TANF benefits. This strategy will reduce the TANF rolls. It may be a necessary condition for reducing poverty among TANF clients, but it is unlikely to be sufficient, for three important reasons. First, the economy must generate enough jobs for TANF clients; no welfare program can do this. Second, TANF clients appear to need help in order to successfully transition from welfare to work, especially with childcare and medical expenses. Third, the jobs that TANF clients get must pay an adequate wage.

Unemployment Policy

Since the passage of the legislation establishing TANF, there has been more than a 25 percent increase in the percentage of single mothers who are working. Proponents of TANF claim this as an accomplishment of TANF. TANF was born, however, in the midst of the longest peacetime economic expansion in the last century so it is arguable whether the precipitating factor behind the rise in employment rates of single mothers was TANF or the economy.

One way to analyze the issue is to compare the pre-transfer poverty rate and the unemployment rate. The pre-transfer poverty rate is a measure of what the poverty rate would be without government transfers or, alternatively, a measure of the ability of low-income households to escape poverty primarily by working. As indicated in Figure 12.8, the pre-transfer poverty rate has hovered between 19 and 23 percent for the last two decades. As Figure 12.8 also shows, however, the variations that have occurred in the pre-transfer rate virtually mimic the unemployment rate over the same period. This relationship strongly suggests that the ability of the economy to generate jobs is an important determinant of the poverty rate. The persistence of the pre-transfer rate also suggests that the market can solve only *part* of the poverty problem by generating jobs.

Figure 12.9 shows that variations in the unemployment rate and variations in the poverty rates for selected groups were similar from 1979 to 1993–1994, but that poverty rates for blacks, Hispanics, and female-headed households fell more rapidly than the unemployment rate after 1994. This suggests that something other than the robust performance of the economy was at work, such as the new work requirements imposed

FIGURE 12.8 Pre-Transfer Poverty Rate and Unemployment Rate, 1979–2001

Variations in the pre-transfer poverty rate occur at about the same time, and in the same direction, as variations in the unemployment rate. This suggests, but does not prove, that the variations in the unemployment rate cause the variations in the poverty rate.

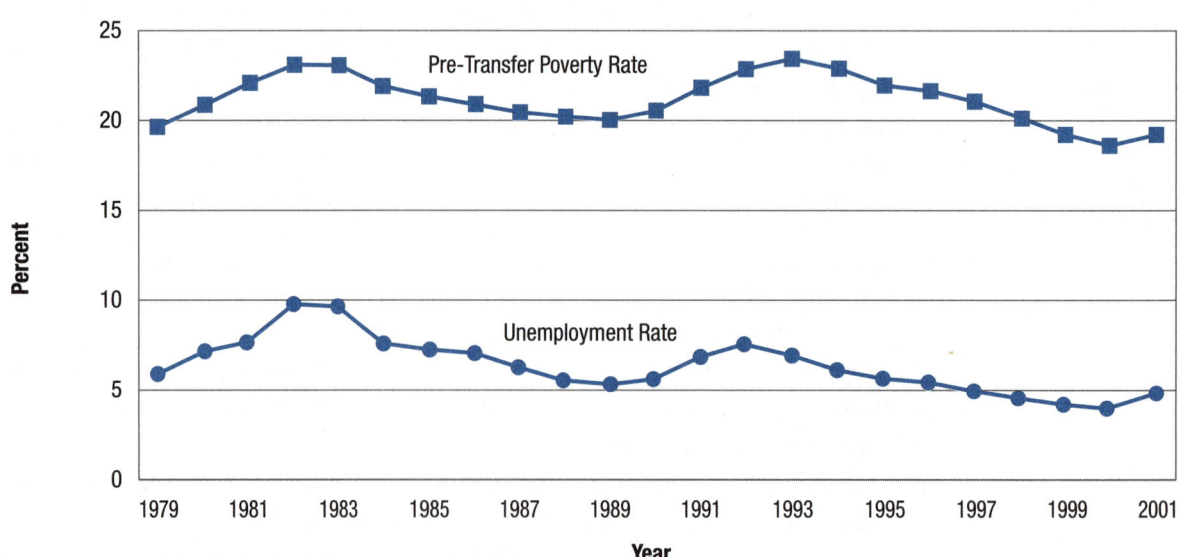

FIGURE 12.9 The Unemployment Rate and Poverty Rates for Selected Groups, 1973–2001

Variations in the poverty rate for female-headed families, blacks and Hispanics tend to match variations in the unemployment rate except during the last decade. The relatively more rapid decline in the poverty rate for these groups may reflect a generally tighter labor market in the 1990s.

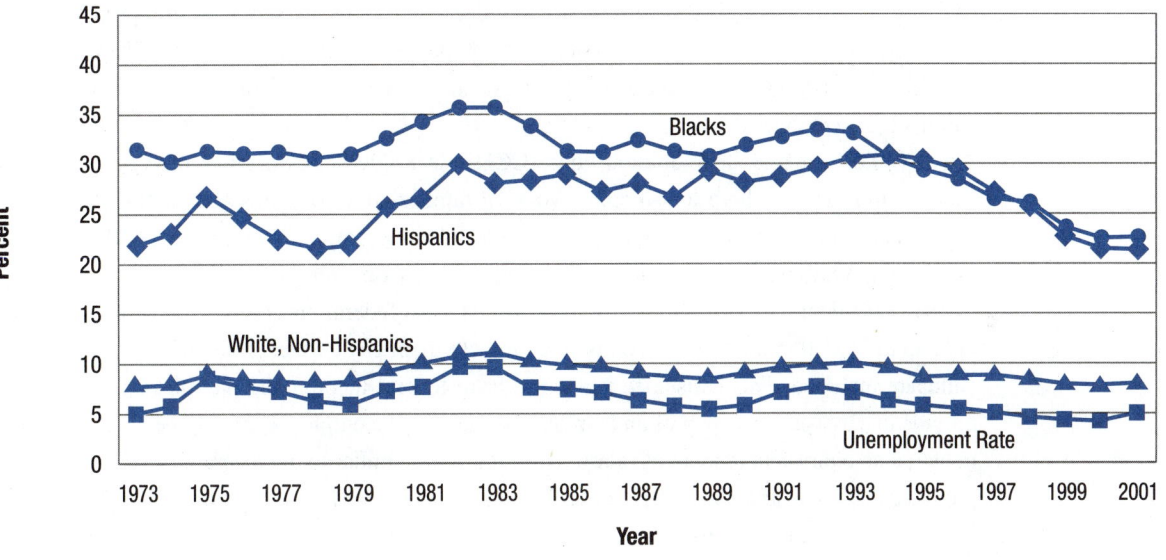

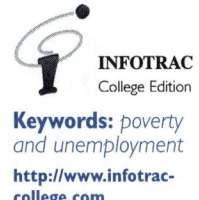

INFOTRAC
College Edition

Keywords: *poverty and unemployment*
http://www.infotrac-college.com

by TANF. The reduction in unemployment that occurred in the 1990s began, however, when the economy was already at a lower level of unemployment than it was at the beginning of the fall of the unemployment rate in the 1980s. The fact that labor markets were much tighter in the 1990s than in the 1980s may account for the relatively rapid gains for blacks, Hispanics, and female-headed households.

Researchers will eventually sort out the relative importance of the economic expansion and TANF in explaining the reduction in poverty recorded in the 1990s. In the meantime, it is hard to escape the conclusion that a robust economy is a precondition for the success of government efforts to reduce poverty by increasing income from earnings among low-income families. The macroeconomic policies designed to reduce unemployment that are discussed in Chapter 14 are rarely considered an antipoverty tool. Yet they may be vital in any effort to make lasting progress against the poverty of the working poor.

Childcare Assistance

Over 20 percent of the mothers who leave the TANF rolls for work return to TANF within 2 years. Although they encounter a variety of obstacles while working, two of the more prominent are the costs of childcare and loss of Medicaid benefits.

The lack of affordable childcare can significantly hinder the labor market participation of adults in poor families. Childcare in organized facilities is expensive. In the absence of subsidies, a single mother moving from welfare to work will find that childcare costs eat up a substantial share of her income; thus, childcare costs can reduce her incentive to work.

Both the federal government and state governments have programs that provide some form of childcare assistance. The most prominent of these are the Child and Dependent Care Tax Credit, the Child Care and Development Fund, the Dependent Care Assistance Program, and the Child Tax Credit.

Both the federal government and about half of the state governments have a Child and Dependent Care Tax Credit (CDCTC) that provides a credit against income tax liability for childcare expenses for working taxpayers. Eligible expenses for the federal credit are limited to $2,400 per child under age 13 for the first two children. The credit is equal to 30 percent of eligible expenses. The maximum credit is $1,440. The credit can be claimed by working heads of one-parent families or by families in which both parents are working.

The Child Care and Development Fund (CCDF) is a federal government bloc grant that provides the states with money to help low-income working families pay for childcare. States use this money, and sometimes some of their own money, to provide subsidies for childcare. Like TANF benefit payments, the amount available and conditions of eligibility vary from state to state.

The Dependent Care Assistance Program (DCAP) is a federal program that allows an employer to provide up to $5,000 in assistance to employees to help them pay certain child and dependent care expenses, childcare included. This assistance is exempt from federal income and payroll taxes. An employer may provide this assistance as part of an employee's salary or the employee may agree to receive the assistance in lieu of an equivalent amount of salary. This program is similar to the federal tax exemption for employer-provided health insurance (EPHI) described in Chapter 7. The DCA lowers the cost of child-related expenses to the employee just as the exemption for EPHI lowers the cost of health insurance. The value of the DCA to an employee depends on the employee's marginal tax rate. Thus, like the EPHI, the value of the exemption is greater for taxpayers at higher income levels.

The federal tax code also provides a Child Tax Credit (CTC) of up to $500 per dependent child under age 17 for single taxpayers with income of $84,000 or less, and for married taxpayers with income of $119,000 or less.

Although these programs reflect something of an awakening to the childcare problem, they have not significantly reduced the difficulty that the poor have in working and paying for childcare at the same time. The CDCTC provides virtually no benefits to the poor; less than 1 percent of the total credit goes to families with adjusted gross incomes less than $10,000. It is doubtful that the working poor can afford childcare in the first place. Moreover, in many poor two-parent families, only one parent works (probably because of high childcare expenses in many cases), making the family ineligible for the credit. To top it off, the CDCTC is not refundable. The CCDF is better targeted to the poor, but the amount available to a poor family depends on where it lives. DCA has been adopted by only a small percentage of employers and employees. The CTC is available to the working poor, but, by itself, will cover only 10 to 15 percent of the costs of childcare.

INFOTRAC
College Edition

Keywords: *childcare and poverty, childcare assistance*

http://www.infotrac-college.com

Proponents of these approaches to reducing poverty generally argue for an expansion of the amount of money provided the states by the CCDF. They also argue for making the CDCTC refundable and adjusting the maximum amount to cover a larger percentage of childcare expenses. Expanding the percentage of childcare expenses covered by the credit, as is often suggested, would largely help the non-poor and significantly increase program costs. It would be more target-efficient to provide vouchers for childcare services directly to the poor.

Medical Protection

Policy makers have long feared that the potential loss of Medicaid benefits deters families from leaving welfare for work. Accordingly, Congress, under the Family Support Act of 1988, required states to expand Medicaid coverage for up to 12 months for families leaving AFDC for work. Under waivers, some states have expanded coverage for up to 24 months.

The law that established TANF broke the direct link between eligibility for cash assistance and Medicaid. Families who leave TANF for work are still eligible, however, to receive 12 months of transitional medicaid assistance (TMA). Once transitional Medicaid benefits are exhausted, Medicaid now provides coverage to all children younger than 6 living in families with incomes below 133 percent of the federal poverty level. If the parent in a family of 3 worked 35 hours a week and earned $9 per hour, the family's earnings would still fall below 133 percent of the poverty threshold, and any children ages 6 and younger would still be covered by Medicaid. Given this coverage, it is unlikely that Medicaid regulations should deter a parent from moving from no work to at least a part-time job.

Keywords: *TANF and Medicaid*
http://www.infotrac-college.com

The bigger problem is that the parent would need to find health insurance for herself before the end of the first year of employment when TMA runs out. After a year of steady employment, she might get employer-provided health insurance or be able to purchase reasonably priced individual coverage. But there are many instances in which these options are not available. There is a need, then, for the expansion of health insurance coverage to adults in low-income families.

Minimum Wage

The working poor are poor partly because their wages are so low. Considerable interest exists, then, in policies that increase the rewards that workers realize from their efforts. The three most-discussed policies are (1) expanding the EITC, (2) raising the minimum wage and (3) providing wage subsidies. The features of the EITC have been examined previously. Here we concentrate on the minimum wage and wage subsidies.

The federal minimum wage is currently $5.15 per hour. Even full-time work at this wage cannot eliminate poverty. Thus, even though Congress increased the minimum wage in 1996, political pressure for further increases cannot be ruled out.

Although few people—economists included—question the motive for raising the minimum wage, economists note that a higher minimum wage generates unemployment. Empirical studies show that the minimum wage increases unemployment primarily in low-wage industries and among teenagers. Apparently, no studies have discovered a significant effect on the full-time working poor. Nevertheless, their employment prospects may be adversely affected because the working poor are concentrated in low-wage industries.

Keywords: *minimum wage and poverty, minimum wage and unemployment*
http://www.infotrac-college.com

A further difficulty with a higher minimum wage is its target inefficiency. A policy is target inefficient when a large share of the benefits it provides is distributed to individuals other than those whom the policy is designed to assist. Of the 3.9 million workers who earned the minimum wage when it was $3.35 per hour, less than 10 percent were household heads of poor families. A further increase in the minimum wage would probably go largely to nonpoor individuals as well.

Wage Subsidies

In a program of wage subsidies, low-wage workers would receive a subsidy for each hour worked. The wage subsidy would equal some percentage of the difference between a designated maximum wage and the worker's wage. To illustrate, suppose that the designated maximum wage is $8 per hour and the subsidy percentage is 50 percent. Someone earning a wage of $5.15 per hour would receive a wage subsidy of $1.43 per hour [= 0.5 ($8 − $5.15)], thus increasing the effective wage to $6.58 per hour. If a person were earning $6 per hour, the wage subsidy would be $1, and the effective wage would be $7.

A wage subsidy can be more effectively targeted to the poor than can the minimum wage, provided it is restricted to principal family workers. Unlike the minimum wage, a wage subsidy probably would not reduce employment. It does not require employers to pay workers more than they are worth as employees, as does the minimum wage. The prospect of the government picking up part of the tab for labor costs, however, may provide employers with an incentive to reduce the wage they are willing to pay.

Paradoxically, a wage subsidy does not guarantee increased work effort, as one would expect a higher effective wage to do. On the one hand, the higher wage increases the opportunity cost of leisure, inducing people to work more. On the other hand, a higher wage enables an individual to maintain a given standard of living by working less. The net effect is uncertain.

Labor Market Discrimination Policy

We have noted previously that poverty rates are higher in families headed by females, blacks, and Hispanics than in families headed by non-Hispanic whites. Such differences raise the specter of discrimination and suggest that poverty may be, at least to some extent, caused by discrimination.

The purpose of this section is to explore the relationship between poverty and discrimination. We begin by examining the extent of labor market discrimination. We then look more closely at possible links between labor market discrimination and poverty and briefly examine some of the implications of those linkages for public policy toward discrimination.

THE EXTENT OF LABOR MARKET DISCRIMINATION.
Table 12.6 contains data for full-time wage and salary workers in the third quarter of 2002, as compiled by the Bureau of Labor Statistics. The data are reported as earnings ratios—the ratios of the average earnings by individuals in selected groups to the average earnings of white males. They indicate, for example, that average white female earnings were 78 percent of those of the average white male, the average black male earned 73 percent of the average white male's pay, and so on.

Although these data represent only one recent year, the general pattern displayed here has persisted for as long as reliable data have been collected; that is, white males have always out-earned the other groups

INFOTRAC
College Edition

Keywords: *wage subsidy, wage subsidy and poverty*
http://www.infotrac-college.com

TABLE 12.6 Ratio of Average Earnings of Full-Time Workers in Selected Groups to Average Earnings of Full-Time White Male Workers, Third Quarter, 2002

Group	Ratio
White women	.78
Black men	.73
Black women	.63
Hispanic men	.64
Hispanic women	.55

SOURCE: Calculated from data in U.S. Department of Labor, Bureau of Labor Statistics, *Usual Weekly Earnings of Wage and Salary Workers: Third Quarter of 2002.*

represented in Table 12.6. As a general rule, differences in earnings reflect a host of factors that distinguish one worker, or group of workers, from another. Discrimination is one of these factors, but the list also includes education, training, work experience, occupation, location, hours worked, work effort, industry, marital status, verbal skills, intelligence, and others. The trick is to separate the effect of discrimination from the effects of all of the other factors that could explain differences in earnings.

Many economists have attempted to do this, using various empirical or statistical techniques. No reliable measure exists, however, for discrimination. Thus, using these approaches economists can determine only the share of observed earnings differentials that can be attributed to factors other than discrimination. The portion not explained by factors other than discrimination could be a result of discrimination; it is not possible to know for certain.

According to the data in Table 12.6, black males appear to pay a 27 percent earnings penalty for being black. Empirical studies indicate, however, that as much as half of this penalty can be attributed to differences in experience, education, location, veteran and marital status, number of children, and hours worked.[3] Thus, the earnings differential between black males and white males produced by discrimination is probably no larger than around 13 percent of white male earnings—and possibly less (some of the differential may be due to other omitted factors).

According to the data in Table 12.6, white females appear to pay a 22 percent earnings penalty for being female. Time on the job is interrupted more often and for longer periods of time for women than for men, however, primarily for child rearing. This puts women at a disadvantage in the labor market in terms of work experience. In fact, the evidence suggests that perhaps half of the observed pay difference between white women and men can be explained by differences in experience.[4] Another 5 to 6 percent of the 22 percent differential can probably be attributed to occupational segregation.[5] Simply put, women are overrepresented in relatively lower-paying clerical and service occupations and underrepresented in relatively higher-paying precision production, crafts, and repair occupations, and also among operators, fabricators, and laborers. Several studies have shown that at least half of the occupational wage differential is eliminated when job characteristics are held constant; that is, higher pay by occupation in part reflects compensation for less attractive working conditions.[6]

As was the case for differences between black peoples' earnings and white peoples' earnings, we do not know for certain how much of the differential in male and female earnings reflects labor market discrimination. Differences in work experience and working conditions, however, appear to account for more than half of the observed earnings differential. Some of the unexplained variation, moreover, can be attributed to pre–labor market discrimination—that is, to gender differences in socialization. Overall, it seems reasonable to infer that labor market discrimination produces no more, and possibly less, than a 10 percent difference in male and female earnings.

The data in Table 12.6 also suggest substantial earnings penalties for Hispanic males and females. The evidence indicates, however, that the wages of Hispanics living in the United States are only slightly below

---

[3] Francine Blau and Andrea Beller, "Black–White Earnings over the 1980s: Gender Differences in Trends," *Review of Economics and Statistics* 74 (1992), 276–286.

[4] Mary Corcoran, "The Structure of Female Wages," American Economic Association, *Papers and Proceedings* 68 (1978), 165–170.

[5] Erica Groshen, "The Structure of the Female/Male Wage Differential," *Journal of Human Resources* 26 (1991), 457–472.

[6] See, for example, David MacPherson and Barry Hirsch, "Wages and Gender Composition: Why Do Women's Jobs Pay Less?" *Journal of Labor Economics* 13 (1995), 426–471.

(5 percent at most) those of non-Hispanic whites after adjusting for differences in education, age, hours worked, marital status, region, fluency in English, and place of birth.[7] Lack of fluency in English has been an especially important factor keeping Hispanics out of higher-paying professional and managerial occupations.

This quick review of the evidence indicates that unexplained differences in pay do exist between apparently identical white and black workers, between male and female workers, and between Hispanic and non-Hispanic white workers. The unexplained pay differences appear no larger, however, than the 13 percent penalty paid by blacks, and they are probably less for both females and Hispanics. These differences should be viewed, moreover, as upper limits; they may represent the effects of discrimination, but they may also result from unmeasured differences in productivity.

These results are not surprising when viewed in the context of economic theory. Wage discrimination can arise from the unwillingness of employers to hire members of a certain race, ethnic group, or gender. Such choices, however, inevitably require employers to pass up more productive employees in favor of less productive employees. This will elevate costs of production above the level achievable in the absence of discrimination and eventually drive discriminating firms from the market. Thus, economic theory suggests that normal market forces will tend to moderate the extent of labor market discrimination.

HOW MUCH DOES LABOR MARKET DISCRIMINATION CONTRIBUTE TO POVERTY?

Frankly, we doubt that discrimination has much to do with poverty for several reasons. First, although poverty rates are higher among blacks, Hispanics, and female-headed families, 48 percent of the poor live in families headed by white males. Thus at the very least, nearly half of the poor are not subjected to labor market discrimination.

Second, some evidence indicates that the earnings differential between white males and others is smaller for lower-paying occupations than it is for higher-paying occupations. For example, women's wages were 88 percent of men's wages in service occupations (except private household and protective) in the third quarter of 1996, according to the data in U.S. Bureau of Labor Statistics, *Usual Weekly Earnings of Wage and Salary Workers: Third Quarter of 1996*. This is a significant fact because the poor will be working, if at all, in the lower-paid occupations. In fact, evidence of discrimination against the so-called average worker is irrelevant in determining the contribution of discrimination to poverty in the United States.

Third, evidence suggests that the earnings differential between white males and others is smaller among individuals with less education—that is, among individuals more likely to be poor. For example, in 1993, the black–white earnings ratio for full-time male workers with less than a high school education was 0.97.[8] Discrimination seems to be a bigger factor in creating wage differences among more-educated workers competing for higher-paying jobs than among less-educated workers competing for lower-paying jobs.

Fourth, poverty rates have persisted even though earnings differentials have narrowed over time. We have already presented evidence of the failure of the poverty rate to fall appreciably since 1975. During the same period, however, female–male earnings ratios (white female/white male, black female/black male, Hispanic female/Hispanic male) in the United States rose from 0.58 to 0.78 for whites, from 0.75 to 0.86 for blacks, and from 0.68 to 0.86 for Hispanics.[9]

---

[7] Leonard Carlson and Caroline Swartz, "The Earnings of Women and Ethnic Minorities, 1959–1979," *Industrial and Labor Relations Review* 41 (1988), 530–546.

[8] R. K. Filer, D. S. Hammermesh, and A. S. Rees, *The Economics of Work and Pay*, 6th ed. (New York: HarperCollins, 1996), 552.

[9] Ibid.

Fifth, the earnings penalty imposed by discrimination would be too small in most cases to cause poverty—that is, to lower a family's income from above the poverty threshold to below the poverty threshold. In other words, if the income lost because of discrimination were somehow restored to the victims of discrimination, it would not be enough in most cases to raise their income above the poverty threshold.

Whether such a restoration would be sufficient to raise a family's income above the poverty threshold depends on (1) how close the family's income is to the poverty threshold, (2) how much of that income is derived from wages, and (3) how large the restoration would be (or the size of the discrimination penalty). It is impossible to apply a combination of all of these factors to the poverty data short of a lengthy study, but we can suggest an upper limit by using some general characteristics of the poverty population.

The typical poverty family in the United States has between three and four people. The poverty thresholds in 2001 for families of three and four were $14,128 and $18,104, respectively. Assuming a discrimination penalty of 13 percent, the largest possible penalty would have been $2,353 (= 0.13 × $18,104). But this is the penalty for a worker whose entire income is from wages and whose hourly wage is at least $9 per hour. Most poor workers do not do nearly this well in the labor market. This computation is based, moreover, on a penalty percentage (13 percent) that our previous discussion suggests is too high for many victims of discrimination. Let us assume, however, that every female-headed, black, or Hispanic family with an income below the poverty threshold suffers from a discrimination penalty of $2,000. If even this much income were given to each family in these three categories, only about 17 percent of the families would be elevated above the poverty threshold.

POLICY IMPLICATIONS. Much of the preceding discussion suggests that labor market discrimination is not a significant source of poverty in the United States. Thus, even if policies aimed at reducing labor market discrimination, such as affirmative action, were successful in reducing discrimination, they would have little effect on the poverty rate. A stronger link is probable between poverty and occupational segregation, and some hope that reducing the latter will also lower the poverty rate. So far, however, we have failed to accomplish this through public policy. The one approach that has been suggested most often is paying workers according to pay scales based on comparable worth, or inherent job requirements. This approach has failed, however, to generate much political support in the United States.

INFOTRAC
College Edition

Keywords: *poverty and discrimination*

http://www.infotrac-college.com

■ Making Fathers Pay

The increase in female-headed families has focused attention on the poor record of absent fathers in supporting the children they leave behind. Nearly one of every two children born today will become eligible for child support by an absent parent at some point before reaching age 18. Currently, however, courts award child support to only 58 percent of eligible parents. The process of setting the award is expensive and contentious. The size of the award as a percentage of the noncustodial parent's income varies greatly. Awards are extremely difficult to collect; fewer than 30 percent of awardees receive the full amount awarded on a regular basis.

Even if welfare parents were fully employed, many of them could earn no more than their annual welfare grant. It seems unreasonable in view of this fact to expect these parents to be totally self-supporting. One way to reduce poverty without creating total dependency is to supplement, rather than replace, the earnings of single parents who have custody of minor children. Some of this supplement must come from public assistance, but some can (and should) come from private child support.

Child Support Assistance

Child support is an important strategy in making work pay because it increases and stabilizes the income of low-income working adults. Combined with a mother's earnings, regular child support is a key income support that can help move families out of poverty. To the extent that fathers have the ability to pay, strengthened child support enforcement means that more low-income families will be able to leave welfare and sustain low-wage employment, and those who are already working will benefit from a higher standard of living.

To this end, the federal government has moved to develop new enforcement tools and to compel states to strengthen their individual child support programs. In addition, some states have introduced pass-through legislation, which allows for a portion of the noncustodial parent's payment to go directly to custodial parents who are recipients of cash assistance.

The first step in this direction at the federal level was the establishment of the Child Support Enforcement program, which created a bureaucracy to enforce private child support obligations for all AFDC recipients and for others on request. Legislation passed in 1984 required the states to adopt expedited procedures for obtaining child support orders from the courts, to establish child support guidelines for the courts, and to initiate automatic paycheck withholding for child support beginning one month after failure to pay.

The Family Support Act of 1988 stiffened federal resolve on this issue. Starting in November 1990, states were required to provide for immediate wage withholding for all cases handled by the Office of Child Support Enforcement. Starting in 1994, withholding was required for all support orders.

The Personal Responsibility and Work Opportunity Reconciliation Act of 1996 (P.L.104-193) included strict child support enforcement and paternity establishment policies. The law requires state agencies operating the federal child support program to use a range of enforcement tools. States failing to comply with these requirements are penalized by deductions from their TANF bloc grants. The law also provides for the development of a National Directory of New Hires, which requires employers to report all new hires to child support enforcement authorities; the development of a Financial Institutions Data Match Program, which requires all states to enter into agreements with financial institutions to match the records of parents who are delinquent in their child support obligations; and the application of the Uniform Interstate Family Support Act, which seeks to consolidate and simplify the process of collecting child support across state lines.

States may apply penalties for failure to pay child support obligations. Penalties vary by state but they include revoking licenses, imposing work requirements on delinquent parents, denying food stamps to delinquent parents, withholding federal income tax refunds, and denying passports. The 1996 legislation also strengthened penalties for TANF recipients who failed to cooperate in child support collection activities and established new performance goals for paternity establishment.

These federal initiatives along with state and local pressure have helped increase child support collections. The federal and state child support enforcement program collected $15.5 billion in fiscal year 1999, nearly doubling the amount collected in 1992. The federal government collected over $1.3 billion in overdue child support from federal income tax refunds for tax year 1998, an 18 percent increase over the previous year and a 99 percent increase since 1992.

Child Support Assurance

Some believe that government should go beyond simply collecting money from absent fathers; that child support *assistance* should become child support *assurance*. In a child support assurance (CSA) system, a family would be guaranteed a certain amount of child support regularly and on time each month. To fund the guaranteed payment, the state would collect the child support owed by the noncustodial parent. If it were unable to collect, the state would still provide child support to the family at the guaranteed level and continue to pursue collection. If a low-income noncustodial parent paid support but the amount were less than the guaranteed level, then the state would supplement that parent's payment up to the guaranteed level.

To see how CSA would work, suppose that a state determines that the minimum amount required to meet a child's basic needs is $250 a month and establishes this as the guaranteed payment. It also recognizes that absent fathers are likely to be low-wage employees and determines that they should be required to pay no more than 20 percent of their monthly after-tax income in child support. A mother with one child would receive $250 a month. The amount the absent father would pay would depend on his income. If he were employed full-time at the minimum wage, his monthly income after the Social Security payroll tax would be $794 (167 hours per month at $5.15 per hour, minus 7.65 percent for the payroll tax). The government would collect $159 a month from him for child support, supplement this amount with $91 from tax collections, and pay $250 a month to the custodial parent.

INFOTRAC
College Edition

Keywords: *child support assistance, child support assurance*

http://www.infotrac-college.com

New York has run a CSA-like program for more than a decade. The New York Child Assistance Program (CAP) began as a demonstration project to test CSA as an alternative to welfare. The project was judged to be so successful that any county that wishes to do so can now offer CAP as an alternative to TANF. The success of CAP persuaded the California legislature to authorize a similar demonstration project beginning in 2003. Minnesota has a grant from the U.S. Department of Health and Human Services (HHS) to design a CSA project in the context of TANF. HHS has recently solicited proposals from states for additional feasibility studies and demonstration projects.

Summary

This chapter begins by developing an historical perspective on the poverty problem. The primary focus is on the official measure of poverty and the official poverty rate. The official poverty rate declined significantly during the 1990s, nearly reaching an all-time low in 2000. Even then, 11.3 percent of the population lived in a family with income below the official poverty threshold. The elderly have a poverty rate below the official rate, but people living in black, Hispanic, and female-headed households experience poverty at a much higher rate than the average.

In the absence of government transfers, around 20 percent of the population would normally live in poverty. Government cash transfers normally provide enough income to the poor to reduce the poverty rate by 7 to 8 percentage points. Accounting for taxes increases the poverty rate, but accounting for noncash transfers more than offsets the effect of taxes. In fact, the poverty rate after all transfers (cash and noncash) and taxes are accounted for is usually 2 to 3 percentage points below the official poverty rate.

The three most common sources of support for poverty families, other than income from work, are food stamps, the EITC, and TANF payments. Each of these is a means-tested transfer. None is generous enough, by itself, to elevate very many families above the poverty threshold. Benefits from both the food stamp and TANF programs fall as income from work increases above a deduction for essential needs, raising the possibility that the loss of benefits discourages people from working. The EITC increases as AGI increases from $0 to $10,020 and remains constant from $10,020 to $13,090, encouraging work. Beyond that level, the EITC falls as AGI increases, discouraging work. The net effect of the three programs together probably does not discourage the poor from working at low wages but may adversely affect the transition from low to higher wages.

The establishment of the TANF program is a clear signal that Congress wants to increase the percentage of income that the poor receive from work. Accordingly, this chapter reviews several programs or policies designed to achieve that objective.

An examination of the relationship between unemployment and poverty suggests that policies to reduce unemployment are an important part of any strategy to reduce poverty.

Data gathered to date on people who return to TANF after leaving TANF for work indicate that there is a need for more effective childcare assistance. It is believed that TANF clients are reluctant to leave TANF for work because of a fear that they will lose Medicaid benefits. This may be the case for adults, but not for children.

Increases in the minimum wage are often mentioned as a means of increasing the rewards from work. These suggestions are unlikely to come from economists, who emphasize the unemployment-creating effects of the minimum wage and its poor target efficiency.

Wage subsidies are also mentioned as a means of increasing the rewards from work. They find greater favor with economists because they may encourage work and can be made target efficient.

The relatively high incidence of poverty among blacks, Hispanics, and female-headed households raises the possibility that poverty may be reduced further by policies that discourage labor market discrimination. This prospect arises because of the higher wages received by non-Hispanic white males relative to non-Hispanic females, black males, black females, Hispanic males, and Hispanic females. We conclude, however, that labor market discrimination accounts for very little of actual wage differentials, and that dramatic reductions in labor market discrimination would have a small impact on poverty. Therefore, fighting poverty through policies to reduce labor market discrimination is not a promising route.

The final programs we consider are government efforts to assist single mothers with collecting child support payments from absent fathers. Efforts to date have resulted in significant increases in the amount of child support collected. Some believe, however, that the government should assure or guarantee child support payments while making further efforts to get fathers to pay.

Key Terms

Poor person
Official poverty threshold
Gross money income
Poverty rate
Pre-transfer poverty rate
Means-tested transfer
Basic benefit
Deduction for essential needs
Benefit reduction rate
Break-even gross income (BEGI)
Target efficiency

Review Questions

1. Currently, in-kind transfers are not included in the official measure of resources that individuals have available to meet their basic needs. Do you believe these transfers should be included? Defend your answer.
2. "Instead of enacting new transfer programs to eliminate poverty, we should concentrate on policies that would reduce unemployment." Do you agree or disagree with this statement? Defend your answer.
3. What government program or programs has (have) been the most effective poverty-reducer(s)? Justify your answer.
4. The average female earned 78 percent as much as the average male in 2001. Explain why this comparison overstates the degree of labor market discrimination against females.

5. Evidence indicates that there is some labor market discrimination against blacks, Hispanics, and females, but such discrimination has little to do with poverty. Explain why.

6. Congressperson Smith argues that government transfers have worked to alleviate poverty. Congressperson Jones argues that these transfers have worked to increase poverty. Who is correct? Defend your answer.

7. Using the benefit equations for food stamps and TANF, solve the following problem for each program considered separately.

    Suppose the basic benefit is $500 per month and the deduction for essential needs is $150. What is the benefit that will be received?

8. Suppose that a person works 1,800 hours a year at the minimum wage. How large will this person's EITC be? Assume that total income from wages and AGI are equal. Show your calculations.

9. Repeat question 8 for someone who earns $10 per hour. Assume again that total income from wages and AGI are equal.

10. Congress is currently debating the pros and cons of the various methods of increasing the earnings of the poor: increasing the minimum wage, expanding the earned income tax credit, and granting wage subsidies. You are called before the House to testify. Briefly outline your views on these various programs.

11. The prospect of paying childcare expenses and the fear of losing Medicaid are both barriers to leaving TANF for work. Which of these two is really the bigger barrier? Explain.

12. What factors would you consider in designing a child support assurance program? Why?

Economic Issues on the Internet

– Making Wages Work—http://www.makingwageswork.org
This Web page focuses on providing information on the various approaches to child support enforcement and provides information on the evaluations of those approaches. It includes research, state and federal programs, expert contact, and general publications that look at the various dimensions of child support enforcement

– U.S. Census Bureau, *Census Historical Poverty Tables*—http://www.census.gov/hhes/www/censpov.html
These tables are the best source of data on various measures of poverty in the United States.

– U.S. Census Bureau, *Poverty in the United States: 2001*—http://www.census.gov/hhes/www/poverty.html
Proctor, Bernadette, and Joseph Dalaker. *Poverty in the US: 2001*. U.S. Census Bureau. Current Population Reports P60-219, September 2002. The latest in the Census Bureau's annual survey of poverty in the United States.

– U.S. Department of Agriculture, Food and Nutrition Information Center—http://www.nal.usda.gov/fnic
For information on the Food Stamp Program.

CHAPTER 13

Tracking the Macroeconomy

Outline:

Gross Domestic Product (GDP)
GDP's Components
   Consumption
   Gross Investment
   Government Purchases
   Net Exports
Nominal GDP, Real GDP, and the GDP Deflator

The Nation's Economic Performance
Determining the Nation's Output and Price Level
   Aggregate Demand
   Aggregate Supply
   Aggregate Demand and Supply Interaction

This chapter introduces many of the concepts used to measure the economy's performance. As measures of the economy's performance, they provide helpful information to households, firms, and policy makers, which is why the news media bombard us with data based on these concepts.

Information on the performance of the economy can improve decision making for households, firms, and policy makers. With regard to households, suppose a person is considering quitting his job to search for a better one. If the economy is performing well, his chances of success are better than if the economy is performing poorly. Similarly, suppose a graduating college senior is considering attending graduate school to obtain her master's degree. If the economy is performing well with good jobs relatively plentiful, she may wish to postpone her graduate education. On the other hand, if it is performing poorly, with good jobs relatively scarce, she may wish to continue her education.

With regard to firms, suppose you wish to start your own firm. If the economy is performing well, you have a better chance of succeeding than if it is performing poorly. Similarly, suppose a firm is considering increasing its output and employment. If the economy is performing well, this may be a wise decision. If it is performing poorly, however, increasing output and employment may be unwise.

Finally, information on the economy's performance is important to policy makers, who compare the nation's economic performance with both its past performance and that of other countries. If the economy is performing poorly, policy makers can try to enact policies to improve its performance. If the economy is performing well, no policy action is necessary. Instead, policy makers can concentrate on taking credit, whether it is deserved or not.

The performance of the economy is always an important issue at election time. Indeed, it can be decisive in presidential elections. Most experts believe that President Bush lost his bid for reelection in 1992 primarily because of the economy's mediocre performance. They also believe that President Clinton's bid for reelection in 1996 was successful partly because of the economy's strength. You can be sure that in the 2004 presidential elections, politicians will attempt to focus our attention on the economy, making it a major issue. Understanding the validity of the political claims made about the economy is crucial in casting an informed vote.

In addition to discussing various concepts used to measure the economy's performance, this chapter introduces aggregate demand–aggregate supply analysis. As we shall see, aggregate demand and aggregate supply determine the nation's output and price level. Because aggregate demand and supply change over time, output and the price level also change.

Because they determine output and the price level, aggregate demand and supply are important in determining the nation's unemployment and inflation rates. We consider unemployment in Chapter 14 and inflation in Chapter 15. Aggregate demand and supply also help to determine the nation's budget and balance of payments surpluses and deficits. We cover the federal government's budget in Chapter 16 and the nation's balance of payments in Chapter 18.

■ GROSS DOMESTIC PRODUCT (GDP)

Gross Domestic Product (GDP) – The market value of all final goods and services produced in the economy over the relevant time span, usually one year.

Final Goods – Goods purchased (or available to be purchased) for final use.

Intermediate Goods – Goods purchased for resale or for use in producing other goods.

In judging the nation's economic performance, measuring the nation's output is clearly important. Various measures of output exist, but the one most frequently cited is gross domestic product. **Gross domestic product (GDP)** is the market value of all final goods and services produced in the economy over a year.

Only final goods and services are counted in GDP. **Final goods** are those purchased (or available to be purchased) for final use. By definition, final goods are not used to produce other goods. In contrast, **intermediate goods** are purchased for resale or for use in producing other goods. Automobiles and bread are final goods because they are typically purchased for final use. Steel and flour are intermediate goods because they are used in the production of other goods.

If all goods—intermediate and final—were counted as part of GDP, part of the nation's output would be counted twice. To illustrate, part of the steel industry's output is used in the production of automobiles. If the outputs of both the steel and automobile industries were included in GDP, the part of the

INSIGHTS

MEASURED GDP AND THE UNDERGROUND ECONOMY

Over the years, many economists have become concerned that measured GDP may drastically underestimate the nation's level of economic activity because of the existence of an underground economy. The *underground economy* consists of economic activity that avoids official detection and measurement. The activities are either inherently illegal or not reported to avoid taxes, detection by the Immigration and Naturalization Service, or for other reasons. Examples of the former include illegal drug trafficking, bookmaking, and prostitution. Examples of the latter include the nondeclaration of receipts by owners or managers of restaurants, bars, and various retail establishments, the failure to report income from tips and casual or part-time work, particularly by people who would lose such benefits as unemployment compensation, welfare payments, or, in the case of illegal migrants, residency. Although an underground economy has always existed, studies show that its share of GDP has increased substantially since 1960. Estimates for Germany, Sweden, and the United States put its share in 1960 at 2 percent, 3.5 percent, and 2 percent, respectively. Although by its nature the exact size of underground economy is difficult to measure, the evidence is overwhelming that it increased after 1960. By 1995, comparable estimates of its size were 13.2 percent for Germany, 16 percent for Sweden, and for the United States, 9.5 percent. It is not surprising that the underground economy is larger in Germany and Sweden than in the United States because these countries' economies are more heavily taxed and regulated.[a] In general, higher payroll and other taxes and increased regulations of all types have caused the underground economy to grow.

The incentives to avoid taxes and to evade costly regulations existed in 1960, just as they do today. Even if the incentives had not increased substantially, underground economic activity might still have increased. The incentive to "cheat" the government is offset by the disincentive offered by potential punishment and perhaps more importantly by the disincentive created by a guilty conscience. If one can convince himself that everyone else is doing it, or herself that government regulates and taxes unfairly, then the disincentive is reduced. It is likely that the increased size of the underground economy is due both to increased taxes and regulations and to less concern about obeying the law.

The existence of a large underground economy implies that a disproportionate share of the tax burden is carried by those not participating in the underground economy. If those who participate in the underground economy paid taxes, tax rates could be reduced significantly without loss of tax revenue. In addition, the underground economy may be less efficient. The various activities must be carried out covertly, which often precludes the most efficient means of production and distribution. Also, most or all transactions must be conducted with cash, which is disadvantageous in many instances. These factors, however, are offset to some degree by the lack of government regulation and by the greater flexibility, including part-time and at-home work, in the underground economy.

Various suggestions have been made to reduce the size of the underground economy. These include reducing tax rates, making the tax system more equitable, devoting more resources to law enforcement, and increasing the penalties for participating in the underground economy. It must be recognized, however, that with existing tax rates (or even lower ones) a strong economic incentive exists for people to participate in the underground economy. Moreover, given its shadowy nature, it is difficult to reduce its size by devoting more resources to law enforcement. For these reasons, a large underground economy is likely to persist for the foreseeable future.

---

[a]Bruno Frey and Friedrich Schneider, "Informal and Underground Economy," Orley Ashenfelter: *International Encyclopedia of Social and Behavioral Science*, Bd. 12 Economics, Amsterdam: Elsevier Science Publishing Company, 2001.

INFOTRAC
College Edition
Keywords: underground economy
http://www.infotrac-college.com

---

steel industry's output that is used in the production of automobiles would be counted twice, first as part of the steel industry's output and second as part of the automobile industry's output. The same would happen if the outputs of both the flour and bread industries were included in GDP. To prevent multiple counting of the nation's output, only final goods and services are included in GDP.

GDP is an estimate of the market value of all final goods and services. It is the sum of the market value of each final good or service. The sum must be in value, or dollar, terms because it is not meaningful to add the physical units of the various goods and services. In estimating the nation's output, it would, for example, make no sense to add together the numbers of automobiles and toothbrushes produced because automobiles are worth much more than toothbrushes.

The GDP summation must be in value, or dollar, terms, but it need not be in terms of market prices. The market price of each good or service is used, however, because it represents the value that people place on that good or service, making market prices less arbitrary than any other set of prices. Even with the use of market prices, however, accurate comparisons the nation's output in different time periods are difficult.

Finally, GDP is a measure of production, not sales. All goods produced during the year are counted in GDP, regardless of whether they are sold or added to business inventories. Suppose firms produced $100 billion worth of automobiles in 2003, but they sold only $90 billion worth. The automobile industry's contribution to GDP in that year would be $100 billion, with $90 billion sold and $10 billion added to business inventories.

As defined, GDP excludes many transactions. It excludes purchases of used or secondhand goods because these goods were counted when they were produced. It also excludes financial transactions such as the purchase of stocks or bonds because they involve an exchange of financial assets, not production.

■ GDP'S COMPONENTS

GDP has four parts: personal consumption expenditures, gross private domestic investment, government purchases of goods and services, and net exports of goods and services.

Consumption

Personal Consumption Expenditures – Household purchases of durable and nondurable goods and services.

Personal consumption expenditures (consumption) consist of household purchases of durable goods (such as automobiles, appliances, and furniture), nondurable goods (such as food, clothing, and cigarettes), and services (such as medical and dental care, legal advice, and hairstyling). Of these expenditures, most are for nondurable goods and services. The distinguishing characteristic of these goods and services is that they last only a short time. Durable goods, on the other hand, last much longer; even so, their contribution to GDP is recorded when they are produced rather than over their life span.

As shown in Table 13.1, personal consumption expenditures account for almost 70 percent of GDP. Thus, they make up the largest part of GDP by a wide margin. As a percentage of GDP, these expenditures vary little from year to year; they are a relatively stable component of GDP.

Gross Investment

Gross Private Domestic Investment – Firms' purchases of new equipment, purchases of all newly produced structures, and changes in business inventories.

Gross private domestic investment (gross investment) is (1) the purchases of new equipment by firms, (2) the purchases of all newly produced structures, and (3) changes in business inventories. Thus, a firm's purchase of a new lathe or drill press is treated as investment. The construction of a factory is also classified as investment. The construction of residential housing, including apartment houses and homes, is treated as investment. Finally, changes in business inventories are included in investment because GDP is a measure of production, not sales. As discussed earlier, suppose that firms produced $100 billion worth

TABLE 13.1 Gross Domestic Product and Its Components, 2001 (Billions of Current Dollars)

GDP has four components: personal consumption expenditures, gross private domestic investment, government purchases of goods and services, and net exports of goods and services. The largest component by a wide margin is personal consumption expenditures.

			Percent of GDP
Gross domestic product		$10,082.2	69.3
Personal consumption expenditures		6,897.0	15.7
Gross private domestic investment		1,586.0	18.4
Government purchases of goods and services		1,858.0	−3.5
Net exports of goods and services		−348.9	10.3
Exports of goods and services	1,034.1		13.7
Imports of goods and services	1,383.0		

SOURCE: U.S. Department of Commerce, Bureau of Economic Analysis, *Survey of Current Business* 79 (Washington, DC: Government Printing Office, August 2002), D–2.

INFOTRAC
College Edition

Keywords: consumption and GDP, GDP and economic analysis

http://www.infotrac-college.com

Capital Stock – The nation's accumulated stock of structures, producers' durable equipment, and business inventories.

of automobiles in 2003 but sold only $90 billion worth in that year. If the automobiles were sold to households, the $90 billion would be counted as consumption and included in GDP. Because $10 billion worth of automobiles were not sold, business inventories increased by that amount. This $10 billion increase in inventories is investment and is part of GDP. It must be included to measure accurately the contribution of the automobile industry to GDP in 2003.

So far, we have discussed gross private domestic investment, or gross investment. Part of gross investment merely replaces structures and equipment that have worn out or been destroyed during the period. To determine the part of gross investment that adds to the existing stock of structures and equipment, we subtract consumption of fixed capital from gross investment to obtain *net private domestic investment*, or net investment. *Consumption of fixed capital* consists of depreciation, an estimate of the deterioration of the nation's structures and equipment, and an allowance for accidental damage to them. To illustrate, gross investment was $1,574.6 billion in 2001. Of this amount, $1,110.7 billion was used to replace structures and equipment that had deteriorated or been destroyed during the year, yielding net investment of only $463.9 billion, obtained by subtracting consumption of fixed capital from gross investment.

Net investment is an important concept because it implies a change in the nation's capital stock. The nation's **capital stock** is its accumulated stock of structures, producers' durable equipment, and business inventories. Gross investment is the amount of newly produced structures and producers' durable equipment plus changes in business inventories. Because part of gross investment simply replaces structures and equipment that wear out or are destroyed during the period, only net investment adds to the nation's capital stock.

The capital stock is important because it is a major determinant of the nation's productive capacity. All other things equal, an increase in the nation's capital stock (positive net investment) implies an increase in the nation's productive capacity. With the increase, the economy will be capable of producing more goods and services, as discussed in Chapter 1.

In 2001, gross investment accounted for approximately 16 percent of GDP. In contrast, net investment was only about 5 percent. In addition to constituting a smaller proportion of GDP than consumption, investment also exhibits greater fluctuations from year to year.

Government Purchases

Government Purchases of Goods and Services – The purchases of federal, state, and local governments.

Government purchases of goods and services are simply the purchases of federal, state, and local governments.[1] These purchases include procurement of military hardware; construction of dams, highways, and schools; and payment for the services of accountants, teachers, and other government employees. State and local governments account for most governmental purchases.

In 2001, government purchases accounted for approximately 18 percent of GDP—a surprisingly low percentage. The primary reason for the low percentage is that *government transfer payments* are excluded from GDP.

Government transfer payments include Social Security benefits, Medicare and Medicaid payments, and unemployment compensation. Like purchases of goods and services, transfer payments involve payments by government; unlike them, the government receives no goods or services in return. Because transfer payments involve no production of goods and services, they are excluded from GDP. Although excluded, these payments are obviously important.

Net Exports

Net Exports of Goods and Services – The amount by which foreign spending on domestically produced goods and services is greater (or less) than domestic spending on goods and services produced abroad.

Exports – Goods and services produced in this country and purchased by foreigners.

Imports – Goods and services produced abroad and bought by persons in this country.

Net exports of goods and services is the difference between exports of goods and services and imports of goods and services. **Exports** are produced in this country and purchased by foreigners. **Imports** are produced abroad and purchased by persons in this country. Because GDP is a measure of domestic production, exports are included in GDP. Consequently, exports are added to consumption, gross investment, and government purchases to arrive at GDP. Because imports are produced abroad, they are excluded from GDP. They are subtracted from consumption, gross investment, and government purchases because those components include the purchases of goods produced both here and abroad. Suppose a household purchases a new car made in Japan. The purchase is counted as consumption. Similarly, suppose a firm purchases machine tools made in Sweden. The purchase is included in gross investment. Because the various components of GDP include both domestic and foreign production, imports must be subtracted from those components to guarantee that only domestic production is included in GDP. If the subtraction was not made, the nation's output of goods and services would be greatly overstated.

Rather than treating exports and imports separately, we take the difference between them to arrive at net exports. This concept may be interpreted as the amount by which foreign spending on domestically produced goods and services (exports) is greater (or less) than domestic spending on goods and services produced abroad (imports). This difference may be either positive or negative. In recent years, exports have been less than imports. The difference, therefore, has been negative.

In 2001, exports of goods and services totaled $1,034.1 billion, approximately 14 percent of GDP. Imports of goods and services were $1,383.0 billion, about 14 percent of GDP. Net exports of goods and services equaled a minus $348.9 billion, obtained by subtracting $1,383.0 billion from $1,034.1 billion.

■ NOMINAL GDP, REAL GDP, AND THE GDP DEFLATOR

GDP is calculated by adding the market values of various goods and services. Unfortunately, quantities *and* prices change over time. Because GDP reflects changes in both quantities and prices, it is difficult to compare the output of goods and services in different years by comparing GDP in different years.

---

[1] With regard to government purchases, the U.S. Department of Commerce distinguishes between government consumption and investment. For convenience, however, we shall refer to government purchases rather than government consumption expenditures and gross investment.

To illustrate the problem and its resolution, consider the following example. We will assume, for simplicity, only one good (good A) and two years (2003 and 2004). The relevant quantities and prices are shown in Table 13.2.

As indicated in the table, 6 million units of good A were produced in 2003. The price per unit was $1,000. With only one good, the nation's GDP in that year was $6 billion, obtained by multiplying 6 million (the number of units produced) by $1,000 (the price per unit). In contrast, 6.3 million units were produced in 2004 at a price per unit of $1,100. GDP in that year was therefore $6.93 billion, obtained by multiplying 6.3 million by $1,100.

A GDP of $6 billion in 2003 and $6.93 billion in 2004 seems to indicate that the nation's output of goods and services increased by about 15 percent. Thus, a person might conclude, incorrectly, that 15 percent more goods and services were available to members of society in 2004 than in 2003. Table 13.2 shows that the number of units produced increased from 6 million to 6.3 million, which is only a 5 percent increase in the number of goods available in 2004.

Why does GDP overstate the increase in output? It does so because most of the increase in GDP is due to the increase in good A's price. In 2003, the price was $1,000. In 2004, it was $1,100. This 10 percent increase in price and the 5 percent increase in quantity adds to the increase in GDP.

This example illustrates the problem. To show the resolution, we first construct a price index and then divide, or deflate, GDP by the appropriate price index number to compensate for the change in the price level.

Price Index – A measure of the price level for a given period relative to the base period.

A **price index** measures the price level for a given period relative to the base period. By definition, it is the price for the period in question divided by the price in the base period multiplied by 100:

$$\text{Price index} = \frac{\text{Price for period in question}}{\text{Price in base period}} \times 100$$

To explain this index, we start by selecting a base period; let's select 2003. We first compute the price index for the base period. In this case, the price for the period in question, the numerator, is the same as the price in the base period, the denominator: $1,000. This is because the base period is the period in question. Therefore, the price index for the base period (2003) is 100. We can now compare the price level in other periods with the base period, and we do so according to the preceding formula. To illustrate, the price of good A was $1,100 in 2004 and $1,000 in 2003 (the base period), so we have $1,100 divided by $1,000 equal to 1.1. Following the formula, we multiply this by 100, making the 2004 price index number 110. Because the price index for the base period is standardized to be 100, it is easy to see that the price level in 2004 is 110 percent of the price level in 2003 (the base period).

The price index numbers for 2003 and 2004, along with the data from Table 13.2, are shown in Table 13.3. Note that GDP from column 4 of Table 13.2 now appears as nominal GDP in column 5 of Table 13.3.

TABLE 13.2 Quantities, Prices, and GDP: A Simple Example

This table shows that output increased by 5 percent and price increased by 10 percent from 2003 to 2004. Consequently, GDP increased by about 15 percent.

Year	Number of Units Produced	Price per Unit	GDP
2003	6 million	$1,000	$ 6 billion
2004	6.3 million	1,100	6.93 billion

TABLE 13.3 Deflating GDP

By deflating, or dividing, nominal GDP by the price index, we obtain real GDP. Adjusting for the price change indicates that output increased by 5 percent from 2003 to 2004.

Year	Number of Units Produced	Price per Unit	Price Index	Nominal GDP	Real GDP
2003	6 million	$1,000	100	$ 6 billion	$ 6 billion
2004	6.3 million	1,100	110	6.93 billion	6.3 billion

Nominal GDP — GDP measured on the basis of current, or nominal, prices.

Nominal GDP is GDP measured on the basis of current, or nominal, prices. In this example, nominal GDP in 2003 is calculated using 2003 prices; nominal GDP in 2004 is calculated using 2004 prices.

As we have seen, prices may change. If they do, nominal GDP gives a false impression of the nation's output of goods and services. To correct for price changes, we can divide, or deflate, nominal GDP by the price index. The result is real GDP. In equation form, the relationship is

$$\text{Real GDP} = \frac{\text{Nominal GDP}}{\text{Price index (in decimal form)}}$$

Note that we divide nominal GDP by a price index written as a decimal rather than as a percentage. Conversion from percentage to decimal form requires moving the decimal point two places to the left or, what amounts to the same thing, dividing by 100.

Real GDP — GDP measured on the basis of constant prices; reflects only changes in quantities.

Real GDP is GDP measured on the basis of constant prices. To calculate real GDP in 2003, we divide nominal GDP in 2003 ($6 billion) by the price index number for that year (100). Before making the calculation, however, we convert the 100 (percentage form) to 1.00 (decimal form). Thus,

$$\text{Real GDP} = \frac{\$6 \text{ billion}}{1} = \$6 \text{ billion}$$

Real GDP in 2003 is $6 billion, the same as nominal GDP.

To calculate real GDP in 2004, we repeat the procedure. We divide nominal GDP in 2004 ($6.93 billion) by the price index number, in decimal form, for that year (1.10). Thus,

$$\text{Real GDP} = \frac{\$6.93 \text{ billion}}{1.10} = \$6.3 \text{ billion}$$

INFOTRAC College Edition
Keywords: *real gross domestic product*
http://www.infotrac-college.com

Real GDP in 2004 is $6.3 billion, which is less than nominal GDP in that year. This occurs because by dividing nominal GDP in 2004 by the price index for that year, we have eliminated the effect of higher prices on GDP. Recall that the price of good A increased from $1,000 in 2003 to $1,100 in 2004, a 10 percent increase. By dividing nominal GDP in 2004 by 1.10—the price index (in decimal form) in 2004—we have calculated GDP *as if* price had not changed.

By adjusting nominal GDP in this manner, we obtain real GDP, a measure of the nation's output that reflects only changes in quantities. (Nominal GDP reflects changes in both quantities and prices.) Because real GDP reflects only changes in quantities, real GDP is a better measure of the nation's output of goods and services than is nominal GDP.

In our example, we assumed only one good.[2] To deflate nominal GDP, a price index for *all* final goods and services must be used. This index is called the implicit price deflator for GDP, or the GDP deflator. The relationship between nominal GDP, real GDP, and the GDP deflator is

$$\text{Real GDP} = \frac{\text{Nominal GDP}}{\text{GDP deflator}}$$

GDP Deflator – A weighted average of the prices of all final goods and services produced in the economy.

The **GDP deflator** is a weighted average of the prices of all final goods and services produced in the economy. It is a weighted average because the various goods and services are not of equal importance. At present, the GDP deflator has 1996 as its base. Nominal GDP, real GDP, and the GDP deflator for 1979 to 2001 are shown in Table 13.4.

TABLE 13.4 Nominal GDP, Real GDP, and the GDP Deflator; 1979–2001

Nominal GDP and the GDP deflator increased annually from 1979 to 2001. Except for decreases in 1980, 1982, 1991, and 2001, real GDP also increased. Real GDP may be obtained by dividing nominal GDP by the GDP deflator.

Year	Nominal GDP (Billions of Current Dollars)	Real GDP (Billions of 1996 Dollars)	GDP Deflator
1979	2566.4	4912.1	52.2
1980	2795.6	4900.9	57.0
1981	3131.3	5021	62.4
1982	3259.2	4919.3	66.3
1983	3534.9	5132.3	68.9
1984	3932.7	5505.2	71.4
1985	4213	5717.1	73.7
1986	4452.9	5912.4	75.3
1987	4742.5	6113.3	77.6
1988	5108.3	6368.4	80.2
1989	5489.1	6591.5	83.3
1990	5803.2	6707.9	86.5
1991	5986.2	6676.4	89.7
1992	6318.9	6880	91.8
1993	6642.3	7062.6	94.0
1994	7054.3	7347.7	96.0
1995	7400.5	7543.8	98.1
1996	7813.2	7813.2	100.0
1997	8318.4	8159.5	101.9
1998	8781.5	8508.9	103.2
1999	9274.3	8856.5	104.7
2000	9824.6	9224	106.9
2001	10082.2	9214.5	109.4

SOURCE: U.S. Department of Commerce, Bureau of Economic Analysis, *Survey of Current Business* (Washington, DC: Government Printing Office, August 2002).

---

[2]With many goods and services, it becomes more difficult to calculate real GDP and the GDP deflator. For a discussion of the U.S. Department of Commerce's procedures, see J. Steven Landefeld, Robert P. Parker, and Jack E. Triplett, "Preview of the Comprehensive Revision of the National Income and Product Accounts: BEA's New Featured Measures of Output and Prices," *Survey of Current Business* 75 (July 1995), 31–38.

■ THE NATION'S ECONOMIC PERFORMANCE

Over the years, the U.S. economy has performed well. From 1929 to 2001, the nation's output of goods and services increased at an average annual rate of 3 percent. At first glance, a 3 percent growth rate appears modest, but it implies that output doubles every 24 years.

Despite its upward trend, output does not grow steadily; in fact, it sometimes declines. The 1930s saw dramatic changes in GDP. With the advent of the Great Depression, U.S. output decreased at a 7 percent rate from 1929 to 1933. As the nation recovered from the depression, it increased at a 10 percent rate from 1933 to 1941. Since 1960, GDP has continued its long-run upward trend accompanied by sharp short-run fluctuations. Figure 13.1 shows GDP on an annual basis from 1960, with GDP measured on the left axis. Although the upward-sloping line may give an impression of steady growth, this impression is misleading. The jagged line in the figure shows the annual percentage growth rate, with the growth rate measured on the right axis. Examining the jagged line, it is easy to see that during some years, output grew relatively rapidly, while in others, it grew less rapidly or even declined. Calculations for some longer periods show that real GDP grew at a 1 percent rate from 1988 to 1991, but that it grew at a 4 percent rate from 1982 to 1988 and at a 3.6 percent rate from 1991 to 2000.

As measured by real GDP, the nation's level of economic activity has fluctuated throughout its history. The recurring fluctuations in the level of economic activity are **business cycles**. A business cycle has four phases: expansion, peak, contraction, and trough (see Figure 13.2). During the **expansion phase**,

Business Cycles – Recurring fluctuations in the general level of economic activity.

Expansion Phase – The business cycle phase during which real GDP, employment, productive capacity use, and profits increase while unemployment falls.

FIGURE 13.1 REAL GDP: 1960–2001

Real GDP, as measured in 1996 prices, increased substantially from 1960–2001, as can be seen in the relatively smooth line, with its measure on the left vertical axis. It did not, however, increase steadily. As the jagged line with its measure on the right vertical axis clearly shows, real GDP increased more rapidly in some years than in others. This jagged line also shows the declines in real GDP (negative growth) in 1970, 1974, 1975, 1980, 1982, 1991, and 2001.

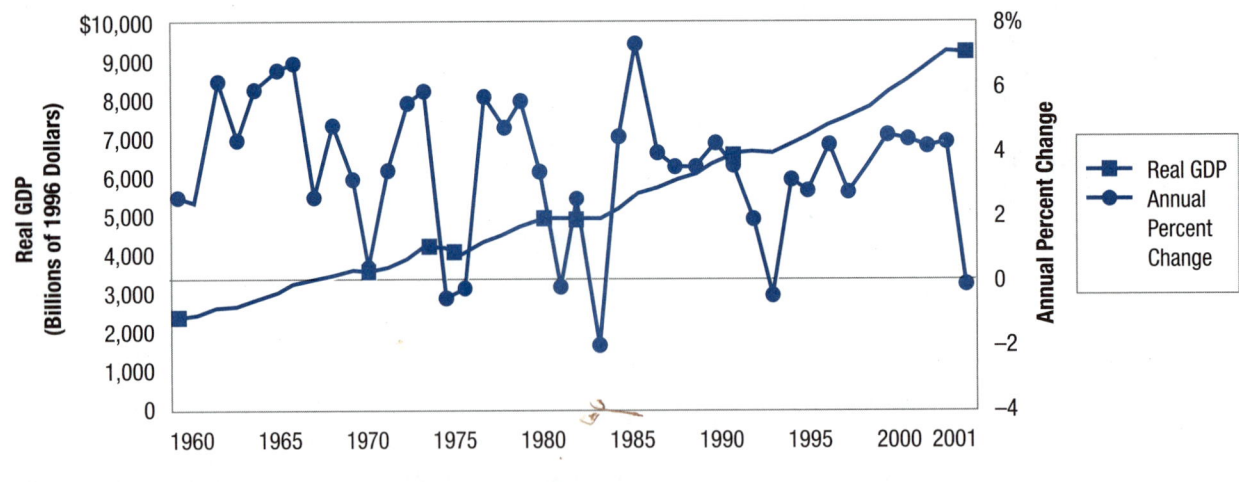

SOURCE: U.S. Department of Commerce, Bureau of Economic Analysis, *Survey of Current Business* (Washington, DC: Government Printing Office, August 2002).

FIGURE 13.2 Phases of the Business Cycle

Although real GDP increases over time, it does not increase steadily. Instead, it grows rapidly, reaches a peak, falls, reaches a trough, and repeats the cycle. This figure shows the four phases of the business cycle: expansion, peak, contraction, and trough.

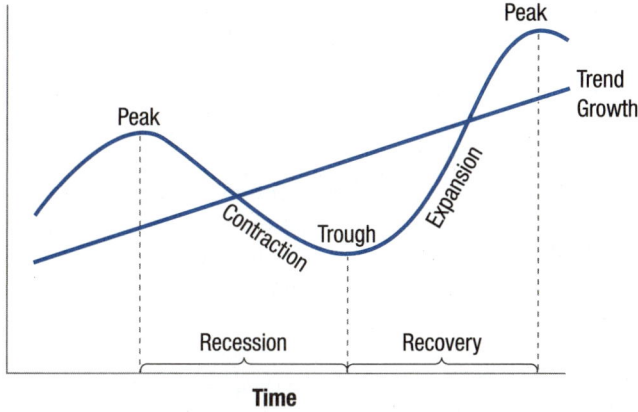

Peak –
The highest point in the business cycle, during which real GDP is at a maximum and employment, profits, and productive capacity use are high.

Contraction Phase –
The phase of the business cycle during which real GDP, employment, productive capacity use, and profits decrease while unemployment rises.

Trough –
The lowest point of the business cycle, during which real GDP is at a minimum and employment, profits, and productive capacity use are low.

real GDP increases relatively rapidly. As it does, employment increases and the unemployment rate decreases. Also, a higher percentage of the nation's productive capacity is used and profits increase. As the unemployment rate falls and a higher percentage of productive capacity is used, however, wages and prices start increasing or increase more rapidly.

Eventually, a **peak** occurs. At the peak, real GDP is at a maximum. Employment, capacity use, and profits are high; unemployment is low. With unemployment low and capacity use high, wages and prices will increase more rapidly, and inflation may become a problem.

After the peak, the economy enters the **contraction phase**. During the contraction, real GDP decreases. With the decline, employment decreases and the unemployment rate rises. The percentage of the nation's productive capacity used falls. Profits also fall. With the increase in the unemployment rate and reduction in capacity use, wages and prices increase less rapidly or fall.

Eventually, a **trough** will be reached. At the trough, GDP is at its low point. Employment, capacity use, and profits are low. The unemployment rate, however, is high. With high unemployment and low capacity use, there is little or no upward pressure on wages and prices. Indeed, wages and prices may fall.

The expansion phase is sometimes called a *recovery*. The contraction phase is often referred to as a *recession*. When a recession is particularly severe and prolonged, it is called a *depression*. The Great Depression of the 1930s is an example of the latter. Although we have had a number of recessions since the 1930s, none is in the same class as the Great Depression, when output decreased by about 30 percent from 1929 (peak) to 1933 (trough) and the unemployment rate increased from 3.2 percent to 24.9 percent.

Although each business cycle (as measured from peak to peak or trough to trough) has the same four phases, they *differ* in duration and intensity. Historically, contractions have averaged 18 months in length with the longest contraction lasting 65 months and the shortest lasting only 6 months. Expansions have averaged 35 months, with the longest lasting 120 months and the shortest, 10 months. The most recent

>
>
> ## INSIGHTS
>
> ### REAL GDP AND SOCIAL WELFARE
>
> Real GDP measures an economy's or society's production of final goods and services in a year at market value. Is it also a measure of social welfare? Or to ask a slightly different question, if GDP increases, can we conclude that a society is better off? With regard to the first question, the answer is no. GDP has nothing to say about many important elements of the good life—freedom, equality of opportunity, justice, and human development. With regard to the second question, the answer is a qualified yes. Most economists and perhaps most people would agree that an increase in goods and services available to a society's members will increase social welfare, assuming that no individual has an associated decrease in goods and services.
>
> As recent terrorist acts have emphasized, not all measured final goods and services in GDP result in people having a greater availability of goods and services. According to the national accounts, terrorists destroyed over $16 billion of physical assets on September 11, 2001, in New York City. Their destruction did not affect measured GDP in 2001 and will never be a direct offset to GDP. (It enters the national accounts as consumption of fixed capital, affecting net domestic product.) The cost of dealing with the crisis—rescue, cleanup, and so on—amounted to at least $11 billion, which in turn was part of GDP for 2001. Although it was part of GDP, no one would suggest that because the terrorist act caused this economic activity that it made people better off.
>
> One effect of the terrorist threat is to increase the demand for security. In response, the federal government is expected to increase its spending on defense and security from 3.1 percent of GDP to 3.4 percent. This 10 percent increase will be supplemented by a substantial increase in private spending for security from its base of about $40 billion. This increased spending will draw resources away from other uses in the public and private sectors. Just as GDP makes no adjustment for environmental pollution or resource depletion, it makes no adjustment for reduced well-being because of the perception of a greater risk of terrorist activity. Just as the economic activity associated with cleaning up the environment contributes to GDP, so does the economic activity associated with enhanced security measures.[a]
>
> Furthermore, GDP does not include a significant amount of production of final goods and services. The output produced by the family outside the scope of the market is not included in GDP. This includes all aspects of managing a household, child care, do-it-yourself

contraction, or recession, began in March 2001, and as we write its official end has not been determined. The previous contraction began in July 1990 and ended in March 1991. At 8 months, it was shorter than average; it was also milder than most. The longest expansion in American economic history began in March 1991 and continued to March 2001. From 1991 through 2000, GDP grew at 3.6 percent per year, while unemployment fell to 4 percent and inflation remained low.

Like the long-run trend, cyclical movements in real GDP have important implications for the economy. In addition to representing fluctuations in the nation's output, they have implications for unemployment and inflation. As the economy enters the contraction phase, unemployment increases and becomes a major problem at or near the trough. As the economy recovers, unemployment decreases. As the recovery continues, however, the price level may rise. Indeed, as the economy approaches the peak, inflation may become a major problem.

Both the long-run trend and cyclical movements of real GDP are determined by aggregate demand and aggregate supply. Because of their importance, we shall devote the rest of this chapter to a careful development of these concepts.

Keywords: *United States economic conditions*

http://www.infotrac-college.com

INSIGHTS (continued)

projects, gardening, and so on. In principle, this production could be included in GDP, but assembling accurate data would be very costly. Because these activities do not go through the market, market prices would have to be estimated. Because this production is not included in GDP, an increase in GDP can occur without any increase in production. If people went to restaurants for all of their meals, GDP would increase. If we assume that they purchase the exact meals that would have been prepared at home, no increase in production occurs, even though GDP increases. Over time, a larger and larger percentage of meals have been procured in the market, which lends an upward bias to measured GDP.

Real GDP has other defects as a social welfare measure. In particular, it provides no information as to the distribution of that output. Suppose GDP increased by, say, 5 percent. We might conclude that society's welfare increased. Assume, however, that the increase in GDP was accompanied by a significant redistribution of income from the poor to the rich. In particular, suppose households with above-average incomes received large increases in income and those with below-average incomes experienced large decreases. Given the reduction in incomes for those at lower income levels, we would probably conclude welfare decreased, not increased.

GDP is a measure of the nation's output of goods and services, and social welfare depends, in part, on this output. Social welfare also depends on leisure. Over time, the length of the workweek has declined. In 1900, the average nonagricultural workweek was more than 50 hours. Today, it is about 40. In addition, we now have longer paid vacations and more holidays. The increase in leisure is widely regarded as having a positive effect on welfare. As before, suppose GDP increases by 5 percent. Suppose, however, that the increase in output is accomplished by significantly lengthening the workweek. Given the reduction in leisure, it is not clear that the increase in output is an improvement in social welfare.

GDP is a measure of the market value of goods and services produced in a year. Although an increase in GDP, other things equal, makes members of society better off, other things may not be equal. Consequently, GDP is an imprecise measure of social welfare. On its own terms, GDP provides a useful measure of market production in an economy. It is an element of social welfare, but it must be supplemented by many other factors.

[a] "Economic Consequences of Terrorism," Ch. 4, *OECD Economic Outlook* 71 (June 2002).

Keywords: *economic aspects of terrorism*
http://www.infotrac-college.com

■ Determining the Nation's Output and Price Level

Over time, the nation's output increases, but not steadily. It increases more rapidly in some years than in others. Similarly, the price level increases, but not steadily. As we shall see, aggregate demand and aggregate supply determine the nation's output and price level. By determining output and the price level, aggregate demand and supply also help to determine the nation's unemployment, inflation, and output growth rates. Finally, aggregate demand and supply help to determine the nation's budget and balance of payments surpluses or deficits. Because aggregate demand and supply are extremely important in determining the nation's economic performance, we must master those concepts.

Aggregate Demand

Aggregate Demand Curve — A curve showing the quantity of final goods and services (real GDP) that will be purchased at each price level (GDP deflator).

An **aggregate demand curve** shows the quantity of final goods and services (real GDP) that will be purchased at each price level (the GDP deflator). As discussed earlier, the quantity of final goods and services purchased can be divided into the amounts spent for consumption, investment, government purchases, and net exports.

MOVEMENTS ALONG AN AGGREGATE DEMAND CURVE. An aggregate demand curve, AD in Figure 13.3, like the demand curve for a single product, slopes downward and to the right. As the price level (as measured by the GDP deflator) decreases, the quantity of final goods and services purchased (as measured by real GDP) increases.

Both the demand curve for a single product and the aggregate demand curve are negatively sloped, but for different reasons. As you may recall from Chapters 2 and 4, nominal income and the prices of other goods and services are assumed constant in deriving the demand curve for a single product. As the price of the product falls, the product becomes less expensive relative to other goods and services. Consequently, individuals buy more of it.

This explanation is *not* appropriate for the derivation of the aggregate demand curve. When the price level falls, the prices of *all* final goods and services fall. Consequently, we cannot argue that more will be purchased because one product is becoming less expensive relative to other goods and services.

The aggregate demand curve owes its negative slope to three effects:

- The effect of the price level on real balances and hence consumption
- The effect of the price level on interest rates and hence investment and consumption
- The effect of the price level on exports and imports

The first effect has to do with the impact of the price level on financial assets that have fixed dollar values. These assets include currency and checking account balances. As the price level rises, their purchasing power declines. As the real value of these assets erodes, households can be expected to reduce the real amount that they spend on consumption. To illustrate, suppose you have a balance of $1,000 in currency and in your checking account. If the price level is 100, the real value of these money balances is $1,000. If the price level were to double (to 200), the real value would be only $500. If your real money

FIGURE 13.3 The Aggregate Demand Curve

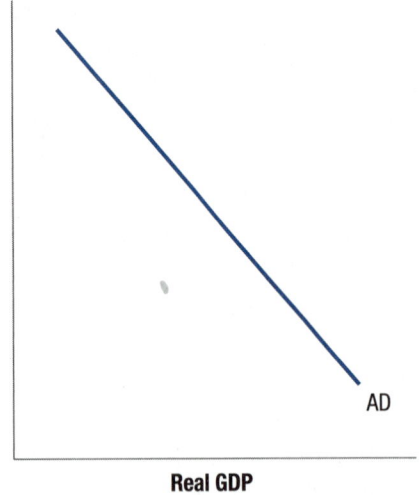

An aggregate demand curve shows the quantity of final goods and services (real GDP) that will be purchased at each price level (the GDP deflator). The aggregate demand curve is negatively sloped.

Real Balance Effect – The change in consumption caused by a change in the price level that changes the real value of financial assets that have fixed dollar values.

balances decline in this way, you are likely to reduce the real amount that you spend on consumption. We call the effect of changes in real balances on consumption the **real balance effect**.

As we have just seen, an increase in the price level tends to reduce consumption—one component of aggregate demand—through its impact on real balances. The increase in the price level and decrease in real balances also have an impact on aggregate demand through the interest rate. When a reduction in real money balances occurs, households and firms may attempt to maintain their spending by borrowing more. As they borrow more, interest rates rise. The increase in interest rates increases the cost of borrowing. As a result of this **interest rate effect**, firms will invest less in new plants and equipment. Higher interest rates also discourage housing construction and purchases of new automobiles and other consumer durables. Thus, an increase in the price level tends to reduce investment and consumption—two components of aggregate demand—through its impact on interest rates.

Interest Rate Effect – The change in consumption and investment caused by a change in the price level that ultimately causes interest rates to change.

The third and final effect of the price level on aggregate demand is through exports and imports. As discussed earlier, exports and imports are important to the U.S. economy. The amounts that the United States exports and imports depend, in part, on the price level in the United States relative to the price level abroad. Suppose the price level in the United States rises and the price level abroad is constant. U.S. exports will be less competitive in world markets and will therefore decline. Similarly, as the price level rises in the United States relative to the price level abroad, households and firms will buy fewer goods produced in this country and more goods produced abroad because goods produced here are now relatively more expensive. Like the reduction in exports, this increase in imports reduces net exports and, therefore, aggregate demand. We can conclude that an increase in the U.S. price level results in the **foreign trade effect** that tends to reduce net exports, a component of aggregate demand, by increasing the price of U.S. products relative to foreign products.

Foreign Trade Effect – The change in net exports caused by a change in the price level that causes a change in the relative desirability of domestic and foreign goods and services.

SHIFTS IN THE AGGREGATE DEMAND CURVE. We have just explained why the aggregate demand curve is negatively sloped. We now consider the causes of shifts in the aggregate demand curve. One factor is changes in the degree of optimism (or pessimism) among households and firms. Suppose households were to become more optimistic about the future state of the economy. They may, as a result, spend more of their incomes on consumption. If they do, consumption will increase, and because consumption is a component of aggregate demand, aggregate demand will increase. This increase in aggregate demand is shown in Figure 13.4 as a shift in the aggregate demand curve from AD_0 to AD_1. With the shift, aggregate demand is now greater at each price level. A similar shift occurs if firms become more optimistic about the future state of the economy. The only difference is that if firms become more optimistic, investment increases.

Fiscal Policy – Use of government purchases and taxes to achieve full employment and other economic goals.

The aggregate demand curve will shift for other reasons. For our purposes, we focus on changes caused by changes in the nation's fiscal and monetary policies. **Fiscal policy** is the use of government purchases and taxes to achieve full employment and other economic goals. Government purchases are one component of aggregate demand. If government purchases increase, the aggregate demand for goods and services increases and the aggregate demand curve, as shown in Figure 13.4, shifts to the right. If taxes are reduced, households find that their after-tax income, or disposable income, is higher. Because of the increase in their disposable income, households will increase their consumption. Because consumption is one component of aggregate demand, the aggregate demand for goods and services rises and the aggregate demand curve shifts to the right.

FIGURE 13.4 A Shift in the Aggregate Demand Curve

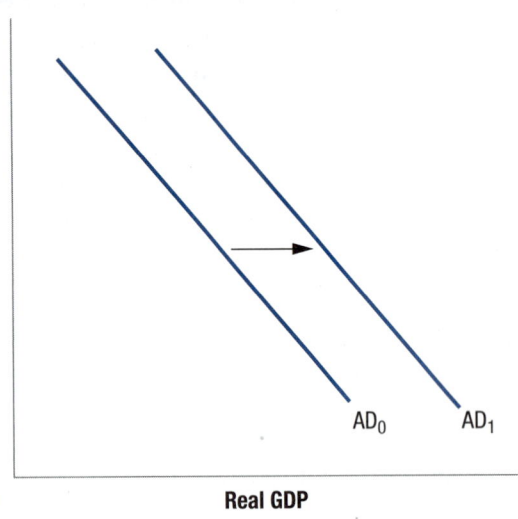

An increase in aggregate demand is shown by a rightward shift in the aggregate demand curve. The aggregate demand curve may shift to the right because policy makers are pursuing an expansionary fiscal or monetary policy.

As demonstrated, both an increase in government purchases and a decrease in taxes cause aggregate demand to increase. Thus we define an expansionary fiscal policy as an increase in aggregate demand brought about by an increase in government purchases, a decrease in taxes, or some combination of the two.

A decrease in government purchases or an increase in taxes has the opposite effect on aggregate demand. Both reduce aggregate demand, thereby causing the aggregate demand curve to shift to the left. Thus we define contractionary fiscal policy as a decrease in aggregate demand brought about by a decrease in government purchases, an increase in taxes, or some combination.

A change in the money supply also affects the aggregate demand for goods and services. For the purposes of this chapter, we define the nation's **money supply** as its currency (including coins), checkable deposits, and travelers' checks. These items are considered money because they are generally accepted as payment for goods and services.

Money Supply – Currency (including coins), checkable deposits, and travelers' checks.

If the nation's money supply increases, the aggregate demand for goods and services increases and the aggregate demand curve shifts to the right. The increase in aggregate demand occurs for at least two reasons. First, the increase in the money supply increases real balances. As a result, households increase their consumption. Second, the increase in the money supply reduces interest rates. Lower interest rates mean firms will invest more in new plant and equipment. Similarly, lower interest rates encourage housing construction and purchases of new automobiles and other consumer durables. The increase in real balances and the decrease in interest rates cause consumption and investment to increase. Because consumption and investment are components of aggregate demand, aggregate demand increases and the aggregate demand curve shifts to the right.

Monetary Policy – Use of the money supply to achieve full employment and other economic goals.

The nation's money supply can be altered by the Federal Reserve, an independent agency of the federal government discussed at length in Chapter 15. The Federal Reserve conducts U.S. monetary policy. **Monetary policy** is the use of the money supply to achieve full employment and other economic goals.

As shown, an increase in the money supply causes aggregate demand to increase. Thus, we define expansionary monetary policy as an action by the Federal Reserve to increase the money supply. In contrast, we define contractionary monetary policy as an action by the Federal Reserve to decrease the money supply. A decrease in the money supply causes aggregate demand to decrease.

Aggregate Supply

Aggregate Supply Curve — A curve showing the quantity of final goods and services (real GDP) that will be produced at each price level (the GDP deflator).

An **aggregate supply curve** shows the quantity of final goods and services (real GDP) that will be produced at each price level (the GDP deflator). Aggregate supply curve AS is depicted in Figure 13.5.

MOVEMENTS ALONG AN AGGREGATE SUPPLY CURVE. The aggregate supply curve in Figure 13.5 has two segments: a positively sloped segment up to price level P_1 and a vertical segment from P_1 up. The positively sloped segment of AS is like the supply curve for a single product. As the price level (as measured by the GDP deflator) increases, the quantity of goods and services (as measured by real GDP) supplied increases. In deriving the positively sloped segment of the aggregate supply curve, it is assumed that wage rates and other input prices (as well as the labor supply, capital stock, and technology) are constant. Consequently, when the price level rises from, say, P_0 in Figure 13.5 to P_1, firms' profits increase at output GDP_0. It is profitable for them to increase production. As firms expand production, they employ more workers and their unit costs increase along the upward-sloping part of the aggregate supply curve. Production continues to increase until GDP reaches its full employment rate, GDP_{FE}. As production expands, the unemployment rate falls.

Keywords: *economic aspects of U.S. monetary policy, economic aspects of U.S. fiscal policy*

http://www.infotrac-college.com

Once price level P_1 is reached, the aggregate supply curve becomes vertical at output GDP_{FE}, the full employment output level. Suppose the price level rises from P_1 to P_2. Wage rates and other input prices can

FIGURE 13.5 The Aggregate Supply Curve

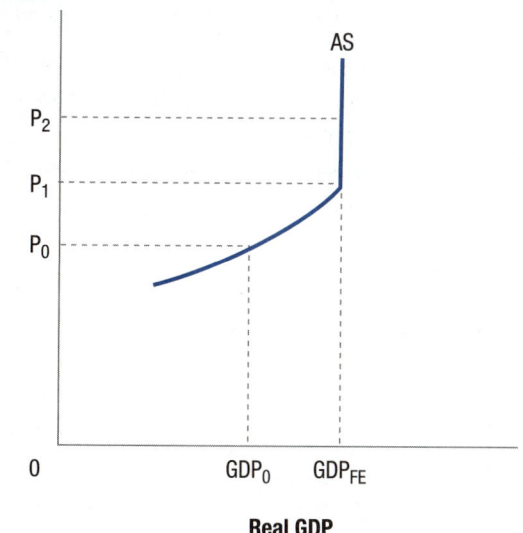

An aggregate supply curve shows the quantity of final goods and services (real GDP) that will be produced at each price level (the GDP deflator). The aggregate supply curve is positively sloped until the full employment level of output, GDP_{FE}, is reached. It then becomes vertical.

no longer be assumed constant. With the economy at full employment, individual firms may increase output by offering higher wage rates to attract workers from other firms. These increases in output are offset by the decreases in output experienced by firms that lose workers. Thus, despite the increase in the price level and wage rates, total output is unchanged.

SHIFTS IN THE AGGREGATE SUPPLY CURVE. We turn now to the causes of shifts in the aggregate supply curve. As discussed, the positively sloped segment of the aggregate supply curve is derived assuming that wage rates and other input prices are constant. For most firms, wages and salaries are the largest expense, typically accounting for 70 to 75 percent of all expenses. Consequently, wage and salary increases cause a major cost increase. This cost increase means firms must receive higher prices to continue producing the same amounts. Thus a wage increase causes the aggregate supply curve to shift from AS_0 to AS_1 in Figure 13.6. An increase in the prices of other inputs will shift the aggregate supply curve in the same manner.

In deriving the aggregate supply curve, the nation's labor supply, capital stock, and technology are assumed constant. If the labor supply or the capital stock increases, the aggregate supply curve shifts to the right. Similarly, if technological progress occurs, the aggregate supply curve shifts to the right. One such shift is shown in Figure 13.7. Note that, with the shift, the full employment level of output increases from GDP_{FE} to GDP'_{FE}. This is because increases in the labor supply and capital stock and technological progress increase the nation's productive capacity. If wage rates or other input prices rise, however, the full employment level of output (see Figure 13.6) does not change, because the nation's productive capacity is unaltered.

Aggregate Demand and Supply Interaction

In Chapter 2, you saw that the demand for and supply of a particular good determine its equilibrium output and price. Similarly, aggregate demand and supply determine the equilibrium levels of real GDP and the GDP deflator. In Figure 13.8, the aggregate demand curve is AD_0 and the aggregate supply curve is AS_0.

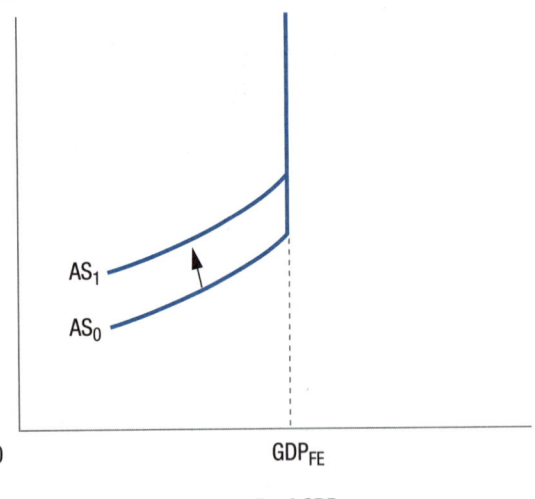

FIGURE 13.6 The Impact of a Wage Rates Increase on the Aggregate Supply Curve

The positive slope of a portion of the aggregate supply curve is due to the assumption that wage rates and other input prices are constant. If wage rates rise, the relevant portion of the aggregate supply curve shifts upward to the left—from AS_0 to AS_1.

FIGURE 13.7 The Impact of an Increase in the Capital Stock on the Aggregate Supply Curve

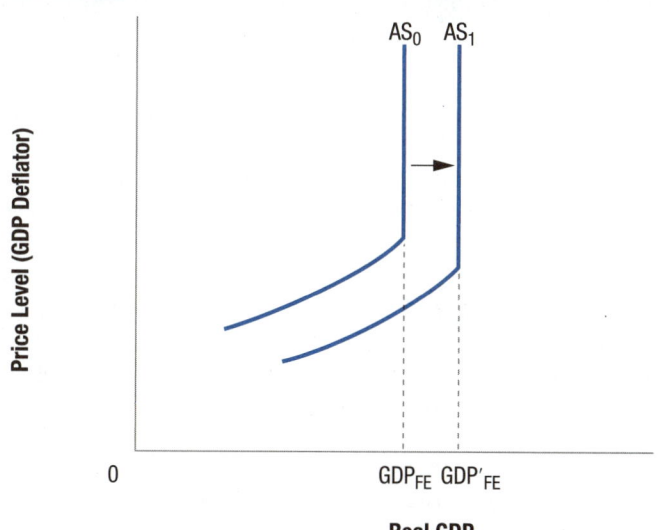

The aggregate supply curve is drawn on the assumption that the economy's labor supply, capital stock, and technology are constant. If the capital stock increases, the aggregate supply curve shifts to the right.

FIGURE 13.8 Aggregate Demand and Supply

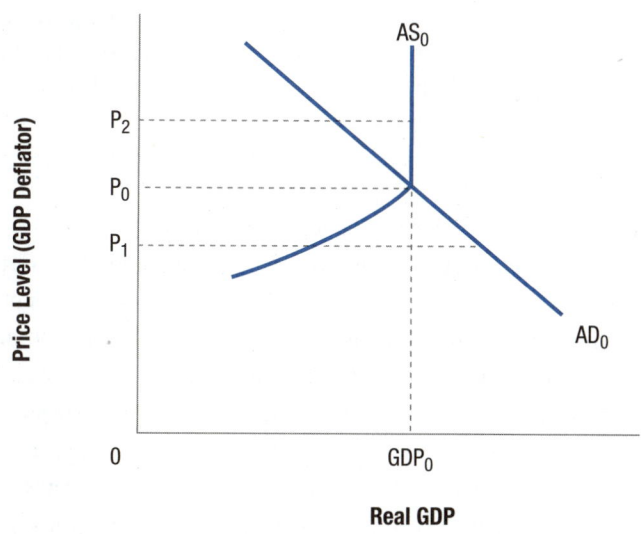

The equilibrium combination of output (real GDP) and the price level (GDP deflator) is given by the intersection of the aggregate demand and supply curves. In this case, the equilibrium level of output is GDP_0 and the equilibrium price level is P_0.

The equilibrium levels of real GDP and the GDP deflator are GDP_0 and P_0, respectively, given by the intersection of these aggregate demand and supply curves.

To show that GDP_0 and P_0 must be the equilibrium combination of real GDP and the GDP deflator, consider alternative price levels. Suppose that the price level is P_1, which is less than the equilibrium

INSIGHTS

THE LONG BOOM

Since 1980, the United States has had three recessions and two expansions. Following the severe recession that began in July 1981 and lasted 16 months, the economy began a long expansion that lasted until June 1990. The mild recession that started in July 1990 and ended in March 1991 provided a brief pause for the U.S. economy, which then began its longest expansion ever—10 years. This expansion ended in March 2001, with the ensuing recession probably ending in less than 1 year. [At this time (November 2002) the economy seems to be in a somewhat shaky expansion, with some economists expecting the recovery to fizzle.]

The severe recession that began in 1981 followed the Federal Reserve's contractionary monetary policy that subdued the rapid inflation of the late 1970s and 1980. The inflation rate did drop, but the nation's output and employment fell, and the unemployment rate increased. Real GDP fell by 2.2 percent in 1982, a large decrease by historical standards. The unemployment rate increased steadily, reaching a high of 10.8 percent in November 1982 (the trough).

Following 1982, the nation's output and employment grew rapidly and the unemployment rate dropped sharply. Both monetary and fiscal policy contributed to the strong recovery. Starting in December 1982, the nation's money supply grew much more rapidly. Also, government spending grew rapidly. Finally, federal personal income tax rates were reduced by 5 percent on October 1, 1981, by 10 percent on July 1, 1982, and by another 10 percent on July 1, 1983.

The economic expansion that followed the November 1982 trough was the nation's third longest expansion, almost 8 years. During the expansion, the unemployment rate fell steadily, reaching 5.3 percent in 1989. With the economy at or near full employment, prices started rising more rapidly. As a result, the Federal Reserve reduced the growth rate of the money supply. Although this policy succeeded in reducing the inflation rate, it was one of the factors causing the recession of 1990–1991. Other factors include (1) increases in debt—household, business, and government—which contributed to cutbacks in spending, (2) cuts in defense and in state and local spending, and (3) the impact of the savings and loan crisis on households and firms.

As previously stated, the 1990–1991 recession was both short and mild. Real GDP increased in 1990 and fell by only 0.7 percent in 1991. Similarly, the unemployment rate in March 1991 (the trough) was only 6.8

price level. At P_1, the aggregate quantity demanded exceeds the aggregate quantity supplied, implying that purchasers would like to buy more goods and services than firms are willing to produce. Firms find that they cannot maintain their desired levels of inventories because purchasers buy their products faster than they are produced. In addition to firms finding that they are not producing fast enough to maintain their sales, some customers are finding that they cannot buy all that they want to buy at the current prices. A general excess demand exists for goods and services. This excess demand puts upward pressure on prices, causing the price level to rise. As the price level rises, firms become willing to produce more and consumers cut back on their purchase plans. The price level will continue to rise until it reaches the equilibrium level, P_0. At P_0, purchasers buy the quantity of goods and services that firms produce. Consequently, neither purchasers nor firms have an incentive to alter their behavior.

Suppose that the price level is P_2, which is above the equilibrium price level. At P_2, the aggregate quantity supplied exceeds the aggregate quantity demanded, implying that purchasers are unwilling to buy as many goods and services as firms are willing to produce. This excess supply of goods and services places downward pressure on prices. As a result, the price level falls until the equilibrium price level, P_0, is reached.

INSIGHTS (continued)

percent, 4 percentage points less than in November 1982. In the first part of the recovery that began in spring 1991, real GDP grew slowly and unemployment continued to increase, reaching a high of 7.8 percent in May 1992. Starting in the third quarter of that year, however, the economy began to grow more rapidly and the unemployment rate finally began to fall.

The recovery that ended the 1990–1991 recession proved to be the longest expansion in American history. Indeed, professor John Taylor of Stanford University notes that the mild recession of the early 1990s was just a blip in what he calls the "Long Boom" that started in November 1982 and continued at least until March 2001, when the economy fell into recession for the first time since the early 1990s. Figure 13.1 nicely illustrates this "Long Boom" and the decreased variability in growth rates that accompanied it. The expansion that began in 1991 started slowly, but soon gained momentum with real GDP growing every year through 2000. The GDP growth rate peaked in 1997, but it continued to grow at a robust rate through 2000. The recession of 2001 turned the annual growth rate slightly negative, but growth appeared to resume for 2002. Remarkably, the unemployment rate continued to fall through 2000, reaching a low of 4.0 percent. A review of Figure 14.1 (in the next chapter) shows that this was the lowest unemployment rate since 1969. Most remarkably, the inflation rate also fell through 1998, even as the unemployment rate fell. A review of Figure 15.2 (in Chapter 15) shows that in the previous expansion the inflation rate had already begun to increase a couple of years before the unemployment rate fell to its minimum in 1989.

What accounts for this remarkable period in American economic history? Professor Taylor, the Under Secretary of the Treasury for International Affairs in the second Bush's administration, attributes it to sound monetary policy. Robert Rubin, Secretary of the Treasury during part of the Clinton administration, attributes much of the 1990s expansion to sound fiscal policy that balanced the federal budget and led to reductions in interest rates. The economic boom of the late 1990s resulted from a surge of investment that led to investment accounting for an unusually large part of GDP growth. Investment was spurred by new technologies and by monetary and fiscal policies that lowered the rate of interest. As the boom progressed, a more restrictive monetary policy and the development of excess capacity in some sectors of the economy caused investment to slow and the recession developed.

In this example, P_0 is the equilibrium price level because it is the only price level at which purchasers are willing to buy the same quantity of goods and services that firms are willing to produce. At any other price level, either excess aggregate demand or excess aggregate supply exists, and the price level changes until the equilibrium price level is restored.

In Figure 13.8, the equilibrium level of real GDP is GDP_0, the full employment level of output. We know that GDP_0 is the full employment level of output because the aggregate supply curve becomes vertical at that output level, indicating that the nation's productive capacity is fully utilized. There is no guarantee, however, that GDP will be at its full employment level. Suppose that, in Figure 13.9, aggregate demand falls from AD_0 to AD_1. With aggregate demand AD_0, real GDP was GDP_0—the full employment level of output. With the reduction in aggregate demand, purchasers now buy less at each price level. As a result, both real GDP and the GDP deflator fall. As real GDP decreases, firms reduce employment and the unemployment rate rises. With wage rates and other input prices constant (or slow to adjust), the unemployment rate may be above the full employment rate of unemployment for a substantial period of time.

FIGURE 13.9 Changes in Aggregate Demand and Their Impact on Real GDP and the Price Level

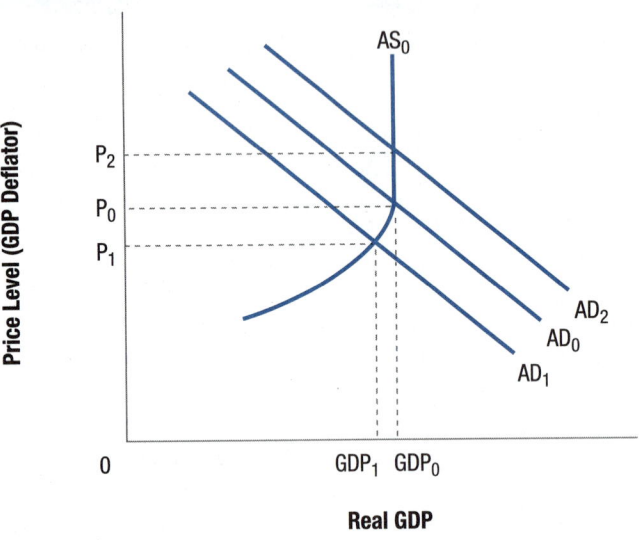

The initial equilibrium combination of output and the price level is GDP_0, P_0. If aggregate demand decreases (to AD_1) with wage rates and other input prices constant, output and the price level fall. If aggregate demand increases (to AD_2), the price level rises. Output, however, remains constant because the economy is already at full employment.

Just as aggregate demand may fall from AD_0 to AD_1, it could increase from AD_0 to AD_2. When aggregate demand increases to AD_2, purchasers buy more at each price level. This increase in aggregate demand causes the price level to rise to P_2. It does not, however, alter real GDP. With the economy already producing at the full employment level of output, GDP_0, the increase in aggregate demand results in higher output and input prices, but not higher output.

Summary

Gross domestic product (GDP) is the market value of all final goods and services produced in the economy over the relevant time span, usually a year. GDP, the most frequently cited measure of the nation's output, is divided into four components: consumption, gross investment, government purchases, and net exports.

In compiling GDP, market prices are used. This makes it difficult to measure the nation's output because both quantities and prices change over time. To overcome this problem, we first construct a price index, a measure of the price level for a given period relative to the base period. Once this price index—the GDP deflator—is constructed, we divide, or deflate, nominal GDP by the GDP deflator to obtain real GDP. Thus, the relationship between real GDP, nominal GDP, and the GDP deflator is

$$\text{Real GDP} = \frac{\text{Nominal GDP}}{\text{Price deflator}}$$

Nominal GDP reflects both quantity and price changes. In contrast, real GDP reflects only quantity changes. Because real GDP reflects only quantity changes, it is a better measure of the nation's output.

The GDP deflator is a weighted average of the prices of all final goods and services produced in the economy. It is the most comprehensive measure of the nation's price level.

Historically, the economy has performed well. Since 1929, output has increased at an average annual rate of about 3 percent. It has not, however, increased steadily. Periods of rapidly increasing real GDP have been followed by periods of slowly rising or even falling real GDP. These fluctuations in the level of economic activity are called business cycles.

An aggregate demand curve shows the quantity of final goods and services that will be purchased at each price level. Similarly, an aggregate supply curve shows the quantity of final goods and services that will be produced at each price level.

The nation's equilibrium output and price level are given by intersection of the aggregate demand and supply curves. Because aggregate demand and supply change over time, output and the price level also change over time.

Fiscal policy is the use of government purchases and taxes to achieve full employment and other economic goals. Similarly, monetary policy is the use of the money supply to achieve those same goals. Through the use of fiscal and monetary policy, policy makers can alter aggregate demand and, hence, the nation's output and price level.

Key Terms

Gross domestic product (GDP)
Final goods
Intermediate goods
Personal consumption expenditures
Gross private domestic investment
Capital stock
Government purchases of goods and services
Net exports of goods and services
Exports
Imports
Price index
Nominal GDP
Real GDP
GDP deflator
Business cycles
Expansion phase
Peak
Contraction phase
Trough
Aggregate demand curve
Real balance effect
Interest rate effect
Foreign trade effect
Fiscal policy
Money supply
Monetary policy
Aggregate supply curve

Review Questions

1. Define GDP. Why are only final goods and services included? Why are changes in business inventories included?
2. List and briefly describe GDP's major components.
3. Describe the effects of each of the following on U.S. GDP:
    a. a terrorist attack that destroys a dam and destroys 1,500 homes downstream
    b. a ban on U.S. imports from Germany
    c. the legalization of marijuana
    d. U.S. involvement in a war in the Middle East.
4. What is the underground economy? Why do people participate in the underground economy? How might its size be reduced?
5. What is the difference between nominal and real GDP?
6. "An increase in nominal GDP means that more goods and services are available to society." Using a specific example, explain why this statement is true or false.
7. Fill in the blanks in the following table:

Year	Nominal GDP (Billions of Current Dollars)	Real GDP (Billions of 1992 Dollars)	GDP Deflator
2002	___	4,800.0	120.0
2003	6,500.0	5,000.0	___
2004	9,000.0	___	150.0

8. Discuss the business cycle and its phases. What are the short- and long-run implications of the business cycle for growth of real GDP?
9. What is the aggregate demand curve? Why is it negatively sloped?

10. What factors may cause the aggregate demand curve to shift? Graphically, illustrate both an increase and a decrease in aggregate demand.
11. Carefully explain why the aggregate supply curve has two segments: a positively sloped segment and a vertical segment.
12. What factors will cause the aggregate supply curve to shift? How will these factors affect the two segments of the curve?
13. Using graphical analysis, explain why the equilibrium levels of GDP and the GDP deflator are determined by the intersection of the aggregate demand and supply curves.
14. Over the last three decades, there have been several episodes of increasing oil prices due to political events. The United States imports much of the oil that it uses. What effect does a large increase in oil prices have on real GDP and the GDP deflator? Defend your answer.

Economic Issues on the Internet

- Econ Data and Links—**http://zimmer.csufresno.edu/~johnsh/econ/econ_EDL.htm**
  A megasite with numerous links to U.S. and world economic data and to other sites with an economic orientation.
- Economic Policy Institute—**http://www.epinet.org**
  The Economic Policy Institute focuses on research and education and seeks to promote a prosperous and fair economy. Among its Web features are Economic Indicators and Economic Snapshots.
- Economic Research—**http://www.research.stlouisfed.org**
  The St. Louis Federal Reserve Bank site for their economics research contains links to data and to the many publications of the bank, many of which are accessible to students.
- Economics Resource Center—**http://www.swcollege.com/bef/economics.html**
  This site by South-Western provides links to other sites through such features as Status of the Economy and Economic Data Online. It also presents debates on current economics topics.

CHAPTER 14

Unemployment: A Recurring Problem

Outline:

Costs of Unemployment
  Economic Costs
  Noneconomic Costs
Counting the Unemployed
Types of Unemployment
  Frictional Unemployment
  Structural Unemployment
  Cyclical Unemployment

Full Employment
Policies to Reduce Unemployment
  Reducing Cyclical Unemployment
  Reducing Structural Unemployment
  Reducing Frictional Unemployment
Unemployment and the Minimum Wage
Unemployment in Europe
  Impediments to Hiring

Impediments to Accepting Employment
Conclusion

Unemployment is often a problem in our society. Many college seniors, for example, do not have a job at graduation. Fortunately, almost all of them find jobs within a few months. This type of unemployment is not a serious problem for either the individual or society. Unfortunately, most unemployment is different. Some people have difficulty finding jobs during economic expansions. More people have difficulty during recessions. During much of the 1981 to 1982 recession, the U.S. unemployment rate was about 10 percent, implying that one person in every 10 who wanted a job was unable to find one. Matters were worse during the Great Depression of the 1930s. In 1933, the unemployment rate averaged about 25 percent, implying that one person in every four could not find a job. The hardships and miseries of the unemployed characterize that period. In the recession that began in March 2001, the unemployment rate apparently peaked at a much lower level, at about 6 percent.

In this chapter, we take up unemployment and related issues. Among other topics, we consider its costs to the individual and to society, the various types of unemployment, and policies to reduce it. Although the chapter emphasizes unemployment in the United States, we also consider unemployment in Japan and Europe.

■ Costs of Unemployment

Keywords: *causes of unemployment*
http://www.infotrac-college.com

Unemployment bears both economic and noneconomic costs. Moreover, these costs differ for the individual and for society.

Economic Costs

For the individual, the most obvious economic cost of unemployment is the income that the person would have received if employed. This lost income may be partially offset by unemployment compensation, food stamps, or other government transfer payments. In general, however, these benefits are less than the income lost. As a result, the individual's economic position deteriorates.

So long as the period of unemployment is short, the impact on the individual is not severe. The individual and family may be able to maintain their standard of living by spending from savings. As time passes, however, the family may be forced to alter its lifestyle by spending less for food, clothing, and entertainment. More drastic changes might include moving to less expensive housing and selling assets. Ultimately, the individual and family may be impoverished.

For society, the cost of unemployment is the goods and services that could have been produced by the unemployed. To illustrate, the U.S. unemployment rate increased from 3.2 percent in 1929 to 24.9 percent in 1933. As a result, the nation's output of goods and services fell by about 30 percent, a tremendous decline.

Noneconomic Costs

In addition to economic costs, individuals experiencing prolonged unemployment are subject to other costs. Many unemployed persons experience anxiety, stress, loss of self-confidence and self-esteem, and depression. It is, after all, frustrating and depressing to apply unsuccessfully for job after job. It is also frustrating to be unable to buy what you and your family want and not to know when you will be able.

Various studies suggest that high unemployment rates are associated with a higher incidence of alcoholism and drug abuse as well as higher crime and suicide rates. Other studies indicate that prolonged unemployment has an adverse effect on physical and mental health. Prolonged unemployment also has an adverse effect on families. Studies suggest that high unemployment rates are associated with higher divorce rates, a higher incidence of child abuse, and increased infant mortality.

Compared to the economic costs of unemployment, these noneconomic costs are very difficult or impossible to quantify. They are, however, no less real and should be taken into account when discussing the costs of unemployment.

■ COUNTING THE UNEMPLOYED

More attention is paid to the unemployment rate than to any other economic statistic. Given the costs associated with unemployment, this is not surprising. The **unemployment rate** is the percentage of the **civilian labor force** that is unemployed. Briefly, the civilian labor force is the number of persons working plus the number of persons not working but looking for work.

The unemployment rate is calculated monthly on the basis of household interviews. Each month, interviewers visit nearly 60,000 households scattered throughout the United States and ask questions about each member of the household 16 years of age and older. The answers to the questions allow the government to classify each member of the household as employed, unemployed, or not in the civilian labor force.

People are defined as employed if they did any work at all as paid employees in the previous week or worked 15 hours or more as unpaid employees in a family business. People also are employed if they have jobs but do not work because of illness, bad weather, vacation, labor management disputes, or personal reasons.

People are unemployed if they had no job, were available for work, and had actively looked for work during the past 4 weeks. Also counted as unemployed are persons waiting to start new jobs within 30 days or waiting to be recalled to jobs from which they had been laid off.

After counting the number of persons employed and unemployed, we can calculate the number of persons in the civilian labor force: persons employed plus persons unemployed. Suppose we tally 135 million employed persons and 7 million unemployed. The civilian labor force is then 142 million.

Persons 16 years of age and older who are neither employed nor unemployed are not in the civilian labor force.[1] Persons not in the labor force include

- College students who do not have jobs (and are not looking for jobs)
- Homemakers and retired persons not looking for jobs
- Persons without jobs who have become discouraged and stopped actively looking for jobs

In calculating the unemployment rate, only people in the civilian labor force are counted. Suppose once more that 7 million persons are unemployed and the civilian labor force is 142 million. The following equation gives the unemployment rate:

$$\text{Unemployment rate} = \frac{\text{Number of persons unemployed}}{\text{Civilian labor force}} \times 100$$

In the equation, the ratio of the number of persons unemployed to the civilian labor force is multiplied by 100 to express the unemployment rate as a percentage. With 7 million persons unemployed and a civilian labor force of 142 million, we have the following:

$$\text{Unemployment rate} = \frac{7}{142} \times 100 = 4.9$$

for an unemployment rate of 4.9 percent.

Unemployment Rate – The percentage of the civilian labor force that is unemployed.

Civilian Labor Force – The number of persons employed plus the number of persons unemployed.

---

[1] Also excluded from the civilian labor force are members of the armed forces and persons institutionalized in mental and correctional facilities.

The unemployment rate, reported monthly,[2] tells much about the labor market, but, as illustrated in Table 14.1, it also conceals important differences among demographic groups. Note that the overall unemployment rate for 2001 is 4.8 percent. Several other rates are significantly higher than this rate.

- First, the unemployment rate for teenagers (persons ages 16 to 19) is approximately three times the overall rate. Teenage unemployment is always much higher than overall.
- Second, the unemployment rate for females is slightly lower than that for males. This has not always been the case. In the 1960s and 1970s, the unemployment rate was much higher for females than for males.
- Third, the unemployment rate for blacks is more than twice that of whites. This differential has been relatively constant over the years. The unemployment rate for persons of Hispanic origin is usually between that for whites and blacks.
- Finally, although not shown in Table 14.1, lower unemployment rates are associated with higher levels of educational attainment. This tendency suggests that although graduating from college does not guarantee that a person will always have a job, it helps.

INFOTRAC
College Edition

Keywords: economic aspects of unemployment, psychological aspects of unemployment.

http://www.infotrac-college.com

These differences in unemployment rates have two important implications. First, they imply that an increase in the overall unemployment rate is not shared equally. Suppose the unemployment rate increases by 1 percentage point. Because the unemployment rates for teenagers and blacks are about three and two times the overall rate, respectively, the increase implies that the teenage unemployment rate will rise about 3 percentage points and the black unemployment rate, about 2 percentage points. Second, the different unemployment rates among demographic groups may indicate the necessity of different policies to reduce the unemployment rates of the various groups, a point discussed later.

TABLE 14.1 Unemployment Rates by Demographic Group: 2001

Although the overall unemployment rate in the United States was 4.8 percent in 2001, the rate was much higher for some demographic groups, particularly teenagers and blacks. The unemployment rate for females was slightly lower than for males.

Demographic Group	Unemployment Rate (Percent)
Overall	4.8
Age	
16–19	14.7
20 and over, males	4.2
20 and over, females	4.1
Sex	
Males	4.8
Females	4.7
Race	
White	4.2
Black	8.7

SOURCE: *Economic Report of the President* (Washington, DC: Government Printing Office, February 2002), 370.

[2] The monthly rates are adjusted to eliminate the effects of holidays and other seasonal influences.

INSIGHTS

JOB OPPORTUNITIES AND DISCRIMINATION

The unemployment rate for blacks is about double that for whites and has been for years. Is this differential in unemployment rates due to discrimination? Before answering, we must analyze the situation.

Employers consider workers' productivity in their hiring decisions. At a given wage, hiring the most productive workers minimizes the firm's costs and maximizes its profits. Unfortunately, blacks typically receive less education and on-the-job training than whites. Moreover, the education that blacks do receive is often inferior to that of whites. With less education and on-the-job training, some blacks are less productive and are denied employment because of their low productivity. In fact, much, perhaps most, of the differential in unemployment rates is due, not to job discrimination, but to differences in productivity, which, in turn, is related to discrimination in the amount and quality of education that blacks receive.

Given that the unemployment rate for blacks is relatively high, the way to reduce it is to eliminate the cause.

The productivity of blacks would be enhanced by more and better—that is, equal—education. Improving access to better schools and ensuring that persons from disadvantaged homes have the financial resources through student loan and other programs would go far to eliminate the differential in unemployment rates between blacks and whites.

Affirmative action programs to provide blacks with greater educational and job opportunities are desirable. Quotas, however, are probably undesirable because they contribute to racial tensions and can result in reverse discrimination.

To the extent that blacks are the last to be hired and the first to be fired, stabilizing output and employment at their full employment levels is another way of reducing the differential in unemployment rates. With stability of employment, blacks will gain valuable experience and on-the-job training. Also, with full employment, employers are less able to discriminate because of the limited number of prospective employees. With less than full employment, employers are more able to discriminate because they can choose from a large number of unemployed workers, both black and white.

INFOTRAC
College Edition

Keywords: unemployed workers, employment discrimination

http://www.infotrac-college.com

■ TYPES OF UNEMPLOYMENT

Economists commonly distinguish among three types of unemployment—frictional, structural, and cyclical—that have different policy implications. First, we consider each type, and later we discuss appropriate policies to deal with each type of unemployment.

Frictional Unemployment

Frictional Unemployment — Temporary unemployment arising from the normal job-search process.

Frictional unemployment is temporary unemployment arising from the normal job-search process. It includes persons entering the job market for the first time (or reentering after an absence). It also includes persons who have quit jobs to search for better ones. Finally, it includes persons who have been laid off or fired. Although some people find jobs almost immediately, for others it may take several months. Consider a young man who has no job when he graduates from college. He must first identify available jobs and apply for them. Then he must wait for prospective employers to examine his credentials, check his references, interview candidates, and decide whom to hire. Even after he receives a job offer, the effective date of employment may be some time in the future. All in all, the job-search process is time consuming, which is one reason why college students are urged to start interviewing early in their senior years.

Because it takes time to find a job, some frictional unemployment is inevitable. Although it may be unpleasant, it is temporary. Moreover, it is an aspect of an efficiently functioning economy because it results from people searching for the best (higher paying?) jobs. Those who are successful in finding higher-paying jobs have also found higher-productivity jobs, and to this extent, the nation's output of goods and services increases. Because frictional unemployment is temporary and serves some useful social functions, it is not a major policy concern.

Structural Unemployment

Structural Unemployment — Unemployment caused by structural changes in the economy that eliminate certain jobs.

A second type of unemployment is structural unemployment. **Structural unemployment** arises when jobs are eliminated by changes in the structure of the economy. These changes occur because of technological progress and shifts in the demand for goods and services. Technological progress creates new jobs and eliminates old ones. The production process in many industries, for example, is becoming increasingly computerized. As a result, some production-line workers are losing their jobs. At the same time, new jobs such as computer repair technician and software engineer are appearing. Even so, displaced production-line workers may lack the skills necessary for these new jobs. Similarly, the demand for some goods and services declines over time, while the demand for others rises. Again, workers who lose their jobs in the declining industries may not have the skills needed in the expanding industries.

As with frictional unemployment, the problem is not caused by a lack of jobs. Jobs are available. Structural unemployment reflects a mismatch between the skills of prospective workers and the skills needed in the vacant jobs. Michigan may have unemployed automobile workers and unfilled computer science jobs. Similarly, Oklahoma may have a surplus of oil field workers and a shortage of airplane mechanics.

Although structural unemployment resembles frictional unemployment in that the problem is not lack of jobs, it differs in two important (and related) respects. First, a person who is frictionally unemployed has marketable job skills. A person who is structurally unemployed does not and might benefit from substantial retraining or additional education to become employable. Second, a frictionally unemployed person can look forward to obtaining a job soon. A structurally unemployed person—without new training or additional education—faces a bleak future of long-term unemployment broken, perhaps, by sporadic employment spells. Because it is long term, policy makers regard structural unemployment as a more serious problem than frictional unemployment.

INFOTRAC
College Edition

Keywords: *structural unemployment, technological unemployment*

http://www.infotrac-college.com

Cyclical Unemployment

Cyclical Unemployment — Unemployment caused by the drop in economic activity that occurs during the contraction phase of the business cycle.

The third and final type of unemployment is cyclical unemployment. **Cyclical unemployment** occurs when the level of economic activity falls. As firms reduce output, they also lay off or discharge workers, causing the unemployment rate to rise. (Unlike frictional and structural unemployment, cyclical unemployment is characterized by a job shortage.) The unemployment rate continues to increase during the contraction phase of the business cycle and reaches a maximum at or near the trough. As the economy enters the expansion phase of the business cycle, firms increase output and employment, and the unemployment rate falls. The unemployment rate continues to decrease during the expansion phase and reaches a minimum at or near the peak. At the peak of the business cycle, cyclical unemployment is negligible.

The U.S. unemployment rate for 1960 through 2001 is plotted in Figure 14.1. As the figure shows, it has varied considerably over this time span, with most of the variation due to cyclical unemployment. As a result, policy makers are concerned with cyclical unemployment.

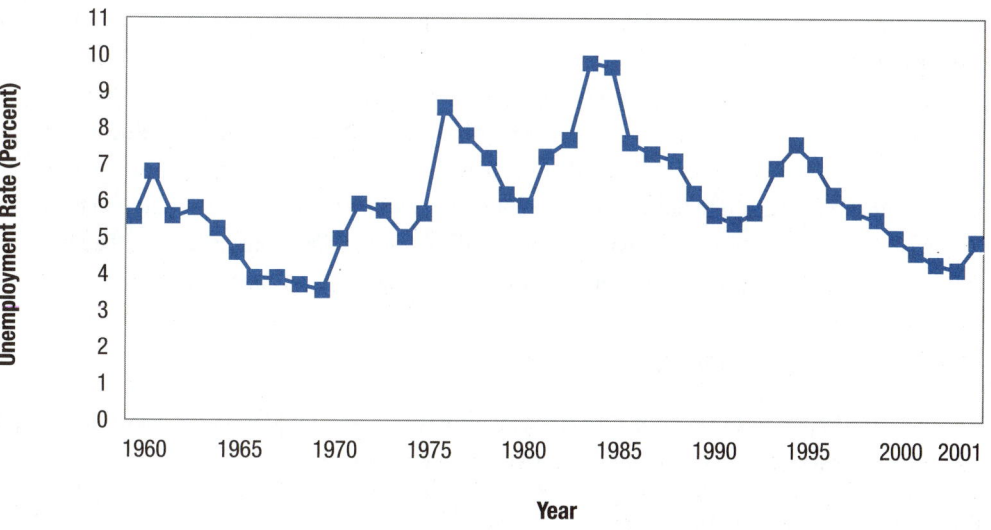

FIGURE 14.1 The U.S. Unemployment Rate: 1960–2001

The U.S. unemployment rate varied appreciably over the 1960–2001 period. It ranged from 3.5 percent in 1969 to 9.7 percent in 1982. In 2000, the unemployment rate decreased to 4.0 percent, the lowest rate since 1969.

■ Full Employment

Full Employment Rate of Unemployment — The frictional rate of unemployment plus the structural rate of unemployment; the lowest unemployment rate consistent with a nonaccelerating inflation rate.

Natural Rate of Unemployment — The full employment rate of unemployment.

Full employment is defined in terms of frictional and structural unemployment. The **full employment rate of unemployment** is the frictional rate of unemployment plus the structural rate of unemployment. To put it differently, it is the lowest unemployment rate consistent with a nonaccelerating inflation rate. If aggregate economic policies force the unemployment rate below the full employment rate, the price level will rise more and more rapidly.

Economists often refer to the full employment rate of unemployment as the **natural rate of unemployment**. This choice of terminology does not mean that the rate of unemployment is constant or unchanging. The natural rate of unemployment does change slowly over time because of changes in the composition of the labor force and other factors. In the 1960s, the natural unemployment rate was widely regarded to be 4 percent. During that period, however, teenagers started entering the labor force in record numbers. Given their significantly higher unemployment rate, they drove up the natural unemployment rate. Women also began entering the labor force in record numbers. At that time, the unemployment rate for females was much higher than for males. Because of their higher unemployment rate, increased numbers of women in the labor force also caused the natural unemployment rate to rise.

The natural rate increased in the 1960s and 1970s in part because of changes in the composition of the labor force. Most economists believe, however, that the natural rate has peaked and is now declining. Ironically, some of the factors that led to its increase are now leading to its decline.[3] The baby bust has

---

[3] For discussions of various factors causing the decline in the unemployment rate, see Robert Shimer, "Why Is the U.S. Unemployment Rate So Much Lower?" *NBER Macroeconomics Annual 1998*, edited by Ben S. Bernanke and Julio J. Rotemberg, 11–61, Cambridge: MIT Press, 1999; and Lawrence F. Katz and Alan B. Krueger, "The High-Pressure U.S. Labor Market of the 1990s," *Brookings Papers on Economic Activity*, No. 1 (1999), 1–65.

resulted in fewer teenagers entering the labor force. As a result, teenagers now account for a smaller part of the labor force. Even though the teenage unemployment rate remains high, the natural unemployment rate is lower because they are a smaller part of the labor force. Women continue to participate in the labor force in record numbers. Fortunately, however, the unemployment rate for females is about the same as that for males. The elimination of this unemployment rate differential has also reduced the natural unemployment rate.

INFOTRAC
College Edition
Keywords: *full employment*
http://www.infotrac-college.com

The full employment rate of unemployment increased from 4 percent in the 1960s to 6 percent or more in the 1980s and early 1990s. Starting in 1993, however, the unemployment rate decreased, and in the mid-1990s, various economists argued that the natural unemployment rate had decreased to 5.5 percent. With the unemployment rate falling to 4 percent in 2000 with little or no acceleration in the inflation rate, it appears that the natural unemployment rate has decreased to 5 percent or less. In the absence of information about future inflation and unemployment rates, however, we cannot be precise.

■ Policies to Reduce Unemployment

We now turn to policies to reduce unemployment. Because most of the variation in the unemployment rate is due to variations in cyclical unemployment, we start with it.

Reducing Cyclical Unemployment

Most economists believe that changes in the unemployment rate over the business cycle are caused by changes in aggregate demand.[4] During the expansion phase of the business cycle, aggregate demand increases, thereby increasing output and employment and decreasing the unemployment rate. During the contraction phase, aggregate demand decreases, thereby decreasing output and employment and increasing the unemployment rate.

In Figure 14.2, we consider the impact of a decrease in aggregate demand. Suppose initially that aggregate demand is AD_0 and aggregate supply is AS_0, so that the price level is P_0 and real GDP is GDP_0, the full employment level. Next, suppose that aggregate demand falls to AD_1. At P_0, the amount firms plan to produce, the quantity of aggregate supply, is greater than the amount that purchasers plan to buy, the quantity of aggregate demand. When firms produce at the planned rate, they are unable to sell all that they produce. As inventories pile up, firms are pressured to cut their prices and to reduce output. As they do so, they find that they can get by with fewer employees, so some employees are laid off. With wage rates and other input prices constant, the price level falls to P_1 while real GDP falls to GDP_1. The reduction in aggregate demand also causes employment to fall and unemployment to rise.

As just demonstrated, a reduction in aggregate demand can cause unemployment. Whether it persists depends, in part, on the flexibility of wage rates and other input prices. If wage rates fall in response to the increase in unemployment, aggregate supply in Figure 14.2 increases from AS_0 to AS_2 and eventually AS_3; in the process, output and employment return to their full employment levels.

---

[4]Proponents of the real business cycle theory do not share this view. For an introduction to this theory, see Charles I. Plosser, "Understanding Real Business Cycles," *Journal of Economic Perspectives* 3 (Summer 1989), 51–77.

FIGURE 14.2 The Impact of a Decrease in Aggregate Demand on the Unemployment Rate

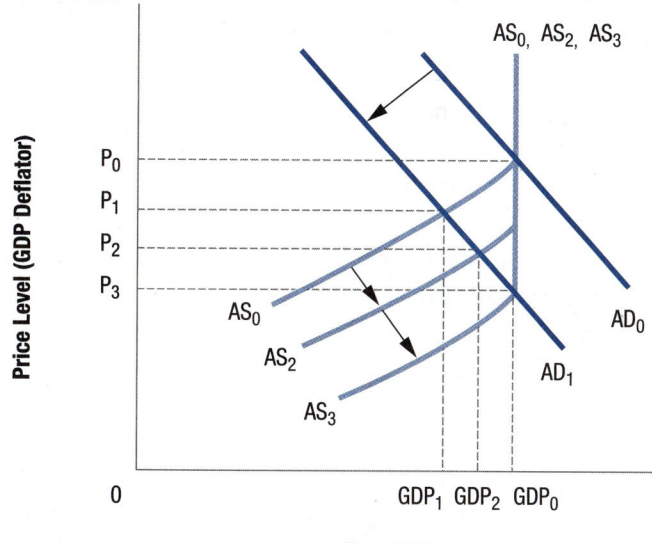

If aggregate demand is AD_0 and aggregate supply is AS_0, the equilibrium price and output levels are P_0 and GDP_0, respectively. If aggregate demand falls to AD_1, the price level falls to P_1 and output falls to GDP_1, assuming wages and other input prices remain constant. As the price level and output fall, employment also falls and the unemployment rate rises. In contrast, if we assume that wages fall in response to the unemployment, aggregate supply shifts from AS_0 to AS_3, restoring full employment.

Most economists believe that wage rates are "sticky"; that is, they respond slowly to change in labor market conditions. One reason they are sticky is that long-term contracts establish the wage rates of many workers.[5] Most labor union contracts, for example, cover 3 years. Even in industries where wage rates are not set by contract, they usually are adjusted only once a year. Most workers receive wage rates well above the legal minimum wage. But some workers receive only the minimum wage, which cannot legally be reduced. For these and other reasons, wage rates are sticky—especially downward. Because wage rates are slow to respond to an increase in unemployment, economists believe that unemployment caused by a reduction in aggregate demand may persist for 2 or 3 years.

Rather than letting this slow adjustment process run its course, policy makers can implement expansionary fiscal or monetary policies to reduce or eliminate the unemployment. With expansionary fiscal policy, either government purchases increase or taxes are reduced (or some combination of the two). Because government purchases are a component of aggregate demand, an increase in government purchases results in an increase in aggregate demand. A tax cut, on the other hand, increases disposable income, causing households to increase their consumption. Because consumption is a component of aggregate demand, aggregate demand increases. Consequently, expansionary fiscal policy acts to increase aggregate demand, say from AD_1 to AD_0 in Figure 14.2. The increase in aggregate demand in turn causes output and employment to rise and the unemployment rate to fall, returning to their full employment levels. If aggregate demand increases by a smaller amount, output and employment increase, but by smaller amounts, leaving the econ-

---

[5]Other input prices may be fixed by long-term contracts. Examples include the prices paid for raw materials and rental prices of buildings and machinery.

omy in an unemployment equilibrium. Consequently, some cyclical unemployment will remain. If it increases by a larger amount, output and employment increase to the original level, but the price level increases, perhaps setting the stage for inflation, which is analyzed in the next chapter. Now suppose instead that expansionary monetary policy is applied. An increase in the money supply results in increased investment and consumption. Because investment and consumption are components of aggregate demand, aggregate demand increases, thereby increasing output and employment and reducing the unemployment rate. If aggregate demand increases to AD_0 (or some higher level), full employment will be restored. If it increases by a smaller amount, some unemployment will remain.

In conclusion, unemployment due to inadequate aggregate demand can be alleviated by expansionary fiscal or monetary policies. If pursued vigorously, either of these two policies can increase aggregate demand enough to restore full employment.

In the foregoing analysis, the price level increased from P_1 to P_0 with the increase in aggregate demand from AD_1 to AD_0. Although the price increase may be undesirable, most economists believe that the benefits of reducing the unemployment rate are well worth the costs associated with the price increase. If the economy is at full employment, however, the situation is different. Suppose aggregate demand as shown in Figure 13.9 on page 342 is initially AD_0 and that it increases to AD_2. This increase in aggregate demand causes the price level to rise to P_2, but output, employment, and the unemployment rate are unaltered. At first glance, the increase in aggregate demand appears to do no harm; the price level is higher, but the other variables are unchanged. As we shall see in the next chapter, however, an increase in the price level imposes costs on society. For that reason, it is important that aggregate demand be stabilized at AD_0. To keep aggregate demand from rising, either contractionary fiscal or monetary policy can be applied.

To prevent or reduce cyclical unemployment while maintaining a reasonably stable price level, policy makers can pursue stabilization policy. **Stabilization policies** are government policies—usually fiscal and monetary policies—intended to maintain full employment and a reasonably stable price level. Indeed, policy makers in the United States have actively pursued stabilization policy since 1946. Many economists believe that since World War II government stabilization policy has reduced economic instability. At the same time, we still observe cyclical movements in the economy and fluctuations in output and employment. These fluctuations occur for at least two reasons.

First, policy makers are uncertain as to the magnitude of the changes in government purchases, taxes, and the money supply necessary to restore or maintain full employment. Is a $20 billion increase in government purchases sufficient to restore full employment, or is a larger increase necessary? Even if policy makers accurately estimate the necessary increase, political and other considerations may prevent adoption of the appropriate policy. Members of Congress, for example, are often reluctant to reduce government spending or raise taxes in an election year.

Second, stabilization policy must be timely to reduce the instability of the economy. Suppose the unemployment rate rises. If policy makers act in a timely manner, they can use expansionary fiscal and monetary policies to reduce the unemployment rate. Suppose, however, that they are slow to act. By the time they agree on a new set of policies to reduce the unemployment rate and these policies have an impact, the economy may once again be at full employment. If it is, these new policies will result in a higher price level rather than higher levels of output and employment.

Stabilization Policies – Government policies (generally fiscal or monetary) undertaken to maintain full employment and a reasonably stable price level.

INFOTRAC
College Edition

Keywords: *economic aspects of fiscal policy, economic aspects of monetary policy*

http://www.infotrac-college.com

INTERNATIONAL PERSPECTIVE

UNEMPLOYMENT IN JAPAN

Following World War II, the Japanese economy grew rapidly. Indeed, from its devastation in World War II, the Japanese economy became the world's second largest economy. In the 1990s, however, it stagnated. From 1991 through 2001, its real GDP increased at a meager 1 percent annual rate. Moreover, Japan's unemployment rate increased, reaching 5 percent in 2001. (Japan's unemployment rate averaged 2.5 percent in the 1980s.) This is the highest unemployment rate Japan has experienced since it started keeping statistics in 1953. This rate was also higher than the corresponding rate in the United States, an unusual phenomenon. The unemployment rate in the United States had been higher than in Japan, sometimes as much as four times higher.

The stagnation of the 1990s occurred for a variety of reasons. Households in Japan, typically more frugal than those in the United States, were slow to increase their consumption. Japan's banking system was hobbled by bad loans. (In total, bad loans were estimated to be $1 trillion.) In view of these bad loans, many banks were unable or unwilling to make business loans. The Asian financial crisis in 1998, discussed in Chapter 18, and its effect on Japanese exports had an adverse effect on the Japanese economy. Finally, the lack of aggressive fiscal and monetary policies prolonged the stagnation.

Japanese policy makers initiated various programs to stimulate the economy during the 1990s, including higher government spending and lower taxes. These programs, however, were not aggressive because the government was experiencing large budget deficits. (The Japanese government's budget deficit as a percentage of GDP is among the highest in the developed world.) In fact, the government raised taxes in 1997 to reduce the deficit. The tax hike, of course, was counterproductive in terms of stimulating the economy.

Interest rates declined and reached a low level, more because of the stagnation of the Japanese economy rather than a rapid increase in the nation's money supply. Many, if not most, economists believe that Japan's money supply should be increased more rapidly. This increase, they believe, would increase aggregate demand and, therefore, output and employment.

Economists also believe that banks with many bad loans should be either allowed to fail or be absorbed by banks in better financial condition. In the long run, a healthy banking system would be beneficial to the economy.

Finally, many economists believe that the Japanese economy should be deregulated and opened up to foreign competition. Deregulation would greatly increase the range of business opportunities. A reduction in international trade barriers would reduce the cost of imports and bring competition to various sectors of the Japanese economy. Of course, deregulating and reducing trade barriers may initially have an adverse effect on unemployment, but these policies are important for the long-run vitality of the Japanese economy.

Japan has a huge stake in increasing its growth rate and reducing its unemployment rate. Its trading partners, particularly its Asian partners, also have a big stake in Japan's prosperity. The healthier the Japanese economy, the more it will buy from its trading partners.

INFOTRAC
College Edition

Keyword: *Japan's unemployment*
http://www.infotrac-college.com

Most economists believe that stabilization policy plays a valuable role in reducing the economy's instability. They concede that policy makers have made mistakes in the past but, on balance, are optimistic that policy makers can do better in the future. Some economists believe, however, that stabilization policy actually increases the economy's instability and that policy makers should abandon its use.

Reducing Structural Unemployment

In the late 1950s and early 1960s, the U.S. unemployment rate increased. Most economists believed that the increase was due to inadequate aggregate demand. But some argued that rapid structural change was causing structural unemployment to rise.

With structural unemployment, the problem is not caused by a lack of jobs. As old jobs are destroyed, new ones are created. Instead, the problem is that the displaced workers fail to meet the skill and educational requirements of the new jobs. In this situation, expansionary fiscal and monetary policies are ineffective because the jobs created are like those already available.

In retrospect, it is clear that the increased unemployment of the late 1950s and early 1960s was cyclical rather than structural. Even so, there is little doubt that mismatches between the skill and educational levels of unemployed workers and those of existing job vacancies are a problem. To put it differently, even if no cyclical unemployment exists, the nation's unemployment rate will still be 4 to 5 percent. Most economists think this is too high. What can be done to reduce the full employment rate of unemployment?

Expansionary fiscal and monetary policies cannot help. As we observed earlier, if aggregate demand increases when the economy is operating at full employment, only prices and wage rates rise. Output and employment are unchanged.

Instead of stabilization policy, other policies must be used. One possibility is government programs to retrain displaced workers. With new job skills, these workers should be able to compete successfully in the job market. Another possibility is to provide subsidies to firms that will employ these workers and train them on the job. Still another possibility is to help workers relocate to areas where jobs exist. Without assistance, prospective workers may be reluctant or unable to relocate. Alternatively, firms may be given favorable tax or other treatment to induce them to build or expand plants in areas with labor surpluses. Finally, prospective workers might be induced to continue or resume their educations. Without more education, many of them will have great difficulty in finding jobs—or at least good jobs—in a technologically advanced society.

INFOTRAC
College Edition
Keywords: *vocational education*
http://www.infotrac-college.com

Starting in the 1960s, the federal government has sponsored various job training programs. Unfortunately, the results have been mixed.[6] In some programs, many enrollees failed to complete their training. In others, the enrollees were trained for jobs that were virtually nonexistent. In still others, the enrollees were trained with obsolete equipment. Finally, the placement record of many of these programs is disappointing.

Despite the mixed results to date, job training programs are probably necessary to reduce structural unemployment. Because we live in a dynamic society, some structural unemployment will always be present. Even so, many economists believe we can reduce it and thus reduce the full employment rate of unemployment.

Reducing Frictional Unemployment

For the most part, frictional unemployment exists because searching for a job is time consuming. Job seekers have imperfect information about vacancies, salaries, retirement and fringe benefits, and working conditions. Similarly, prospective employers have imperfect information about job seekers and their qualifications. With imperfect information, job seekers and prospective employers must search for the best matches of jobs and job seekers' qualifications.

---

[6] For discussions of the impact of training programs, see Robert J. LaLonde, "The Promise of Public Sector–Sponsored Training Programs," *Journal of Economic Perspectives* 9 (Spring 1995), 149–168; Duane E. Leigh, *Assisting Workers Displaced by Structural Change* (Kalamazoo, MI: W. E. Upjohn Institute for Employment Research, 1995); Yolanda K. Kodrzycki, "Training Programs for Displaced Workers: What Do They Accomplish?" Federal Reserve Bank of Boston, *New England Economic Review* (May/June 1997), 39–59; and Daniel Friedlander, David H. Greenberg, and Philip K. Robins, "Evaluating Government Training Programs for the Economically Disadvantaged," *Journal of Economic Literature* 35 (December 1997), 1809–1855.

To reduce frictional unemployment, job seekers and prospective employers require better information about job vacancies and job seekers' qualifications. In an attempt to reduce the cost of this information, the United States Department of Labor's Employment and Training Administration in cooperation with the states has established One-Stop Career Centers that pull together all employment, training, and education programs designed to help job seekers find jobs. These centers provide access to Internet information about jobs, such as the publicly supported America's Job Bank, which in October 2002 listed more than 900,000 jobs and over 400,000 resumes. Many other sites exist, providing information both about jobs and applicants.

Although providing job seekers and prospective employers with more information is desirable, it may have the unintended effect of increasing worker turnover. If it is easier to find another job, workers are more likely to quit their current jobs. If it is easier for employers to find new workers, they are more likely to fire current employees. The increases in the number of people who quit jobs and in the number of firings result in a higher turnover rate. The effects of the higher turnover rate, in turn, tend to offset the effects of the faster placement of job seekers.

INFOTRAC
College Edition

Keywords: *analysis of job hunting*
http://www.infotrac-college.com

Another approach to reducing frictional unemployment is to implement apprenticeship programs similar to those in Austria and Germany. These programs ease the transition from high school to full-time employment and provide some on-the-job training. The apprenticeship programs in those countries, however, have existed for many years. It may prove difficult, therefore, to adopt them in the United States, at least on a large-scale basis.

In conclusion, reducing frictional unemployment will not be easy. Fortunately, frictional unemployment is not a major problem, because it is temporary and serves some useful social functions.

■ Unemployment and the Minimum Wage

Earlier, we observed that one of the reasons for a high full employment rate of unemployment is that some prospective workers lack the skills necessary to fill the existing job vacancies. The imposition of a minimum wage makes this problem worse. A minimum wage discourages firms from hiring persons with minimal skills.

A federal minimum wage—25 cents per hour—was first imposed in 1938. Over the years, the minimum wage has been increased and the covered number of workers expanded. It was $3.35 per hour from January 1, 1981, to April 1, 1990. It increased to $3.80 on April 1, 1990, and to $4.25 on April 1, 1991. More recently, the minimum wage increased to $4.75 on October 1, 1996, and to $5.15 on September 1, 1997. More than 80 percent of the nonagricultural labor force is now covered. In addition to the federal legislation, many states have passed minimum wage legislation. In some states, the state-imposed minimum wage exceeds the federal minimum wage.

The expressed intent of increasing the minimum wage is to help the working poor. It is possible for a family headed by a person working full time at the minimum wage to have an income below the poverty line. By raising the minimum wage, it is argued, the worker's income will be increased and the family's standard of living improved. To politicians, increasing the minimum wage is a particularly attractive way to alleviate poverty because it does not require an increase in transfer payments and accompanying tax hike.

Although advocates of a high minimum wage have the best of intentions, the outcome is likely to be different from what they expect. In Figure 14.3, we plot the demand for and supply of low-skill workers. We focus on low-skill workers because the equilibrium wage rate for high-skill workers is likely to be well above the minimum wage. Consequently, the minimum wage will have no direct effect on them. Suppose a minimum wage higher than the equilibrium wage is imposed. The increase in the wage causes the quantity of labor demanded in Figure 14.3 to fall from N_0 to N_1 while the quantity of labor supplied increases to N_2. Because firms cannot pay less than the minimum wage, they will hire only N_1 workers. As a result, unemployment increases.[7]

The imposition of the minimum wage causes firms to discharge or decline to hire workers with minimal skills and experience. Many teenagers fall into this category, so it is not surprising that they are among those most adversely affected by the minimum wage. It is believed that a 10 percent increase in the minimum wage reduces teenage employment by 1 to 3 percent.[8]

The impact of the minimum wage on teenagers is unfortunate. Many teenagers lack work experience and have few skills. Consequently, they have difficulty getting jobs. But without jobs, they cannot get experience and upgrade their skills—a vicious circle. Because the minimum wage can make it prohibitively expensive for firms to hire teenagers, many economists believe that the minimum wage should not apply to them or that they should receive a lower minimum wage.

In addition to teenagers, structurally unemployed persons may be adversely affected. A minimum wage reduces firms' incentive to offer on-the-job training, making it more difficult for structurally unemployed persons to find jobs. To ease this problem, some economists have recommended that the long-term unemployed either be exempt from the legislation or face a lower minimum wage.

FIGURE 14.3 The Demand for and Supply of Low-Skill Workers

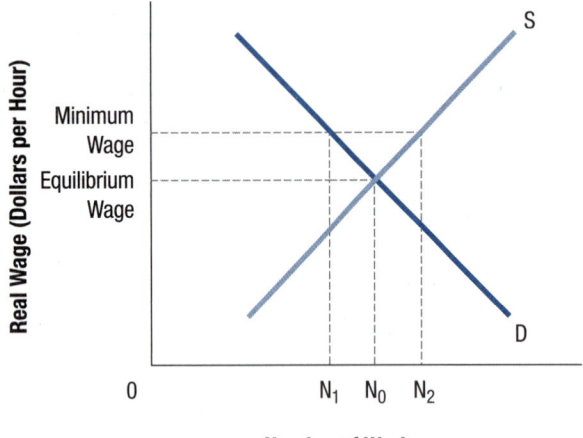

The demand for and supply of low-skill workers determine the equilibrium wage for low-skill workers. If minimum-wage legislation results in a wage higher than the equilibrium wage, fewer low-skill workers will be employed. In this case, employment is reduced from N_0 to N_1.

---

[7] The imposition of—or a significant increase in—the minimum wage has other adverse effects. The minimum wage raises the costs of producing goods and services. In general, some of this increase in costs will be passed on to purchasers in the form of higher prices. At the same time, firms may reduce fringe benefits and allow working conditions to deteriorate to offset, or partially offset, the costs imposed on them by the minimum wage.

[8] Young adults (ages 20 to 24) are adversely affected, but to a lesser extent. Women and blacks are also adversely affected. See Charles Brown, Curtis Gilroy, and Andrew Kohen, "The Effect of the Minimum Wage on Employment and Unemployment," *Journal of Economic Literature* 20 (June 1982), 487–528.

Another problem has to do with the excess supply of labor generated by imposing a minimum wage. At the minimum wage, firms wish to hire only N_1 workers (refer to Figure 14.3). On the other hand, N_2 prospective workers are seeking jobs. This excess supply of workers, N_2–N_1, provides employers with the opportunity to choose among the job seekers. As a result, they are in a position to discriminate—if they desire to do so—against blacks and others. If the wage rate is the equilibrium rate, the quantity of labor demanded equals the quantity supplied, and employers are not in a position to choose among applicants.

Those workers who remain employed after the imposition of a higher minimum wage have higher incomes. But does this mean that the lot of the working poor has improved? Unfortunately, increases in the minimum wage are less beneficial to the working poor than supposed. More than half of the low-wage workers in the United States are members of households with *above average* family incomes. These workers include high school and college students with part-time jobs and spouses with low-wage jobs. Consequently, only part of the increase in incomes accrues to the working poor.

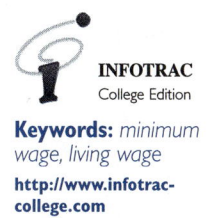

INFOTRAC
College Edition

Keywords: *minimum wage, living wage*
http://www.infotrac-college.com

If the goal is to help the working poor, the earned income tax credit approach is a better solution. As discussed in Chapter 12, working families with low incomes may deduct the credit from the taxes they owe. For families with very low incomes, the credit will exceed the tax liability. Consequently, they will receive a payment from the federal government. Because the earned income tax credit does not raise labor costs to firms, it does not reduce the quantity of labor demanded and, hence, employment. On the other hand, the tax credit does reduce tax revenue.

■ UNEMPLOYMENT IN EUROPE

Although unemployment is a problem in the United States, it is an even greater problem in parts of Europe. As shown in Table 14.2, the unemployment rate for the European countries that use the euro,

TABLE 14.2 Standardized Unemployment Rates for Various Countries: 2001

The unemployment rate for some European countries is higher than for the United States. For the Euro area (countries that have adopted the euro as their currency), it is over 70 percent higher than for the United States: 8.3 compared to 4.8.

Country	Unemployment Rate (Percent)	Country	Unemployment Rate (Percent)
Netherlands	2.4	New Zealand	5.3
Austria	3.6	Hungary	5.8
Norway	3.6	Belgium	6.6
Ireland	3.8	Australia	6.7
Korea	3.9	Canada	7.2
Portugal	4.1	Germany	7.9
Denmark	4.3	France	8.6
United States	4.8	Finland	9.1
Japan	5.0	Italy	9.5
United Kingdom	5.0	Spain	13.0
Sweden	5.1	Euro area	8.3

SOURCE: Organization for Economic Cooperation and Development, *Main Economic Indicators* (April 2002), 26.

the Euro area, is significantly higher than for the United States. Some of the largest European countries, including France, Germany, and Italy, are among the individual European countries with unemployment rates much higher than in the United States. Although the United States has had more favorable unemployment rates since the mid-1970s, before that the unemployment rate for most European countries was significantly lower than the U.S. rate.

In addition to higher unemployment rates, long-term unemployment is a greater problem in most European countries. In many of those countries, over half of the persons classified as unemployed have been unemployed for 1 year or more. In the United States, only about 10 percent of those classified as unemployed have been unemployed for that long.

To reduce the unemployment rate, European policy makers could implement expansionary monetary and fiscal policies. Most economists, however, believe that such policies would have little or no effect on unemployment rates. Instead, these policies would cause prices to rise more rapidly.

Many of these economists believe that unemployment rates are high in many European countries because of structural impediments that discourage employment. For convenience, we divide these impediments into two categories: (1) those that discourage firms from hiring more workers and (2) those that discourage unemployed persons from accepting jobs.

Impediments to Hiring

As in the United States, European governments have set minimum wages that employers must pay. These minimum wages are higher in France and most European countries than in the United States. As previously discussed, a minimum wage discourages firms from hiring persons with minimal job skills and experience.

Labor unions in most European countries are more powerful than those in the United States. These unions have used the collective bargaining process to achieve high wages for their members. Unfortunately, the effect is to reduce the number of workers that firms hire.

In addition to the effects of minimum-wage legislation and labor unions on wages, European firms must pay relatively high social security, unemployment compensation, and other payroll taxes. Also, government regulations often mandate numerous vacation days and other paid leaves. These taxes and paid leaves add greatly to the cost of employing workers. As a result, they discourage hiring.

In many European countries, it is both costly and time consuming to discharge workers. Often, firms must make large severance payments. In the United States, the typical discharged worker gets a week's severance pay for each year of service. In Germany, the average worker gets four times as much—one month's pay for each year of service. In addition, notification must be given well in advance. In the United States, a discharged worker usually gets a 1-month notice, whereas in Germany, the worker gets almost a 7-month notice. In some countries, firms must get outside approval to discharge workers.

At first glance, it appears that these requirements regarding dismissal increase employment. As employees retire or quit, however, firms are reluctant to replace them because it is so costly to discharge workers.

Finally, in many European countries, government regulations and controls make it difficult for entrepreneurs to start new firms or expand existing ones. In the German state of North Rhine-Westphalia, a firm must obtain permission from almost 90 federal, state, and local government offices to open a new plant. In the United States, firms are subject to fewer regulations. As a result, new firms and the growth of small firms have made an important contribution to the increase in employment in the United States.

INFOTRAC
College Edition
Keywords: *unemployment in Europe*
http://www.infotrac-college.com

INTERNATIONAL PERSPECTIVE

MORE ON EUROPEAN LABOR MARKETS

Since 1980, the full employment rate of unemployment has increased from 5.5 percent to 8.8 percent in the Euro area countries, while it has fallen from 6.1 to 5.2 for the United States, according to one estimate. Thus, structural unemployment has been increasing in the former and decreasing in the latter.[a] Although we discuss this topic in the text, we do not discuss some of the other differences in the European and United States labor markets. A recent issue of the U.S. Department of Labor's *Monthly Labor Review* provides a number of additional comparisons.[b] These comparisons show that U. S. employment growth far exceeded that of three large euro-zone countries—France, Germany, and Italy—called here the EU3.

Although employment growth is ultimately limited by population growth, the U. S. advantage in employment growth was due to more than faster population growth. The employment ratio (employment as a proportion of population) has increased steadily in the United States and fallen steadily in the EU3. Starting from a higher employment ratio in 1960, by 2000 in the EU3 countries less than 50 per hundred of the working age population was actually working, whereas in the United States the ratio had increased from 56 per hundred working age people to 64 per hundred.

It is important to note that diversity in labor market performance exists among the EU3 and more generally among European economies. The unemployment rate in the Netherlands, for instance, has fallen substantially, with its full employment rate of unemployment dropping to less than 5 percent; in addition, its employment ratio has risen and it now above that of the United States. Part of its success is due to a tremendous growth in part-time and temporary employment. Indeed, one of the ways that employers get around the impediments to hiring new "permanent" employees is through part-time and temporary jobs. Although the Netherlands has had quite successful policies to promote youth employment, the employment rate of people age 55 to 64 is low, perhaps because of a generous disability program. About 15 percent of the country's working age population receives disability payments, which reflects both a system with generous benefits and one in which it is not difficult to qualify for the benefit.

In general, European labor markets are subject to more regulation than U.S. labor markets, with the regulations designed to increase the security of the employed. Some European countries have engaged in significant labor-market deregulation with the result that the (full-employment) unemployment rates in some countries have fallen from their peaks and, as noted earlier, fallen below that of the United States. As *The Economist* has noted, part of the improved performance is based on the increasing importance of part-time and temporary employment, which, as in the Netherlands, permits employers to avoid some of the regulations while providing the types of employment desired by many, but not all, of the part-time workers.[c] As a result of this and other factors, the European employment growth rate has exceeded the U.S. rate for several years. Even though the part-time employment has led to a fall in average hours worked per employee, total hours have also increased every year since 1995.[d]

---

[a]Dave Turner et al., "Estimating the Structural Rate of Unemployment for the OECD Countries," *OECD Economic Studies* 33, 2001/II: 171–216.

[b]Constance Sorrention and Joyannna Moy, "U.S. Labor Market Performance in International Perspective," *Monthly Labor Review*, June 2000, 125 (6), 15–35;.

[c]"Economic Illusions," *The Economist*, May 2, 2002.

[d]"Starting to Work: European Jobs," *The Economist*, May 18, 2002.

Impediments to Accepting Employment

In both the United States and Europe, unemployed persons can draw unemployment benefits. Although these benefits serve a useful social purpose, they reduce the incentive to work. The problem is more acute in Europe than it is in the United States because (1) benefits abroad are relatively higher and (2) unemployed persons can draw benefits for a longer period. (Normally, unemployed persons in the United States can draw unemployment benefits for only 6 months.)

In addition, tax rates are relatively high in European countries. High tax rates, combined with loss of unemployment and other benefits, sharply reduce the incentive for unemployed persons to take jobs. Finally, unemployed persons in Europe have little or no incentive to work to obtain health insurance and other benefits because these are usually provided by the state.

Conclusion

For various reasons, unemployment rates in most European countries are higher than in the United States. To reduce those rates, European policy makers must reduce or eliminate the impediments that discourage firms from hiring and unemployed persons from accepting jobs. Because the causes of the high unemployment rates vary from country to country, one should not expect the same set of policies to be successful in all countries.

Summary

Unemployment is costly both to the individual and to society. The societal cost of unemployment is the goods and services that could have been produced by the unemployed.

The unemployment rate is the percentage of the civilian labor force that is unemployed. Unemployment rates vary among demographic groups. Teenage and black unemployment rates are well above the overall rate.

Economists distinguish three types of unemployment: frictional, structural, and cyclical. Because of its temporary nature, frictional unemployment is a minor policy concern. In contrast, the structurally unemployed face long-term unemployment unless they retrain or obtain additional education. Structural unemployment is, therefore, a serious problem. In recessions and early stages of recoveries, cyclical unemployment is also a serious problem.

The full employment, or natural, rate of unemployment is the frictional rate of unemployment plus the structural rate of unemployment. It is the lowest unemployment rate consistent with a nonaccelerating inflation rate. Currently, this rate is estimated to be about 5 percent.

Aggregate demand and supply determine the equilibrium combination of real GDP and the GDP deflator. If the aggregate demand curve cuts the aggregate supply curve at the full employment level of output, cyclical unemployment is zero. If aggregate demand falls, real GDP decreases. As firms reduce output, they also reduce employment, and the unemployment rate rises. Policy makers may use either expansionary fiscal or monetary policy to increase aggregate demand, thereby causing output and employment to rise and the unemployment rate to fall.

Most economists believe that stabilization policy may be used to maintain full employment and a reasonably stable price level. Stabilization policy can do little, however, to reduce structural unemployment. Other government programs may be needed here, such as retraining workers, subsidizing firms to hire structurally unemployed workers and train them on the job, and helping workers relocate to areas where jobs exist.

By forcing the wage rate above the equilibrium wage rate, the minimum wage causes unemployment—particularly among those with minimal job skills and experience.

Unemployment rates in most European countries are higher than those in the United States. These higher unemployment rates stem from structural impediments that reduce the incentives for firms to hire and for unemployed persons to take jobs. These impediments include high minimum wages, high tax rates, high unemployment benefits, and excessive government regulation.

Key Terms

Unemployment rate

Civilian labor force

Cyclical unemployment

Full employment rate of unemployment

Frictional unemployment
Structural unemployment
Natural rate of unemployment
Stabilization policies

Review Questions

1. Briefly discuss both the economic and noneconomic costs of unemployment to the individual and society.

2. Suppose you are given the following information about the Simplistic economy:

Persons over 65 years not actively seeking employment	20,000
Homemakers	40,000
School-age children under 16 years	60,000
Military personnel	15,000
Persons 16 years and older working	85,000
Persons 16 years and older not working because of illness, labor disputes, vacation, bad weather, or personal reasons	5,000
Persons between 16 and 65 years actively seeking employment	6,000

   a. Calculate the number of persons in the civilian labor force.
   b. Calculate the number of persons who are unemployed.
   c. Calculate the unemployment rate.

3. "A decrease in the unemployment rate will benefit society; however, these benefits will not be shared equally by all groups in society." Explain why this statement is true.

4. List and briefly discuss the different types of unemployment. Should policy makers regard each type as equally detrimental to society?

5. "Full employment means that everyone who wants a job is able to find one." Is this statement true or false? Defend your answer.

6. Why isn't the natural rate of unemployment constant over time? Is this rate likely to increase or decrease over time? Defend your answer.

7. "So long as the economy tends to move toward the equilibrium level of GDP, there is no need to be concerned about unemployment." Is this statement true or false? Defend your answer.

8. Should government undertake stabilization policies if wage rates and other input prices are flexible? Suppose wage rates and other input prices are "sticky." What policies should government pursue in the face of unemployment caused by a drop in aggregate demand?

9. "If pursued vigorously, expansionary fiscal or monetary policies can be used to reduce unemployment caused by inadequate aggregate demand." If this statement is true, why do we still experience periods of cyclical unemployment?

10. Can stabilization policy help deal with structural unemployment? Why or why not? If we cannot use stabilization policy, what—if anything—can policy makers do to reduce structural unemployment?

11. Suppose the economy is experiencing full employment. In response to political pressure, Congress reduces taxes. What are the effects of this tax cut on GDP, the GDP deflator, and employment? Defend your answers.

12. Discuss the impact of an increase in the minimum wage on the market for low-skill workers. Use graphical analysis to assist you.

13. "Even though some low-skill workers are laid off as the minimum wage increases, the economic situation of the working poor is improved because those low-skill workers who retain their jobs are receiving a higher wage." Is this statement true or false? Defend your answer.

14. Compare and contrast unemployment in the United States and Europe. If unemployment in Europe is caused by structural factors, what will be the effect of an increase in aggregate demand?
15. Based on the European experience, list and briefly discuss the factors that discourage
    a. firms from hiring
    b. unemployed persons from accepting jobs

    How might these factors be altered to reduce unemployment?

Economic Issues on the Internet

- Bureau of Labor Statistics, U.S. Department of Labor—http://www.bls.gov

  The site of choice for information about the U.S. labor market. It has several online publications, including the *Monthly Labor Review*, and has large data bases.

- European Employment Observatory—http://www.eu-employment-observatory.net/introframeset_en.htm

  This site provides information on European labor markets and labor market policy.

- Institute for Labour Market Policy Evaluation—http://www.ifau.se/eng

  This Swedish government institute focuses on evaluation of Swedish labor market policy and dissemination of the results. It is of particular interest because the Swedish government has one of the most extensive sets of labor market policies.

- International Labour Organization—http://www.ilo.org

  This United Nations agency promotes social justice and human rights with respect to labor.

CHAPTER 15

Inflation: A Monetary Phenomenon

Outline:

Defining Inflation
Measuring Inflation
   The GDP Deflator
   The Consumer Price Index
   Calculating the Inflation Rate
   Recent Experience
Effects of Inflation
   The Redistribution of Income and Wealth
   Inflation and Government

Inflation and Net Exports
   Other Effects
Money and the Money Supply
   Money's Functions
   The Money Supply
   The Federal Reserve
Causes of Inflation
   The Quantity Theory of Money
   Inflation Is a Monetary Phenomenon

Inflation as a Monetary Phenomenon: Two Qualifications
   Labor Unions, Monopolies, and Inflation
Inflation and Policy
   Monetary Policy
   Fiscal Policy
   Supply-Side Policies
   Incomes Policy
Appendix: Money Creation and Monetary Policy

During the expansion of the 1990s, prices in the United States increased about 2 percent per year. Some prices, including college tuition, increased at a higher rate; others increased at a lower rate or, like desktop computers, even decreased. Although prices increased, they increased at a lower rate than the 3 percent rate of the 1980s and particularly the approximate 7 percent rate of the 1970s. They also increased at a more moderate rate than in many other countries.

With prices rising, the costs to society seem obvious. Rising prices erode the purchasing power of people's wages, salaries, and pensions. It is not this simple, however, because, as prices rise more rapidly, wages and salaries also rise more rapidly.

In this chapter, we show that inflation helps some individuals and harms others. Among those who benefit are persons whose incomes rise more rapidly than prices. Those who are harmed include persons whose incomes rise less rapidly than prices. Although some people benefit from inflation, inflation—like unemployment—is costly to society. For that reason, policies to reduce or eliminate it are important. To find such policies, we must determine the causes of inflation.

■ Defining Inflation

Inflation is commonly defined as any increase in the price level. This definition fails to serve, though, because it includes both once-and-for-all increases in the price level and continuing increases. It is better to refer to a once-and-for-all increase in the price level as a *rise* in the price level and to refer to a continuing rise in the price level as **inflation**.

> **Inflation** – A continuing rise in the price level.

The distinction is important because once-and-for-all increases in the price level require no monetary policy action, but inflation does. Suppose, for instance, that an earthquake destroys part of the nation's capital stock. The decrease in capital stock reduces the aggregate supply of goods and services. As the aggregate supply curve shifts left, the price level rises. Once the economy adjusts to the lower capital stock, however, the price level stops rising. Consequently, policies to keep the price level from rising are unnecessary. On the other hand, if inflation occurs, the price level continues to rise until action is taken to stop it.

> **Deflation** – A continuing fall in the price level.

Deflation, the opposite of inflation, is a continuing fall in the price level. Deflations—usually associated with depressions—are rare. The last deflation in the United States occurred during the Great Depression of the 1930s. Nevertheless, deflation has reappeared in Japan, and some analysts see it as a threat to the German and U.S. economies.

■ Measuring Inflation

This section discusses two price indexes used to measure inflation.[1] They are (1) the implicit price deflator for GDP (the GDP deflator) and (2) the consumer price index (CPI).

The GDP Deflator

As defined in Chapter 13, the GDP deflator is a weighted average of the prices of all final goods and services produced in the economy. It is, therefore, the broadest-based measure of the nation's price level. Price deflators are also available for the various components of GDP, such as consumption and investment. Like the GDP deflator, these deflators are available quarterly. Because of its comprehensiveness, most economists consider the GDP deflator to be the best measure of a nation's inflation rate.

The Consumer Price Index

> **Consumer Price Index (CPI)** – A weighted average of the prices of goods and services purchased by a typical urban household.

The **consumer price index (CPI)** is a weighted average of the prices of goods and services purchased by a typical urban household. It includes the prices of food, clothing, housing, transportation, medical care, and

---

[1] In this context, the producer price indexes deserve mention. These indexes measure the prices received by domestic producers of commodities at various stages of production (finished goods, intermediate goods, and crude materials). These indexes are important because movements in them usually foreshadow movements in the CPI. For that reason, the indexes receive widespread attention when they are released each month.

entertainment. The current market basket of goods and services was determined by a 1999–2000 survey of urban household purchases. In addition to the CPI, subindexes for such specific goods as food and energy are also compiled. Like the CPI, these subindexes are available monthly.

Although the GDP deflator provides the best overall measure of inflation, the CPI is the most widely cited measure of inflation in the United States. The main reason for its popularity is that the CPI focuses on the prices of goods and services purchased by households. The GDP deflator, in contrast, focuses on the prices of *all* final goods and services produced in the economy, including those purchased by firms and government.

Because it is based on the prices of goods and services purchased by households, the CPI is widely regarded as a cost-of-living index. As a measure of the cost of living, however, it has several shortcomings. First, it is an index for the *typical* urban household. Consequently, we would not expect it to be accurate for the atypical household. To illustrate, suppose the typical urban household allocates 40 percent of its expenditures to housing. If the price of housing was to rise relatively rapidly, households allocating more than 40 percent of their expenditures to housing would find their cost of living rising more rapidly than the CPI. By the same token, households allocating less than 40 percent to housing would find their cost of living rising less rapidly.

Second, the CPI overstates the increase in the cost of living because it is based on a fixed market basket of goods and services. In actuality, when households find that some prices rise more rapidly than others, they substitute goods and services that have risen less in price for those that have risen more. The CPI does not take this substitution into account, and so it overstates the increase in the cost of living.

Third, the CPI also overstates the increase in the cost of living because it does not fully account for changes in quality. The quality of many goods and services (such as televisions, personal computers, and medical care) has improved over the years. If it took these changes into account, the CPI would increase less rapidly. Although the U.S. Bureau of Labor Statistics, the government bureau responsible for the CPI, does an excellent job in calculating the CPI, the problems that we have mentioned or others are, in the end, unavoidable. For instance, when a new product comes on the market, it may not be represented in the index for several years. Most new products experience rapidly falling prices in their first years on the market. The CPI usually fails to capture these initial price decreases.

INFOTRAC
College Edition

Keywords: *measure of inflation, CPI*

http://www.infotrac-college.com

Despite its shortcomings as a measure of the cost of living, the CPI plays an important role in our economy. As the most common measure of inflation, it is often a basis for policy making. As a measure of the cost of living, it is a basis for labor negotiations. In addition, millions of workers have *cost-of-living adjustment (COLA)* clauses in their contracts. Under these clauses, wage rates increase automatically as the CPI rises. Similarly, tens of millions of retirees find that their Social Security benefits increase automatically as the CPI rises. Finally, the CPI is used to adjust the federal personal income tax system to eliminate the effects of inflation.

Calculating the Inflation Rate

To determine the inflation rate (the percentage rate of increase in the price level) from one period to the next period, we apply the following formula:

$$(15.1) \quad \text{Inflation rate} = \frac{\text{Current period's price level} - \text{Previous period's price level}}{\text{Previous period's price level}} \times 100$$

We first subtract the previous period's price level from the current period's price level to obtain the change in the price level from one period to the next. Then we divide the change in the price level by the previous period's price level and multiply the result by 100. (Multiplying by 100 expresses the inflation rate as a percentage.)

To illustrate, we can find the inflation rate for 2001. Taking 1996 as the base year, in 2000, the GDP deflator was 107 and the CPI was 109.7; in 2001, they were 109.4 and 112.9, respectively. Because the base year is the same, the different index numbers for the two price indexes for the same year shows that they give different price level measures. Recall that the GDP deflator is a price index for all final goods and services and the CPI is a price index for consumer goods purchased by a typical urban consumer. Consequently, there is no reason for them to be the same. We substitute the GDP deflator numbers in the formula to get a measure of the inflation rate: Inflation rate = $((109.4 - 107) \div 107) \times 100$, equals 2.2 percent. If you calculate the inflation rate using the CPI, you will find it different from the rate based on the GDP deflator. How much different is it? As we discussed in Chapter 1, the CPI is often used to put incomes in "real" terms. Because the CPI generally overstates inflation, using the CPI to get real income tends to result in a downward bias in the measurement of real income.

INFOTRAC
College Edition

Keywords: *inflation, cost of living, standard of living*

http://www.infotrac-college.com

Recent Experience

Since 1940, inflation has been the norm in the United States. Before then, periods of continuing price increases were followed by periods of continuing price decreases. The price level rose during World War II and the immediate postwar period. It rose again during the Korean War. From 1953 to 1965, the price level increased at a moderate rate. Starting in 1966, it increased more rapidly, as we can see in Figure 15.1. Inflation was high, by U.S. standards, throughout the 1970s. The inflation rate, as measured by the GDP deflator, peaked in 1975 at 9.4 percent. In the early 1980s, the inflation rate decreased, but by the late 1980s, it accelerated once more, peaking at 4.3 percent in 1990. Since the early 1990s, the inflation rate has been relatively low. In 1998, it was only 1.2 percent, the lowest rate since 1959. Even though the expansion continued until 2001, the inflation rate remained around 2 percent, its average for the 1990s.

The inflation rate in the United States averaged 1.8 percent for the 1995 to 2001 period; the United States experienced less inflation than most countries over that time. Some countries, including Mexico and Turkey as shown in Table 15.1, had double-digit inflation. The Euro Zone had a slightly lower inflation rate than the United States. One surprise in the table is the emergence of deflation in Japan and isolated incidences of it in other countries. Whether here or abroad, inflation or deflation always has adverse effects.

 EFFECTS OF INFLATION

The effects of inflation (or deflation) depend largely on whether it is unanticipated or anticipated. **Unanticipated inflation** is inflation that is unexpected or higher than expected. For example, people might expect no inflation and instead experience an actual inflation rate of 5 percent. **Anticipated inflation** is inflation that is expected. For instance, people might expect inflation to occur at a 5 percent rate and the price level might, in fact, rise at that rate.

Unanticipated Inflation – Inflation that is unexpected or higher than expected.

Anticipated Inflation – Inflation that is expected.

The Redistribution of Income and Wealth

One effect of inflation is a redistribution of income and wealth—a substantial redistribution if the inflation is unanticipated. Some individuals gain because their wages and salaries rise more rapidly than the

FIGURE 15.1 The GDP Deflator and the Inflation rate: 1960–2001

The price level, as measured by the GDP deflator, on the left axis increased substantially during 1960–2001. It increased more rapidly in the 1970s and 1980s than in the 1960s and 1990s. Graphing the inflation rate, the rate of change of the price level, on the right axis, the inflation rate and its fluctuations are more easily seen. It reached 9 percent in both 1974 and 1975 and in 1980 and 1981, illustrating the economic difficulties in that period. In contrast, the inflation rate was only about 1 percent in the beginning of the 1960s and about 2 percent at the end of the 1990s.

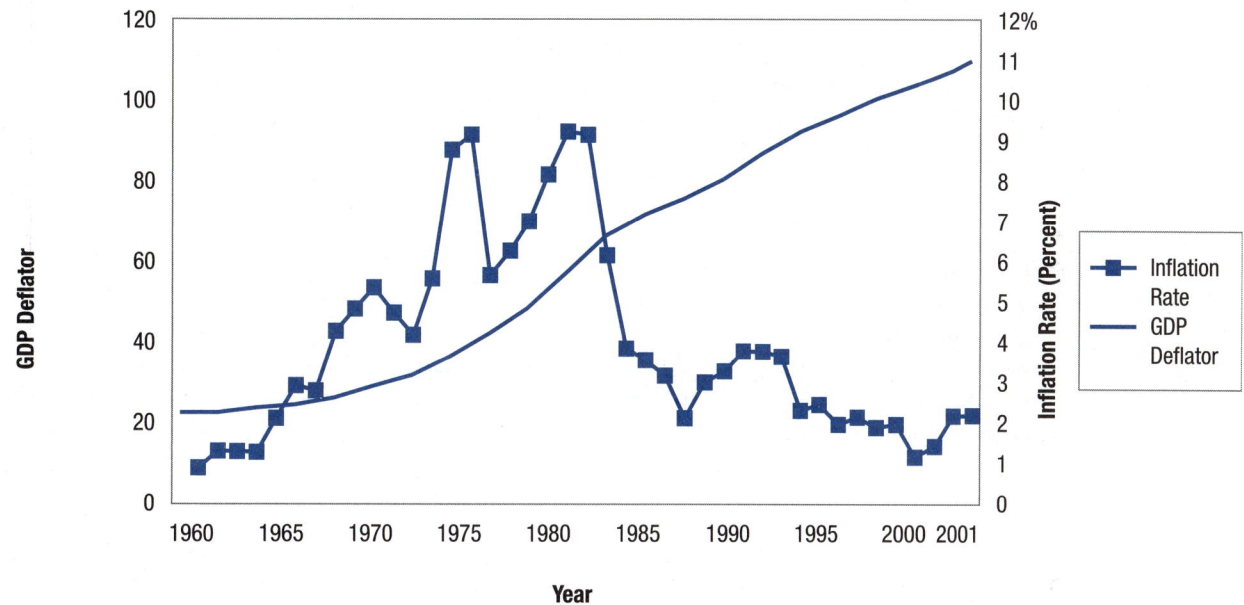

price level. Others lose because their wages, salaries, and pensions rise less rapidly than the price level. In this sense, real income is redistributed from some individuals to others. To illustrate, suppose workers in a particular industry, expecting no inflation, agree to a long-term contract calling for annual 4 percent wage increases. By most standards, 4 percent wage increases are very satisfactory if no inflation is occurring. Suppose, however, inflation occurs at an 8 percent rate. With wage rates rising less rapidly than prices, income is redistributed—in this case, from the workers to the owners of the firms in the industry.

In the preceding illustration, the workers received 4 percent wage increases that partially offset the 8 percent price increases. Inflation is a more serious problem for those living on fixed incomes. Consider someone who retired in 1985 on a fixed income. From 1985 to 2002, the CPI increased by about two-thirds, which means that a retiree's fixed income in 2002 would buy only 60 percent of what it bought in 1985. This 40 percent reduction in the purchasing power of a fixed income occurred with inflation averaging just 3 percent. If inflation had averaged 7 percent, as it did in the 1970s, the price level would triple over the same 18 years, reducing the purchasing power of a fixed income to 30 percent.

High inflation rates, clearly, have a disastrous impact on persons living on fixed incomes. Fortunately, most retirees do not live on fixed incomes. Social Security benefits constitute the bulk of the typical

TABLE 15.1 — Inflation Rates for Various Countries: 1996–2001

During 1996–2001, the U.S. inflation rate (as measured by the GDP deflator) averaged 1.8 percent. Some other countries, such as Turkey and Mexico, experienced double-digit inflation over these years. The Euro Zone had a slightly lower rate than the United States, averaging 1.6 percent. Several countries experienced a year or two when the overall price level fell, but Japan has had deflation of about 1 percent per year.

Country	1996	1997	1998	1999	2000	2001	Average*
Turkey	77.8	81.5	75.7	55.6	50.7	54.6	66.0
Mexico	30.6	17.7	15.4	14.8	10.8	6.0	15.9
Norway	4.0	3.0	−0.6	6.2	16.3	2.1	5.2
Greece	7.4	6.8	5.2	3.0	3.4	3.8	4.9
Spain	3.5	2.3	2.4	2.9	3.4	4.1	3.1
Malaysia	3.7	3.5	8.5	0.0	4.7	−2.7	3.0
United Kingdom	3.3	2.9	2.9	2.6	1.7	2.4	2.6
Netherlands	1.2	2.0	1.7	1.7	3.7	4.7	2.5
United States	1.9	2.0	1.2	1.4	2.3	2.2	1.8
Korea	3.8	3.0	5.2	−2.0	−0.9	1.3	1.7
Euro Zone	2.9	−0.1	1.2	1.8	1.2	2.3	1.6
Canada	1.6	1.2	−0.4	1.7	3.9	1.1	1.5
Sweden	1.4	1.7	0.9	0.5	0.8	1.7	1.2
France	1.4	1.3	0.9	0.5	0.5	1.4	1.0
Germany	1.0	0.7	1.1	0.5	−0.4	1.4	0.7
Japan	−0.8	0.3	−0.1	−1.4	−1.9	−1.5	−0.9

* The arithmetic average.
SOURCE: Federal Reserve Bank of St. Louis, *International Economic Trends* (July 2002), 6.

Indexing – Linking benefits to the CPI so that they increase automatically as the CPI rises.

Creditor – A person to whom money is owed.

Debtor – A person who owes money.

retiree's income, and these benefits are **indexed**. That is, they are linked to the CPI so that they increase automatically as the CPI rises. If the CPI rises by, say, 5 percent, Social Security benefits increase by 5 percent. Consequently, the effects of inflation on retired persons are not as disastrous as one might think.

Just as income is redistributed with inflation, wealth is also redistributed. Inflation causes many asset prices to rise, some more than the price level and others less. People whose assets appreciate more in price gain from the inflation; those whose assets appreciate less lose.

One important type of redistribution is that from creditors to debtors. A **creditor** is a person to whom money is owed. A **debtor** is a person who owes money. Suppose you borrow at a fixed interest rate to buy a home and that your monthly payment on the principal and interest is $800. Then, over time, the price level doubles. The prices of the goods and services that you typically buy double, but, with the inflation, so does your income. Consequently, you can continue to buy the same amount of food, clothing, and so on. What about your mortgage payment? It remains the same. Because your income has doubled, this $800 payment is much less burdensome than before. To put it differently, the inflation means you are able to repay the loan in dollars with substantially less purchasing power than those that you borrowed. You benefit from the inflation.

Just as debtors gain from inflation, creditors lose. They are repaid with dollars that have less purchasing power than the dollars that they lent. In the example, the institution from which you borrowed finds that the $800 monthly payment will buy only half as much as before because the price level has doubled.

Unanticipated inflation causes a substantial redistribution of income and wealth. With anticipated inflation, however, the redistribution is much less dramatic. When people anticipate inflation, they can take action to protect themselves. Consider once more the workers who agreed to a contract calling for 4 percent wage increases and then experienced 8 percent inflation. If the 8 percent inflation continues, these workers will expect the inflation rate to be 8 percent, and the inflation will become anticipated inflation. At the expiration of their contract, the workers will bargain for wage increases that take the anticipated inflation into account.

With anticipated inflation, the redistribution of wealth from creditors to debtors is also less dramatic. When they expect no inflation, creditors are willing to lend money at relatively low interest rates. A lender might be willing to lend $100 for a year at a 4 percent interest rate, which means that the borrower must pay the lender $104 at the end of the year. If the price level rises by 8 percent during the year, the $104 that the lender receives at the end of the year will buy less than the $100 would have at the start of the year. Under these circumstances, the lender will no longer agree to lend at a 4 percent rate. Instead, the lender will insist on a rate that will compensate for the expected deterioration in the purchasing power of money. If the inflation rate is anticipated to be 8 percent, the lender will insist on a 12 percent rate. The additional 8 percent is to compensate for the anticipated inflation.

It is easy to see why the lender will insist on a higher interest rate when the anticipated inflation rate rises. It is perhaps less easy to see why borrowers will agree to it. To the typical borrower, however, a 12 percent interest rate with 8 percent inflation is no more burdensome than a 4 percent rate with no inflation. This is because, with 8 percent inflation, the typical wage earner can expect his or her income to rise 8 percent faster. Of course, not all wage earners will find their incomes rising 8 percent faster.

Thus, the switch from unanticipated to anticipated inflation causes interest rates to rise. The rise in interest rates protects lenders so that no redistribution of wealth occurs between lenders and borrowers. (People who borrowed at relatively low interest rates before the increase in the inflation rate still benefit.)

Even with anticipated inflation, some redistribution of income and wealth occurs. Persons who retire often have part of their income that is fixed; for instance, they may have a pension that is fixed in nominal dollars, i.e., that it not indexed. Moreover, those who have lent money at a low interest rate can do little or nothing when they realize that the inflation rate has increased. Consequently, they are adversely affected by inflation. Others, however, gain at their expense, so that society as a whole is unaffected.

In one important case, society is adversely affected by an increase in the inflation rate. Inflation hurts people who hold money, because it erodes purchasing power. Consequently, as the inflation rates rise, people attempt to reduce the amount of money that they hold. To the extent that they devote more time and effort to reducing their holdings of money, fewer resources are devoted to the production of goods and services. The reduced production represents a cost to society. Studies suggest that this cost is small at low inflation rates but increases as the inflation rate rises.

Inflation and Government

Inflation affects government in two important ways. First, the federal government is a huge debtor, owing more than *$6 trillion*. As a debtor, the federal government gains from inflation. Creditors, on the other hand, lose.

Second, under inflation the federal government gains additional real tax revenue at the expense of taxpayers because part of our nation's tax system is based on nominal income rather than real income. Before 1985, the federal personal income tax system had many tax brackets (for example, $20,000–$22,000). Moreover, as the taxpayer's income (and thus income tax bracket) increased, the tax rate on the incremental income also increased. Suppose the tax law levies a 10 percent tax on the first $20,000 of income and a 20 percent rate on the next $20,000. As we have seen, inflation results in higher incomes. If the price level doubles over some time span, the income of a typical household also doubles. Suppose Sarah had income of $20,000 before the inflation and $40,000 afterward. She would pay $2,000 income tax before the inflation and $6,000 after the inflation. Before inflation, her after-tax income was $18,000; after it was $34,000. But because prices doubled, her after-tax real-income went from $18,000 to $17,000. This reduction in real after-tax income occurred because the increase in *nominal* income moved Sarah into a tax bracket with a higher tax rate, even though her real income had not changed. Her real tax payment increased from $2,000 to $3,000.

Under the pre-1985 personal income tax system, inflation automatically raised tax rates on personal income, redistributing real income from taxpayers to government and, ultimately, to the beneficiaries of government spending. This redistribution may or may not have been desirable. It must be recognized, however, that it took place without congressional action to raise taxes. Consequently, it was not possible for voters to properly "reward" those in Congress responsible for higher taxes. Moreover, because inflation increases real tax revenue, Congress may have had less of an incentive to pursue anti-inflationary policies than it would otherwise have had.

To prevent the redistribution of income through the personal income tax system, Congress passed and President Reagan signed legislation in 1981 to index the personal income tax system, starting in 1985. The system is now adjusted each year to eliminate the effects of inflation on real tax revenue.

Unfortunately, although the federal personal income tax system is now indexed, the rest of the federal tax system is not. This is particularly unfortunate with regard to the federal corporate income tax system. When inflation occurs, corporations find that their real tax liability increases. The reduction in real after-tax profits makes it less profitable for them to invest in new plant and equipment. As a result, they reduce investment. Less investment means the nation's capital stock increases less rapidly, which in turn means the nation's output and standard of living also increase less rapidly.

To the extent that politicians focus on the short term, they have incentives to allow inflation. First, unanticipated inflation reduces the real value of its debt, making it easier for the government to repay it. Second, because taxes are not completely indexed, an increase in the inflation rate increases governments real tax revenues, allowing it to spend more without raising nominal tax rates.

Inflation and Net Exports

Inflation also can affect exports and imports. Suppose the United States is experiencing more inflation than the rest of the world. All other things equal, U.S. exports will become less competitive in world markets. Consequently, the United States will export less. This will have an adverse impact on output and employment in the economy's export-producing sectors (such as the agricultural and airplane industries).

With prices rising more rapidly in the United States, imports become relatively less expensive. As a result, purchasers will buy fewer domestically produced goods and services and more imports. The increase in imports has an adverse impact on output and employment in the economy's import-competing sector (such as the automobile and steel industries).

We find that a higher inflation rate in the United States than in the rest of the world decreases U.S. exports and increases U.S. imports. (A lower inflation rate would have the opposite effect.) Over time, the dollar will depreciate (decrease) in value in terms of foreign currencies. The depreciation in the dollar will compensate for the higher inflation rate in the United States, although it may take years. In the interim, both the export-producing and import-competing sectors of the U.S. economy will endure economic hardship.

Other Effects

As the inflation rate rises, it becomes more variable, making planning for the future more difficult. Under these circumstances, more resources will be devoted to predicting the inflation rate. Similarly, people will devote more resources to devising ways to protect their real income and wealth. To the extent that fewer resources are allocated to the production of goods and services, the nation's output of goods and services will be reduced.

A high and variable inflation rate also may lead to speculation in real estate, gold, antiques, and art. During periods of rising prices, these assets often appreciate significantly in value. Although buying these assets may prove profitable, it does not increase the nation's capital stock. Indeed, to the extent that resources are diverted from investment in plant and equipment, the nation's capital stock will grow less rapidly. As a result, the GDP growth rate will be reduced and the nation's standard of living will improve less rapidly.

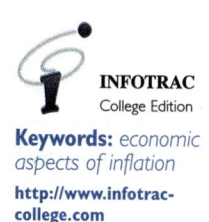

INFOTRAC
College Edition

Keywords: *economic aspects of inflation*
http://www.infotrac-college.com

Finally, when the inflation rate becomes dangerously high, a nation's monetary system may disintegrate. When prices rise very rapidly, the purchasing power of money deteriorates sharply. As a result, people will hold little or no money. They also will insist on being paid often so that they can buy goods before they increase further in price. At some point, money will become worthless, and people will exchange goods and services only for other goods and services. Barter is extremely inefficient because it takes much time and effort to find people who both have what you want and are willing to trade for what you have. The nation's output of goods and services will decline, and the economy may collapse.

History has provided many examples. The most famous involves Germany after World War I. In 1922, its inflation rate was over 5,000 percent. In 1923, in just four months, prices increased by more than a million times. Prices increased almost continuously. Diners at restaurants found, for example, that they had to pay more for their meals than was listed on the menu when they ordered. Prices became astronomical, with meat and butter costing millions of marks per pound. Money became worthless or virtually worthless. It was used as kindling to start fires.

Hyperinflation – Extremely high inflation rates.

Although we could mention many examples of **hyperinflation**—extremely high inflation rates—inflation need not and typically does not reach such high proportions. The hyperinflation in post–World War I Germany was caused by the government's printing huge amounts of money. Most governments are much more prudent.

■ Money and The Money Supply

As just discussed, hyperinflations are caused by huge increases in the money supply. What about more moderate inflation rates? Are they caused by increases in the money supply? This is a very important question. Before answering it, however, we must consider money, its functions, and the money supply.

Money's Functions

Money has three functions. Money serves as (1) a unit of account, (2) a medium of exchange, and (3) a store of value. With regard to money's *unit of account* function, we keep track of the value of things in terms of money. A pizza costs $5.00, a hamburger $2.50, a hot dog $1.00, and so on. By using a common measure, we can easily compare relative costs. A pizza costs twice as much as a hamburger and five times as much as a hot dog. This ease of comparison greatly aids decision making.

Money's medium of exchange function is extremely important. A **medium of exchange** is something that can be used to purchase goods and services and pay debts. In ancient times, households were largely self-sufficient. They grew and cooked their own food, made their own clothes, built their own dwellings, and so on. Few goods and services were exchanged. Little need existed, therefore, for a medium of exchange. As time passed, however, households found it in their interest to specialize in relatively few activities and trade or barter the goods that they produced for other goods and services. As a result, a need for a medium of exchange developed. Money greatly simplified the exchange of goods and services. It would be almost impossible for a modern economy to function without a medium of exchange, because the alternative—barter—is extremely inefficient.

With regard to its *store of value* function, money is a way for households to hold their savings. They may hold their savings in other forms, including bonds, common stock, and real estate. Money, therefore, is not unique as a store of value. Moreover, during periods of inflation, money is an unsatisfactory store of value because rising prices erode its purchasing power. For this reason, households and firms seek to reduce their holdings of money during periods of inflation.

The Money Supply

Money usually is defined in terms of its medium of exchange function. **Money** is anything generally accepted as final payment for goods, services, and debt. **Currency (cash)**—paper money and coins—is money because it is generally accepted as payment for goods, services, and debt. Similarly, **demand deposits**—checking accounts at commercial banks—are money because checks are generally accepted as payment for goods, services, and debt. The same is true of other checkable deposits, including those at savings and loan associations and credit unions. Based on this definition, however, savings and time deposits are not money because we cannot use them as final payment for goods, services, and debt. We must first convert them to currency or some other form of money. The same is true of other assets such as bonds and stocks. Those assets are not generally accepted as final payment for goods, services, and debt.

Given the definition of money, we are now in a position to define the nation's **money supply**. The money supply is defined as currency, travelers' checks, demand deposits, and other checkable deposits. Like the other components of the money supply, travelers' checks are included in the money supply because they are generally accepted as final payment for goods, services, and debt. As shown in Table 15.2, currency accounts for 51.6 percent of the money supply, and demand and the other checkable deposits account for 47.7 percent. Travelers' checks account for the remaining 1 percent of the nation's money supply.

Medium of Exchange – Anything used to purchase goods and services and pay debts.

Money – Anything generally accepted as final payment for goods, services, and debt.

Currency (Cash) – Paper money and coins.

Demand Deposits – Checking accounts at commercial banks.

Money Supply – Currency (including coins), checkable deposits, and travelers' checks.

INSIGHTS

CURRENCY HOLDINGS AND THE UNDERGROUND ECONOMY

Although currency is convenient for small transactions, checkable deposits have many advantages as a medium of exchange. Currency can be lost, destroyed, or stolen. For large transactions, it is bulky. Checks can be made for any amount, large or small. They also provide a record of the transactions. Finally, checkable deposits are typically insured.

With these advantages, it is not surprising that checkable deposits account for almost half of the nation's money supply. Even so, both on a per capita basis and as a percentage of the money supply, currency is more important now than it was in 1960. Indeed, more than $2,100 in cash is in circulation for every man, woman, and child in the United States. For those of us who rarely have more than $20 or $30 in cash, this statistic is astounding.

What accounts for this increase in cash balances? Is it because we have more coin-operated machines and the like? Most experts believe that this explanation can account for only a small part of the increase in cash balances. One reason for the increase, they believe, is the growth of the underground economy, especially the part that deals with illegal drugs.

When people participate in the underground economy, they want no records of their transactions. After all, records can be used to identify them and as evidence in a court of law. Also, honor among thieves aside, there is unlikely to be trust. People engaged in illegal activities usually insist on payment in cash.

The large influx of immigrants may have contributed to the increase in cash balances. For various reasons, many immigrants prefer to hold cash rather than open checking accounts at banks.

Finally, much U.S. currency is held abroad. Individuals in foreign countries often prefer to hold dollars because they distrust their own currency. Large amounts of U.S. currency are held in Central and South America, Eastern Europe (particularly Russia), and the Middle and Far East. Although some U.S. currency has always been held abroad, the trend toward foreign ownership has become more pronounced in recent years.

TABLE 15.2 The Money Supply and Its Components: October 2002

The nation's money supply (M1) was $1,201.3 billion in October 2002. Currency accounted for 51.6 percent of the money supply. Demand and other checkable deposits accounted for almost all (47.7 percent) of the remainder.

Component	Amount (Billions of Dollars)[a]	Relative Importance (Percent)
Currency	619.8	51.6
Travelers' checks	7.7	0.6
Demand deposits	295.9	24.6
Other checkable deposits	277.8	23.1
Totals	1201.3	100.0

[a]Average of daily figures (seasonally adjusted).

SOURCE: Board of Governors of the Federal Reserve System, *Federal Reserve Bulletin* or http://www.federalreserve.gov/releases.

The money supply, as defined here, corresponds to one of the monetary aggregates published by the Federal Reserve. This aggregate is referred to as M1. The other aggregates—M2 and M3—are defined more broadly.

M2 includes the various components of M1. It also includes savings and (small-denomination) time deposits, money market deposit accounts, and money market mutual funds. Savings and time deposits are included because they are easily converted to cash or checkable deposits. Persons with money market deposit accounts can, within certain limits, write checks on these accounts. Persons participating in money market mutual funds also have that privilege. M2 is of importance because the Federal Reserve often emphasizes M2 in conducting monetary policy.

M3 is defined even more broadly. Many of its components, however, are not easily convertible to cash or checkable deposits. Consequently, it is not important for our purposes. In addition, the Federal Reserve places more emphasis on M1 and M2 than on M3 in conducting monetary policy.

The Federal Reserve

The Federal Reserve, an independent agency of the federal government, is the United States' central bank. By **central bank**, we mean a government-established agency that controls the nation's money supply, conducts monetary policy, and, in general, supervises the nation's monetary system. Because these functions are so important, countries typically have central banks. In England, the central bank is the Bank of England; in the Euro Zone, it is the European Central Bank; and so on.

The Federal Reserve controls the nation's money supply. If policy makers at the Federal Reserve believe that the money supply should increase or decrease more rapidly, they can take the appropriate action. The Federal Reserve and the nation's monetary system are discussed in greater detail in the appendix to this chapter.

Central Bank – A government-established agency that controls the nation's money supply, conducts monetary policy, and supervises the monetary system.

■ CAUSES OF INFLATION

After defining and discussing the nation's money supply, we now turn to the causes of inflation. Inflation is a continuing rise in the price level. In the absence of policies to reduce or eliminate it, inflation will continue indefinitely. Inflation, therefore, is a long-run phenomenon.

The Quantity Theory of Money

Inflation can best be explained in terms of the **quantity theory of money**. This theory emphasizes that the money supply is the principal determinant of nominal GDP. The quantity theory of money, in turn, can be explained with reference to the equation of exchange. The **equation of exchange** shows the relationship among the money supply (M), the income velocity of money (V), the GDP deflator (P), and real GDP. It is

(15.2) $$M \times V = P \times GDP$$

(The money supply was defined earlier in this chapter; the GDP deflator and real GDP were defined in Chapter 13.) The **income velocity of money** is the number of times the money supply is used to purchase final goods and services during a year. It is calculated by dividing nominal GDP ($P \times GDP$) by the money supply (M). Suppose that nominal GDP is $1 trillion and that the money supply is $100 billion. The income velocity of money is 10, obtained by dividing $1 trillion by $100 billion.

As the equation stands, it is a tautology—something that is true by definition. This is so because the velocity of money is defined in terms of the other variables ($V = $ Nominal GDP/M). In the example, the

Quantity Theory of Money – A theory emphasizing that the money supply is the principal determinant of nominal GDP.

Equation of Exchange – An equation showing the relationships among the money supply, the income velocity of money, the GDP deflator, and real GDP.

Income Velocity of Money – The number of times the money supply is used to purchase final goods and services during a year.

money supply is $100 billion. If that much money is used to purchase $1 trillion worth of goods and services, it must be used 10 times. Another way to view it is to note that the left side of the equation of exchange (M × V) represents the amount spent on final goods and services, and the right side (P × GDP) represents the amount received for those final goods and services. These two amounts must be equal.

The quantity theory of money assumes that the velocity of money is constant or approximately so. Although velocity varies to some extent from year to year, it shows greater stability in the long run. Because inflation is a long-run phenomenon, we shall assume initially that it is constant.

Chapter 13 shows that an increase in the money supply, through its impact on aggregate demand, results in an increase in nominal GDP. The same is true in the quantity theory. Moreover, the increase in nominal GDP is proportional to the increase in the money supply, provided that the velocity of money is constant. Suppose the money supply increases from $100 billion to $200 billion. With the velocity of money constant, nominal GDP must increase from $1 trillion to $2 trillion. If unemployment existed initially, both the GDP deflator and real GDP will rise. If full employment prevailed, only the GDP deflator will rise.

To determine the impact of an increase in the money supply on the inflation rate, we rewrite equation 15.2 to obtain

$$\frac{\Delta M}{M} + \frac{\Delta V}{V} = \frac{\Delta P}{P} + \frac{\Delta GDP}{GDP}$$

In the equation, $\Delta M/M$, the change in the money supply (ΔM) divided by the money supply, is the growth rate of the money supply; $\Delta V/V$, the change in velocity (ΔV) divided by velocity, is the growth rate of velocity; $\Delta P/P$, the change in the GDP deflator (ΔP) divided by the GDP deflator, is the inflation rate; and $\Delta GDP/GDP$, the change in real GDP (ΔGDP) divided by real GDP, is the output growth rate. If the velocity of money is constant (ΔV and therefore $\Delta V/V$ equal zero) we have

(15.3) $$\frac{\Delta M}{M} = \frac{\Delta P}{P} + \frac{\Delta GDP}{GDP}$$

Equation 15.3 states that the growth rate of the money supply equals the inflation rate plus the output growth rate. Rearranging terms gives

(15.4) $$\frac{\Delta P}{P} = \frac{\Delta M}{M} - \frac{\Delta GDP}{GDP}$$

Equation 15.4 states that the inflation rate equals the growth rate of the money supply less the output growth rate.

The growth rate of the money supply is determined by the Federal Reserve. In the long run, the growth rate of output is determined by the growth rates of the nation's resources and by the rate of technological progress. Over the business cycle, the growth rate of real GDP varies. In the long run, however, aggregate supply and real GDP increase by about 3 percent per year.

The growth rate of the money supply that is consistent with a stable price level, or a zero inflation rate, can now be determined. To do so, substitute zero for the inflation rate and 3 percent for the output growth rate in equation 15.4, and then solve for $\Delta M/M$. The solution is 3 percent, implying that the money supply can grow at a 3 percent rate and the price level will still remain constant.

INTERNATIONAL PERSPECTIVE

DEFLATION IN JAPAN: THE REEMERGENCE OF AN OLD ISSUE

As we saw in Table 15.1, the Japanese economy experienced deflation from 1996 to 2001. In fact, the Japanese economy has stagnated since the beginning of the 1990s, when its stock market crashed. Its output growth has averaged less than 1 percent a year, while its unemployment rate is approaching 6 percent. Although its current unemployment rate is below the European Union's unemployment rate, the Japanese economy had been accustomed an unemployment rate of around 2 percent in the 1980s, a period when the annual output growth was about 4 percent per year.

The economic causes of Japan's lost decade of economic growth or its decade of stagnation are complex and not well understood by economists or other analysts. Its stock market crash is sometimes referred to as a burst bubble. The analogy to a bubble is an attempt to explain a sudden collapse after a period when investment in the stock market (financial investment), in plant and equipment (physical capital), and in new enterprises frenetically feeds upon itself. The recent dot-com bubble that preceded the collapse in U. S. investment—stock market, physical capital, and new enterprises—provides another example of the phenomenon.

Although the Japanese economy grew at 1 percent over this period, its industrial production stagnated and fell by 15 percent in 2001. As a result, in 2002, 12 years after its stock market collapse, Japan's industrial production was about 10 percent below that at the beginning of the 1990s. In comparison, U.S. industrial production fell by much more than this after the stock market crash of 1929, but it returned to its pre-crash level in about 8 years. Thus, the Japanese economy did not go as deeply into depression as the U.S. economy did in the Great Depression; Japan's overall loss in output, however, is comparable to the U.S. loss because its still ongoing economic collapse lasted much longer than the U.S. collapse.

Deflation has caused tremendous problems in the Japanese economy and has increased the difficulty of finding a solution. An unexpected deflation creates losses for debtors because they must repay their loans with money that is worth more than it was when they borrowed. With deflation, or lower than expected inflation, debtors find that their debts are much more burdensome. Some debtors have to sell physical assets to meet their obligations, increasing the downward pressure on asset prices. In addition to the downward pressure on asset prices, indebted consumers find it difficult to make their payments, which may decrease aggregate demand. Moreover, when consumers realize that prices are falling, they may postpone purchases in order to get a "better buy" later. It's like waiting for the price of a new generation of computers to fall before making the purchase. This adds to the downward pressure on aggregate demand. Firms, therefore, postpone investment because their sales are weak and also because they expect prices of capital equipment to fall. These decreases in aggregate demand intensify the deflation, creating a feedback effect that makes it difficult to halt a deflationary process.[a]

---
[a] Suggested by various articles in *The Economist*, including "Terrible Twins? Economic Parallels Between America and Japan." June 13, 2002, and "Comparing Symptoms. The Risk of Deflation," November 7, 2002.

The aggregate supply–aggregate demand framework can illustrate this result. Suppose that, in Figure 15.2, aggregate demand is AD_1 and aggregate supply is AS_1. (For convenience, the aggregate demand and supply curves are assumed to be linear.) The price level, given by the intersection of AD_1 and AS_1, is P_1. As the nation's capital stock and labor supply increase and technological progress occurs, aggregate supply increases. Suppose the new aggregate supply curve is AS_2. If aggregate demand increases at the same rate to AD_2, the price level, given by the intersection of AD_2 and AS_2, will be P_1, the same as the original price level. Should aggregate demand and supply continue to grow over time at the same rate, the price level will remain constant.

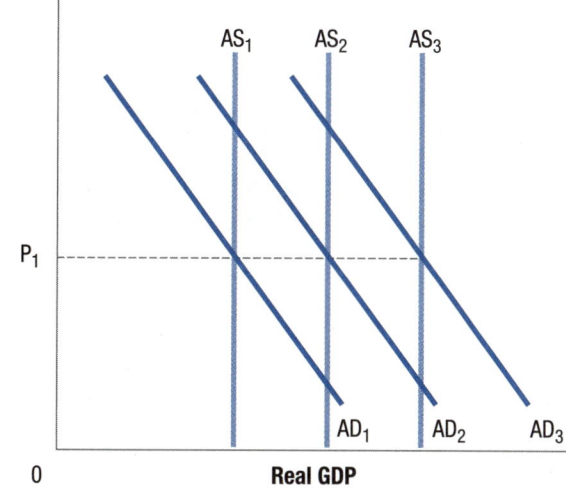

FIGURE 15.2 Aggregate Demand, Aggregate Supply, and the Price Level

The price level is determined by aggregate demand and supply. The initial price level is P_1, given by the intersection of the initial aggregate demand curve AD_1 and aggregate supply curve AS_1. If aggregate demand and supply grow at the same rate—such as the shift from AD_1 to AD_2 and the shift from AS_1 to AS_2—the price level remains constant.

In the example, the money supply can grow at 3 percent without causing inflation. Suppose the money supply were to grow at, say, 8 percent. What would be the impact of the increased growth rate of the money supply on the inflation rate? Equation 15.4 gives the answer. With 8 percent growth in the money supply and 3 percent output growth, the inflation rate is 5 percent (8 percent − 3 percent).

Once again, the aggregate supply–aggregate demand framework can demonstrate this result. Suppose that, in Figure 15.3, aggregate demand is AD_1 and aggregate supply is AS_1. The price level, given by the intersection of AD_1 and AS_1, is P_1. As the nation's capital stock and labor supply increase and technological progress occurs, aggregate supply increases, say to AS_2. Previously, aggregate demand increased at the same rate as aggregate supply and the price level was constant. The money supply, however, is now increasing at an 8 percent rate rather than a 3 percent rate. With the velocity of money constant, aggregate demand also grows at 8 percent. Therefore, in period 2 the new aggregate demand curve has shifted farther to the right than the aggregate supplied has shifted. Measured at the price level P_1, AD_2 is farther to the right than AS_2. The new price level P_2, given by the intersection of AD_2 and AS_2, is higher than the original price level, P_1.

With aggregate demand growing more rapidly than aggregate supply, the price level will continue to rise. With aggregate demand growing at an 8 percent rate and aggregate supply at a 3 percent rate, the price level will rise at a 5 percent rate.

Inflation Is a Monetary Phenomenon

The inflation rate rises from 0 percent to 5 percent when the growth rate of the money supply rises from 3 percent to 8 percent. This demonstrates a very important proposition: The higher the growth rate of the money supply, the higher the inflation rate. Excessive rates of growth of the money supply cause inflation; therefore, inflation is a monetary phenomenon. Figure 15.4 shows the relationship between the inflation rate and the money supply growth rate for 110 countries during the period 1960 to 1990. The

INFOTRAC
College Edition
Keywords: *quantity theory of money*
http://www.infotrac-college.com

FIGURE 15.3 Aggregate Demand, Aggregate Supply, and Inflation

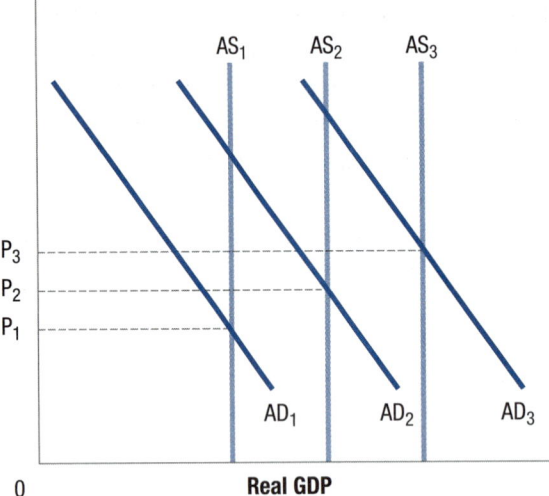

The price level is determined by aggregate demand and supply. The initial price level is P_1, given by the intersection of the initial aggregate demand curve AD_1 and aggregate supply curve AS_1. If aggregate demand grows more rapidly than aggregate supply—such as the shift from AD_1 to AD_2 compared to the larger shift from AS_1 to AS_2—the price level rises.

money supply growth rate and the inflation rate are measured for periods of 10 to 30 years, depending upon the country. The average growth rates over the long time period are used because inflation is a long-run phenomenon. The points surround an imaginary line that slopes up to the right. It says as the money supply growth rate increases, the inflation rate increases. The fact that actual data trace out a positive relationship between the money supply and the inflation rate supports the quantity theory of money and the proposition that inflation is a monetary phenomenon. Before examining the policy implications of this explanation of inflation, we consider two qualifications.

Inflation as a Monetary Phenomenon: Two Qualifications

Based on equation 15.4, an increase in the growth rate of the money supply causes the inflation rate to rise. This conclusion assumes that (1) the output growth rate is constant and (2) the velocity of money is constant. If these assumptions are relaxed, the relationship between the growth rate of the money supply and the inflation rate is not as strong.

THE OUTPUT GROWTH RATE. Previously, we assumed that real GDP grew at 3 percent. Although the output growth rate has averaged about 3 percent since 1929, the growth rate varies over the business cycle. Typically, it exceeds 3 percent during expansions (particularly during the early stages) and is less than 3 percent during contractions. Given this variation in growth rates, the inflation rate will vary over the business cycle even if the growth rate of the money supply is constant.

Suppose the economy is beginning to recover from a recession. During a recession, unemployment is high and firms have excess capacity. Because they have idle equipment and easily can hire more workers, firms can increase output relatively rapidly. Suppose the money supply is growing at 8 percent. If output grows at 3 percent (the long-run average), the inflation rate will be 5 percent. With excess capacity and high unemployment, output may grow at a higher rate, say, 5 percent. With the money supply growing at 8 percent and output growing at 5 percent, the inflation rate is only 3 percent.

FIGURE 15.4   The Long-Run Relation Between Inflation and Money Supply Growth: Cross-Country Data

These data show the inflation rate for a country and its relationship with money supply growth. The period covered is somewhere between 1960 and 1990, is at least 10 years, and it varies with country depending upon data availability. The point in the upper-right corner is for Argentina. It shows that Argentina had a money supply growth rate of about 80 percent (reading on the horizontal axis) and also an inflation rate of about 80 percent (reading on the vertical axis). The next highest inflation rate, for Poland, is about 55 percent, and the associated money supply growth rate is about 50 percent. The second highest money supply growth rate is for Chile, about 52 percent, with an associated inflation rate of about 40 percent. The specific numbers and countries are not the point of the figure. The point is that there is a strong association between money supply growth and inflation, just as the quantity theory predicts.

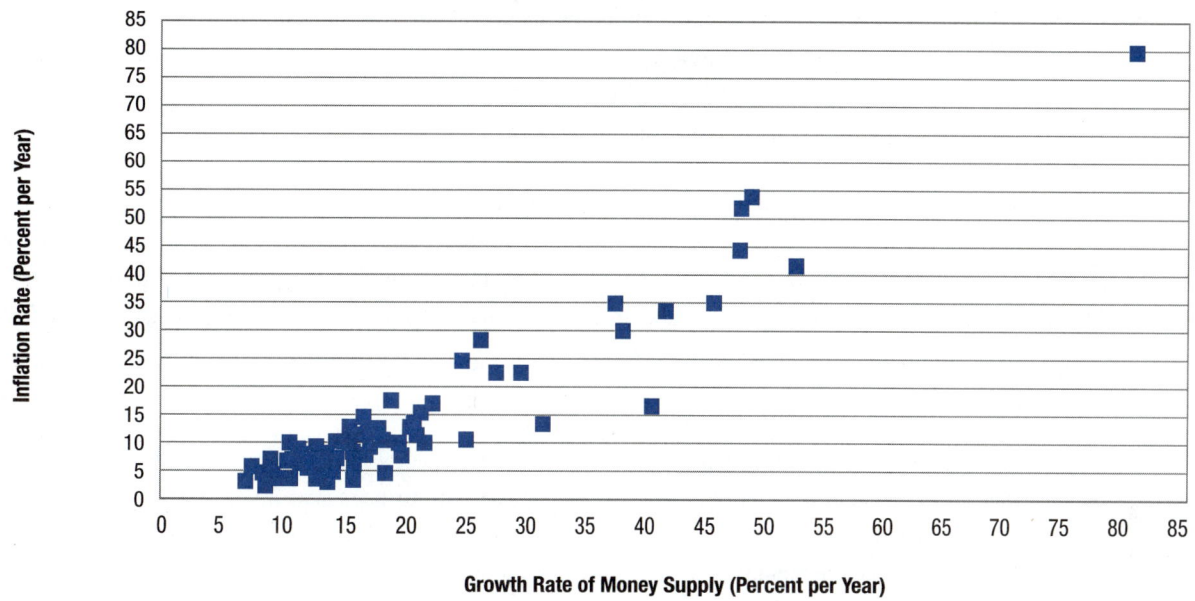

SOURCE: George T. McCandless, Jr., and Warren E. Weber, "Some Monetary Facts," Federal Reserve Bank of Minneapolis, *Quarterly Review*, Vol. 25, No. 4, Fall 2001. Reprinted from *Quarterly Review*, Summer 1995.

Output cannot grow at 5 percent indefinitely. Sooner or later, full employment will be achieved and output will grow less rapidly. If the money supply continues to grow at 8 percent and the output growth rate falls, the inflation rate will rise.

With variable output growth, the inflation rate varies even if the growth rate of the money supply is constant. Because the output growth rate varies in the short run, we find that the relationship between the growth rate of the money supply and the inflation rate is not as strong as originally stated. The long-run relationship, however, is clear. If the money supply grows faster than the long-run output growth rate, inflation will ensue. Thus, the short-run variation in the output growth rate does not modify the conclusion that inflation is a monetary phenomenon. Instead, it merely obscures the relationship between the growth rate of the money supply and the inflation rate.

THE VELOCITY OF MONEY. Just as the output growth rate varies in the short run, the velocity of money varies. Suppose the growth rate of the money supply increases. With velocity and the output growth rate constant, the inflation rate rises. If the velocity of money falls at the same time the growth rate of the money supply increases, the inflation rate will rise but by a smaller amount. In both situations, the increase in growth rate of the money supply is the same. In the second situation, the money supply circulates less rapidly. It, therefore, has less of an impact on the inflation rate.

In the short run, the velocity of money may fall in response to an increase in the growth rate of the money supply. In the long run, however, the velocity of money is relatively constant. Consequently, the short-run variation in velocity does not alter the conclusion that inflation is a monetary phenomenon. Like the short-run variation in the output growth rate, it merely obscures the relationship between the growth rate of the money supply and the inflation rate.

Similarly, suppose government purchases increase while the money supply is constant. With the increase in government purchases, aggregate demand increases and the price level rises. With the money supply constant, the increase in the price level must stem from an increase in the velocity of money caused by the increase in government purchases.

Although factors other than the money supply (in this case, government purchases) affect the price level through variations in the velocity of money in the short run, these factors are much less important in the long run because of the relative constancy of the velocity of money in the long run. If the velocity of money is constant (or approximately so), it is the growth rate of the money supply that determines the growth rate of aggregate demand and, with a constant growth rate of aggregate supply, the inflation rate. Inflation is a monetary phenomenon.

Labor Unions, Monopolies, and Inflation

Economists generally agree that inflation is a monetary phenomenon. Some economists, however, argue that the exercise of monopoly power by labor unions and firms causes inflation.

LABOR UNIONS. According to the argument, labor unions—through the collective bargaining process—force wages up more rapidly than they would otherwise increase. Firms, in turn, pass their higher labor costs on to their customers in the form of higher prices. In terms of the aggregate demand–aggregate supply model, a general increase in wage rates causes the aggregate supply curve to shift to the left, at least over part of its range (see Figure 13.6 on page 338). With a reduction in aggregate supply and with aggregate demand constant, the price level rises. In this situation, labor unions cause the price level to rise.

But is this a likely occurrence? Most economists think not. First, many labor unions lack significant bargaining power and therefore cannot force up the wages of their members more rapidly than they would otherwise increase. Second, even if labor unions can force up union wages, it is unlikely that they will alter wages in general. Less than 15 percent of nonagricultural workers belong to unions. Consequently, the overwhelming majority of workers are not covered by union contracts. In addition, unions can force up wages only by limiting employment opportunities in the unionized sector of the economy. Those unable to find employment in the unionized sector will turn to the nonunionized sector, thereby depressing wages there. Consequently, even if unions can force up union wages, average wages are unlikely to be altered significantly. Labor unions, therefore, are an unlikely cause of inflation.

FIRMS. Like labor unions, firms often are accused of causing inflation by exercising monopoly power. That is, firms are accused of raising prices even in the absence of increased demand or rising costs.

This could not happen in a purely competitive economy. In a purely competitive economy, each product has many sellers. A single seller would be unable to raise prices above the market price and retain its customers. Moreover, because many sellers exist, it is impossible for them to collude. Thus, the argument that firms cause inflation cannot hold in a purely competitive economy.

Although part of the U.S. economy is purely competitive, part of it is not. In industries characterized by imperfect competition, firms have discretion regarding the prices of their products. Even so, inflation is not inevitable. Indeed, economic theory suggests that a monopolist (to take the simplest case) will set a price that maximizes profits. Once the monopolist sets the profit-maximizing price, however, management has no incentive to raise price further. (As explained in Chapter 5, a higher price would reduce profits.)

In conclusion, monopolists are interested in charging "high" prices. Inflation, however, is not about high prices; it is about rising prices. Consequently, although we would expect prices to be higher under monopoly than under pure competition, we would *not* expect price to rise indefinitely because of market power. Thus we would not expect inflation to be a greater problem in an economy where some industries have market power than in an economy where all industries are competitive.

■ Inflation and Policy

The appropriate cure for inflation depends upon its cause. Monetary policy, fiscal policy, supply-side policies, and incomes policy are proposed cures. Monetary and fiscal policies are government actions designed to control aggregate demand. **Supply-side policies** are government actions aimed at increasing aggregate supply. **Incomes policy** is government action, other than monetary and fiscal policies, to restrain or control wages, prices, and other forms of income.

Supply-Side Policies – Government actions aimed at increasing aggregate supply.

Incomes Policy – Government action, other than monetary and fiscal policies, to restrain or control wages, prices, and other forms of income.

Monetary Policy

Earlier, we concluded that inflation is a monetary phenomenon; that is, it is caused by excessive rates of growth of the money supply. To reduce the inflation rate, the growth rate of the money supply must therefore be reduced. Reducing the growth rate of the money supply will cause aggregate demand to grow less rapidly. With aggregate supply growing at a constant rate in the long run, slower growth in aggregate demand will lower the inflation rate. We found earlier that an 8 percent growth rate in the money supply implies an inflation rate of 5 percent. If the money supply growth rate was reduced to 5 percent, the inflation rate would drop to 2 percent (see equation 15.4).

Reducing the money supply growth rate reduces the inflation rate. Because the Federal Reserve controls the money supply, this would seem to be an easy matter. Unfortunately, two problems exist. One is that an unexpected reduction in the inflation rate causes a redistribution of income and wealth in much the same manner as an unexpected increase in the inflation rate. Firms that agreed to large wage increases in anticipation of continued inflation will find that the prices of their products increase less rapidly if the inflation rate falls, making it more difficult for them to fulfill their contractual obligations. People who borrowed at high interest rates in anticipation of continued inflation also will find themselves worse off if the inflation rate falls. Because some firms and households will be adversely affected, they will resist policies aimed at reducing inflation.

INSIGHTS

THE FED AS INFLATION FIGHTER

The Federal Reserve, or Fed, has primary responsibility for achieving and maintaining a low inflation rate. When inflation threatens, the Fed significantly reduces the money supply growth rate and raises short-term interest rates. This is designed to reduce the growth rate of aggregate demand, thereby reducing the upward pressure on prices.

Except for the discount rate, the Federal Reserve has no direct control over interest rates.[a] The Fed, however, can alter the federal funds rate. *Federal funds* are loans between banks of their deposits at the Federal Reserve. The interest rate on these loans is called the *federal funds rate*. By increasing or decreasing bank reserves, the Fed can lower or raise the federal funds rate.

In 1994 and again in 1999 and 2000, the Fed raised interest rates to keep inflation from rising. In 1994, the Fed raised the federal funds rate on six occasions for a total increase in the rate of 2.5 percentage points. In 1999 and 2000, the Fed again raised the federal funds rate six times, for a total of 1.75 percentage points. As the federal funds rate increased, other interest rates increased.

Critics of the Federal Reserve's actions note that the inflation rate did not rise substantially in either 1994 or 1999 to 2000. This, however, does not necessarily imply that the Fed's actions were unwarranted. Like an ocean liner, the U.S. economy has considerable momentum. If an ocean liner is headed toward a reef, the helmsman cannot wait until the last moment to turn the rudder. Because of the ship's momentum, the rudder must be turned well in advance. The same is true for the economy. If the Federal Reserve is to avoid a significant increase in the inflation rate, it must act before the inflation rate rises. Moreover, once the inflation rate rises, it is extraordinarily difficult to reduce it without causing a recession.

In January 2001, the Fed, suspecting that the economy was slowing, began a series of 11 cuts in 2001 that totaled a decrease of 4.75 percentage points. Although a recession began in March 2001, the Fed's actions may have reduced the length and severity of the recession. In November 2002, almost a year after the last cut in 2001, the Fed cut the federal funds rate by another one-half percentage point, in an attempt to ensure economic recovery.

Should the economy grow rapidly in the future and inflation threaten, we can expect the Federal Reserve to reduce the growth rate of the money supply and raise interest rates.

---

[a]The discount rate is the interest rate at which banks and other depository institutions borrow from the Federal Reserve. It is discussed in the appendix to this chapter.

INFOTRAC
College Edition

Keywords: *federal funds rate*

http://www.infotrac-college.com

Another problem is that the reduction in the inflation rate is likely to be accompanied by an increase in the unemployment rate in the short run. This is especially true if the inflation has continued for some time. One reason for the increase in unemployment is the contractual obligations of firms to pay higher wages. These contracts were presumably signed when it appeared that the inflation would continue. The reduction in the inflation rate means that firms will see the prices of their products increase less rapidly or not at all. Consequently, they may be forced to discharge workers in order to meet their contractual obligations to the remaining employees. Such reductions in employment cause the unemployment rate to rise.

Historically, reductions in inflation are often accompanied by increases in unemployment. This happened, for example, in the early 1980s. During President Carter's administration, the price level increased more rapidly each year. In 1979 and 1980, inflation (as measured by the CPI) reached double-digit levels. To reduce the inflation rate, the Federal Reserve sharply reduced the growth rate of the money supply in

Keywords: *monetary policy and inflation, deflation*

http://www.infotrac-college.com

1981. The inflation rate fell dramatically in 1982 and 1983. At the same time, the unemployment rate increased dramatically. As time passed, the unemployment rate returned to its full employment level.

During the transition period from a high inflation rate to a lower one, the unemployment rate tends to be above its full employment level. This increased unemployment with its attendant hardships is perhaps the most important reason why the Federal Reserve sometimes fails to take action to reduce the growth rate of the money supply to a level consistent with price stability.

Fiscal Policy

Because fiscal policy can alter aggregate demand, it is appropriate to examine its role in reducing inflation. In the short run, contractionary fiscal policy can hold the price level in check. As before, suppose the money supply and, hence, aggregate demand are growing at 8 percent. With aggregate supply growing at 3 percent, the inflation rate is 5 percent. To slow the rate of increase in aggregate demand, government spending may be reduced or taxes increased. If policy makers enact a contractionary fiscal policy, the effect of the growth of the money supply on aggregate demand will be at least partially offset. As a result, the price level will rise less rapidly. Unfortunately, so long as the money supply continues to grow, policy makers must continue to reduce government spending or raise taxes. Most government spending is for Social Security, national defense, interest on the national debt, and various programs to assist the poor. These programs cannot be cut indefinitely. Similarly, taxes cannot be raised indefinitely.

Thus, although contractionary fiscal policy may achieve temporary relief from increases in the price level, it cannot indefinitely offset the effects of the growth in the money supply on aggregate demand. Consequently, fiscal policy cannot be regarded as a serious alternative to monetary policy in fighting inflation. In the long run, contractionary monetary policy must be applied.

Keywords: *fiscal policy and inflation*

http://www.infotrac-college.com

Supply-Side Policies

A potential cure of inflation is an increase in the growth rate of aggregate supply. If aggregate supply was to grow more rapidly, the inflation rate would fall. As before, suppose the money supply and aggregate demand are growing at 8 percent. If aggregate supply is growing at 3 percent, the inflation rate is 5 percent. Suppose the growth rate of aggregate supply could be increased to 6 percent. The inflation rate would then fall to 2 percent.

Are policies to increase the growth rate of aggregate supply—supply-side policies—effective? Unfortunately, no. It is very difficult to increase the growth rate of aggregate supply, which depends on the growth rate of the labor supply, the rate of capital accumulation, and the rate of technological progress. Labor supply growth depends, ultimately, on population growth. Barring changes in immigration laws, little can be done, at least in the short run, to change the population growth rate. The nation's tax laws could be altered to favor investment in plant and equipment. Even if politically feasible, such a change might have a small impact on investment. Similarly, the tax laws could be altered to encourage firms to devote more resources to research and development. This might increase the rate of technological progress; however, the impact could be small.

In view of the U.S. experience, most economists believe that an increase in the growth rate of aggregate supply from 3 to 4 percent (a $33^{1}/_{3}$ percent increase) would be a tremendous achievement. If the growth rate of aggregate supply was to increase by 1 percentage point, the inflation rate would fall by 1 percentage point. If the inflation rate is low (say, 2 or 3 percent), the increase in the growth rate of aggregate supply would significantly reduce the inflation rate. If the inflation rate is higher, the reduction would be much less significant.

Suppose the money supply and aggregate demand are growing at 13 percent and aggregate supply at 3 percent. The inflation rate is 10 percent. Now suppose the growth rate of aggregate supply increases from 3 percent to 4 percent. If the money supply and aggregate demand continue to grow at 13 percent, the inflation rate falls—but only to 9 percent. Thus, despite the tremendous achievement (by historical standards) of increasing the growth rate of aggregate supply by $33^{1}/_{3}$ percent (from 3 to 4 percent), the inflation rate falls by only 10 percent (from 10 to 9 percent). Given its variation over time, a reduction in the inflation rate from 10 to 9 percent is barely noticeable.

It is apparent that increasing the growth rate of aggregate supply is unlikely to reduce the inflation rate significantly. If policy makers are serious about reducing inflation, they must focus on reducing the growth rate of aggregate demand. In particular, they must concentrate on reducing the growth rate of the money supply.

Although increasing the growth rate of aggregate supply is unlikely to have a major impact on the inflation rate, it is nevertheless extremely important. The growth rate of aggregate supply determines the nation's output growth rate and hence the standard of living. If the growth rate of aggregate supply could be increased from 3 to 4 percent, the nation's output of goods and services would increase $33^{1}/_{3}$ percent more rapidly, and living standards would improve much more rapidly than at present.

Incomes Policy

Incomes policy is governmental action, other than fiscal and monetary policy, aimed at influencing or controlling the rate of increase of prices, wages, and other forms of income. Although incomes policy takes various forms, the most common are wage-price guidelines and controls.

Either explicitly or implicitly, advocates of incomes policy usually believe that inflation is caused by the exercise of monopoly power by labor unions and firms. Although few economists share this view, it is important to become familiar with incomes policies and their effects.

The U.S. economy has been subjected to wage-price guidelines and controls during part of its history, most recently in 1979–1980. During the Carter administration, the price level increased more rapidly each year. To restrain inflation, President Carter announced a set of voluntary pay and price standards. Under these standards, firms and workers were to slow the rate at which prices and wages increased.

These standards proved ineffective. In fact, prices and wages increased even more rapidly after their imposition. Some economists claimed that inflation would have been even worse in the absence of the standards. Yet it was generally agreed that the program was not working, and it was dropped.

The Kennedy and Johnson administrations had earlier subjected the U.S. economy to wage-price guidelines, starting in 1962. These guidelines suffered the same fate as the Carter pay and price standards. When inflationary pressure became intense, they became ineffective and were abandoned. For all practical purposes, they ended in 1966.

Rather than voluntary guidelines, some people advocate the use of wage-price controls. With controls, firms cannot legally raise prices or wages more than the maximum permissible amount. The U.S. economy was subjected to wage-price controls during World War II and again during the 1970s. In August 1971, President Nixon imposed a 90-day freeze on prices and wages. The freeze was the first phase of a wage-price control program that ended in 1974. This program, like the others, ended in failure.

Economists oppose wage and price controls for at least four reasons. First, they tend to be ineffective. Second, to the extent that they are effective, controls distort the allocation of resources. Third, they are costly to administer. Finally, they are likely to cause inequities.

Controls often prove ineffective. Unless the money supply growth rate is reduced, we have strong upward pressure on prices and wages. In response, firms may reduce the size of their products or allow quality to deteriorate. Both actions are price hikes in disguise. With regard to wage hikes, firms usually may give wage increases to workers who are promoted. If a firm wishes to give a worker a raise, it can create a position and then "promote" the person.

To the extent that price controls are effective, they are likely to lead to a misallocation of resources. Consider the demand, D_0, and supply, S_0, curves for product A in Figure 15.5. The equilibrium price is P_0, and the equilibrium quantity is Q_0. Next, suppose the demand for product A increases. In the absence of price controls, the equilibrium price rises to P_1, giving firms an incentive to increase production. They will buy more raw materials, hire more workers, and so on. As they do so, production increases to Q_1.

Suppose, however, that price controls fix the price of the product at P_0. As a result, firms have no incentive to expand production. Indeed, output will remain at Q_0. A misallocation of resources occurs. Consumers would like to buy more of the product and are willing to pay a higher price. Legally, however, they cannot.[2]

FIGURE 15.5 Demand, Supply, and Price Controls

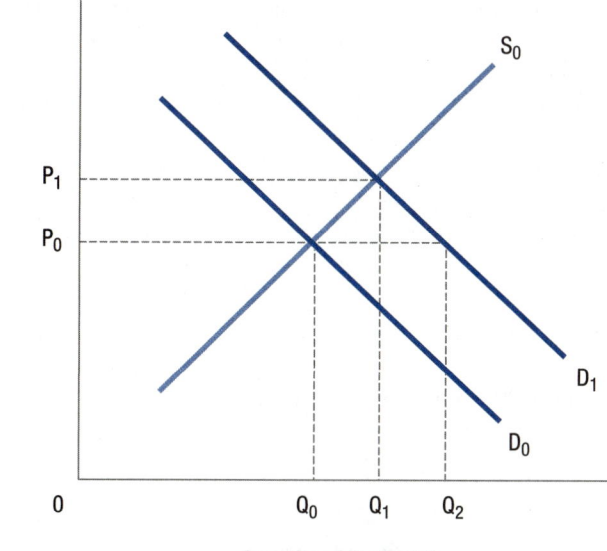

In the absence of price controls, an increase in the demand for good A results in a higher price, P_1. The increase in price induces firms to produce more of good A. With price controls, however, the price remains P_0. Firms have no incentive, therefore, to increase production. Consequently, too few resources will be devoted to the production of good A and, by implication, too many resources will be devoted to the production of other goods and services.

---

[2] After the increase in demand, a shortage, Q_2Q_0, exists at price P_0. The limited supply, Q_0, must be allocated in some way. During World War II, rationing was used. Despite widespread support of the war effort, black markets developed. In these markets, products were exchanged at prices well above the official price.

From society's standpoint, too few resources are devoted to the production of product A and, by implication, too many resources are devoted to the production of other goods.

Controls are costly to administer. During World War II, a large government bureaucracy administered the program. The Nixon controls were less costly to administer, both because existing government employees administered them and because the program was viewed as temporary. Even so, the controls were costly to taxpayers.

Controls are also costly to firms, which must keep better records and make them available for scrutiny. Controls do have one beneficial effect: They greatly increase the demand for accountants, lawyers, and economists!

Finally, controls are likely to be inequitable. Firms and labor unions in high-profile industries are likely to be scrutinized more closely than those in other industries. Because of the huge numbers of firms, controls often apply only to large firms. Both tendencies lead to inequities.

Summary

Inflation is a continuing rise in the price level, which means that it is a long-run phenomenon. Although the GDP deflator is the most comprehensive of the various price indexes used to measure inflation, the CPI usually receives more attention.

Unanticipated inflation causes a substantial redistribution of income and wealth. With anticipated inflation, the redistribution is less dramatic because people take action to protect themselves.

Inflation is costly to society because it results in fewer resources being devoted to the production of goods and services and reduces investment in new plant and equipment.

The nation's money supply—currency, travelers' checks, and checkable deposits—is controlled by the Federal Reserve.

With a constant income velocity of money, the inflation rate equals the growth rate of the money supply less the output growth rate. With the velocity of money and the output growth rate constant, the growth rate of the money supply determines the inflation rate. Inflation, therefore, is a monetary phenomenon.

In the short run, the velocity of money and the output growth rate vary, implying that the short-run relationship between the growth rate of the money supply and the inflation rate is not as strong as the long-run relationship.

To reduce the inflation rate, the growth rate of the money supply must be reduced. Reduced inflation is likely to be accompanied by increased unemployment in the short run.

Reducing government spending or raising taxes can keep the price level from rising in the short run. Because government spending cannot be cut or taxes raised indefinitely, fiscal policy cannot be regarded as a serious alternative to monetary policy in reducing inflation.

Because it is very difficult to increase the growth rate of aggregate supply, supply-side policies are unlikely to reduce inflation significantly.

The U.S. economy was subjected to wage-price guidelines under the Carter and Kennedy–Johnson administrations and wage-price controls under the Nixon administration. These programs were unsuccessful.

Economists generally oppose controls because they are ineffective, distort the allocation of resources, are costly to administer, and result in inequities.

Key Terms

Inflation	**Debtor**	**Central bank**
Deflation	**Hyperinflation**	**Quantity theory of money**
Consumer price index (CPI)	**Medium of exchange**	**Equation of exchange**

Unanticipated inflation	Money	Income velocity of money
Anticipated inflation	Currency (cash)	Supply-side policies
Indexing	Demand deposits	Incomes policy
Creditor	Money supply	

Review Questions

1. What is the difference between an increase in the general price level and inflation? Why is it necessary to make this distinction?
2. Why is the CPI the most widely cited measure of inflation in the United States? Why is this index an imprecise measure of the cost of living?
3. "Inflation will always cause some economic agents to gain and others to lose." Is this statement true or false? Defend your answer.
4. How might unanticipated inflation result in a redistribution of income and wealth?
5. Inflation can be detrimental to the economy. Therefore, the proper role of government is to enact policies to deal with inflation. Why might government be reluctant to undertake anti-inflationary policies?
6. Aside from its effects on income, wealth, and the government, in what other ways might inflation affect the economy?
7. What is money? What basic functions does it perform?
8. "Inflation is a long-term phenomenon caused by too-rapid growth in the money supply." Is this statement true or false? Use the quantity theory of money in defense of your answer.
9. Use the aggregate demand–aggregate supply framework to demonstrate how increases in the money supply can result in inflation.
10. "If the growth rate of the money supply is constant, there will be no inflation." Is this statement true or false? Defend your answer.
11. Using the aggregate demand–aggregate supply model, explain how labor unions can cause inflation. Is such a scenario likely? Why or why not?
12. "A monopolist charges higher prices for its products than does a pure competitor; hence, an economy characterized by a large number of monopolies is more likely to experience inflation than an economy characterized by a large number of competitive firms." Is this statement true or false? Defend your answer.
13. Explain and graphically show how monetary policy may be used to reduce inflation. Are any problems associated with the use of this policy?
14. In the long term, why can't fiscal policy reduce the inflation rate?
15. Show and explain how supply-side policies could lessen inflation. Are such policies a viable alternative for policy makers? Why or why not?
16. What is an incomes policy? Why have such policies generally been unsuccessful in dealing with inflation?
17. Go to http://www.swcollege.com/bef/econ_news.html—Economic News Online—and choose either Employment, Unemployment, and Inflation or Monetary Policy under the Macroeconomics category; choose an EconNews story that interests you. Read the full summary, and answer the questions posed.

Economic Issues on the Internet

– Board of Governors of the Federal Reserve System—**http://www.federalreserve.gov**
  The official site of the Federal Reserve System's Board of Governors. Several parts of the site are of interest, including Testimony and Speeches, Monetary Policy, Economic Research and Data, and Publications and Education Resources. It also has links to each of the 12 Federal Reserve Banks, all of which have material of interest on their Web sites.

- The European Central Bank—http://www.ecb.int/index.html
  Euros, European monetary policy and more.
- Economic-Indicators.com—http://www.economic-indicators.com
  R. Mark Rogers, author of the *Handbook of Key Economic Indicators*, Second Edition (McGraw Hill) 1998 has developed a Web site that allows users to keep up to date on economic data—a one-stop shop—with links to numerous other policy and central bank sites.
- Million Dollar Babies—http://www.milliondollarbabies.com
  Alan Kaim's site has some photographs of some of the currency that has been printed during hyperinflations.

Appendix to Chapter 15

Money Creation and Monetary Policy

Outline:

The Money Creation Process
   Depository Institutions
   The Federal Reserve
   The Federal Reserve and the Money Supply

The Federal Reserve and Control of the Money Supply
   Open Market Operations
   Reserve Requirements
   The Discount Rate

This appendix first examines the money creation process and then considers the various ways in which the Federal Reserve can alter the money supply.

■ THE MONEY CREATION PROCESS

The actions of depository institutions and of the Federal Reserve are important in creating money. This section discusses both.

Depository Institutions

Depository Institutions – Financial institutions that accept checkable and savings deposits.

By **depository institutions**, we mean financial institutions that accept checkable and savings deposits. Commercial banks, savings and loan associations, mutual savings banks, and credit unions are depository institutions.

National Banks – Banks chartered by the federal government.

State Banks – Banks chartered by state governments.

Member Banks – Banks that are members of the Federal Reserve System.

COMMERCIAL BANKS. Of these institutions, commercial banks are the second most numerous (after credit unions) and account for most of the deposits. There are about 10,000 commercial banks in the United States. Each bank is organized as a corporation and has a charter authorizing it to engage in banking. Banks offer a variety of services. For a start, they accept demand and time deposits, make business and consumer loans, and finance home mortgages. A commercial bank is either a national or a state bank. **National banks** are banks chartered by the federal government. **State banks** are those chartered by state governments. State banks outnumber national banks almost two to one, but national banks are typically larger.

By law, national banks must belong to the Federal Reserve System. State banks may join if they meet the requirements. Most have elected not to do so. In fact, fewer than half of the nation's commercial banks are members of the Federal Reserve System. But these banks, called **member banks**, account for well over half of total deposits.

Member banks are subject to the rules and regulations of the Federal Reserve System, including its reserve requirements. Member banks must hold a percentage of their deposits as cash and deposits at Federal Reserve Banks. Prior to the passage of the Depository Institutions Deregulation and Monetary Control Act of 1980, nonmember banks were required by state law to hold reserves, but the requirements were usually less restrictive than those of the Federal Reserve. Today, both member and nonmember banks are subject to the same reserve requirements.

OTHER DEPOSITORY INSTITUTIONS. Although commercial banks account for most deposits, the other depository institutions—savings and loan associations, mutual savings banks, and credit unions—are important. Savings and loan associations accept both checkable and savings deposits. Historically, they specialized in home mortgage lending, but they now make other types of loans as well. Like other depository institutions, mutual savings banks accept checkable and savings deposits and make loans. Geographically, they are concentrated in New York and New England. Credit unions differ from other depository institutions in that their depositors typically have the same employer or belong to the same labor union. Credit unions make loans, mostly consumer, but only to their depositors.

Since the 1970s, many of the distinctions among commercial banks, savings and loan associations, mutual savings banks, and credit unions have become blurred. Also, since the implementation of the Depository Institutions Deregulation and Monetary Control Act of 1980, the reserve requirements are the same for all depository institutions.

The Federal Reserve

After a long history of monetary crises in the United States, Congress created the Federal Reserve in 1913. The Federal Reserve is responsible for controlling the nation's money supply and conducting monetary policy.

A seven-person board of governors oversees the Federal Reserve. Members are appointed by the president (with Senate confirmation) to 14-year terms. The appointments are staggered so that one member is appointed every two years. The president also appoints a chairman of the board to a four-year term. Historically, that person has commonly been referred to as the second most powerful person in the nation. Currently, Alan Greenspan is chairman of the Federal Reserve Board of Governors. He succeeded Paul Volcker in 1987.

Rather than having a single central bank, as is common in other countries, the United States is divided into 12 Federal Reserve Districts, each with its own Federal Reserve Bank. Each of these district banks has its own board of directors. The district banks are located in Atlanta, Boston, Chicago, Cleveland, Dallas, Kansas City, Minneapolis, New York, Philadelphia, Richmond, St. Louis, and San Francisco. Some of these district banks have branch banks. The Federal Reserve Bank of Chicago, for example, has a branch bank in Detroit. For the most part, these Federal Reserve Banks (and their branch banks) do not deal directly with the general public. Instead, they provide services to commercial banks and other financial institutions.

Primary authority over control of the money supply rests with the Federal Open Market Committee (FOMC). The FOMC has 12 members. Each of the seven members of the Federal Reserve Board of Governors is a member of the FOMC. The other five members of the FOMC are presidents of Federal

Reserve Banks. Because New York City is the nation's financial center, the president of the Federal Reserve Bank of New York is a permanent member. The presidents of the 11 other Federal Reserve Banks rotate.

In addition to controlling the money supply and conducting monetary policy, the Federal Reserve (1) assists in the check-clearing process, (2) supervises the operations of member banks, and (3) acts as the federal government's fiscal agent. Although these three functions are important, the Federal Reserve's role as manager of the nation's money supply is crucial if the nation is to achieve its economic goals.

The Federal Reserve and the Money Supply

As discussed previously, depository institutions must hold reserves against their deposits. Member banks, for example, hold their reserves in cash and deposits at their Federal Reserve Banks. (Cash held by banks and other depository institutions is usually referred to as **vault cash**. Because it is not actively circulating, vault cash is *not* counted as part of the nation's money supply.) **Required reserves** are reserves that depository institutions are required to hold. **Excess reserves** are reserves over and above those that are required. The **reserve requirement** is the ratio of required reserves to deposits.

Vault Cash – Cash held by banks and other depository institutions.

Required Reserves – Reserves that depository institutions are required to hold.

Excess Reserves – Reserves over and above required reserves.

Reserve Requirement – The ratio of required reserves to deposits.

Open Market Operations – The purchase or sale of U.S. Treasury securities by the Federal Reserve.

Suppose Sunshine National Bank has demand deposits of $5 million. If the reserve requirement is 20 percent, its required reserves are $1 million ($5 million × 20 percent). If its actual reserves against demand deposits are $1.2 million, Sunshine Bank has required reserves of $1 million and excess reserves of $0.2 million ($1.2 million − $1.0 million). Because reserves earn no interest, depository institutions have a strong economic incentive to lend their excess reserves. (Like other firms, depository institutions are in business to make profits.)

Although the Federal Reserve can alter the money supply in several ways, it almost always uses open market operations to do so. **Open market operations** are the purchase or sale of U.S. Treasury securities. When the U.S. Treasury borrows, it issues Treasury securities. These securities are in effect IOUs indicating, in part, when the Treasury will repay the loan. The Treasury issues three types of securities: bills, notes, and bonds. Treasury bills mature in 1 year or less. Notes mature in 2 to 10 years. Bonds mature in 10 or more years.

THE CREATION OF MONEY. We now consider the purchase of a U.S. Treasury security by the Federal Reserve and its impact on the money supply. In doing so, we have two purposes in mind. The first is to show that an open market purchase of Treasury securities results in an increase in the money supply. The second is to show that the purchase results in the creation of money by commercial banks or, more generally, depository institutions.[1] This money creation process results in an increase in the money supply that exceeds the initial increase.

Suppose the Federal Reserve buys a U.S. Treasury security from Melanie for $10,000. It will pay for the security with a check drawn on a Federal Reserve Bank. If Melanie deposits this $10,000 check in her checking account at Sunshine National Bank, Sunshine Bank's demand deposits increase by $10,000.

---

[1] In describing the money creation process, we focus on the behavior of commercial banks because most people are more familiar with banks than with other types of depository institutions. Because all depository institutions are subject to the same reserve requirements, we would arrive at the same conclusions if both banks and other depository institutions were taken into account. Similarly, we focus on demand deposits. Because other checkable deposits are subject to the same reserve requirement as demand deposits, we would reach the same conclusions if both demand and other checkable deposits were considered.

This increase in demand deposits constitutes an increase in the nation's money supply. (Recall that demand deposits are one component of the money supply.) This increase in the money supply, however, is only the beginning of the money creation process.

As the check that Melanie deposited at Sunshine Bank clears, the Federal Reserve credits Sunshine Bank's deposits at its Federal Reserve Bank. Consequently, Sunshine Bank's reserves increase by $10,000. With an increase in demand deposits of $10,000 and a reserve requirement of 20 percent, Sunshine Bank's required reserves increase by $2,000 ($10,000×0.20). Its excess reserves increase by $8,000 ($10,000−$2,000).

Sunshine Bank has excess reserves of $8,000. Because reserves earn no interest, it has a strong incentive to lend these excess reserves. Suppose Sunshine Bank lends Joe the $8,000 to pay for a car. If Joe's check is deposited in the car dealership's checking account at Moonbeam National Bank, Moonbeam Bank's demand deposits increase by $8,000.

This increase in demand deposits at Moonbeam Bank represents an increase in the money supply. With an increase in demand deposits of $10,000 at Sunshine Bank and $8,000 at Moonbeam Bank, the total increase in the money supply is now $18,000 ($10,000+$8,000). The money supply will continue to increase because, in addition to the increase in demand deposits, Moonbeam Bank experiences an increase in excess reserves. Sunshine Bank no longer has excess reserves. (It lent them to Joe.) Moonbeam Bank, however, has excess reserves. As the check that the car dealership deposited at Moonbeam Bank clears, the Federal Reserve credits Moonbeam Bank's deposits at its Federal Reserve Bank. With an $8,000 increase in both demand deposits and reserves and a reserve requirement of 20 percent, Moonbeam Bank's required reserves increase by $1,600 ($8,000×0.20) and its excess reserves increase by $6,400 ($8,000−$1,600). Because reserves earn no interest, Moonbeam Bank has a strong incentive to lend these excess reserves.

Suppose Moonbeam Bank lends the $6,400 to Andrea and Greg to pay for remodeling their home. If Andrea and Greg's check is deposited in the builder's checking account at Starlight National Bank, Starlight Bank's demand deposits increase by $6,400.

This increase in demand deposits at Starlight Bank constitutes an increase in the money supply. With increases in demand deposits of $10,000 at Sunshine Bank, $8,000 at Moonbeam Bank, and $6,400 at Starlight Bank, the total increase in the money supply is now $24,400 ($10,000+$8,000+$6,400). The money supply will continue to increase, however, because in addition to the increase in demand deposits, Starlight Bank experiences an increase in excess reserves.

Although Sunshine and Moonbeam Banks no longer have excess reserves, Starlight Bank does. As the check that the builder deposited at Starlight Bank clears, the Federal Reserve credits Starlight Bank's deposits at its Federal Reserve Bank. With a $6,400 increase in both demand deposits and reserves and a reserve requirement of 20 percent, Starlight Bank's required reserves increase by $1,280 ($6,400×0.20) and its excess reserves increase by $5,120 ($6,400−$1,280). Starlight Bank has a strong incentive to lend these excess reserves. And so it goes.

THE CHANGE IN THE MONEY SUPPLY. Instead of following the money creation process indefinitely, we can derive an equation to determine the total increase in demand deposits and, hence, the money supply. Two simplifying assumptions are made. First, depository institutions do not hold excess reserves. Second, the public does not add to its holdings of cash.

In the illustration, demand deposits and reserves first increased by $10,000. This increase in demand deposits was followed by successive increases of $8,000 and $6,400. As demand deposits increased, more and more of the initial $10,000 increase in reserves was used as required reserves. Sunshine Bank's required reserves increased by $2,000 to support its $10,000 increase in demand deposits. Moonbeam Bank's required reserves increased by $1,600, and Starlight Bank's by $1,280. Given the assumptions, depository institutions will continue to make loans until all of the initial increase in reserves becomes required reserves. Thus, the initial change in reserves, denoted as ΔR, ultimately becomes a change in required reserves, denoted as ΔRR. In equation form,

$$\Delta R = \Delta RR$$

The change in required reserves, in turn, equals the ratio of required reserves to demand deposits (the reserve requirement) multiplied by the total change in demand deposits. If the ratio of required reserves to demand deposits is denoted as r and the total change in demand deposits as DDD, we have

$$\Delta R = \Delta RR = r\Delta DD$$

Dividing both sides of the equation by r and rearranging terms yields

$$\Delta DD = \frac{\Delta R}{r}$$

This equation indicates that the total change in demand deposits equals the initial change in reserves divided by the reserve requirement. In the illustration, the initial change in reserves is $10,000 and the reserve requirement is 20 percent. Consequently, the total change in demand deposits is calculated by dividing $10,000 by 0.20. Thus, the total change in demand deposits is $50,000. We know that this must be the case because with an initial increase in reserves of $10,000 and a 20 percent reserve requirement, demand deposits must ultimately increase by $50,000 for all of the increase in reserves to become required reserves.

The foregoing analysis indicates that the initial increase in reserves of $10,000 results in an increase in demand deposits of $50,000. Because demand deposits are a component of the nation's money supply, we find that the money supply also increases by $50,000. If the change in the money supply is denoted by ΔM, the relationship between the change in the money supply and the change in reserves is

(15A.1) $$\Delta M = \frac{\Delta R}{r}$$

Equation 15A.1 indicates that a change in reserves, ΔR, results in a change in the money supply, ΔM, equal to the change in reserves divided by the reserve requirement, r.

Equation 15A.1 holds for both increases and decreases in the money supply. In our illustration, we showed that an open market purchase of U.S. Treasury securities by the Federal Reserve increases the money supply. Equation 15A.1 indicates that the total increase in the money supply is equal to the increase in reserves divided by the reserve requirement. By the same token, an open market sale of U.S. Treasury securities by the Federal Reserve decreases the money supply.

To illustrate, suppose the Federal Reserve sells a U.S. Treasury security to Tiffany for $10,000. Tiffany pays for the security with a check drawn on Boomtown National Bank. Boomtown Bank's

Key words: *Fed and money supply*
http://www.infotrac-college.com

demand deposits decrease by $10,000. As the check clears, Boomtown Bank's reserves also decrease by $10,000. The decrease in reserves will force Boomtown Bank to curtail its loans. This loss of reserves and curtailment of loans will lead to successive decreases in demand deposits and the money supply just as an increase in reserves leads to successive increases in demand deposits and the money supply (see review question 3 following this appendix). Equation 15A.1 indicates that the total decrease in the money supply equals the decrease in reserves divided by the reserve requirement.

THE CHANGE IN THE MONEY SUPPLY: TWO QUALIFICATIONS. The change in the money supply indicated by equation 15A.1 is the maximum possible change. Again, the equation assumes that (1) depository institutions do not hold excess reserves and (2) the public does not add to its holdings of cash. If these assumptions are met, the money supply will change by the amount indicated by equation 15A.1. If the assumptions are not met, the change in the money supply will be less than the amount indicated by the equation.

To demonstrate that the change in the money supply indicated by equation 15A.1 represents the maximum possible change, we now relax each of the assumptions. Previously, we assumed that depository institutions hold no excess reserves. Based on this assumption, institutions with excess reserves will lend them and the money creation process will be as described earlier. Suppose depository institutions lend only part of their excess reserves. If so, the corresponding increases in demand deposits will be smaller. As a result, the total increase in demand deposits and hence the money supply will be smaller, too.

Thus, if depository institutions hold excess reserves, the money supply increases in response to the purchase of U.S. Treasury securities by the Federal Reserve, but not by the maximum possible amount. The same is true if the public adds to its holdings of cash during the money creation process. If the public adds to its holdings of cash, depository institutions lose some of their reserves and so will not be able to increase their loans by as much as before. The corresponding increases in demand deposits will be smaller. As a result, the total increase in demand deposits and hence the money supply will be smaller.

In conclusion, we find that the money supply increases in response to an open market purchase. If the simplifying assumptions are met, the money supply increases by the maximum possible amount; if they are not met, the money supply increases by a smaller amount. We could develop an equation to determine the increase in the money supply when the assumptions are not met, but this is unnecessary for our purposes and beyond the scope of this text.

■ THE FEDERAL RESERVE AND CONTROL OF THE MONEY SUPPLY

The Federal Reserve can alter the money supply by (1) conducting open market operations, (2) changing reserve requirements, and (3) changing the discount rate.

Open Market Operations

As defined earlier, open market operations are the purchase or sale of U.S. Treasury securities. Suppose the Federal Reserve decides to increase the money supply by purchasing U.S. Treasury securities. It pays for these securities with checks drawn on Federal Reserve Banks. These checks will be deposited at various depository institutions. The Federal Reserve will credit these institutions' deposits at Federal

Reserve Banks, and these increased deposits will constitute an increase in reserves. Banks and other depository institutions will respond by making new loans, and the money creation process will begin.

Just as the Federal Reserve increases the money supply by purchasing U.S. Treasury securities, it can reduce the money supply by selling Treasury securities. Those buying the securities pay for them with checks drawn on various depository institutions. During the check-clearing process, the Federal Reserve will reduce those institutions' deposits at Federal Reserve Banks. Banks and other depository institutions will respond to the decrease in reserves by curtailing their loans. Fewer loans will cause demand and other checkable deposits to decline. Because these deposits are part of the money supply, the nation's money supply will fall.

INFOTRAC
College Edition
Keywords: *Fed and interest rate*
http://www.infotrac-college.com

The ultimate authority regarding the conduct of open market operations rests with the Federal Open Market Committee. Once the committee decides on the appropriate course of action, it issues a directive to the appropriate person at the Federal Reserve Bank of New York. This person actually supervises the purchase and sale of the Treasury securities. The Federal Reserve almost *always* uses open market operations to control the nation's money supply.

Reserve Requirements

The Federal Reserve can also alter the money supply by changing the reserve requirements for depository institutions. If the Federal Reserve wants to increase the money supply, it can reduce reserve requirements, thereby creating excess reserves in the monetary system. As a result, depository institutions will make new loans, resulting in the creation of demand and other checkable deposits. The increase in these deposits constitutes an increase in the money supply.

In the illustration, it was assumed that depository institutions were required to have reserves equal to 20 percent of their deposits. Suppose that Sunshine Bank initially had $1 million in reserves and $5 million in deposits. As a result, it was not in a position to make new loans. Now suppose the reserve requirement was reduced to 10 percent. Sunshine Bank would be required to hold only $500,000 in reserves. It would be free to lend up to $500,000 (its excess reserves), and the money creation process would begin.

Just as the Federal Reserve can increase the money supply by reducing reserve requirements, it can decrease the money supply by raising them. By raising requirements, it can make depository institutions hold more reserves, forcing them to curtail loans. As fewer loans are made, demand deposits and therefore the nation's money supply fall. In the illustration, suppose the reserve requirement was raised from 20 to 30 percent. Sunshine Bank's required reserves would now be $1.5 million. With reserves of only $1 million, Sunshine Bank would have to curtail its loans. Fewer loans lead to fewer demand and other checkable deposits and therefore a smaller money supply.

Although changes in reserve requirements are a powerful means to alter the money supply, they are rarely used. For one thing, changing reserve requirements is a very blunt way to alter the nation's money supply. Even small changes in reserve requirements cause large changes in required reserves and the money supply. For another, changes in reserve requirements are not easily reversed. Suppose reserve requirements are lowered in order to increase the money supply. Should the increase in the money supply prove too large, the Federal Reserve could raise reserve requirements to reduce the money supply. But these new reserve requirements would be disruptive, especially for depository institutions not sufficiently liquid to meet them.

The Discount Rate

Discount Rate — The interest rate at which depository institutions can borrow from Federal Reserve Banks.

In addition to using open market operations and altering reserve requirements, the Federal Reserve may alter the money supply by changing the discount rate. The **discount rate** is the interest rate at which depository institutions can borrow from Federal Reserve Banks. Each Federal Reserve Bank's rate is determined by that bank's board of directors. The rate must be approved, however, by the Federal Reserve Board of Governors.

If the Federal Reserve wishes to increase the money supply, it could reduce the discount rate, thus giving depository institutions a greater incentive to borrow. If the depository institutions borrow more, their reserves increase, permitting an expansion in the money supply. If the Federal Reserve wishes to reduce the money supply, it could raise the discount rate, thereby discouraging depository institutions from borrowing. If they borrow less, their reserves decrease and the money supply falls.

INFOTRAC
College Edition

Keywords: *Fed and discount rate*

http://www.infotrac-college.com

Although changing the discount rate is a means to alter the money supply, it is rarely altered for that purpose. Depository institutions are discouraged from borrowing from their Federal Reserve Banks except as a last resort. Consequently, the discount rate may change significantly without altering depository institution borrowing from the Federal Reserve.

Unlike reserve requirements, the discount rate is altered frequently. On most occasions, the intent is to bring it into line with other interest rates, not to alter the money supply. Consequently, when the discount rate is changed, we cannot be sure that the Federal Reserve is altering its monetary policy.

Summary

Depository institutions—financial institutions that accept checkable and savings deposits—include commercial banks, savings and loan associations, mutual savings banks, and credit unions. All depository institutions are subject to the same reserve requirements.

The Federal Reserve, an independent government agency, is the United States' central bank. It controls the nation's money supply, conducts monetary policy, and, in general, supervises the nation's monetary system.

A board of governors oversees the Federal Reserve. The Federal Open Market Committee, which includes the board of governors as members, has primary responsibility for the conduct of monetary policy.

Open market operations are the purchase or sale of U.S. Treasury securities by the Federal Reserve. If the Federal Reserve wishes to increase (decrease) the nation's money supply, it can do so by buying (selling) U.S. Treasury securities. By buying U.S. Treasury securities, the Federal Reserve adds to the reserves of the monetary system. The increase in reserves causes depository institutions to make new loans, increasing the nation's money supply.

The money creation process increases the money supply beyond the initial increase in reserves. The maximum possible increase in the money supply equals the initial increase in reserves divided by the reserve requirement.

The Federal Reserve can also alter the money supply by changing reserve requirements. If it wishes to increase (decrease) the money supply, it can lower (raise) the reserve requirement. Finally, the Federal Reserve can alter the money supply by changing the discount rate—the interest rate at which depository institutions can borrow from Federal Reserve Banks. If it wishes to increase (decrease) the money supply, it can lower (raise) the discount rate.

Key Terms

Depository institutions	**Vault cash**	**Open market operations**
National banks	**Required reserves**	**Discount rate**
State banks	**Excess reserves**	
Member banks	**Reserve requirement**	

Review Questions

1. Briefly discuss the structure of the Federal Reserve.
2. Suppose the required reserve ratio is 10 percent. Assume that the banking system has $20 million in deposits and $5 million in reserves. Find the required reserves, excess reserves, and the maximum amount by which demand deposits could expand.
3. Suppose the required reserve ratio is 25 percent. Assume that banks lend all of their excess reserves and the public does not add to its cash holdings. Briefly explain how the Federal Reserve's purchase of a $1,000 U.S. Treasury security will affect the money supply. Suppose the Federal Reserve had instead sold a $1,000 security. How would this action affect the money supply?
4. What factors could cause the increase in the money supply to be less than the maximum possible increase?
5. What actions can the Federal Reserve undertake if it wishes to increase the money supply?
6. "An increase in the discount rate means that the Federal Reserve is attempting to decrease the money supply." Is this statement true or false? Defend your answer.

CHAPTER 16

Deficits, Surpluses, and Debt: Past, Present, and Future

Outline:

Budgets and Budget Concepts
Historical Budget Perspective
The Public Debt
Long-Run Budget and Debt Projections
   The Incredible Shrinking Surplus
   The Deficit and the Debt in the Coming Decade
   The Really Long Run

Measurement Issues
   Inflation
   Business Cycles
   Government Investment
   State and Local Government Deficits and Surpluses
Economic Effects of a Deficit
   The Keynesian View: A Deficit Can Help to Cure Recessions

The Modern View: The Strength of the Cure Depends on How the Deficit Is Financed
The Burden of the Debt
Taking Stock

In 1998, 1999, 2000, and 2001, the federal government achieved a surplus in the unified budget. This was such a dramatic break from the past—an almost unbroken string of deficits between 1962 and 1997—that the Congressional Budget Office has called it one of Congress' 50 greatest achievements. Looking forward from the spring of 2001, moreover, it appeared that the successes of the 1998 to 2001 period were a mere preview of more surpluses to come. Then came a major tax cut, a recession, and growing demands for money to fight terrorism, and the projected surpluses disappeared—almost overnight. In fact, it now appears that budget deficits are once more the order of the day and that deficits will be an important subject of policy discussion in Washington. If they are, there is a good chance that many of the people participating in the discussion will not have their facts straight or their concepts clearly defined; this has certainly been the case in the past. This chapter is written to help you avoid the same fate.

It is important to cut through the rhetoric surrounding the deficit, because whatever is done about it will have real effects on your life. It is a pocketbook issue, because it will partly determine how much you will pay in taxes. It is a productivity and economic-growth issue, because it will influence how much is invested in physical and human capital. It is a fairness issue, because it will affect how much government provides for America's underprivileged. Finally, it is an international issue, because it will impact what Congress devotes to national defense and international programs.

■ BUDGETS AND BUDGET CONCEPTS

Budget –
A statement of income (or receipts) and expenditures (or outlays) for a specific period of time (a year).

Unified Budget –
The federal budget with Social Security included.

Like all budgets, the federal **budget** is a statement of income (or receipts) and expenditures (or outlays) for a specific period of time (a year). The federal budget you will be dealing with is recorded in Table 16.1, with actual numbers for the year 2001. This is the **unified budget** of the federal government. The unified budget includes Old Age, Survivors, and Disability Insurance (OASDI—better known as Social Security) receipts. It also includes the uses of these funds; namely, outlays for Social Security. With these items included, the budget surplus or deficit is a measure that indicates how much the government has to borrow from the public (in the case of a deficit) or how much past borrowing could be repaid (in the case of a surplus).

TABLE 16.1 — Federal Government Unified Budget, 2001 (in Billions of Dollars)

Receipts		Outlays	
Individual income taxes	994.3	Discretionary, total	649.3
		National defense	306.1
Corporation income taxes	151.1	International affairs	22.5
		Domestic	320.8
Social insurance and retirement receipts, total	694.0	Entitlements and other mandatory, total	1095.2
Social Security (OASDI)	508.0	Means-tested, total	248.7
Medicare (HI)	150.0	Medicaid	129.4
Unemployment insurance	28.0	Other	119.3
Other	9.0	Non–means-tested, total	846.5
		Medicare (HI and SMI)	237.9
Excise taxes, total	66.1	Social Security (OASDI)	429.4
		Other retirement and disability	92.7
Estate and gift taxes	28.4	Unemployment compensation	27.9
		Farm price supports	22.4
Customs duties	19.4	Other	23.8
Miscellaneous receipts	37.8	Net interest	206.2
		Offsetting receipts	–86.8
Total receipts	1991.0	Total outlays	1863.9
Budget Balance (receipts – outlays)			
Unified budget	127.1		
Social Security (off-budget)	78.6		
On-budget	48.5		

SOURCE: U.S. Office of Management and Budget, *Historical Tables*.

INFOTRAC
College Edition

Keywords: *federal budget, unified budget*
http://www.infotrac-college.com

Net Budget Balance – Total revenues minus total outlays.

Budget Surplus – A positive net budget balance—total revenues exceed total outlays.

Budget Deficit – A negative net budget balance—total outlays exceed total revenues.

Off-Budget Surplus – Total revenues in excess of total outlays in the Social Security portion of the unified budget.

On-Budget Surplus – Total revenues in excess of total outlays in the non–Social Security portion of the unified budget.

INFOTRAC
College Edition

Keywords: *budget deficit, budget surplus*
http://www.infotrac-college.com

The right-hand side of Table 16.1 displays government outlays. Total outlays are divided into two types: discretionary and mandatory. A discretionary program is one for which government sets a spending limit annually. For mandatory programs, government defines eligibility criteria for benefits or "entitlements." Annual expenditures depend on how many people meet the criteria and on legislated benefits per person. This distinction is important because it indicates that government currently has control of less than 35 percent of its outlays—and nearly half of that amount is allocated to national defense. In this environment, most of the debate over the budget normally revolves around relatively small annual changes in spending. Most of that attention is focused on what to do with the extra revenues produced by annual growth and not on a reallocation of funds committed to specific programs in the past.

The "bottom line" of the budget is the **net budget balance**—total revenues minus total outlays. If receipts exceed outlays, as in the 2000 budget, there is a positive net balance or **budget surplus**. If receipts are less than outlays, there is a negative net balance or **budget deficit**. If receipts and outlays are equal, the net balance is zero and the budget is balanced.

Congress actually distinguishes three net balances. One is the net balance in the unified budget. When it is positive, as in Table 16.1 ($127.1 billion), it is usually referred to as the unified budget surplus. The other net balances are (1) the net balance in the Social Security portion of the budget and (2) the net balance in the non–Social Security portion of the budget. The Social Security portion of the budget in Table 16.1 had a surplus of $78.6 billion ($508 billion in Social Security receipts minus $429.4 billion in outlays for Social Security). This surplus is also called the **off-budget surplus**. The non–Social Security portion of the budget accounts for the remainder of the unified budget surplus, or $48.5 billion. This portion of the surplus is also called the **on-budget surplus**. The unified budget surplus is equal, then, to the sum of the on-budget (non–Social Security) surplus and the off-budget (Social Security) surplus. (Actually, the off-budget portion of the unified budget also includes receipts and outlays of the U.S. Postal Service, but the postal service balance is so small relative to the Social Security balance that it is not misleading to refer to the off-budget balance as the Social Security balance.) Congress distinguishes between on-budget and off-budget net balances primarily to keep separate books on Social Security. The unified budget, however, includes all receipts and expenditures. Thus, it presents a more accurate picture of the claims made, and programs delivered, by the federal government.

■ HISTORICAL BUDGET PERSPECTIVE

Figure 16.1 depicts the behavior of the unified budget net balances over the past 40 years. It is a picture dominated by deficits, with surpluses realized only in 1969 and 1998 to 2001.

Figure 16.2 distinguishes between the net balances in the unified budget and net balances in the budget without Social Security (on-budget net balances). We noted in the discussion of Table 16.1 that the inclusion of the Social Security net balance made the unified budget surplus larger in 2001. According to Figure 16.2, this has been the case for the last 4 years. Prior to that, the inclusion of Social Security in the unified budget made the unified budget deficit smaller from 1985 to 1997. People who argue that Social Security should not be included in the federal budget do so partly on the grounds that its inclusion helps Congress to understate the size of the budget deficit. Figure 16.2 illustrates their point, but it

| FIGURE 16.1 | Unified Federal Budget Deficits (−) and Surpluses (+), 1962–2001 |

The net balance of the unified budget was negative (a budget deficit) every year from 1962 through 1997, except 1969. The net balance was positive (a budget surplus) from 1998 through 2001.

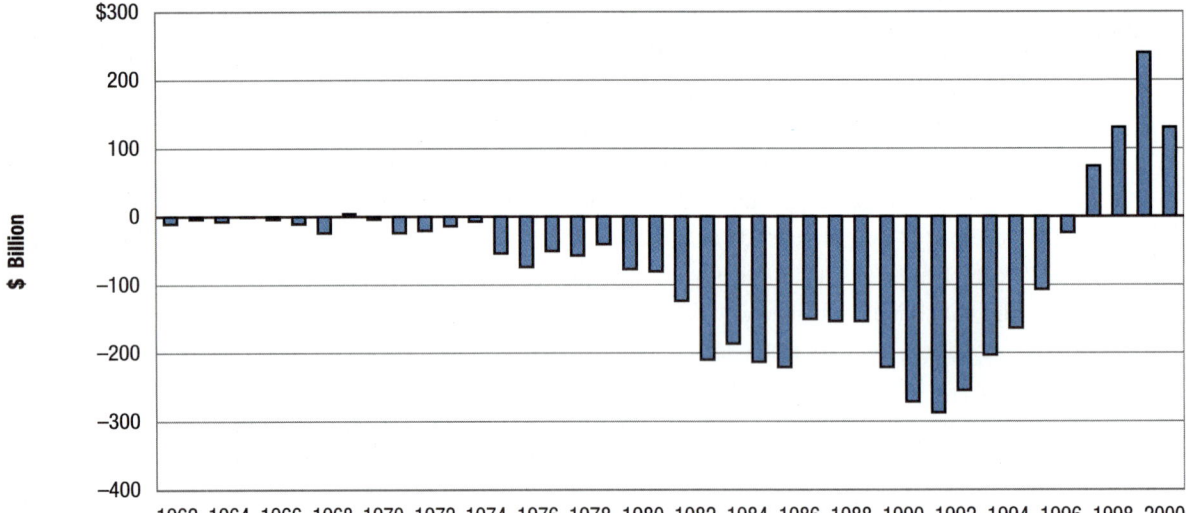

SOURCE: Office of Management and Budget, *Historical Tables, Budget of the United States Government, Fiscal 2003*.

INSIGHTS

FROM DEFICIT TO SURPLUS

After peaking in 1992, the federal government's budget deficit decreased, eventually becoming a surplus in 1998. After running a record deficit in 1992, why did the federal government experience a surplus in 1998? The answer is straightforward. Government revenue increased much more rapidly than government expenditures over the 1992 to 1998 span.

On a fiscal year basis, revenue grew at an astounding 9.6 average annual percentage rate from 1992 to 1998. In contrast, government expenditures increased at a modest 3.3 average annual percentage rate. The higher growth rate of revenue stemmed partly from tax hikes that occurred during the Bush and Clinton administrations and partly from rapid economic growth.

Government expenditures increased less rapidly at 3.3 percent. Expenditures for national defense actually decreased. They declined at an average annual rate of 1.7 percent. Expenditures for the other major categories increased. Spending for Social Security grew at a 5.3 percent rate; spending for Medicare at a 10.3 percent rate; and net interest at a 3.7 percent rate.

The lower growth rate in spending was due mostly to decisions by Congress and Presidents Bush and Clinton to reduce spending. (When the president and members of Congress refer to spending cuts, they usually mean reductions in the projected rate of increase.) The demise of the Soviet Union and end of the Cold War allowed President Clinton and Congress to reduce spending on defense. Had defense spending increased at the same rate as non-defense spending, 4.6 percent, government expenditures would have increased more rapidly. Instead of a 1998 budget surplus of $69.2 billion, the federal government would have had a $46.8 billion budget deficit.

FIGURE 16.2 Unified Budget and On-Budget Net Balances, 1962–2001

Unified budget and on-budget net balances were virtually the same from 1962 through 1984 because the Social Security budget was balanced (annual income and outgo were about the same; Social Security was on a pure pay-as-you-go basis). Social Security accumulated surpluses from 1985 through 2001, increasing unified budget net balances, which include Social Security, relative to on-budget net balances, which do not include Social Security.

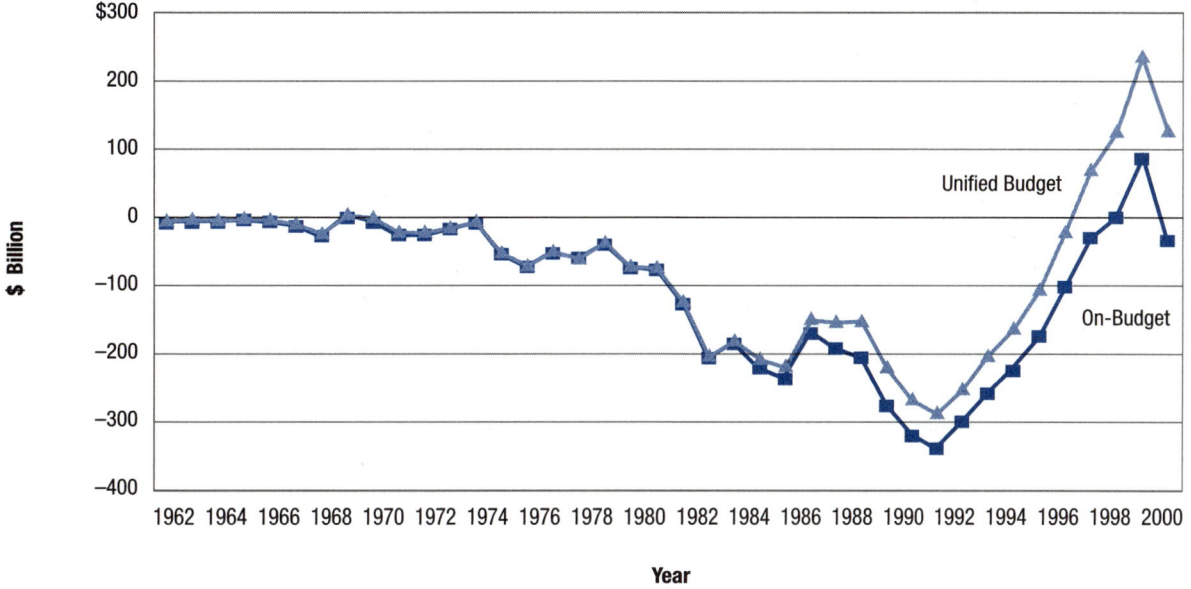

SOURCE: Office of Management and Budget, *Historical Tables, Budget of the United States Government, Fiscal 2003*.

also shows that, prior to 1998, the inclusion of the Social Security surpluses had offset only a small portion of the on-budget (non–Social Security) deficits. We appear to have been plagued most of the time with a tendency toward budget deficits, regardless of the treatment of Social Security surpluses.

■ THE PUBLIC DEBT

Gross Federal Debt – Also known as the national debt; the debt of the federal government held by both the public and government agencies.

Public Debt – The portion of the gross federal debt held by the public.

The total outstanding debt of the federal government—the **gross federal debt**—stood at approximately $6.2 trillion in November 2002. That figure consists of $3.5 trillion in debt that the government owes to the public and $2.7 trillion in debt that the government owes to itself. Debt held by the public—the **public debt**—is the value of all the federal securities that have been sold to the public and are still outstanding; it represents the government's borrowing from the public to finance past deficits *less* past surpluses that have been used to retire the public debt. Businesses and the financial markets pay close attention to the public debt (but not the gross federal debt) because of its impact on the economy. When the Department of the Treasury sells securities or borrows from the public, it acquires resources that otherwise might be invested in the private sector. Conversely, when the Treasury Department redeems securities, it increases the resources available for private investment.

INTERNATIONAL PERSPECTIVE

THE RELATIVE IMPORTANCE OF BUDGET DEFICITS AND SURPLUSES FOR VARIOUS COUNTRIES: 1998

Many countries had budget deficits more than 2 percent of GNP[a] in 1998. The United States and many other countries had a surplus. Indonesia balanced its budget.

Country	Deficit (−) or Surplus as a Percentage of GNP	Country	Deficit (−) or Surplus as a Percentage of GNP
Turkey	−7.0	Netherlands	−0.7
Japan	−6.0	United Kingdom	−0.4
Venezuela	−4.7	South Korea	−0.2
South Africa	−3.3	Indonesia	0.0
France	−2.9	Switzerland	0.1
Italy	−2.7	Australia	0.5
Thailand	−2.6	Chile	0.7
Greece	−2.4	New Zealand	0.9
Israel	−2.4	Denmark	1.0
Austria	−2.1	Canada	1.3
Germany	−2.0	United States	1.6
Philippines	−1.9	Sweden	1.9
Spain	−1.8	Ireland	2.4
Mexico	−1.6	Norway	3.9
China	−1.2	Malaysia	4.4

[a]GNP is a measure of output similar to GDP.

SOURCE: Federal Reserve Bank of St. Louis, *International Economic Trends* (July 1999), 9.

Keywords: *public debt, national debt, gross federal debt*
http://www.infotrac-college.com

The portion of the debt that the government owes itself largely consists of federal securities credited to various trust fund accounts. Those securities represent the balances of either excess receipts collected to finance specific programs (for example, Social Security taxes) or reserve spending authority that has been allocated for a particular activity (for example, appropriations for the military retirement system). Like federal securities sold to the public, they are legal obligations of the government and are backed by its full faith and credit. However, unlike federal securities sold to the public, which are assets of the holder, Treasury obligations held by federal trust funds are not assets of the government as a whole. A member of the public who holds a Treasury security has a legal claim against the government; a federal trust fund holding a Treasury security is simply a case of the government having a claim against itself.

Adding federal securities to and subtracting them from the government's trust fund accounts have no direct impact on businesses and the financial markets. Such activity does not cause money to flow between the government and individuals, private businesses, or other institutions; it has no impact on bond prices and yields; and it does not change the economic worth of any entity. The securities also do not represent the future benefits that individuals are potentially entitled to under federal programs. Just as importantly, they are not resources that the government can use to pay beneficiaries. When the trust funds encounter cash inflows that are less than cash outflows, they can redeem their securities to make up the difference (at least for awhile), but the Treasury will either have to borrow the money to redeem them or use existing tax revenues. The true resources available to pay beneficiaries, then, are either the savings of the public or the taxes collected from the public.

Figure 16.3 shows how the public debt grew between 1962 and 1998 as a consequence of the virtually uninterrupted budget deficits of that period. Figure 16.4 shows the public debt as a percentage of GDP. Although there has been tremendous growth in the public debt, the **burden of the public debt**, as measured by size of the debt relative to GDP, is smaller than it was in 1962. This reflects not only the budget surpluses attained from 1998 through 2001, but also the rapid growth in GDP experienced by the U.S. in the 1990s.

Burden of the Public Debt –
The public debt as a percentage of GDP.

FIGURE 16.3 Debt Held by the Public, 1962–2001

Debt held by the public (the public debt) grew from 1962 through 1997 as the U.S. Treasury borrowed from (i.e., sold securities to) the public to finance the deficits in the unified budget during that period. The public debt fell from 1998 through 2001 as the Treasury used the surpluses in the unified budget to redeem maturing securities.

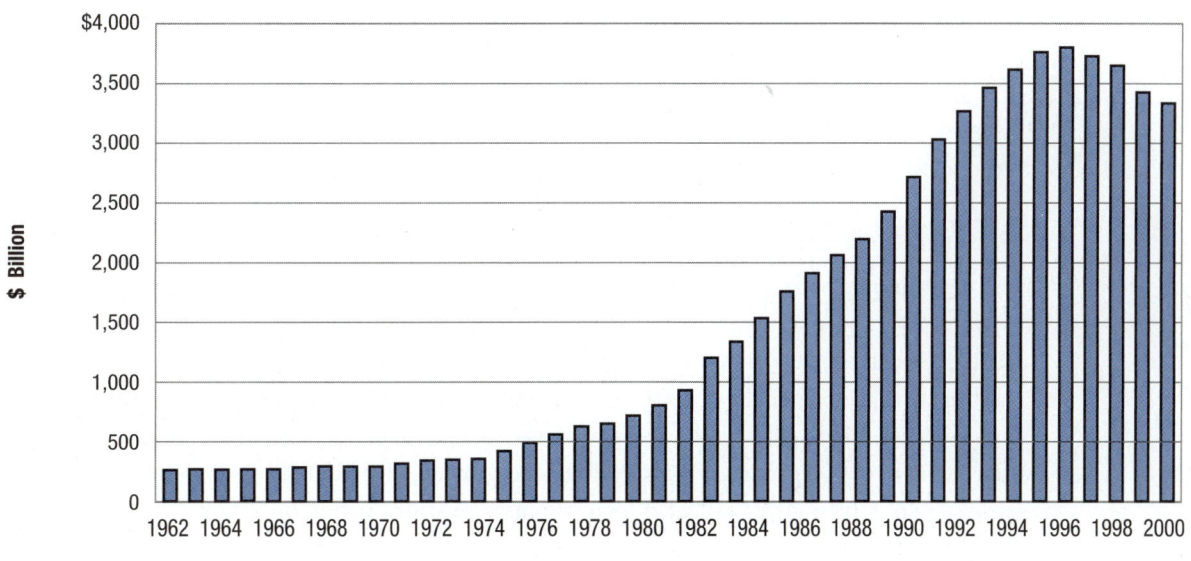

SOURCE: Office of Management and Budget, *Historical Tables, Budget of the United States Government, Fiscal 2003.*

FIGURE 16.4 Debt Held by the Public as Percent of GDP, 1962–2001

The public debt as a percent of GDP—(Public Debt/GDP)×100—fluctuated between 25 and 50 percent from 1962 through 2001. It was smaller in 2001 than in 1962 primarily because the deficit in the unified budget was shrinking while GDP was rising rapidly from 1992 through 2000.

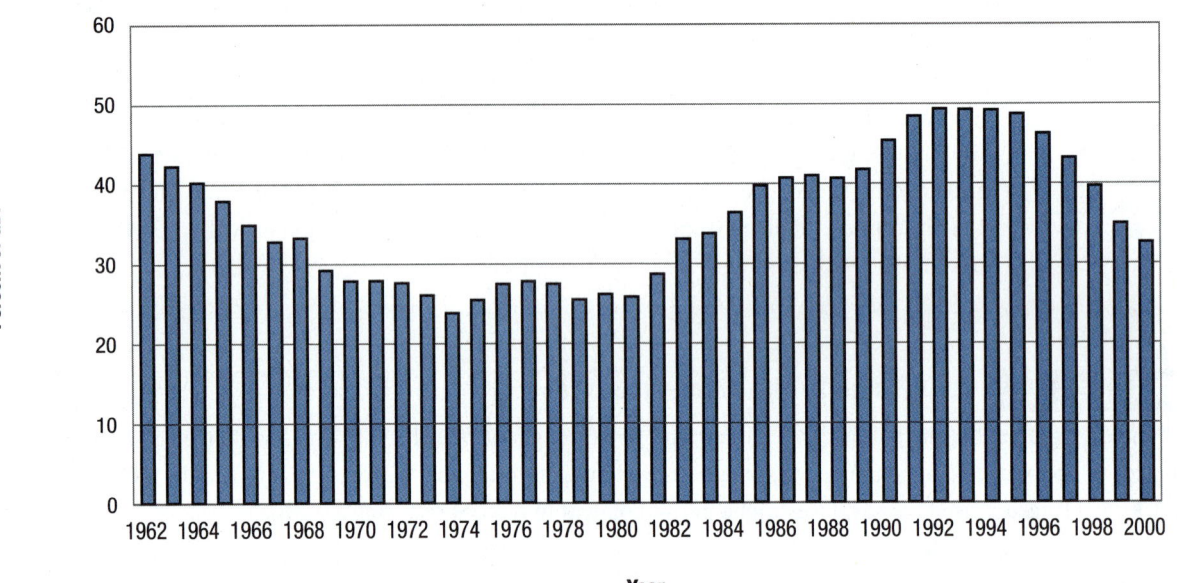

SOURCE: Office of Management and Budget, *Historical Tables, Budget of the United States Government, Fiscal 2003.*

■ LONG-RUN BUDGET AND DEBT PROJECTIONS

The Incredible Shrinking Surplus

Given the progress made in reducing the deficit between 1992 and 1997 and the surpluses achieved from 1998 to 2001, have we turned the corner in the battle against budget deficits? Many people thought so in 2001, including analysts at the Congressional Budget Office (CBO). In their long-run (10-year) forecast made at the beginning of 2001, they anticipated a decade of unprecedented surpluses. What they saw in their looking glass, in the absence of any changes in tax or expenditure policies, were surpluses starting at over $300 billion a year in 2002 and growing steadily until 2011, when they would reach nearly $900 billion. They expected total surpluses over this period of $5.6 trillion. The upper line in Figure 16.5 depicts the trajectory they had in mind.

The expectation of such surpluses ushered in a lengthy debate in Congress about how to use them. Some argued for using the surpluses to reduce the national debt; some favored using them to expand existing spending programs or to spawn new ones; and still others favored using them to provide a tax cut. Those favoring a tax cut were the clear winners; the Bush administration got congressional approval for a tax cut amounting to nearly $1.3 trillion over the next decade. This was a tax cut with strings

FIGURE 16.5 — Projected Federal Unified Budget Net Balances Projections of January 2001 (for 2002–2011) and August 2002 (for 2002–2012)

This figure depicts two projections made by the Congressional Budget Office of net balances in the unified budget—one in January 2001 and the other in August 2002. The lower projection in 2002 reflects lower expected revenues, due to the tax cut of 2001 and the slowdown in the economy in 2001–2002, and higher expected outlays for fighting the war in Afghanistan and the war on terrorism.

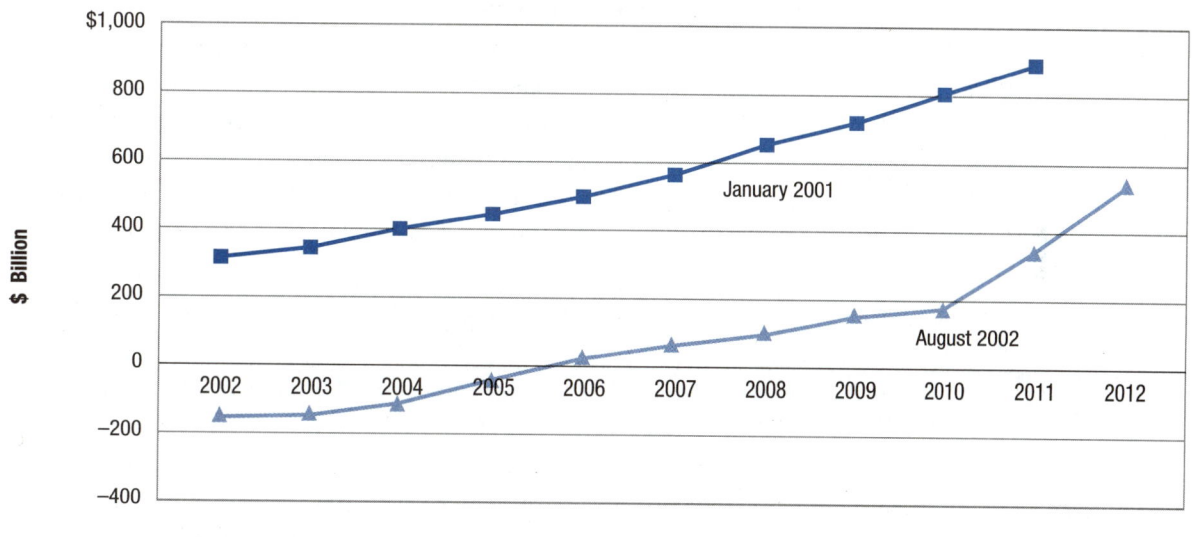

SOURCE: Congressional Budget Office, *The Budget and Economic Outlook: An Update*, August 2002.

attached, however. Various provisions of the legislation were to be phased in over several years, and the entire tax cut was scheduled to expire in December 2010.

Shortly after the CBO issued its January 2001 projections, the economy slipped into a recession, and then terrorists struck the World Trade Center and the Pentagon in September 2001. The first two of these events—the tax cut and the recession—combined to drastically reduce tax revenues; the last event—the terrorist attacks on the World Trade Center and the Pentagon—served as a catalyst for additional spending on international military ventures and homeland security. Analysts at the CBO and elsewhere began to revise their projections of future surpluses downward. In August 2002, they issued the forecast of the net balances in the unified budget for 2002–2012 that appears as the lower line in Figure 16.5. What emerged was a picture of net balances that averaged over $300 billion a year less than they had expected 18 months earlier. The $5.6 trillion 2002–2011 surplus had shrunk to a 2002–2012 surplus of only $859 billion. Given this projected outcome, Figure 16.5 probably should be relabeled "The Incredible Shrinking Surplus."

In addition to lower surpluses, Figure 16.5 also portrays the return of deficits in the unified budget from 2002 to 2005. These are followed by surpluses, however, over the balance of the forecast period, 2006–2012. It appears that the return to deficit finance is only temporary.

INFOTRAC
College Edition

Keywords: federal budget projections, budget surplus and projections

http://www.infotrac-college.com

The trajectory for the unified budget net balances is the summation, however, of the trajectories for the on-budget and off-budget (Social Security) net balances. As Figure 16.6 illustrates, on-budget net balances are expected to be negative through 2010. They would remain negative through 2012 if Congress decided to extend the 2010 deadline for reversing the tax cut of 2001. Thus, the unifed budget eventually records a surplus only because of the surplus in Social Security and the lack of action by Congress to make the tax cut of 2001 permanent.

The Deficit and the Debt in the Coming Decade

Table 16.2 illustrates the data behind the lower line in Figure 16.6. The projected on-budget and unified net balances are shown in columns 2 and 4. Column 3 provides the numbers for the off-budget or Social Security surplus. Columns 5 and 6 indicate how the projected on-budget deficit will be financed. Columns 7 through 9 show the effect that the financing of the on-budget deficit has on the publicly-held debt.

The law requires Social Security to use its surpluses to purchase U.S. government securities from the Treasury. The Treasury will use the proceeds from the sale of securities to Social Security to finance a significant portion of the on-budget deficit—77.6 percent from 2002 to 2010 (column 5). The Treasury will fund the remaining 22.4 percent of the 2002 to 2010 on-budget deficit by selling securities to the public.

FIGURE 16.6 Projected Federal Budget Net Balances, Projection of August 2002 Unified Budget and On-Budget, 2002–2012

The Congressional Budget Office projects that the unified budget will record a deficit from 2002 through 2005 and a surplus from 2006 through 2012. On-budget net balances are expected to be negative from 2002 through 2010. Net balances in the unified budget are higher because it includes Social Security surpluses and because the tax cut of 2001 expires at the end of 2010, providing a boost in revenues in 2011 and 2012.

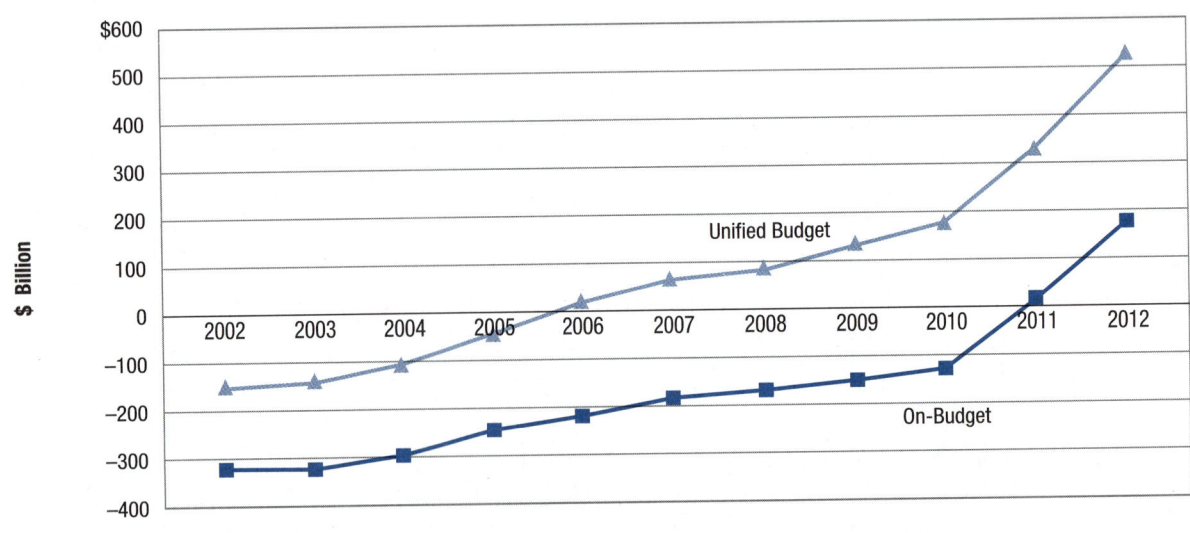

SOURCE: Congressional Budget Office, *The Budget and Economic Outlook: An Update*, August 2002.

TABLE 16.2 Federal Budget Net Balances, Means of Funding On-Budget Deficit and Effects on Public Debt, 2002–2012

	Federal Budget Net Balances			Funding of On-Budget Deficit		Effects on Publicly-Held Debt		
	On Budget (Non–Soc Sec) Net Balance	Off-Budget (Soc Sec) Net Balance	Unified Budget Net Balance	On-Budget Deficit Funded by Soc Sec	On-Budget Deficit Funded by Public	Public Debt Retired with SS Surplus	Public Debt Retired with OB Surplus	Change in Public Debt
Year	$ Billion	$ Billion	$ Billion	$ Billion	$ Billion	$ Billion	$ Billion	$ Billion
1	2	3	4	5	6	7	8	9
2002	−314	157	−157	157	157	0	0	157
2003	−315	170	−145	170	145	0	0	145
2004	−299	188	−111	188	111	0	0	111
2005	−246	207	−39	207	39	0	0	39
2006	−209	224	15	209	0	15	0	−15
2007	−190	242	52	190	0	52	0	−52
2008	−173	262	89	173	0	89	0	−89
2009	−147	280	133	147	0	133	0	−133
2010	−122	299	177	122	0	177	0	−177
2011	4	319	323	0	0	319	4	−323
2012	185	337	522	0	0	337	185	−522
Totals	−1826	2685	859	1563	452	1122	189	−859
			Percent of Total	77.6%	22.4%	85.6%	14.4%	

SOURCE: Congressional Budget Office, *The Budget and Economic Outlook: An Update*, August 2002.

During the period 2002 to 2005, all of the Social Security surplus must be used to help finance the on-budget deficit. (Compare columns 3 and 5 for this time period.) These surpluses are not large enough, however, to finance all of the on-budget deficits, and it is necessary to borrow also from the public (see column 6). As a result, the public debt will increase by the amount borrowed from the public (column 9). During this period, none of the Social Security surplus will be saved.

The Social Security surplus is considered saved whenever it results in a reduction in the public debt. The reason is straightforward. When the public debt is falling, the Treasury can reduce the amount it borrows each year to refinance the portion of the debt that comes due that year (the government bonds that have matured). When the Treasury borrows less, it indirectly increases the amount of money that can be used to finance private investment, instead. The act of borrowing less is equivalent to providing new funds for private investment or, what is the same thing, equivalent to an increase in the supply of savings to the private sector.

During the period 2006 to 2010, the Social Security surplus will be larger than the on-budget deficit so all of the latter will be financed by Treasury sales of bonds to Social Security. The excess Social Security surpluses will also be lent to the Treasury, and the Treasury will use these proceeds to refinance the existing public debt instead of borrowing the funds from the public. Thus, the public debt will fall by the same amount as the excess Social Security surpluses (see column 9), and the excess Social Security surpluses will be saved.

In the last two years, both the on-budget and Social Security surpluses will replace borrowing from the public, the public debt will fall, and the federal budget (including Social Security) will be the source of significant savings. The gross federal debt is projected to rise substantially over the next 10 years, however, from $6.2 trillion in November 2002 to $9.1 trillion at the end of 2012; the budget is expected to run cumulative surpluses of more than $800 billion during that period.

How can that be; shouldn't budget surpluses cause the federal debt to shrink? In fact, as we have just shown, part of it does: the part owed to the public. The public debt is projected to rise until 2006, but then, as budget surpluses emerge, it falls to a level lower than it is now. However, the portion that the government owes to itself (not shown in Table 16.2) is projected to increase by more than the portion it owes to the public. Thus, the gross debt will rise. The public debt is projected to drop from $3.5 trillion today to $2.7 trillion by the end of 2012; the debt held in government accounts is projected to rise from $2.7 trillion to $6.4 trillion.

Keywords: *federal budget, federal trust funds*

http://www.infotrac-college.com

The Really Long Run

What happens, though, after 2012? The CBO has a long-run projection model that provides the general parameters of what we might expect. This model combines historical data from 1950 to 2002 and assumptions about future revenues and expenditures to produce the actual and projected trend in the unified budget from 1950 to 2075. One key assumption behind the projections is that tax policy after 2010 will remain unchanged (including the expiration of the provisions of the tax cut of 2001). On the expenditure side, the largest federal entitlement programs—Social Security, Medicare, and Medicaid—and net interest are the primary drivers. Social Security spending is assumed to reflect growth in both the number of recipients and wages, upon which benefits are calculated. Medicare and Medicaid spending reflects an increasing number of recipients as well as higher costs for medical care. For these projections, the rise in health care cost per recipient is assumed to be about 1 percentage point faster than per capita GDP—a conservative assumption in light of past cost increases.

Figure 16.7 shows the CBO's view of the long-run trajectory of the unified budget's net balances. According to this view, surpluses are expected to begin in 2006 and last until 2025. After that, the unified budget balance will turn negative, and the deficit will continue to grow as a percent of GDP for the next 50 years.

Keywords: *population aging and federal budget, long-run federal budget*

http://www.infotrac-college.com

Figure 16.8 illustrates projected outlays, by major type, for the same 125-year period. It is clear that the farther one looks into the future, the more important are the commitments to Social Security, Medicare and Medicaid, and interest on the debt. In fact, the projected outlays for these functions, alone, are so large that they will seriously constrain and ultimately eliminate choices in other areas of the budget. This point is illustrated in Figure 16.9, which shows outlays for these functions increasing relative to projected revenues and eventually commanding all available revenues by 2050.

■ MEASUREMENT ISSUES

Some economists argue that federal budget deficits are overstated. According to economists like Robert Eisner, past president of the American Economics Association, and Alan Blinder, former vice chairman of the Federal Reserve, the way the federal deficit is currently computed does not account for some impor-

FIGURE 16.7 Federal Unified Budget Net Balance, 1950–2001, and Projections, 2002–2075, Percent of GDP

This figure shows both past (1950–2002) and projected future (2002–2075) net balances in the unified budget as a percentage of GDP. A budget surplus is expected from 2006 through 2024, followed by a deficit for the remainder of the forecast period. The steep descent in net balances is due to a growing gap between income and outgo for Social Security and Medicare and the rising costs of Medicaid and interest on the public debt.

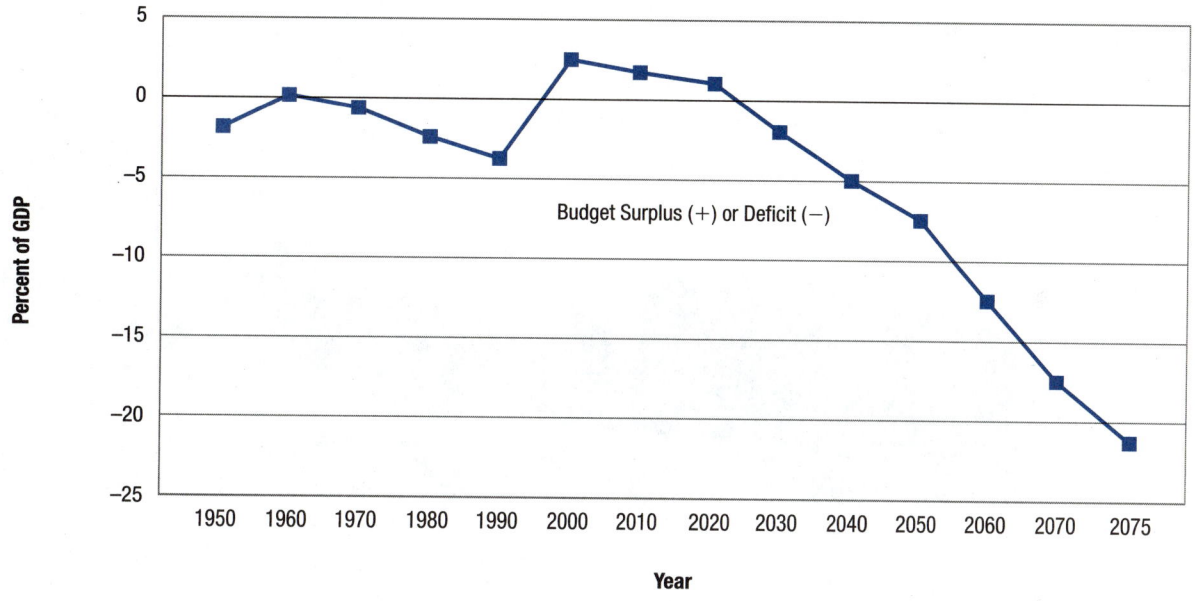

SOURCE: Congressional Budget Office, *A 125-Year Picture of the Federal Government's Share of the Economy, 1950 to 2075*, Revised, July 3, 2002.

tant factors that make the deficit less onerous that it would otherwise appear. These factors are (1) inflation, (2) business cycles, (3) government investment, and (4) state and local government net balances.

Inflation

The federal government does not calculate the effect of inflation on its accounts, but it is an important adjustment where the deficit is concerned. To see why, consider this example. Suppose that the government borrows $100 million from the public when the annual inflation rate is 5 percent and plans to pay it back in a year's time. Given the inflation rate, the $100 million repayment costs the government only $95.24 million ($100/1.05) in real purchasing power. The public, in effect, has given the government $4.76 in inflation "taxes." Some economists therefore adjust the value of the federal deficit to account for the implicit government revenue that is generated by the effect of inflation on the real value of the outstanding federal debt. Adjusted for inflation, deficits are smaller than they are under current accounting procedures. Indeed, by this measure the federal government achieved budget surpluses in 9 of the years between 1962 and 1998, instead of the 1 year in that time period according to the official measure of the deficit.

FIGURE 16.8   Federal Outlays, by Category, 1950–2075, Percent of GDP

In 2000, Social Security, Medicare, Medicaid, and interest on the debt accounted for roughly half of total federal outlays. The share attributable to these programs will increase dramatically in the future, reaching over 80 percent by 2075. This trend reflects the expected aging of the population, medical care costs increasing relative to increases in GDP, and deficits that must be financed by borrowing from the public.

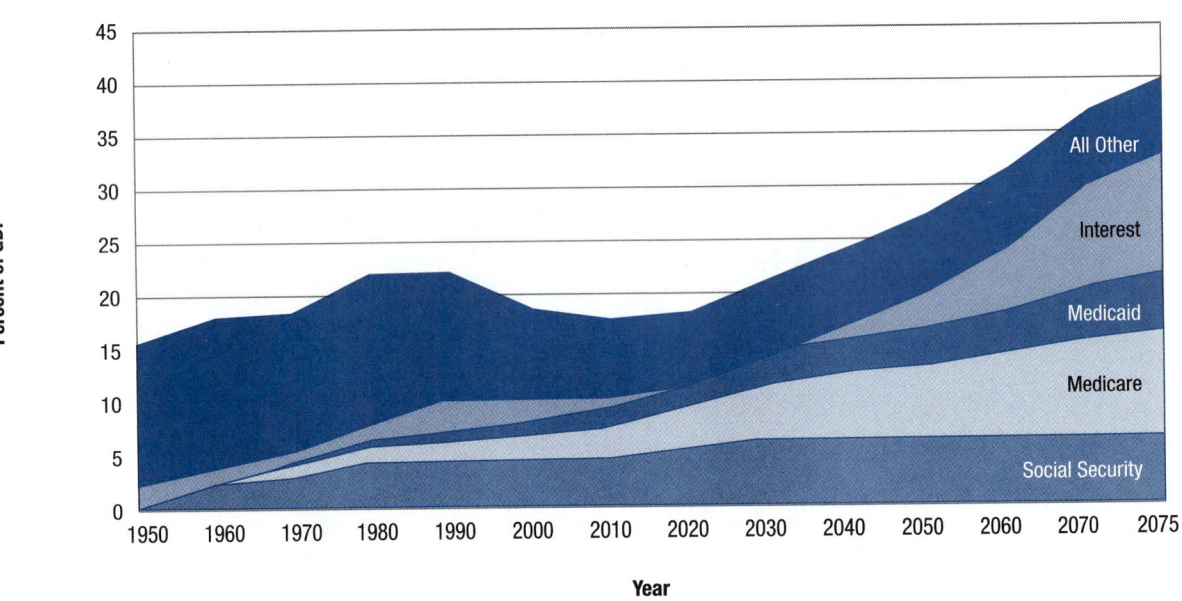

SOURCE: Congressional Budget Office, *A 125-Year Picture of the Federal Government's Share of the Economy, 1950 to 2075,* Revised, July 3, 2002.

Business Cycles

Structural Deficit – The deficit at full employment.

Actual Deficit – The amount by which actual government expenditures exceed actual government revenues.

Economists distinguish two types of deficits. The first is the structural, or full employment, deficit. The **structural deficit** is the deficit that would occur if the economy were at full employment. To calculate the structural deficit, economists estimate the government's expenditures and revenues as if full employment prevailed. The second is the **actual deficit**, the difference between the government's actual expenditures and revenue. At full employment, the structural and actual deficits are equal; if a recession occurs, however, the actual deficit will be greater than the structural deficit because a recession triggers automatic government expenditure increases and tax revenue decreases. Government expenditures increase as unemployment increases, because the government pays more in unemployment compensation and other transfer payments. Tax revenue decreases because those who become unemployed pay less in taxes. Those who remain employed but experience declining incomes also pay less in taxes. Firms pay less in taxes because profits fall during recessions.

From our perspective, the structural deficit is more important than the actual deficit for two reasons. First, the automatic changes in government expenditures and revenue that occur when the economy

FIGURE 16.9 Actual and Projected Revenues and Outlays for Social Security, Medicare, Medicaid, and Interest, 1950–2075

In 1950, outlays for Social Security, Medicare, Medicaid, and interest on the public debt (SSMMI) were about 15 percent of federal revenues. By 2000, SSMMI absorbed almost half of available revenues. In the absence of changes in tax policy and benefits provided by Social Security, Medicare, and Medicaid, SSMMI will claim all available revenues by 2050.

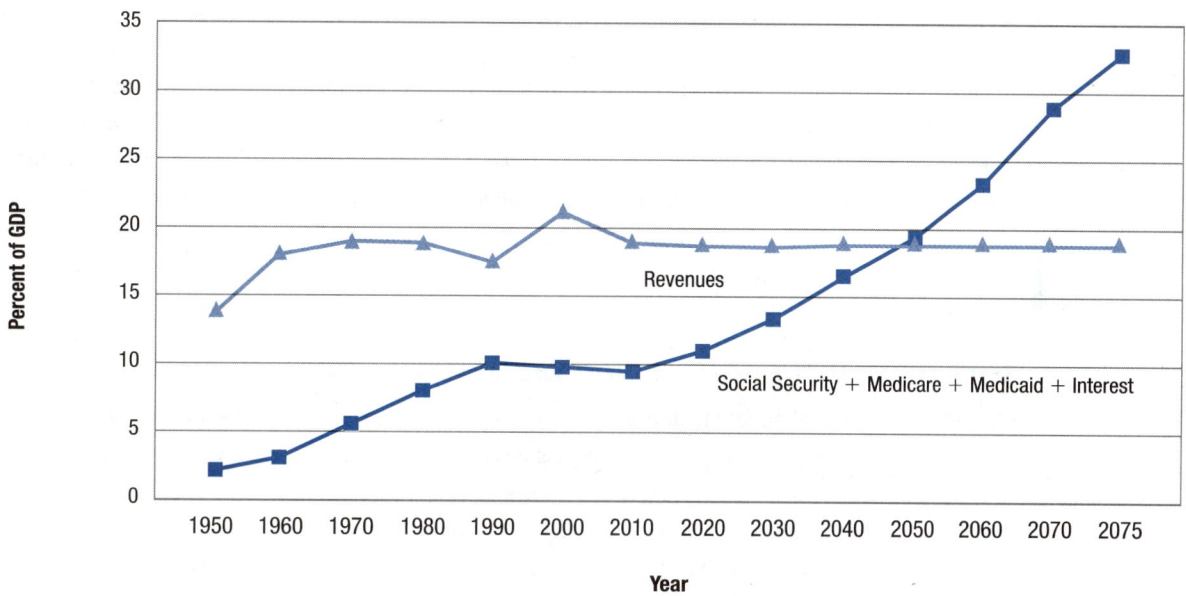

SOURCE: Congressional Budget Office, *A 125-Year Picture of the Federal Government's Share of the Economy, 1950 to 2075*, Revised, July 3, 2002.

enters a recession help to stabilize the economy. The increase in expenditures and decrease in tax revenue provide households with more disposable income, thereby maintaining consumption at a higher level than it otherwise would be. As a result, the recession is less severe.

Second, the portion of a deficit resulting from a depressed economy is of little concern because it will become smaller as the economy recovers and disappear completely when the economy reaches full employment. On the other hand, the structural portion of a deficit will remain even after the economy reaches full employment. To illustrate, huge government deficits developed in the early 1980s. Much of the deficit was due to the depressed state of the economy—particularly in 1981 and 1982, when the United States experienced a severe recession. Economists were not particularly concerned with this portion because they realized that it would disappear when full employment was restored. Thus, they would argue, the portion of a deficit due to the business cycle should be subtracted from the official deficit.

Government Investment

Concern about the deficit is rooted in the notion that federal government borrowing is a bad thing. Generally speaking, the federal government can borrow for two purposes: (1) to pay for consumption-type expenditures (e.g., food stamps, farm subsidies, and armaments) and (2) to pay for investment-type expenditures (e.g., education, research, and highways). Outside the federal government, borrowing to pay for investment-type purchases is viewed as a sound business practice. The same standard should be applied to the federal government.

If it were, the deficit, which currently combines borrowing for both consumption and investment, would be split into its investment and consumption components. Investment expenditures would be deducted from the official deficit to get a more accurate picture of the deficit of concern. The only proviso is that the investment expenditures that are deducted should be productive investments from which the public can expect a reasonable return on their tax dollars. The measurement stakes are large. In 1996, for example, the government invested an estimated $229 billion in physical assets, research and development, and education and training. Some of this—$93 billion—was invested in national defense, but the remainder—$136 billion—was invested in nondefense activities. It is the latter portion of the investment budget that most economists would argue should be viewed as a legitimate object of government borrowing and not counted as part of the deficit. This portion, alone, was larger than the official deficit of $107.5 billion in 1996.

State and Local Government Deficits and Surpluses

One reason the federal government runs a deficit is the large amounts that it gives to state and local governments in the form of grants-in-aid. Such largess has enabled state and local governments to run substantial budget surpluses. In fact, state and local governments achieved a surplus in 37 of the 40 years between 1962 and 2001. The combined deficits of all levels of government have therefore been smaller than the deficits of the federal government, alone. If the deficit is intended as a measure of government borrowing from the public, the relevant deficit is the combined deficit, and state and local governments surpluses should be added to federal government deficits to get a true picture of government borrowing.

Keywords: *real deficits, deficits and inflation, structural deficits, government investment*

http://www.infotrac-college.com

If federal net balances are adjusted to account for all four factors—inflation, business cycles, government investment, and state and local government surpluses—federal budget deficits become much smaller, and federal budget surpluses become much larger. Figure 16.10 illustrates the difference that these adjustments make when they are combined. They not only reduce the magnitude of the federal deficits, but they change deficits to surpluses in 29 of the 36 years from 1962 to 1997. In fact, the unadjusted deficit averaged $97 billion over this period; the adjustments turn this into a surplus of $34 billion a year.

It is impossible to know if these kinds of adjustments would significantly reduce the deficits projected for 2002 to 2005, but they would still be relevant. They would still be relevant, as well, for the long-run deficits projected for the 2025 to 2075 time frame, but it seems extremely unlikely that they would significantly reduce these deficits. The deficits in that time frame appear much too large to be adjusted away.

■ ECONOMIC EFFECTS OF A DEFICIT

The Keynesian View: A Deficit Can Help to Cure a Recession

Over the years, attitudes toward budget deficits have changed. Prior to the 1930s, most people believed that the government's budget should be balanced annually—that government expenditures should equal tax revenue regardless of the state of the economy. With the advent of the Great Depression and the pub-

FIGURE 16.10 — Federal Budget Net Balances, Unified and Adjusted, 1962–2001 (Adjusted for Inflation, Business Cycles, Nondefense Investment, and S & L Surpluses)

Net balances in the unified budget were negative in 35 of the 40 years from 1962 through 2001. Adjustments for inflation, business cycles, nondefense investment, and state and local government net balances (primarily surpluses) change deficits to surpluses in 29 of the 36 years from 1962 through 1997.

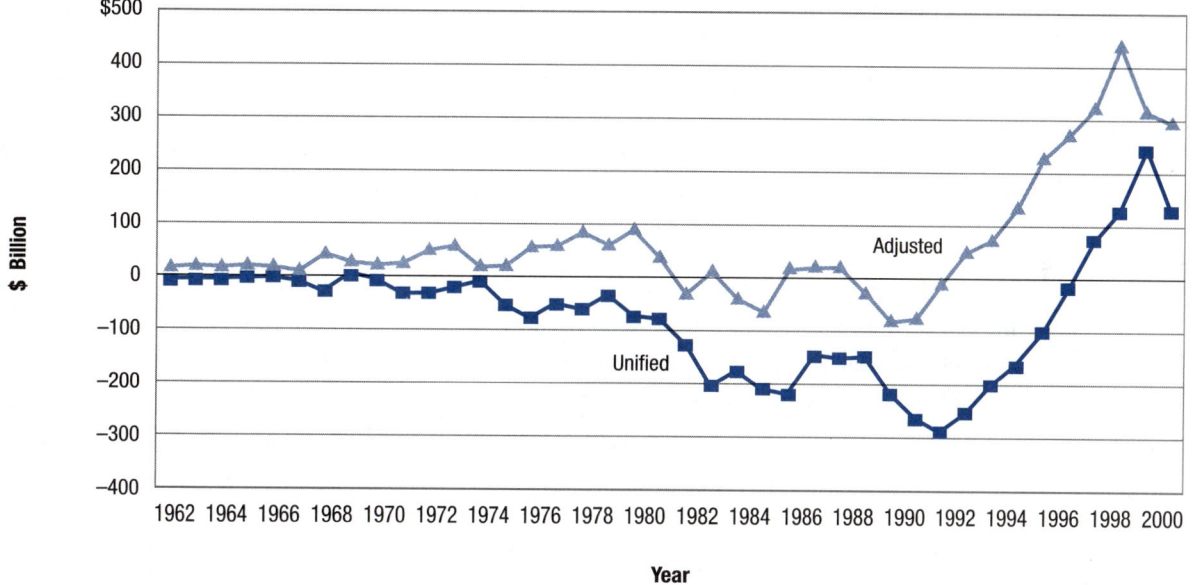

SOURCES: Office of Management and Budget, *Historical Tables, Budget of the United States Government, Fiscal 2003*. Adjusted net balances from authors' calculations.

lication of John M. Keynes's *The General Theory of Employment, Interest, and Money* in 1936, this view faded.

According to Keynesian economics, deficits are desirable during recessions. We already know that government expenditures increase and tax revenues decrease automatically as the economy enters a recession. Despite their impact on the budget, these changes provide households with additional disposable income, thus maintaining consumption at a higher level than it would be otherwise. Because these automatic changes moderate the recession, government should not act to offset them by reducing expenditures or increasing taxes to maintain a balanced budget. In fact, Keynesian economics suggests that the appropriate fiscal policy during a recession is to increase expenditures, reduce taxes, or do both. These changes cause aggregate demand to increase, thereby increasing the nation's output and employment. The increase in government expenditures or decrease in tax revenue helps to restore prosperity despite the growing budget deficit

The Modern View: The Strength of the Cure Depends on How the Deficit Is Financed

The Keynesians are right; running a budget deficit will increase output and employment—provided that the economy is at less than full employment. How much output and employment will increase, however, depends on how the deficit is financed.

The U.S. Treasury must borrow to finance a budget deficit. It can borrow what it needs from the public (households, firms, financial institutions, or governments), from Social Security, or from the Federal Reserve. The public is normally a dependable source of funds; Treasury securities are always in demand as a safe, income-earning asset. Social Security is a source of funds as long as there is a surplus in the Social Security budget. The Federal Reserve is a source of funds only if they are planning to increase the nation's money supply.

The effect of a deficit on output and employment will be affected by the sale of securities to the public—for reasons to be explained. The effect of a deficit on output and employment is not affected at all by sales of Treasury securities to Social Security. The Treasury simply gives Social Security special-issue securities in exchange for Social Security revenues. No market transaction is involved. Therefore, there is no effect on the economy. The effect of a deficit on output and employment is unlikely to be affected, either, by the sale of securities to the Federal Reserve—but for much different reasons.

BOND SALES TO THE PUBLIC SECTOR. Suppose the deficit is financed by selling U.S. Treasury securities to the public sector. The effect is expansionary, but less than the Keynesians thought, because this method of financing causes higher interest rates. Interest rates increase because the government must compete with the private sector for **loanable funds** and, other things equal, an increased demand for loanable funds causes the interest rate to rise (see Figure 16.11).

Loanable funds are funds available for borrowing by households and firms and by government. In Figure 16.11, the D_0 curve represents the demand for loanable funds. It is negatively sloped because, as the interest rate falls, firms and households wish to borrow more funds. Firms may desire more funds to finance an increase in their productive capacity. Similarly, households may wish to borrow to buy homes

Loanable Funds – Funds available for borrowing by households, firms, and government.

FIGURE 16.11 The Impact of an Increase in the Demand for Loanable Funds on the Interest Rate

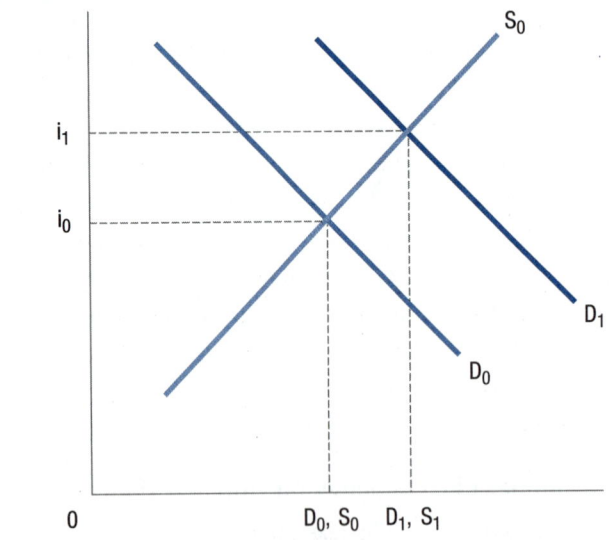

If the demand for loanable funds is D_0 and the supply of loanable funds is S_0, the equilibrium interest rate is i_0. If the federal government develops a deficit and finances it by borrowing from the public, the demand for loanable funds increases to D_1. As a result, the equilibrium interest rate increases to i_1.

Demand for and Supply of Loanable Funds

or automobiles. The S_0 curve represents the supply of loanable funds. It is positively sloped because, as the interest rate rises, households and firms are more willing to lend funds. Given the demand for and supply of loanable funds, the initial equilibrium interest rate is i_0.

Suppose that a deficit develops in the federal government's budget. Because we are assuming that the federal government finances this deficit by borrowing from the private sector, the demand for loanable funds increases. This increase is depicted in Figure 16.11 by the shift in the demand curve from D_0 to D_1. The increase in demand causes the interest rate to increase from i_0 to i_1. Thus, if the federal government finances the deficit by borrowing from the private sector, the interest rate will be higher than it would be otherwise.

The increase in the interest rate has important implications for the economy. A higher interest rate reduces investment. Firms invest less in plant and equipment because of the increased cost of borrowing funds. The reduction in investment causes the nation's capital stock to grow less rapidly. As a consequence, the nation's output and employment grow more slowly and productivity gains lag. In short, the reduction in investment and, therefore, in the rate of capital accumulation mean our living standard improves less rapidly than it would otherwise.

Higher interest rates also affect exports and imports. If U.S. interest rates rise relative to those in other countries, people in other countries will take advantage of the situation by buying U.S. Treasury and other securities. As a result, the demand for dollars and dollar-denominated assets will increase. With flexible exchange rates (discussed in Chapter 18), the dollar will appreciate (increase) in value in terms of one or more foreign currencies.

The appreciation of the dollar will make U.S. goods more expensive to foreigners and, as a result, less competitive in world markets. U.S. exports will decrease, adversely affecting output and employment in the export-producing sector of the economy.

The appreciation of the dollar has the opposite effect on imports, causing foreign goods to become less expensive to people in the United States. Consequently, U.S. imports increase, adversely affecting output and employment in the import-competing sector of the economy.

This problem was particularly acute in the early 1980s. Interest rates increased in the United States relative to other countries—largely due to the big budget deficits of that period. These higher interest rates increased the demand for dollars, and the dollar appreciated significantly over the 1981 to 1985 period. As a result, exports decreased and imports increased, causing economic hardship in the export-producing and import-competing sectors of the U.S. economy.

As we have observed, a government deficit financed by selling bonds to the private sector raises interest rates, which discourages investment and reduces the nation's growth rate. At the same time, output and employment do increase, provided the economy is at less than full employment. Moreover, if the economy is operating at less than full capacity, the increase in interest rates may be small. With excess capacity, firms have less incentive to borrow to invest in new plant and equipment, and they may reduce their demand for loanable funds at the same time that the Treasury is increasing its demand for loanable funds to finance a deficit. With a reduction in private demand, the increase in interest rates resulting from the federal government's increased demand for loanable funds may be small.

Given the increases in output and employment and provided that the increase in interest rates is small, budget deficits may be justified when the economy is at less than full employment. If the economy is at full employment, however, they are not. In this situation, the growth in government expenditures and subsequently in aggregate demand increases the price level, not output and employment. As a result, no increase in economic activity occurs. Moreover, interest rates increase by a larger amount at full employment. With little or no excess capacity, firms have a greater incentive to borrow to invest in new plant and equipment. They may, therefore, increase their demand for loanable funds. This increase, along with the federal government's increase in demand for loanable funds, results in a larger increase in interest rates. These higher interest rates curtail investment. Consequently, the rate of capital accumulation slows, reducing the growth rate and retarding improvement in the standard of living.

BOND SALES TO THE FEDERAL RESERVE. Instead of financing the deficit by selling bonds to the private sector, suppose the federal government finances it by selling bonds to the Federal Reserve. The effect is more expansionary than if the deficit had been financed by selling them to the private sector. The reason is that the purchase of bonds by the Federal Reserve increases the money supply. This effect is expansionary; thus it reinforces the effect of the deficit.

The change in the government's budget and increase in the money supply cause aggregate demand to increase. If the economy is experiencing unemployment, output and employment increase. Moreover, the increase in economic activity is unlikely to be accompanied by significantly higher interest rates. On the one hand, an increase in the deficit increases the demand for loanable funds. On the other hand, an increase in the money supply increases the supply of loanable funds. The net result will be little or no change in interest rates and, therefore, little or no change in investment and the value of the dollar.

Thus, given less than full employment, an increase in government expenditures has no harmful effects on the economy, provided that the deficit is financed by selling bonds to the Federal Reserve. Indeed, it has a positive effect by increasing output and employment. (The same effect could have been achieved with lower interest rates by merely increasing the money supply.) When the economy is at full employment, this justification for deficits disappears. Under full employment, the increase in aggregate demand causes the price level—not output and employment—to increase because the economy is already fully using its productive capacity. Moreover, if the deficit persists and the Federal Reserve continues to buy U.S. Treasury securities, the inflation rate will rise. With no increase in output and employment and with rising inflation, the deficit—especially if financed by selling bonds to the Federal Reserve—is clearly undesirable.

INFOTRAC
College Edition

Keywords: *crowding out*

http://www.infotrac-college.com

■ THE BURDEN OF THE DEBT

Given its magnitude, many people are concerned about the federal debt. As you will see, this concern is warranted. We start, however, with some arguments that have little or no merit. One of the arguments is that the federal government should not borrow, thereby increasing the public debt. Instead, the government should balance its budget annually just as households and firms must balance their budgets annually. Households and firms, however, often do not balance their budgets on an annual basis. Students borrow to help finance their college educations. Households borrow to purchase homes and automobiles. Firms borrow to construct plants or to purchase new equipment. To say, therefore, that the federal government must balance its budget because households and firms must balance theirs is incorrect.

To go further, it is often desirable to borrow (incur debt). By borrowing to complete their college educations, students may significantly increase their future earnings. Part of these additional earnings can be used to repay their loans. Similarly, a home provides a flow of services over time. Borrowing to purchase a home may be desirable because a household can pay off the mortgage with the income that would otherwise be used to pay rent. Finally, by building a new plant or purchasing new equipment, a firm may increase its future sales receipts. Part of these proceeds can then be used to pay off the loan.

In each of these examples, borrowing provides an increased flow of income in the future, part of which could be used to pay off the loan. The same is true for the federal government. It is desirable for the federal government to borrow (increase the public debt), provided that the money is spent on projects that yield a flow of future benefits sufficient to repay the loan. Such projects might include roads, dams, irrigation projects, and schools.

It is sometimes asserted that federal government debt, like private debt, ultimately must be repaid. This is true in the sense that part of the debt falls due each year. The Treasury, however, can simply refund the debt; that is, borrow new money to pay the holders of the securities as they mature. Thus, the government's debt need not be repaid in the sense of ultimately being reduced to zero.

Neither of these two arguments regarding the public debt—(1) the government should balance its budget each year because households and firms must balance their budgets each year and (2) the debt must ultimately be reduced to zero—is valid.

Another invalid argument is as follows: The national debt is owed to ourselves. In truth, some of it is and some of it isn't. The part that we do owe to ourselves is the part held by the U.S. public. This part of the debt is a liability to taxpayers, but it is an asset to those who hold the debt. Interest payments on the debt redistribute income from taxpayers to debt holders. Because taxpayers generally have lower incomes than persons who hold the national debt, the transfer of income from taxpayers to the debt holders may result in a more unequal distribution of income. But this redistribution does not directly reduce the nation's productive capacity, output, or available goods and services. Consequently, it does not represent a burden to either current or future generations.

However, one-third of the public debt is held by foreigners. We do not, therefore, owe the entire debt to ourselves. Interest payments and repayment of principal to foreign investors involve more than a transfer of dollars. The dollars represent a potential claim against goods and services produced in the United States. If foreigners use them to buy goods and services produced in this country, the quantity of goods and services available to U.S. citizens decreases. This reduction in goods and services represents a burden to both present and future generations.

In addition, a large public debt places a heavy burden on taxpayers. Interest on the public debt is the third largest item in the federal budget after Social Security and defense. Tax rates must be sufficiently high to pay this interest. High marginal tax rates may dampen incentives to work, save, invest, and innovate. High marginal tax rates reduce the after-tax rate of return to work, thereby reducing the supply of labor. They also reduce the after-tax rate of return to saving, which discourages saving. If saving falls, interest rates rise. The higher interest rates—combined with a reduced after-tax rate of return to investment due to higher marginal tax rates—reduce investment and, therefore, the rate of capital accumulation. Finally, high marginal tax rates reduce the after-tax rate of return to innovation which, in turn, reduces the nation's growth rate.

If the tax rates necessary to finance the interest on the public debt (and various government programs) are high enough to reduce incentives to work, save, invest, and innovate, the nation's productive capacity and output will be lower than otherwise. Smaller output represents a burden to the current generation.

A reduction in productive capacity means that output will be less in the future, representing a burden to future generations.

Even if tax rates are not high enough to reduce the incentives to work, save, invest, and innovate, the public debt is still a burden to society. Although the federal government will once again have budget surpluses (from 2006 to 2026), they will not be large enough to retire all of the debt; in fact, in the really long run, the debt will begin to soar again as the deficit becomes larger. Consequently, the U.S. Treasury will eventually be a net borrower. Interest rates, therefore, will be higher than they would be otherwise. With higher interest rates, investment will be less, causing a slower rate of capital accumulation. More distant generations will inherit a smaller capital stock and productive capacity. As a result, their incomes will be lower.

INFOTRAC
College Edition

Keywords: *burden of the debt*

http://www.infotrac-college.com

■ TAKING STOCK

The public debt cannot be reduced, of course, unless Congress achieves tight control over future deficits. Federal budget deficits are potentially serious problems, even though their magnitudes have often been overestimated. Congress can do a better job of measuring the deficit by incorporating the adjustments suggested here. A useful step in this direction would be the establishment of separate capital and operating budgets, similar to those used in most state governments and in private businesses.

If the CBO's long-run projections are right, however, it will difficult to engage Congress in serious pursuit of deficit reduction. As we have seen, the federal government is likely to experience deficits only in the next 4 years, and these should be relatively small as a percentage of GDP. After that, surpluses may prevail for another 20 years before the combined effect of commitments for health care and Social Security plunge the budget into ever growing deficits. Congress's interest span is rarely this long.

The expected 20 years of surpluses will be realized, moreover, only if (1) Congress allows the 2001 tax cut to expire as scheduled, (2) the economy stays on a steady growth path, and (3) there are no new major program initiatives. All of these are problematic, but the payoff from realizing the projected surpluses is substantial. If they are saved or, what is the same thing, channeled into productive investment, future GDP will be larger, future tax receipts will be higher, and future interest payments on the debt will be lower. In other words, if the surpluses are turned into productive investments, future deficits will be smaller.

There are three principal ways to channel both the expected on-budget and Social Security surpluses (Social Security will have positive net balances through 2017, according to the intermediate projections in the *2002 Annual Report* of the Social Security Trustees) into productive investment: (1) by using them to reduce the public debt, (2) by using them to finance government investment, and (3) by turning them into tax relief that increases private investment. These are not necessarily equivalent alternatives, but they all deserve serious consideration; reducing the public debt is not the only way to achieve higher future living standards.

However, the stark truth is that, although savings from surpluses are important, they will not be sufficient by themselves to achieve the kind of deficit reduction that will be needed. They must be coupled with action to slow the long-term drivers of the projected deficits, i.e., Social Security and health programs. We have reviewed some of the possibilities in the chapters in this book on Social Security and medical care.

Reducing the relative future burdens of Social Security and federal health programs is critical to promoting a sustainable budget for the very long run. Absent prior reform, the impact of federal health and retirement programs on budget choices will be felt as the baby boom generation begins to retire. Although much of the public debate concerning the Social Security and Medicare programs focuses on trust fund balances, the net cash impact of the trust funds on the budget—not trust fund solvency—is the important measure. The Social Security Trust Fund (OASDI), for example, is projected to be exhausted in 2041, and virtually all of the long-run attention to Social Security focuses on that date. Under the trustees' intermediate assumptions, however, Social Security is projected to have cash deficits beginning in 2018. At that point, the program becomes a net claimant on the federal budget; that is, the Treasury will have to start borrowing from the public, or Congress will have to increase taxes or reduce other spending, in order to pay the interest on the debt held by Social Security. In another 5 or 6 years after that, the Treasury will have to borrow even more to buy back the securities that Social Security will have to sell to finance the growing obligations to the baby boom generation of retirees.

The truth is that, when the long-run prospects for Social Security (and Medicare and Medicaid, as well) are viewed in the context of the federal budget, Congress has much less time to deal with the long-run financing problems of these programs than is commonly thought. The accumulation of federal securities in trust funds will not mitigate the future strains that programs such as Social Security and Medicare will impose on the federal budget and the economy. When trust fund balances are drawn down, these programs will not be using resources that have been saved for a rainy day, as is commonly believed. They will be using resources generated at that time, and those resources can only be provided either from a surplus in the rest of the federal budget or by borrowing from the public.

Summary

The U.S. Congress distinguishes between two budgets, one that includes Social Security—the unified budget—and one that does not—the non–Social Security budget. The bottom line of the budget is the net balance—revenues minus expenditures. A positive net balance is a budget surplus; a negative net balance is a deficit. Net balances in the unified budget were negative from 1962 through 1997 (except 1969) and positive from 1998 through 2001.

The gross federal debt was $6.2 trillion at the end of 2001; $3.5 trillion of this was debt held by the public. The public debt impacts the economy; the gross federal debt does not. The public debt grew steadily during the period 1962 to 1997, reflecting the nearly unbroken string of deficits in the unified budget. These deficits were often so large that they could not be financed entirely with Social Security surpluses, and the Treasury had to borrow from the public. In spite of this, the burden of the debt (the public debt relative to GDP) is less in 2002 than it was in 1962.

According to future scenarios developed by the CBO, we are facing a deficit from 2002 through 2005, followed by relatively small surpluses through 2012. This is far different from the decade of record surpluses forecasted in January 2001. Part of this deficit will be financed by Social Security surpluses and part by borrowing from the public, so the public debt will increase for the next 4 years. From 2006 through 2012, Social Security surpluses are large enough, by themselves, to finance the on-budget deficit, allowing the Treasury to reduce the public debt or save the Social Security surpluses.

After 2012, the CBO expects another decade of budget surpluses, followed by about a half-century of steadily increasing deficits. These deficits will be fueled primarily by cash deficits in Social Security, Medicare, and Medicaid and by rising interest payments on the debt. In fact, these programs will become so large relative to projected revenues that they will eventually claim all of them.

The way the federal deficit is currently computed does not account for some important factors that make the deficit less onerous that it would otherwise appear. These factors are (1) inflation, (2) business cycles, (3) government non-defense investment, and (4) state and local government net balances. Application of these adjustments to historical data changes the net balance in the unified budget from deficit to surplus in 29 of the 36 years from 1962 to 1997.

Prior to the 1930s, most people believed that the government's budget should be balanced annually. With the spread of Keynesian economics, a new view developed—namely, to run deficits during recessions to stimulate the economy.

Although expansionary, deficits may also have adverse effects on the economy, depending on how the deficit is financed. If the deficit is financed by borrowing from the private sector, it causes higher interest rates and lower investment. If the deficit is financed by borrowing from the Federal Reserve, the nation's money supply increases so that the net effect on interest rates may be negligible. If the deficit is financed by borrowing from Social Security, there is no adverse effect on the economy.

If the economy is at less than full employment, the deficit results in higher output and employment regardless of the method of financing. Thus, at less than full employment, some justification for running deficits exists. With full employment, the deficit results in higher prices, but not higher output and employment. At full employment, no justification exists for a deficit.

The federal debt is large enough to be a legitimate source of concern. A large debt should not be viewed as a good reason, however, to avoid budget deficits. If the federal government borrows for productive purposes, and it can afford the interest costs associated with servicing the debt, it is simply following good financial practices. Although the debt is large, it need never be repaid; the full faith and credit of the federal government is good enough to permit continual refunding of the debt as it matures. About a third of the public debt is held by foreign individuals or institutions. This portion of the debt is more troublesome than the portion owned by US citizens and institutions. Finally, a large debt can necessitate higher taxes, causing adverse effects on work, saving, and investment.

Key Terms

Budget	**Off-budget surplus**	**Structural deficit**
Unified budget	**On-budget surplus**	**Actual deficit**
Net budget balance	**Gross federal debt**	**Loanable funds**
Budget surplus	**Public debt**	
Budget deficit	**Burden of the public debt**	

Review Questions

1. Explain the differences between the unified budget and the non–Social Security budget.
2. How are a unified budget deficit, an on-budget deficit, and an off-budget deficit related?
3. Briefly describe the history of the unified budget and on-budget net balances for the period 1962 to 2001.
4. Briefly describe what is in store for net balances in the unified budget, the non–Social Security budget, and the public debt for the period 2002 to 2012. Carefully explain why the public debt is expected to grow and then decline.
5. Explain how the public debt can decline while the gross federal debt grows (as is expected to happen from 2006 to 2012).
6. Suppose that the public debt is $3 trillion at the end of a year, that during that year the unified budget deficit was $200 billion and the rate of inflation was 3 percent. What is the real value of the deficit after adjusting for inflation?
7. When are structural and actual deficits the same? How do these deficits differ if the economy is experiencing a recession? Which deficit should be a greater source of concern?

8. Is it possible for budget deficits and surpluses to stabilize the economy? On the basis of your response, evaluate the argument for an annually balanced federal budget.
9. Suppose the economy is currently at full employment and the federal government's budget is showing a surplus. How would balancing the budget (eliminating the surplus) affect the economy?
10. Carefully describe the differences in the effects on the economy of financing a deficit by selling Treasury bonds to the private sector and selling bonds to the Federal Reserve.
11. Why is it undesirable for the federal government to run a deficit with the economy at full employment?
12. Briefly explain why economists are more concerned about the public debt than about the gross federal debt, although the latter is significantly larger than the former.
13. Explain how the federal government saves the Social Security surplus.
14. The federal government has two important advantages over households and firms when it comes to reducing or financing budget deficits. What are these advantages? With these advantages in mind, evaluate the following statement: "Like households that go too deeply in debt, the federal government with its large deficits may be forced into bankruptcy."
15. During the 1980s and 1990s, the proportion of the national debt held by foreigners increased. How does this affect the burden of the debt?
16. Describe the ways in which the Social Security surplus can be channeled into productive investment.
17. Explain why Social Security and Medicare are more immediate problems when viewed in the context of the federal budget than when they are viewed as independent programs.

Economic Issues on the Internet

- Congressional Budget Office—**http://www.cbo.gov**

  The Budget and the Economic Outlook, An Update, August 2002, contains the CBO's projections of the federal unified and Social Security budgets for 2002 to 2012. All of the CBO's studies can be downloaded from the Web site.

- Office of Management and Budget—**http://www.omb.gov**

  Historical Budget Tables, Budget of the United States Government, Fiscal Year 2003, is an excellent source of historical data on deficits and debt. All Office of Management and Budget information can be downloaded from the Web site.

Chapter 17

The Global Economy: Trade

Outline:

U.S. Participation in World Trade
Comparative Advantage and International Trade
Net Gains from International Trade
Barriers to International Trade
   Tariffs
   Quotas
   Voluntary Export Restraints

The Case for Free Trade
   Decreasing Costs
   Increased Competition
   Diversity of Products
The Case for Protection
   Infant Industry
   National Defense
   Save American Jobs

   Cheap Foreign Labor
Reducing Trade Barriers
   The Global Approach
   The Regional Approach

The U.S. economy is becoming increasingly internationalized. Exports and imports are rising relative to GDP. Travel to and from the United States is commonplace. U.S. and foreign investors participate in domestic and international financial markets by purchasing each others' stocks and bonds.

International trade touches us all. Many of the foods that we eat, many of the clothes that we wear, and many of the cars that we drive come from foreign countries. The incomes and jobs of many workers in manufacturing and agriculture depend crucially on their ability to compete in world markets.

In this chapter, we consider U.S. participation in the world economy. After discussing the basis for trade, we examine existing barriers to international trade. We then consider the case for and against reducing those barriers. Finally, we discuss global and regional approaches to reducing trade barriers.

■ U.S. Participation in World Trade

U.S. exports and imports have increased significantly over the past four decades. As shown in Figure 17.1, exports rose from $25 billion in 1960 to $1,034 billion in 2001, and imports increased from $23 billion to $1,383 billion.

The U.S. economy also grew rapidly over the same time period. GDP was $527 billion in 1960 and $10,082 billion in 2001. The growth of international trade outpaced GDP, however. As shown in Figure 17.2, the U.S. economy has become increasingly internationalized. Measured by exports, foreign trade increased from almost 5 percent of GDP in 1960 to nearly 12 percent in 1997, then fell back to about 10 percent of GDP by 2001. Measured by imports, international trade grew from a little over 4 percent of GDP in 1960 to a peak of 15 percent of GDP in 2000, then fell back to about 14 percent of GDP in 2001.

The United States exports a variety of goods, including commercial aircraft, computers, scientific equipment, machinery, chemicals, and grain. It also imports a variety of goods, including automobiles, steel, clothing, footwear, various foodstuffs (such as coffee, bananas, cocoa, and tea), crude oil, and various raw materials (such as bauxite and natural rubber). The United States' main trading partner is Canada, followed by Japan and Mexico.

From 1960 to 1976, U.S. exports closely matched U.S. imports. Since then, the United States has had a **trade deficit** (imports greater than exports). As shown in Figure 17.3, the trade deficit reached a record level of more than $350 billion—3.5 percent of GDP in 2000. Many people see exports as a source of

INFOTRAC
College Edition

Keywords: *trade deficit, balance of trade*

http://www.infotrac-college.com

Trade Deficit — A negative net balance in the international trade account; imports greater than exports.

FIGURE 17.1   U.S. Exports and Imports, 1960–2001

U.S. exports and imports, measured in current dollars, increased rapidly from 1960 to 2000 and declined slightly in 2001.

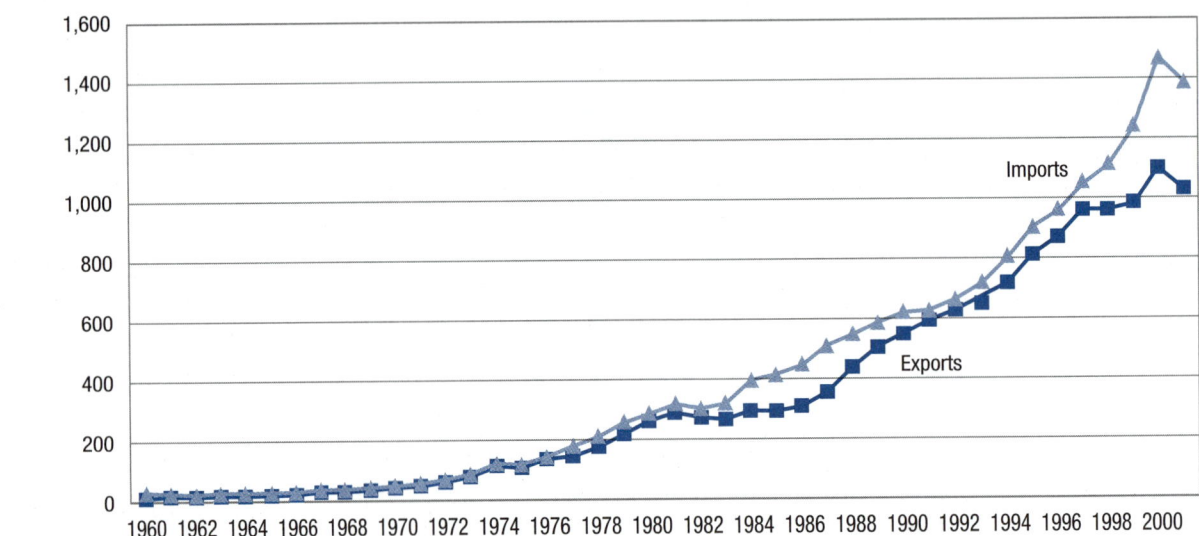

SOURCE: Bureau of Economic Analysis, *GDP and Other Major Series, 1929–2002.1*, August 2002.

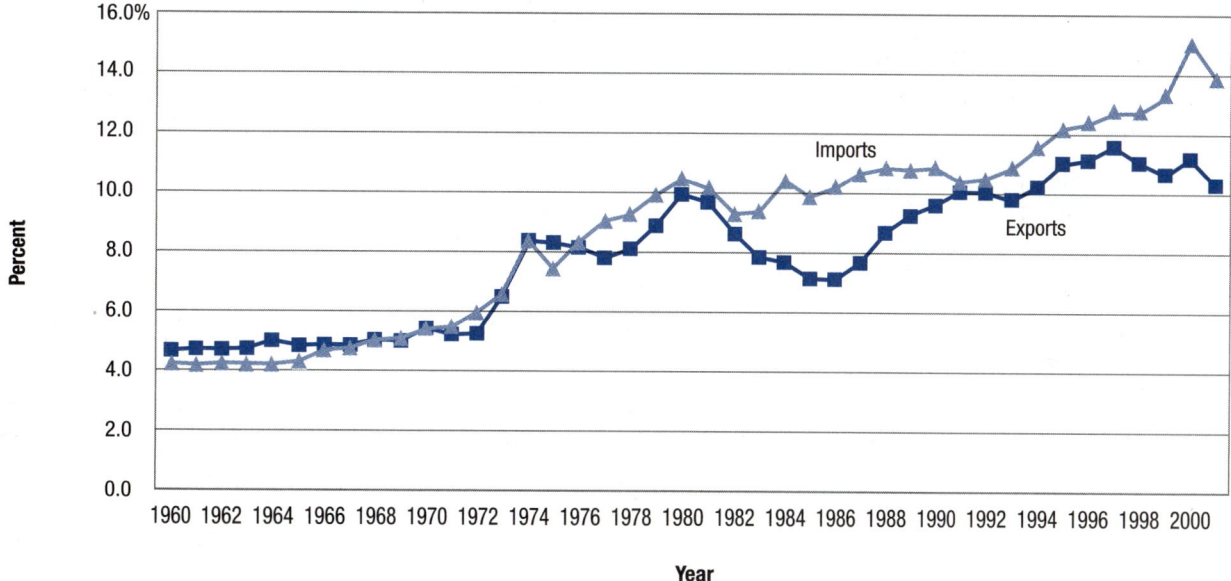

FIGURE 17.2 Exports and Imports as a Percent of GDP, 1960–2001

Both exports and imports have increased as a percentage of GDP over the last four decades. Since 1976, imports have increased at a faster rate than exports.

SOURCE: Bureau of Economic Analysis, *GDP and Other Major Series, 1929–2002.1*, August 2002.

jobs and imports as a loss of jobs—in the sense that imported goods and services would have provided jobs in the United States if they had been produced here. They view the trend in Figure 17.3 as evidence that foreign trade destroys more jobs than it creates and push for various restrictions on trade as a means of protecting U.S. workers.

Economists do not normally subscribe to this view. They argue, first, that, as a consequence of something called comparative advantage, free international trade makes both countries better off. Second, although they acknowledge that jobs will be lost in industries that produce products that compete with imports, they argue that U.S. consumers will gain from the lower prices of imports, and that the gains to consumers will exceed the losses to workers. Based on these arguments, they generally oppose restrictions on trade as a means of saving U.S. jobs.

■ COMPARATIVE ADVANTAGE AND INTERNATIONAL TRADE

Comparative Advantage – The advantage a country has if it produces a good or service at a lower opportunity cost than its trading partner.

Comparative Disadvantage – The disadvantage a country has if it produces a good or service at a higher opportunity cost than its trading partner.

Trade among nations is based on comparative advantage. A country has a **comparative advantage** (or a **comparative disadvantage**) in a good or service if it can produce the good or service at a lower (higher) opportunity cost than its trading partner. Countries gain by producing goods and services for which they have a comparative advantage and exchanging them for goods and services for which they have a comparative disadvantage.

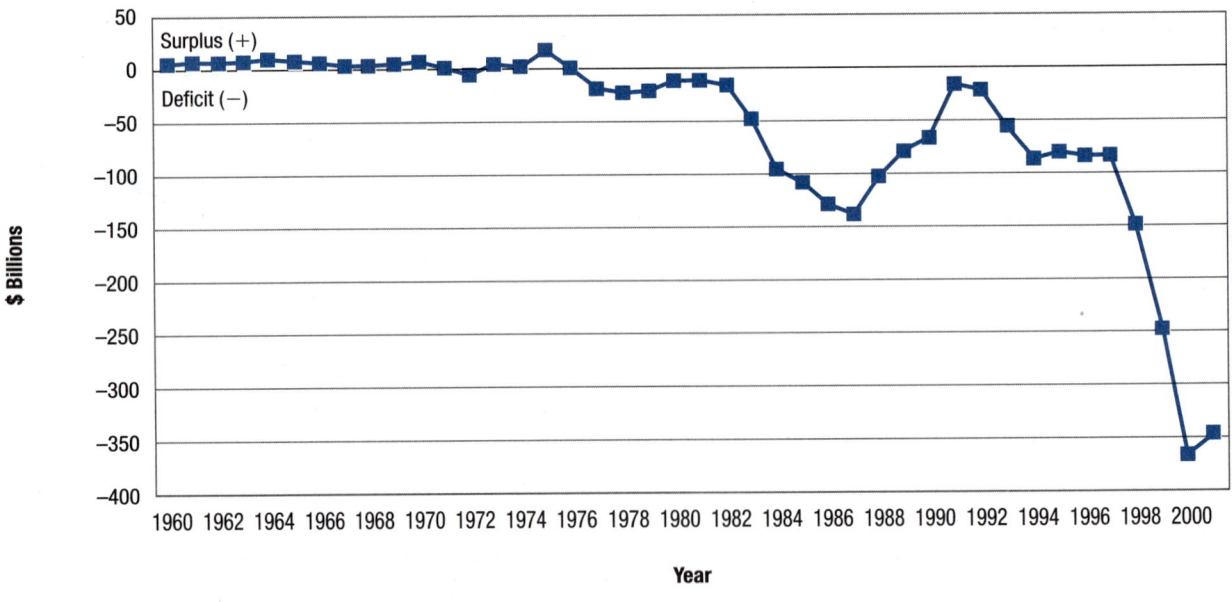

FIGURE 17.3 The U.S. Balance of Trade, 1960–2001

The United States has had a trade deficit every year since 1976. It grew especially fast in the 1990s and reached a record level of $365 billion in 2000.

SOURCE: Bureau of Economic Analysis, *GDP and Other Major Series, 1929–2002.1*, August 2002.

Absolute Advantage – The advantage a country has if it can produce a good or service at a lower cost than its trading partner.

Absolute Disadvantage – The disadvantage a country has if it produces a good or service at a higher cost than its trading partner.

The principle of comparative advantage was developed early in the nineteenth century by David Ricardo, a famous English economist. Following Ricardo, we construct a simple example of trade based on comparative advantage. The example assumes two countries, the United States and the United Kingdom; two goods, wheat and cloth; and one factor of production, labor. Although the volume of international trade depends on transportation costs, they do not alter the principle of comparative advantage, so they are ignored in this example.

Table 17.1 assumes that a U.S. worker can produce either 6 bushels of wheat or 6 yards of cloth per day. In contrast, a U.K. worker can produce either 1 bushel of wheat or 3 yards of cloth. Because the output of both goods is higher in the United States, it has an **absolute advantage** in the production of both wheat and cloth. Correspondingly, the United Kingdom has an **absolute disadvantage** in the production of both goods.

It may appear that no basis for mutually advantageous trade exists. After all, output per worker is higher in the United States for both goods. Nevertheless, a basis for trade exists because the United States is relatively more efficient in the production of wheat, and the United Kingdom is relatively more efficient in the production of cloth. A worker in the United States can produce 6 times as much wheat per day as a worker in the United Kingdom, but only 2 times as much cloth.

Because the United States is relatively more efficient in producing wheat, it can specialize in wheat production, export wheat to the United Kingdom in exchange for cloth, and be better off. Similarly,

TABLE 17.1	Output per Worker in the United States and the United Kingdom

Because output per worker is higher for both wheat and cloth in the United States, it has an absolute advantage in the production of those goods and the United Kingdom has an absolute disadvantage. Because the United States is relatively more efficient in the production of wheat, it has a comparative advantage in wheat production and the United Kingdom has a comparative advantage in cloth production.

Country	Wheat (Bushels per Day)	Cloth (Yards per Day)
United States	6	6
United Kingdom	1	3

because the United Kingdom is relatively more efficient in producing cloth, it can specialize in cloth production, export cloth to the United States in exchange for wheat, and be better off.

To demonstrate that both countries will be better off, we first note that the opportunity cost of 1 bushel of wheat is 1 yard of cloth in the United States. (In the U.S. economy, it is necessary to give up 1 bushel of wheat to obtain an additional yard of cloth.) In contrast, the opportunity cost of 1 bushel of wheat is 3 yards of cloth in the United Kingdom.

Although we cannot say exactly what the terms of trade will be, trade will be mutually advantageous if the United States can get more than 1 yard of cloth in exchange for 1 bushel of wheat and the United Kingdom can get 1 bushel of wheat for less than 3 yards of cloth. Suppose the international exchange ratio is 1 bushel of wheat for 2 yards of cloth. The United States is better off because it can now get 2 yards of cloth from the United Kingdom by giving up 1 bushel of wheat. Domestically, it can get only 1 yard of cloth by giving up 1 bushel of wheat. The United Kingdom is also better off because it can now get 1 bushel of wheat by giving up 2 yards of cloth. Domestically, it must give up 3 yards of cloth to get 1 bushel of wheat.

The example shows that both countries gain from international trade by producing goods in which they have a comparative advantage and exchanging them for goods in which they have a comparative disadvantage. We can demonstrate this result in a slightly different manner, one that shows that specialization with international trade results in a higher level of consumption for both countries.

With full employment, the United States can, by assumption, produce 600 bushels of wheat (and no cloth), 600 yards of cloth (and no wheat), or some combination of wheat and cloth (see Table 17.2). Suppose, in the absence of international trade, it produces and consumes 400 bushels of wheat and 200 yards of cloth.

With full employment, the United Kingdom can, by assumption, produce 600 yards of cloth (and no wheat), 200 bushels of wheat (and no cloth), or some combination. Suppose, in the absence of international trade, the United Kingdom produces and consumes 300 yards of cloth and 100 bushels of wheat.

Next, suppose that trade opens up between the United States and the United Kingdom. Because of its comparative advantage in wheat production, the United States will specialize in wheat production and export wheat to the United Kingdom in exchange for cloth. Similarly, the United Kingdom has a comparative advantage in

| TABLE 17.2 | Production and Consumption Before and After the Introduction of International Trade |

Before the introduction of international trade, the United States produced and consumed 400 bushels of wheat and 200 yards of cloth, while the United Kingdom produced and consumed 300 yards of cloth and 100 bushels of wheat. After the introduction of international trade, the United States specializes in wheat production and exports wheat to the United Kingdom in exchange for cloth. The United Kingdom specializes in cloth production and exports cloth to the United States in exchange for wheat. With specialization and international trade, both countries consume more wheat and cloth.

	United States	United Kingdom
Production at full employment	600 bushels of wheat or 600 yards of cloth (or some combination)	600 yards of cloth or 200 bushels of wheat (or some combination)
Consumption before international trade	400 bushels of wheat and 200 yards of cloth	300 yards of cloth and 100 bushels of wheat
Consumption after international trade[a]	475 bushels of wheat and 250 yards of cloth	350 yards of cloth and 125 bushels of wheat

[a] Assumes an international exchange ratio of 1 bushel of wheat for 2 yards of cloth.

cloth production. It will specialize in cloth production and export cloth to the United States in exchange for wheat. As before, assume that 1 bushel of wheat exchanges for 2 yards of cloth.

After the introduction of international trade, the United States will produce 600 bushels of wheat (and no cloth) and export, say, 125 bushels to the United Kingdom in exchange for 250 yards of cloth. As a result, consumption in the United States will be 475 bushels of wheat and 250 yards of cloth. Thus, after the trade, the United States will consume more wheat and more cloth.

The United Kingdom will produce 600 yards of cloth (and no wheat) and export 250 yards to the United States in exchange for 125 bushels of wheat. Consequently, consumption in the United Kingdom will be 350 yards of cloth and 125 bushels of wheat. After trade, the United Kingdom also will consume more wheat and more cloth.

In this example and in general, international trade is advantageous. It allows countries to specialize in the production of goods in which they have a comparative advantage and exchange those goods for goods in which they have a comparative disadvantage. In this way, countries achieve higher levels of consumption.

■ NET GAINS FROM INTERNATIONAL TRADE

But what about textile producers and workers in textile firms? We know that the United States can produce cloth, so if textiles are imported from the United Kingdom, U.S. firms will suffer from losses in sales and some textile workers will lose their jobs. This is true, as far as it goes, but it is only part of the story. Textiles will not be imported in the real world unless U.S. consumers value them more highly relative to their price than domestically-produced textiles. So, although textile imports create losses for workers and producers, they also create gains for consumers. It turns out, moreover, that gains to consumers exceed losses to workers and producers.

INFOTRAC
College Edition

Keywords: *gains from trade*
http://www.infotrac-college.com

Consumers' Surplus — The difference between the price that consumers are willing to pay (their demand price) and the price that they must pay.

Producers' Surplus — The difference between the price that producers receive and the price that they must receive (their supply price).

This result can be demonstrated using supply and demand analysis and some of the measures related to that analysis that we have used previously. Figure 17.4 shows the domestic market for cloth. In the absence of supply from the United Kingdom, the market would clear at Qb (the quantity before international trade) and Pb (the price before international trade). Given that the United Kingdom has a comparative advantage in cloth production, however, its opportunity cost of cloth production is generally lower than in the United States. This means it can offer its cloth on the U.S. market at a price below that of most U.S. cloth producers. This is indicated in the figure by a U.K. price (Pa—the price after trade) that is below the U.S price of Pb. Given the lower U.K. price, U.S. consumers will buy Qd from domestic producers, some of whom are more efficient than their U.K. counterparts. They will consume Qc, however, importing Qc−Qd from lower-cost producers in the United Kingdom.

Before the U.K. cloth is available, consumers reap net benefits in this market equal to the difference between what they *would* pay for the cloth they buy, their demand price, and the price they *must* pay, Pb. Their net benefit, or **consumers' surplus**, is equal to area A. Before the U.K. cloth is available, U.S. producers enjoy net benefits equal to the difference between the price they *receive*, Pb, and what they *must receive* to cover costs, i.e, their supply price. Their net benefit, or **producers' surplus**, is equal to area B+C.

After cloth is imported from the United Kingdom, consumers gain additional consumers' surplus of B+D and producers lose producers' surplus of B. The gain in consumers' surplus is larger than the loss in producers' surplus by the area D. Area D represents the net gains from trade for cloth with the United Kingdom.

U.S. production will fall from Qb to Qd, however. Because of this, some U.S. workers will lose their jobs. There is a net loss to workers, however, only to the degree that they are unable to find alternative employment. Under normal conditions, an economy at or close to full employment, they will find other jobs and net losses to workers will be small.

FIGURE 17.4 The U.S. Market for Cloth, with Imports from the United Kingdom

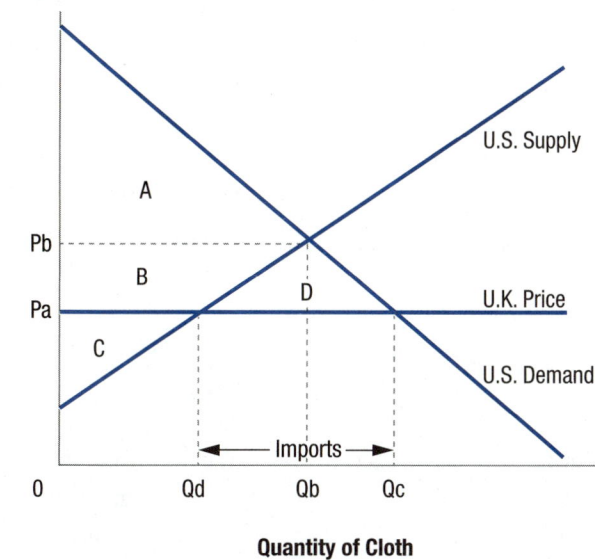

With no imports, the market would clear at Qb and Pb, producing net gains to consumers (consumers' surplus) equal to area A and net gains to producers (producers' surplus) equal to area B+C. With trade, the price will fall to Pa, and consumers will buy Qc; Qd from domestic producers and Qc−Qd from U.K. producers. Trade will increase the net gains of consumers by the area B+D and reduce the net gains of producers by area B, leaving a net gain from trade of area D.

INSIGHTS

THE COST OF SAVING U.S. JOBS

Often, people argue that the United States should impose tariffs or quotas to save jobs. As argued elsewhere, trade restrictions are not the best way to achieve or maintain full employment.

In addition, saving jobs by imposing trade restrictions is costly. Trade restrictions raise prices, costing consumers billions of dollars. The U.S. International Trade Commission has estimated the cost to consumers of saving a job in various industries. The commission found, for example, that it costs $63,500 to save a job in the U.S. bicycle industry (see table). This cost is well above the typical worker's salary in the bicycle industry, making it costly to society to save a worker's job through trade restrictions. To put it differently, consumers could pay a former bicycle worker $40,000 a year to do nothing, and still be $23,500 better off than if the government had restored the worker's job in the bicycle industry through trade restrictions.

The Cost of Saving a Job: Selected Industries

Industry	Consumer Cost per Job
Ceramic tiles	$225,000
Earthenware	173,500
Rubber footwear	113,400
Luggage	103,500
Women's footwear	92,900
Costume jewelry	86,700
Women's purses	84,000
Canned tuna	76,600
Chinaware	73,000
Bicycles	63,500
Leather gloves	46,800

The cost of saving jobs through trade restrictions is even higher in other industries. In the ceramic tile industry, the cost to consumers of saving a job is $225,000; in the earthenware industry, $173,500; and so on.

SOURCE: U.S. International Trade Commission, *The Economic Effects of Significant U.S. Import Restraints, Phase I: Manufacturing* (Washington, DC: Government Printing Office, October 1989), x.

■ BARRIERS TO INTERNATIONAL TRADE

The principle of comparative advantage makes a strong case for unrestricted, or free, international trade. An examination of the relative size of gains and losses in the textiles market also indicates that unrestricted trade will generate positive net benefits. The real world doesn't work quite as smoothly as Figure 17.4 implies, however. Some workers will probably not find alternative employment quickly and some firms will probably go out of business. Thus, some of the costs of free trade will be highly visible. This is likely to lead to restrictions on trade, such as tariffs, quotas, and voluntary export restraints.

Tariffs

Tariff –
A tax levied on a good when it crosses a nation's border.

A **tariff** is a tax levied on a good when it crosses a nation's border. The United States has tariffs on many imported goods, including textiles, apparel, and footwear. Historically, the United States has had high tariffs. With the passage of the Smoot–Hawley Act in 1930, the average tariff on imported goods reached 60 percent. Since then, tariffs have been reduced. Today, the average tariff on imports into the United States is only about 5 percent. Some goods, however, are subject to much higher tariffs.

The imposition of a tariff causes the domestic price of the good to rise. Consumers buy less of the product and imports fall. Domestic producers, not subject to the tariff, receive a higher price for the good. As a result, they expand production, implying that more domestic resources are devoted to the production of the good.

When it imposes a tariff, the federal government experiences an increase in tax revenue (unless the tariff is so high that no imports enter the country). Indeed, for much of our nation's history, tariffs were an important source of federal tax revenue. Today, tariff revenue is only a small part of total tax revenue, and few tariffs are levied for that purpose.

The imposition of a tariff makes consumers worse off because they must pay a higher price for the product. Domestic producers, however, are better off. They receive a higher price for their product; they are also able to increase production. (Foreign producers are, of course, worse off.) Because domestic producers are better off, it is not surprising that many domestic firms favor tariffs or other trade restrictions and lobby strongly for such measures.

Because consumers are worse off and domestic producers are better off, what can be said for society as a whole? Society is worse off. The imposition of tariffs causes resources to flow to industries that have a comparative disadvantage. Some of these resources come from industries that have a comparative advantage. When more resources are engaged in less efficient productive activities and fewer resources in more efficient productive activities, people experience a lower standard of living.

Quotas

Quota –
An upper limit on the amount of a good that may be imported during any time period.

An import **quota** specifies the maximum amount of a good that may be imported during any time period. Although tariffs are more common than quotas, the United States has set quotas for various goods, including steel, textiles, sugar, and beef.

By limiting the amount that can be imported, a quota—like a tariff—results in a higher price for the product. Indeed, the price may be higher with a quota than with a tariff. With a tariff, imports can increase in response to an increase in demand. The increase in imports limits the rise in price. But with a quota, it is not possible to import more.

Because of the increase in price, domestic producers increase their output. As a result, more domestic resources are used to produce this good, implying that fewer resources are available to produce other goods.

So far, the effects of tariffs and quotas are similar. They both raise prices, thus hurting consumers and helping domestic producers. Yet they do differ in one important respect. Tariffs usually generate revenue for the federal government; quotas do not.

Although domestic producers benefit from quotas, society as a whole is worse off. Like tariffs, quotas shift resources from industries that have a comparative advantage to those that have a comparative disadvantage. The result is a reduction in peoples' standard of living.

Voluntary Export Restraints

Voluntary Export Restraints (VERs) –
Agreements whereby exporting nations limit the amounts of goods that they ship to importing nations.

Voluntary export restraints (VERs) are agreements whereby exporting nations agree to limit the amounts of goods that they ship to importing nations. The United States negotiated a VER with Japan on automobiles in the early 1980s. Under this agreement, the Japanese "volunteered" to limit the number of automobiles that they ship to the United States. (As with most VERs, the Japanese agreed because they feared that even more stringent import restrictions might be imposed.) The United States has negotiated VERs on steel, machine tools, televisions, VCRs, and lumber, thus limiting U.S. imports of those products.

Keywords: *restraints on trade, tariffs, trade quotas*

http://www.infotrac-college.com

VERs reduce imports, thereby raising the prices of goods subject to VERs. Consumers are, of course, worse off. Domestic producers, however, are better off because they can charge higher prices for their products. They also benefit from increased production.

Although domestic producers benefit from VERs, society as a whole is worse off. Like tariffs and quotas, VERs shift resources from industries that have a comparative advantage to those that have a comparative disadvantage. The result is a reduction in the nation's standard of living.

■ The Case for Free Trade

The case for free trade based on the principle of comparative advantage is strong. When other factors are taken into account, the case is even stronger.

Decreasing Costs

In many industries, the average cost of production decreases as output increases. Large-scale production may, for example, make for more efficient use of machinery and lower costs per unit. In industries with decreasing costs, a higher volume of output enables firms to sell their products at lower prices.

In the absence of international trade, an industry's market may be too small for firms to achieve the lowest possible average cost. With international trade, these firms may be able to increase production and sell the extra output abroad, resulting in lower average costs and price. Both producers and consumers benefit from the increased production and lower price.

Although markets in the United States are typically large, international markets enable some industries to produce more, thus lowering average costs and prices. The commercial aircraft industry is an example. If that industry's sales were confined to the United States, the average cost and price of aircraft would be higher than they are today.

The possibility of increasing output and selling the extra output abroad is important, even for a large country like the United States. It is even more important for smaller countries with limited domestic markets.

Increased Competition

As discussed in Chapter 5, competition among firms results in higher output and lower prices. The same analysis applies to competition between domestic and foreign firms.

Domestically, one or a few firms may dominate an industry. A case in point is the automobile industry in the United States. For all practical purposes, the domestic industry consists of only three firms. If foreign competition did not exist, these firms would be able to restrict output and raise prices.

Domestic producers, however, are subject to considerable competition from foreign automobile manufacturers, especially firms from Japan and Western Europe. This competition forces domestic producers to charge lower prices. It also forces them to compete in terms of quality, gas mileage, and other dimensions that are important to consumers.

In conclusion, free trade is desirable because competition from foreign firms is often the only way to keep markets from being dominated by one or a few domestic firms.

Diversity of Products

Another argument for free trade is that it increases the diversity of products available to consumers. With trade, consumers in the United States can buy many goods that might not otherwise be available, such as coffee, tea, cocoa, bananas, spices, and silk.

Trade also enhances choice among competing models of the same good. With trade, consumers can choose among many types of automobiles. Besides domestically produced automobiles, consumers in the United States can choose among various foreign automobiles, including expensive models from Japan and Germany and inexpensive models from South Korea.

■ THE CASE FOR PROTECTION

Despite the strength of the arguments for free trade, some people argue that government should act to protect domestic industries by imposing tariffs, quotas, or similar measures. Indeed, many arguments have been advanced to restrict international trade. We shall consider some of the most common.

Infant Industry

Some people argue that new, or infant, industries should be protected. They claim that these industries, after they are established, will have a comparative advantage. Initially, however, they will be unable to compete with industries already established in other countries. According to this argument, protection would only be temporary. It would be eliminated as the industry becomes competitive in world markets.

Although this view may have some relevance for less-developed countries, it is not particularly relevant for mature industrial economies like the United States. In the United States, mature industries (such as the steel and automobile industries) typically request protection. These industries often claim that they need time to modernize in order to become more competitive, and that protection will provide them that time. Once the modernization is complete, they claim, the protection can be removed.

Industries may use that time to modernize. On the other hand, protection reduces or eliminates the incentive to modernize. Indeed, experience suggests that little modernization occurs unless competition forces it.

Even if we concede that new industries need help in establishing themselves, tariffs and quotas are not the best means to that end. Economists agree that direct government subsidies would be a better approach. With subsidies, price remains low to consumers. Subsidies also make it clear which industries are being helped and to what extent. Finally, a subsidy may be easier to eliminate than a tariff or quota.

National Defense

Some people argue that industries producing goods important to national security should be protected. They claim, for example, that steel, petroleum, and military hardware are crucial for national defense and so should be protected. Proponents of this argument recognize that protectionist measures raise the prices of these products. They believe, however, that the benefits of increased military preparedness outweigh the costs associated with the higher prices.

Even if we concede the validity of this argument, protectionist measures are not the best means by which to strengthen the industries in question. If increased national security is a benefit, it is shared by society as a whole—not just the persons who buy the industries' goods. Consequently, government should assist the industries by providing direct subsidies. Because subsidies are financed from tax revenue, the costs of the subsidization (as well as its benefits) would be shared by society as a whole.

Save American Jobs

Another argument for protection has to do with jobs. It is claimed that foreign competition can reduce output and employment in import-competing industries. Consequently, some form of protection is necessary to maintain employment in those industries.

As noted previously, there is little doubt that imports can cause unemployment in import-competing industries. Over time, some industries lose their comparative advantage and become vulnerable to foreign competition. To maintain full employment, however, the solution is not the imposition of tariffs and quotas. Instead, it is to use fiscal and monetary policy (see Chapters 14 and 15). Because some workers who lose their jobs may not have the skills and education necessary to fill the jobs available, government may need to assist them in upgrading their skills and relocating.

The U.S. experience in the 1990s suggests strongly that it is possible to reduce trade barriers and at the same time reduce unemployment. Despite reductions in trade barriers following the so-called Uruguay Round of international trade negotiations and the implementation of NAFTA (both are discussed later in this chapter), U.S. unemployment decreased, reaching a 30-year low in 2000.

The best way to protect American jobs is to pursue monetary and fiscal policies that provide for full employment and, at the same time, pursue policies to help the structurally unemployed. With this approach, resources will flow from industries that have lost their comparative advantage to those that have gained a comparative advantage. The imposition of protectionist measures to preserve an old and inefficient allocation of resources would result in a lower standard of living.

INFOTRAC
College Edition
Keywords: *saving American jobs, exporting jobs*
http://www.infotrac-college.com

Cheap Foreign Labor

Still another argument for protection has to do with the importation of goods from countries with low wages. It is claimed that many U.S. industries cannot compete because wages are much higher in the United States than in foreign countries. Therefore, tariffs or quotas—so the argument goes—must be imposed to protect those industries.

High wages do not necessarily imply high costs. Wages in the United States are high because labor productivity is high. Workers in the United States are well trained and work with relatively large amounts of capital. It is not surprising, therefore, that they are very productive and earn high wages. Because of their high productivity, their high wages don't necessarily mean that the United States is a high-cost producer.

Suppose it is true that high wages give the United States an absolute disadvantage in all industries. Would it be advantageous to the United States to trade with other nations? Of course. Trade among nations is based on comparative advantage, not absolute advantage. It is desirable for the United States to concentrate on goods it produces more efficiently and export those goods in exchange for goods that it produces less efficiently.

■ REDUCING TRADE BARRIERS

Since World War II, barriers to international trade have been reduced significantly. In reducing these barriers, countries have taken two approaches: (1) trade negotiations on a global basis and (2) formation of regional trading blocs.

The Global Approach

Since World War II, eight rounds of international trade negotiations have been conducted under the auspices of the General Agreement on Tariffs and Trade (GATT), an international organization founded in

INTERNATIONAL PERSPECTIVE

THE WTO: AN INTERNATIONAL CONSPIRACY?

In 1995, the World Trade Organization (WTO) was formed as successor to the General Agreement on Tariffs and Trade (GATT).[a] Approximately 120 nations, including the United States, belong to the WTO; these nations account for most of the world's trade. Like GATT, the WTO provides a framework for multilateral trade negotiations, issues ground rules for the conduct of international trade, and helps resolve trade disputes.

With regard to international trade, the WTO has an important role. Even so, some people are critical of the WTO. In many cases, this criticism dates back to the GATT. Environmentalists were particularly upset with GATT's ruling regarding tuna imported from Mexico. In 1976, Congress passed and the president signed the Marine Mammal Protection Act. In part, the act outlawed the practice of catching tuna with large nets that also snared dolphins who were feeding on the tuna. (Most of the dolphins failed to escape from the nets and died.) U.S. fishing fleets, of course, had to abide by the law; foreign fleets did not. Subsequently, the United States imposed an embargo on tuna caught by foreign fishing fleets that did not follow the U.S. practice.

Mexico protested the embargo, and in 1991 GATT ruled against the United States. Under GATT rules, it is the product (in this case, tuna) that is relevant, not the process by which it is produced. (Under GATT rules, the only time that the process becomes relevant is when the good is produced by prison labor.) Mexico also protested on other grounds, noting, for example, that dolphins are not an endangered species.

In 1998, environmentalists were again upset when the WTO ruled against U.S. restrictions on imports of shrimp caught in nets without adequate means to exclude sea turtles. The WTO conceded that measures to protect endangered species were consistent with WTO rules, but ruled that the U.S. approach was implemented in a discriminatory and arbitrary fashion.

Although the WTO has disappointed environmentalists and other groups in the United States from time to time, no evidence indicates an international conspiracy against the United States. The WTO has ruled in favor of the United States in various disputes, including several with the European Union. The WTO for the most part continues to perform the same functions as GATT, including provision of a framework for trade negotiations and resolution of trade disputes. In resolving disputes, it is rarely possible to please everyone.

---

[a]For a discussion of the WTO, see Mordechai E. Kreinin, *International Economics: A Policy Approach*, 8th ed. (Fort Worth: Dryden, 1998), 192–200.

Keywords: *GATT, World Trade Organization, WTO*
http://www.infotrac-college.com

1947 to establish rules of conduct for international trade. Each of these rounds resulted in reductions in tariff rates.

The Uruguay Round, called that because the initial discussions were held in Punta del Este, Uruguay, is the most recent round of GATT negotiations. The negotiations were both long and difficult. They began in 1986, and agreement was not reached until December 1993.

The 1993 agreement is more comprehensive than past agreements. It covers trade in services as well as trade in goods. It also covers trade-related intellectual property rights (such as patents and copyrights) and trade-related investment. Finally, it created the World Trade Organization (WTO), which monitors trade among the 120 countries that signed the agreement (see box).

Under the agreement, many tariffs and nontariff barriers (quotas, VERs, and so forth) will be reduced or eliminated. Although the agreement took effect on January 1, 1995, these reductions in trade barriers will occur over a number of years.

Insights

Trade Negotiations, Labor, and the Environment

Multilateral trade negotiations are complex and time consuming. It takes years or even decades to reach an agreement to reduce tariffs and other trade barriers. In the future, these negotiations promise to become even more complex as some parties attempt to link the negotiations to labor and environmental standards.

Individuals favoring a linkage argue that many countries, particularly those less developed, have labor and environmental standards less stringent than those in the United States. Trade agreements offer an opportunity, therefore, to raise those standards. True, working conditions are worse in most countries than in the United States. In those countries, the workplace is often unpleasant and perhaps unsafe, the workweek is long, wages are low, and retirement and fringe benefits are minimal or nonexistent. However, many of these countries are at the same stage of development that the United States was 100 years ago. To impose the United States' current labor standards on those countries, even if it were possible, could have a devastating effect on their development. Raising the cost of employing workers would reduce employment, causing further impoverishment or even starvation.

Indeed, policy makers in less-developed countries overwhelmingly believe that linking trade negotiations to labor standards serves only to keep their citizens among the downtrodden.

With regard to environmental standards, some individuals claim that without safeguards, policy makers will allow environmental standards in their countries to deteriorate in order to entice multinational corporations to locate plants there. The evidence, however, is that most of these corporations use environment-friendly technologies.

In addition, much evidence indicates that as a country's income per capita rises, more of its resources go to reducing pollution. This has been the case in the United States and elsewhere. Because lowering barriers to international trade helps countries develop, emphasis should be placed on reducing those barriers.

Finally, to the extent that labor and environmental standards diverge among countries in an unsatisfactory manner, international institutions already exist that monitor and advocate higher standards. These include the International Labor Organization and the United Nations Environmental Protection Agency. Rather than linking trade negotiations to labor and environmental standards, it is better to rely on the expertise of these existing organizations.

The Regional Approach

Rather than relying entirely on the global approach, many countries have formed regional trading blocs. That is, they have agreed to reduce or eliminate trade barriers among themselves while maintaining barriers against countries outside the bloc.

THE NORTH AMERICAN FREE TRADE AREA. In 1988, the United States and Canada ratified an agreement to gradually eliminate trade barriers between the two countries beginning January 1, 1989.

Following the agreement between the United States and Canada, the two countries began talks with Mexico regarding the formation of a free-trade area to include Mexico. President Bush announced in August 1992 that the leaders of the three nations had reached an agreement—the North American Free Trade Agreement (NAFTA). The agreement was later approved by Congress and the other countries' legislative bodies and took effect January 1, 1994. At its inception, the free-trade area encompassed 362 million people and had a combined GDP that was 25 percent greater than that of the European Union.

Keywords: *customs unions, NAFTA and trade, EU and trade*

http://www.infotrac-college.com

The agreement called for the elimination of tariffs over a 15-year period, although many tariffs were scheduled to be eliminated much sooner than this. It also called for the elimination of quotas and other trade barriers. While eliminating trade barriers within the free-trade area, each country was to remain free to maintain trade barriers against nonmember countries. Finally, the agreement called for opening investment opportunities within each country to member countries.

THE EUROPEAN UNION. The European Union (EU) is another important trading bloc. It was founded in 1957 with six members: Belgium, France, Italy, Luxembourg, the Netherlands, and West Germany. Nine other countries—Austria, Denmark, Finland, Greece, Ireland, Portugal, Spain, Sweden, and the United Kingdom—joined later. The EU has eliminated most trade barriers between member countries. As a result, trade within the EU has increased tremendously. The EU, however, still maintains trade barriers against nonmember nations. We discuss the European Union's evolution in Chapter 18.

Summary

U.S. participation in world trade has been increasing. The United States exports and imports more than any other country in the world. It has had a trade deficit every year since 1976. The size of the deficit has grown rapidly in the last decade.

Trade among nations is based on the principle of comparative advantage, whereby countries produce and export goods and services in which they have a comparative advantage and import goods and services in which they have a comparative disadvantage. Trade based on the principle of comparative advantage makes both trading partners better off.

Not everyone gains from international trade. Domestic consumers normally gain, domestic producers normally lose, but the gains to consumers outweigh the losses to producers. Some workers may lose their jobs as U.S. imports rise, but they would normally find alternative employment.

Most countries—including the United States—restrict trade in various ways. Among other measures, they impose tariffs, quotas, and voluntary export restraints.

These protectionist measures raise domestic prices by restricting imports. As a result, consumers are worse off. Domestic producers, however, receive higher prices and are better off. Society as a whole is worse off because trade restrictions shift resources from industries with a comparative advantage to those with a comparative disadvantage. As a result, the nation's standard of living declines.

The case for free trade is based partly on the principle of comparative advantage. Some other arguments favoring free trade are that (1) specialization allows firms to produce higher levels of output, enabling them to produce at lower average cost; (2) free trade increases competition; and (3) international trade increases the diversity of goods and services available to consumers.

Despite the strong case for free trade, many argue that domestic industries should be protected. The most common arguments stress that (1) new industries should be protected until they can become competitive, (2) industries essential for national defense should be protected, (3) protection is necessary to save jobs, and (4) American workers must be protected from cheap foreign labor. To the extent that these arguments are valid, the goals can best be accomplished in ways other than trade restrictions.

Since World War II, countries have significantly reduced barriers to international trade. In reducing these barriers, countries have followed both global and regional approaches.

Key Terms

Trade deficit
Comparative advantage
Comparative disadvantage
Absolute advantage
Absolute disadvantage
Consumers' surplus
Producers' surplus
Tariff
Quota
Voluntary export restraints (VERs)

Review Questions

1. Describe the relationship between U.S. exports and imports since 1960.
2. Describe the behavior of the trade deficit since 1976. What is the political significance of this trend?
3. Distinguish between absolute advantage and comparative advantage.
4. Suppose that a worker in the United States is able to produce more beef and more steel than a worker in Japan. Does this mean that Japan will be unable to trade with the United States? Defend your answer.
5. Use the information in the table to answer parts a, b, and c.

Country	Car Production per Day	Wine Production per Day
United States	6	2
France	1	1

    a. Which country has the absolute advantage in cars? In wine? Explain.
    b. Which country has the comparative advantage in cars? In wine? Explain.
    c. Is there a basis for trade between the two countries? Explain in detail why or why not.

6. International trade affects consumers, producers, and workers. Illustrate and explain why economists normally conclude that free international trade is a good thing for society, on balance, referring to the effects of international trade on each of these parties.
7. Compare and contrast the different restrictions that the United States might place on steel imports.
8. How is each of the following affected by a tariff? By an import quota?
    a. consumers
    b. domestic producers
9. What is the infant-industry argument? Is it likely to be valid for a mature economy like that of the United States? If valid, what would be a better solution than imposing trade restrictions?
10. "If we allow free trade in the automobile industry, some automobile workers will lose their jobs. This unemployment will make society worse off." What advantages of free trade does this argument overlook? How might the unemployment be alleviated at lower cost than the cost imposed by a tariff?
11. Suppose U.S. wage rates are higher than those abroad. Does this preclude trade between the United States and the rest of the world? Defend your answer.
12. Despite the fact that society is generally better off with free trade, governments often impose trade barriers. Why might a government take such action?
13. Compare and contrast the global and regional approaches to reducing barriers to international trade.
14. What is the World Trade Organization (WTO)? Why are environmentalists and other groups disappointed in the WTO?
15. Trade negotiations are complex and lengthy. Explain why they may be even more complex and time consuming in the future.

Economic Issues on the Internet

- *Economic Report of the President*—**http://www.access.gpo.gov/eop**
  Washington, DC: Government Printing Office, published annually. Contains data on foreign trade.

- U.S. Census Bureau, Foreign Trade Division. *Foreign Trade Statistics*—**http://www.census.gov/foreign-trade**
  Washington, DC: World Wide Web, updated periodically. Contains data on U.S. foreign trade.

CHAPTER 18

The Global Economy: Finance

Outline:

The Balance of Payments
Exchange Rates and Their Determination
   Flexible Exchange Rates
   Fixed Exchange Rates
The Current International Financial System
The Case for Flexible Exchange Rates
The Case for Fixed Exchange Rates
Should Capital Flows Be Controlled?
The Asian Financial Crisis

In the previous chapter, we focused on trade in the global economy. In this chapter, we focus on finance in the global economy. There is a flow of financial capital from one country to another to pay for imports of goods and services, and also to pay for stocks, bonds, and other assets. For the United States, international capital flows equal trillions of dollars annually.

    We start our discussion with a consideration of the U.S. balance of payments. We then consider exchange rates and their determination in the contexts of both flexible and fixed exchange rates. After discussing the advantages and disadvantages of flexible and fixed exchange rates, we address the question of whether capital flows should be controlled. Finally, we consider the recent Asian financial crisis and its lessons.

The Balance of Payments

Balance of Payments – A summary of all economic transactions between the residents of one country and those of all other countries during a given period of time.

The **balance of payments** is a summary of all economic transactions between the residents of one country and those of all other countries during a given period of time. These transactions include exports, imports, and various capital flows. Table 18.1 summarizes the U.S. balance of payments in 2001.

The transactions in Table 18.1 are divided into two categories: those that give rise to dollar inpayments and those resulting in dollar outpayments. Inpayments are recorded as plus (credit) items; outpayments as minus (debit) items. Exports of goods and services (line 1) are recorded as a plus item because they generate dollar inpayments; imports of goods and services (line 2) are entered as a minus item because they require dollar outpayments.

In 2001, exports were $1,005 billion and imports were $1,371 billion. Imports, therefore, exceeded exports by $366 billion. Unilateral transfers (line 3) include foreign aid as well as private monetary gifts to residents of foreign countries. In 2001, net unilateral transfers were −$51 billion.

The balance on current account (line 4) is obtained by adding exports (line 1), imports (line 2), and net unilateral transfers (line 3). In 2001, this balance was −$417 billion.

We now turn from the current account (lines 1 through 4) to the capital account (lines 5 through 8). Private capital flows are summarized in line 5. They include direct private investment abroad by U.S. corporations (such as the establishment of foreign subsidiaries) and purchases of foreign securities (such as stocks and bonds) by U.S. citizens. They also include direct private investment in the United States by foreign corporations and purchases of U.S. securities by foreigners. In 2001, these private capital flows totaled +$455 billion, indicating that more capital was flowing from other countries to the United States than from the United States to other countries.

TABLE 18.1   U.S. Balance of Payments: 2001 (Billions of Dollars)

In 2001, the United States' current account deficit was $417 billion. This deficit, due primarily to an excess of imports over exports, was offset by a capital account surplus of $417 billion. The overall balance, therefore, was 0.0. (The overall balance is *always* zero.)

Current Account		
1. Exports of goods and services	+1,005	
2. Imports of goods and services	−1,371	
3. Unilateral transfers, net	−51	
4. Balance on current account (1+2+3)		−417
Capital Account		
5. Private capital flows, net	+455	
6. Official capital flows, net	+1	
7. Statistical discrepancy	−39	
8. Balance on capital account (5+6+7)		+417
9. Overall Balance (4+8)		0.0

SOURCE: "U.S. International Transactions in 2001," *Federal Reserve Bulletin* 88 (May 2002) 235–247.

> ## INSIGHTS
>
>
>
> ### THE UNITED STATES: THE WORLD'S LARGEST DEBTOR
>
> Usually when we think of debtor nations, we have less-developed countries in mind. The United States, however, owes more to foreign creditors than any other nation.[a] In 2000, its net debt was estimated at $1.8 trillion, based on the cost of replacing capital assets, and at $2.2 trillion dollars, measured by the stock market value of owners' equity. The U.S. net foreign debt will continue to rise as long as the country has a current account deficit and a capital account surplus.
>
> That foreign households, firms, and governments wish to invest in the United States is not surprising. The United States is the largest market in the world. Moreover, its market for goods and services is growing rapidly. The United States is also a safe place to invest. Its government is stable, inflation is low, and from 1995 to 1999, stock prices increased rapidly.
>
> The magnitude of the debt raises some concerns. So long as creditors believe that the United States is capable of servicing this debt, however, they will continue to invest here. Thus, the United States could continue to be the world's largest debtor more or less indefinitely.
>
> The ability of a country to service its debt is often judged on the basis of its ratio of international indebtedness to GDP. The higher this ratio, the greater the likelihood that the country will have problems in paying the interest on this debt and paying the principle as it falls due.
>
> In 2000, the United States' net indebtedness was 18 to 20 percent of its GDP. This percentage continues to rise. Other countries—including Canada and Australia—have much higher ratios of net foreign indebtedness to GDP and continue to prosper. Based on the experience of these countries, the United States is in no imminent danger.
>
> Suppose foreign investors were to doubt the ability of the United States to service its debt. They would invest less in the United States. With the reduced capital inflow, the demand for dollars and dollar-denominated assets would decrease, causing the dollar to depreciate. As a consequence, U.S. exports would rise as U.S. goods and services became less expensive to foreigners. Similarly, U.S. imports would fall as foreign goods and services became more expensive to U.S. households and firms. The end result would be a smaller current account deficit and a smaller capital account surplus. Whether the adjustments would take place gradually or abruptly depends in large part on how quickly foreigners might adjust their expectations regarding the United States' ability to service its debt.
>
> ---
>
> [a]For more detail, see Owen F. Humpage, "Is the Current-Account Deficit Sustainable?" Federal Reserve Bank of Cleveland, *Economic Commentary* (October 15, 1998), 1–4.

Official capital flows are summarized in line 6. These flows include the purchase and sale of dollars, dollar-denominated assets (such as U.S. Treasury securities), and foreign currencies by the U.S. and foreign governments. In 2001, the net official capital flow was very small, only +$1 billion.

The statistical discrepancy is recorded in line 7. It is difficult to maintain accurate records of the nation's exports, imports, and capital flows. In some cases, the data are inaccurate; in other cases, they are not available. The statistical discrepancy adjusts for these errors and omissions. Because most of the errors and omissions relate to capital flows, the statistical discrepancy is included in the capital account.

The balance on capital account, shown in line 8, is obtained by summing lines 5 through 7. For 2001, this balance was +$417 billion.

Finally, the overall balance is given in line 9. It is obtained by summing lines 4 and 8. Note that this balance is 0.0. It is always zero because the balance of payments must always balance. All international transactions must be financed in some way. In 2001, the United States imported $366 billion more than it exported. The other entries in Table 18.1 indicate how this trade deficit was financed.

Because the overall balance must be zero, a country cannot have an *overall* deficit or surplus. It can, however, have a deficit or surplus in various *portions* of its balance of payments. In 1998, the United States had a deficit of $417 billion in its current account (line 4) and a surplus of $417 billion in its capital account (line 8).

The United States has had deficits in its current account every year since 1981, with the single exception of 1991 when it had a very small surplus (see Figure 18.1). In 1982, the deficit started to rise. In 1987, it reached $160.7 billion. After decreasing from 1987 to 1991, the deficit increased.[1] As already noted, it reached $417 billion—the all-time high—in 2001. Throughout the last 20 years, most of the deficit has occurred because the United States imports more than it exports.

Much concern exists about the magnitude and duration of this deficit. Most of the deficit is financed by foreign investment in the United States. So long as this foreign investment continues, more and more of the nation's assets will become the property of foreigners. The increase in foreign ownership means that foreigners will receive more income and interest from the United States, and U.S. citizens will receive less (see Insights: "The United States: The World's Largest Debtor").

FIGURE 18.1 U.S. Balance on Current Account: 1960–2001

For about half of the 1960–2001 period, the United States had small surpluses and deficits in its current account. Starting in 1983, it began running large deficits. The deficit reached $160.7 billion in 1987 and then declined. It has been rising rapidly since 1991, reaching a record high of $417 billion in 2001.

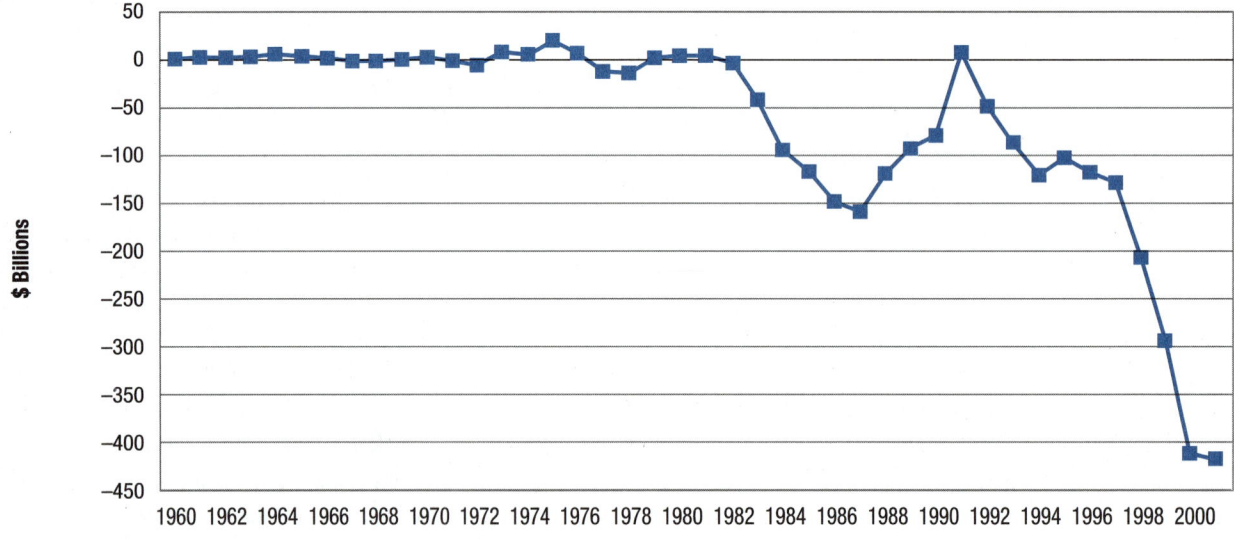

[1] The current account surplus of $3.7 billion in 1991 occurred primarily because certain countries—including Kuwait and Japan—reimbursed the United States for expenses incurred during Operation Desert Storm.

Exchange Rates and Their Determination

Exchange Rate – The number of units of one currency exchangeable for one unit of another.

An **exchange rate** is the number of units of one currency exchangeable for a unit of another. Suppose 100 Japanese yen exchange for a dollar; the exchange rate is 100 yen per dollar. Similarly, suppose 10 Mexican pesos exchange for a dollar—an exchange rate of 10 pesos per dollar. If 100 yen exchange for a dollar and 10 pesos for a dollar, the exchange rate between the Japanese and Mexican currencies is 10 yen per peso.

Exchange rates are important; they help determine the cost of internationally traded goods, services, and assets. Suppose you are planning a vacation in Canada. If the vacation costs 6,000 Canadian dollars and the exchange rate is 1.5 Canadian dollars per American dollar, you will pay 4,000 American dollars. If the exchange rate is only 1.2 Canadian dollars per American dollar, the same vacation will cost you 5,000 American dollars. Thus, seemingly small changes in exchange rates can significantly alter the cost of foreign goods and services.

Flexible Exchange Rates

Flexible (Floating) Exchange Rates – Exchange rates determined by demand and supply.

Under a **flexible (floating) exchange rate** system, exchange rates are determined by the demand for and supply of the various currencies. To illustrate, we consider two countries, the United States and Japan. The Japanese have a demand for dollars in terms of their price in yen. This is shown in Figure 18.2. The demand for dollars is based on the demand by Japanese consumers, business firms, and governments for goods and services produced in the United States, for U.S. stocks and bonds, and so on. As the exchange rate (the number of yen necessary to purchase one dollar) rises, the quantity of dollars demanded decreases. If the exchange rate rises from 100 yen per dollar to 110 yen per dollar, the quantity of dollars demanded decreases from $180 billion to $160 billion.

FIGURE 18.2 Flexible Exchange Rates

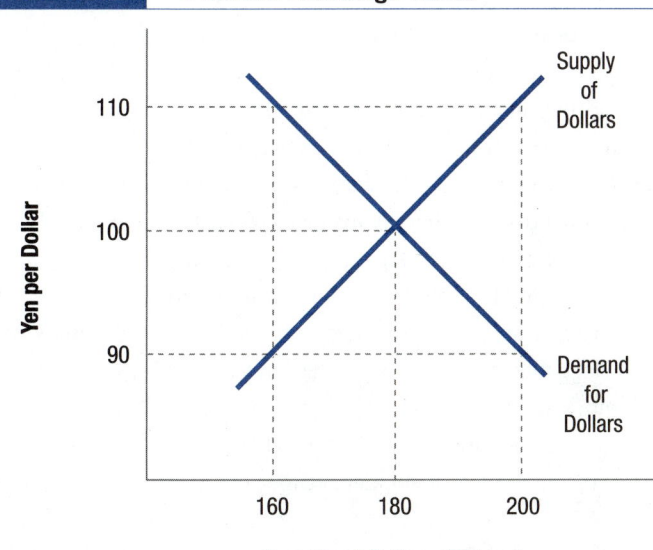

In a flexible exchange rate system, exchange rates are determined by demand and supply. In this figure, the equilibrium exchange rate—given by the intersection of the demand and supply curves—is 100 yen per dollar.

The supply of dollars is based on American demand for Japanese goods and services, Japanese stocks and bonds, and so on. As the exchange rate rises, the quantity of dollars supplied increases. If the exchange rate rises from 100 yen per dollar to 110 yen, the quantity of dollars supplied increases from $180 billion to $200 billion.

In Figure 18.2, the equilibrium exchange rate is 100 yen per dollar. At that exchange rate, the quantity of dollars demanded by the Japanese, $180 billion, equals the quantity of dollars supplied to them, also $180 billion. Because the quantity demanded equals the quantity supplied, no tendency exists for the exchange rate to change. Suppose, however, that the exchange rate was temporarily at 110 yen per dollar. At that exchange rate, the quantity of dollars demanded by the Japanese is only $160 billion and the quantity supplied to them is $200 billion. Given the excess supply of dollars, the exchange rate would fall. As the exchange rate fell, U.S. goods, services, and assets would become less expensive to the Japanese. If the exchange rate were 110 yen per dollar, 110 yen would buy a dollar's worth of U.S. goods. If the exchange rate fell to 100 yen per dollar, the same goods would cost only 100 yen. Because U.S. goods, services, and assets would be cheaper to the Japanese, they would increase the quantity of dollars demanded with a view to buying more American goods.

Just as the quantity of dollars demanded by the Japanese increases as the exchange rate falls, the quantity of dollars supplied to them decreases. As the exchange rate falls, Japanese goods, services, and assets become more expensive to Americans. If the exchange rate is 110 yen per dollar, a dollar will buy 110 yen's worth of Japanese goods. If the exchange rate fell to 100 yen per dollar, a dollar would buy only 100 yen's worth of Japanese goods. Because Japanese goods, services, and assets would become more expensive to Americans, they would buy less of them, and the quantity of dollars supplied to the Japanese would decrease.

So long as the quantity of dollars supplied exceeds the quantity of dollars demanded, the yen–dollar exchange rate falls. In Figure 18.2, it will fall to 100 yen per dollar. At that rate, the quantity supplied equals the quantity demanded, and the exchange rate is in equilibrium.

Suppose the exchange rate were 90 yen to the dollar. At that rate, the quantity of dollars demanded by the Japanese would be $200 billion and the quantity supplied would be only $160 billion. Given the excess demand for dollars, the exchange rate would rise. As the exchange rate increased, U.S. goods, services, and assets would become more expensive to the Japanese. Therefore, they would have an incentive to buy fewer of them, and the quantity of dollars demanded by the Japanese would decrease.

At the same time, the quantity of dollars supplied to the Japanese would increase. As the exchange rate rises, Japanese goods, services, and assets would become less expensive to Americans. Because they are less expensive, Americans would buy more of them, thereby increasing the quantity of dollars supplied.

As we have seen, the yen–dollar exchange rate is determined by the demand for and supply of dollars. If the exchange rate is above the equilibrium rate, it would fall; if below, it would rise. When the yen–dollar exchange rate falls in a flexible exchange rate system, the yen **appreciates** in value because it now takes fewer yen to purchase a dollar. The dollar, on the other hand, **depreciates** because it now takes more dollars to buy the same quantity of yen.

When the yen–dollar exchange rate rises in a flexible exchange rate system, the yen depreciates because it takes more yen to purchase a dollar. The dollar appreciates because it takes fewer dollars to buy the same quantity of yen.

Appreciation – Under a flexible exchange rate system, a rise in the value of one currency relative to another.

Depreciation – Under a flexible exchange rate system, a fall in the value of one currency relative to another.

THE IMPACT OF AN INCREASE IN U.S. OUTPUT. Under a flexible exchange rate system, the yen–dollar exchange rate is determined by Japanese demand for dollars and supply of dollars to them. The exchange rate, therefore, will change if either the demand for or supply of dollars changes. Suppose GDP in the United States rises while GDP in Japan remains constant. As U.S. GDP rises, domestic households and firms buy more from abroad. Consequently, the United States will import more from Japan, causing the supply of dollars to the Japanese to increase.

In Figure 18.3, the initial dollar demand and supply curves are D_0 and S_0, respectively. The exchange rate, therefore, is e_0. If U.S. households and firms buy more Japanese goods and services, the supply of dollars to the Japanese increases to S_1. With the increase in the supply of dollars, the yen–dollar exchange rate falls to e_1. Because it now takes more dollars to buy the same quantity of yen, the dollar depreciates. The yen, in turn, appreciates.

THE IMPACT OF AN INCREASE IN U.S. INTEREST RATES. Suppose that interest rates rise in the United States relative to interest rates in Japan. Because interest rates are higher in the United States, the Japanese have an incentive to buy U.S. Treasury securities and other dollar-denominated assets. Therefore, the Japanese demand for dollars increases. Similarly, because interest rates are now relatively higher in the United States, Americans have less incentive to buy yen-denominated assets. Therefore, the supply of dollars to the Japanese decreases.

In Figure 18.4, the initial demand and supply curves are D_0 and S_0, respectively; the exchange rate, therefore, is e_0. With the increase in the demand for dollars and the decrease in supply, the new demand and supply curves are D_1 and S_1, respectively. As a result, the new exchange rate is e_1. With the rise in the exchange rate, the yen depreciates and the dollar appreciates.

FIGURE 18.3 Effect of an Increase in Real GDP on the Exchange Rate

An increase in real GDP causes the United States to import more from Japan. As a result, the U.S. supply of dollars increases. The shift in the supply curve from S_0 to S_1 causes the exchange rate to fall from e_0 to e_1 and the dollar to depreciate.

FIGURE 18.4 Effect of a Higher Interest Rate on the Exchange Rate

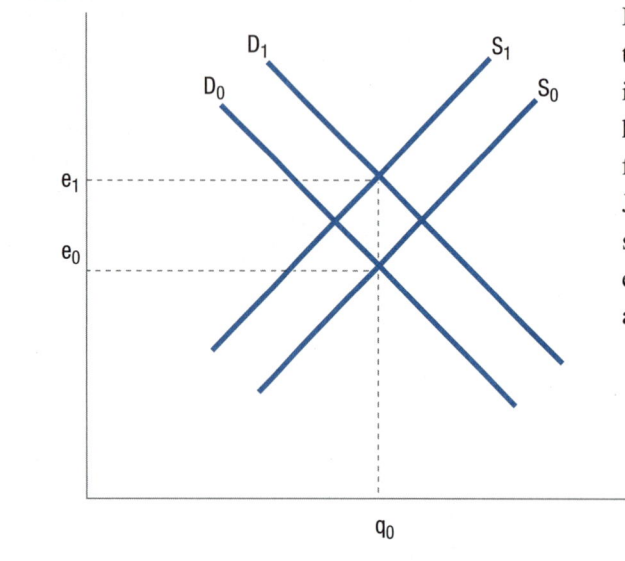

If interest rates in the United States rise relative to those in Japan, the Japanese will invest more heavily in the United States and Americans will invest less heavily in Japan. Consequently, the Japanese demand for dollars will increase and the supply of dollars to Japan will decrease. The shifts in the demand and supply curves to D_1 and S_1, respectively, cause the exchange rate to rise from e_0 to e_1 and the dollar to appreciate.

Because of the yen's depreciation, U.S. goods and services are now more expensive to the Japanese, whereas Japanese goods and services are cheaper to Americans. As a result, the United States will export less to Japan and import more from Japan. Output and employment, therefore, will fall in both the U.S. export and import-competing sectors.

In 1981 and 1982, interest rates in the United States increased relative to those in most of the world's major trading nations. The main reason for the increase was the combination of expansionary fiscal and contractionary monetary policies pursued by the United States. Both policies resulted in higher interest rates. With higher interest rates, the dollar appreciated against most major currencies. The appreciation depressed U.S. exports and stimulated U.S. imports, resulting in large current account deficits in the early and mid-1980s, and a downturn in the export and import-competing sectors of the economy.

Fixed Exchange Rates

Fixed Exchange Rates – Exchange rates kept constant through central bank purchases and sales of foreign currencies.

In a flexible exchange rate system, exchange rates are determined by the demand for and supply of currencies. Should demand or supply change, exchange rates also change. In a **fixed exchange rate** system, this is not the case. Central banks intervene in foreign exchange (currency) markets to keep exchange rates constant.

In Figure 18.5, we illustrate a fixed exchange rate system. If the yen–dollar exchange rate is 100, the quantities of dollars demanded and supplied are equal. The exchange rate, therefore, has no tendency to change and neither the United States' nor Japan's central bank need intervene to keep the exchange rate at 100 yen per dollar. Suppose, however, that the exchange rate is 110 yen per dollar and that government officials are committed to keeping it at that level. With an excess supply of dollars, the exchange rate would tend to fall. The Federal Reserve, the United States' central bank, would have to intervene to keep

| FIGURE 18.5 | Fixed Exchange Rates |

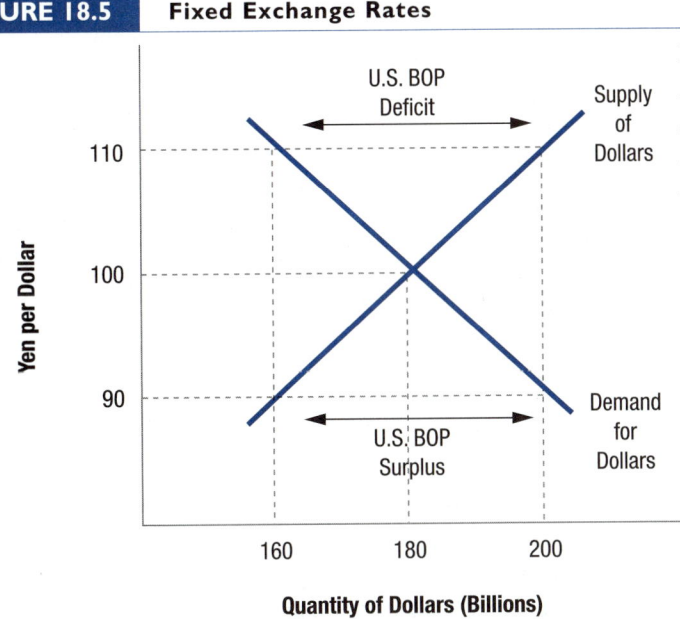

In a fixed exchange rate system, central banks buy and sell foreign currencies to keep exchange rates constant. If the exchange rate is 110 yen per dollar, the Federal Reserve must use its holdings of yen to buy dollars to keep the dollar from depreciating. If the exchange rate is 90 yen per dollar, it must use its holdings of dollars to buy yen to keep the dollar from appreciating.

Balance of Payments Deficit – At a given exchange rate, the amount by which the home country's purchases of foreign goods, services, and assets exceed the rest of the world's purchases from it.

Devaluation – Under a fixed exchange rate system, a fall in the value of one currency relative to another.

Balance of Payments Surplus – At a given exchange rate, the amount by which the rest of the world's purchases of the home country's goods, services, and assets exceed its purchases from the rest of the world.

it from falling. To keep the exchange rate at 110 yen per dollar, the Federal Reserve would have to buy, or increase the demand for, dollars. In this case, it would have to use 4.4 trillion Japanese yen to buy $40 billion in foreign exchange markets.

A supply of dollars greater than the demand for dollars in the absence of government intervention is a sign of a **balance of payments (BOP) deficit** for the United States in its international transactions with Japan. U.S. consumers and investors want to supply more dollars to buy Japanese goods and services or to invest in Japanese assets than Japanese consumers and investors want to acquire in order to buy U.S. goods, services, and assets. If the balance of payments deficit persists, the Federal Reserve will eventually exhaust its holdings of yen. At that point, it may allow the yen–dollar exchange rate to fall. If it does, a **devaluation** of the dollar would occur. This would reduce the price of U.S. goods, services, and assets to Japanese buyers and increase the price of Japanese goods, services, and assets to U.S. buyers. U.S. exports of goods and services to Japan would increase relative to U.S. imports of Japanese goods and services. Japanese investment in the United States would also increase relative to U.S. investment in Japan. Eventually, the balance of payments deficit would disappear.

Suppose, alternatively, that the exchange rate is 90 yen per dollar and that government officials are committed to keeping it at that level. With an excess demand for dollars, the exchange rate would tend to rise and the Federal Reserve would have to intervene to keep it from rising. To keep the exchange rate at 90 yen per dollar, the Federal Reserve would have to sell, or increase the supply of, dollars. In this case, it would have to supply $40 billion to buy $4 trillion yen in foreign exchange markets.

A demand for dollars greater than the supply of dollars in the absence of government intervention is a sign of a **balance of payments (BOP) surplus** for the United States in its international transactions with Japan. Japanese consumers and investors want to supply more yen to buy U.S. goods or to invest in U.S. assets than U.S. consumers and investors want to acquire in order to buy Japanese goods and assets. If the balance of payments surplus persists, the Federal Reserve will have to continue to buy yen. Although the Federal Reserve can use dollars to buy yen more or less indefinitely, it may become reluctant to do so, or the Japanese may become reluctant to accumulate more dollars. At that point, the Federal Reserve may allow the exchange rate to rise. If it does, a **revaluation** of the dollar would occur. This would increase the price of U.S. goods, services, and assets to Japanese buyers and reduce the price of Japanese goods, services, and assets to U.S. buyers. U.S. imports of goods and services from Japan would increase relative to U.S. exports of goods and services to Japan. U.S. investment in Japan would also increase relative to Japanese investment in the United States. Eventually, the balance of payments surplus would disappear.

Revaluation – Under a fixed exchange rate system, a rise in the value of one currency relative to another.

■ THE CURRENT INTERNATIONAL FINANCIAL SYSTEM

From the end of World War II to 1973, the international financial system was a fixed exchange rate system. This system is often called the Bretton Woods system because it was organized at a conference held at Bretton Woods, New Hampshire, in 1944. Under the Bretton Woods system, central banks bought and sold various currencies to keep exchange rates constant. To be sure, some countries devalued or revalued their currencies, but they supposedly did so only when their countries experienced a "fundamental disequilibrium" in their balance of payments.

By the early 1970s, many countries, including the United States, had abandoned the fixed exchange system. Today's international financial system is a mixture of flexible and fixed exchange rate systems, with many countries, including the United States, Canada, Japan, and the United Kingdom, allowing their currencies to fluctuate or "float" as in a flexible exchange rate system. Even so, these countries sometimes intervene to moderate fluctuations in exchange rates. Other countries, like Mexico, allow their currencies to float, but only within certain limits. Still others peg their currencies to the American dollar, the French franc, or some other currency or bundle of currencies, and allow them to fluctuate in concert with these currencies.

Starting in 1979, countries in the European Monetary System (EMS) began to keep exchange rates among members within a narrow range. Each country's currency, however, was free to float against those of non–EMS countries. In 1992, the 15 EMS countries signed the Treaty on European Union, commonly called the Maastricht Treaty. In this treaty, the countries agreed in principle to form a monetary union with a common currency and monetary policy. On January 1, 1999, 11 countries (Austria, Belgium, Finland, France, Germany, Ireland, Italy, Luxembourg, the Netherlands, Portugal, and Spain) formally launched the euro as a common currency and instituted the European Central Bank (ECB). Greece joined this group on January 1, 2001. Sweden plans to join as soon as it has fulfilled all of the conditions for membership. When it does, Denmark and the United Kingdom will be the only European Union countries outside the jurisdiction of the ECB. The euro is now the common currency for the 12 member countries and it floats against other currencies (see International Perspective: "The Euro").

■ THE CASE FOR FLEXIBLE EXCHANGE RATES

Strong arguments support both flexible exchange rates and fixed exchange rates. We start with arguments for flexible exchange rates.

INTERNATIONAL PERSPECTIVE

THE EURO

As noted in the text, the 11 countries of the European Economic and Monetary Union (EMU) formally introduced the euro on January 1, 1999. A single currency was intended to ease the problems of traveling from one country to another and make trade much easier.

The initial transition period ran from January 1, 1999, to December 31, 2001. During this period, the euro did not circulate as a currency. For cash transactions, each EMU country used its own currency. To buy something with euros, however, a person could write a check or use a credit card or travelers' check. Bank accounts, credit cards, and travelers' checks denominated in euros have been available since January 1, 1999.

Starting January 1, 2002, each EMU country's currency and coins were withdrawn from circulation. They were replaced with euro notes and coins. The replacement process was completed by March 1, 2002.

Why did these countries adopt a single currency and form a monetary union? As previously stated, it is more convenient to use one currency when traveling from one country to another or conducting business with parties in other countries. (Think of how inconvenient it would be if each of the 50 U.S. states had a separate currency!)

In addition to reducing transactions costs, a single currency eliminates risk associated with fluctuations in exchange rates. Less risk should encourage increased trade among member countries.

Although the move to a single currency will lead to significant benefits, costs will also occur. With a single currency and common monetary policy, individual countries will be unable to conduct an independent monetary policy. Suppose a shock occurs that affects some countries more than others. The countries more adversely affected will be unable to respond with an independent monetary policy.

In addition, individual countries will be unable to alter exchange rates vis-à-vis other EMU countries. This eliminates another policy that could be used to stimulate output and employment. By eliminating independent monetary and exchange rate policy, individual countries must rely on fiscal policy, which may prove a slender reed.

Given limited migration among EMU countries and inflexible European labor markets, unemployment could increase (see Chapter 14 for a fuller discussion of the unemployment problem in Europe). If it does, relations among the EMU countries will be strained.

INFOTRAC
College Edition

Keywords:
European Union, euro
http://www.infotrac-college.com

Proponents argue that flexible exchange rates result in greater economic stability. Suppose that the United States' major trading partners experience a recession. As a consequence, the demand for U.S. exports falls. If exchange rates are free to adjust, the dollar will depreciate, making American goods and services less expensive to foreigners. As a result, they will buy more U.S. goods and services, at least partially offsetting the initial decrease in U.S. exports.

In contrast, suppose that the United States had fixed exchange rates. Despite the decrease in exports, exchange rates would remain constant. The dollar would not depreciate. Consequently, American goods and services would not become less expensive to foreigners and no offsetting increase in exports would occur. As a result, the U.S. export and import-substitution sectors, and the economy as a whole, would suffer a loss in jobs and income.

Another argument for flexible exchange rates has to do with monetary policy. In a fixed exchange rate system, central banks must buy or sell their nation's currencies to keep exchange rates constant. To keep a country's currency from depreciating, its central bank must use foreign currencies to buy the domestic currency. When it does this, it reduces the nation's currency in circulation—a principal component of its money supply. This effect on the money supply may be the opposite of what the central bank would like to have to reduce unemployment.

INFOTRAC
College Edition

Keywords: *flexible exchange rates*
http://www.infotrac-college.com

In a flexible exchange rate system, central banks have no commitment to keep exchange rates constant. As discussed in earlier chapters, they can alter the domestic money supply to achieve or maintain full employment and price stability.

■ THE CASE FOR FIXED EXCHANGE RATES

Proponents of fixed exchange rates argue that less risk and uncertainty exist under that system. In a flexible exchange rate system, rates can and do change day to day. These fluctuations can result in too-frequent reallocations of domestic resources between export and import-competing sectors of the economy. They may also lead to less international trade and investment.

Proponents of flexible exchange rates concede that exchange rates do fluctuate under that system. They note, however, that firms can take action to protect themselves against unforeseen changes in exchange rates. They also note that central banks in many countries have acted successfully to moderate exchange-rate fluctuations and that there is little reason to doubt their ability to do so in the future.

Proponents of fixed exchange rates argue that flexible exchange rates may lead to destabilizing speculation. Suppose a currency is depreciating. If speculators believe that it will depreciate further, they will sell the currency, causing it to depreciate even more. To the extent that destabilizing speculation does occur, exchange rates in a flexible exchange rate system will fluctuate even more.

Opponents of fixed exchange rates argue that destabilizing speculation is less likely to occur when exchange rates adjust continuously than when a country is forced to devalue because of a balance of payments deficit. If a country has a balance of payments deficit and meager foreign currency holdings to defend the domestic currency, speculators may sell the domestic currency, perhaps forcing a devaluation or a larger devaluation than otherwise would take place.

Finally, proponents of fixed exchange rates assert that fixed exchange rates provide a discipline to central banks. With fixed exchange rates, central banks must act to keep exchange rates constant. This prevents them from increasing the money supply rapidly, which would cause inflation.

Opponents of fixed exchange rates concede that the flexible exchange rate system can be more inflationary than a fixed exchange rate system. Even so, they argue that central banks should not be committed to keeping exchange rates constant. Instead, they should be free to pursue whatever policies are necessary for full employment. Flexible exchange rates allow central banks this freedom.

As we have seen, strong arguments exist both for and against flexible exchange rates. Even so, many countries have switched from fixed to flexible exchange rates in recent years.

Keywords: *fixed exchange rates*
http://www.infotrac-college.com

■ SHOULD CAPITAL FLOWS BE CONTROLLED?

In addition to foreign exchange markets, the allocation of resources across countries depends heavily on the global capital market, the market that facilitates the flow of funds for the purchase and sale of financial and real assets. Historically, economists have favored free international capital movements. Various countries, however, limited or banned capital flows during World Wars I and II. Following World War II, many of these countries dropped their controls. With the advent of the Mexican and Asian financial crises, policy makers and economists alike began reconsidering the desirability of limiting capital flows.

INTERNATIONAL PERSPECTIVE

THE MEXICAN PESO CRISIS

When the North American Free Trade Agreement (NAFTA) went into effect on January 1, 1994, it was widely anticipated that trade between the United States and Mexico would grow rapidly. In 1994, trade did grow rapidly. In December 1994, however, the peso depreciated vis-à-vis the dollar, depressing U.S. exports to Mexico and stimulating U.S. imports from Mexico.

In 1994, Mexican authorities were maintaining an approximately constant exchange rate between the peso and dollar by buying and selling pesos in foreign exchange markets. At the same time, Mexico was experiencing a current account deficit that was largely financed by foreign investment in Mexico. As time passed, the deficit became larger. Moreover, events within Mexico—including a rebellion in Chiapas province and the assassination of the ruling party's presidential candidate, Luis Donaldo Colosio—caused concern abroad. As a result, the peso began to depreciate. To keep the peso from depreciating further, Mexican authorities used their international reserves (including dollars) to buy pesos in foreign exchange markets. By December 1994, Mexico's holdings of international reserves were low.

On December 20, the Mexican peso was devalued by 20 percent. This devaluation proved insufficient and by December 27 the exchange rate was 5.7 pesos per dollar, a decline of nearly 40 percent since just before the initial devaluation. With the assistance of a direct-loan package that included $20 billion from the United States, the situation eventually stabilized, but not before interest rates soared and the Mexican economy experienced a severe recession.

The depreciation of the peso made Mexican goods and services much cheaper to Americans. It also made American goods and services much more expensive to Mexicans. Consequently, U.S. imports from Mexico increased in 1995 while its exports to Mexico decreased. In addition to the depreciation of the peso, the recession in Mexico contributed to the decrease in imports from the United States.

For the United States, the net effect of these changes was to go from a trade surplus with Mexico, averaging about $4 billion from 1991 through the third quarter of 1994, to a trade deficit of about $15 billion. Even so, output in the United States continued to rise and the unemployment rate continued to fall. In 1994, the U.S. unemployment rate was 6.1 percent. In 1995, it was only 5.6 percent.

With the Mexican economy now expanding, U.S. exports to Mexico are at record levels and are expected to grow in the future. Indeed, in the absence of another peso crisis, the growth in trade between the United States and Mexico that was anticipated with the signing of the North American Free Trade Agreement is likely to occur.

INFOTRAC
College Edition

Keywords: *peso crisis*
http://www.infotrac-college.com

Controls may be applied to either capital outflows or capital inflows (or both). An increase in net capital outflows causes a balance-of-payments deficit. In a country with a fixed exchange rate, the central bank must use its holdings of foreign currencies to buy the domestic currency to keep exchange rates from rising. If the central bank's holdings of currencies are meager, the country may be forced to devalue its currency. Similarly, if the country's exchange rates are flexible and capital starts flowing from the country, the domestic currency will depreciate. To prevent a devaluation or depreciation of its currency, a country may impose controls to reduce the capital outflow.

If capital starts flowing to a country with fixed exchange rates, the demand for its currency increases, causing a balance of payments surplus. The country's central bank must use its holdings of domestic currency to buy foreign currencies to keep exchange rates constant. This increases the domestic money supply, causing prices to rise. An increase in the price level makes the country's goods and services less competitive in world markets, thereby decreasing exports. The rise in the price level also makes foreign goods and services relatively cheaper, thereby increasing imports.

Rather than buying foreign currencies to keep exchange rates constant, the country's central bank could revalue its currency. The revaluation, however, would make its goods and services more expensive to foreigners and foreign goods and services less expensive to its citizens. Consequently, the country's exports would fall and its imports would rise, imposing hardships on its export and import-competing sectors.

If capital starts flowing to a country with flexible exchange rates, the demand for its currency increases, causing an appreciation of the currency. As before, the appreciation would make its goods and services more expensive to foreigners and foreign goods and services less expensive to its citizens. Consequently, the country's exports would fall and its imports would rise, imposing hardships on its export and import-competing sectors.

To prevent prices from rising or a revaluation of its currency, a country with fixed exchange rates may elect to impose controls to limit or prevent capital inflows. To keep its currency from appreciating, a country with flexible exchange rates may decide to impose controls on capital inflows. Finally, a country may impose controls on capital inflows because of the volatility of these flows or because the government prefers local ownership of its assets.

Capital controls vary considerably; they range from taxing capital transactions to an outright ban. Perhaps the best-known tax approach is the Tobin plan, named after James Tobin, a Nobel Prize winner in economics, who proposed it in 1972. To reduce the short-term volatility of capital flows, he proposed that a tax be applied to foreign-currency transactions.

Should countries impose capital controls? Strong arguments exist on both sides of the debate. The traditional view is that capital should be free to flow from countries offering low prospective returns to countries offering higher prospective returns. Barring distortions caused by tax systems and the like, this will ensure an efficient global allocation of resources. Critics of the traditional view note, however, that distortions do exist. They also claim that investors and speculators exhibit herd-like behavior, giving rise to greater volatility of capital flows than warranted.

Proponents of the traditional view also claim that capital controls are ineffective. In today's high-tech world, many ways exist for households and firms to evade controls. Witness the flow of drug money from the United States to Colombia. Moreover, controls invite corruption among government officials and disrespect for the law. Critics, on the other hand, claim that controls are effective. The debate over their effectiveness continues with no resolution in sight.

INFOTRAC
College Edition
Keywords: *international capital flows*
http://www.infotrac-college.com

Proponents of controls claim that unimpeded capital flows can result in large changes in prices and exchange rates that destabilize the economy. Capital flows have undoubtedly contributed to the instability of some economies. For countries with sound banking systems and well-developed financial markets, however, capital flows have been less of a problem.

Proponents of controls also argue that capital controls allow time for countries to initiate new policies and undertake fundamental reforms in their banking systems and financial markets. The evidence on this point is mixed. Some countries have used this time wisely to initiate new policies. Others have simply procrastinated.

In conclusion, capital controls may benefit some countries, particularly in the short run, but they are no substitute for appropriate economic policies and a sound banking system and smoothly functioning financial markets.

■ THE ASIAN FINANCIAL CRISIS

The importance of a sound banking system is illustrated clearly by the Asian financial crisis of 1997–1999. Throughout most of the 1970s, 1980s, and 1990s, the economies of Thailand, Malaysia, Indonesia, South Korea, and the Philippines were the envy of the rest of the world. They were growing rapidly. Unemployment was low and inflation was moderate. In general, they enjoyed government budget surpluses and moderate current account deficits.

Their apparent successes masked some underlying financial weaknesses, however. The ratio of short-term foreign debt to foreign exchange reserves in most of the countries was high, and banks had engaged in large-scale foreign lending. Many of these loans were risky, with a high proportion in real estate, rather than in ventures that increased productive capacity.

In 1997, several events occurred that triggered a financial crisis. In Korea, two large conglomerates failed and Kia, Korea's third largest automaker, was in great difficulty. In Thailand, non-bank financial companies experienced difficulty because of bad real estate loans. In May, Thailand's largest finance company failed.

INFOTRAC
College Edition
Keywords: *Asian crisis, Asian financial crisis*
http://www.infotrac-college.com

In July, the Bank of Thailand announced that they would no longer maintain a fixed exchange rate, and their currency, the baht, would be allowed to float. As a result, the baht depreciated significantly. Speculators attacked other currencies, including the Philippine peso, the Malaysian ringgit, the Indonesian rupiah, and the Korean won. The values of these currencies plummeted as speculators sold them and capital flowed from the countries. By January 1998, the rupiah, for example, had lost 80 percent of its value against the dollar. The crisis spread to stock markets and stock prices dropped dramatically.

As time passed, the various economies turned downward. What had started as mainly a financial crisis spread to the real economy. Output decreased and unemployment increased. By 1999, the worst of the crisis appeared to have passed. Although still shaky, the East Asian economies began to grow once more.

Summary

Since the early 1980s, the United States has experienced large current account deficits, caused primarily by an excess of imports over exports. For the most part, the deficits have been financed by foreign investment in this country. As these deficits have occurred, the United States' foreign indebtedness has risen, making the United States the world's largest debtor nation.

An exchange rate is the number of units of one currency exchangeable for a unit of another. Exchange rates are important because they help to determine the relative prices of internationally traded goods, services, and assets.

In a flexible exchange rate system, exchange rates are determined by demand and supply. The United States is part of the flexible exchange rate system, but the Federal Reserve does intervene occasionally to smooth fluctuations in exchange rates.

In a fixed exchange rate system, central banks intervene to keep exchange rates constant. If the dollar is depreciating, the Federal Reserve can use its holdings of foreign currencies to buy dollars, thereby keeping it from depreciating. Conversely, if the dollar is appreciating, the Federal Reserve can use dollars to buy foreign currencies, thus keeping the dollar from appreciating.

Disagreement exists regarding the appropriate exchange rate system. Even so, more countries are switching to flexible exchange rates.

The Asian financial crisis had a significant impact on certain countries, including Thailand, Malaysia, Indonesia, South Korea, and the Philippines. Prior to the crisis, these countries were growing rapidly. With the crisis, they experienced severe recessions.

The traditional view is that capital should flow freely from one nation to another. As a result of the Mexican, East Asian, and other financial crises, various economists have questioned this view. It is clear, however, that capital controls are no substitute for appropriate economic policies, a sound banking system, and smoothly functioning financial markets.

Review Questions

1. Even though the United States has a large current account deficit, it has an overall balance of payments of zero. Why, then, is there concern about the large current account deficit?
2. With regard to the balance of payments, classify each of the following as to whether they fall in the current or capital accounts. Also, indicate whether they are a credit or debit.
    a. U.S. purchases of beef from Argentina
    b. Japanese purchases of IBM stock
    c. your spring break vacation in Mexico
    d. a U.S. fast-food chain opening a series of restaurants in Canada
3. If the yen–dollar exchange rate is 100 yen per dollar, what is the dollar–yen exchange rate?
4. Explain how exchange rates are determined in
    a. a flexible exchange rate system
    b. a fixed exchange rate system
5. Suppose the British pounds for U.S. dollar exchange rate falls. Does the dollar appreciate or depreciate? Defend your answer.
6. Suppose the U.S. dollar appreciates relative to the Japanese yen. How will the exports and imports of the two countries be affected?
7. Assuming flexible exchange rates, how will each of the following affect the home country's currency?
    a. an increase in real GDP abroad
    b. an increase in the home country's inflation rate
    c. an increase in foreign interest rates
    d. renewed confidence in the home country's economy
8. What is the euro? Why should Americans be interested in it?
9. Summarize the advantages and disadvantages of flexible and fixed exchange rates.
10. Suppose a country suddenly experiences a capital outflow. Describe the impact on the country assuming
    a. flexible exchange rates
    b. fixed exchange rates
11. Critically evaluate the following statement: "The Asian financial crisis was about financial transactions; the countries involved continued to grow."
12. What impact did the Asian financial crisis have on U.S. exports to that region? Defend your answer.
13. What are capital controls? Why might a country wish to impose them?
14. What is the traditional view regarding capital movements? Why are economists reassessing this view?

Key Terms

Balance of payments
Exchange rate
Flexible (floating) exchange rates
Appreciation
Depreciation
Fixed exchange rates
Balance of payments deficit
Devaluation
Balance of payments surplus
Revaluation

Economic Issues on the Internet

- Euro Essentials—**http://europa.eu.int/comm/economy_finance/euro_en.htm**
  This site provides basic information on the evolution and current status of the euro.

- Federal Reserve Bank of New York—**http://www.x-rates.com**
  This bank Web site provides data on current exchange rates for the world's major currencies.

- Global Macroeconomic and Financial Policy Site—**http://www.stern.nyu.edu/globalmacro**
  This site by Nourial Roubini provides access to basic readings and references on the causes and consequences of the Asian financial crisis. (Click on "Asian Crisis" in the left-hand menu.)

- PACIFIC Exchange Rate Service—**http://pacific.commerce.ubc.ca/xr**
  This site, provided by the University of British Columbia, provides access to current exchange rates, information on each country's exchange rate regime (fixed or floating), and trend projections for the Canadian dollar, the U.S. dollar, and the euro.

- U.S. Department of Commerce, Bureau of Economic Analysis—**http://www.bea.gov/bea/di1.htm**
  The BEA's international accounts data, including information on the balance of payments, the current account, and the capital account, can be accessed.

Glossary

Absolute advantage- The advantage a country has if it can produce a good or service at a lower cost than its trading partner.

Absolute disadvantage- The disadvantage a country has if it produces a good or service at a higher cost than its trading partner.

Acid rain- A solution of sulfuric acid and precipitation.

Actual deficit- The amount by which actual government expenditures exceed actual government revenues.

Adverse selection- Self-selection by policyholders that results in a pool of insured individuals dominated by high-risk individuals.

Aggregate demand curve- A curve showing the quantity of final goods and services (real GDP) that will be purchased at each price level (GDP deflator).

Aggregate supply curve- A curve showing the quantity of final goods and services (real GDP) that will be produced at each price level (the GDP deflator).

Ambient concentrations- Concentrations of pollutants in the atmosphere.

Anticipated inflation- Inflation that is expected.

Appreciation- Under a flexible exchange rate system, a rise in the value of one currency relative to another.

Average indexed monthly earnings (AIME)- Actual average monthly earnings for the highest 35 years of earnings, adjusted by an indexing factor.

Balance of payments- A summary of all economic transactions between the residents of one country and those of all other countries during a given period of time.

Balance of payments deficit- At a given exchange rate, the amount by which the home country's purchases of foreign goods, services, and assets exceed the rest of the world's purchases from it.

Balance of payments surplus- At a given exchange rate, the amount by which the rest of the world's purchases of the home country's goods, services, and assets exceed its purchases from the rest of the world.

Barrier to entry- Any condition that prevents new firms from entering an industry with the same cost conditions as existing firms.

Basic benefit- The benefit paid by a means-tested transfer program when gross income is zero.

Benefit reduction rate- The decrease in benefits paid by a means-tested transfer program when gross income increases.

Best technology- The technology that requires the fewest resources to produce a given combination of goods and services.

Break-even gross income (BEGI)- The gross income at which benefits become zero in a means-tested transfer program.

Budget- A statement of income (or receipts) and expenditures (or outlays) for a specific period of time (a year).

Budget deficit- A negative net budget balance—total outlays exceed total revenues.

Budget surplus- A positive net budget balance—total revenues exceed total outlays.

Burden of the public debt- The public debt as a percentage of GDP.

Business cycles- Recurring fluctuations in the general level of economic activity.

Capital gain- The market price of an asset minus the purchase price of that asset.

Capital intensity- The ratio of capital to labor in production; units of capital per unit of labor.

Capital stock- The nation's accumulated stock of structures, producers' durable equipment, and business inventories.

Cartel- An organized group of producers who manage their output and pricing as if they were a monopoly.

Central bank- A government-established agency that controls the nation's money supply, conducts monetary policy, and supervises the monetary system.

Civilian labor force- The number of persons employed plus the number of persons unemployed.

Coase's Theorem- The thesis that the assignment and enforcement of property rights can lead to the efficient level of pollution.

Coefficient of the price elasticity of demand- The percentage change in quantity demanded divided by the percentage change in price; it is a measure of the responsiveness of consumers to price changes.

Common property resource- A resource that is the property of all.

Commutative justice- A norm for a market economy based on voluntary exchange. Voluntary exchange means exchange of equal market value.

Comparative advantage- The advantage a country has if it produces a good or service at a lower opportunity cost than its trading partner.

Comparative disadvantage- The disadvantage a country has if it produces a good or service at a higher opportunity cost than its trading partner.

Competitive market- A market is competitive if it has many buyers and sellers, so that both buyers and sellers are price takers, and easy entry of new producers, so that new firms enter in response to economic profit and compete that profit away.

Complement- A good used with another good. An increase in the price of a good results in a decrease in demand for its complement.

Consumer price index (CPI)- A weighted average of the prices of goods and services purchased by a typical urban household.

Consumers' surplus- The difference between the price that consumers are willing to pay (their demand price) and the price that they must pay.

Contraction phase- The phase of the business cycle during which real GDP, employment, productive capacity use, and profits decrease while unemployment rises.

Cost Disease of the Services Sector- A theory developed by William Baumol that explains why costs in the services sector of the economy will rise faster than costs in the rest of the economy.

Creditor- A person to whom money is owed.

Criteria pollutants- Pollutants that are subject to the National Ambient Air Quality Standards (NAAQS).

Currency (cash)- Paper money and coins.

Cyclical unemployment- Unemployment caused by the drop in economic activity that occurs during the contraction phase of the business cycle.

Deadweight loss- Another name for efficiency loss.

Deadweight loss from taxation- Same as the efficiency loss from taxation.

Debtor- A person who owes money.

Decrease in demand- A situation in which, at each price, consumers plan to purchase less of a good; it is depicted by a leftward shift of the demand curve. It may also be interpreted as a reduction in the value of an additional unit of the good, which emphasizes the downward shift of the curve.

Decrease in supply- A situation in which, at each price, producers plan to sell less of a good; it is depicted by a leftward shift of the supply curve. It may also be interpreted as an increase in the supply price for each quantity of the good, which emphasizes the upward shift of the curve.

Deduction for essential needs- An allowance for essential needs that is disregarded in determining benefits from a transfer program.

Defensive medicine- Medical procedures performed to reduce the risk of a lawsuit.

Deflation- A continuing fall in the price level.

Delayed retirement credit- The amount by which retirees' benefits are increased for each year that retirement is delayed up to age 70.

Demand curve- A curve (line) showing the quantity demanded of a good for each possible price, holding constant other factors that affect demand.

Demand deposits- Checking accounts at commercial banks.

Demand price- The price at which consumers will just buy the exact quantity on the market. It is the maximum price that anyone will pay for a unit.

Depository institutions- Financial institutions that accept checkable and savings deposits.

Depreciation- Under a flexible exchange rate system, a fall in the value of one currency relative to another.

Devaluation- Under a fixed exchange rate system, a fall in the value of one currency relative to another.

Discount factor- The value of the divisor, $(1+i)^t$, used to discount a future value.

Discount rate- The interest rate at which depository institutions can borrow from Federal Reserve Banks.

Distributive justice- Equality among people, providing a norm of equal opportunity, with the hope that equal opportunity combined with commutative justice will move people toward equality.

Dynamic efficiency- An efficient allocation of resources in the long run.

Early retirement penalty- The amount by which Social Security benefits are reduced for people who retire before the normal retirement age.

Economic approach to organization- An approach that mimics the market in designing a profit or nonprofit organization. In particular, it assigns decision rights to people who have relevant specific knowledge, evaluates those decisions in relation to the organization's objective, and rewards decisions that advance the objective.

Economic efficiency- An allocation of resources that satisfies wants as fully as possible.

Economic profit- A rate of earning in excess of the minimum necessary to attract economic resources into a particular use.

Economic rent seeking- Attempt by people to gain an economic advantage through production of new or better products or through production of products at a lower cost.

Efficiency improvement- A change from less than the best to the best technology. It allows more output to be produced with the same resources.

Efficiency loss- Maximum total net benefits minus actual total net benefits.

Efficiency loss from pollution- Marginal social cost (MSC) minus marginal benefit (MB), summed over all units produced for which MSC>MB.

Efficiency loss from taxation- The wedge between maximum total net benefits and actual net benefits created by some feature of the tax, such as the marginal rate or exemptions from the tax base.

Efficient output- The output where marginal social benefit equals marginal social cost.

Emissions reduction credit- A credit for reducing emissions more than required by regulations.

Emissions tax- A tax charged polluters for each unit of pollutants emitted.

Equation of exchange- An equation showing the relationships among the money supply, the income velocity of money, the GDP deflator, and real GDP.

Equilibrium- A state of rest for the economy or market. Market equilibrium occurs at the price at which quantity demanded equals quantity supplied. This price is referred to as the equilibrium price, and this quantity is referred to as the equilibrium quantity.

Excess demand- A situation in which quantity demanded exceeds quantity supplied at a given price.

Excess reserves- Reserves over and above required reserves.

Excess supply- A situation in which quantity supplied exceeds quantity demanded at a given price.

Exchange rate- The number of units of one currency exchangeable for one unit of another.

Expansion phase- The business cycle phase during which real GDP, employment, productive capacity use, and profits increase while unemployment falls.

Exports- Goods and services produced in this country and purchased by foreigners.

External benefits- Benefits created in a market that are realized by individuals other than the buyers and sellers.

External costs- Costs created in a market that are paid by individuals other than the buyers and sellers, or costs created by producers or consumers, but paid by others.

Fertility rate- The average number of children born to women in their lifetime.

Final goods- Goods purchased (or available to be purchased) for final use.

Fiscal policy- Use of government purchases and taxes to achieve full employment and other economic goals.

Fixed exchange rates- Exchange rates kept constant through central bank purchases and sales of foreign currencies.

Flexible (floating) exchange rates- Exchange rates determined by demand and supply.

Foreign trade effect- The change in net exports caused by a change in the price level that causes a change in the relative desirability of domestic and foreign goods and services.

Free rider- An individual who uses goods or services provided by others without paying for them.

Frictional unemployment- Temporary unemployment arising from the normal job-search process.

Full employment rate of unemployment- The frictional rate of unemployment plus the structural rate of unemployment; the lowest unemployment rate consistent with a nonaccelerating inflation rate.

Fully-funded fund- A fund with a balance that can cover future benefits and expenses for many years.

Future value (FV)- The value at a future date of a sum of money now.

GDP deflator- A weighted average of the prices of all final goods and services produced in the economy.

General knowledge- Knowledge that is easy to transfer to another person, including people in another part of the organization or the economy.

Government purchases of goods and services- The purchases of federal, state, and local governments.

Greenhouse gas- A gas that helps the Earth retain heat from the sun.

Gross domestic product (GDP)- The market value of all final goods and services produced in the economy over the relevant time span, usually one year.

Gross federal debt- Also known as the national debt; the debt of the federal government held by both the public and government agencies.

Gross money income- Earnings (before taxes), interest, dividends, and private and government cash transfers, such as alimony and child support payments, Social Security benefits, unemployment benefits, and payments from TANF.

Gross private domestic investment- Firms' purchases of new equipment, purchases of all newly produced structures, and changes in business inventories.

High-stakes testing- Focuses on achievement testing with demonstration of achievement important for completing high school and for subsequent employment opportunities and college admission.

Human capital- The knowledge and skills embodied in people, as used in the production process.

Hyperinflation- Extremely high inflation rates.

Imports- Goods and services produced abroad and bought by persons in this country.

Income effect of a wage decrease- The increase in hours worked to replace the decrease in income resulting from a wage rate reduction.

Income elasticity of demand (IED)- The percentage change in the quantity purchased of a good or service resulting from a given percentage change in income.

Income velocity of money- The number of times the money supply is used to purchase final goods and services during a year.

Incomes policy- Government action, other than monetary and fiscal policies, to restrain or control wages, prices, and other forms of income.

Incomplete market- A market in which the good or service is available to only some of the potential customers.

Increase in demand- A situation in which, at each price, consumers plan to purchase more of a good, depicted by a rightward shift of the demand curve. It may also be interpreted as an increase in the demand price, which emphasizes the upward shift of the curve.

Increase in supply- A situation in which, at each price, producers plan to sell more of a good; it is depicted by a rightward shift of the supply curve. It may also be interpreted as a reduction in supply price for each quantity of the good, which emphasizes the downward shift of the curve.

Indexing- Linking benefits to the CPI so that they increase automatically as the CPI rises.

Indexing factor- A ratio of average national wages in two different years used to index actual annual earnings.

Induced retirement effect- The increase in household savings to offset early retirement induced by Social Security.

Inferior good- A good that consumers purchase less of when their income rises; a good with an income elasticity of demand less than zero.

Inflation- A continuing rise in the price level.

GLOSSARY

Inflation indexing- Annual upward adjustment in Social Security benefits to cover the increase in the consumer price index.

Inflation protection benefit- The value of the inflation indexing of Social Security benefits.

Interest rate effect- The change in consumption and investment caused by a change in the price level that ultimately causes interest rates to change.

Intermediate goods- Goods purchased for resale or for use in producing other goods.

Labor- All physical and mental abilities used by people in production.

Land- Resources found in nature, such as land, water, forests, mineral deposits, and air.

Law of demand- As the price of some good changes with other factors constant, the quantity demanded for that good changes in the opposite direction.

Law of supply- As the price of some good changes with other factors constant, the quantity supplied for that good changes in the same direction.

Loanable funds- Funds available for borrowing by households, firms, and government.

Managed care- Health care that is reviewed by someone other than the patient or provider to determine whether the right services are being provided and whether the cost of provision is minimized.

Marginal abatement cost- The cost of abating or eliminating an additional unit of pollutants.

Marginal benefit- The satisfaction or value received from consumption of an additional unit of a good or service.

Marginal benefit curve- A curve that depicts the benefits from each additional, or marginal, unit.

Marginal cost- The opportunity cost of producing an additional unit of a good.

Marginal cost curve- A curve that depicts the costs of providing each additional, or marginal, unit.

Marginal external benefits (MEB)- External benefits on the additional, or marginal, unit.

Marginal external costs (MEC)- External costs on the additional, or marginal, unit, or external costs attributable to each additional unit of production.

Marginal principle- To maximize profits, the producer should choose the output that equates marginal revenue and marginal cost.

Marginal product- The change in output associated with a 1-unit change in an input, for example labor.

Marginal revenue- The change in total revenue associated with a 1-unit change in the output sold by a producer.

Marginal social benefits (MSB)- The sum of marginal benefits and marginal external benefits.

Marginal social costs (MSC)- The sum of marginal costs and marginal external costs.

Market failure- A situation in which a market fails to achieve efficiency.

Market power- A situation in which a firm or a few firms can affect the price received for their product, and new firms do not enter the industry in response to economic profit.

Marketable pollution permit- A permit that can be bought and sold that allows a polluter to emit a specified quantity of a pollutant or pollutants.

Means-tested transfer- A transfer that decreases in value as a recipient's means or income increases.

Medium of exchange- Anything used to purchase goods and services and pay debts.

Member banks- Banks that are members of the Federal Reserve System.

Monetary benefits and costs- Benefits and costs valued in dollars.

Monetary policy- Use of the money supply to achieve full employment and other economic goals.

Money- Anything generally accepted as final payment for goods, services, and debt.

Money supply- Currency (including coins), checkable deposits, and travelers' checks.

Monopoly- An industry with a single producer of a good that has no close substitutes.

Moral hazard- The risk that insurance for an event will increase the probability of the event occurring.

National banks- Banks chartered by the federal government.

Natural monopolies- Monopolies that exist if demand and cost conditions are such that only one firm can survive in an industry.

Natural rate of unemployment- The full employment rate of unemployment.

Net budget balance- Total revenues minus total outlays.

Net cost of health insurance- The difference between the subsidized cost of insurance and the value of claims paid.

Net exports of goods and services- The amount by which foreign spending on domestically produced goods and services is greater (or less) than domestic spending on goods and services produced abroad.

Nominal GDP- GDP measured on the basis of current, or nominal, prices.

Nonexcludable good- A good that is impossible or extremely difficult to exclude nonpayers from consuming.

Nonexistent markets- Markets that cannot be organized or created.

Nonmonetary benefits and costs- Benefits and costs not valued in dollars.

Nonrival good- A good that one person can consume without reducing the amount available for others to consume, such as a feeling of security in a safe city.

Nonstudent benefits- Benefits of a college education to nonstudents.

Nonstudent costs- Costs of a college education paid by nonstudents.

Normal good- A good that consumers purchase more of when their income rises.

Off-budget surplus- Total revenues in excess of total outlays in the Social Security portion of the unified budget.

Official poverty threshold- The annual cost of a nutritionally adequate diet multiplied by three.

Oligopoly- An industry with only a few producers or sellers of a good.

On-budget surplus- Total revenues in excess of total outlays in the non–Social Security portion of the unified budget.

Open market operations- The purchase or sale of U.S. Treasury securities by the Federal Reserve.

Opportunity cost- The value of the best alternative sacrificed when a choice is made.

Pay-as-you-go fund- A fund with a balance that can cover future benefits and expenses for only a few years.

Peak- The highest point in the business cycle, during which real GDP is at a maximum and employment, profits, and productive capacity use are high.

Personal consumption expenditures- Household purchases of durable and nondurable goods and services.

Physical capital- Man-made, durable items used in the production process, such as factories, equipment, dams, and transportation systems.

Physician-induced demand- Clearly ineffective health care prescribed by physicians to increase their own wealth.

Political rent seeking- Attempt by certain individuals or groups to encourage government activity that will result in an economic advantage for them.

Poor person- A person who lives in a family with income below the poverty threshold

Poverty rate- The number of poor people divided by the U.S. population.

Pre-transfer poverty rate- An estimate by the Census Bureau of what the poverty rate would be without the income provided by government cash transfers, except the earned income tax credit (EITC)

Present value (PV)- The value now of a future sum of money.

Present value decision rule- A rule used to determine if an investment is financially sound; an investment is financially sound according to this rule if the sum of the present value of benefits is equal to or greater than the sum of the present value of costs.

Price elastic- Demand is price elastic if the elasticity coefficient is greater than 1.0.

Price floor- A minimum price set by government, below which the market price is not allowed to go.

Price index- A measure of the price level for a given period relative to the base period.

Price inelastic- Demand is price inelastic if the elasticity coefficient is less than 1.0.

Primary Insurance Amount (PIA)- Monthly Social Security benefits at the normal retirement age.

Privatization- The investment of Social Security trust fund balances in private securities.

Producers' surplus- The difference between the price that producers receive and the price that they must receive (their supply price).

Production possibilities curve- A curve showing the maximum combinations of two goods or services that can be produced by an economy when resources are fully used and the best technology is applied.

Profit- Total revenue minus total cost.

Progressive tax- A tax with marginal tax rates that increase as the tax base increases.

Property right- A legally defined and enforceable right to use property for specific purposes.

Public debt- The portion of the gross federal debt held by the public.

Public good- A good from which no one can be excluded, even if they pay nothing for its provision; a good that is nonexcludable and nonrival.

Quantity demanded- The quantity of a good that consumers plan to buy at each possible price, holding constant other factors that affect demand.

Quantity supplied- The quantity of a good that producers will plan to sell at each possible price, holding constant other factors that affect supply.

Quantity theory of money- A theory emphasizing that the money supply is the principal determinant of nominal GDP.

Quota- An upper limit on the amount of a good that may be imported during any time period.

Rate of return (ROR)- The discount rate, r, at which the sum of the present value of costs is equal to the sum of the present value of benefits.

Rate of return decision rule- A rule used to determine if an investment is financially sound; an investment is financially sound according to this rule if the rate of return on the investment is equal to or greater than the rate of return on the best alternative use of funds.

Ration- To allocate a limited supply of goods and services to people.

Real balance effect- The change in consumption caused by a change in the price level that changes the real value of financial assets that have fixed dollar values.

Real GDP- GDP measured on the basis of constant prices; reflects only changes in quantities.

Regressive tax- A tax with marginal tax rates that decrease as taxable income decreases.

Relative price- The price of one good in terms of another good. It measures what must be given up to obtain a good.

Required reserves- Reserves that depository institutions are required to hold.

Reserve requirement- The ratio of required reserves to deposits.

The residual- In a health expenditures context, the proportion of health expenditures that cannot be attributed to factors other than technology.

Revaluation- Under a fixed exchange rate system, a rise in the value of one currency relative to another.

Risk reduction benefit- The value of the lower risk of loss of Social Security benefits relative to the risk of loss of income from private securities.

Scarcity- The common situation for all economies, in which aggregate wants exceed the economy's ability to meet them because of limited resources.

Social benefits- Benefits that accrue to all individuals; applied to college education, benefits to students and nonstudents.

Social costs- Costs paid by all individuals; applied to college education, costs to students and nonstudents.

Social rate of return (ROR)- Rate of return realized by students and nonstudents from investing in a college education; the discount rate at which the sum of the present value of social benefits is equal to the sum of the present value of social costs.

Social Security wealth- The present value of Social Security benefits minus the present value of Social Security taxes.

Specific knowledge- Knowledge that is costly to transfer to another person and is particularly costly to transfer to someone in another part of the organization or the economy.

Stabilization policies- Government policies (generally fiscal or monetary) undertaken to maintain full employment and a reasonably stable price level.

State banks- Banks chartered by state governments.

Static efficiency- An efficient allocation of resources in the short run.

Structural deficit- The deficit at full employment.

Structural unemployment- Unemployment caused by structural changes in the economy that eliminate certain jobs.

Student benefits- Benefits of a college education to students.

Student costs- Costs of a college education paid by students.

Student rate of return (ROR)- Rate of return realized by students from investing in a college education; the discount rate at which the sum of the present value of student benefits is equal to the sum of the present value of student costs.

Student rate of return without government support- The student rate of return from investing in a college education when government pays none of the cost.

Substitute- A good used in place of another good. An increase in the price of one good results in an increase in demand for the substitute good.

Substitution effect of a wage decrease- The decrease in hours worked because of a fall in the wage rate.

Superior good- A good with an income elasticity of demand greater than one.

Supply curve- A curve (line) showing the quantity supplied of a good for each possible price, holding constant other factors that affect supply

Supply price- The price at which sellers will just put a specific quantity of a good or service on the market. It is the minimum price that a seller will accept in return for selling one more unit of a good or service.

Supply-side policies- Government actions aimed at increasing aggregate supply.

Target efficiency- The degree to which transfer program benefits are confined to the poor.

Target price- A guaranteed price for a product. The product is sold at the market price, and the government pays the producer the difference between it and the guaranteed price.

Tariff- A tax levied on a good when it crosses a nation's border.

Technical change- Technological and efficiency improvements combined.

Technological improvement- An improvement in best technology that allows more output with a given amount of resources.

Third-party payment- A payment made directly to the provider of a good or service by a party other than the buyer.

Total benefit- The sum of marginal benefits; also the area under the marginal benefit or demand curve.

Total cost- The sum of marginal costs; also the area under the marginal cost or supply curve.

Total net benefit- Total benefit minus total cost; also the area between the demand and supply curves.

Total revenue- Number of units sold times price per unit; also the rectangle under the demand curve, where height is the price per unit and base is the quantity sold.

Trade deficit- A negative net balance in the international trade account; imports greater than exports.

Transactions costs- The costs of finding willing buyers and sellers and negotiating a mutually acceptable price.

Trough- The lowest point of the business cycle, during which real GDP is at a minimum and employment, profits, and productive capacity use are low.

Unanticipated inflation- Inflation that is unexpected or higher than expected.

Unemployment rate- The percentage of the civilian labor force that is unemployed.

Unified budget- The federal budget with Social Security included.

Unit elastic- Demand is unit elastic if the elasticity coefficient equals 1.0.

Utilization review- A process used to determine if the medical care prescribed by a physician is appropriate.

Value of a life- The value people put on their own lives, inferred from what they must be paid to incur small but predictable increases in the risk of death.

Vault cash- Cash held by banks and other depository institutions.

Voluntary export restraints (VERs)- Agreements whereby exporting nations limit the amounts of goods that they ship to importing nations.

Voucher- A coupon for a good or service that is used as a means of payment.

Wealth substitution effect- The reduction in household savings caused by the substitution of Social Security wealth for other types of wealth.

Index

Absolute advantage, 430
Absolute disadvantage, 430
Absolute poverty, 3
ACE (agreement, cooperation, and enforcement), 139
Achievement tests, 256–262
Acid rain, 155
Actual deficit, 414
Adverse selection, 74
Affirmative action programs, 349
Africa, economic growth in, 22
African Americans
    See Blacks
Aggregate demand and supply interaction, 338–342
Aggregate demand curve
    defined, 333
    movements along, 334–335
    shifts in, 335–337
Aggregate supply curve
defined, 337
movements along, 337–338
shifts in, 338, 339
Aging population, 178
Agricultural policy
    output constraints, 116–117
    price floor, 114–115
    rent seeking, 119–120
    sugar prices (Insights), 118
    target prices and deficiency payments, 117–119
Agricultural price supports, 76, 77, 87–88
Agriculture
    breaking even in farming (Insights), 113
    competition in, 111–114
    competitive markets and economic profits, 109–114
    economic and historical characteristics, 106–109
    Internet sites regarding, 122
    risks in, 109–111
Agriculture, competitive markets and, 93–95
    demand and supply analysis, 96–103
    equilibrium price and quantity, 103–106
Aid to Families with Dependent Children (AFDC), 304, 305
    See also Temporary Assistance for Needy Families (TANF)
Air pollution, 153
    acid rain, 155
    economic perspective, 156–158
    emissions reductions, 162–163
    emissions taxes, 166–167
    global warming, 155, 169–171
    hazardous air pollutants, 156
    Internet sites regarding, 173–174
    marketable pollution permits, 167–169
    market failure and government action, 158–160
    stratospheric ozone depletion, 155
    urban air quality, 154

Air pollution regulation
    See Clean Air Act of 1963
Albania, 53
Alcohol, 215
    abuse of, 219
Algeria, 23
Ambient concentrations, 161
Anticipated inflation, 368, 371
Appreciation, 448
Argentina, 22n
    economic growth in, 22
Asia, 24
    economic growth in, 22–24
Asian financial crisis, 457
Assembled knowledge, 265
Austria, 441, 452
Average indexed monthly earnings (AIME), 274–275
Balance of payments (BOP), 444–446
Balance of payments (BOP) deficit, 451
Balance of payments (BOP) surplus, 451–452
Bangladesh, 22n
Banks, 391–392
Barriers to international trade
    quotas, 435
    tariffs, 434–435
    voluntary export restraints (VERs), 435–436
Barrier to entry, 136–138
Basic benefit, 302
Baumol, William, 177–178
Becker, Gary, 201–202
Belarus, 51, 53
Belgium, 441, 452
Benefit reduction rate, 302
Benefits and Costs of the Clean Air Act, 1970 to 1990, The, 162, 163
Benefits and Costs of the Clean Air Act, 1990 to 2010, The, 162, 163
Bennett, William J., 211–212, 219
Berry, Marion, 95
Best technology, 9
Bishop, John, 260
Blacks
    labor market discrimination and, 312–315
    poverty rates, 298, 301, 308–309
    unemployment rate for, 348, 349
Bond sales
    to the Federal Reserve, 420
    to the public sector, 418–420
Boskin, Michael, 286
Brazil, 22n
    economic growth in, 3–6, 7
Break-even gross income (BEGI), 302
Bretton Woods system, 452
Budget deficit, 403
Budget, federal, 401

467

business cycles and, 414–415
debt, burden of, 420–422
deficit and, economic effects of, 416–420
deficits and surpluses for various countries (International Perspective), 406
from deficit to surplus (Insights), 404
defined, and concepts of, 402–403
future of, 422–423
government investment, 415–416
historical perspective, 403–405
inflation and, 413
Internet sites regarding, 425
long-run, and debt projections, 408–412, 413, 414
measurement issues, 412–416
public debt, 405–408
state and local government deficits and surpluses, 416
U.S. deficit yearly since 1981, 446
Budget surplus, 403
Burden of the public debt, 407–408
Bush, George H. W., 404, 440
Bush, George W., 408
Business cycle, 330–332
deficits and, 414–415
Canada, 285, 440, 452
Capital flows, control of, 454–456
Capital gains, 84
Capital intensity, 17
contribution of, 18
Capital stock, 325
Carbon monoxide, 154
Cartels
defined, 128
determinants of success of, 140–141
formation of, 139–140
OPEC, problems of, 141–145
Carter, Jimmy, 386
Cash transfers, 297, 299–301
Central bank, 376
Centrally planned economic systems
price system and, 50
See also Command systems
Checkable deposits, 375
Chernick, Howard, 305
Child and Dependent Care Tax Credit (CDCTC), 310
Child Care and Development Fund (CCDF), 310
Childcare assistance, Temporary Assistance for Needy Families (TANF), 309–310
Child support assistance, 316–317
Child support assurance, 317
Child Support Enforcement program, 316
Child Tax Credit (CTC), 310
Chile, 22n, 23, 159
economic growth in, 22
China, 22n, 28, 262
economic growth in, 3–6, 7, 33
Chlorofluorocarbons, 155
Civilian labor force, 347
Clayton Act, 149
Clean Air Act of 1963 (amended 1965, 1970, 1977, 1990), 163
benefits and costs, 1970 to 1990, 164–165
benefits and costs, 1990 to 2010, 165–166
economics of, 163–166

effects of, on air quality, 162–163
emissions limits, 161
emissions trading, 162
monitoring and compliance, 162
National Ambient Air Quality Standards (NAAQS), 161
new source performance standards, 161
offset requirements, 162
prescribed fuels, 162
prevention of significant deterioration, 162
restricted technology, 161
Clinton, Bill, 304, 404
Coase, Ronald, 159–160
Coase's theorem, 160
Cocaine, 212–215, 218, 221
Coefficient of the price elasticity of demand, 123
College education, 227
college reputation matters (Insights), 235
education and economic growth (International Perspective), 236
government support of, 238–243
Internet sites regarding, 245
investment decision, analysis of, 228–230
monetary benefits and costs, 230–236
nonmonetary external benefits, 237–238
nonmonetary external costs, 238
nonmonetary student benefits, 236–237
nonmonetary student costs, 237
rates of return around the world, in education (International Perspective), 238
Colombia, 22n
Colosio, Luis Donaldo, 455
Command economy
information in, 48
motivation in, 48–49
rationing in, 48
See also Comparative systems
Command systems
compared to market systems, 28–29
coordination of economic activity by, 49
See also Centrally planned systems; Command economy
Commercial banks, 391–392
Common property resource, 159
Communism, 51
Community benefit spillovers, 237
Commutative justice, 254
Comparative advantage, international trade and, 429–432
Comparative disadvantage, 429
Comparative systems
command economy: information, rationing, and motivation in, 48–49
market economy: information, rationing, and motivation in, 45–48
price system, 44–45
socialism and the price system (Insights), 50
systems and coordination, 49
Competition
in agriculture, 111–114
among physicians, 188
foreign, 135
monopoly and, compared, 132–135
Competitive markets, 36, 111

efficiency in resource allocation and, 66–68
   See also Agriculture
Complement, 99
Congestion pricing, 159
Congo, 23
Constitution, U.S., 1, 198
Consumer price index (CPI), 286, 294
   inflation and, 366–368
Consumers' surplus, 433
Consumption, 324
   versus growth, 10–12
Consumption of fixed capital, 325
Contraction phase (business cycle), 331
Controls, wage-price, 386–388
Coordination, by an economic system, 34
   market and command economies compared, 49
   market systems and, 36
Costa Rica, 23
Cost Disease of the Services Sector, 177–178
Cost-of-living adjustment (COLA), 367
Costs
   economic, of unemployment, 346
   external, 156
   implicit, 113
   marginal abatement, 166–167
   marginal external, 156
   marginal social, 156
   monetary benefits and, 230–236
   net, of health insurance, 190
   noneconomic, of unemployment, 346
   nonmonetary external, 238
   nonmonetary student, 237
   nonstudent, 231
   social, 231
   social, of the automobile (pollution; International Perspective), 158–159
   student, 231
   transactions, 169
   up-front, 145–146
   See also Health expenditures; Medical care
Cote d'Ivoire, 22n
Crack cocaine, 218
Creditor, 370
Credit unions, 392
Crime and crime control, 201
   drug control and, competing views, 219–224
   economic approach to, 202–206
   falling rates in the United States, 208
   Internet sites regarding, 226
   scientific method in economics (Insight), 210
   trends in the United States and England, 206–209
Criteria pollutants, 165–166
Currency (cash), 374
   underground economy and (Insights), 375
Cutler, David, 178, 182–183
Cyclical unemployment, 350
   reducing, 352–355
Czech Republic, 51, 53
Deadweight loss, 70
   from taxation, 82
Debtor, 370
Debt projection and the long-run budget, 408–412
Declaration of Independence, 1, 23

Decrease in demand, 98
Decrease in supply, 103
Deduction for essential needs, 302
Default (of college loans), 240–242
Defensive medicine, 189
Deficiency payments, 117–119
Deficit
   actual, 414
   financing of, 417–420
   future, 422–423
   help for a recession, 416–420
   overall, 446
   Social Security and, 283–290
   state and local government, 416
   structural, 414
   See also Budget, federal
Deficit measurement issues
   business cycles, 414–415
   government investment, 415–416
   inflation, 413
   state and local government deficits and surpluses, 416
Deflation, 366
Delayed retirement credit, 276
Demand, 36–39
   changes in, affecting equilibrium price and quantity, 104–105
   decrease in, 98
   for drugs, reducing, 216
   excess, 44
   for higher education (Insights), 242
   income (farming), 100–101
   increase in, 100
   physician-induced, 186–189
   related goods (farming), 98–100
Demand and supply, 41–44
   farming analysis, 96–103
   how changes in affect equilibrium price and quantity, 103–106
Demand curve, 38
Demand deposits, 374
Demand price, 38
Demand schedule, 37–38
Denmark, 441
Dependent Care Assistance Program (DCAP), 310
Depository institutions, 391
Depository Institutions Deregulation and Monetary Control Act of 1980, 392
Depreciation, 448
Depression, 331
Deregulation, government, 135–136
Devaluation, 451
Discount factor, 229
Discount rate, 398
Discretionary program, 403
Discrimination
   See Labor market discrimination
Disney, Walt, 50
Distributive justice, 254
Division of labor, 34–36
Drug control and its relationship with crime control, 219–224
Drug legalization
   arguments against, 211–212

arguments for, 210–211
consequences of, 219
Drug policy, 212–214
    Internet sites regarding, 226
    prohibition, consequences of, 216–219
    to reduce demand, 216
    to reduce supply, effects of, 215–216
    in the United States (Insights), 224
Durable goods, 324
Dynamic efficiency, 66
Early retirement, 278
Early retirement penalty, 275
Earned income tax credit (EITC), 299, 303–305, 311
    TANF + food stamps + EITC, 306–307
E-commerce, 13
Economic approach
    to crime and crime control, 202–206
    to organization, 265
Economic costs of unemployment, 346
Economic efficiency, 65
    See also Efficiency; Market power
Economic Freedom of the World (Gwartney and Lawson), 23
Economic growth
    consumption versus, 10–12
    in developing countries after 1950, 22–24
    education and (International Perspective), 236
    efficiency improvement, 12
    in Europe and Japan, 20–22
    government, efficiency, and (International Perspective), 87
    Internet sites regarding, 26
    market power and, 145–148
    production possibilities, 7–10
    recent global experiences, 3–6
    resource accumulation, 12, 13
    technological improvement, 12, 13–14
    transformation of life in industrialized countries, 2
    in the United States, 34
    See also Productivity growth
Economic inefficiency, monopoly and, 134
Economic profit, 47, 111
Economic Reform Today (Gwartney and Lawson), 23
Economic rent seeking, 119, 149, 150
Economics of student achievement, 254–256
Economic systems
    Internet sites regarding, 63–64
    rules of (five), 32–34
    See also Command systems; Market system; Price system
Economy
    importance of information on performance of, 321–322
    performance of, 330–333
    underground, 323, 375
Education
    arguments for public support of schools, 251–254
    blacks, unemployment rate, and, 349
    economics of student achievement, 254–256
    as a factor in poverty rates, 314
    high-stakes testing, 256–262
    Internet sites regarding, 272
    unemployment rate and, 348
    See also College education

Educational reform, 247
    nature of the problem, 248–251
    See also Public education
Efficiency
    dynamic, 66
    equity and, 87–88
    versus equity: tax trade-offs, 85–86
    government and growth (International Perspective), 87
    versus innovation, 86
    Internet sites regarding, 91
    offsets to inefficiency, 88
    of public education, 252
    in resource allocation, 66–68
    static, 66
    target, 303
    See also Economic efficiency; Inefficiency
Efficiency improvement, 13–14
Efficiency loss, 70
    from pollution, 157
    from taxation, 82
Efficient output, 134
Egypt, 23
EITC
    See Earned income tax credit (EITC)
Elderly
    reduction in poverty rate for, 295, 296
    Social Security, poverty and, 297
Emissions limits, 161
Emissions reduction credits, 162
Emissions reductions, 162–163
Emissions taxes, 166–167
Emissions trading, 162
Employer-provide health insurance (EPHI), 181, 189–190, 192, 310
Employment, full, 351–352
England, crime trends in, compared to the United States, 206–209
Environmentalists, 439, 440
Equation of exchange, 376
Equilibrium, 44
Equilibrium price and quantity, how changes in demand and supply affect, 103–106
Equimarginal principle, 222
Equity
    efficiency and, 87–88
    versus efficiency: tax trade-offs, 85–86
Estonia, 51, 53
Ethics, physician, 189
Euro (International Perspective), 453
Europe
    economic and productivity growth in, 20–22
    unemployment in, 359–362
European Bank for Reconstruction and Development (EBRD), 54
European Central Bank (ECB), 452
European Common Market, 21
European Economic and Monetary Union (EMU), 453
European Monetary System (EMS), 452
European Union, 21, 441
Excess demand, 44
Excess reserves, 393
Excess supply, 43–44
Exchange rates
    defined, 447

fixed, 450–452, 454
flexible, 447–450, 452–454
Expansion phase (business cycle), 330–331
   of 1991-2001 (Insights), 340–341
Exports
   See International trade
External benefits, 70–72
External costs, 36, 72, 73–74, 156
Family farms, 94–95
Family Support Act of 1988, 311, 316
Farm Bill of 1996, 93, 94
Farming
   See Agriculture
Federal Agriculture Improvement and Reform Act of 1996, 93
Federal funds, 384
Federal funds rate, 384
Federal Open Market Committee (FOMC), 392–393
Federal Reserve, 376, 392
   bond sales to, 420
   change in the money supply, 394–396
   creation of money, 393–394
   discount rate, 398
   as inflation fighter (Insights), 384
   open market operations, 396–397
   reserve requirements, 397
Female-headed families, poverty rate and, 297
   See also Women
Fertility rate, 284–286
Final goods, 322
Finance in the global economy, 443
   Asian financial crisis, 457
   balance of payments, 444–446
   capital flows, control of, 454–456
   current system, 452
   euro (International Perspective), 453
   exchange rates and their determination, 447–452
   fixed exchange rates, 450–452, 454
   flexible exchange rates, 447–450, 452–454
   Internet sites regarding, 459
   Mexican peso crisis (International Perspective), 455
   United States as world's largest debtor (Insights), 445
Finland, 441, 452
Fiscal policy, 335, 385
Fixed exchange rates, 450–452, 454
Flexible (floating) exchange rate, 447–450, 452–454
Food stamp program (FSP), 302–303
   TANF + food stamps + EITC, 306–307
Ford, Henry, 13, 50
Foreign-trade effect, 21, 335
France, 158, 159, 441, 452
Freedom to Farm bill, 93
Free rider, 201
Free trade
   decreasing costs, 436
   diversity of products, 436–437
   increased competition, 436
Frictional unemployment, 349–350
   reducing, 356–357
Friedman, Milton, 210–211, 212, 219
Full employment rate of unemployment, 351–352
Fully-funded fund, 274
Future value (FV), 182, 229
Gasoline prices, 158–159

Gasoline taxes, 159
Gates, Bill, 50
Gateway hypothesis, 220
GDP
   See Gross domestic product (GDP)
GDP deflator, 329, 366
GDP per capita, 2
   in developing countries after 1950, 22–24
   in Europe and Japan, 20–22
   recent global experiences, 3–6, 7
Gender issues
   See Women
General Agreement on Tariffs and Trade (GATT), 438–439
General knowledge, 263–264
General Theory of Employment, Interest, and Money, The (Keynes), 417
Germany, 158, 159, 285, 323, 452
   inflation after World War I, 373
   unemployment in, 360
Gettysburg Address, 1
Ghana, 22n
   economic growth in, 22
Global economy
   See Finance in the global economy; International trade
Global warming, 155, 169–171
Globerman, Steven, 187
Goods
   inferior, 100, 179
   intermediate, 322
   nonexcludable, 200
   nonrival, 200
   normal, 100
   public, 72, 200–201
Goods and services
   combination of, 10–12
   government purchases of, 326
   net exports of, 326
   quantities of, produced in an economy, 32–33
Government
   as barrier to entry, 138
   deregulation, 135–136
   enforcement of property rights, 200–201
   inflation and, 372
   investment, deficit, and, 415–416
   market power and, 148–150
   public goods, 200–201
   role of, in a market economy, 197–199
   support of college education, 238–243
Government failure
   agricultural price supports, 76, 77
   government-subsidized medical care, 76–78, 88
   minimum wage, 78, 79
   rent controls, 75–76
   See also Taxes
Government outlays, 402–403
Government purchases of goods and services, 326
Government-subsidized medical care, 76–78, 88
Government transfers, 297, 299–301, 326
Great Depression, 27, 93, 331, 345, 366, 416–417
Greece, 441
Greenhouse gas, 155
Greenspan, Alan, 392
Gross domestic product (GDP), 2, 321
   aggregate demand and supply interaction, 338–342

aggregate demand curve, 333–337
aggregate supply curve, 337–338, 339
business cycle, 330–332
defined, 322–324
economic performance of the nation, 330–333
expansion phase of 1991-2001 (Insights), 340–341
GDP deflator, 329
government purchases of goods and services, 326
gross private domestic investment (gross investment), 324–325
Internet sites regarding, 344
measured, and the underground economy (Insights), 323
net exports of goods and services, 326
nominal, 328
output and price level of the nation, 333–342
personal consumption expenditures, 324, 325
price index, 327
real, 328–329, 330
real, and social welfare (Insights), 332–333
worldwide, 3–6, 7
Gross federal debt, 405
Gross money income, 294
Gross private domestic investment (gross investment), 324–325
Gwartney, James D., 23
Hanushek, Eric, 250–251
Harrington, Michael, 293
Haveman, Robert, 236–237, 305
Hazardous air pollutants, 156
Health care
    See Medical care
Health care vouchers, 193
Health expenditures, 176
    Cost Disease of the Services Sector, 177–178
    income elasticity of demand for health care, 179
    insurance coverage, increases in, 179–180
    the medically uninsured (Insights), 181
    population aging, 178
    technological change, 180–181
Health maintenance organizations (HMOs), 190–192
Heroin, 214, 215
High-stakes testing
    absolute grading scale, 257
    additional earnings to come from, 261
    benefits and costs of higher achievement, 260–261
    connection between school performance and prospects for employment and college, 256
    economics of investing in, 259–261
    effect of, on achievement, 260
    expectations for all students, 257
    for grade promotion and graduation, 258–259
    in Japan (International Perspective), 261
    labor market of the future, 257–259
    mathematics achievement (Insights), 257
    test scores have consequences, 258
Hispanics
    labor market discrimination and, 312–315
    poverty rates, 298, 301, 308–309
    unemployment rate for, 348
Honduras, 23
Hong Kong, 23, 28
Household savings, 278–279

Human capital, 7
    contribution to growth, 15
    intensity, 17
Hungary, 51–53, 56, 57, 62
Hyperinflation, 373
Implicit cost, 113
Imports
    See International trade
Incentives, 29
    in a command economy, 50
    in transition economies, 57–58
Income disregard, 302
Income effect of a wage decrease, 276
Income elasticity of demand (IED)
    for health care, 179
Income, farming analysis, 100–101
Incomes policy, 383, 386–388
Income taxes, 80–84
Income velocity of money, 376
Incomplete markets, 74–75
Increase in demand, 100
Increase in supply, 102
Independent practice associations (IPAs), 190
Indexing, 370
Indexing factor, 274
Index of Economic Freedom, 23
India, 22n
    economic growth in, 2, 3–5
Individual income tax, 84–85
Individual rates of return (Social Security benefits), 279–282
Indonesia, 23, 457
Induced retirement effect, 279
Industrial concentration, 136
Industrial Revolution, 35, 106–107
Inefficiency
    efficiency as offset to, 88
    Internet sites regarding, 91
    of public school system, 270
    See also Economic efficiency; Efficiency
Inefficiency in the private sector (market failure)
    external benefits, 70–72
    external costs, 72–74
    incomplete markets, 74–75
    monopoly, 68
    nonexistent markets, 74
    public goods, 72
Inefficiency in the public sector (government failure)
    agricultural price supports, 76, 77
    government-subsidized medical care, 76–78
    minimum wage, 78, 79
    rent controls, 75–76
    See also Taxes
Inferior good, 100, 179
Inflation, 365
    anticipated, 368, 371
    causes of, 376–383
    consumer price index (CPI), 366–368
    deficit and, 413
    defined, 30, 366
    deflation in Japan (International Perspective), 378
    disintegration of monetary system and, 373
    effects of, 368–373

Federal Reserve, 376, 384
fiscal policy, 385
GDP deflator, 366
government and, 372
incomes policy, 386–388
Internet sites regarding, 389–390
labor unions, monopolies, and, 382–383
measuring, 366–368
monetary phenomenon, 379–382
monetary policy, 383–385
money's functions, 374
money supply, 374–376
net exports and, 372–373
planning for the future, difficulty of, 373
quantity theory of money, 376–379
recent experience, 368
redistribution of income and wealth, 368–371
speculation as a result of, 373
supply-side policies, 385–386
unanticipated, 368, 371
See also Inflation rate; Money
Inflation indexing, 276
Inflation protection benefit, 283
Inflation rate
calculation of, 367–368
for various countries (table), 370
Information
in a command economy, 48, 50
in a market economy, 45–46
Information revolution, 136
Information technology (IT), 18–20
Innovation, versus efficiency, 86
Insights
breaking even in farming, 113
carbon taxes, 171
college reputation matters, 235
cost of saving U.S. jobs, 434
from deficit to surplus, 404
demand for higher education, 242
drug policy in the United States, 224
economic approach to crime and crime control, 205
economic expansion of 1991-2001 (the Long Boom), 340–341
efficiency loss from taxation, 85
Federal Reserve as inflation fighter, 384
higher education, demand for, 242
income inequality (poverty), 301
international trade negotiations, labor, and the environment, 440
Jefferson, Smith, and public schools, 253
living standards, past and present, 16
measured GDP and the underground economy, 323
price of sugar, 118
real GDP and social welfare, 332–333
scientific method in economics (crime and crime control), 210
socialism and the price system, 50
standards for mathematics achievement, 257
technology and market power, 149
underground economy, currency holdings and, 375
unemployment, job opportunities, and discrimination, 349
United States as world's largest debtor, 445

welfare reform, 304–305
Insurance coverage
health care, increases in, 179–180
health, federal tax exemption for, 189–190, 192
the medically uninsured (Insights), 181
Interest rate effect, 335
Interest rate liberalization, 58
Intermediate farms, 94
Intermediate goods, 322
International Labor Organization, 440
International Perspective
American and Japanese automobile firms, 137
budget deficits and surpluses for various countries, 406
criminal activity in Russia, 59
deflation in Japan, 378
Dutch drug policy, 220
economic freedom and growth in developing countries, 23
economic growth and poverty in China, 3
economic growth in China, 33
education and economic growth, 236
euro, 453
European labor markets, 361
Mexican peso crisis, 455
New Zealand farming, 97
public pension plans, 285
rates of return around the world, in education, 238
total social cost of the automobile (pollution), 158–159
unemployment in Japan, 355
World Trade Organization (WTO), 439
International trade, 427
barriers to, 434–436
barriers to, reducing, 438–441
comparative advantage and, 429–432
cost of saving U.S. jobs (Insights), 434
Internet sites regarding, 442
negotiations, labor, and the environment (Insights), 440
net gains from, 432–433
quotas, 435
tariffs, 434–435
U.S. participation in, 428–429, 430
voluntary export restraints (VERs), 435–436
World Trade Organization (WTO) (International Perspective), 439
See also Free trade; Protection
Internet sites
agriculture, 122
air pollution, 173–174
college education, 245
crime and crime control, 224
drug issues, 224
economic and price systems, 63–64
for economic and productivity growth, 26
economic issues, 152
education, 272
federal budget, 425
finance in the global economy, 459
gross domestic product (GDP), 344
inflation, 389–390
international trade, 442
market power, 152
medical care, 195
poverty, 319

Social Security, 291
  unemployment, 364
Iran, 23, 138
Ireland, 441, 452
Italy, 158, 159, 441, 452
Jamaica, 23
Japan, 22n, 158, 159, 285, 452
  automobile firms (International Perspective), 137
  deflation in (International Perspective), 378
  economic and productivity growth in, 20–22
  economic growth in, 2, 3–6
  global financial example, 447–452
  high-stakes testing in (International Perspective), 261
  unemployment in (International Perspective), 355
Jefferson, Thomas, 1, 2
  on education, 251, 253
Job Opportunities and Basic Skills (JOBS), 304
Johnson, Lyndon, 293, 386
Johnson, Paul, 198
Kadiyala, Srikanth, 182–183
Kaplan, John, 211, 214
Kazakhstan, 51
Kennedy, John F., 293, 386
Kenya, 22n
Keynes, John M., 417
Khrushchev, Nikita, 27
Knowledge, 145–146
  assembled, 265
  economy's dependence on, 247
  general, 263–264
  local, 265
  specific, 263–264
  tacit, 35, 264
Knowledge spillovers, 237
Korea, 22n
  economic growth in, 3–6, 7, 22
Kristol, Irving, 211–212
Kuwait, 138–139
Kyoto protocol, 169–171
Kyrgyzstan, 53
Labor, 7
  division of, 34–36
  specialization of, 34–36
Labor market discrimination
  contributions to poverty, 314–315
  extent of, 312–314
  (Insights), 349
  policy implications, 315
Labor unions, inflation and, 382
Land, 7
Landau, Daniel, 87
Latin America, 24
  economic growth in, 22
Law of demand, 38
  See also Demand
Law of supply, 41
  See also Supply
Lawson, Robert A., 23
Lead, 154
Liberalization
  interest rate, 58
  price, 55
Life expectancy, 182

Lincoln, Abraham, 1, 2
Loanable funds, 418
Local knowledge, 265
Lock in, 149
Logrolling, 119–120
Long-run budget and debt projections, 408–412
Lucas, Robert, 2, 3
Luxembourg, 441, 452
M1, M2, and M3 aggregate, 375–376
Maastricht Treaty, 452
Macroeconomy
  See Gross domestic product (GDP)
Maddison, Angus, 20–22, 24
Malaysia, 23, 457
Managed care (medical care), 190–192
Mandatory program, 403
Marginal abatement cost, 166–167
Marginal benefit, 11
Marginal benefit curve, 67
Marginal cost, 9–10
Marginal cost curve, 67
Marginal external benefits (MEB), 70
Marginal external costs (MEC), 72, 156
Marginal principle, 131–132
Marginal product, 12
Marginal revenue, 130
Marginal social benefits (MSB), 70
Marginal social costs (MSC), 72, 156
Marijuana, 211, 215, 218, 220, 221, 222–223
Marine Mammal Protection Act, 439
Marketable pollution permits, 167–169
Market economy
  government's role in, 197–199
  information in, 45–46
  motivation in, 47–48
  rationing in, 46–47
  See also Comparative systems
Market exchanges, 29
Market failure
  defined, 68
  external benefits, 70–72
  external costs, 72–74
  incomplete markets, 74–75
  monopoly, 68–70
  nonexistent markets, 74
  pollution and, 158–160
  public goods, 72
Market power, 127
  barriers to entry, 136–138
  cartels and, 139–145
  defined, 128
  dominating firms and, 145
  economic efficiency and, 135–138
  economic growth and, 145–148
  government and, 148–150
  Internet sites regarding, 152
  OPEC and, 138–145
  trend in, 135–136
  See also Cartels; Monopoly
Market risk, in agriculture, 110
Market systems
  compared to command systems, 28–29
  coordination of economic activity by, 49

economic coordination in, 36
successful, 31–32
well-functioning, 30–31
See also Market economy
Marsden, Keith, 87
Marshall, Alfred, 2, 3, 50
Mauritius, 23
Means-tested transfers, 302
Medicaid, 76–77, 88, 311, 326
Medical care, 175
   defensive medicine, 189
   federal tax exemption for health insurance, 189–190, 192
   government-subsidized, 76–78
   health care vouchers, 193
   Internet sites regarding, 195
   managed care, 190–192
   physician-induced demand, 186–189
   for the poor, 311
   rising cost of, 176
   technological change, worth of, 181–183
   third-party payments, 184–186, 187
   wasteful expenditures, reducing, 190–193
   See also Health expenditures
Medicare, 76–77, 88, 191, 273, 326
Medium of exchange, 374
Member banks, 391
Mexico, 22n, 139, 142, 144–145, 440, 452
   peso crisis (International Perspective), 455
Microsoft, 45, 146–150
Mill, John Stuart, 210–211, 212
Minimum wage, 78, 79, 88
   TANF + food stamps + EITC, 307
   unemployment and, 357–359
   working poor and, 311
Minorities
   See Blacks; Hispanics; Women
Monetary benefits and costs, of a college education, 230–236
Monetary policy, 383–385
   defined, 336–337
Monetary system
   in transition economies, 51–54
   well-functioning, 32
Money
   change in the supply of, 394–396
   creation of, 393–394
   defined, 374
   functions of, 374
   See also Money supply
Money creation process, 391–396
Money supply, 374–376
   defined, 336
   Federal Reserve and, 393–396
Monopoly, 21
   competition and, compared, 132–135
   defined, 128
   inflation and, 382–383
   marginal principle, 131–132
   marginal revenue, 130–131
   natural, 136
   OPEC: sellers acting like, 138–145
Monopoly profit, 134, 148

Moore's Law, 18
Moral hazard, 74
Morocco, 22n, 23
Motivation
   in a command economy, 48–49
   in a market economy, 47–48
Murphy, Kevin, 183
Mutual savings banks, 392
National Ambient Air Quality Standards (NAAQS), 161
National banks, 391
National Center on Addiction and Substance Abuse, 224
National Council of Teachers of Mathematics, 257
National health expenditures (NHE), 176–177
National health insurance, 187
Natural monopolies, 136
Natural rate of unemployment, 351–352
Net budget balance, 403
Net cost of health insurance, 190
Net exports
   of goods and services, 326
   inflation and, 372–373
Net gains from international trade, 432–433
Netherlands, the, 441, 452
   drug policy in (International Perspective), 220
Net private domestic investment, 325
New Zealand, farming analysis, 97
Nicaragua, 23
Nigeria, 22n
   economic growth in, 22
Nitrogen dioxide emissions, 154
Nixon, Richard, 387–388
Nominal GDP, 328, 329
Noneconomic costs of unemployment, 346
Nonexcludable good, 200
Nonexistent markets, 74
Nonmonetary benefits and costs, 231
Nonmonetary external benefits, 237–238
Nonmonetary external costs, 238
Nonmonetary student benefits, 236–237
Nonmonetary student costs, 237
Nonrecourse loan, 114–115
Nonrival good, 200
Nonstudent benefits, 231
Nonstudent costs, 231
Normal good, 100
North American Free Trade Agreement (NAFTA), 440–441, 455
North Korea, 28
Norway, 139, 144–145, 159
OASI (old-age and survivors insurance)
   See Social Security
OASI Trust Fund (Social Security), 274, 283–286
   exhausted in 2041, 423
Occupational segregation, 313, 315
Off-budget surplus, 403
Official poverty threshold, 294
Old-age and survivors insurance (OASI)
   See Social Security
Oligopoly, 138
   defined, 128
Olson, Mancur, 87
On-budget surplus, 403
OPEC (Organization of Petroleum Exporting Countries), 138

cartel formation, 139–140
cartel success, 140–141
dominating firms, 145
problems of OPEC cartel, 141–145
Open market operations, 396–397
  defined, 393
Opportunity cost, 8
Organization for Economic Cooperation and Development, 94
O'Rourke, P.J., 119
Ose, Doug, 95
Other America, The (Harrington), 293
Output constraints, 116–117
Output growth rate, 380–381
Output, national
  See Gross domestic product
Overall deficit or surplus, 446
Ozone, 154
Pakistan, 22n, 23
Panama, 23
Parking cash-outs, 159
Patents, 148
Pay-as-you-go funds, 274
Peak phase (business cycle), 331
Pell grant program, 242–243
Personal consumption expenditures, 324, 325
Personal Responsibility and Work Opportunity Reconciliation Act (1996), 304, 316
Personal saving, 84–85
Peru, 22n
Philippines, 457
Physical capital, 7
  contribution to growth, 15–16, 17
Physician ethics, 189
Physician-induced demand, 186–187
  conditions necessary for, 188
  limits to, 188–189
Planning
Play-or-pay insurance schemes, 181
Point of service plans (POSs), 190
Poland, 50, 51, 53
Political rent seeking, 119, 149, 150
Poor person, 294
Population, aging of, 178
Population growth, 13
Portugal, 23, 441, 452
Poverty, 293
  after rate adjustments, 301
  childcare assistance for workers, 309–310
  child support assistance, 316–317
  child support assurance, 317
  in China, 3
  earned income tax credit (EITC), 303–305
  of the elderly, 295–296
  fathers and child support, 315–317
  female-headed households, 296
  food stamps, 302–303
  government transfers, 297–301
  income inequality (Insights), 301
  Internet sites regarding, 319
  labor market discrimination policy, 312–315
  means-tested transfers, 302–307
  measures of, 294
  medical protection for workers, 311
  minimum wage, 311
  number of people in, 1959-2001, 294–295
  official poverty threshold, 294
  poor person, 294
  poverty rate, 295–296
  by race, 297
  TANF + food stamps + EITC, 306–307
  Temporary Assistance for Needy Families (TANF), 305–306
  typical family in, 315
  unemployment policy for workers, 308–309
  wage subsidies, 311–312
  welfare reform (Insights), 304–305
  working and, 307–315
Poverty rate, 295, 296
Preferred provider organizations (PPOs), 190
Prescribed fuels, 162
Present value decision rule, 229–230
Present value of net benefits (PVNB), 230
  social, 234–236
  student, 232–234
Present value (PV), 182, 229
Pre-transfer poverty rate, 299
Price elastic, 123
Price elasticity of demand
  determinants of, 124–125
  elasticity coefficient, 123–124
  total revenue and, relationship between, 124
Price floor, 114
Price index, 327
Price inelastic, 124
Price level, national
  See Gross domestic product
Price liberalization, 55
Prices
  flexible, in transition economies, 55–56
  gasoline, 158–159
  relative, 29
  stable, in transition economies, 51–54
Price searcher, 129
Price supports, agricultural, 76, 77, 87–88
Price system
  as coordinator, 36–44
  demand, 36–39
  demand and supply, 41–44
  Internet sites regarding, 63–64
  market and command economies compared, 44–45
  socialism and, 50
  supply, 39–41
  See also Market system
Price takers, 45, 129
Primary insurance amount (PIA), 275
Principles of Economics (Marshall), 2
Private ownership, 29
Private property, in transition economies, 56–58
Private sector
  See Inefficiency in the private sector
Privatization
  of the public school system, 262
  of Social Security, 288–289
Producer price indexes, 366n
Producers' surplus, 433

INDEX

Product differentiation, 137–138
Production, methods of, 32
Production possibilities curve, 9
Production possibilities for the economy, 7–10
Productivity growth, 16–17
    capital intensity growth, 18
    in developing countries after 1950, 22–24
    in Europe and Japan, 20–22
    importance of, 14–15
    Internet sites regarding, 26
    technical change, 18–20
Profit, 68
    in agriculture, 109–111
    as motivation, 47–48
Profit-maximizing equilibrium, 132, 133
Progressive tax, 80
Property rights, 159
    government enforcement of, 200–201
    in transition economies, 56–57
Protection
    cheap foreign labor, 438
    infant industry, 437
    national defense, 437
    save American jobs, 437–438
Pryor, Frederic, 87
Public debt, 405–408
Public education
    current system, alternatives to, 268–270
    decision making and, 266–267
    economic organization of, 262–270
    privatization of, 262
    spending, per pupil, 248–251
    U.S., compared to rest of world, 248–251
Public goods, 72, 200–201
Public pension plans (International Perspective), 285
Public sector
    See Inefficiency in the public sector
Quantity demanded, 37
Quantity supplied, 40
Quantity theory of money, 376–379
Quotas, 349, 435
Rate of return decision rule, 230
Rate of return (ROR), 230
    deficit, Social Security, and, 289–290
    social, 232, 234–236
    student, 232–234
Ration, 47
Rationing
    in a command economy, 48
    in a market economy, 46–47
Real balance effect, 335
Real GDP, 328–329, 330
Recession, 331
    deficit help for, 416–417
Recovery, 331
Regressive tax, 80
Related goods, farming analysis, 98–100
Relative price, 29
Rent controls, 75–76
Rent seeking, 119–120, 149
Required reserves, 393
Reschovsky, Andrew, 305
Research spillovers, 237

Reserve requirement, 393, 397
Residual, 180
Resource accumulation, 12, 13
    efficiency in, rules for achieving, 66
Resource allocation, 65
    competitive market example, 66–68
Resources available (measure of poverty), 294
Retirement age, 287
    See also Social Security
Reuter, Peter, 219, 221
Revaluation, 452
Reynolds, Morgan, 208
Ricardo, David, 430
Risk
    in agriculture, 109–111
    defaulting on student loans, 240–242
Risk reduction benefit, 283
Rivkin, Steven, 250
Romania, 51, 53
Ross, Randy, 87
Rural residence farms, 94
Russia, 51, 56, 57, 58, 60–61, 145
    criminal activity in, 59
    index number of, 55
    inflation rate from 1996 to 2001, 54
Sales taxes, 84
Satisfaction maximization, 188
Saudi Arabia, 143–144
    oil and, 138–139
Saving, personal, 84–85
Savings and loan associations, 392
Scarcity, 7, 10, 47
Scientific method in economics (Insights), 210
Second opinions (medical care), 188
Senior citizens
    See Elderly
September 11, 2001, 332, 409
Sherman Act, 149
Simons, Henry, 254
Singapore, 23
Slovenia, 53, 55, 56, 57, 60
Smith, Adam, 1–2, 3, 24, 34–35, 50, 197–198, 253
Social benefits, 231
Social cost of the automobile (pollution; International Perspective), 158–159
Social costs, 231
Socialism, price system and, 50
Social rate of return (ROR), 232
Social Security, 273, 326
    as an antipoverty program, 297
    deficit remedies, 286–289
    early retirement and, 278
    household savings and, 278–279
    individual rates of return, 279–282
    Internet sites regarding, 291
    long-run deficit, 283–286
    lower deficits and lower rates of return, 289–290
    principal features, 274–276
    privatization of, 290
    public pension plans (International Perspective), 285
    surplus funds, federal budget and, 410–412, 418
    value to "investors," 282–283
    who pays, 276–278

Social Security wealth, 278
Social welfare, real GDP and (Insights), 332–333
Somalia, 23
South Africa, 22n
South Korea, 28, 457
Soviet Union, 138–139, 262
Spain, 441, 452
Specialization of labor, 34–36
Specific knowledge, 263–246
Spillovers, 237
Stabilization policies, 354–355
Standard of living, 2
State appropriations, for higher education, 243
State banks, 391
State-owned enterprises (SOEs), 56–57, 60
    education and, 262–266
Static efficiency, 66
Stratospheric ozone depletion, 155
Structural deficit, 414
Structural unemployment, 350
    reducing, 355–356
Student benefits, 231
Student costs, 231
Student rate of return (ROR), 232
Student rate of return without government support, 239
Subsidies
    for farmers, 94–96
    government-subsidized medical care, 76–78
    wage-subsidies, 311–312
Subsitute, 99
Subsitution effect of a wage decrease, 276
Sulfur dioxide, 154, 155
Superior good, 179
Supply, 39
    changes in, affecting equilibrium price and quantity, 105
    decrease in, 103
    of drugs, reducing, 215–216
    farming analysis, 101–103
    increase in, 102
Supply and demand, 41–44
Supply curve, 40
Supply price, 40
Supply schedule, 39–40
Supply-side policies, 383, 385–386
Surplus
    consumers', 433
    federal, shrinking, 408–410
    overall, 446
    producers', 433
    state and local government, 416
    See also Budget, federal
Suspended particulates, 154
Sweden, 323, 441
Tacit knowledge, 35, 264
Taiwan, 22n
    economic growth in, 22
TANF
    See Temporary Assistance for Needy Families
Tanzania, 22n, 23
Target efficiency, 303
Target price, 117

Tariffs, 138, 434–435
Taxes, 78–79
    capital gains, 84
    carbon, 171
    deadweight loss from taxation, 82
    efficiency loss from taxation, 82, 85
    emissions, 166–167
    federal exemption for health insurance, 189–190, 192
    gasoline, 159
    income, 80–84
    individual income and personal saving, 84–85
    progressive, 80
    regressive, 80
    sales, 84
    trade-offs, 85–86
Technical change, 17–20
Technological change, medical care costs and, 180–183
Technological improvement, 13–14
    (Insights), 149
Technology, 7
    best, 9
    economy's dependence on, 247
    restricted (air pollution), 161
Teenage unemployment, 348
Tellez, Luis K., 144
Temporary Assistance for Needy Families (TANF), 294, 304, 305–306
    insufficiency of work requirement, 307–315
    problems in funding, 305
    TANF + food stamps + EITC, 306–307
Thailand, 22n, 23, 158, 457
Thatcher, Margaret, 198
Third International Mathematics and Science Study (TIMSS), 248
Third-party payments (medical care), 184–186, 187
Topel, Robert, 183
Total benefit, 67
Total cost, 68
Total net benefit, 68
Total revenue, 68
    price elasticity and, 124
Toyoda, Eiji, 13
Trade agreements, 440
Trade barriers, 21
    global approach to reducing, 438–439
    regional approach to reducing, 440–441
Trade deficit, 428–429
Transactions costs, 169
Transitional Medicaid assistance (TMA), 311
Transition economies, 29
    criminal activity in Russia (International Perspective), 59
    culture of honesty and trust, 60–61
    flexible prices, 55–56
    incentives, 57–58, 60
    liberalization, 55, 58
    private property and property rights, establishment of, 56–57
    reforms, 54–61
    stable prices and the monetary system, 51–54
    summary, 61–62
Treaty on European Union, 452

Trough phase (business cycle), 331
Turkey, 23
Ukraine, 51–54, 56, 57, 58, 60–61
Unanticipated inflation, 368, 371
Underground economy, 323
    currency holdings and (Insights), 375
Unemployment, 345
    counting the unemployed, 347–348
    cyclical, 350
    cyclical, reducing, 352–355
    economic costs, 346
    in Europe, 359–362
    frictional, 349–350
    frictional, reducing, 356–357
    full employment, 351–352
    Internet sites regarding, 364
    in Japan (International Perspective), 355
    job opportunities and discrimination (Insights), 349
    minimum wage and, 357–359
    noneconomic costs, 346
    structural, 350
    structural, reducing, 355–356
    Temporary Assistance for Needy Families (TANF) and, 308–309
Unemployment benefits, 361–362
Unemployment compensation, 326
Unemployment rate
    1960-2001 (figure), 351
    for blacks, 348, 349
    calculation of, 347
    defined, 347
    demographic groups, 348
    Temporary Assistance for Needy Families (TANF) and, 308–309
Unified budget
    defined, 402
    See also Budget, federal
United Arab Emirates, 139
United Kingdom, 139, 158, 159, 285, 441, 452
    economic growth in, 3–6
United Nations Environmental Protection Agency, 440
Unit elastic, 124
Up-front costs, 145–146

Urban air quality, 154
Uruguay Round, 439
Utilization review, 191
Value of a life, 182
Vault cash, 393
Velocity of money, 376, 381–382
Venezuela, 23, 138–139
Volcker, Paul, 392
Voluntary exchange, 36, 254
Voluntary export restraints (VERs), 435–436
Vouchers, health care, 193
Wage-price controls, 386–388
Wage subsidies, 311–312
Wales, 206
Wal-Mart, 20
Walton, Sam, 13
War on poverty, 293
Washington, George, 251
Wealth of Nations, The (Smith), 1, 23, 34, 197
Wealth substitution effect, 278
Welfare reform (Insights), 304–305
West Germany, 28, 441
Wilson, James Q., 211–212
Winfrey, Oprah, 50
Winners, Losers, and Microsoft: Competition and Antitrust in High Technology (Leibowitz and Margolis), 147
Wolf, Charles, 87
Wolfe, Barbara, 236–237
Women
    childcare assistance, 309–310
    child support assistance, 316–317
    child support assurance, 317
    family medical protection, 311
    as head of household, poverty and, 297, 301, 308–309
    labor market discrimination and, 312–315
    unemployment rate for, 348
World trade
    See Finance in the global economy; International trade
World Trade Organization (WTO), 439
World Wide Web, 136
Zambia, 23